ACCA

STUDY TEXT

PAPER P7

ADVANCED AUDIT AND ASSURANCE

(INTERNATIONAL)

BPP Learning Media is the **sole ACCA Platinum Approved Learning Partner – content** for the ACCA qualification. In this, **the only Paper P7 study text to be reviewed by the examiner**:

- We **discuss** the **best strategies** for studying for ACCA exams

- We **highlight** the **most important elements** in the syllabus and the **key skills** you will need

- We **signpost** how each chapter links to the syllabus and the study guide

- We **provide** lots of **exam focus points** demonstrating what the examiner will want you to do

- We **emphasise** key points in regular **fast forward summaries**

- We **test your knowledge** of what you've studied in **quick quizzes**

- We **examine your understanding** in our **exam question bank**

- We **reference all the important topics** in our **full index**

BPP's **i-Pass** product also supports this paper.

FOR EXAMS IN 2012

First edition 2007

Sixth edition October 2011

ISBN 9781 4453 7774 2
(Previous ISBN 9780 7517 8934 8)
e-text ISBN 9780 7517 8701 6

British Library Cataloguing-in-Publication Data
A catalogue record for this book
is available from the British Library

Published by

BPP Learning Media Ltd
BPP House, Aldine Place
London W12 8AA

www.bpp.com/learningmedia

Printed in the United Kingdom

We are grateful to the Association of Chartered Certified
Accountants for permission to reproduce past
examination questions. The suggested solutions in the
exam answer bank have been prepared by BPP Learning
Media Ltd, unless where otherwise stated.

Your learning materials, published by BPP
Learning Media Ltd, are printed on paper
sourced from sustainable, managed forests.

Contents

A note about copyright

How the BPP ACCA-approved Study Text can help you pass

BPP Learning Media – the sole Platinum Approved Learning Partner - content

As ACCA's **sole Platinum Approved Learning Partner – content**, BPP Learning Media gives you the **unique opportunity** to use **examiner-reviewed** study materials for the 2012 exams. By incorporating the examiner's comments and suggestions regarding the depth and breadth of syllabus coverage, the BPP Learning Media Study Text provides excellent, **ACCA-approved** support for your studies.

NEW FEATURE – the PER alert!

Before you can qualify as an ACCA member, you do not only have to pass all your exams but also fulfil a three year **practical experience requirement** (PER). To help you to recognise areas of the syllabus that you might be able to apply in the workplace to achieve different performance objectives, we have introduced the '**PER alert**' feature. You will find this feature throughout the Study Text to remind you that what you are **learning to pass** your ACCA exams is **equally useful to the fulfilment of the PER requirement**.

Tackling studying

Studying can be a daunting prospect, particularly when you have lots of other commitments. The **different features** of the text, the **purposes** of which are explained fully on the **Chapter features** page, will help you whilst studying and improve your chances of **exam success**.

Developing exam awareness

Our Texts are completely **focused** on helping you pass your exam.

Our advice on **Studying P7** outlines the **content** of the paper, the **necessary skills** the examiner expects you to demonstrate and any **brought forward knowledge** you are expected to have.

Exam focus points are included within the chapters to highlight when and how specific topics were examined, or how they might be examined in the future.

Using the Syllabus and Study Guide

You can find the syllabus and Study Guide on page xi of this Study Text

Testing what you can do

Testing yourself helps you develop the skills you need to pass the exam and also confirms that you can recall what you have learnt.

We include **Questions** – lots of them – both within chapters and in the **Exam Question Bank**, as well as **Quick Quizzes** at the end of each chapter to test your knowledge of the chapter content.

Chapter features

Each chapter contains a number of helpful features to guide you through each topic.

Topic list

Topic list	Syllabus reference

Tells you what you will be studying in this chapter and the relevant section numbers, together the ACCA syllabus references.

Introduction

Puts the chapter content in the context of the syllabus as a whole.

Study Guide

Links the chapter content with ACCA guidance.

Exam Guide

Highlights how examinable the chapter content is likely to be and the ways in which it could be examined.

Knowledge brought forward from earlier studies

What you are assumed to know from previous studies/exams.

FAST FORWARD

Summarises the content of main chapter headings, allowing you to preview and review each section easily.

Examples

Demonstrate how to apply key knowledge and techniques.

Key terms

Definitions of important concepts that can often earn you easy marks in exams.

Exam focus points

Tell you when and how specific topics were examined, or how they may be examined in the future.

Formula to learn

Formulae that are not given in the exam but which have to be learnt.

PER alert

This is a new feature that gives you a useful indication of syllabus areas that closely relate to performance objectives in your Practical Experience Requirement (PER).

 Question

Give you essential practice of techniques covered in the chapter.

 Case Study

Provide real world examples of theories and techniques.

Chapter Roundup

A full list of the Fast Forwards included in the chapter, providing an easy source of review.

Quick Quiz

A quick test of your knowledge of the main topics in the chapter.

Exam Question Bank

Found at the back of the Study Text with more comprehensive chapter questions. Cross referenced for easy navigation.

Studying P7

As the name suggests, this paper examines advanced audit and assurance topics. Paper P7 is one of the professional level Options papers and as such candidates must consider carefully whether they have the required competencies.

The P7 examiner

The examiner, Lisa Weaver, expects you to demonstrate a highly **professional approach** to all questions – not just presenting information in a professional manner, but also **integrating knowledge and understanding** of topics from across the syllabus. The examiner is also very keen for students to demonstrate evidence of **wider reading** and to demonstrate an understanding of current issues as they affect audit and assurance. At the absolute minimum you should read *student accountant*. The examiner often examines topics that she has written about in *student accountant*.

Syllabus update

The P7 syllabus has been updated for the June 2012 sitting onwards. The full syllabus and study guide can be found in this Study Text on pages xi to xxi.

1 What P7 is about

The aim of the syllabus is to analyse, evaluate and conclude on the assurance engagement and other audit and assurance issues in the context of best practice and current developments.

The paper builds on the topics covered in Paper F8 *Audit and Assurance* but as an advanced paper it tests much more than just your knowledge of ISAs and your ability to list standard audit procedures. You must be able to apply your knowledge to more complex audit and assurance scenarios, identifying and formulating the work required to meet the objectives of audit and non-audit assignments and to evaluate the findings and results of work performed. Accounting knowledge examined in Paper P2 *Corporate Reporting* is also assumed. Therefore, candidates studying for P7 should refer to the Accounting Standards listed under P2.

The syllabus is divided into **SEVEN** main sections:

(a) **Regulatory environment**

This section introduces the legal and regulatory environment including **corporate governance** issues. It also examines the topics of **money laundering** and the consideration of law and regulation.

(b) **Professional and ethical considerations**

The details of the various **ethical codes** should be familiar to you from your earlier studies, however the importance of this topic should not be underestimated. The examiner has indicated that ethical and professional issues are likely to feature in every sitting. This section also covers **fraud and professional liability** both of which are topical issues.

(c) **Practice management**

This part of the syllabus covers quality control, tendering and professional appointments. It also covers advertising, publicity, obtaining professional work and fees.

(d) **Audit of historical financial information**

This is the largest section of the syllabus looking in detail at the procedures involved in a range of audit and assurance assignments. The examiner has indicated that evidence gathering is a key part of the syllabus and is likely to feature at each sitting. Requirements are likely to focus on **specific assertions, balances or transactions**.

(e) **Other assignments**

This section also covers a range of **audit-related and assurance services**. The examiner has stressed the need for candidates to be able to tackle these types of scenario.

(f) **Reporting**

The detail of audit reports should be familiar to you from your earlier studies. At this level you will be expected to **apply this knowledge** to more complex scenarios. The examiner has also stressed the importance of the **relationship between financial reporting and auditing**. This will be particularly important when forming an appropriate audit opinion. This section of the syllabus also includes reports to management and other reports.

(g) **Current issues and developments**

Current issues and developments includes a wide range of topics including the IAASB clarity project, professional, ethical and corporate governance, information technology, going concern transnational audits and social and environmental auditing. The examiner has indicated that this is likely to be examined at each sitting, and that candidates are expected to have read around the issues for themselves. You will need to be able to discuss current issues topics **in the context of a client scenario**.

2 What skills are required?

- A thorough understanding of the relevant audit, assurance and financial reporting regulations that fall within the syllabus
- The ability to apply knowledge to specific client scenarios
- The ability to have an independent opinion, backed by reasoned argument
- An appreciation of commercial factors which influence practice management
- An appreciation of fast-moving developments in audit and assurance practices

3 How to improve your chances of passing

- Study the **entire** syllabus. Although Section B of the paper contains an optional element, the two questions in Section A are compulsory and could cover a range of topics from across the syllabus. Question spotting at this level is unwise and not recommended.
- **Practise** as many questions as you can under **timed conditions** – this is the best way of developing good exam technique. Make use of the **Question Bank** at the back of this text. **BPP's Practice and Revision Kit** contains numerous exam standard questions (many of them taken from past exam papers) as well as three mock exams for you to try.
- Section A questions will be the case study type of question – make sure you relate your answers to the scenario rather than being generic. Answers that are simply regurgitated from texts are unlikely to score highly.
- Present your answers in a **professional** manner – there are between four and six **professional marks** available for setting answers out properly and for coherent, well structured arguments and recommendations. You should be aiming to achieve all of these marks.
- Consider the **question requirement** carefully so that you answer the actual question set.
- **Answer plans** will help you to focus on the requirements of the question and enable you to manage your time effectively
- Answer the question that you are most comfortable with first – it will help to settle you down if you feel you have answered the first question well.
- **Answer all parts** of the question – leaving out a five mark discursive element for example may mean the difference between a pass and a fail.
- Read the financial press and relevant web sites for real life examples – the examiner is specifically looking for evidence of **wider reading**.
- Read **Student Accountant** (the ACCA's student magazine) regularly – it often contains technical articles written either by or on the recommendation of the examiner which can be invaluable for future exams.

The P7 examiner made the same comment in a number of her recent examiner's reports which is so important that we will quote it here:

> "Similar factors as detailed in previous examiner's reports continue to contribute to the unsatisfactory pass rate:
>
> - Failing to answer the specific question requirements
> - Not applying knowledge to question scenarios
> - Not explaining or developing points in enough detail
> - Lack of knowledge on certain syllabus areas
> - Illegible handwriting."

> "As seen in previous sittings, **what makes the difference between a pass and a fail script is usually the level of application skills which have been demonstrated. Candidates who answer the specific question requirement, and tailor their answers to the scenarios provided are likely to do well.**"

4 Brought forward knowledge

The P7 syllabus assumes knowledge brought forward from F8 *Audit and Assurance*. It also assumes knowledge from Paper F7 *Financial Reporting* and Paper P2 *Corporate Reporting*. It is very important to be comfortable with your financial reporting studies because such aspects are likely to come up in scenario-based questions in Sections A and B of this paper.

> The P7 examiner, Lisa Weaver, has written a number of articles relevant to the P7 exam and it is highly recommended that you read them. A list of these articles can be found after chapter 18 of this study text.

The exam paper

Format of the paper

Section A:	Two compulsory questions	50-70
Section B:	Choice of two from three questions	30-50
		100

Time allowed: 3 hours

Guidance

Section A will consist of two compulsory 'case study' style questions. These will include detailed information including, for example extracts from financial statements and audit working papers. The questions will include a range of requirements covering different syllabus areas.

Exams in 2011 will feature a new style of question requirement in Section A, with the requirement being embedded within the scenario. For more information on the change, see the examiner (Lisa Weaver)'s article in the February 2010 edition of *Student accountant*.

Section B questions will tend to be more focussed towards specific topic areas, such as ethical issues and auditor's reports. Short scenarios will be provided as a basis for these questions.

Syllabus and Study Guide

The P7 syllabus and study guide can be found below.

Syllabus

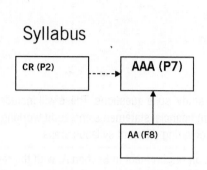

AIM

To analyse, evaluate and conclude on the assurance engagement and other audit and assurance issues in the context of best practice and current developments.

MAIN CAPABILITIES

On successful completion of this paper candidates should be able to:

A   Recognise the legal and regulatory environment and its impact on audit and assurance practice

B   Demonstrate the ability to work effectively on an assurance or other service engagement within a professional and ethical framework

C   Assess and recommend appropriate quality control policies and procedures in practice management and recognise the auditor's position in relation to the acceptance and retention of professional appointments

D   Identify and formulate the work required to meet the objectives of audit assignments and apply the International Standards on Auditing

E   Identify and formulate the work required to meet the objectives of non-audit assignments

F   Evaluate findings and the results of work performed and draft suitable reports on assignments

G   Understand the current issues and developments relating to the provision of audit-related and assurance service

RELATIONAL DIAGRAM OF MAIN CAPABILITIES

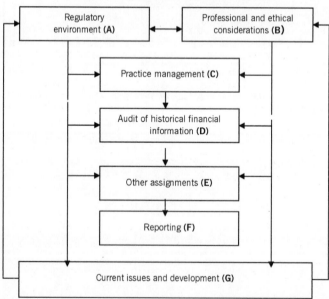

4

RATIONALE

The Advanced Audit and Assurance syllabus is essentially divided into seven areas.

The syllabus starts with the legal and regulatory environment including money laundering, and professional and ethical considerations, including the Code of Ethics and professional liability. This then leads into procedures in practice management, including quality control and the acceptance and retention of professional engagements.

The syllabus then covers the audit of financial statements, including planning, evidence and review. It then covers other assignments including prospective financial information, and other assurance assignments, as well as the reporting of these assignments.

The final section covers current issues and developments relating to the provision of audit-related and assurance services.

DETAILED SYLLABUS

A   Regulatory Environment

1.   International regulatory frameworks for audit and assurance services

2.   Money laundering

3.   Laws and regulations

B   Professional and Ethical Considerations

1.   Code of Ethics for Professional Accountants

2.   Fraud and error

3.   Professional liability

C   Practice Management

1.   Quality control

2.   Advertising, publicity, obtaining professional work and fees

3.   Tendering

4.   Professional appointments

D   Audit of historical financial information

1.   The audit of historical financial information including;
    i)   Planning, materiality and assessing the risk of misstatement
    ii)   Evidence
    iii) Evaluation and review

2.   Group audits

E   Other assignments

1.   Audit-related services

2.   Assurance services

3.   Prospective financial information

4.   Forensic audits

5.   Internal audit

6.   Outsourcing

F   Reporting

1.   Auditor's reports

2.   Reports to those charged with governance and management

3.   Other reports

G   Current Issues and Developments

1.   Professional and ethical

2.   Information technology

3.   Transnational audits

4.   Social and environmental auditing

5.   Other current issues

5

APPROACH TO EXAMINING THE SYLLABUS

The examination is a three hour paper constructed in two sections. Questions in both sections will be almost entirely discursive. However, candidates will be expected, for example, to be able to assess materiality and calculate relevant ratios where appropriate.

Section A questions will be based on 'case study' type questions. That is not to say that they will be particularly long, rather that they will provide a setting within a range of topics, issues and requirements can be addressed. Different types of question will be encountered in Section B and will tend to be more focussed on specific topics, for example 'auditor's reports', 'quality control' and topics of ISAs which are not examinable in Paper F8, *Audit and Assurance*. (This does not preclude these topics from appearing in Section A). Current issues will be examined across a number of questions.

Section A: 2 compulsory questions   50-70 marks

Section B: Choice of 2 from 3   30-50 marks
            questions   100

6

Study Guide

A REGULATORY ENVIRONMENT

1. International regulatory frameworks for audit and assurance services

a) Explain the need for laws, regulations, standards and other guidance relating to audit, assurance and related services.[2]

b) Outline and explain the need for the legal and professional framework including:[2]
   i) public oversight to an audit and assurance practice
   ii) the role of audit committees and impact on audit and assurance practice.

2. Money laundering

a) Define 'money laundering'.[1]

b) Explain how international efforts seek to combat money laundering.[2]

c) Explain the scope of criminal offences of money laundering and how professional accountants may be protected from criminal and civil liability.[2]

d) Explain the need for ethical guidance in this area.[2]

e) Describe how accountants meet their obligations to help prevent and detect money laundering including record keeping and reporting of suspicion to the appropriate regulatory body.[2]

f) Explain the importance of customer due diligence (CDD).[2]

g) Recognise potentially suspicious transactions and assess their impact on reporting duties.[2]

h) Describe, with reasons, the basic elements of an anti-money laundering program.[2]

3. Laws and regulations

a) Compare and contrast the respective responsibilities of management and auditors concerning compliance with laws and regulations in an audit of financial statements.[2]

b) Describe the auditors considerations of compliance with laws and regulations and plan audit procedures when possible non-compliance is discovered.[2]

c) Discuss how and to whom non-compliance should be reported.[2]

d) Recognise when withdrawal from an engagement is necessary.[2]

B PROFESSIONAL AND ETHICAL CONSIDERATIONS

1. Code of Ethics for Professional Accountants

a) Explain the fundamental principles and the conceptual framework approach.[1]

b) Identify, evaluate and respond to threats to compliance with the fundamental principles.[3]

c) Discuss and evaluate the effectiveness of available safeguards.[3]

d) Recognise and advise on conflicts in the application of fundamental principles.[3]

2. Fraud and error

a) Define and clearly distinguish between the terms 'error', 'irregularity', 'fraud' and 'misstatement'.[2]

b) Compare and contrast the respective responsibilities of management and auditors for fraud and error.[2]

c) Describe the matters to be considered and procedures to be carried out to investigate actual and/or potential misstatements in a given situation.[2]

d) Explain how, why, when and to whom fraud and error should be reported and the circumstances in which an auditor should withdraw from an engagement.[2]

7

e) Discuss the current and possible future role of auditors in preventing, detecting and reporting error and fraud.[2]

3. Professional liability

a) Recognise circumstances in which professional accountants may have legal liability.[2]

b) Describe the factors to determine whether or not an auditor is negligent in given situations.[2]

c) Explain the other criteria for legal liability to be recognised (including 'due professional care' and 'proximity') and apply them to given situations.[2]

d) Compare and contrast liability to client with liability to third parties.[3]

e) Evaluate the practicability and effectiveness of ways in which liability may be restricted.[3]

f) Discuss liability limitation agreements.[2]

g) Discuss and appraise the principal causes of audit failure and other factors that contribute to the 'expectation gap' (e.g. responsibilities for fraud and error).[3]

h) Recommend ways in which the expectation gap might be bridged.[2]

C PRACTICE MANAGEMENT

1. Quality control

a) Explain the principles and purpose of quality control of audit and other assurance engagements.[1]

b) Describe the elements of a system of quality control relevant to a given firm.[2]

c) Select and justify quality control procedures that are applicable to a given audit engagement.[3]

d) Assess whether an engagement has been planned and performed in accordance with professional standards and whether reports issued are appropriate in the circumstances.[3]

2. Advertising, publicity, obtaining professional work and fees

a) Recognise situations in which specified advertisements are acceptable.[2]

b) Discuss the restrictions on practice descriptions, the use of the ACCA logo and the names of practising firms.[2]

c) Discuss the extent to which reference to fees may be made in promotional material.[2]

d) Outline the determinants of fee-setting and justify the bases on which fees and commissions may and may not be charged for services.[3]

e) Discuss the ethical and other professional problems, for example, lowballing, involved in establishing and negotiating fees for a specified assignment.[3]

3. Tendering

a) Discuss the reasons why entities change their auditors/professional accountants.[2]

b) Recognise and explain the matters to be considered when a firm is invited to submit a proposal or fee quote for an audit or other professional engagement.[2]

c) Identify the information to be included in a proposal.[2]

4. Professional appointments

a) Explain the matters to be considered and the procedures that an audit firm/professional accountant should carry out before accepting a specified new client/engagement including:[3]
   i) client acceptance
   ii) engagement acceptance
   iii) establish whether the preconditions for an audit are present
   iv) agreeing the terms of engagement.

b) Recognise the key issues that underlie the agreement of the scope and terms of an engagement with a client.[2]

D AUDIT OF HISTORICAL FINANCIAL INFORMATION

1(i) Planning, materiality and assessing the risk of misstatement

a) Define materiality and performance materiality and demonstrate how it should be applied in financial reporting and auditing.[2]

b) Identify and explain business risks for a given assignment.[3]

c) Identify and explain audit risks for a given assignment.[3]

d) Identify and explain financial statement risks for a given assignment.[3]

e) Discuss and demonstrate the use of analytical procedures in the planning of an assignment.[3]

f) Explain how the result of planning procedures determines the relevant audit strategy.[2]

1(ii) Evidence

a) Identify and describe audit procedures to obtain sufficient audit evidence from identified sources.[2]

b) Identify and evaluate the audit evidence expected to be available to
   i) support the financial statement assertions and accounting treatments (including fair values)
   ii) support disclosures made in the notes to the financial statements.[3]

c) Apply analytical procedures to financial and non-financial data.[2]

d) Explain the specific audit problems and procedures concerning related parties and related party transactions.[2]

e) Recognise circumstances that may indicate the existence of unidentified related parties and select appropriate audit procedures.[2]

f) Evaluate the use of written management representations to support other audit evidence.[2]

g) Recognise when it is justifiable to place reliance on the work of an expert (e.g. a surveyor employed by the audit client).[2]

h) Assess the appropriateness and sufficiency of the work of internal auditors and the extent to which reliance can be placed on it.[2]

1(iii) Evaluation and review

a) Evaluate the matters (e.g. materiality, risk, relevant accounting standards, audit evidence) relating to:[3]
   i) inventory and construction contracts
   ii) standard costing systems
   iii) statement of cash flows
   iv) changes in accounting policy
   v) taxation (including deferred tax)
   vi) segmental reporting
   vii) non-current assets
   viii) fair value
   ix) leases
   x) revenue recognition
   xi) employee benefits
   xii) government grants
   xiii) related parties
   xiv) earnings per share
   xv) impairment
   xvi) provisions, contingent liabilities and contingent assets
   xvii) intangible assets
   xviii) financial instruments
   xix) investment properties
   xx) share-based payment transactions
   xxi) business combinations
   xxii) assets held for sale and discontinued operations
   xxiii) events after the end of the reporting period
   xxiv) the effects of foreign exchange rates
   xxv) borrowing costs.

b) Explain the use of analytical procedures in evaluation and review.[3]

c) Explain how the auditor's responsibilities for corresponding figures, comparative financial statements, and 'other information', are discharged.[3]

d) Apply the further considerations and audit procedures relevant to initial engagements.[2]

9

e) Discuss the courses of action available to an auditor if an inconsistency or misstatement of fact exists in relation to other information.[2]

f) Specify audit procedures designed to identify subsequent events that may require adjustment to, or disclosure in, the financial statements of a given entity.[2]

g) Identify and explain indicators that the going concern basis may be in doubt and recognise mitigating factors.[2]

h) Recommend audit procedures, or evaluate the evidence that might be expected to be available and assess the appropriateness of the going concern basis in given situations.[3]

i) Assess the adequacy of disclosures in financial statements relating to going concern and explain the implications for the auditor's report with regard to the going concern basis.[3]

2. **Group audits**

a) Recognise the specific matters to be considered before accepting appointment as principal auditor to a group in a given situation.[3]

b) Justify the situations where a joint audit would be appropriate.[2]

c) Recognise the audit problems and describe audit procedures specific to a business combination, including goodwill, accounting policies, inter-company trading, the classification of investments, equity accounting for associates, and accounting for a foreign subsidiary.[3]

d) Identify and explain the audit risks, and necessary audit procedures relevant to the consolidation process.[3]

e) Identify and describe the matters to be considered and the procedures to be performed at the planning stage, when a principal auditor considers the use of the work of component auditors.[3]

f) Consider how the principal auditor should evaluate the audit work performed by a component auditor.[2]

g) Explain the implications for the auditor's report on the financial statements of an entity where the opinion on a component is qualified or otherwise modified in a given situation.[2]

E OTHER ASSIGNMENTS

1. **Audit-related services**

a) Describe the nature of audit-related services, the circumstances in which they might be required and the comparative levels of assurance provided by professional accountants and distinguish between:[2]
   i) audit-related services and an audit of historical financial statements
   ii) an attestation engagement and a direct reporting engagement.[2]

b) Plan review engagements, for example:[2]
   i) a review of interim financial information
   ii) a 'due diligence' assignment (when acquiring a company, business or other assets).

c) Explain the importance of enquiry and analytical procedures in review engagements and apply these procedures.[2]

2. **Assurance services**

a) Describe the main categories of assurance services that audit firms can provide and assess the benefits of providing these services to management and external users.[3]

b) Justify a level of assurance (reasonable, high, moderate, limited, negative) for an engagement depending on the subject matter evaluated, the criteria used, the procedures applied and the quality and quantity of evidence obtained.[3]

c) Recognise the ways in which different types of risk (e.g. strategic, operating, information) may be identified and analysed and assess how management should respond to risk.[3]

3. **Prospective financial information**

a) Define 'prospective financial information' (PFI) and distinguish between a 'forecast', a 'projection', a 'hypothetical illustration' and a 'target'.[1]

10

b) Explain the principles of useful PFI.[1]

c) Identify and describe the matters to be considered before accepting a specified engagement to report on PFI.[2]

d) Discuss the level of assurance that the auditor may provide and explain the other factors to be considered in determining the nature, timing and extent of examination procedures.[1]

e) Describe examination procedures to verify forecasts and projections.[2]

f) Compare the content of a report on an examination of PFI with reports made in providing audit-related services.[2]

4. Forensic audits

a) Define the terms 'forensic accounting', 'forensic investigation' and 'forensic audit'.[1]

b) Describe the major applications of forensic auditing (e.g. fraud, negligence, insurance claims) and analyse the role of the forensic auditor as an expert witness.[2]

c) Apply the fundamental ethical principles to professional accountants engaged in forensic audit assignments.[2]

d) Plan a forensic audit engagement.[2]

e) Select investigative procedures and evaluate evidence appropriate to determining the loss in a given situation.[3]

5. Internal audit

a) Evaluate the potential impact of an internal audit department on the planning and performance of the external audit.[2]

b) Explain the benefits and potential drawbacks of outsourcing internal audit.[2]

c) Consider the ethical implications of the external auditor providing an internal audit service to a client.[2]

6. Outsourcing

a) Explain the different approaches to 'outsourcing' and compare with 'insourcing'.[2]

b) Discuss and conclude on the advantages and disadvantages of outsourcing finance and accounting functions.[3]

c) Recognise and evaluate the impact of outsourced functions on the conduct of an audit.[3]

F   REPORTING

1   Auditor's reports

a) Critically appraise the form and content of a standard unmodified auditor's report.[3]

b) Recognise and evaluate the factors to be taken into account when forming an audit opinion in a given situation and justify audit opinions that are consistent with the results of audit procedures.[3]

c) Assess whether or not a proposed audit opinion is appropriate.[3]

d) Recognise when the use of an emphasis of matter paragraph and other matter paragraph would be appropriate.[3]

2.   Reports to those charged with governance and management

a) Critically assess the quality of a report to those charged with governance and management.[3]

b) Advise on the content of reports to those charged with governance and management in a given situation.[3]

3.   Other reports

a) Analyse the form and content of the professional accountant's report for an assurance engagement as compared with an auditor's report.[2]

b) Discuss the content of a report on examination of prospective financial information.[2]

c) Discuss the effectiveness of the 'negative assurance' form of reporting and evaluate situations in which it may be appropriate to express a reservation or deny a conclusion.[3]

G   CURRENT ISSUES AND DEVELOPMENTS

Discuss the relative merits and the consequences of different standpoints taken in current debates and express opinions supported by reasoned arguments.

1.   Professional and ethical

a) Discuss the relative advantages of an ethical framework and a rulebook.[2]

b) Identify and assess relevant to emerging ethical issues and evaluate the safeguards available.[3]

c) Discuss IFAC developments.[2]

2.   Information technology

a) Describe recent trends in IT and their current and potential impact on auditors (e.g. the audit implications of 'cyberincidents' and other risks).[2]

b) Explain how IT may be used to assist auditors and discuss the problems that may be encountered in automating the audit process.[2]

3.   Transnational audits

a) Define 'transnational audits' and explain the role of the Transnational Audit Committee (TAC) of IFAC.[1]

b) Discuss how transnational audits may differ from other audits of historical financial information (e.g. in terms of applicable financial reporting and auditing standards, listing requirements and corporate governance requirements). [2]

4.   Social and environmental auditing

a) Plan an engagement to provide assurance on performance measures and sustainability indicators.[2]

b) Describe the difficulties in measuring and reporting on economic, environmental and social performance and give examples of performance measures and sustainability indicators.[2]

c) Explain the auditor's main considerations in respect of social and environmental matters and how they impact on entities and their financial statements (e.g. impairment of assets, provisions and contingent liabilities).[2]

d) Describe substantive procedures to detect potential misstatements in respect of socio-environmental matters.[2]

e) Discuss the form and content of an independent verification statement (e.g. on an environmental management system (EMS) and a report to society).[2]

5.   Other current issues

a) Explain current developments in auditing standards including the need for new and revised standards and evaluate their impact on the conduct of audits. [3]

b) Discuss other current legal, ethical, other professional and practical matters that affect accountants, auditors, their employers and the profession. [3]

READING LIST

This section only contains examiner suggested reading which is in addition to the study texts and/or revision materials and/or other reading listed within the learning content provider directory.

Additional examiner suggested reading:

Forensic accounting and fraud investigation for non-experts, H Silverstone and M Sheetz, 2nd edition, Wiley, 2007

Please note, the following text is only relevant for students studying in Singapore

AUDIT COMMITTEE GUIDANCE COMMITTEE GUIDEBOOK FOR AUDIT COMMITTEES IN SINGAPORE

Further details on reading lists and Approved Learning Content can be found in the first few sections of this guide and on the following link.

http://www.accaglobal.com/learningproviders/alpc/content_provider_directory/search/

13

Analysis of past papers

The table below provides details of when each element of the syllabus has been examined and the question number and section in which each element appeared. Further details can be found in the Exam Focus Points in the relevant chapters.

Covered in Text chapter		June 2011	Dec 2010	June 2010	Dec 2009	June 2009	Dec 2008	June 2008	Dec 2007	Pilot Paper
	Regulatory environment									
1	International regulatory frameworks for audit and assurance services			2(d)					5(b)	
1	Money laundering				2(c)				4(a)	5(a), 5(b)
1	Laws and regulations					4(b)				
	Professional and ethical considerations									
2	Code of ethics for professional accountants	3(a)	2(a), 4(b)	3(b), 4	4(b)	4	4	4, 5(b)	4(b), 4(c)	5(b)
3	Fraud and error			2(d)		5(a)				
3	Professional liability			5(b)					5(c)	
	Practice Management									
4	Quality control				2(b)	5(c)		3(c)	1(c)	3, 5(b)
5	Advertising, publicity, obtaining professional work and fees		4(a)		4(b)					
5	Tendering					2(b), 2(c)				
5	Professional appointments	3(a)	4(a)			2(a), 2(c)		1(c)		
	Assignments									
6,7,8, 9,10	The audit of historical financial information including: planning, materiality and assessing the risk of misstatement / Evidence / Evaluation and review	1, 2, 3(b)	1(a), 2(c), 3(a)-(c),	1, 3(b), 5(a)	1, 2(a)-(b), 5	1(a), 1(b), 1(c), 3(a), 3(b)	1(a), 1(b), 3, 5	1(a), 1(b), 3(a), 3(b)	1(a), 1(b), 2(b), 2(c), 2(d)	
11	Group audits	5(b)				2(d)		2(b), 2(c)		1(a), 1(b), 1(c), 1(d)
	Other assignments									
12	Audit-related services	4				3(b)			5(c)	
12	Assurance services		2(a), 2(b)			3(b)		2(a)	3(a), 3(b)	
13	Prospective financial information	2(a)			3					
14	Forensic audits			2(c)			2		3(c)	2(a), 2(b), 2(c), 2(d)
15	Social and environmental auditing		2(a), 2(b)				1(c)			

Covered in Text chapter		June 2011	Dec 2010	June 2010	Dec 2009	June 2009	Dec 2008	June 2008	Dec 2007	Pilot Paper
16	Internal audit and outsourcing	4(a)		2(b), (b)					2(a)	
	Reports									
17	Auditor's reports	5(a)	5(a)	5(a)		5(b)			5(a)	4
17	Reports to management		5(b)					5(a)		
17	Other reports					3(b)				
	Current issues and developments									
1,2,3	Professional, ethical and corporate governance		4(b)			4				
6	Information technology									
11	Transnational audits					2(d)				
15	Social and environmental auditing									
18	Other current issues			3(a)	4(a)	5(a)				

Regulatory environment

International regulatory environments for audit and assurance services

Topic list	Syllabus reference
1 International regulatory frameworks for audit and assurance services	A1
2 Audit committees	A1
3 Internal control effectiveness	A1
4 Money laundering	A2
5 Laws and regulations	A3

Introduction

This chapter covers a wide range of regulations that affect the work of audit and assurance professionals. You need to be aware of the international nature of the audit and assurance market and the main issues driving the development of regulatory frameworks.

The detailed requirements relating to money laundering are then discussed. You should be prepared to explain the responsibilities of professional accountants in this area and to outline the procedures that audit firms should implement.

The final section looks at the auditor's responsibilities in respect of laws and regulations that apply to an audit client. This is a topic that could be built in to a practical case study question.

Study guide

		Intellectual level
A	**Regulatory environment**	
A1	**International regulatory frameworks for audit and assurance services**	
(a)	Explain the need for laws, regulations, standards and other guidance relating to audit, assurance and related services	2
(b)	Outline and explain the legal and professional framework including: (i) Public oversight to an audit and assurance practice (ii) The role of audit committees and impact on audit and assurance practice	2
A2	**Money laundering**	
(a)	Define 'money laundering'	1
(b)	Explain how international efforts seek to combat money laundering	2
(c)	Explain the scope of criminal offences of money laundering and how professional accountants may be protected from criminal and civil liability	2
(d)	Explain the need for ethical guidance in this area	2
(e)	Describe how accountants meet their obligations to help prevent and detect money laundering including record keeping and reporting of suspicion to the appropriate regulatory body	2
(f)	Explain the importance of customer due diligence (CDD)	2
(g)	Recognise potentially suspicious transactions and assess their impact on reporting duties	2
(h)	Describe, with reasons, the basic elements of an anti-money laundering program	2
A3	**Laws and regulations**	
(a)	Compare and contrast the respective responsibilities of management and auditors concerning compliance with laws and regulations in an audit of financial statements	2
(b)	Describe the auditor's considerations of compliance with laws and regulations and plan audit procedures when possible non-compliance is discovered	2
(c)	Discuss how and to whom non-compliance should be reported	2
(d)	Recognise when withdrawal from an engagement is necessary	2

Exam guide

The technical content of this part of the syllabus is mainly drawn from your earlier studies. Questions in this paper are unlikely to ask for straight repetition of this knowledge, but rather to require explanation or discussion of the reasons behind the regulations.

1 International regulatory frameworks for audit and assurance services

Major developments in international regulation of audit and assurance have recently concluded, with far-reaching effects on ISAs.

1.1 The need for laws, regulations, standards and other guidance

Corporate scandals, such as Enron and Worldcom in the USA, and Parmalat in Italy have brought the audit profession under close scrutiny from investors, businesses, regulators and others.

Businesses have become more complex and global, and firms of accountants have expanded their range of services well beyond traditional assurance and tax advice. This has led to a great deal of re-examination of regulatory and standard-setting structures both nationally and internationally in recent years.

1.2 The legal and professional framework

One of the competencies you require to fulfil performance objective 18 of the PER is the ability to describe the audit regulatory and legal framework. You can apply the knowledge you obtain from this section of the text to help you demonstrate this competency.

You have studied the regulatory framework in earlier papers. The following summaries will provide a quick reminder. Note that the UK regulatory framework is given in this International-stream Study Text as an example only.

1.2.1 Overview of the UK regulatory framework

The EU 8th Directive on company law requires that persons carrying out statutory audits must be approved by the authorities of EU member states. The authority to give this approval in the UK is delegated to Recognised Supervisory Bodies (RSBs). An auditor must be a member of an RSB and be eligible under its own rules. The ACCA is a RSB.

The RSBs are required to have rules to ensure that persons eligible for appointment as a company auditor are either (Companies Act):

- Individuals holding an appropriate qualification
- Firms controlled by qualified persons

The Financial Reporting Council

The Financial Reporting Council (FRC) is the UK's independent regulator for corporate reporting and governance.

Its aim is to promote confidence in corporate reporting and governance.

In pursuit of this aim its six objectives are to promote:
- High quality corporate reporting
- High quality auditing
- High quality actuarial practice
- High standards of corporate governance
- The integrity, competence and transparency of the accountancy and actuarial professions
- Its effectiveness as a unified independent regulator The functions it exercises in pursuit of these six objectives can be summarised as follows:
- Promoting high standards of corporate governance
- Setting, monitoring and enforcing accounting and auditing standards
- Setting actuarial standards

- Statutory oversight and regulation of auditors
- Operating an independent investigation and discipline scheme for public interest cases
- Overseeing the regulatory activities of the professional accountancy and actuarial bodies

1.2.2 International standard setting

International Standards on Auditing are produced by the International Auditing and Assurance Standards Board (IAASB), a technical standing committee of the International Federation of Accountants (IFAC). An explanation of the workings of the IAASB, the authority of the ISAs and so on are laid out in the *Preface to International Standards on Quality Control, Auditing, Assurance and Related Services*.

The *Preface* restates the mission of IFAC as set out in its constitution: 'The development and enhancement of an accountancy profession with harmonised standards able to provide services of consistently high quality in the public interest'.

Within each country, local regulations govern, to a greater or lesser degree, the practices followed in the auditing of financial or other information. Such regulations may be either of a statutory nature, or in the form of statements issued by the regulatory or professional bodies in the countries concerned.

National standards on auditing and related services published in many countries differ in form and content. The IAASB takes account of such documents and differences and, in the light of such knowledge, issues ISAs which are intended for international acceptance.

1.2.3 The IAASB clarity project

In 2003 the IAASB reviewed the drafting conventions used in its ISAs, with a view to improving the clarity and overall understandability, and therefore the consistent application of its ISAs.

With this in mind, the IAASB reissued its *Preface to International Standards on Quality Control, Auditing, Review, other Assurance and Related Services* in January 2007 in order to establish the conventions to be used by the Board in drafting future ISAs. In accordance with this redrafted ISAs are structured as follows:

- **Objective.** This provides the context in which the requirements of the ISA are met.
- **Requirements.** These are contained in a separate section and expressed using the word 'shall'.
- **Application and other explanatory material.** This is an integral part of the ISA.

1.2.4 Current ISAs

No	Title
200	Overall Objective of the Independent Auditor, and the Conduct of an Audit in Accordance with International Standards on Auditing
210	Agreeing the Terms of Audit Engagements
220	Quality Control for an Audit of Financial Statements
230	Audit documentation
240	The Auditor's Responsibilities Relating to Fraud in an Audit of Financial Statements
250	Consideration of Laws and Regulations in an Audit of Financial Statements
260	Communication with Those Charged with Governance
265	Communicating Deficiencies in Internal Control to Those Charged with Governance and Management
300	Planning an Audit of Financial Statements
315	Identifying and Assessing the Risks of Material Misstatement through Understanding the Entity and Its Environment
320	Materiality in Planning and Performing an Audit
330	The Auditor's Responses to Assessed Risks
402	Audit Considerations Relating to an Entity Using a Service Organization
450	Evaluation of Misstatements Identified during the Audit

No	Title
500	Audit Evidence
501	Audit – Specific Considerations for Selected Items
505	External Confirmations
510	Initial Audit Engagements-Opening Balances
520	Analytical Procedures
530	Audit Sampling
540	Auditing Accounting Estimates, Including Fair Value Accounting Estimates, and Related Disclosures
550	Related Parties
560	Subsequent Events
570	Going Concern
580	Written Representations
600	Special Considerations—Audits of Group Financial Statements (Including the Work of Component Auditors)
610	Using the Work of Internal Auditors
620	Using the Work of an Auditor's Expert
700	Forming an Opinion and Reporting on Financial Statements
705	Modifications to the Opinion in the Independent Auditor's Report
706	Emphasis of Matter Paragraphs and Other Matter Paragraphs in the Independent Auditor's Report
710	Comparative Information—Corresponding Figures and Comparative Financial Statements
720	The Auditor's Responsibilities Relating to Other Information in Documents Containing Audited Financial Statements
ISQC 1	Quality Controls for Firms that Perform Audits and Reviews of Financial Statements, and Other Assurance and Related Services Engagements

Notes

1   Students should be aware of the nature and meaning of the audit report and should be able to discuss the contents and wording of the report. Students would not be asked to reproduce the audit report in full in an exam question, but they may be requested to prepare explanatory paragraphs for inclusion in the report particularly in situations leading to a modified report.

2   Students are advised that questions will be based on the principles and good practice set out in the International Standards on Auditing.

Exam focus point

International standards are quoted throughout this text and you must understand how they are applied in practice. Make sure you refer to auditing standards when answering questions.

1.3 Public oversight

FAST FORWARD

Public oversight of the audit profession and of standard-setting has been a trend in recent regulatory developments internationally.

1.3.1 Public oversight internationally

In February 2005 the **Public Interest Oversight Board (PIOB)** was launched to exercise oversight for all of IFAC's 'public interest activities' including its standard-setting bodies such as the IAASB. Its work involves:

- Monitoring the standard-setting boards
- Overseeing the nomination process for membership of these boards
- Co-operation with national oversight authorities.

The objective of the international PIOB is to increase the confidence of investors and others that the public interest activities of IFAC are properly responsive to the public interest. The PIOB is based in Madrid, Spain, where it operates as a non-profit Spanish foundation.

1.3.2 Other examples of public oversight

An example of public oversight is the UK's Professional Oversight Board (POB) of the FRC, the independent regulator of corporate governance and reporting in the UK, is a regulatory body whose aim is to provide assurance that the professional accountancy bodies in the UK are properly setting standards and enforcing discipline for their members in accordance with UK-specific companies legislation and other statutory requirements.

 Case Study

Amongst other significant scandals in America in recent years was the Enron scandal, when one of the country's biggest companies filed for bankruptcy. The scandal also resulted in the disappearance of Arthur Andersen, one of the Big Five accountancy firms who had audited Enron's accounts. The main reasons why Enron collapsed were over-expansion in energy markets, eventually too much reliance on derivatives trading which eventually went wrong, breaches of federal law, and misleading and dishonest behaviour. However enquiries into the scandal exposed a number of deficiencies in the company's governance.

(a)   A lack of the transparency in the accounts especially in relation to certain investment vehicles that were kept off balance sheet.

(b)   The non-executive directors were weak, and there were conflicts of interest.

(c)   Inadequate scrutiny by the external auditors. Arthur Andersen failed to spot or failed to question dubious accounting treatments. Since Andersen's consultancy arm did a lot of work for Enron, there were allegations of conflicts of interest.

(d)   Information asymmetry where the directors and managers knew more than the investors.

(e)   Executive compensation methods were meant to align the interests of shareholders and directors, but seemed to encourage the overstatement of short-term profits. Particularly in the USA, where the tenure of Chief Executive Officers is fairly short, the temptation is strong to inflate profits in the hope that share options will have been cashed in by the time the problems are discovered.

In the US, the response to the breakdown of stock market trust caused by perceived inadequacies in corporate governance arrangements and the Enron scandal was the **Sarbanes-Oxley Act 2002.** The Act applies to all companies that are required to file periodic reports with the Securities and Exchange Commission (SEC).

The **Public Company Accounting Oversight Board (PCAOB)** is a private sector body in the USA created by Sarbanes-Oxley. Its aim is to oversee the auditors of public companies. Its stated purpose is to 'protect the interests of investors and further the public interest in the preparation of informative, fair and independent audit reports'. Its powers include setting auditing, quality control, ethics, independence and other standards relating to the preparation of audit reports by issuers. It also has the authority to regulate the non-audit services that audit firms can offer.

Sarbanes-Oxley has been criticised in some quarters for **not being strong enough** on certain issues, for example the selection of external auditors by the audit committee, and at the same time being over-rigid on others. Directors may be less likely to consult lawyers in the first place if they believe that legislation could override lawyer-client privilege.

In addition, it has been alleged that a Sarbanes-Oxley compliance industry has sprung up focusing companies' attention on complying with all aspects of the legislation, significant or much less important. This has distracted companies from **improving information flows** to the market and then allowing the market to make well-informed decisions. The Act has also done little to address the temptation provided by generous stock options to inflate profits, other than requiring possible forfeiture if accounts are subsequently restated.

Most significantly perhaps, there is recent evidence of companies turning away from the US Stock markets and towards other markets such as London. An article in the *Financial Times* suggested that this was partly due to companies tiring of the **increased compliance costs** associated with Sarbanes-Oxley implementation. In addition the nature of the **regulatory regime** may be an increasingly significant factor in listing decisions.

2 Audit committees

Audit committees are made up of non-executive directors and are perceived to increase confidence in financial reports.

Point to note

The detail on corporate governance issues in this chapter is based on UK law and regulations. It is included as an example of how law and regulations affect the auditor in this area.

2.1 UK Corporate Governance Code provisions

FRC Guidance on audit committees was first published in 2003 and updated in December 2010. The key requirement is that the board **would establish** an audit committee of **at least three, or in the case of smaller companies, two members**. The main role and responsibilities of the audit committee are listed below.

- To monitor the integrity of the financial statements of a company, and any formal announcements relating to the company's performance, reviewing significant financial reporting judgements contained in them.

- To review the company's internal financial controls and, unless expressly addressed by a separate board risk committee composed of independent directors or by the board itself, to review the company's internal control and risk management systems.

- To monitor and review the effectiveness of the company's internal audit function.

- To make recommendations to the board, for it to put to shareholders for their approval in general meeting, in relation to the appointment, re-appointment and removal of the external auditor and to approve the remuneration and terms of engagement of the external auditor.

- To review and monitor the external auditor's independence and objectivity and the effectiveness of the audit process, taking into consideration relevant UK professional and regulatory requirements.

- To develop and implement policy on the engagement of the external auditor to supply non audit services, taking into account relevant ethical guidance regarding the provision of non-audit services by the external audit firm and to report to the board, identifying any matters in respect of which it considers that action and improvement is needed and making recommendations as to the steps to be taken.

2.2 Advantages and disadvantages of audit committees

The key advantage to an auditor of having an audit committee is that such a committee of independent non-executive directors provides the auditor with an independent point of reference other than the executive directors of the company, in the event of disagreement arising.

Other **advantages** that are claimed to arise from the existence of an audit committee include:

(a) It will lead to **increased confidence** in the credibility and objectivity of financial reports.

(b) By specialising in the problems of financial reporting and thus, to some extent, fulfilling the directors' responsibility in this area, it will allow the **executive** directors to **devote their attention to management**.

(c) In cases where the interests of the company, the executive directors and the employees conflict, the audit committee might provide an **impartial body** for the auditors to consult.

(d)   The internal auditors will be able to report to the audit committee.

Opponents of audit committees argue that:

(a)   There may be **difficulty selecting** sufficient non-executive directors with the necessary competence in auditing matters for the committee to be really effective.

(b)   The establishment of such a **formalised reporting procedure** may **dissuade** the **auditors** from raising matters of judgement and limit them to reporting only on matters of fact.

(c)   **Costs** may be **increased**.

2.3 Role and function of audit committees

An appendix to the Cadbury Report, expands on the role and function of the audit committee.

'If they operate effectively, audit committees can bring significant benefits. In particular, they have the potential to:

(a)   Improve the quality of financial reporting, by reviewing the financial statements on behalf of the Board

(b)   Create a climate of discipline and control which will reduce the opportunity for fraud

(c)   Enable the non-executive directors to contribute an independent judgement and play a positive role

(d)   Help the finance director, by providing a forum in which he can raise issues of concern, and which he can use to get things done which might otherwise be difficult

(e)   Strengthen the position of the external auditor, by providing a channel of communication and forum for issues of concern

(f)   Provide a framework within which the external auditor can assert his independence in the event of a dispute with management

(g)   Strengthen the position of the internal audit function, by providing a greater degree of independence from management

(h)   Increase public confidence in the credibility and objectivity of financial statements.'

Question

Audit committees

Since 1978 all public companies in the United States of America have been required to have an audit committee as a condition of listing on the New York Stock Exchange.

(a)   Explain what you understand by the term audit committee.

(b)   List and briefly describe the duties and responsibilities of audit committees.

(c)   Discuss the advantages and disadvantages of audit committees.

Answer

(a)   An **audit committee** reviews financial information and liaises between the auditors and the company. It normally consists of the non-executive directors of the company, though there is no reason why other senior personnel should not also be involved.

(b)   (i)   To monitor the integrity of the financial statements of the company, reviewing significant financial reporting issues and judgements contained in them

(ii)   To review the company's internal financial control system and, unless expressly addressed by a separate risk committee or by the board itself, risk management systems

(iii)   To monitor and review the effectiveness of the company's internal audit function

(iv)   To make recommendations to the board in relation to the appointment of the external auditor and to approve the remuneration and terms of engagement of the external auditors

(v)   To monitor and review the external auditor's independence, objectivity and effectiveness, taking into consideration relevant professional and regulatory requirements

(vi) To develop and implement policy on the engagement of the external auditor to supply non-audit services, taking into account relevant ethical guidance regarding the provisions of non-audit services by the external audit firm

In addition to these responsibilities, any responsible audit committee is likely to want:

(1) To **ensure that the review procedures** for interim statements, rights documents and similar information are **adequate**

(2) To **review both the management accounts** used internally and the **statutory accounts** issued to shareholders for reasonableness

(3) To make **appropriate recommendations for improvements in management control**

(c) There are a number of advantages and disadvantages.

Disadvantages

(i) Since the findings of audit committees are rarely made public, it is **not** always **clear what they do** or how effective they have been in doing it.

(ii) It is possible that the audit committee's **approach** may prove somewhat **pedestrian,** resolving little of consequence but acting as a drag on the drive and entrepreneurial flair of the company's senior executives.

(iii) Unless the requirement for such a body were made compulsory, as in the US, it is likely that those **firms most in need** of an audit committee would nevertheless **choose not to have one.** (Note that the UK Corporate Governance Code requires listed companies to have an audit committee.)

Advantages

(i) By its very existence, the audit committee should make the **executive directors more aware of their duties and responsibilities.**

(ii) It could act as a **deterrent to the committing of illegal acts** by the executive directors and may discourage them from behaving in ways which could be prejudicial to the interests of the shareholders.

(iii) Where **illegal or prejudicial acts** have been carried out by the executive directors, the **audit committee** provides an **independent body** to which the auditor can turn. In this way, the problem may be resolved without the auditor having to reveal the matter to the shareholders, either in his report or at a general meeting of shareholders.

3 Internal control effectiveness

FAST FORWARD

Internal control is a key part of good corporate governance. Directors are responsible for maintaining a system of control that will safeguard the company's assets.

3.1 Importance of internal control and risk management

Internal controls are essential to management, as they contribute to:

- Safeguarding the company's assets
- Helping to prevent and detect fraud
- Therefore, safeguarding the shareholders' investment

Good internal control helps the business to run efficiently. A control system reduces identified risks to the business. It also helps to ensure reliability of reporting, and compliance with laws.

3.2 Directors' responsibilities

The **ultimate responsibility** for a company's system of internal controls lies with the board of directors. It should set procedures of internal control and regularly monitor that the system operates as it should.

Part of setting up an internal control system will involve **assessing the risks** facing the business, so that the **system** can be **designed** to ensure those **risks are avoided**. As you know from your earlier studies in auditing the system of internal control in a company will reflect the **control environment**, which includes the attitude of the directors towards risk, and their awareness of it.

Internal control systems will always have **inherent limitations**, the most important being that a system of internal control cannot eliminate the possibility of human error, or the chance that staff will collude in fraud.

Once the directors have set up a system of internal control, they are responsible for **reviewing** it regularly, to ensure that it **still meets its objectives**.

The board may decide that in order to carry out their review function properly they have to employ an **internal audit function** to undertake this task. The role of internal audit is discussed in more detail in Chapter 16, but this is potentially part of its function.

If the board does not see the need for an internal audit function, the UK Corporate Governance Code suggests that it revisits this decision on an annual basis, so that the **need for internal audit is regularly reviewed**.

The UK Corporate Governance Code recommends that the board of directors of listed companies **reports** on its review of internal controls as part of the annual report. The statement should be based on an annual assessment of internal control which should confirm that the board has considered **all significant aspects** of internal control. In particular the assessment should cover:

(a)   The **changes** since the last **assessment** in **risks** faced, and the company's **ability** to **respond** to **changes** in its business environment

(b)   The **scope** and **quality** of management's monitoring of risk and internal control, and of the work of internal audit, or consideration of the need for an internal audit function if the company does not have one

(c)   The **extent** and **frequency** of reports to the board

(d)   **Significant controls**, **failings** and **deficiencies** which have or might have material impacts upon the accounts

(e)   The effectiveness of the public reporting processes

3.3 Auditors' responsibilities

In response to a statement on internal controls by directors, auditors should concentrate on the review carried out by the board. The objective of the auditors' work is to assess whether the company's summary of the process that the board has adopted in reviewing the effectiveness of the system of internal control is supported by the documentation prepared by the directors and reflects that process.

The auditors should make appropriate enquiries and review the statement made by the board in the accounts and the supporting documentation.

Auditors will have gained some understanding of controls due to their work on the accounts; however what they are required to do by auditing standards is narrower in scope than the review performed by the directors.

Auditors therefore are not expected to assess whether the directors' review covers all risks and controls, and whether the risks are satisfactorily addressed by the internal controls. To avoid misunderstanding of the scope of the auditors' role, the auditors are recommended to use the following wording in the audit report.

'We are not required to consider whether the board's statements on internal control cover all risks and controls, or form an opinion on the effectiveness of the company's corporate governance procedures or its risk and control procedures.'

It is particularly important for auditors to communicate quickly to the directors any significant deficiencies they find, because of the requirements for the directors to make a statement on internal control.

The directors are required to consider the material internal control aspects of any significant problems disclosed in the accounts. Auditors' work on this is the same as on other aspects of the statement; the auditors are not required to consider whether the internal control processes will remedy the problem.

The auditors may report by exception if problems arise such as:

(a) The **board's summary** of the process of review of internal control effectiveness does **not reflect** the **auditors' understanding** of that process.

(b) The **processes** that **deal with** material internal control aspects of **significant problems** do **not reflect** the **auditors' understanding** of those processes.

(c) The board has **not made** an **appropriate disclosure** if it has **failed** to **conduct** an **annual review**, or the disclosure made is not consistent with the auditors' understanding.

The report should be included in a separate paragraph below the opinion paragraph. For example:

> **Other matter**
>
> We have reviewed the board's description of its process for reviewing the effectiveness of internal control set out on page x of the annual report. In our opinion the boards comments concerning... do not appropriately reflect our understanding of the process undertaken by the board because...

Critics of recent developments have argued that listed company directors ought to be able to report on the effectiveness of internal controls, and that this is part of the responsibility and accountability expected of listed company directors. The debate is likely to continue over the next few years.

3.4 Assurance services

Accountants may also provide assurance services relating to internal control systems. This is discussed in Chapter 12.

4 Money laundering   Pilot paper, 12/07, 12/09

FAST FORWARD Money laundering law is an increasingly important issue for auditors to be aware of.

Point to note This section is based on UK law and regulation. It is included as an example of how law and regulation affects the auditor in this area.

Key term 'ced**Money laundering** is the process by which criminals attempt to conceal the true origin and ownership of the proceeds of their criminal activity, allowing them to maintain control over the proceeds and, ultimately, providing a legitimate cover for their sources of income.'   ACCA *Code of Ethics and Conduct*

Money laundering is a particularly hot topic internationally. Clearly, auditors should consider it when assessing compliance risks at a client.

4.1 What is money laundering?

4.1.1 Background

Once they have gotten hold of money through crime, criminals face a difficulty when it comes to actually using it. For example, a group of organised criminals might generate huge amounts of money from dealing illegal drugs, but as soon as they try to spend it they end up drawing attention to the fact that they obtained the money from drug dealing. Usually the money to be laundered is in the form of **cash**.

Money laundering is the attempt to conceal the origin of this money by making it look legitimate or 'clean'. This is a big problem for the world economy: the IMF has stated that something like 2-5% of world GDP is likely to be related to money laundering.

4.1.2 How money is laundered

There are essentially three stages in laundering money:

1. **Placement**. This is the introduction or placement of the illegal funds into the financial system. Examples include (amongst many possibilities):

    - making **lots of small cash deposits** in numerous **bank accounts**;

    - using a **cash-intensive business**, such as a betting shop or a used car dealership, to disguise 'dirty' money as legitimate revenue.

2. **Layering**. This is passing the money through a large number of transactions or 'layers', so that it becomes very difficult to trace it to its original source. Examples include:

    - **transferring** the money **through multiple bank accounts**, perhaps across several **different national jurisdictions**;

    - making numerous purchases and sales of **investments**;

    - making fake sales between controlled companies (this can often be extremely subtle, eg through the use of invoices that do involve a transfer of goods, but which exaggerate the price).

Integration. This is the final integration of funds back into the legitimate economy. The criminal now has 'clean' money which can be spent or invested.

4.2 International recommendations and UK law

An inter-governmental body, the Financial Action Task Force on Money Laundering (FATF) was established to set standards and develop policies to combat money laundering and terrorist financing. In 1990, FATF issued 49 recommendations for governments on how to combat these offences and these recommendations have now been endorsed by more than 130 countries.

Relevant legislation in the UK includes:

- The Terrorism Act 2000
- The Proceeds of Crime Act 2002
- Money Laundering Regulations 2007 In Singapore, there are various pieces of legislation:
- Corruption, Drug Trafficking and Other Serious Crimes (Confiscation of Benefits) Act 1992
- Terrorism (Suppression of Financing) Act 2002
- United Nations Act 2001
- United Nations (Anti-Terrorism Measures) Regulations 2001

In Australia, the Anti-Money Laundering and Counter-Terrorism Financing Act 2006 is relevant.

4.3 Ethical guidance

4.3.1 Need for ethical guidance

Ethical guidance on money laundering is needed because applying the law involves making difficult judgements, particularly if there are confidentiality issues.

The ACCA has issued *Technical Factsheet 145* on *Anti-money laundering for the accounting sector* as guidance for its members on their responsibilities under this legislation. The ACCA's *Code of Ethics and Conduct* also includes detailed guidance for members on money laundering. Its requirements are very similar to those in the Technical Factsheets, but less detailed. The Technical Factsheet gives guidance in the context of current UK law, whereas the ethical guidance emphasises the international nature of money laundering and the need for ACCA members to be aware of local legal frameworks and the basic procedures to be applied, irrespective of where in the world their work is taking place.

4.3.2 Confidentiality and ethical conflict

'Ethical conflict' means conflict between the auditor's duty to be ethical and the auditor's relationship with the client. This conflict may be particularly sharp where an auditor suspects the client of money laundering. In the UK, there is a **legal requirement to report** even a **suspicion** of money laundering (see section 4.6 below), which would be likely to **conflict** with the auditor's **duty of confidentiality** to their client.

The situation is further complicated by the need to avoid 'tipping off' the client that the auditor suspects money laundering (see section 4.6.3 below), which could make it very difficult for an auditor to decide whether they have a duty to report their suspicions, as it would be hard to gather evidence of money laundering without tipping the client off.

If such an ethical conflict cannot be resolved then the auditor may consider **obtaining professional advice** from the ACCA or from legal advisors. This can generally be done without breaching the fundamental principle of confidentiality if the matter is discussion anonymously with the ACCA, or under legal privilege with a legal advisor.

4.4 Accountants' obligations

Many countries have now made money laundering a criminal offence. In some countries, such as the UK, Australia, Singapore and the USA, the criminal offences include those directed at accountants. It is useful to look in detail at the obligations of UK accountants in relation to the law regarding money laundering as an example.

In the UK, the basic requirements are for accountants to keep records of clients' identity and to report suspicions of money laundering to the **Serious Organised Crime Agency (SOCA)**. These obligations apply both to firms and to individuals. A firm must establish an anti-money laundering programme such as that set out below, which includes appointing a Money Laundering Reporting Officer (MLRO) who is responsible for reporting to SOCA. Individuals within the firm are then legally required to report any offences to the MLRO.

Elements of a money-laundering programme:

Procedures	Explanations
• Appoint a Money Laundering Reporting Officer (MLRO) and implement internal reporting procedures	• The MLRO should have a suitable level of seniority and experience. • Individuals should make internal reports of money laundering to the MLRO. • The MLRO must consider, and document the process, whether to report to SOCA, and document the process
• Train *individuals* to ensure that they are aware of the relevant legislation, know how to recognise and deal with potential *money laundering*, how to report suspicions to the *MLRO*, and how to identify *clients*	• Individuals should be trained in the firm's obligations under law, and their personal obligations. • They must be made aware of the firm's identification, record-keeping and reporting procedures.

Procedures	Explanations
• Establish internal procedures appropriate to forestall and prevent *money laundering*, and make relevant *individuals* aware of the procedures	• Procedures should cover – Client acceptance – Gathering 'know your client' (KYC) / 'Customer Due Diligence' (CDD) information (see section 4.4.1 below) – Controls over client money and transactions through the client account – Advice and services to clients that could be of use to a money launderer – Internal reporting lines – The role of the MLRO
• Verify the identity of new and existing *clients* and maintain evidence of identification (ie customer due diligence measures)	• The firm must be able to establish that new clients are who they claim to be • Typically, this will include taking copies of evidence such as passports, driving licences and utility bills • For a company this will include identities of directors and certificates of incorporation
• Maintain records of *client* identification, and any transactions undertaken for or with the *client*	• Special care needs to be taken when handling clients' money to avoid participation in a transaction involving money laundering.
• *Report* suspicions *of money laundering* to SOCA	• SOCA has designed standard disclosure forms.

4.4.1 'Customer due diligence' information

The firm must gather 'know your client' information. This includes:

- Who the client is
- Who controls it
- The purpose and intended nature of the business relationship
- The nature of the client
- The client's source of funds
- The client's business and economic purpose

KYC enables the audit firm to understand their client's business well enough to spot any unusual business activity. This assists the firm in identifying suspicions of money laundering.

In the UK the Money Laundering Regulations 2007 extended the circumstances under which Customer due diligence (CDD) must be carried out from new to existing clients.

Customer due diligence is the term used in the Money Laundering Regulations for the steps that businesses must take to:

(a) Identify the customer and verify their identity using documents, data or information obtained from a reliable and independent source.

(b) Identify any beneficial owner who is not the customer. This is the individual (or individuals) behind the customer who ultimately own or control the customer or on whose behalf a transaction or activity is being conducted.

(c) Where a business relationship is established, you will need to understand the purpose and intended nature of the relationship, for example details of customer's business or the source of the funds.

Businesses must also conduct ongoing monitoring to identify large, unusual or suspicious transactions as part of CDD.

The requirement to confirm the identity of customers and other individuals clearly links to the concept of KYC described above.

4.5 Risk-based approach

On any assignment, the auditor should assess the risk of money laundering activities. Clearly, every circumstance is different, but the following diagram illustrates some key risk factors.

Question

You are the audit manager of Loft Co, a chain of nightclubs across the north-west of England. During the course of the audit Mr Roy, an employee of the company, informed you that a substantial cash deposit was paid into the company's bank account and a month later, the same amount was paid by direct transfer into a bank account in the name of Evissa, a company based overseas. The employee also informed you that Mr Fox, the managing director of Loft Co had instructed him not to record the transaction in the accounting records as it had nothing to do with Loft Co's business.

Required

Comment on the situation outlined above.

Answer

The transaction described in the scenario raises suspicion of money laundering for several reasons.

(a)   It has been alleged by Mr Roy that the purpose of the transaction has nothing to do with the nightclub business. This could be a sign that Mr Fox is attempting to legitimise the proceeds of a crime through Loft Co by concealing the illegal source of the cash.

(b)   The amount of the transaction is substantial for Loft Co. An unusually large transaction should alert the auditor to the possibility of money laundering, especially as it does not seem to relate to the business of Loft Co.

(c)   The cash amount paid into Loft Co's bank account is the same as the amount paid to Evissa. This could be an attempt by Mr Fox to make the cash appear legitimate by moving it through several companies and jurisdictions.

(d)   Mr Roy was instructed not to record the transaction in the accounting records of Loft Co. Increased secrecy over transactions is another indicator of money laundering.

Loft Co's bank statement should be checked to confirm Mr Roy's assertion. The suspicious transaction should be reported to the firm's MLRO or SOCA as soon as possible and any 'tipping off' (see 4.5.3) must be avoided. It is a criminal offence to not report suspicions of money laundering.

4.6 The scope of criminal offences

The firm requires these procedures to avoid committing any of the wide range of offences under the UK's Money Laundering Regulations.

4.6.1 Money laundering offences

These include:

- Concealing criminal property
- 'Arranging' – becoming involved in an arrangement which is known or is suspected of facilitating the acquisition of criminal property
- Acquiring using or possessing criminal property.

Defences to these offences include:

- Reporting to SOCA or the MLRO before the act took place
- Reporting to SOCA or the MLRO after the act took place if there was good reason for the failure to report earlier

4.6.2 Failure to report offences under the legislation

Key term

Knowledge

- Actual knowledge
- Shutting one's mind to the obvious
- Deliberately deterring a person from making disclosures, the content of which one might not care to have
- Knowledge of circumstances which would indicate the facts to an honest and reasonable person
- Knowledge of circumstances which would put an honest and reasonable person on inquiry and failing to make the reasonable inquiries which such a person would have made

Suspicion

Suspicion is not defined in existing legislation. Case law and other sources indicate that suspicion is more than speculation but it falls short of proof or knowledge. Suspicion is personal and subjective but will generally be built on some objective foundation and so there should be some degree of consistency in how a *business's MLRO* treats possible causes of suspicion.

- Failure by an individual in the regulated sector to inform SOCA or the MLRO as soon as practicable of knowledge or suspicion of money laundering.
- Failure by the MLRO to pass on a report to SOCA as soon as possible.

  The defences here for an individual would include that there was a reasonable excuse for not having made a report, or that the person did not know or suspect money laundering and their employer has not provided them with appropriate training.

  The defence for the MLRO is that there is a reasonable excuse for not having made a report. The Court would consider whether relevant guidance, such as the ACCA Technical Factsheet, had been followed.

4.6.3 Tipping off and other offences

Tipping off is when the MLRO or any individual discloses something that might prejudice any investigations. It is a defence if the person did not know or suspect that it was likely to prejudice the investigation.

Other offences include:

- Falsifying, concealing, destroying or disposing of documents relevant to the investigation
- Consenting to a transaction which they know or suspect is money laundering, where consent has not been received from SOCA

5 Laws and regulations

FAST FORWARD

Auditors must be aware of laws and regulations as part of their planning and must be aware of any statutory duty to report non-compliance by the company.

5.1 Legal requirements relating to the company

Companies are increasingly subject to laws and regulations with which they must comply. Some examples are given in the following diagram.

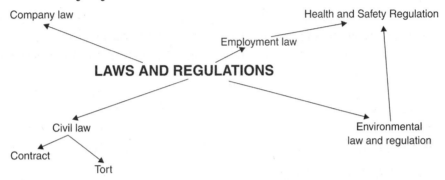

An auditor must be aware of the effect that non-compliance with the laws and regulations would have on the financial statements.

ISA 250 *Consideration of laws and regulations in an audit of financial statements* provides guidance on the auditor's responsibility to consider laws and regulations in an audit of financial statements.

5.2 Responsibility of management for compliance

It is the responsibility of management (with oversight from those charged with governance) to ensure a client's operations are conducted in accordance with laws and regulations.

The following policies and procedures, among others, may be implemented to assist management in the prevention and detection of non-compliance with laws and regulations.

- **Monitor legal requirements** and ensure that operating procedures are designed to meet these requirements
- **Institute and operate** appropriate systems of **internal control** including internal audit and an audit committee
- **Develop, publicise and follow a code of conduct**
- Ensure **employees** are properly **trained** and **understand the code of conduct**
- **Monitor compliance** with the code of conduct and act appropriately to **discipline** employees who fail to comply with it
- **Engage legal advisors** to assist in monitoring legal requirements
- **Maintain a register** of significant laws with which the entity has to comply within its particular industry and a record of complaints

'Non-compliance' refers to acts of omission or commission by the entity, either intentional or unintentional, which are contrary to the prevailing laws or regulations. Such acts include transactions entered into by the entity, or on its behalf by its management or employees. It does **not** include personal misconduct.

5.3 Responsibility of the auditor

As with fraud and error, the auditor is not, and cannot be held responsible for preventing non-compliance. There is an unavoidable risk that some material misstatements in the financial statements go undetected, even though the audit is properly planned and performed.

Certain factors will increase the risk of material misstatements due to non-compliance with laws and regulations not being detected by the auditor.

(a) There are many laws and regulations, relating principally to the operating aspects of an entity, that typically do **not affect the financial statements** and are not captured by the entity's information systems relevant to financial reporting.

(b) Non-compliance may involve conduct **designed to conceal** it, such as collusion, forgery, deliberate failure to record transactions, management override of controls or intentional misrepresentations being made to the auditor.

(c) Whether an act constitutes non-compliance is ultimately a matter for legal determination by a court of law.

Laws and regulations governing a business entity can vary enormously (financial disclosure rules, health and safety, pollution, employment, etc). Whether an act constitutes non-compliance is a legal matter that may be beyond the auditor's professional competence, although the auditor may have a fair idea in many cases through his knowledge and training. Ultimately such matters can only be decided by a court of law.

The further removed non-compliance is from the events and transactions normally reflected in the financial statements, the less likely the auditor is to become aware of it or recognise non-compliance.

ISA 250.10

The objectives of the auditor are:

(a) To obtain sufficient appropriate audit evidence regarding compliance with the provisions of those laws and regulations generally recognised to have a direct effect on the determination of material amounts and disclosures in the financial statements;

(b) To perform specified audit procedures to help identify instances of non-compliance with other laws and regulations that may have a material effect on the financial statements; and

(c) To respond appropriately to non-compliance or suspected non-compliance with laws and regulations identified during the audit.

5.4 The auditor's consideration of compliance

ISA 250.12

As part of obtaining an understanding of the entity and its environment in accordance with ISA 315, the auditor shall obtain a general understanding of:

(a) The legal and regulatory framework applicable to the entity and the industry or sector in which the entity operates; and

(b) How the entity is complying with that framework.

The auditor may obtain a general understanding of laws and regulations affecting the entity in the following ways.

- **Use the auditor's existing understanding** of the entity's industry, regulatory and other external factors
- **Update the understanding** of those laws and regulations that **directly** determine the reported amounts and disclosures in the financial statements.
- **Enquire of management** as to other laws or regulations that may be expected to have a fundamental effect on the operations of the entity

- **Enquire of management** concerning the entity's **policies and procedures** regarding compliance with laws and regulations
- **Enquire of management** the **policies or procedures** adopted for identifying, evaluating and accounting for **litigation claims.**

The auditor should obtain sufficient appropriate audit evidence of compliance with those **laws and regulations which have a direct effect on the determination of material amounts** and disclosures in the financial statements. These laws and regulations will be well-established, known to the entity and within the entity's industry and be relevant to the entity's financial statements. They could relate to the following.

- The form and content of financial statements
- Industry specific financial reporting issues
- Accounting for transactions under government contracts
- The accrual or recognition of expenses for income tax or pension costs

In obtaining this general understanding the auditor should obtain an understanding of the procedures followed by the entity to ensure compliance. The auditor should recognise that some laws and regulations may have a **fundamental effect** on the operations of the entity, ie they may cause the entity to cease operations or call into question the entity's continuance as a going concern. For example, non-compliance with the requirements of the entity's licence or other title to perform its operations could have such an impact (for example, for a bank, non-compliance with capital or investment requirements).

The auditor would usually obtain a general understanding of laws and regulations affecting the entity in the following ways.

- **Use the existing knowledge** of the entity's industry and business
- **Enquire of management** concerning the entity's **policies and procedures** regarding compliance with laws and regulations
- **Enquire of management** as to the laws or regulations that may be expected to have a fundamental effect on the operations of the entity
- **Discuss with management** the **policies or procedures** adopted for identifying, evaluating and accounting for **litigation claims and assessments**

ISA 250.14

The auditor shall perform the following audit procedures to help identify instances of non-compliance with **other laws and regulations that may have a material effect** on the financial statements:

(a)   Inquiring of management and, where appropriate, those charged with governance, as to whether the entity is in compliance with such laws and regulations; and

(b)   Inspecting correspondence, if any, with the relevant licensing or regulatory authorities.

ISA 250.15

During the audit, the auditor shall remain alert to the possibility that other audit procedures applied may bring instances of non-compliance or suspected non-compliance with laws and regulations to the auditor's attention.

Examples include the following.

- Reading minutes
- Enquiring of the entity's management and in-house legal counsel or external legal counsel concerning litigation, claims and assessments
- Performing substantive tests of details of classes of transactions, account balances or disclosures

In the absence of identified or suspected non-compliance, the auditor is not required to perform audit procedures other than those detailed above.

5.4.1 Audit procedures when non-compliance is identified or suspected

The ISA sets out examples of the type of information that might come to the auditor's attention that may indicate non-compliance.

- **Investigation** by a **regulatory organisation** or **government department** or payment of fines or penalties
- **Payments** for **unspecified services** or loans to consultants, related parties, employees or government employees
- **Sales commissions** or agents' fees that appear excessive in relation to those normally paid by the entity or in its industry or to the services actually received
- **Purchasing** at **prices significantly above** or **below market price**
- **Unusual payments** in **cash**, purchases in the form of cashiers' cheques payable to bearer or transfers to numbered bank accounts
- **Unusual transactions** with companies registered in **tax havens**
- **Payments for goods or services made other than to the country from which** the goods or services **originated**
- **Payments without proper exchange control documentation**
- **Existence** of an **information system** that **fails**, whether by design or by accident, to **provide an adequate audit trail** or sufficient evidence
- **Unauthorised transactions** or improperly recorded transactions
- **Adverse media comment**

When evaluating the possible effect on the financial statements, the auditor should consider the following.

- The **potential financial consequences**, such as fines, penalties, damages, threat of expropriation of assets, enforced discontinuation of operations and litigation
- Whether the **potential financial consequences** require **disclosure**
- Whether the potential financial consequences are so serious as to call into question the **fair presentation** given by the financial statements, or otherwise make the financial statements misleading.

Such discussions are subject to the laws concerning 'tipping off' (see Section 4.5.3). If information provided by management is not sufficient, the auditor may find it appropriate to consult the entity's lawyer and, if necessary, his own lawyer on the application of the laws and regulations to the particular circumstances.

> **ISA 250.20/21**
>
> If sufficient information about suspected non-compliance cannot be obtained, the auditor shall evaluate the effect of the lack of sufficient appropriate audit evidence on the auditor's opinion
>
> The auditor shall evaluate the implications of non-compliance in relation to other aspects of the audit, including the auditor's risk assessment and the reliability of written representations, and take appropriate action.

On this last point, as with fraud and error, the auditor must reassess the risk assessment and the validity of written representations. In exceptional cases, the auditor may consider whether withdrawal from the engagement is necessary. If withdrawal from the engagement is not possible under applicable law or regulation, the auditor may consider alternative actions including describing the non-compliance in an Other Matters paragraph in the auditor's report.

5.5 Reporting of identified or suspected non-compliance

5.5.1 To those charged with governance

> **ISA 250.22/23/24**
>
> ...the auditor shall communicate with those charged with governance matters involving non-compliance with laws and regulations that come to the auditor's attention during the course of the audit, other than when the matters are clearly inconsequential.
>
> If, in the auditor's judgment, the non-compliance... is believed to be intentional and material, the auditor shall communicate the matter to those charged with governance as soon as practicable.
>
> If the auditor suspects that management or those charged with governance are involved in non-compliance, the auditor shall communicate the matter to the next higher level of authority at the entity, if it exists, such as an audit committee or supervisory board.

In relation to the last point, where no higher authority exists, or if the auditor believes that the communication may not be acted upon or is unsure as to the person to whom to report, the auditor shall consider seeking legal advice.

5.5.2 To the users of the auditor's report

> **ISA 250.25/26/27**
>
> If the auditor concludes that the non-compliance has a material effect on the financial statements, and has not been adequately reflected in the financial statements, the auditor shall... express a qualified opinion or an adverse opinion on the financial statements.
>
> If the auditor is precluded by management or those charged with governance from obtaining sufficient appropriate audit evidence to evaluate whether non-compliance that may be material to the financial statements has, or is likely to have, occurred, the auditor shall express a qualified opinion or disclaim an opinion on the financial statements on the basis of a limitation on the scope of the audit...
>
> If the auditor is unable to determine whether non-compliance has occurred because of limitations imposed by the circumstances rather than by management or those charged with governance, the auditor shall evaluate the effect on the auditor's opinion...

5.5.3 To regulatory and enforcement authorities

Confidentiality is an issue again here, but it may be overridden by the law, statute or the courts of law. The auditor should obtain legal advice. If the auditor has a statutory duty to report, a report should be made without delay.

Alternatively, it may be necessary to make disclosures in the public interest. In practice it will often be extremely difficult for an auditor to decide whether making a disclosure in the public interest is warranted. As elsewhere, the auditor should obtain professional advice, either anonymously from the ACCA, or under legal privilege from a legal advisor.

5.6 Withdrawal from the engagement

As is the case for fraud or error, withdrawal may be the only option if the entity does not take the remedial action the auditor thinks is necessary, even for non-material matters.

5.7 Documentation

The auditor must document identified or suspected non-compliance with laws and regulations and the results of discussions with management and, where applicable, those charged with governance and other parties outside the entity.

5.8 Practical problems with ISA 250

5.8.1 Distinction between types of law

The most difficult distinction in practice is between:

- Laws which have a **direct effect** on the determination of material amounts in the financial statements

- Other laws and regulations In practice:

(a) For some businesses, certain laws and regulations have a direct effect on material amounts in the financial statements, for other businesses the **same** laws and regulations will not.

(b) For some businesses, laws and regulations which did not have a direct or material effect last year may have this year, (for example, where the maximum penalty for a first offence is a warning, but subsequent infringements may lead to closure of the business).

5.8.2 Procedures that should be performed

There is a distinction between checking systems of compliance and checking actual compliance. An example would be emissions from a chemical factory; auditors would review the company's systems for keeping these under control, and would also review correspondence with the environmental authority. However, the auditors would not be expected to check the actual emissions.

Chapter Roundup

- Major developments in international regulation of audit and assurance have recently concluded, with far-reaching effects on ISAs.

- Public oversight of the audit profession and of standard-setting has been a trend in recent regulatory developments internationally.

- Audit committees are made up of non-executive directors and are perceived to increase confidence in financial reports.

- Internal control is a key part of good corporate governance. Directors are responsible for maintaining a system of control that will safeguard the company's assets.

- Money laundering law is an increasingly important issue for auditors to be aware of.

- Auditors must be aware of laws and regulations as part of their planning and must be aware of any statutory duty to report non-compliance by the company.

1   ISAs are set by the .... This is a technical standing committee of the .... Oversight for all of IFAC's public interest activities is undertaken by the ....

2   List four potential duties of the audit committee.

    (1)   ....

    (2)   ....

    (3)   ....

    (4)   ....

3   Auditors are responsible for a company's system of internal controls.

    True   ☐

    False ☐

4   List the main elements of an anti-money-laundering program that should be followed by a firm of professional accountants.

    (1)   ....

    (2)   ....

    (3)   ....

    (4)   ....

    (5)   ....

    (6)   ....

5   Name four areas of law which might affect a company.

    (1)   ....

    (2)   ....

    (3)   ....

    (4)   ....

6   It is the responsibility of the auditor to ensure a client's operations are conducted in accordance with laws and regulations.

    True   ☐

    False ☐

Answers to Quick Quiz

1   International Auditing and Assurance Standards Board, International Federation of Accountants, Public Interest Oversight Board.

2
- (1) Review of financial statements
- (2) Liaison with external auditors
- (3) Review of internal audit
- (4) Review of internal controls

3   False – this is the directors' duty.

4
- (1) Appoint a Money Laundering Reporting Officer (MLRO) and set up internal reporting procedures
- (2) Train individuals about the legal requirements and the firm's procedures
- (3) Establish appropriate internal procedures
- (4) Verify the identity of new clients/existing clients
- (5) Maintain records of client identification
- (6) Report suspicions of money laundering to SOCA (in the UK)

5   From:
- (1) Company law
- (2) Contract law
- (3) Tort law
- (4) Employment law
- (5) Environmental law

6   False – it is the responsibility of management (with oversight from those charged with governance)

Now try the questions below from the Exam Question Bank

Number	Level	Marks	Time
Q9	Introductory	N/A	N/A

Professional and ethical considerations

Code of ethics and conduct

Topic list	Syllabus reference
1 Fundamental principles and the conceptual framework approach	B1
2 Specific guidance: Independence	B1
3 Specific guidance: Confidentiality	B1
4 Specific guidance: Conflicts of interest	B1
5 Conflicts in application of the fundamental principles	B1

Introduction

You have already learnt about ethical rules for auditors in your earlier studies. We will examine the issues in more detail and consider some of the complex ethical issues that auditors may face.

We also refer to the ethical guidance of the International Federation of Accountants. This is similar to the ACCA's guidance. Both approach issues of ethics in a conceptual manner.

ISQC 1 *Quality control for firms that perform audits and reviews of financial statements and other assurance and related services engagements*, is also relevant in providing the ethical aspects of quality control and review.

Some of this chapter is likely to be revision, but that does not mean you should ignore it. Ethics is a key syllabus area. Complex ethical issues are introduced in this chapter. You particularly need to work through the questions given so that you practise **applying** ethical guidelines in given scenarios as this is how this topic will be tested in the exam.

Study guide

		Intellectual level
B1	**Code of ethics for professional accountants**	
(a)	Explain the fundamental principles and the conceptual framework approach	1
(b)	Identify, evaluate and respond to threats to compliance with the fundamental principles	3
(c)	Discuss and evaluate the effectiveness of available safeguards	3
(d)	Recognise and advise on conflicts in the application of fundamental principles	3
G1	**Current issues and developments**	
(a)	Discuss the relative advantages of an ethical framework and a rulebook.	2
(b)	Identify and assess relevant emerging ethical issues and evaluate the safeguards available.	3
(c)	Discuss IFAC developments.	2

Exam guide

Professional ethics are of vital importance to the audit and assurance profession so this area is likely to be a regular feature of the exam.

Questions are likely to be practical, giving scenarios where you are required to assess whether the situations are acceptable. Some of these can be answered by reference to specific guidance in the ACCA *Code of Ethics and Conduct* but others may require you to apply your understanding of the fundamental principles underlying the Code.

You may also have to suggest appropriate safeguards that the audit firm should implement.

1 Fundamental principles and the conceptual framework approach
Pilot paper, 12/07, 6/09

FAST FORWARD

Accountants require an ethical code because they hold positions of trust, and people rely on them.

1.1 The importance of ethics

The IESBA's *Code of Ethics for Professional Accountants* gives the key reason why accountancy bodies produce ethical guidance: **the public interest**.

'A distinguishing mark of the accountancy profession is its acceptance of the responsibility to act in the public interest. Therefore, a professional accountant's responsibility is not exclusively to satisfy the needs of an individual client or employer.'

The public interest is considered to be the collective well-being of the community of people and institutions the professional accountant serves, including clients, lenders, governments, employers, employees, investors, the business and financial community and others who rely on the work of professional accountants.

The **key reason** that **accountants need** to have an **ethical code** is that **people rely on them and their expertise.**

Accountants deal with a range of issues on behalf of clients. They often have access to confidential and sensitive information. Auditors claim to give an independent view. It is therefore critical that accountants, and particularly auditors, are, and are seen to be, independent.

1.2 Sources of ethical guidance

As the auditor is required to be, and seen to be, ethical in his dealings with clients, ACCA publishes guidance for its members in its *Code of Ethics and Conduct*. This guidance is given in the form of fundamental principles, guidance and explanatory notes.

The IESBA (International Ethics Standards Board for Accountants), a body of IFAC, also lays down fundamental principles in its *Code of Ethics for Professional Accountants*. The fundamental principles of the two associations are extremely similar.

One of the competencies you require to fulfil performance objective 1 of the PER is the ability to uphold (and be seen to uphold) professional ethics, values and standards. You can apply the knowledge you have obtained from this chapter of the text to help demonstrate this competence.

1.3 The fundamental principles

ACCA

Integrity. Members should be **straightforward** and **honest** in all professional and business relationships.

Objectivity. Members **should not allow bias, conflict of interest or undue influence of others** to override professional or business judgements.

Professional competence and due care. Members have a continuing duty to maintain professional knowledge and skill at a level required to ensure that a client or employer receives the advantage of competent professional service based on current developments in practice, legislation and techniques. Members should act diligently and in accordance with applicable technical and professional standards when providing professional services.

Confidentiality. Members should respect the confidentiality of information acquired as a result of professional or business relationships **and should not disclose** any such information to third parties without proper and specific authority **unless there is a legal or professional right or duty to disclose**. Confidential information acquired as a result of professional and business relationships should not be used for the personal advantage of the professional accountant or third parties.

Professional behaviour. Members should **comply with relevant laws and regulations and should avoid any action that discredits the profession**.

1.4 The conceptual framework

The ethical guidance discussed above is in the form of a conceptual framework. It contains some rules, for example, ACCA prohibits making loans to clients, but in the main it is flexible guidance. It can be seen as a **framework rather than a set of rules**. There are a number of advantages of a framework over a system of ethical rules. These are outlined in the table below.

Advantages of an ethical framework over a rules based system

A framework of guidance places the onus on the auditor to **actively consider** independence for every given situation, rather than just agreeing a checklist of forbidden items. It also requires him to **demonstrate** that a responsible conclusion has been reached about ethical issues.

The framework **prevents auditors interpreting legalistic requirements narrowly** to get around the ethical requirements. There is an extent to which rules engender deception, whereas principles encourage compliance.

A framework **allows for** the variations that are found in every **individual situation**. Each situation is likely to be different.

A framework can accommodate a **rapidly changing environment**, such as the one that auditors are constantly in.

However, a **framework can contain prohibitions** (as noted above) where these are necessary as safeguards are not feasible.

1.5 Threats to compliance with the fundamental principles

There are five general sources of threat:

- **Self-interest** threat (for example, having a financial interest in a client)
- **Self-review** threat (for example, auditing financial statements prepared by the firm)
- **Advocacy** threat (for example, promoting shares in a listed entity when that entity is a financial statement audit client)
- **Familiarity** threat (for example, an audit team member having family at the client)
- **Intimidation** threat (for example, threats of replacement due to disagreement)

1.6 Available safeguards

There are three general categories of safeguard:

- Safeguards created by the profession, legislation or regulation
- Safeguards in the work environment
- Safeguards created by the individual

Examples of safeguards created by the **profession**, **legislation** or **regulation**:

- Educational training and experience requirements for entry into the profession
- Continuing professional development requirements
- Corporate governance regulations
- Professional standards
- Professional or regulatory monitoring and disciplinary procedures
- External review by a legally empowered third party of the reports, returns, communication or information produced by a professional accountant.

IFAC issues ethical standards (through the IESBA), quality control standards and auditing standards which work together to ensure independence is safeguarded and quality audits are carried out. The regulatory framework was discussed in Chapter 1.

Examples of safeguards in the **work environment**:

- Involving an additional professional accountant to review the work done or otherwise advise as necessary
- Consulting an independent third party, such as a committee of independent directors, a professional regulatory body or another professional accountant
- Appropriate disciplinary processes
- Timely communication of the employing organisation's policies and procedures, including any changes to them, to all employees and appropriate training and education on such policies and procedures
- Using different partners and engagement teams with separate reporting lines for the provision of non-assurance services to clients
- Discussing ethical issues with those in charge of client governance
- Disclosing to those charged with governance the nature of services provided and extent of fees charged
- Involving another firm to perform or reperform part of the engagement

Example of safeguards created by **the individual**:

- Complying with continuing professional development requirements
- Keeping records of contentious issues and approach to decision-making
- Maintaining a broader perspective on how similar organisations function through establishing business relationships with other professionals
- Using an independent mentor
- Maintaining contact with legal advisors and professional bodies

The **specific** threats arising within these general areas and the effectiveness of the available safeguards will be considered in Section 2.

2 Specific guidance: Independence   6/08, 12/08, 6/09, 6/10

The ACCA's guidance was designed to comply with the requirements of the IESBA Code

2.1 Objective of the guidance

You should be familiar with the concept of independence from your earlier studies.

The IESBA Code discusses independence requirements for audit and review engagements in section 290.

The guidance states its purpose in a series of steps. It aims to help firms and members:

Step 1   **Identify threats** to independence

Step 2   **Evaluate** the **significance** of the threats identified

Step 3   **Apply safeguards** when necessary to eliminate the threats and reduce them to an acceptable level.

It also recognises that there may be occasions **where no safeguard is available**. In such a situation, it is only appropriate to:

- **Eliminate the interest** or activities causing the threat
- **Decline the engagement**, or discontinue it

Exam focus point

You should apply the three steps set out above when approaching questions of independence, and show the examiner that you have done so in your answer. Remember, if there appears to be no safeguard, you must consider the fallback option of not continuing with the professional relationship.

2.1.1 Current issues in ethical guidance

This is currently a very topical area within the profession. Auditor independence has been under intense outside scrutiny since the financial crisis of 2007-8. Recent debate has focused on the provision of non-audit services alongside the external audit. In September 2011 details were made public of EC proposals to ban non-audit work for auditors of larger companies, along with mandatory auditor rotation and mandatory joint audits for companies with balance sheets larger than €1bn. You need to keep an eye on the professional press for any developments in this fast-changing area.

The IESBA (and IFAC) revised its *Code of Ethics for Professional Accountants* in July 2009. The revised IFAC *Code of Ethics for Professional Accountants* was effective on 1 January 2011. In 2011 the ACCA revised its *Code of Ethics and Conduct* to reflect these changes. The ACCA Code reproduces much of the IESBA Code guidance, and then augments it with stricter requirements for ACCA members in some areas.

2.1.2 Public interest entities

The revised IESBA Code introduced the concept of a public interest entity , which effectively replaced the older notion of a 'listed entity'. To be precise, the Code (290.25-26) defines a public interest entity as:

(i)   Any listed entity; and

(ii)   Any entity defined by regulation or legislation as a public interest entity; or

(iii)   Any entity that is required by legislation or regulation to have an audit that is as independent as an audit of a listed entity would be; and

(iv)   Any other entity the firm determines to be a public interest entity, because it has a large number and wide range of stakeholders. Factors to be considered include:

- The nature of the business, such as the holding of assets in a fiduciary capacity for a large number of stakeholders. Examples may include financial institutions, such as banks and insurance companies, and pension funds;

- Size; and

- Number of employees.

The distinction between 'public interest entities' and other entities then allows the Code to prescribe stricter requirements for the public interest entities.

Exam focus point

At P7 level you must be able to do more than just recite this definition in your exam. You should be able to recognise a public interest entity in a question, and adapt your answer accordingly.

2.2 What is independence?

A provider of assurance services must be, and be seen to be, independent. What is required for this to be the case?

Key terms

Independence of mind: The state of mind that permits the provision of an opinion without being affected by influences that compromise professional judgement, allowing an individual to act with integrity, and exercise objectivity and professional scepticism.

Independence in appearance: The avoidance of facts and circumstances that are so significant that a reasonable and informed third party, having knowledge of all relevant information, including safeguards applied, would reasonably conclude a firm's, or a member of the assurance team's, integrity, objectivity or professional scepticism had been compromised.

The degree of independence required is less stringent for a low level assurance engagement to non-audit clients than for audit. This is summarised in the following table:

	Audit	Non-audit, general use	Non-audit, restricted use
Audit client	The assurance team, the firm and the network firm must all be independent of the client.	The assurance team, the firm and the network firm must all be independent of the client.	The assurance team, the firm and the network firm must all be independent of the client.
Non-audit assurance client	N/A	The assurance team and the firm must be independent of the client.	The assurance team and the firm must have no material financial interest in the client.

2.3 When must the assurance provider be independent?

The team and the firm should be independent 'during the period of the engagement'.

The period of the engagement is from the commencement of work until the signing of the final report being produced. For a **recurring audit**, independence may only cease on **termination of the contract** between the parties.

Both the ACCA and the IESBA codes give examples of a number of situations where independence might be threatened and suggest safeguards to independence.

2.4 Revision of threats to independence

The area of threats to independence should not be new to you. You should be aware of many of the threats to independence from your earlier studies in auditing. To refresh your memory about independence issues, try the following question.

Question   Revision of audit independence

From your knowledge brought forward from your previous studies, and any practical experience of auditing you may have, write down as many potential ethical risk areas as you can in the areas below. (Some issues may be relevant in more than one column.)

Personal interests	Review of your own work	Disputes	Intimidation

Answer

Personal interests	Review of your own work	Disputes	Intimidation
Undue dependence on an audit client due to fee levels	Auditor prepares the accounts	Actual litigation with a client	Any threat of litigation by the client
Overdue fees becoming similar to a loan	Auditor participates in management decisions	Threatened litigation with a client	Personal relationships with the client
An actual loan being made to a client	Provision of any other services to the client	Client refuses to pay fees and they become long overdue	Hospitality
Contingency fees being offered			Threat of other services provided to the client being put out to tender
Accepting commissions from clients			Threat of any services being put out to tender
Provision of lucrative other			

Personal interests	Review of your own work	Disputes	Intimidation
services to clients			
Relationships with persons in associated practices			
Relationships with the client			
Long association with clients			
Beneficial interest in shares or other investments			
Hospitality			

The ACCA and IESBA codes give extensive lists of examples of threats to independence and applicable safeguards. In the rest of this section, these threats and some relevant factors and potential safeguards will be outlined. Definite rules are shown in bold. You should learn these.

Exam focus point

It is important that you read through this section and think about the issues raised in each example, rather than just turning to Section 3 and trying to learn rules for each situation. In this exam, it is important that you can apply the spirit of the guidance to a given situation, using the three steps given in Section 2.

2.5 Self-interest threat   12/10

The ACCA *Code of Ethics and Conduct* highlights a great number of areas in which a self-interest threat might arise.

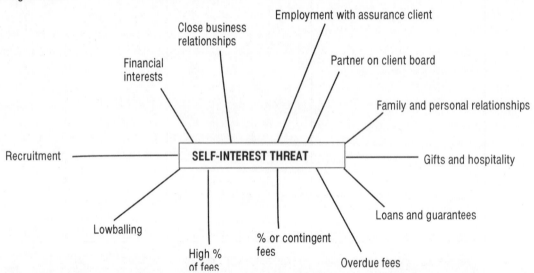

2.5.1 Financial interests

Key term

A **financial interest** exists where an audit firm has a financial interest in a client's affairs, for example, the audit firm owns shares in the client, or is a trustee of a trust that holds shares in the client.

A financial interest in a client constitutes a substantial self-interest threat. According to both the ACCA and the IESBA, **the parties listed below are not allowed to own a direct financial interest or an indirect material financial interest in a client**:

- The assurance firm
- A member of the assurance team
- An immediate family member of a member of the assurance team

The following safeguards will therefore be relevant:

- Disposing of the interest
- Removing the individual from the team if required
- Keeping the client's audit committee informed of the situation
- Using an independent partner to review work carried out if necessary

Such matters will involve judgement on the part of the partners making decisions about such matters. For example, what constitutes a material interest? A small percentage stake in a company might be material to its owner. How does the firm judge the closeness of a relationship between staff and their families, in other words, what does immediate mean in this context?

Audit firms should have quality control procedures requiring staff to disclose relevant financial interests for themselves and close family members. They should also foster a culture of voluntary disclosure on an on-going basis so that any potential problems are identified on a timely basis.

Question   Financial interests

You are the Ethics Partner at Stewart Brice, a firm of Chartered Certified Accountants. The following situations exist.

Teresa is the audit manager assigned to the audit of Recreate, a large quoted company. The audit has been on-going for one week. Yesterday, Teresa's husband inherited 1,000 shares in Recreate. Teresa's husband wants to hold on to the shares as an investment.

The Stewart Brice pension scheme, which is administered by Friends Benevolent, an unconnected company, owns shares in Tadpole Group, a listed company with a number of subsidiaries. Stewart Brice has recently been invited to tender for the audit of one of the subsidiary companies, Kermit Co.

Stewart Brice has been the auditor of Kripps Bros, a limited liability company, for a number of years. It is a requirement of Kripps Bros' constitution that the auditor owns a token $1 share in the company.

Required

Comment on the ethical and other professional issues raised by the above matters.

Answer

(a) Teresa is at present a member of the assurance team and a member of her immediate family owns a direct financial interest in the audit client. This is unacceptable.

In order to mitigate the risk to independence that this poses on the audit, Stewart Brice needs to apply one of two safeguards:

- Ensure that the connected person divests the shares
- Remove Teresa from the engagement team

Teresa should be appraised that these are the options and removed from the team while a decision is taken whether to divest the shares. Teresa's husband appears to want to keep the shares, in which case, Teresa should be removed from the team immediately.

The firm should appraise the audit committee of Recreate of what has happened and the actions they have taken. The partners should consider whether it is necessary to bring in an independent partner to review audit work. However, given that Teresa's involvement is subject to the review of the existing engagement partner and she was not connected with the shares while she was carrying out the work, a second partner review is likely to be unnecessary in this case.

(b) The audit firm has an indirect interest in the parent company of a company it has been invited to tender for by virtue of its pension scheme having invested in Tadpole Group.

This is no barrier to the audit firm tendering for the audit of Kermit Co.

Should the audit firm win the tender and become the auditors of Kermit Co they should consider whether it is necessary to apply safeguards to mitigate against the risk to independence on the audit as a result of the indirect financial interest.

The factors that the partners will need to consider are the materiality of the interest to either party and the degree of control that the firm actually has over the financial interest.

In this case, the audit firm has no control over the financial interest. An independent pension scheme administrator is in control of the financial interest. In addition, the interest is unlikely to be substantial and is therefore immaterial to both parties. Only if the threat is significant should the interest be divested.

It is likely that this risk is already sufficiently minimal so as not to require safeguards. However, if the audit firm felt that it was necessary to apply safeguards, they could consider the following:

- Notifying the audit committee of the interest
- Requiring Friends Benevolent to dispose of the shares in Tadpole Group

(c)   In this case, Stewart Brice has a direct financial interest in the audit client, which is technically forbidden by ACCA guidance. However, it is a requirement of any firm auditing the company that the share be owned by the auditors.

The interest is not material. The audit firm should safeguard against the risk by not voting on its own re-election as auditor. The firm should also strongly recommend to the company that it removes this requirement from its constitution as it is at odds with ethical requirements for auditors.

2.5.2 Close business relationships

Examples of when an audit firm and an audit client have an inappropriately close business relationship include:

- Having a material financial interest in a joint venture with the assurance client
- Arrangements to combine one or more services or products of the firm with one or more services or products of the assurance client and to market the package with reference to both parties
- Distribution or marketing arrangements under which the firm acts as distributor or marketer of the assurance client's products or services or *vice versa*

Again, it will be necessary for the partners to judge the materiality of the interest and therefore its significance. However, **unless the interest is clearly insignificant, an assurance provider should not participate in such a venture with an assurance client**. Appropriate safeguards are therefore to end the assurance provision or to terminate the (other) business relationship.

If an individual member of an audit team had such an interest, he should be removed from the audit team.

However, if the firm or a member (and immediate family of the member) of the audit team has an interest in an entity when the client or its officers also has an interest in that entity, the threat might not be so great.

Generally speaking, **purchasing goods and services from an assurance client on an arm's length basis does not constitute a threat to independence**. If there are a substantial number of such transactions, there may be a threat to independence and safeguards may be necessary.

2.5.3 Employment with an audit client

It is possible that staff might transfer between an assurance firm and a client, or that negotiations or interviews to facilitate such movement might take place. Both situations are a threat to independence:

- An audit staff member might be motivated by a desire to impress a future possible employer (objectivity is therefore affected – self-interest threat)

- A former partner turned Finance Director has too much knowledge of the audit firm's systems and procedures

In general there may be **familiarity** and **intimidation threats** when a member of the audit team joins an audit client. If a **'significant connection'** still **remains** between the audit firm and the former employee/partner, **then no safeguards could reduce the threat to an acceptable level**. This would be the case where:

- The individual is entitled to benefits from the audit firm (unless fixed and predetermined, and not material to the firm)
- The individual continues to participate in the audit firm's business or professional activities.

If there is no significant connection, then the threat depends on:

- The **position** the individual has taken at the client;
- Any **involvement** the individual will have **with the audit team**;
- The **length of time** since the individual was a member of the audit team or partner of the firm; and
- The **former position** of the individual **within the audit team or firm**, for example, whether the individual was responsible for maintaining regular contact with the client's management or those charged with governance.

Safeguards could include:

- **Modifying** the **audit plan**;
- **Assigning individuals** to the audit team **who have sufficient experience** in relation to the individual who has joined the client; or
- Having an independent professional accountant **review** the work of the former member of the audit team.

If the **audit client** is a **public interest entity**, 'cooling off' periods are required. Both the ACCA and IESBA Codes state that **when a key audit partner joins such a client**, either as a director or as an employee with significant influence on the financial statements, the client must have issued audited financial statements covering at least 12 months before the employment can begin.

In the case of a **senior or managing partner joining an audit client**, 12 months must have passed (ie there is no requirement for audited financial statements to have been issued).

Key term

> The **key audit partner** is the:
>
> - engagement partner
> - individual responsible for the engagement quality control review
> - other audit partners on the engagement team
>
> **who make key decisions or judgments on significant matters with respect to the audit** of the financial statements on which the firm will express an opinion. Depending upon the circumstances and the role of the individuals on the audit, "other audit partners" may include, for example, audit partners responsible for significant subsidiaries or divisions.

2.5.4 Temporary staff assignments

Staff may be loaned to an audit client, but only **for a short period of time. Staff must not assume management responsibilities**, or undertake any assurance work that is prohibited elsewhere in the Code. The audit client must be responsible for directing and supervising the activities of the loaned staff.

Possible safeguards include:

- Conducting an additional review of the work performed by the loaned staff;

- Not giving the loaned staff audit responsibility for any function or activity on the audit, that they performed during the temporary staff assignment; or

- Not including the loaned staff in the audit team.

2.5.5 Partner on client board

A partner or employee of an assurance firm should not serve on the board of an assurance client.

It may be acceptable for a partner or an employee of an assurance firm to perform the role of company secretary for an assurance client, if the role is essentially administrative.

2.5.6 Family and personal relationships

Family or close personal relationships between assurance firm and client staff could seriously threaten independence. Each situation has to be evaluated individually. Factors to consider are:

- The individual's responsibilities on the assurance engagement
- The closeness of the relationship
- The role of the other party at the assurance client

When an immediate family member of a member of the assurance team is a director, an officer or an employee of the assurance client in a position to exert direct and significant influence over the subject matter information of the assurance engagement, the individual should be removed from the assurance team.

The audit firm should also consider whether there is any threat to independence if an employee who is not a member of the assurance team has a close family or personal relationship with a director, an officer or an employee of an assurance client.

A firm should have quality control policies and procedures under which staff should disclose if a close family member employed by the client is promoted within the client.

If a firm inadvertently violates the rules concerning family and personal relationships they should apply additional safeguards, such as undertaking a quality control review of the audit and discussing the matter with the audit committee of the client, if there is one.

2.5.7 Compensation and evaluation policies

There is a self-interest threat when a member of the audit team is evaluated on selling non-assurance services to the client. The significance of the threat depends on:

- The proportion of the individual's compensation or performance evaluation that is based on the sale of such services;

- The role of the individual on the audit team; and

- Whether promotion decisions are influenced by the sale of such services.

The firm should either revise the compensation plan or evaluation process, or put in place appropriate safeguards. Safeguards include:

- Removing the member from the audit team; or

- Having the team member's work reviewed by a professional accountant.

A **Key audit partner shall not be evaluated based on their success in selling non-assurance services to their audit client**.

Point to note

In the UK, the Audit Inspection Unit (AIU)'s annual report for 2010-11 expressed concern over the selling of non-audit services to audited entities, The report stated that partners and staff were too often compromised by an inappropriate focus on this area, with the result that firms sometimes failed to identify the nature and extent of threats, and therefore failed to apply appropriate safeguards.

2.5.8 Gifts and hospitality

Unless the value of the gift/hospitality is clearly insignificant, a firm or a member of an assurance team should not accept.

2.5.9 Loans and guarantees

The advice on loans and guarantees falls into two categories:

- The client is a bank or other similar institution
- Other situations

If a lending institution client lends an immaterial amount to an audit firm or member of the assurance team on normal commercial terms, there is no threat to independence. If the loan were material it would be necessary to apply safeguards to bring the risk to an acceptable level. A suitable safeguard is likely to be an independent review (by a partner from another office in the firm).

Loans to members of the assurance team from a bank or other lending institution client are likely to be material to the individual, but provided that they are on normal commercial terms, these do not constitute a threat to independence.

An audit firm or individual on the assurance engagement should not enter into any loan or guarantee arrangement with a client that is not a bank or similar institution.

2.5.10 Overdue fees

In a situation where there are overdue fees, the auditor runs the risk of, in effect, making a loan to a client, whereupon the guidance above becomes relevant.

Audit firms should guard against fees building up and being significant by discussing the issues with those charged with governance, and, if necessary, the possibility of resigning if overdue fees are not paid.

2.5.11 Percentage or contingent fees   12/10

Key term

> **Contingent fee** A fee calculated on a predetermined basis relating to the outcome of a transaction or the result of the services performed by the firm. A fee that is established by a court or other public authority is not a contingent fee.

A firm shall not enter into a contingent fee arrangement in respect of an assurance engagement. For both audit and assurance engagements, a contingent fee would carry a threat so great that no safeguards could reduce it to an acceptable level.

For non-assurance engagements (eg tax services), where the client is not also an audit client, the significance of the threat depends on:

- The range of possible fee amounts;
- Whether an appropriate authority determines the outcome of the matter upon which the contingent fee will be determined;
- The nature of the service; and
- The effect of the event or transaction on the subject matter information.

Possible safeguards include:

- Having a **professional accountant review** the relevant assurance work or otherwise advise as necessary; or
- Using professionals who are not members of the assurance team to perform the non-assurance service.

2.5.12 High percentage of fees

When a firm receives a high proportion of its fee income from just one audit client, there is **a self-interest** or **intimidation threat**, as the firm will be concerned about losing the client. This depends on:

- The **structure** of the **firm**
- Whether the **firm** is established or **new**
- The **significance of the client** to the firm.

It is important not to overlook these caveats: a high % fee income from a client does not by itself create an insurmountable threat. The threat from the % fee income might be mitigated by the structure of the firm, or by the fact that the audit firm is new (so the fee dependence is likely to be temporary).

A recent exam question tested this point in the context of a new audit firm. The examiner commented in her report that many students were not aware of the Code's provisions in this area.

These kinds of caveats are important for all of the threats to independence in this chapter. You should know most of the rules from your previous studies, but at P7 level you will need to be able to apply them in detail.

Possible safeguards include:

- **Reducing** the **dependency** on the client;
- **External** quality control **reviews**; or
- **Consulting a third party**, such as a professional regulatory body or a professional accountant, **on key audit judgments**.

It is not just a matter of the audit firm actually **being** independent in terms of fees, but also of it being **seen to be independent by the public**. It is as much about public perception as reality.

The Code also states that a threat may be created where an individual partner or office's % fees from one client is high. The safeguards are as above, except that internal quality control reviews are also relevant.

For audit clients that are **public interest entities**, the Code states that where **total fees** from the client represent **more than 15% of the firm's total fees for two consecutive years**, the firm shall:

- **Disclose** this to **those charged with governance.**
- **A review will be conducted**, either by an external professional accountant or by a regulatory body. This review can be either before the audit opinion on the second year's financial statements is issued (a "**pre-issuance review**"), or after it is issued (a "**post-issuance review**").

If total fees **significantly exceed 15%,** then a post-issuance review may not be sufficient, and a **pre-issuance review** will be required.

2.5.13 Lowballing

When a firm quotes a significantly lower fee level for an assurance service than would have been charged by the predecessor firm, there is a significant self-interest threat. If the firm's tender is successful, the firm must apply safeguards such as:

- Maintaining records such that the firm is able to demonstrate that appropriate staff and time are spent on the engagement
- Complying with all applicable assurance standards, guidelines and quality control procedures

2.5.14 Recruitment

Recruiting senior management for an assurance client, particularly those able to affect the subject matter of an assurance engagement creates a self-interest threat for the assurance firm.

Assurance providers must not make management decisions for the client. Their involvement could be limited to reviewing a shortlist of candidates, providing that the client has drawn up the criteria by which they are to be selected.

2.6 Self-review threat

The key area in which there is likely to be a self-review threat is where an assurance firm provides services other than assurance services to an assurance client (providing multiple services). There is a great deal of guidance in the ACCA and IESBA rules about various other services accountancy firms might provide to their clients, and these are dealt with below.

Exam focus point

In exam questions, bear in mind the nature of the entity being audited. Is it a small owner-managed business where the auditor is in effect an all-round business adviser and accountant, or is it a listed company where the above rule is relevant?

In the United States rules concerning auditor independence for **listed** companies state that an accountant is not independent if they provide certain non-audit services to an audit client. The relevant services are:

- Bookkeeping
- Financial information systems design and implementation
- Appraisal or valuation services or fairness opinions
- Actuarial services
- Internal audit services
- Management functions
- Human resources
- Broker-dealer services
- Legal services

The rules, found in the Sarbanes-Oxley Act, apply to **any** company listed on the US Stock Exchange so they have an international impact. They also apply to companies based outside of the US but who are part of groups who are listed on the US Stock Exchange.

2.6.1 Recent service with an assurance client

Individuals who have been a director or officer of the client, or an employee in a position to exert direct and significant influence over the subject matter information of the assurance engagement in the period under review or the previous two years should not be assigned to the assurance team.

If an individual had been closely involved with the client prior to the time limits set out above, the assurance firm should consider the threat to independence arising and apply appropriate safeguards, such as:

- Obtaining a quality control review of the individual's work on the assignment
- Discussing the issue with the audit committee

2.6.2 General other services

For assurance clients, accountants are not allowed to:

- Authorise, execute or consummate a transaction
- Determine which recommendation of the company should be implemented
- Report in a management capacity to those charged with governance

Having custody of an assurance client's assets, supervising client employees in the performance of their normal duties, and preparing source documents on behalf of the client also pose significant self-review threats which should be addressed by safeguards. These could be:

- Ensuring non-assurance team staff are used for these roles
- Involving an independent professional accountant to advise
- Quality control policies on what staff are and are not allowed to do for clients
- Making appropriate disclosures to those charged with governance
- Resigning from the assurance engagement

2.6.3 Preparing accounting records and financial statements 6/11

There is clearly a significant risk of a self-review threat if a firm prepares accounting records and financial statements and then audits them.

On the other hand auditors routinely assist management with the preparation of financial statements and give advice about accounting treatments and journal entries.

Therefore, assurance firms must analyse the risks arising and put safeguards in place to ensure that the risk is at an acceptable level. Safeguards include:

- Using staff members other than assurance team members to carry out work
- Obtaining client approval for work undertaken

The rules are more stringent when the client is listed or public interest. **Firms should not prepare accounts or financial statements for listed or public interest clients**, unless an emergency arises.

For any client, assurance firms are also not allowed to:

- **Determine or change journal entries without client approval**
- **Authorise or approve transactions**
- **Prepare source documents**

2.6.4 Valuation services

Key term

> A **valuation** comprises the making of assumptions with regard to future developments, the application of certain methodologies and techniques, and the combination of both in order to compute a certain value, or range of values, for an asset, a liability or for a business as a whole.

If an audit firm performs a valuation which will be included in financial statements audited by the firm, a self-review threat arises.

Audit firms should not carry out valuations on matters which will be material to the financial statements. If the valuation is for an immaterial matter, the audit firm should apply safeguards to ensure that the risk is reduced to an acceptable level. Matters to consider when applying safeguards are the extent of the audit client's knowledge of the relevant matters in making the valuation and the degree of judgement involved, how much use is made of established methodologies and the degree of uncertainty in the valuation. Safeguards include:

- Second partner review
- Confirming that the client understands the valuation and the assumptions used
- Ensuring the client acknowledges responsibility for the valuation
- Using separate personnel for the valuation and the audit

2.6.5 Taxation services

The Code divides taxation services into four categories:

(a) Tax return preparation;
(b) Tax calculations for the purpose of preparing the accounting entries;
(c) Tax planning and other tax advisory services; and
(d) Assistance in the resolution of tax disputes.

Guidance in respect of each of these categories is as follows.

(a) **Tax return preparation does not generally threaten independence**, as long as management takes responsibility for the returns.

(b) **Tax calculations for the purpose of preparing the accounting entities may not prepared for public interest entities**, except in emergency situations. For non-public interest entities, it is acceptable to do so provided that safeguards are applied.

(c) **Tax planning may be acceptable in certain circumstances**, eg where the advice is clearly supported by tax authority or other precedent. However, if the effectiveness of the tax advice depends on a particular accounting treatment or presentation in the financial statements, the audit team has reasonable doubt about the accounting treatment, and the consequences of the tax advice would be material, then the service should not be provided.

Assistance in the resolution of tax disputes may be provided, depending on whether the firm itself provided the service which is the subject of the dispute, and whether the effect is material to the financial statements. Safeguards include using professionals who are not members of the audit team to perform the service, and obtaining advice on the service from an external tax professional.

2.6.6 Internal audit services

A firm may provide internal audit services to an audit client. However, it should ensure that the client acknowledges its responsibility for establishing, maintaining and monitoring the system of internal controls. It may be appropriate to use safeguards such as ensuring that an employee of the client is designated responsible for internal audit activities and that the client approves all the work that internal audit does.

If the client is a **public interest entity**, then internal audit services must not be provided if they relate to:

(a) A **significant** part of **the internal controls** over **financial reporting**;

(b) Financial accounting systems generating information which is significant to the financial statements; or

Amounts or disclosures which are **material** to the financial statements.

2.6.7 Corporate finance

Certain aspects of corporate finance will create self-review threats that cannot be reduced to an acceptable level by safeguards. Therefore, **assurance firms are not allowed to promote, deal in or underwrite an assurance client's shares. They are also not allowed to commit an assurance client to the terms of a transaction or consummate a transaction on the client's behalf**.

Other corporate finance services, such as assisting a client in defining corporate strategies, assisting in identifying possible sources of capital and providing structuring advice may be acceptable, providing that safeguards, such as using different teams of staff, and ensuring no management decisions are taken on behalf of the client.

2.6.8 Other services

The audit firm might sell a variety of other services to audit clients, such as:

- IT services
- Litigation support
- Legal services

The assurance firm should consider whether there are any barriers to independence, such as if the firm were asked to design internal control IT systems, which it would then review as part of its audit. The firm should consider whether the threat to independence could be reduced by appropriate safeguards.

2.7 Advocacy threat   12/10

An advocacy threat arises in certain situations where the assurance firm is in a position of taking the client's part in a dispute or somehow acting as their advocate. The most obvious instances of this would be when a firm offered legal services to a client and, say, defended them in a legal case or provided evidence on their behalf as an expert witness. Advocacy threat might also arise if the firm carried out corporate finance work for the client, for example, if the audit firm was involved in advice on debt reconstruction and negotiated with the bank on the client's behalf.

> The June 2010 exam contained a scenario in which the auditor was asked to attend a meeting with the client's bank relating to a matter that was crucial to the client's ability to continue as a going concern. Although many students would have sensed that this was wrong, not many would have gotten the marks for saying that it was an advocacy threat.

As with the other threats above, the firm has to appraise the risk and apply safeguards as necessary. Relevant safeguards might be using different departments in the firm to carry out the work and making disclosures to the audit committee. Remember, the ultimate option is always to withdraw from an engagement if the risk to independence is too high.

Question   Advocacy threat

Explain why contingent fees represent an advocacy threat.

Answer

If an accountant is paid fees on a contingency basis, then his will and the client's become too closely aligned. They will both want the same thing to occur (ie the thing the fee is contingent on) and the risk is that the accountant will act in the interests of the client to ensure it happens.

A familiarity threat arises where independence is jeopardised by the audit firm and its staff becoming over familiar with the client and its staff. There is a substantial risk of loss of professional scepticism in such circumstances.

We have already discussed some examples of when this risk arises, because very often a familiarity threat arises in conjunction with a self-interest threat.

2.8.1 Long association of senior personnel with assurance clients

Having an audit client for a **long period of time may create a familiarity threat** to independence. The severity of the threat depends on factors such as how long the individual has been on the audit team; how senior the person is; whether the client's management has changed; whether the client's accounting issues have changed in nature or complexity.

Possible **safeguards** include:

- **Rotating** the **senior personnel** off the **audit team**;

- Having a **professional accountant** who was not a member of the audit team **review** the work of the senior personnel; or

- **Regular** independent **internal or external quality reviews** of the engagement.

The rules for **public interest entities** are stricter. If an individual is a **key audit partner** for **seven years**, they must be rotated off the audit for **two years**. During this time they cannot be on the audit team, and cannot consult with the audit team or the client on any issues that may affect the engagement (including giving just general industry advice).

The Code does allow some flexibility here: **if** key partner **continuity** is particularly beneficial to **audit quality**, and there is some **unforeseen circumstance** (such as the intended engagement partner becoming seriously ill), then the key audit partner **can remain on the audit for an additional year**, making eight years in total.

If a client that was not a public interest entity becomes one, then the seven year limit still applies, starting from the date when the key audit partner originally became the key partner for that audit client.

Finally, it is possible for an independent regulator to give permission for an audit partner to remain a key audit partner indefinitely, provided alternative safeguards are applied (eg external review).

The December 2010 exam contained four marks for evaluating the advantages and disadvantages of compulsory **firm** rotation. The candidates who score well on questions of this sort are those who don't just know the rules, but are also able to think through the issues underlying them.

That being said, you don't need to be intimidated by questions like this: they are within reach of virtually every P7 candidate, provided that you can come up with some sensible points both for and against, and can then draw a reasonable conclusion from what you have written.

2.9 Intimidation threat

An intimidation threat arises when members of the assurance team have reason to be intimidated by client staff.

These are also examples of self-interest threats, largely because intimidation may only arise significantly when the assurance firm has something to lose.

2.9.1 Actual and threatened litigation

The most obvious example of an intimidation threat is when the client threatens to sue, or indeed sues, the assurance firm for work that has been done previously. The firm is then faced with the risk of losing the client, bad publicity and the possibility that they will be found to have been negligent, which will lead to further problems. This could lead to the firm being under pressure to produce an unmodified audit report when they have been modified in the past, for example.

Generally, assurance firms should seek to avoid such situations arising. If they do arise, factors to consider are:

- The materiality of the litigation
- The nature of the assurance engagement
- Whether the litigation relates to a prior assurance engagement

The following safeguards could be considered:

- Disclosing to the audit committee the nature and extent of the litigation
- Removing specific affected individuals from the engagement team
- Involving an additional professional accountant on the team to review work

However, if the litigation is at all serious, it may be necessary to resign from the engagement, as the threat to independence is so great.

2.9.2 Second opinions

Another way that auditors can suffer an intimidation threat is when the audit client is unhappy with a proposed audit opinion, and seeks a **second opinion** from a different firm of auditors.

In such a circumstance, the second audit firm will not be able to give a formal audit opinion on the financial statements – only an appointed auditor can do that. However, the problem is that if a different firm of auditors indicates to someone else's audit client that a different audit opinion might be acceptable, the appointed auditor may feel under pressure to change the audit opinion. In effect, a self-interest threat arises, as the existing auditor may feel that he will lose next year's audit if he does not change this year's opinion.

There is nothing to stop a company director talking to a second firm of auditors about treatments of matters in the financial statements. However, the firm being asked for a second opinion should be very careful, because it is very possible that the opinion they form could be incorrect anyway if the director has not given them all the relevant information. For that reason, firms giving a second opinion should ensure that they seek permission to communicate with the existing auditor and they are appraised of all the facts. If permission is not given, the second auditors should decline to comment on the audit opinion.

Given that second opinions can cause independence issues for the existing auditors, audit firms should generally take great care if asked to provide one anyway.

Increasingly, new standards do not give a choice of accounting treatments, meaning that second opinions might be less called for.

Question

Threats to independence

You are a partner in a firm of chartered certified accountants. The following issues have emerged in relation to three of your clients:

(a)   Easter is a major client. It is listed on a major Stock Exchange. The audit team consists of eight members, of whom Paul is the most junior. Paul has just invested in a personal pension plan that invests in all the listed companies on the exchange.

(b)   You are at the head of a team carrying out due diligence work at Electra, a limited company which your client, Powerful, is considering taking over. Your second in command on the team, Peter, has confided in you that in the course of his work he has met the daughter of the managing director of Electra, and he is keen to invite her on a date.

(c)   Your longest standing audit client is Teddies, which you have been involved in for ten years, four as engagement partner. You recently went on an extended cruise with the managing director on his yacht.

Required

Comment on the ethical and other professional issues raised by the above matters. Your answer should outline the threat arising, the significance of the threat, any factors you have taken into account, and, if relevant, any safeguards you could apply to eliminate or mitigate against the threat.

Answer

(a)   In relation to Easter, there is a threat of self-interest arising, as a member of the audit team has an indirect financial interest in the client.

The **relevant factors** are as follows:

- The interest is unlikely to be **material** to the client or Paul, as the investment is recent and Paul's interest is in a pool of general investments made in the exchange on his behalf
- Paul is the **audit junior** and **does not have a significant role** on the audit in terms of drawing audit conclusions or audit risk areas

The risk that arises to the independence of the audit here is **not significant**. It would be inappropriate to require Paul to divest his interest in the audit client. If I wanted to eliminate all elements of risk in this situation, I could simply change the junior assigned to my team, but such a step is not vital in this situation.

(b) In relation to Powerful, two issues arise. The first is that the firm appears to be providing multiple services to Powerful, which could raise a **self-interest threat**. The second is that the manager assigned to the due diligence assignment wants to engage in a personal relationship with a person connected to the subject of the assignment, which could create a **familiarity or intimidation threat**.

With regard to the issue of multiple services, **insufficient information** is given to draw a conclusion as to the significance of the threat. **Relevant factors** would be matters such as the nature of the services, the fee income and the team members assigned to each. **Safeguards** could include using different staff for the two assignments. The risk is likely to be significant only if one of the services provided is **audit**, which is not indicated in the question.

In relation to the second issue, the **relevant factors** are these:

- The assurance team member has a significant role on the team as second in command
- The other party is closely connected to a key staff member at the company being reviewed
- Timing

In this situation, the firm is carrying out a one-off review of the company, and **timing is a key issue**. Presently Peter does not have a personal relationship which would significantly threaten the independence of the assignment. In this situation, the **safeguard is to request that Peter does not take any action in that direction until the assignment is completed**. If he refuses, then I may have to consider rotating my staff on this assignment, and removing him from the team.

(c) In relation to Teddies, there is a risk that my long association and personal relationship with the client will result in a **familiarity** threat. This is compounded by my acceptance of significant hospitality on a personal level.

The **relevant factors** are:

- I have been involved with the client for ten years and have a personal relationship with client staff
- The company is not a listed or public interest company
- It is an audit assignment

The risk arising here is **significant**, but as the client is not listed, it is not insurmountable. However, it would be a good idea to implement some safeguards to mitigate against the risk. I could invite a second partner to provide a **hot review** of the audit of Teddies, or even consider requesting that I am **rotated** off the audit of Teddies for a period, so that the engagement partner is another partner in my firm. In addition, I must cease accepting hospitality from the directors of Teddies unless it is clearly insignificant.

Exam focus point

> When answering exam questions do not just identify the ethical threats in a given scenario. You must also be able to **explain why** the issue is an ethical threat.

2.10 Quality control: Independence

The quality control standard for firms, ISQC 1 *Quality control for firms that perform audits and reviews of financial statements, and other assurance and related services engagements*, which we shall look at in detail in Chapter 4, contains a section looking at the firm's procedures with regard to ethics and, in particular, independence.

> **ISQC 1.20**
>
> The firm shall establish policies and procedures designed to provide it with reasonable assurance that the firm and its personnel comply with relevant ethical requirements.

The policies and procedures should be in line with the fundamental principles, which should be reinforced by:

- The leadership of the firm
- Education and training
- Monitoring
- A process for dealing with non-compliance

The standard sets out some detailed requirements with regard to independence:

ISQC 1.21

Such policies and procedures shall require:

(a) Engagement partners to provide the firm with relevant information about client engagements, including the scope of services, to enable the firm to evaluate the overall impact, if any, on independence requirements.

(b) Personnel to promptly notify the firm of circumstances and relationships that create a threat to independence so that appropriate action can be taken, and

(c) The accumulation and communication of relevant information to appropriate personnel so that:

    (i) The firm and its personnel can readily determine whether they satisfy independence requirements

    (ii) The firm can maintain and update its records relating to independence, and

    (iii) The firm can take appropriate action regarding identified threats to independence that are not at an acceptable level

ISQC 1.23

The firm shall establish policies and procedures designed to provide it with reasonable assurance that it is notified of breaches of independence requirements, and to enable it to take appropriate actions to resolve such situations. The policies and procedures shall include requirements for:

(a) Personnel to promptly notify the firm of independence breaches of which they become aware

(b) The firm to promptly communicate identified breaches of these policies and procedures to:

    (i) The engagement partner who, with the firm, needs to address the breach, and

    (ii) Other relevant personnel in the firm and, where appropriate, the network, and those subject to the independence requirements who need to take appropriate action, and

(c) Prompt communication to the firm, if necessary, by the engagement partner and the other individuals referred to in subparagraph (b)(ii) of the actions taken to resolve the matter, so that the firm can determine whether it should take further action.

ISQC 1.24

At least annually, the firm shall obtain written confirmation of compliance with its policies and procedures on independence from all firm personnel required to be independent by relevant ethical requirements.

2.10.1 Familiarity threat

Lastly, the ISQC sets out some specific guidance in relation to the threat of over-familiarity with clients.

ISQC 1.25

The firm shall establish policies and procedures:

(a) Setting out criteria for determining the need for safeguards to reduce the familiarity threat to an acceptable level when using the same senior personnel on an assurance engagement over a long period of time, and

(b) Requiring, for audits of financial statements of listed entities, the rotation of the engagement partner and the individuals responsible for engagement quality control review, and where applicable, others subject to rotation requirements, after a specified period in compliance with relevant ethical requirements.

3 Specific guidance: Confidentiality

FAST FORWARD

Both the IESBA and the ACCA recognise a duty of confidence and several exceptions to it.

3.1 Duty of confidence

The ACCA gives guidance relating to confidentiality in the *Code of Ethics and Conduct*. A member acquiring information in the course of his professional work should not use, nor appear to use, that information for his personal advantage or for the advantage of a third party. A member must make clear to a client that he may only act for him if the client agrees to disclose in full to the member all information relevant to the engagement.

Where a member agrees to serve a client in a professional capacity both the member and the client should be aware that it is an implied term of that agreement that the member will not disclose the client's affairs to any other person save with the client's consent within the terms of certain recognised exceptions.

3.2 Recognised exceptions to the rule of confidentiality

ACCA STATEMENT

Obligatory disclosure. If a member knows or suspects his client to have committed an offence of treason he is obliged to disclose all the information at his disposal to a competent authority. Local legislation may also require auditors to disclose other infringements.

Voluntary disclosure. In certain cases voluntary disclosure may be made by the member:

- To protect the member's interests
- Where it is in the public's interest
- Where it is authorised by statute
- To non-governmental bodies

The IESBA extends this list in its guidance.

IESBA *Code of Ethics for Professional Accountants*

- To comply with technical standards and ethical requirements
- To comply with the quality review of a member or professional body
- To respond to an inquiry or investigation by a member body or regulatory body

Also, having decided that confidential information can be disclosed, accountants should consider:

- Whether all relevant facts are known and substantiated
- What type of communication is expected and to whom it should be addressed
- Whether the accountant will incur legal liability as a result of disclosure
- Whether the parties to whom the communication is addressed are appropriate recipients

If an ACCA member is requested to assist the police, the tax authorities or any other authority by providing information about a client's affairs in connection with enquiries being made he should enquire under what **statutory authority** the information is demanded.

Unless he is satisfied that such statutory authority exists he should decline to give any information until he has obtained his client's authority. If the client's authority is not forthcoming and the demand for information is pressed, he should not accede unless advised to by a solicitor.

If an ACCA member knows or suspects that a client has committed a wrongful act he must give careful thought to his own position. He is under no obligation, even in a criminal matter (excluding treason, money-laundering and terrorist offences), to convey his information to a competent authority, but he must ensure that he has not prejudiced himself by, for example, relying on incorrect information.

However, it would be a criminal offence for a member to act positively, without lawful authority or reasonable excuse, in such a manner as to impede with intent the arrest or prosecution of a client whom he knows or believes to have committed an arrestable offence.

3.3 Disclosure in the public interest

The ACCA gives further guidance on disclosure 'in the public interest'. Accountants should usually seek legal advice before making disclosures.

The courts have never given a definition of 'the public interest'. This means that again, the issue is left to the judgement of the auditor. It is often therefore appropriate for the member to seek legal advice.

It is only appropriate for information to be disclosed to certain authorities, for example, the police.

The ACCA guidance states that there are several factors that the member should take into account when deciding whether to make disclosure.

ACCA guidance

- The size of the amounts involved and the extent of likely financial damage
- Whether members of the public are likely to be affected
- The possibility or likelihood of repetition
- The reasons for the client's unwillingness to make disclosures to the authority
- The gravity of the matter
- Relevant legislation, accounting and auditing standards
- Any legal advice obtained

Under ISA 250, if auditors become aware of a suspected or actual instance of non-compliance with law and regulation which gives rise to a statutory right or duty to report, they should report it to the proper authority immediately. They should also seek legal advice.

Exam focus point

If you are required to make judgements about whether such a disclosure should be made in a given scenario, you should apply a checklist like this to the scenario to ensure you have shown evidence of your consideration of all the relevant factors.

4 Specific guidance: Conflicts of interest   6/09, 6/11

Auditors should identify potential conflicts of interest as they could result in the ethical codes being breached.

Audit firms should take reasonable steps to identify circumstances that could pose a conflict of interest. This is because a conflict of interest could result in the ethical code being breached (for example, if it results in a self-interest threat arising).

4.1 Conflicts between members' and clients' interests

A conflict between members' and clients' interests might arise if members compete directly with a client, or have a joint venture or similar with a company that is in competition with the client.

The rules state that **members and firms should not accept or continue engagements in which there are, or are likely to be, significant conflicts of interest between members, firms and clients**.

Members should evaluate the threats arising from a conflict of interest, and unless they are clearly insignificant, they should apply safeguards. The test of whether a threat is significant is whether a reasonable and informed third party, having knowledge of all relevant information, including the safeguards applied, would consider the conflict of interest as likely to affect the judgement of members and firms.

4.2 Conflicts between the interests of different clients

Assurance firms are at liberty to have clients who are in competition with each other. However, the firm should ensure that it is not the subject of a dispute between the clients. It must also manage its work so that the interests of one client do not adversely affect the client. **Where acceptance or continuance of an engagement would, even with safeguards, materially prejudice the interests of any client, the appointment should not be accepted or continued**.

Auditors often give their clients business advice unrelated to audit. In such a position, they may well become involved when clients are involved in issues such as:

- Share issues
- Takeovers

Neither situation is inherently wrong for an auditor to be in. With regard to **share issues**, audit firms should not underwrite an issue of shares to the public of a client they audit. In a **takeover situation**, if the auditors are involved in the audits of both predator and target company, they must take extra care. They must not:

- Be the principal advisors to either party
- Issue reports assessing the accounts of either party other than their audit report

If they find they possess material confidential information, they should contact the appropriate regulator.

4.2.1 Managing conflicts between clients' interests

When considering whether to accept a client or when there is a change in a client's circumstances, assurance firms should take reasonable steps to ascertain whether there is a conflict of interest or if there is likely to be one in the future. Relationships that ended two or more years earlier are unlikely to create a conflict. Disclosure is the most important safeguard, which would usually include:

- Notifying the client of the interest/activities that may cause a conflict of interest and obtaining their consent to act in the circumstances, or
- Notifying all known relevant parties that the member is acting for two or more parties in respect of a matter where their respective interests are in conflict, and obtaining their consent so to act, or
- Notifying the client that the member does not act exclusively for any one client in the provision of proposed services, and obtaining their consent so to act

Other safeguards:

- Using separate engagement teams
- Procedures to prevent access of information (such as special passwords)
- Clear guidelines for the respective teams on issues of security and confidentiality
- The use of confidentiality agreements signed by the partners and staff
- Regular review of the safeguards by an independent partner
- Advising one or both of the clients to obtain additional independent advice

5 Conflicts in application of the fundamental principles

The *Code of Ethics and Conduct* gives some general guidance to members who encounter a conflict in the application of the fundamental principles.

5.1 Matters to consider

The resolution process should include consideration of:

- Relevant facts
- Ethical issues involved
- Fundamental principles related to the matter in question
- Established internal procedures
- Alternative courses of action

5.1.1 Unresolved conflict

If the matter is unresolved, the member should consult with other appropriate persons within the firm. They may wish to obtain advice from the ACCA or legal advisers. If after exhausting all relevant possibilities the ethical conflict remains unresolved, members should consider withdrawing from the engagement team, a specific assignment, or to resign altogether from the engagement.

5.2 Example

Chapter Roundup

- Accountants require an ethical code because they hold positions of trust, and people rely on them.

- The ACCA's guidance is designed to comply with the requirements of the IESBA Code.

- Both the ACCA and the IESBA codes give examples of a number of situations where independence might be threatened and suggest safeguards to independence.

- Both the IESBA and the ACCA recognise a duty of confidence and several exceptions to it.

- The ACCA gives further guidance on disclosure 'in the public interest'. Accountants should usually seek legal advice before making disclosures.

- Auditors should identify potential conflicts of interest as they could result in the ethical codes being breached.

Quick Quiz

1   Match the fundamental principle to the characteristic.

    (a)   Integrity

    (b)   Objectivity

        (i)   Members should be straightforward and honest in all professional and business relationships.

        (ii)   Members should not allow bias, conflict of interest or undue influence of others to override professional or business judgements.

2   Name five general threats to independence.

    (1)   ....

    (2)   ....

    (3)   ....

    (4)   ....

    (5)   ....

3   Name four relevant safeguards against a financial interest in a client.

    (1)   ....

    (2)   ....

    (3)   ....

    (4)   ....

4   Complete the definition.

    .... are fees calculated on a pre-determined basis relating to the outcome or result of a transaction or the result of the work performed.

5   Complete the following definition.

    Insider dealing can be described as .... in .... whilst in possession of .... as an insider, the securities being .... – .... by the information.

Answers to Quick Quiz

1   (a)(i), (b)(ii)

2   (1)   Self-review
     (2)   Self-interest
     (3)   Familiarity
     (4)   Intimidation
     (5)   Advocacy

3   (1)   Disposing of the interest
     (2)   Removing the relevant individual from the assurance team
     (3)   Informing the audit committee of the situation
     (4)   Independent partner review of work undertaken

4   Contingent fees

5   Dealing, securities, insider information, price-affected

Now try the questions below from the Exam Question Bank

Number	Level	Marks	Time
Q1	Examination	15	27 mins
Q2	Examination	15	27 mins

3

Professional liability

Topic list	Syllabus reference
1 Legal liability	B3
2 Negligence	B3
3 Restricting liability	B3
4 Current issues in auditor liability	B3
5 Fraud and error	B2
6 The expectations gap	B3

Introduction

Auditors have responsibilities to several parties. This chapter explores the various **responsibilities** and the **liability that can arise** in respect of them. It also looks at ways of restricting liability, including professional indemnity insurance.

The auditors' responsibility to members and other readers of the accounts in tort and contract can give rise to **liability,** particularly in the event of **negligence.** Case law on this matter is complex and not wholly satisfactory. It results in auditors being liable to some readers and not others. However, **auditors' liability** is a dynamic issue in that it **evolves as cases are brought to court**.

There are some interesting **current developments** for auditors with regard to liability, for example **limited liability partnerships**. This and other current issues pertaining to the topics covered in this chapter are discussed in Section 4.

Critically, and contrary to widespread public belief, **auditors do not have a responsibility to detect and prevent fraud.** The responsibilities that auditors do have with regard to fraud and error are outlined in Section 5. Auditors are required to follow the guidance of ISA 240 *The auditor's responsibilities relating to fraud in an audit of financial statements*.

Reasons for audit failure and other factors contributing to the 'expectation gap' are covered in Section 6.

Study guide

		Intellectual level
B2	**Fraud and error**	
(a)	Define and clearly distinguish between the terms 'error', 'irregularity', 'fraud' and 'misstatement'	2
(b)	Compare and contrast the respective responsibilities of management and auditors for fraud and error	2
(c)	Describe the matters to be considered and procedures to be carried out to investigate actual and/or potential misstatements in a given situation	2
(d)	Explain how, why, when and to whom fraud and error should be reported and the circumstances in which an auditor should withdraw from an engagement	2
(e)	Discuss the current and possible future role of auditors in preventing, detecting and reporting error and fraud	2
B3	**Professional liability**	
(a)	Recognise circumstances in which professional accountants may have legal liability	2
(b)	Describe the factors to determine whether or not an auditor is negligent in given situations	2
(c)	Explain the other criteria for legal liability to be recognised (including 'due professional care' and 'proximity') and apply them to given situations	2
(d)	Compare and contrast liability to client with liability to third parties	3
(e)	Evaluate the practicability and effectiveness of ways in which liability may be restricted	3
(f)	Discuss liability limitation agreements	2
(g)	Discuss and appraise the principal causes of audit failure and other factors that contribute to the 'expectation gap' (eg responsibilities for fraud and error)	3
(h)	Recommend ways in which the expectation gap might be bridged	2

Exam guide

Auditors' liability is a key issue facing the profession globally, and ways of restricting liability are being compared and debated. This area can be examined in topical discussion questions, or in practical scenarios considering whether an auditor may be held to have been negligent in specific circumstances.

The extent of auditors' responsibilities in relation to fraud and error is a critical element of the public's perception of the auditor's role. The requirements of ISA 240 in this regard are core knowledge for this paper and may have to be applied in practical scenarios.

1 Legal liability

FAST FORWARD

Professional accountants may have professional liability under statutory law.

Under certain legislation, notably **insolvency** legislation, auditors may be found to be officers of the company and could be charged with criminal offences or found liable for civil offences in connection with the winding up of the company.

Auditors may also be found guilty of the offence of **insider dealing**, which is a criminal offence, since they are privy to inside information.

Auditors could be found guilty of a criminal offence if they knew or suspected a person was laundering money and they failed to report their suspicions to the proper authority.

2 Negligence

> Auditors may have professional liability in the tort of negligence.

Negligence is a common law concept. It seeks to provide compensation to a person who has suffered loss due to another person's wrongful neglect. To succeed in an action for negligence, an injured party must prove three things:

(a) A **duty of care** which is enforceable by law existed.

(b) This duty of care was **breached**.

(c) The breach caused the injured party **loss**. In the case of negligence in relation to financial advisers/auditors, this loss must be pecuniary (ie financial) loss.

2.1 Who might bring an action for negligence?

The parties likely to want to bring an action in negligence against the auditors, for example, if they have given the wrong audit opinion through lack of care, include:

- The company
- Shareholders
- The bank
- Other lenders
- Other interested third parties

A key difference between the various potential claimants is the extent of the **proximity** between the auditor and the potential claimant, and whether the relationship is sufficiently **proximal** for the auditor to owe them a **duty of care**.

2.2 The audit client

> The auditor owes a duty of care to the audit client automatically under law.

The audit client is the **company**. It is a basic maxim of company law that the company is all the shareholders acting as a body. In other words, the company in this respect, cannot be represented by a single shareholder.

| COMPANY | = | SHAREHOLDERS AS A BODY |

| COMPANY | ≱ | SHAREHOLDER | + | SHAREHOLDER |

The **company** has a **contract** with the audit firm. In the law of many countries, a contract for the supply of a service such as an audit has a duty of reasonable care implied into it by statute.

In other words, whatever the express terms of any written contract between the company and the audit firm, the law always implies a duty of care into it. Therefore, if the company (all the shareholders acting as a body) want to bring a case for negligence, the situation would be as follows.

Client	
Duty of care exists?	AUTOMATIC
Breached?	MUST BE PROVED
Loss arising?	MUST BE PROVED

In order to prove whether a duty of care had been breached, the court has to give further consideration to what the duty of 'reasonable' care means in practice.

2.2.1 The auditors' duty of care

The standard of work of auditors is generally as defined by legislation. A number of judgements made in law cases show how the auditors' duty of care has been gauged at various points in time because legislation often does not state clearly the manner in which the auditors should discharge their duty of care. It is also not likely that this would be clearly spelt out in any contract setting out the terms of an auditors' appointment.

 Case Study

Re Kingston Cotton Mill

When Lopes L J considered the degree of skill and care required of an auditor he declared:

'... it is the duty of an auditor to bring to bear on the work he has to perform that skill, care and caution which a reasonably competent, careful and cautious auditor would use. What is reasonable skill, care and caution, must depend on the particular circumstances of each case.'

Lopes was careful to point out that what constitutes reasonable care depends very much upon the **facts** of a particular case. Another criteria by which the courts will determine the adequacy of the auditors' work is by assessing it in relation to the generally accepted auditing standards of the day.

 Case Study

The courts will be very much concerned with accepted advances in auditing techniques, demonstrated by Pennycuick J in *Re Thomas Gerrard & Son Ltd 1967* where he observed:

'... the real ground on which *Re Kingston Cotton Mill...* is, I think, capable of being distinguished is that the standards of reasonable care and skill are, upon the expert evidence, more exacting today than those which prevailed in 1896.'

 Case Study

Lord Denning in the case of *Fomento (Sterling Area) Ltd v Selsdon Fountain Pen Co Ltd 1958* sought to define the auditors' proper approach to their work by saying:

'... they must come to it with an inquiring mind – not suspicious of dishonesty .... – but suspecting that someone may have made a mistake somewhere and that a check must be made to ensure that there has been none.'

The auditors have a responsibility to keep themselves abreast of professional developments. Auditing Standards are likely to be taken into account when the adequacy of the work of auditors is being considered in a court of law or in other contested situations.

When the auditors are exercising judgement they must act both honestly and carefully. Obviously, if auditors are to be 'careful' in forming an opinion, they must give due consideration to all relevant matters. Provided they do this and can be seen to have done so, then their opinion should be above criticism.

However if the opinion reached by the auditors is one that no reasonably competent auditor would have been likely to reach then they would still possibly be held negligent. This is because however carefully the auditors may appear to have approached their work, it clearly could not have been careful enough, if it enabled them to reach a conclusion which would be generally regarded as unacceptable.

If the auditors' suspicions are aroused, they must conduct further investigations until such suspicions are either confirmed or allayed. Over the years, there have been many occasions where the courts have had to consider cases in which it has been held, on the facts of those cases, that the auditors ought to have been put upon enquiry.

2.3 Third parties

FAST FORWARD

The auditor only owes a duty of care to parties other than the audit client if one has been established.

'Third parties' in this context means anyone other than the company (audit client) who wished to make a claim for negligence. It therefore includes any individual shareholders in the company and any potential investors. It also includes, importantly, the bank, who is very often a key financier of the company.

The key difference between third parties and the company is that third parties have no contract with the audit firm. There is therefore no implied duty of care. The situation is therefore as follows.

Third parties	
Duty of care exists?	MUST BE PROVED
Breached?	MUST BE PROVED
Loss arising?	MUST BE PROVED

Traditionally the courts have been **averse** to **attributing a duty of care to third parties** to the auditor. We can see this by looking at some past cases that have gone to court.

A **very important case** is *Caparo Industries plc v Dickman and Others 1990*, which is described here.

 Case Study

The **facts as pleaded** were that in 1984 Caparo Industries purchased 100,000 Fidelity shares in the open market. On June 12 1984, the date on which the accounts (audited by Touche Ross) were published, they purchased a further 50,000 shares. Relying on information in the accounts, further shares were acquired. On September 4, Caparo made a bid for the remainder and by October had acquired control of Fidelity. Caparo alleged that the accounts on which they had relied were misleading in that an apparent pre-tax profit of some £1.3 million should in fact have been shown as a loss of over £400,000. The plaintiffs argued that Touche owed a duty of care to investors and potential investors.

The conclusion of the **House of Lords** hearing of the case in February 1990 was that the auditors of a public company's accounts owed **no duty of care** to members of the public at large who relied upon the accounts in deciding to buy shares in the company. And as a purchaser of further shares, while relying upon the auditors' report, a shareholder stood in the same position as any other investing member of the public to whom the auditor owed no duty. The purpose of the audit was simply that of fulfilling the statutory requirements of the Companies Act. There was nothing in the statutory duties of company auditors to suggest that they were intended to protect the interests of investors in the market. And in particular, there was no reason why any special relationship should be held to arise simply from the fact that the affairs of the company rendered it susceptible to a takeover bid.

In its report *The Financial Aspects of Corporate Governance*, the Cadbury Committee gave an opinion on the situation as reflected in the *Caparo* ruling. It felt that *Caparo* did not lessen auditors' duty to use skill and care because auditors are **still fully liable in negligence** to the companies they audit and their shareholders collectively. Given the number of different users of accounts, it was impossible for the House of Lords to have broadened the boundaries of the auditors' legal duty of care.

The decision in *Caparo v Dickman* considerably **narrowed the auditors' potential liability to third parties**. The judgement appears to imply that members of various such user groups, which could include suppliers, potential investors or others, will not be able to sue the auditors for negligence by virtue of their placing reliance on audited annual accounts, as their relationship with the auditor is **insufficiently proximate**.

 Case Study

In *James McNaughton Paper Group Ltd v Hicks Anderson & Co 1990,* Lord Justice Neill set out the following position in the light of *Caparo* and earlier cases:

(a) 'In England a restrictive approach was now adopted to any extension of the scope of the duty of care beyond the person directly intended by the maker of the statement to act upon it.

(b) In deciding whether a duty of care existed in any particular case it was necessary to take all the circumstances into account.

(c) Notwithstanding (b), it was possible to identify certain matters which were likely to be of importance in most cases in reaching a decision as to whether or not a duty existed.'

A more recent court case produced a **development** in the subject of audit liability. In December 1995, a High Court judge awarded electronic security group ADT £65m plus interest and costs (£40m) in damages for negligence against the former BDO Binder Hamlyn (BBH) partnership.

 Case Study

The firm had jointly audited the 1988/89 accounts of Britannia Security Group (BSG), which ADT acquired in 1990 for £105m, but later found to be worth only £40m. Although, under *Caparo*, auditors do not owe a duty of care in general to third parties, the judge found that BBH audit partner Martyn Bishop, who confirmed that the firm stood by BSG's accounts at a meeting with ADT in the run-up to the acquisition, had thereby **taken on a contractual relationship** with ADT. This development has occurred, apparently, because (post-*Caparo*) solicitors and bankers are advising clients intent on acquisitions to get direct assurances from the target's auditors on the truth and fairness of the accounts.

BBH appealed this decision; the liable partners, because of a shortfall in insurance cover, were left facing the prospect of coming up with £34m. An out of court settlement was reached with ADT.

A case in 1997 appeared to take a slightly different line, although this case related to some management accounts on which no written report had been issued.

 Case Study

In *Peach Publishing Ltd v Slater & Co 1997* the Court of Appeal ruled that accountants are not automatically liable if they give oral assurances on accounts to the purchaser of a business. The case involved management accounts, which the accountant stated were right subject to the qualification that they had not been audited. The Court held that the purpose of giving the assurance was not to take on responsibility to the purchaser for the accuracy of the accounts. The purchaser's true objective in this case was to obtain a warranty from the accountant's client, the target. Therefore the accountant was not assuming responsibility to the purchaser by giving his client information on which it could decide whether or not to give the warranty. The Court of Appeal also observed that the purchaser should not have relied on the management accounts without having them checked by its advisers.

Case Study

In a further case the Court of Appeal gave guidance on the effect of a disclaimer which stated that the report had been prepared for the client only and no-one else should rely on it. In *Omega Trust Co Ltd v Wright Son & Pepper 1997* (which related to surveyors but the facts of which can be applied to accountants) the court held that the surveyor was entitled to know who his client was and to whom his duty was held. He was entitled to refuse liability to an unknown lender or any known lender with whom he had not agreed.

All this case law raised some **problems**. In spite of the judgement in *Caparo*, the commercial reality is that creditors and investors (especially institutional ones) do use audited accounts. In the UK the Companies Act requires a company to file accounts with the Registrar. Why is this a statutory requirement? It is surely because the public, including creditors and potential investors, have a need for a credible and independent view of the company's performance and position.

It would be unjust if auditors, who have **secondary responsibility** for financial statements being prepared negligently, bore the full responsibility for losses arising from such negligence just because they are insured. It would also be unjust if the auditors could be sued by all and sundry. While the profession has generally welcomed *Caparo*, two obvious problems are raised by the decision.

- Is a restricted view of the usefulness of audited accounts in the profession's long-term interests?

- For private companies there will probably be an increase in the incidence of personal guarantees and warranties given by the directors to banks and suppliers.

Recent developments in the US appear to try to redress the **balance of liability** by highlighting the responsibilities of management with regard to published financial statements. The Sarbanes-Oxley Act requires chief executive officers and finance officers to certify that the accounts of listed companies are not misleading and present the company's financial position and results fairly. In addition, they are required to confirm that they are responsible for internal controls and have reported significant control deficiencies to the auditors/audit committee.

The UK has also seen some recent developments. The UK Companies Act 2006 requires the directors' report to contain a statement to the effect that in the case of each director:

(a)   So far as the director is aware, there is no relevant audit information of which the auditor is unaware.

(b)   He has taken all the steps that he ought to have taken as a director in order to make himself aware of any relevant audit information and to establish that the auditor is aware of that information.

If the statement in the directors' report is false, every director who knew it was false or who was reckless as to whether it was false, and failed to take reasonable steps to prevent the report from being approved, commits an offence.

In addition Companies Act 2006 now makes it possible for auditors to limit their liability by agreement with a company. We will look at this issue in more detail in Section 4.

2.3.1 Banks and other major lenders

Banks and other major lenders have generally been **excluded** from the extent of negligent auditors' liability by the decision in **Caparo**.

Banks often include clauses in loan agreements referring to audited accounts and requesting that they have access to audited accounts on a regular basis or when reviewing the loan facility. In other words, banks may **document a 'relationship'** with the auditors to establish that there is sufficient proximity and that a duty of care exists.

A recent Scottish case involved a situation similar to this and may suggest that judicial thinking on the matter is developing.

In *Royal Bank of Scotland v Bannerman Johnstone Maclay and Others 2002* the bank, who provided an overdraft facility to the company being audited, claimed the company had misstated its position due to a fraud and that the auditors were negligent in not discovering the fraud. The auditors claimed that they had no duty of care to the bank. However, the judge determined that the auditors would have known that the bank required audited accounts as part of the overdraft arrangement and could have issued a disclaimer to the bank. The fact that they had not issued a disclaimer was an important factor in deciding that the auditors did owe a duty of care to the bank.

2.3.2 Assurance services

The audit firm might be able and prepared to **offer assurances** to the bank in relation to financial statements, position, internal controls or other matters of interest to a primary lender. If this is the case, and the service is required by the bank, the **auditor should seek to create an engagement with the bank itself**.

You should bear in mind that providing assurance services to a lender could result in a **conflict of interest** arising, of course.

Exam focus point

> It is vital that you use the right kind of **language** when answering questions in this area. Your correct use of terms such as **duty of care**, **liability**, **negligence**, **proximity** and **third party** can help to demonstrate to the examiner that you are familiar with the subject matter and are simply **applying** it to the circumstances in the question.

2.4 Disclaimers   6/08

FAST FORWARD ⟫ Auditors may attempt to limit liability to clients. This may not always be effective in law.

The cases above suggest that a duty of care to a third party may arise when an accountant does not know that his work will be relied upon by a third party, but only knows that it is work of a kind which is liable in the ordinary course of events to be relied upon by a third party.

Conversely, an accountant may sometimes be informed or be aware, before he carries out certain work, that a third party will rely upon the results. An example is a report upon the business of a client which the accountant has been instructed to prepare for the purpose of being shown to a potential purchaser or potential creditor of that business. In such a case an accountant should assume that he will be held to owe the same duty to the third party as to his client. The Bannermann case suggests this will also be necessary for **audit work**. Since the Bannermann case, many audit firms have included a disclaimer in their audit report.

When ACCA's Council considered the use of disclaimers, its view was:

'Standard disclaimers are not an appropriate or proportionate response to the Bannermann decision. Their incorporation as a standard feature of the audit report could have the effect of devaluing that report.'

However there are areas of professional work (for example when acting as an auditor under the Companies Act on behalf of shareholders and no liability limitation agreement is in place), where it is not possible for liability to be limited or excluded. There are other areas of professional work (for example when preparing reports on a business for the purpose of being submitted to a potential purchaser) where although such a limitation or exclusion may be included, its effectiveness will depend on the view which a court may subsequently form of its reasonableness.

2.5 Litigation avoidance

The other aspect of how firms are trying to deal with litigation is what they are trying to do to avoid litigation. This strategy has various aspects.

- **Client acceptance procedures** are very important, particularly the screening of new clients and the use of engagement letters. This is covered in more detail in Chapter 5.

- **Performance of audit work**. Firms should make sure that all audits are carried out in accordance with professional standards and best practice.

- **Quality control**. This includes not just controls over individual audits but also stricter 'whole-firm' procedures. This is considered in more detail in Chapter 4.

- **Issue of appropriate disclaimers**. We discussed above the importance of these.

In ACCA's view the best way of restricting liability is for auditors to carry out their audit work in accordance with auditing standards. Where work is properly conducted the auditor should not need to subject it to blanket disclaimers.

Exam focus point

> Read the financial and accountancy press on a regular basis between now and your examination and note any new cases or developments in the question of auditor liability.

 ## Question

Negligence claims

Although auditors can incur civil liability under various statutes it is far more likely that they will incur liability for negligence under the common law, as the majority of cases against auditors have been in this area. Auditors must be fully aware of the extent of their responsibilities, together with steps they must take to minimise the danger of professional negligence claims.

Required

(a) Discuss the extent of an auditors' responsibilities to shareholders and others during the course of their normal professional engagement.

(b) List six steps which auditors should take to minimise the danger of claims against them for negligent work.

Answer

(a) *Responsibility under statute*

An auditor of a limited company has a responsibility, imposed upon him by statute, to form and express a professional opinion on the financial statements presented by the directors to the shareholders. He must report upon the truth and fairness of such statements and the fact that they comply with the law. In so doing, the auditor owes a duty of care to the company imposed by statute. But such duty also arises under contract and may also arise under the common law (law of tort).

Responsibility under contract

In the UK the Companies Act does not state expressly the manner in which the auditor should discharge his duty of care; neither is it likely that this would be clearly spelt out in any contract setting out the terms of an auditor's appointment (eg the engagement letter). Although the articles of a company may extend the auditor's responsibilities beyond those envisaged by the Companies Act, they cannot be used so as to restrict the auditor's statutory duties, neither may they place any restriction upon the auditor's statutory rights which are designed to assist him in the discharge of those duties.

The comments of Lopes L J when considering the degree of skill and care required of an auditor in *Re Kingston Cotton Mill* are still relevant.

'... It is the duty of an auditor to bring to bear on the work he has to perform the skill, care and caution which a reasonably competent, careful and cautious auditor would use. What is reasonable skill, care and caution must depend on the particular circumstances of each case.'

Clearly, with the advent of auditing standards, a measure of good practice is now available for the courts to take into account when considering the adequacy of the work of the auditor.

Responsibility in tort

The law of tort has established that a person owes a duty of care and skill to 'our neighbours' (common and well-known examples of this neighbour principle can be seen in the law of trespass, slander, libel and so on). In the context of the professional auditor the wider implications, however, concern the extent to which the auditor owes a duty of care and skill to third parties who rely on financial statements upon which he has reported but with whom he has no direct contractual or fiduciary relationship.

Liability to third parties

In *Caparo Industries plc v Dickman & Others 1990*, it was held that the auditors of a public company's accounts owed no duty of care to members of the general public who relied upon the accounts in deciding to buy shares in the company. Furthermore as a purchaser of more shares, a shareholder placing reliance on the auditors' report stood in the same position as any other investing member of the public to whom the auditor owed no duty. This decision appeared to radically reverse the tide of cases concerning the auditor's duty of care. The purpose of the audit was simply that of meeting the statutory requirements of the Companies Act. There was nothing in the statutory duties of a company auditor to suggest that they were intended to protect the interests of investors in the market. In particular, there was no reason why any special relationship should be held to arise simply from the fact that the affairs of the company rendered it susceptible to a take-over bid.

A case between BDO Binder Hamlyn and ADT seems to have moved the argument on. In this case it was argued that proximity between a prospective investor and the auditors of a company could be created if the investor asked the auditors whether they stood by their last audit. An appeal is likely in this case as the auditors involved face a large shortfall in insurance proceeds. The recent Scottish Bannerman case suggests that judges may be more likely to impute a duty of care to the auditors if they were aware that the bank made use of audited accounts and did not disclaim liability to them.

(b) In order to provide a means of protection for the auditor arising from the comments in (a) above, the following steps should be taken.

(i) Agreements concerning the duties of the auditor should be:

    (1) Clear and precise

    (2) In writing

    (3) Confirmed by a level of engagement, including matters specifically excluded

(ii) Audit work should be:

    (1) Relevant to the system of internal control, which must be ascertained, evaluated and tested. Controls cannot be entirely ignored: for the auditor to have any confidence in an accounting system there must be present and evident the existence of minimum controls to ensure completeness and accuracy of the records.

    (2) Adequately planned before the audit commences

    (3) Reviewed by a senior member of the firm to ensure quality control of the audit and to enable a decision to be made on the form of audit report

(iii) Any queries arising during the audit should be:

    (1) Recorded on the current working papers

    (2) Cleared and filed

(iv)   A management letter should be:

   (1)   Submitted to the client or the Board of Directors in writing immediately following an audit

   (2)   Seen to be acted upon by the client

(v)   All members of an auditing firm should be familiar with:

   (1)   The standards expected throughout the firm

   (2)   The standards of the profession as a whole by means of adequate training, which should cover the implementation of the firm's audit manual and the recommendations of the professional accountancy bodies

(vi)   Insurance should be taken out to cover the firm against possible claims

3 Restricting liability

> **FAST FORWARD**
>
> ACCA requires that auditors take out professional indemnity insurance.

3.1 Professional indemnity insurance

Key terms

> **Professional indemnity insurance** is insurance against civil claims made by clients and third parties arising from work undertaken by the firm.
>
> **Fidelity guarantee insurance** is insurance against liability arising through any acts of fraud or dishonesty by any partner, director or employee in respect of money or goods held in trust by the firm.

It is important that accountants have insurance so that if negligence occurs, the client can be **compensated** for the error by the accountant. The appropriate compensation could be far greater than the resources of the accountancy firm.

Remember that accountants usually trade as **partnerships**, so all the partners are jointly and severally liable to claims made against individual partners.

3.2 ACCA requirements

ACCA requires that firms holding practising certificates and auditing certificates have professional indemnity insurance with a reputable insurance company. If the firm has employees, it must also have fidelity guarantee insurance.

The insurance must cover 'all civil liability incurred in connection with the conduct of the firm's business by the partners, directors or employees'.

The cover must continue to exist for **six years** after a member ceases to engage in public practice.

3.3 Advantages and disadvantages

The key **advantage** of such insurance is that it provides funds for an innocent party to be compensated in the event of a wrong having been done to them.

An **advantage** to the auditor is that it provides some protection against bankruptcy in the event of successful litigation against the firm. This is particularly important for a partnership, as partners may be sued personally for the negligence of their fellow partners.

A key **disadvantage** is that the existence of insurance against the cost of negligence might encourage auditors to take less care than:

- Would otherwise be the case
- Their professional duty requires

Another problem associated with such insurances are that there are limits of cover (linked with the cost of buying the insurance) and any compensation arising from a claim could be higher than those limits. This could lead to partners being bankrupted despite having insurance. A simple disadvantage associated with the above is the regular cost of the insurance to the partnership.

3.4 Incorporation

The major accountancy firms have been interested in methods of reducing personal liability for partners in the event of negligence for some time. For example, some years ago KPMG (one of the big four accountancy firms) incorporated its UK audit practice. This was allowed under the UK's Companies Act 1989.

The new arrangement created 'a firm within a firm'. KPMG Audit plc is a limited company wholly owned by the partnership, KPMG. The reason behind this is to protect the partners from the crushing effects of litigation. The other side of incorporation means that KPMG Audit plc are subject to the statutory disclosure requirements of companies.

An alternative to incorporation as a company is incorporation as a limited liability partnership.

Limited liability partnership can be operated in some countries, for example, some of the states in the USA and the UK, which we will look at briefly below.

3.5 Limited liability partnerships

The Limited Liability Partnership Act 2000 enabled UK firms to establish limited liability partnerships as separate legal entities. These combine the flexibility and tax status of a partnership with limited liability for members.

The effect of this is that the partnership, **but not its members**, will be liable to third parties; however the personal assets of **negligent** partners will still be at risk.

Limited liability partnerships could be formed from 6 April 2001. Several prominent professional partnerships have incorporated as LLPs.

Limited liability partnerships are set up by similar procedures to those for incorporating a company. An incorporation document is sent to the Registrar of Companies. The Registrar will issue a certificate of incorporation to confirm that all statutory requirements have been fulfilled.

In a similar way to traditional partnerships, relations between partners will be governed by internal partner agreements, or by future statutory regulations.

Each member of the partnership will still be an agent of the partnership unless he has no authority to act and an outside party is aware of this lack of authority.

3.6 Advantages and disadvantages of different structures

	Advantages	Disadvantages
Partnership	• Less regulation than for companies • Financial statements not on public record	• Joint and several liability • Personal assets at risk
Incorporation	• Limited liability	• Public filing of audited financial statements • Management must comply with Companies Acts
LLP	• Protection of personal assets • Limited liability of members • Similar tax effect of partnership • Flexible management structures	• Public filing of audited financial statements

4 Current issues in auditor liability

As auditor liability is an important practical issue, there are regular developments in this area.

Even with PII and other means of restricting liability there has been great concern throughout the audit profession globally at the remaining risks to firms' survival in the face of claims which might exceed their insurance cover.

The profession has lobbied for further protection in the form of *proportionate liability* or *capping liability*.

Key terms

> **Proportionate liability** would allow claims arising from successful negligence claims to be split between the auditors and the directors of the client company, the split being determined by a judge on the basis of where the fault was seen to lie. This would require the approval of shareholders.
>
> **Capping liability** would set a maximum limit on the amount that the auditor would have to pay out under any claim.

4.1 UK Companies Act 2006

Chapter 6 of Companies Act 2006 makes it possible for auditors to limit their liability by agreement with a company. It does this by defining a **liability limitation agreement**, which is a contractual limitation of the auditor's liability to a company, requiring shareholder agreement by resolution and only effective if it is **fair and reasonable**.

The agreement can cover liability for negligence, default, breach of duty or breach of trust by the auditor in relation to the audit of accounts for a particular year. For the agreement to be valid it cannot cover more than one financial year. The company can also withdraw its authorisation of the agreement by passing an ordinary resolution.

It is currently open to negotiation between auditors and their client companies as to what form the agreement will take, for example, a liability cap (fixed or variable), or proportionate liability but the Act leaves it open for the government to issue regulations in future as to the nature of these agreements.

Under current legislation, it is possible for auditors to suffer the entire liability for corporate collapse even if they are found to be only partly to blame. The Big Four firms lobbied the then Department of Business, Enterprise and Regulatory Reform (BERR) to get a limit on their exposure in the event of claims from investors and others in the event of a company failure. This was prompted by fears that a blockbuster lawsuit, if successful, could put one or more of them out of business, which in turn could trigger a collapse of the audit market and cause chaos for business.

The Big Four have been pushing for proportionate liability ever since the collapse of Arthur Andersen, then one of the world's five biggest accounting firms, over its involvement in the Enrol scandal in 2002.

4.2 Ongoing debate

There have been concerns that the new regulations may distort competition in the audit market. If the biggest firms set caps at very high levels, mid-tier firms could be disadvantaged. In the UK the government has left a provision for the relevant government ministers to issue specific rules specifying what can and cannot be included in agreements in case competition problems arise.

There are also arguments that capping liability will reduce the value of the audit to investors and may bring pressure on firms to reduce fees.

Overall the profession reacted positively to the new rules. The reaction was less positive to the other major effect of the bill, introducing a criminal offence of 'knowingly or recklessly' including in the auditor's report any matter that is misleading, false or deceptive in a material particular. The government saw this as being a necessary change in order to maintain audit quality.

4.3 Network firms

Several accountancy firms have moved towards network models over recent years. This is where member firms are part of a larger structure, often sharing a name (or using a similar name) and professional resources. As part of a global network, member firms have been able to sell services based on the value and reputation of their global brand name. However in recent liability cases, some network firms have claimed the network is not liable for negligence in an individual member firm even though they appear to be operating under the same brand.

Case Study

In 2009, BDO Seidman, a member firm of the global network BDO International, faced audit negligence claims to the sum of $500m over the audit of ES Bankest, a company owned by the Portuguese bank Banco Espirito Santo. Auditors from BDO Seidman had been accused of being grossly negligent in audits between 1998 and 2002. BDO International had claimed that they should not be held liable as member firm audits are conducted independently.

It is possible that the network model may disappear or be modified in future years. The current situation where network firms advertise under one brand and then claim they are separate firms when things go wrong may not be sustainable given the outcome of current legal activity.

5 Fraud and error 6/09

FAST FORWARD

Misunderstanding of the auditor's responsibilities in respect of fraud is a major component of the 'expectations gap'.

5.1 What is fraud?

Key term

Fraud is an intentional act by one or more individuals among management, those charged with governance (management fraud), employees (employee fraud) or third parties involving the use of deception to obtain an unjust or illegal advantage. Fraud may be perpetrated by an individual, or colluded in with people internal or external to the business.

Fraud is a wide legal concept, but the auditor's main concern is with fraud that causes a material misstatement in financial statements. It is distinguished from error, which is when a material misstatement is caused by mistake, for example, in the application of an accounting policy. Specifically, there are two types of fraud causing material misstatement in financial statements:

- Fraudulent financial reporting
- Misappropriation of assets

5.1.1 Fraudulent financial reporting

This may include:

- Manipulation, falsification or alteration of accounting records/supporting documents
- Misrepresentation (or omission) of events, transactions or other significant information in the financial statements
- Intentional misapplication of accounting principles

Such fraud may be carried out by overriding controls that would otherwise appear to be operating effectively, for example, by recording fictitious journal entries or improperly adjusting assumptions or estimates used in financial reporting.

Aggressive earnings management is a topical issue and, at its most aggressive, may constitute fraudulent financial reporting. Auditors should consider issues such as unsuitable revenue recognition, accruals, liabilities, provisions and reserves accounting and large numbers of immaterial breaches of financial reporting requirements to see whether together, they constitute fraud.

5.1.2 Misappropriation of assets

This is the theft of the entity's assets (for example, cash, inventory). Employees may be involved in such fraud in small and immaterial amounts, however, it can also be carried out by management for larger items who may then conceal the misappropriation, for example by:

- Embezzling receipts (for example, diverting them to private bank accounts)
- Stealing physical assets or intellectual property (inventory, selling data)
- Causing an entity to pay for goods not received (payments to fictitious vendors)
- Using assets for personal use

5.2 Responsibilities with regard to fraud

Management and those charged with governance in an entity are primarily responsible for preventing and detecting fraud. It is up to them to put a strong emphasis within the company on fraud prevention. This will include establishing a strong control environment, with an emphasis on the principles of good corporate governance. In relation to fraud in particular, this would mean eg putting policies in place to help ensure that employees are aware of their responsibilities regarding fraud, issuing guidance for employees on what they should do if they encounter or suspect a fraud.

Auditors are responsible for carrying out an audit in accordance with international auditing standards, one of which is ISA 240 *The auditor's responsibilities relating to fraud in an audit of financial statements*, which we shall look at now.

5.3 The auditor's approach to the possibility of fraud

5.3.1 General

The key responsibility of an auditor is set out early in the ISA.

ISA 240.5

An auditor conducting an audit in accordance with ISAs is responsible for obtaining reasonable assurance that the financial statements taken as a whole are free from material misstatement whether caused by fraud or error.

ISA 240.10

The objectives of the auditor are:

(a)   To identify and assess the risks of material misstatement of the financial statements due to fraud.

(b)   To obtain sufficient appropriate audit evidence regarding the assessed risks of material misstatement due to fraud, through designing and implementing appropriate responses.

(c)   To respond appropriately to fraud or suspected fraud identified during the audit.

An overriding requirement of the ISA is that auditors are aware of the possibility of there being misstatements due to fraud.

> **ISA 240.12**
>
> In accordance with ISA 200 the auditor shall maintain professional scepticism throughout the audit, recognising the possibility that a material misstatement due to fraud could exist, notwithstanding the auditor's past experience of the honesty and integrity of the entity's management and those charged with governance.

The ISA also requires discussion by members of the engagement team of the susceptibility of the entity's financial statements to material misstatement due to fraud, including how fraud might occur.

The engagement partner must consider what matters discussed should be passed on to other members of the team not present at the discussion. The discussion itself usually includes:

- An exchange of ideas between the engagement team about how fraud could be perpetrated
- A consideration of circumstances that might be indicative of aggressive earnings management
- A consideration of known factors that might give incentive to management to commit fraud
- A consideration of management's oversight of employees with access to cash/other assets
- A consideration of any unusual/unexplained changes in lifestyle of management/employees
- An emphasis on maintaining professional scepticism throughout the audit
- A consideration of the types of circumstance that might indicate fraud
- A consideration of how unpredictability will be incorporated into the audit
- A consideration of what audit procedures might be carried out to answer any suspicions of fraud
- A consideration of any allegations of fraud that have come to the auditors' attention
- A consideration of the risk of management override of controls

5.3.2 Risk assessment procedures

The auditor would undertake risk assessment procedures as set out in ISA 315 *Identifying and assessing the risks of material misstatement through understanding the entity and its environment* (see Chapter 6) which would include assessing the risk of fraud. These procedures will include:

- Inquiries of management and those charged with governance
- Consideration of when fraud risk factors are present
- Consideration of results of analytical procedures
- Consideration of any other relevant information

In identifying the risks of fraud, the auditor is required by the ISA to carry out some specific procedures.

> **ISA 240.17**
>
> The auditor shall make enquiries of management regarding:
>
> (a) Management's assessment of the risk that the financial statements may be materially misstated due to fraud, including the nature, extent and frequency of such assessments
>
> (b) Management's process for identifying and responding to the risks of fraud in the entity, including any specific risks of fraud that management has identified or that have been brought to its attention, or classes of transactions, account balances or disclosures for which a risk of fraud is likely to exist
>
> (c) Management's communication, if any, to those charged with governance regarding its processes for identifying and responding to the risks of fraud in the entity, and
>
> (d) Management's communication, if any, to employees regarding its views on business practices and ethical behaviour
>
> **ISA 240.18**
>
> The auditor shall make enquiries of management and others within the entity as appropriate, to determine whether they have knowledge of any actual, suspected or alleged fraud affecting the entity.

> **IAS 240.19**
>
> For those entities that have an internal audit function, the auditor shall make enquiries of internal audit to determine whether it has knowledge of any actual, suspected or alleged fraud affecting the entity, and to obtain its views about the risks of fraud.
>
> **ISA 240.20**
>
> Unless all of those charged with governance are involved in managing the entity the auditor shall obtain an understanding of how those charged with governance exercise oversight of management's processes for identifying and responding to the risks of fraud in the entity and the internal control that management has established to mitigate these risks.
>
> **ISA 240.21**
>
> Unless all of those charged with governance are involved in managing the entity, the auditor shall make inquiries of those charged with governance to determine whether they have knowledge of any actual, suspected or alleged fraud affecting the entity. These inquiries are made in part to corroborate the responses to the inquiries of management.
>
> **ISA 240.24**
>
> The auditor shall evaluate whether the information obtained from the other risk assessment procedures and related activities performed indicates that one or more fraud risk factors are present. While fraud risk factors may not necessarily indicate the existence of fraud, they have often been present in circumstances where frauds have occurred and therefore may indicate risks of material misstatement due to fraud.

The size, complexity and ownership characteristics of the entity have a significant influence on the consideration of relevant fraud risk factors. For example in the case of a large entity there may be factors that generally constrain improper conduct by management including effective oversight by those charged with governance, an effective internal audit function and a written code of conduct. These considerations are less likely in the case of a small entity.

Examples of fraud risk factors

ISA 240 does not attempt to provide a definitive list of risk factors but, in an appendix, identifies and gives examples of two types of fraud that are relevant to auditors:

- Fraudulent financial reporting
- Misstatements arising from misappropriation of assets

For each of these, the risk factors are classified according to three conditions that are generally present when misstatements due to fraud occur:

- Incentives/pressures
- Opportunities
- Attitudes/rationalisations

Fraudulent financial reporting

Incentives/pressures
- Financial stability/profitability is threatened
- Pressure for management to meet the expectations of third parties
- Personal financial situation of management threatened by the entity's financial performance
- Excessive pressure on management or operating personnel to meet financial targets

Opportunities
- Significant related-party transactions
- Assets, liabilities, revenues or expenses based on significant estimates
- Domination of management by a single person or small group
- Complex or unstable organisational structure
- Internal control components are deficient

Attitudes/rationalisations
- Ineffective communication or enforcement of the entity's values or ethical standards by management
- Known history of violations of securities laws or other laws and regulations
- A practice by management of committing to achieve aggressive or unrealistic forecasts
- Low morale among senior management
- Relationship between management and the current or predecessor auditor is strained

Misappropriation of assets

Incentives/pressures
- Personal financial obligations
- Adverse relationships between the entity and employees with access to cash or other assets susceptible to theft

Opportunities
- Large amounts of cash on hand or processed
- Inventory items that are small in size, of high value, or in high demand
- Easily convertible assets, such as bearer bonds, diamonds, or computer chips
- Inadequate internal control over assets

Attitudes/rationalisations
- Overriding existing controls
- Failing to correct known internal control deficiencies
- Behaviour indicating displeasure or dissatisfaction with the entity
- Changes in behaviour or lifestyle

> **ISA 240.26**
>
> When identifying and assessing the risks of material misstatement due to fraud, the auditor shall, based on a presumption that there are risks of fraud in revenue recognition, evaluate which types of revenue, revenue transactions or assertions give rise to such risks.
>
> **ISA 240.27**
>
> The auditor shall treat those assessed risks of material misstatement due to fraud as significant risks and accordingly, to the extent not already done so, the auditor shall obtain an understanding of the entity's related controls, including control activities, relevant to such risks.

Generally, the auditor:

- Identifies fraud risks
- Relates this to what could go wrong at a financial statement level
- Considers the likely magnitude of potential misstatement

You are an audit manager for Elle and Emm, Certified Accountants. You are carrying out the planning of the audit of Sellfones Co, a listed company, and a high street retailer of mobile phones, for the year ending 30 September 20X7. The notes from your planning meeting with Pami Desai, the financial director, include the following:

(1) One of Sellfones' main competitors ceased trading during the year due to the increasing pressure on margins in the industry and competition from online retailers.

(2) A new management structure has been implemented, with 10 new divisional managers appointed during the year. The high street shops have been allocated to these managers, with approximately 20 branch managers reporting to each divisional manager. The divisional managers have been set challenging financial targets for their areas with substantial bonuses offered to incentivise them to meet the targets. The board of directors have also decided to cut the amount that will be paid to shop staff as a Christmas bonus.

(3) In response to recommendations in the prior year's Report to Management, a new inventory system has been implemented. There were some problems in its first months of operation but a report has been submitted to the board by Steven MacLennan, the chief accountant, confirming that the problems have all been resolved and that information produced by the system will be accurate. Pami commented that the chief accountant has had to work very long hours to deal with this new system, often working at weekends and even refusing to take any leave until the system was running properly.

(4) The company is planning to raise new capital through a share issue after the year-end in order to finance expansion of the business into other countries in Europe. As a result, Pami has requested that the auditor's report is signed off by 15 December 20X7 (six weeks earlier than in previous years).

(5) The latest board summary of results includes:

9 months to 30 June 20X7 (unaudited)		Year to 30 September 20X6 (audited)	
	$m		$m
Revenue	320	Revenue	280
Cost of sales	215	Cost of sales	199
Gross profit	105	Gross profit	81
Operating expenses	(89)	Operating expenses	(70)
Exceptional profit on sale of properties	30		–
Profit before tax	46		11

(6) Several shop properties owned by the company were sold under sale and leaseback arrangements.

Required

Identify and explain any fraud risk factors that the audit team should consider when planning the audit of Sellphones Co.

Approaching the answer

Look for key words and ask questions of the information given to you. This is illustrated below.

> Identify the stage of the audit

You are an audit manager for Elle and Emm, Certified Accountants. You are carrying out the planning of the audit of Sellfones Co, a listed company, and a high street retailer of mobile phones, for the year ending 30 September 20X7. The notes from your planning meeting with Pami Desai, the financial director, include the following:

> Indication of level of competition

> Nature of industry – very competitive

(1) One of Sellfones' main competitors ceased trading during the year due to the increasing pressure on margins in the industry and competition from online retailers.

> Is it effective? Do they have the expertise?

> Increased risk?

> Morale?

> Pressure on management to be successful

(2) A new management structure has been implemented, with 10 new divisional managers appointed during the year. The high street shops have been allocated to these managers, with approximately 20 branch managers reporting to each divisional manager. The divisional managers have been set challenging financial targets for their areas with substantial bonuses offered to incentivise them to meet the targets. The board of directors have also decided to cut the amount that will be paid to shop staff as a Christmas bonus.

> Reliability?

> Under pressure

(3) In response to recommendations in the prior year's Report to Management, a new inventory system has been implemented. There were some problems in its first months of operation but a report has been submitted to the board by Steven MacLennan, the chief accountant, confirming that the problems have all been resolved and that information produced by the system will be accurate. Pami commented that the chief accountant has had to work very long hours to deal with this new system, often working at weekends and even refusing to take any leave until the system was running properly.

> Suspicious?

> Pressure on results

(4) The company is planning to raise new capital through a share issue after the year-end in order to finance expansion of the business into other countries in Europe. As a result, Pami has requested that the auditor's report is signed off by 15 December 20X7 (six weeks earlier that in previous years).

> Increased audit risk?

(5) The latest board summary of results includes:

9 months to 30 June 20X7 (unaudited)   *Year to 30 September 20X6 (audited)*

> Changes in margin in line with expectations?

	$m		$m
Revenue	320	Revenue	280
Cost of sales	215	Cost of sales	199
Gross profit	105	Gross profit	81
Operating expenses	(89)	Operating expenses	(70)
Exceptional profit on sale			
of properties	30		–
Profit before tax	46		11

(6) Several shop properties owned by the company were sold under sale and leaseback arrangements.

> Substance

Required

Identify and explain any fraud risk factors that the audit team should consider when planning the audit of Sellphones Co.

Answer plan

Not all the points you notice will necessarily be relevant and you may also find that you do not have time to mention all the points. You may also notice that certain issues are related and should be dealt with together. Prioritise your points in a more formal plan and then write out your answer.

Risk factors

- Nature of industry and operating conditions
- Management structure and incentives
- New inventory system/chief accountant
- Results
- Exceptional gain
- Time pressure
- Theft of assets

Answer

In this scenario there are a large number of factors that should alert the auditors to the possibility of misstatements arising from fraudulent financial reporting, and others that could indicate a risk of misstatements arising from misappropriation of assets.

(1) **Operating conditions within the industry**

The failure of a competitor in a highly competitive business sector highlights the threat to the survival of a business such as Sellphones and this could place the directors under pressure to overstate the performance and position of the company in an attempt to maintain investor confidence, particularly given the intention to raise new share capital.

(2) **Management structure and incentives**

It is not clear in the scenario how much involvement the new divisional managers have in the financial reporting process but the auditors would need to examine any reports prepared or reviewed by them very carefully as their personal interest may lead them to overstate results in order to earn their bonuses.

(3) **New inventory system/chief accountant**

The problems with the implementation of the new inventory system suggest that there may have been control deficiencies and errors in the recording of inventory figures. Misstatements, whether deliberate or not, may not have been identified. The amount of time spent by the chief accountant on the implementation of the new inventory system could be seen as merely underlining the severity of the problems, but the fact that he has not taken any leave should also be considered as suspicious and the auditors should be alert to any indication that he may have been involved in any deliberate misstatement of figures.

(4) **Results**

The year on year results look better than might be expected given the business environment. The gross profit margin has increased to 32.8% (20X6 25.3%) and the operating profit margin has increased to 5% (20X6 3.9%). This seems to conflict with what is known about the industry and should increase the auditors' professional scepticism in planning the audit.

(5) **Exceptional gain**

The sale and leaseback transaction may involve complex considerations relating to its commercial substance. It may not be appropriate to recognise a gain or the gain may have been miscalculated.

(6) **Time pressure on audit**

The auditors should be alert to the possibility that the tight deadline may have been set to reduce the amount of time the auditors have to gather evidence after the end of the reporting period,, perhaps in the hope that certain deliberate misstatements will not be discovered.

(7) **Risk of misappropriation of assets**

The nature of the inventory held in the shops increases the risk that staff may steal goods. This risk is perhaps increased by the fact that the attitude of the staff towards their employer is likely to have been damaged by the cut in their Christmas bonus. The problems with the new inventory recording system increase the risk that any such discrepancies in inventory may not have been identified.

5.3.3 Responding to assessed risks

The auditor must then come up with responses to the assessed risks.

> **ISA 240.28**
>
> In accordance with ISA 330 the auditor shall determine overall responses to address the assessed risks of material misstatement due to fraud at the financial statement level.

In determining overall responses to address the risks of material misstatement due to fraud at the financial statement level the auditor should:

(a) Consider the assignment and supervision of personnel

(b) Consider the accounting policies used by the entity, and

(c) Incorporate an element of unpredictability in the selection of the nature, timing and extent of audit procedures

> **ISA 240.30**
>
> In accordance with ISA 330, the auditor shall design and perform further audit procedures whose nature, timing and extent are responsive to the assessed risks of material misstatement due to fraud at the assertion level.

The auditor may have to **amend** the **nature, timing or extent** of planned audit procedures to address assessed risks. The auditor should also consider the following:

- Audit procedures responsive to management override of controls
- Journal entries and other adjustments
- Accounting estimates
- Business rationale for significant transactions

Examples: specific audit procedures

The auditor might to choose to attend previously unvisited branches to carry out inventory or cash checks.

The auditor might perform detailed analytical procedures using disaggregated data, for example, comparing sales and costs of sales by location.

The auditor might use an expert to assess management estimates in a subjective area.

5.4 Evaluation of audit evidence

The auditor evaluates the audit evidence obtained to ensure it is consistent and that it achieves its aim of answering the risks of fraud. This will include a consideration of results of analytical procedures and other misstatements found. The auditor must also consider the reliability of written representations.

The auditor must obtain written representation that management accepts its responsibility for the prevention and detection of fraud and has made all relevant disclosures to the auditors.

5.5 Documentation

The auditor must document:

- The significant decisions reached as a result of the team's discussion of fraud
- The identified and assessed risks of material misstatement due to fraud
- The overall responses to assessed risks
- Results of specific audit tests
- Any communications with management
- Reasons for concluding that the presumption that there is a risk of fraud related to revenue recognition is not applicable.

5.6 Reporting

There are various reporting requirements in ISA 240.

> **ISA 240.40**
>
> If the auditor has identified a fraud or has obtained information that indicates a fraud may exist, the auditor shall communicate these matters on a timely basis to the appropriate level of management in order to inform those with primary responsibility for the prevention and detection of fraud of matters relevant to their responsibilities.
>
> **ISA 240.41**
>
> Unless all of those charged with governance are involved in managing the entity, if the auditor has identified or suspects fraud involving:
>
> (a)   Management
> (b)   Employees who have significant roles in internal control, or
> (c)   Others, where the fraud results in a material misstatement in the financial statements
>
> the auditor should communicate these matters to **those charged with governance** on a timely basis. If the auditor suspects fraud involving management, the auditor shall communicate these suspicions to those charged with governance and discuss with them the nature, timing and extent of audit procedures necessary to complete the audit.

The auditor should also make relevant parties within the entity aware of significant deficiencies in the design or implementation of controls to prevent and detect fraud which has come to the auditor's attention, and consider whether there are any other relevant matters to bring to the attention of those charged with governance with regard to fraud.

The auditor may have a **statutory duty** to report fraudulent behaviour to **regulators** outside the entity. If no such legal duty arises, the auditor must consider whether to do so would breach their **professional duty of confidence**. In either event, the auditor should take **legal advice**.

5.7 Auditor unable to continue

The auditor should consider the need to withdraw from the engagement if he uncovers exceptional circumstances with regard to fraud.

Exam focus point

Remember the confidentiality issues from Chapter 2. When you are considering whether to make a public interest disclosure, you should always bear it in mind.

5.8 Current issue: fraud in a global economic downturn

The current global economic downturn has resulted in the uncovering of a number of frauds including Satyam Computers in India and Madoff in the USA. Sustaining fraud often relies on incoming cash from investors. As the world economy deteriorates, less cash is available for investment and the fraudulent scheme collapses. This partly explains why more fraud is discovered in a global economic downturn.

Additionally, a tougher economic climate can increase the pressure to carry out fraud. This can be for personal reasons where an employee desires to maintain a higher standard of living than they can now afford. Worries over job security or decreased compensation due to lower bonuses and share values can all add to an employee being able to rationalise and justify fraud. Alternatively, fraud may be perpetrated as management feel pressure to maintain earnings or meet company debt covenants rather than for personal gain.

In the wake of the financial crisis of 2007-8, there has been a lot of discussion in the profession about extending the auditor's responsibilities with regard to fraud. In a global economic downturn the auditor needs to be increasingly aware of the risk of fraud. The audit must be planned and carried out with this in mind.

Two articles in *Student Accountant* have looked at the audit and fraud in the last few years. Both these articles can be accessed through the ACCA website. Make sure you have looked at both of them.

The first article was published in the March 2009 edition and was entitled 'ISA 240 auditors and fraud' and covers some key areas of the updated ISA.

The second article, 'Massaging the figures', was published in the April 2009 edition and was written by the current examiner. It looks at the increased risk of fraudulent financial reporting in a global economic downturn and how this affects the auditor.

Question   Detection of fraud

Required

(a)   Discuss what responsibility auditors have to detect fraud.

(b)   Explain how the auditors might conduct their audit in response to an assessed risk of:

    (i)   Misappropriation

    (ii)   Fraudulent financial reporting

Answer

(a)   The primary responsibility for the prevention and detection of fraud and irregularities rests with management and those charged with governance. This responsibility may be partly discharged by the institution of an adequate system of internal control including, for example, authorisation controls and controls covering segregation of duties.

    The auditors should recognise the possibility of material irregularities or frauds which could, unless adequately disclosed, distort the results or state of affairs shown by the financial statements. ISA 240 states that the auditor is responsible for obtaining reasonable assurance that the financial statements taken as a whole are free from material misstatement whether caused by fraud or error. Auditors are required to carry out their audit with professional scepticism.

    Auditors are required to carry out risk assessment procedures in respect of fraud. This will involve making enquiries of management, considering if any risk factors (such as the existence of pressure for management to meet certain targets) are present and to consider the results of analytical procedures if any method or unexpected relationships have been identified.

    If these is an assessed risk of fraud, the auditor must make suitable responses. Overall responses include considering the personnel for the assignment (for example, using more experienced personnel), considering the accounting policies used by the entity (have they changed? are they reasonable?) and incorporating an element of unpredictability into the audit.

    Specific responses to the risk of misstatement at the assertion level due to fraud will vary depending on the circumstances but could include:

    (i)   Changing the nature of audit tests (for example, introducing CAATs if more detail is required about a computerised system)

    (ii)   Changing the timing of audit tests (for example, testing throughout an audit period, instead of extending audit conclusions from an interim audit)

    (iii)   Changing the extent of audit tests (for example, increasing sample sizes)

(b)   (i)   **Misappropriation**

        Employee frauds such as misappropriation are likely to take place when controls are weak. If controls are weak, auditors may not test controls and hence evidence of employee fraud might go undetected. However, if auditors have identified a risk of employee fraud, they might as a response test controls in the relevant area (such as purchases or sales) in order to identify any unexplained patterns in the company's procedures. For example, if a purchase fraud is suspected, auditors might scrutinise authorisation controls to see if a particular member of staff always authorises certain items/for certain people, where the system does not require that.

Many substantive procedures normally performed by the auditors may assist in isolating employee frauds, if they are occurring. For example, tests performed on the receivables ledger may be aimed at revealing overstatement or bad debts, but the design of such tests also assists with cash understatement objectives and may reveal irregularities such as 'teeming and lading'.

(ii) **Fraudulent financial reporting**

If the auditors conclude that there is a high risk of fraudulent financial reporting by management they will concentrate on techniques such as analytical procedures, scrutiny of unusual transactions and all journal entries, review of events after the reporting period (including going concern evaluation), and review of the financial statements and accounting policies for any changes or material distortions.

6 The expectations gap

ISA 240 sets out the current position on the auditor's responsibility to consider fraud, and in recent years has increased the level of work done by applying the audit risk model. There remains a debate as to whether this is sufficient as the area of fraud is a key part of the expectations gap between what users of auditor's reports believe to be the purposes of the audit compared with the actual nature of the assurance reported to them by auditors.

The issue of the expectations gap is consistently in and out of the financial press. In recent years, there has been a focus on the role of auditors in evaluating whether a company is a going concern. In the USA, the collapse of Lehman Brothers brought with it accusations from some quarters that its auditor, Ernst & Young, had failed to discharge its responsibilities as auditor.

A recent example of such coverage relates to auditors Ernst and Young (EY) expressing a concern over the future of National Express. EY raised concerns that there was significant doubt over the group's ability to continue as a going concern and that there was a material uncertainty about the group's cash flows and its ability to re-pay debts. This news came as National Express reported a first-half pre tax loss of £48.1m, compared to a profit of £52.4m made a year ago.

KPMG's recent going concern statement relating to Liverpool Football Club has also received considerable press coverage. The parent company, Kop Football Holdings suffered a loss last year of £42.6m, and now has been warned by KPMG about its ability to trade as a going concern and instructed to refinance £350m debt.

High profile cases such as these have brought up the question of whether auditors should actually be responsible for the evaluation of whether a company is a going concern, and how this differs from the way that the responsibilities of the auditor are perceived.

6.1 Narrowing the expectations gap

The expectations gap could, theoretically, be narrowed in two ways.

Educating users – the auditor's report as outlined in ISA 700 *Forming an opinion and reporting on financial statements* includes an explanation of the auditor's responsibilities. It is not clear that any further information would help, and it might even have the effect of bringing the value of the audit into question. One suggestion is that auditors could highlight circumstances where they have had to rely on directors' representations.

Extending the auditor's responsibilities – research indicates that extra work by auditors with the inevitable extra costs is likely to make little difference to the detection of fraud because

- Most material frauds involve management.
- More than half of frauds involve misstated financial reporting but do not include diversion of funds from the company.
- Management fraud is unlikely to be found in a financial statement audit.
- Far more is spent on investigating and prosecuting fraud in a company than on its audit.

Suggestions for expanding the auditor's role have included:

- Requiring auditors to report to boards and audit committees on the adequacy of controls to prevent and detect fraud
- Encouraging the use of targeted forensic fraud reviews (see Chapter 14)
- Increasing the requirement to report suspected frauds

- Professional accountants may have professional liability under statutory law.
- Auditors may have professional liability in the tort of negligence.
- The auditor owes a duty of care to the audit client automatically under law.
- The auditor only owes a duty of care to parties other than the audit client if one has been established.
- Auditors may attempt to limit liability to clients. This may not always be effective in law.
- ACCA requires that auditors take out professional indemnity insurance.
- As auditor liability is an important practical issue, there are regular developments in this area.
- Misunderstanding of the auditor's responsibilities in respect of fraud is a major component of the 'expectations gap'.

Quick Quiz

1   Define fraud.

2   Draw a table showing the reporting requirements of ISA 240 *The auditor's responsibilities relating to fraud in an audit of financial statements.*

3   What three matters must a plaintiff satisfy to the court in an action for negligence?

   (1)   ....
   (2)   ....
   (3)   ....

4   Name four aspects of litigation avoidance.

   (1)   ....
   (2)   ....
   (3)   ....
   (4)   ....

5   Professional indemnity insurance is insurance against liability arising through any acts of fraud or dishonesty by partners in respect of money held in trust by the firm.

   True   ☐

   False ☐

Answers to Quick Quiz

1   Fraud is the use of deception to obtain unjust or illegal financial advantage and intentional misrepresentation by management, employees or third parties.

2

Management	If the auditors suspect or detect any fraud (even if immaterial), as soon as they can they should tell management.
Those charged with governance	If the auditor has identified fraud involving management, employees with significant roles in internal control, or others, if it results in a material misstatement, they must report it to those charged with governance.
Third parties	Auditors may have a statutory duty to report to a regulator. Auditors are advised to take legal advice if reporting externally to the company.

3   (1) A duty of care existed
    (2) Negligence occurred
    (3) The client suffered pecuniary loss as a result

4   (1) Client acceptance procedures
    (2) Performance of audit work in line with ISAs
    (3) Quality control
    (4) Disclaimers

5   False. That is fidelity guarantee insurance. Professional indemnity insurance is insurance against civil claims made by clients and third parties arising from work undertaken by the firm.

Now try the questions below from the Exam Question Bank

Number	Level	Marks	Time
Q5	Examination	15	27 mins
Q6	Examination	20	36 mins

Practice management

Quality control

4

Topic list	Syllabus reference
1 Principles and purpose	C1
2 Quality control at a firm level	C1
3 Quality control on an individual audit	C1

Introduction

The role performed by auditors represents an activity of significant public interest. Quality independent audit is crucial, both to users and to the audit profession. Poor audit quality damages the reputation of the firm and leads to loss of clients and subsequently loss of fees as well as increased litigation and professional insurance costs.

Although there are specific standards giving guidance on how auditors should perform their work with satisfactory quality, these can never cater for every situation. There are two standards dealing with quality at a broader level. These are ISQC 1 *Quality control for firms that perform audits and reviews of financial statements, and other assurance and related services engagements*, and ISA 220 *Quality control for an audit of financial statements*.

Study guide

		Intellectual level
C1	**Quality control**	
(a)	Explain the principles and purpose of quality control of audit and other assurance engagements	1
(b)	Describe the elements of a system of quality control relevant to a given firm	2
(c)	Select and justify quality control procedures that are applicable to a given audit engagement	3
(d)	Assess whether an engagement has been planned and performed in accordance with professional standards and whether reports issued are appropriate in the circumstances	3

Exam guide

Issues relating to quality control can be linked with ethics and liability. You could be asked to suggest quality control procedures that a firm should implement in specific circumstances, or to review a firm's procedures and assess their adequacy. A scenario-based question on quality control appeared in the pilot paper.

1 Principles and purpose

Audit quality is not defined in law or through regulations, nor do auditing standards provide a simple definition.

Although each stakeholder in the audit will give a different meaning to audit quality, at its heart it is about delivering an appropriate professional opinion supported by the necessary evidence and objective judgements.

Many principles contribute to audit quality including good leadership, experienced judgement, technical competence, ethical values and appropriate client relationships, proper working practices and effective quality control and monitoring review processes.

The standards on audit quality provide guidance to firms on how to achieve these principles.

2 Quality control at a firm level   Pilot paper, 6/09

FAST FORWARD

> The international standard on quality control (ISQC 1) helps audit firms establish quality standards for their business.

The fact that auditors follow international auditing standards provides a general quality control framework within which audits should be conducted. There are also specific quality control standards.

2.1 Purpose of ISQC 1

ISQC 1.11

The objective of the firm is to establish and maintain a system of quality control to provide it with reasonable assurance that:

(a)   The firm and its personnel comply with professional standards and applicable legal and regulatory requirements; and

(b)   Reports issued by the firm or engagement partners are appropriate in the circumstances.

All quality control policies and procedures should be **documented** and **communicated** to the firm's personnel.

We have already considered the sections of this standard relating to ethics in Chapter 2 and those relating to client acceptance will be covered in Chapter 5 of this Study Text. We shall now consider the requirements of the rest of the standard, which fall into the following areas:

- Firm and leadership responsibilities for quality within the firm
- Human resources
- Engagement performance (see also below, the requirements of ISA 220)
- Monitoring

2.2 Firm and leadership responsibilities for quality within the firm

> **ISQC 1.13**
>
> Personnel within the firm responsible for establishing and maintaining the firm's system of quality control shall have an understanding of the entire text of this ISQC, including its application and other explanatory material, to understand its objective and to apply its requirements properly.

Firms are required to ensure that the appropriate training is provided to ensure there is complete understanding of the objectives and procedures under ISQC 1. The standard stipulates further that some firms may need to apply additional procedures (beyond those of the standard) to ensure that the objectives are met.

The standard requires that the firm implements policies such that the **internal culture** of the firm is one where **quality** is considered **essential**. Such a culture must be inspired by the leaders of the firm, who must sell this culture in their actions and messages. In other words, the entire business strategy of the audit firm should be driven by the need for quality in its operations.

The firm may appoint an individual or group of individuals to oversee quality in the firm. Such individuals must have:

- Sufficient and appropriate experience
- The ability to carry out the job
- The necessary authority to carry out the job

2.3 Human resources

The firm's overriding desire for quality will necessitate policies and procedures on ensuring excellence in its staff, to provide the firm with 'reasonable assurance that it has sufficient personnel with the **capabilities**, **competence**, and **commitment to ethical principles** necessary to perform its engagements in accordance with professional standards and regulatory and legal requirements, and to enable the firm or engagement partners to issue reports that are appropriate in the circumstances'.

These will cover the following issues:

- Recruitment
- Capabilities
- Career development
- Compensation
- Performance evaluation
- Competence
- Promotion
- The estimation of personnel needs

The firm is responsible for the ongoing excellence of its staff, through continuing professional development, education, work experience and coaching by more experienced staff.

2.3.1 Assignment of engagement teams

The assignment of engagement teams is an important matter in ensuring the quality of an individual assignment.

This responsibility is given to the audit engagement partner. The firm should have policies and procedures in place to ensure that:

- Key members of client staff and those charged with governance are aware of the identity of the audit engagement partner
- The engagement partner has appropriate capabilities, competence, authority and time to perform the role
- The engagement partner is aware of his responsibilities as engagement partner

The engagement partner should ensure that he assigns staff of sufficient capabilities, competence and time to individual assignments so that he will be able to issue an appropriate report.

2.4 Engagement performance

The firm should take steps to ensure that engagements are performed correctly, that is, in accordance with standards and guidance. Firms often produce a **manual of standard engagement procedures** to give to all staff so that they know the standards they are working towards. These may be electronic.

Ensuring good engagement performance involves a number of issues:

- Direction
- Supervision
- Review
- Consultation
- Resolution of disputes

Many of these issues will be discussed in the context of an individual audit assignment (see below).

ISQC 1.34

The firm shall establish policies and procedures designed to provide it with reasonable assurance that:

(a) Appropriate consultation takes place on difficult or contentious matters

(b) Sufficient resources are available to enable appropriate consultation to take place

(c) The nature and scope of, and conclusions resulting from, such consultations are documented and are agreed by both the individual seeking consultation and the individual consulted

(d) Conclusions resulting from consultations are implemented

This may involve consulting externally, for example with other firms, or the related professional body (ACCA), particularly when the firm involved is small.

When there are differences of opinion on an engagement team, a report should not be issued until the dispute has been resolved. This may involve the intervention of the quality control reviewer.

Key terms

A **peer review** is a review of an audit file carried out by another partner in the assurance firm.

A **hot review** is a peer review carried out before the audit report is signed.

A **cold review** is a peer review carried out after the audit report is signed.

The firm should have policies and procedures to determine when a quality control reviewer will be necessary for an engagement. This will include all audits of financial statements for listed companies. When required, such a review must be completed before the report is signed.

The firm must also have standards as to what constitutes a suitable quality control review (the nature, timing and extent of such a review, the criteria for eligibility of reviewers and documentation requirements).

Quality control reviews	
Nature, timing and extent	It ordinarily includes discussion with the engagement partner, review of the financial statements/other subject matter information and the report, and consideration of whether the report is appropriate. It will also involve a selective review of working papers relating to significant judgements made.

Quality control reviews	
Eligibility	The reviewer must have sufficient technical expertise and be objective towards the assignment.
Documentation	Documentation showing that the firm's requirements for a review have been met, that the review was completed before the report was issued and a conclusion that the reviewer is not aware of any unresolved issues.
Listed companies	The review should include: • The engagement team's evaluation of the firm's independence in relation to the specific engagement • Significant risks identified during the engagement and the responses to those risks • Judgements made, particularly with respect to materiality and significant risks • Whether appropriate consultation has taken place on matters involving differences of opinion or other difficult or contentious matters, and the conclusions arising from those consultations • The significance and disposition of corrected and uncorrected misstatements identified during the engagement • The matters to be communicated to management and those charged with governance and, where applicable, other parties such as regulatory bodies • Whether working papers selected for review reflect the work performed in relation to the significant judgements and support the conclusions reached • The appropriateness of the report to be issued

2.5 Monitoring

The standard states that firms must have policies in place to ensure that their quality control procedures are:

- **Relevant**
- **Adequate**
- **Operating effectively**
- **Complied with**

In other words, they must monitor their system of quality control. Monitoring activity should be reported on to the management of the firm on an annual basis.

There are two types of monitoring activity, an ongoing evaluation of the system of quality control and period inspection of a selection of completed engagements. An ongoing evaluation might include such questions as, 'has it kept up to date with regulatory requirements?'

A period inspection cycle would usually fall over a period such as three years, in which time, at least one engagement per engagement partner would be reviewed.

The people monitoring the system are required to evaluate the effect of any **deficiencies** found. These deficiencies might be one-offs. Monitors will be more concerned with **systematic or repetitive deficiencies that require corrective action**. When evidence is gathered that an inappropriate report might have been issued, the audit firm may want to take legal advice.

Corrective action

- Remedial action with an individual
- Communication of findings with the training department
- Changes in the quality control policies and procedures
- Disciplinary action, if necessary

3 Quality control on an individual audit

12/07, 6/08, 6/09, 6/11

FAST FORWARD

ISA 220 requires firms to implement quality control procedures over individual audit engagements.

The requirements concerning quality control on individual audits are found in ISA 220 *Quality control for an audit of financial statements*. This ISA applies the general principles of the ISQC we looked at in the previous section to an audit.

ISA 220.6

The objective of the auditor is to implement quality control procedures at the engagement level that provide the auditor with reasonable assurance that:

(a)   The audit complies with professional standards and applicable legal and regulatory requirements; and

(b)   The auditor's report issued is appropriate in the circumstances.

The burden of this falls on the audit engagement partner, who is responsible for the audit and the ultimate conclusion.

3.1 Leadership responsibilities

The engagement partner is required to set an example with regard to the importance of quality.

ISA 220.8

The engagement partner shall take responsibility for the overall quality on each audit engagement to which that partner is assigned.

3.2 Ethical requirements

ISA 220.9

Throughout the audit engagement, the engagement partner shall remain alert, through observation and making enquiries as necessary, for evidence of non-compliance with relevant ethical requirements by members of the engagement team.

This includes the *Code of Ethics and Conduct*, with its fundamental principles and all the other detailed requirements. The ISA also contains some detailed guidance about independence in particular.

ISA 220.11

The engagement partner shall form a conclusion on compliance with independence requirements that apply to the audit engagement. In doing so, the engagement partner shall:

(a)   Obtain relevant information from the firm and, where applicable, network firms, to identify and evaluate circumstances and relationships that create threats to independence

(b)   Evaluate information on identified breaches, if any, of the firm's independence policies and procedures to determine whether they create a threat to independence for the audit engagement

(c)   Take appropriate action to eliminate such threats or reduce them to an acceptable level by applying safeguards, or, if considered appropriate, to withdraw from the audit engagement, where

3.3 Acceptance/continuance of client relationships and specific audit engagements

The partner is required to ensure that the requirements of the ISQC in respect of accepting and continuing with the audit are followed. If the engagement partner obtains information that would have caused him to decline the audit in the first place he should communicate that information to the firm so that swift action may be taken. He must document conclusions reached about accepting and continuing the audit.

3.4 Assignment of engagement teams

As discussed in the previous section, this is also the responsibility of the audit engagement partner. He must ensure that the team is appropriately qualified and experienced as a unit.

3.5 Engagement performance

There are several factors involved in engagement performance, as previously discussed.

3.5.1 Direction

The partner directs the audit. He is required by other auditing standards to hold a meeting with the audit team to discuss the audit, in particular the risks associated with the audit. This ISA suggests that direction includes 'informing members of the engagement team of:

(a)   Their responsibilities (including objectivity of mind and professional scepticism)

(b)   Responsibilities of respective partners where more than one partner is involved in the conduct of the audit engagement

(c)   The objectives of the work to be performed

(d)   The nature of the entity's business

(e)   Risk-related issues

(f)   Problems that may arise

(g)   The detailed approach to the performance of the engagement

3.5.2 Supervision

The audit is supervised overall by the engagement partner, but more practical supervision is given within the audit team by senior staff to more junior staff, as is also the case with review (see below). It includes:

- Tracking the progress of the audit engagement
- Considering the capabilities and competence of individual members of the team, and whether they have sufficient time and understanding to carry out their work
- Addressing significant issues arising during the audit engagement and modifying the planned approach appropriately
- Identifying matters for consultation or consideration by more experienced engagement team members during the audit engagement

3.5.3 Review

Review includes consideration of whether:

- The work has been performed in accordance with professional standards and regulatory and legal requirements
- Significant matters have been raised for further consideration
- Appropriate consultations have taken place and the resulting conclusions have been documented and implemented
- There is a need to revise the nature, timing and extent of work performed
- The work performed supports the conclusions reached and is appropriately documented
- The evidence obtained is sufficient and appropriate to support the auditor's report
- The objectives of the engagement procedures have been achieved

Before the audit report is issued, the engagement partner must be sure that sufficient and appropriate audit evidence has been obtained to support the audit opinion. The audit engagement partner need not review all audit documentation, but may do so. He should review critical areas of judgement, significant risks and other important matters.

3.5.4 Consultation

The partner is also responsible for ensuring that if difficult or contentious matters arise the team takes appropriate consultation on the matter and that such matters and conclusions are properly recorded.

If differences of opinion arise between the engagement partner and the team, or between the engagement partner and the quality control reviewer, these differences should be resolved according to the firm's policy for such differences of opinion.

3.5.5 Quality control review

The audit engagement partner is responsible for **appointing** a reviewer, if one is required. He is then responsible for discussing significant matters arising with the reviewer and for not issuing the audit report until the quality control review has been completed.

A quality control review should include:

- An evaluation of the **significant judgements** made by the engagement team
- An evaluation of the **conclusions** reached in formulating the auditor's report

---

ISA 220.25

The engagement quality control reviewer shall document, for the audit engagement reviewed, that:

(a) The procedures required by the firm's policies on engagement quality control review have been performed.

(b) The engagement quality control review has been completed on or before the date of the auditor's report, and

(c) The reviewer is not aware of any unresolved matters that would cause the reviewer to believe that the significant judgments the engagement team made and the conclusions it reached were not appropriate.

A quality control review for a listed entity will include a review of:

- Discussion of significant matters with the engagement partner

- Review of financial statements and the proposed report

- Review of selected audit documentation relating to significant audit judgements made by the audit team and the conclusions reached

- Evaluation of the conclusions reached in formulating the auditor's report and consideration of whether the auditor's report is appropriate

- The engagement team's evaluation of the firm's independence towards the audit
- Whether appropriate consultations have taken place on differences of opinion/contentious matters and the conclusions drawn
- Whether the audit documentation selected for review reflects the work performed in relation to significant judgements/supports the conclusions reached

Other matters relevant to evaluating significant judgements made by the audit team are likely to be:

- The significant risks identified during the engagement and the responses to those risks (including assessment and response to fraud)
- Judgements made, particularly with respect to materiality and significant risks
- Significance and disposition of corrected and uncorrected misstatements identified during the audit
- Matters to be communicated with management/those charged with governance

Exam focus point

> The June 2011 paper contained a requirement to critically evaluate the planning of an individual audit, including ethical matters. To answer this requirement well, students needed to combine knowledge drawn from a number of different areas of the P7 syllabus, such as quality control, audit planning, ethical & professional matters.

3.6 Monitoring

The audit engagement partner is required to consider the results of monitoring of the firm's (or network's) quality control systems and consider whether they have any impact on the specific audit he is conducting.

Question

Quality control issues

You are an audit senior working for the firm Addystone Fish. You are currently carrying out the audit of Wicker Co, a manufacturer of waste paper bins. You are unhappy with Wicker's inventory valuation policy and have raised the issue several times with the audit manager. He has dealt with the client for a number of years and does not see what you are making a fuss about. He has refused to meet you on site to discuss these issues.

The former engagement partner to Wicker retired two months ago. As the audit manager had dealt with Wicker for so many years, the other partners have decided to leave the audit of Wicker in his capable hands.

Required

Comment on the situation outlined above.

Answer

Several quality control issues are raised in the above scenario:

Engagement partner

An engagement **partner** is usually appointed to each audit engagement undertaken by the firm, to take responsibility for the engagement on behalf of the firm. Assigning the audit to the experienced audit manager is not sufficient.

The lack of an audit engagement partner also means that several of the requirements of ISA 220 about ensuring that arrangements in relation to independence and directing, supervising and reviewing the audit are not in place.

Conflicting views

In this scenario the audit manager and senior have conflicting views about the valuation of inventory. This does not appear to have been handled well, with the manager refusing to discuss the issue with the senior.

ISA 220 requires that the audit engagement partner takes responsibility for settling disputes in accordance with the firm's policy in respect of resolution of disputes as required by ISQC 1. In this case, the lack of engagement partner may have contributed to this failure to resolve the disputes. In any event, at best, the failure to resolve the dispute is a breach of the firm's policy under ISQC 1. At worst, it indicates that the firm does not have a suitable policy concerning such disputes as required by ISQC 1.

3.7 Quality control regulations

The regulation of audit is the same for all audit firms regardless of size. However, it is logical to see that it will impact on large and small firms differently.

For example, a large firm may have international quality control procedures. If not, it will certainly have national and regional ones. In order to meet some of the quality control requirements, small, single-partner firms may need to make extensive use of external experts.

Chapter Roundup

- The international standard on quality control (ISQC 1) helps audit firms establish quality standards for their business.

- ISA 220 requires firms to implement quality control procedures over individual audit engagements.

Quick Quiz

1   The purpose of ISQC 1 is to:

'Establish and maintain a system of .... to provide it with ....
assurance that

   (a)   The firm and its personnel comply with .... standards and ....
         and .... requirements and

   (b)   .... issued by the firm or engagement partners are .... in the
         circumstances.'

2   List five issues relating to good engagement performance that should be addressed in an audit firm's
    procedures manual.

   (1)
   (2)
   (3)
   (4)
   (5)

3   Who reviews audit work in an audit of financial statements?

Answers to Quick Quiz

1   Quality control, reasonable, professional, regulatory and legal, reports, appropriate

2   (1)   Direction
     (2)   Supervision
     (3)   Review
     (4)   Consultation
     (5)   Resolution of disputes

3   Audit work is generally reviewed by the staff member who is more senior on the team than the person who did the work. The partner must carry out a review to ensure there is sufficient and appropriate evidence to support the audit opinion. It might also be necessary under the firm's quality control policies to obtain a quality control review by a suitable person outside the audit team. This will be necessary if the audit is of a listed entity.

Now try the question below from the Exam Question Bank

Number	Level	Marks	Time
Q3	Examination	15	27 mins

Obtaining and accepting professional appointments

Topic list	Syllabus reference
1 Change in auditors	C3
2 Advertising and fees	C2
3 Tendering	C3
4 Acceptance	C4
5 Terms of the engagement	C4

Introduction

It is a commercial fact that companies change their auditors. The question that firms of auditors need to understand the answer to is: why do companies change their auditors? We shall examine some of the common reasons here.

Related to the fact that entities change their auditors is the fact that many auditing firms advertise their services. The ACCA has set out rules for members who advertise their services. We shall examine these rules and the reasons behind them in Section 2.

As we will discover in Section 1, the audit fee can be a very key item for an entity when it makes decisions about its auditors. Determining the price to offer to potential clients can be a difficult process, but it is just one part of the whole process that is tendering. Audits are often put out to tender by companies. We shall examine all the matters firms consider when tendering for an audit in Section 3.

Linked in with the tendering process is the process of determining whether to accept the audit engagement if it is offered. ISQC I *Quality control for firms that perform audits and reviews of financial statements, and other assurance and related services engagements*, sets out some basic requirements for all audit firms accepting engagements. This is discussed in Section 4.

ISA 210 *Agreeing the terms of audit engagements*, sets out the agreement necessary when an audit is accepted and this is covered in Section 5.

Study guide

		Intellectual level
C2	**Advertising, publicity, obtaining professional work and fees**	
(a)	Recognise situations in which specified advertisements are acceptable	2
(b)	Discuss the restrictions on practice descriptions, the use of the ACCA logo and the names of practising firms	2
(c)	Discuss the extent to which reference to fees may be made in promotional material	2
(d)	Outline the determinants of fee-setting and justify the bases on which fees and commissions may and may not be charged for services	3
(e)	Discuss the ethical and other professional problems, for example, lowballing, involved in establishing and negotiating fees for a specified assignment.	3
C3	**Tendering**	
(a)	Discuss the reasons why entities change their auditors/professional accountants	2
(b)	Recognise and explain the matters to be considered when a firm is invited to submit a proposal or fee quote for an audit or other professional engagement	2
(c)	Identify the information to be included in a proposal	2
C4	**Professional appointments**	
(a)	Explain the matters to be considered and the procedures that an audit firm/ professional accountant should carry out before accepting a specified new client/engagement including: (i) Client acceptance (ii) Engagement acceptance (iii) Establish whether the preconditions for an audit are present (iv) Agreeing the terms of engagement	3
(b)	Recognise the key issues that underlie the agreement of the scope and terms of an engagement with a client	2

Exam guide

Ethics is a key topic area and many of the issues in this chapter are ethical. You could be faced with a change in appointment scenario in the exam. The issues surrounding a change in auditors has often been examined in the past with scenarios featuring tendering and audit staffing.

1 Change in auditors   6/09

FAST FORWARD

Common reasons behind companies changing their auditor include audit fee, auditor not seeking re-election and size of company.

1.1 Why do companies change their auditors?

It is a fact of life that companies change their auditors sometimes. Not all new clients of a firm are new businesses, some have decided to change from their previous auditors. Obviously, it is often not in the interests of audit firms to lose clients. Therefore a key issue in practice management for auditors is to understand why companies change their auditors, so that, as far as they are able, they can seek to prevent it.

Question
Change of auditors

Before you read the rest of this chapter, spend a minute thinking about the reasons that companies might change their auditors. You might want to shut the Study Text and write them down and then compare them with the reasons that we give in the rest of this section.

Answer

Read through the rest of Section 1 and compare your answer to ours.

The following diagram shows some of the more common reasons that companies might change their auditors.

1.2 Audit fee

The audit fee can be a very **sensitive issue**. Audit is required by statute for many companies. Many people perceive that it has very little intrinsic value. Therefore, when setting audit fees, auditors must take account of the fact that clients may hold this opinion. Setting fees will be discussed later in the chapter. Here, we shall explore some of the fee-related reasons why companies change their auditors.

1.2.1 Perceived to be too high

This is a common reason for auditors being changed. It is strongly linked to people's perception that audit has no intrinsic value. If directors of a company believe that audit is a necessary evil, they will seek to obtain it for as little money as they can.

Much of the 'value', in cost terms, of an audit is carried out away from a client's premises. This is because the most expensive audit staff (managers and partners) often do not carry out their audit work on site. If the client does not understand this, the following sort of situation may arise.

Bob is the owner-manager of Fixings Co, a small business which manufactures metal fixings. It has a revenue of $4.5 million and the auditors come in for the second week of October every year. Every year a different senior is in charge and he or she asks similar questions to the ones asked the previous year, because the business rarely changes and the audit is low risk. The partner and manager rarely attend the audit itself because it is not considered cost-effective or necessary to do so.

Bob's audit fee was set at $4,500 five years ago when the business was incorporated for tax and inheritance reasons, and has gone up at three per cent a year ever since. It now stands at $5,200. During that time, he has paid the same firm $1,200 a year to organise his tax return and deal with the tax authorities on his behalf. He considers this service far more valuable as he has no understanding of tax issues and is exceedingly nervous of a taxation inspection.

Bob cannot understand how the audit fee is four times the size of the tax fee when the auditors attend for a week and do the same work every year. He is also irritated that it continues to steadily rise while the service does not change.

The example given above is a little exaggerated and generalisations have been made. However, there is some truth in it. An auditor understands the costs that go in to making up the audit fee. It is essential that the client does too.

1.2.2 Perceived not to be value for money

This often goes hand in hand with the audit fee being seen to be too high. In the above example of Bob and Fixings Co, this was certainly the case. However, it is possible that a company could be paying their audit firm a fee that they consider reasonable for an audit, but they just believe that another firm could give them a better audit for a similar fee.

1.2.3 Not competitive

Again, this issue can be linked with the value for money perception. It is true to say that in some cases, audit firms will offer audit services at low prices. This is on the grounds that they then sell other services to the same clients at profitable prices. It is through practices like this that the problem of lowballing can arise. You should remember the issue of lowballing from your earlier studies. In such conditions, a well-set audit fee may not be competitive even if it is a reasonable fee for the service provided.

1.2.4 Interest in whether price is negotiable

This reason may be linked to all of the above fee-related issues, or it may just arise out of interest on the client's part. It costs the client very little except some time on his part to put his audit out to tender. He might even do this with every intention of keeping the present auditor.

Putting the audit out to tender would give him more insight into how competitive his audit fee is and keep his auditor 'honest', in that he will have to justify his fee and risk it being higher than competitors in the tender.

The by-product might be that he receives a competitive tender which offers him far more than he receives from his current auditor and he changes his auditor anyway. It could also mean that, when forced to justify his position, the current auditor reassesses his service and comes up with a far more competitive deal.

1.3 The auditor does not seek re-election

Another key reason for the auditor changing is that the auditor chooses not to stand for election for another year. You should be familiar with many of the reasons behind this:

*   There could be ethical reasons behind the auditor choosing not to stand

- The auditor might have to resign for reasons of competition between clients
- The auditor might disagree with the client over accounting policies
- The auditor might not want to reduce his audit fee

Question

Name three ethical reasons why an auditor might not seek re-election or might resign, explaining the nature of the problem and the reasoning behind the resignation.

Answer

As you know from your earlier studies and from Chapter 2, there are countless ethical issues that could have arisen. Here are some common ones. Refer back to Chapter 2 if you have included any that do not appear here.

(a) **Fee level**

The audit fee which is necessary to carry out the audit at a profit may have reached a level which is inappropriate according to the ACCA's guidance on fee levels. If the audit fee constituted more than 15% of the total practice income, this would be considered to be an independence problem. This is because the audit opinion might be influenced by a fear of losing the client.

In such a situation, or if the practice had a large client below the limits but whose forecast suggested future growth, it might be necessary for the auditor to end the relationship to ensure that he did not become dependent on the client.

(b) **Integrity of management**

The auditor might feel that he has reason to doubt the integrity of management. There are many reasons why this could be the case. It could be as a result of a breakdown in relationship, or an unproven suspected fraud.

However, if the auditor does not feel that the client is trustworthy he should not continue his relationship with him.

(c) **Other services**

The auditor may offer a number of services to the client. He may be offered some lucrative consultancy work by the client which he wants to undertake, but he feels that the independence of the audit will be severely affected by the provision of the consultancy work because of the heavy involvement this would require in the client's business.

As the audit fee is substantially lower than the fees associated with the consultancy work and the auditor is trying to develop his business advice department, he may decide to resign from the audit to take on the consultancy.

1.4 Size of the company

This can be a major reason for a change in auditors. There are two key reasons, one of which has been touched on already.

- Client experiences rapid growth to the point where the audit is no longer practicable for the audit firm.
- Client retrenches or restructures in such a way that it no longer needs a statutory audit

In the first instance, the auditor may no longer be able to provide the audit for several reasons:

- Insufficient resources
- Staff
- Time
- Fee level issue

In the second instance, the client has chosen no longer to take advantage of the audit.

In either situation, there is little that the auditor can do to prevent losing the work.

1.5 Other reasons

These reasons may have been touched on in relation to the other reasons given above. We shall consider them briefly here.

1.5.1 Personality

For many small owner-managed companies, audit is almost a personal service. The relationship between such a client and its auditor may be strongly based on personality, and if relationships break down, it may be necessary for the audit relationship to discontinue.

Personality may not be such an issue for bigger entities and audit firms where the audit engagement partner could be transferred if required, while the audit stayed within the firm.

1.5.2 Audit rotation

Rotation of audit staff was discussed in Chapter 2 as a safeguard to audit independence. However, the partners in a firm may sometimes conclude that the firm as a whole has been associated too long with a client and divest the audit.

1.6 Statement of circumstances

Under the UK Companies Act 2006 for a quoted company an auditor must now always submit a statement of circumstances surrounding his leaving office even where there are no matters which the auditor believes should be brought to the attention of members or creditors. (Previously the auditor was able to submit a negative statement, ie that there were no relevant circumstances.)

Exam focus point

> From the nature of the issues raised above, it is clear that some of them will affect small firms and not larger ones and some will more predominantly affect larger ones. You should bear that in mind when approaching exam questions, and as usual, apply common sense.

Question — Control over re-appointment

(a) Of the reasons for a change in auditors given above, which do you feel that an auditor may have control over and therefore guard against? Ignore the cases when the auditor does not seek re-election or resigns.

(b) What should the auditor do to guard against the issues you have identified in part (a)?

Answer

(a) **Issues auditor may have control over**

There are two key issues identified above that an auditor may have some control over:

(i) **Fees**

    – Perception
    – Competitiveness

(ii) **Personality**

(b) **Actions to guard against issues arising**

(i) With regard to fees, the auditor can ensure that the audit is conducted in such a way as to foster the perception that the audit is good value for the fee. This can be done by encouraging the attitude of audit staff and ensuring that a professional manner is always maintained. It also requires a constant awareness by staff of the need to add value, and to ensure that the audit provides more of a service than fulfilling a statutory requirement. This can be achieved by offering relevant advice to the client as a by-product of the audit, predominantly through the report to management, but also as an integral part of the culture of the audit.

(ii) Also with regard to fees, the auditor can ensure he is competitive in the first instance, by setting reasonable fees and in the second instance by conducting research into what his competitors charge. As companies have to file accounts and the audit fee must be disclosed, this is readily available information.

(iii) Personality is obviously not an issue that an auditor can legislate against. However, part of an auditor's professionalism is to ensure that if personality problems arise, they are handled sensitively and they arise only due to issues on the side of the client.

If serious conflict arises, firms should have a procedure for rotating audits between audit partners.

2 Advertising and fees

ACCA's general rule on advertising is 'the medium used should not reflect adversely on the member, ACCA or the accountancy profession'.

2.1 ACCA guidance

Auditors are in business, and in business it is necessary to advertise. However, accountants are professional people and people rely on their work. It is important therefore that their advertisements do not project an image that is inconsistent with that fact.

ACCA gives guidance about advertising in the *Code of Ethics and Conduct*. In general, ACCA allows members to advertise their work in any way they see fit. In other words, it is a matter of judgement for the member. This is subject to the following general rule:

ACCA STATEMENT

'The medium **should not reflect adversely** on the member, ACCA or the accountancy profession.'

The following guidance is also applicable.

ACCA STATEMENT

Advertisements and promotional material should **not**:

- Bring ACCA into disrepute or bring discredit to the members, firm or the accountancy profession
- Discredit the services offered by others whether by claiming superiority for the member's or firm's own services or otherwise
- Be misleading, either directly or by implication
- Fall short of any local regulatory or legislative requirements, such as the requirements of the United Kingdom Advertising Standard and Authority's code of Advertising and Sales Promotion, notably as to legality, decency, clarity, honesty and truthfulness

2.2 Fees

It is generally inappropriate to advertise fees.

Three issues arise with regard to fees:

- Referring to fees in promotional material
- Commissions
- Setting and negotiating fees

The last two issues are inter-related and are also closely connected with tendering, which is discussed in the next section.

2.2.1 Advertising fees

The fact that it is difficult to explain the service represented by a single fee in the context of an advertisement and that **confusion might arise as to what a potential client might expect to receive in return for that fee** means that it is **seldom appropriate** to include information about fees in short advertisements.

In longer advertisements, where reference is made to fees in promotional material, the **basis** on which those fees are calculated, hourly and other charging rates etc, **should be clearly stated**.

The key issue to remember with regard to advertising fees is that the **greatest care should be taken not to mislead potential clients**. It is appropriate to advertise free consultations to discuss fee issues. This free consultation will allow fees to be explained, thus avoiding the risk of confusion.

2.2.2 Setting and negotiating fees

As this is a key part of the tendering process, this is discussed in Section 3.

2.2.3 Commissions

Members may accept or pay referral fees if appropriate safeguards exist.

ACCA members may offer commission (and by implication receive commission) for introducing clients. However, they should only do so if there are appropriate safeguards such as making full disclosure.

Commissions could be a threat to objectivity – refer back to Chapter 2 for more information on this.

2.3 Use of the ACCA logo

Members of the ACCA may be either associates or fellows, in which case they are allowed to use the designatory letters ACCA or FCCA after their names.

A firm may describe itself as a firm of 'Chartered Certified Accountants' where:

- At least half of the partners are ACCA members, and
- Those partners hold at least 51% of voting rights under the partnership agreement

A firm in which all the partners are Chartered Certified Accountants may use the description 'Members of the Association of Chartered Certified Accountants'.

A firm which holds a firm's auditing certificate from ACCA may describe itself as 'Registered Auditors'.

Felicity Carr and Frank Harrison both qualified as chartered certified accountants five years ago. They have now decided to set up in practice together. Their new firm holds an auditing certificate from ACCA and they intend to undertake small audits and some tax work. They will charge themselves out at $200 per hour initially. They will operate from Frank's home. They are a little rusty on the rules concerning advertising and obtaining professional work and so have asked you to advise them.

They have decided to call their practice Harrison Carr and to advertise in the local paper. As they are launching themselves, they have decided to take out a full page advertisement one week and then run a series of smaller adverts in the future. They have also decided to advertise in a local business newspaper.

Required

(a)   Explain the ACCA guidance on advertising, including advertising fees.

(b)   Advise Harrison Carr how they should proceed in relation to:

    (i)   How they may describe the firm
    (ii)   The adverts in the paper

Answer

(a)   **General guidance on advertising**

Generally members may not advertise in a manner that reflects adversely on themselves and their profession. This means that they should consider the quality of the paper they intend to advertise in. The local paper is appropriate. They should also ensure that they do not discredit the services offered by others in their advert.

Advertising fees

The key issue of importance when advertising fees is to ensure that the reference to fees is not misleading. Generally, it is seldom appropriate to mention fees in a small advert.

(b)   (i)   **Description of firm**

    As both partners are chartered certified accountants it is acceptable to advertise the firm as being a member of the ACCA. They may also describe themselves as registered auditors.

    (ii)   **The proposed advertisements**

    While they are planning a larger advert followed by several smaller ones, it may still not be appropriate to mention fees. This is because while they could refer to charge out rates, it would be impossible in the paper to describe how much each service would cost without estimating the time jobs would take. It is impossible to generalise such matters and the reference to fees could therefore be misleading.

    It would be more appropriate to advertise that they will give free consultations to discuss fees. They may include all the details given above, their name, the membership of the ACCA and their registered auditor status.

3 Tendering

6/09

FAST FORWARD

When approaching a tender, it is important to consider both fees and practical issues.

3.1 Approach

A firm puts together a tender if:

- It has been approached by a prospective client
- The partners have decided that they are capable of doing the work for a reasonable fee

When approached to tender, the auditor has to consider whether he wants to do the work. You should be aware of all the ethical considerations that would go into this decision. The auditor will also have to consider:

- Fees
- Practical issues

3.1.1 Fees

Determining whether the job can be done for a reasonable price will involve a substantial number of estimates. The key estimate will be how long the partner thinks it will take to do the work. This will involve meeting with the prospective client to discuss its business and systems and making the estimate from there.

The first stage of setting the fee is therefore to ascertain **what the job will involve**. The job should be broken down into its respective parts, for example, audit and tax, or if it is a complex and/or pure audit, what aspects of the job would be undertaken by what level of staff.

The second stage is closely linked with the first, therefore. It involves **ascertaining which staff**, or which level of staff, **will be involved** and in what proportions they will be involved.

Once estimates have been made of how long the work will take and what level of expertise is needed in each area, **the firm's standard charge out rates can be applied** to that information, and a **fee estimated**.

Clearly, it is **commercially vital** that the estimates of time and costs are **reasonable**, or the audit firm will be seeking to undertake the work at a loss. However, it is also ethically important that the fee estimate is reasonable, or the result will be that the client is being misled about the sustainable fee level.

3.1.2 Lowballing

Problems can arise when auditing firms appear to be charging less than this, or at least less than the 'market rate' for the audit. The practice of undercutting, usually at tender for the audit of large companies, has been called **lowballing**. In other cases, the audit fee has been reduced even though the auditors have remained the same. The problem here is that, if the audit is being performed for less than it is actually worth, then the auditors' independence is called into question.

This is always going to be a topical debate, but in terms of negotiating the audit fee the following factors need to be taken into account.

(a)   The audit is perceived to have a fluctuating 'market price' as any other commodity or service. In a recession, prices would be expected to fall as companies aim to cut costs everywhere, and as auditors chase less work (supply falls). Audit firms are also reducing staffing levels and their own overhead costs should be lower.

(b)   Companies can **reduce external audit costs** through various legitimate measures:

    (i)   Extending the size and function of internal audit

    (ii)   Reducing the number of different audit firms used world-wide

    (iii)   Selling off subsidiary companies leaving a simplified group structure to audit

    (iv)   The tender process itself simply makes auditors more competitive

    (v)   Exchange rate fluctuations in audit fees

(c)   Auditing firms have increased productivity, partly through the use of more sophisticated information technology techniques in auditing.

The ACCA's guidance on quotations states that it is **not improper** to secure work by **quoting a lower fee** so long as the **client has not been misled** about the level of work that the fee represents.

In the event of investigations into allegations of unsatisfactory work, the level of fees would be considered with regard to member's conduct with reference to the ethical guidelines.

3.1.3 Practical issues

The firm will have to consider the practical points arising from the approach. Common considerations include:

- Does the proposed timetable for the work fit with the current work plan?
- Does the firm have suitable personnel available?
- Where will the work be performed and is it accessible/cost-effective?
- Are (non-accounting) specialist skills necessary?
- Will staff need further training to do the work?
- If so, what is the cost of that further training?

Certain information will be required to put together a proposal document. This has already been touched on briefly, when discussing the audit fee. It is likely that audit staff would have to have a meeting with the prospective client to discuss the following issues:

- What the client requires from the audit firm, (for example, audit, number of visits, tax work)
- What the future plans of the entity are, for example:
    - Is it planning to float its shares on an exchange in the near future?
    - Is growth, or diversification anticipated?
- Whether the entity is seeking its first auditors and needs an explanation of audit
- Whether the entity is seeking to change its auditors
- If the entity is changing its auditors, the reason behind this

3.2 Content of an audit proposal

An audit proposal, or tender, does not have a set format. The prospective client will indicate the format that he wants the tender to take. This may be merely in document form, or could be a presentation by members of the audit firm.

Although each tender will be tailored to the individual circumstances, there are some matters which are likely to be covered in every one. These are set out below.

Matters to be included in audit proposal
<ul><li>The fee, and how it has been calculated</li><li>An assessment of the needs of the prospective client</li><li>An outline of how the firm intends to meet those needs</li><li>The assumptions made to support that proposal</li><li>The proposed approach to the engagement</li><li>A brief outline of the firm</li><li>An outline of the key staff involved</li></ul>

If the tender is being submitted to an **existing client**, some of those details will be unnecessary. However, if it is a competitive tender, the firm should ensure they submit a comparable tender, even if some of the details are already known to the client. This is because the tender must be **comparable** to competitors and must appear professional.

4 Acceptance   6/08, 6/09, 6/11

FAST FORWARD

ISQC 1 sets out what a firm must consider and document in relation to accepting or continuing an engagement, which is the integrity of the client, whether the firm is competent to do the work and whether the firm meets the ethical requirements in relation to the work.

4.1 Ethical requirements

There are a number of ethical procedures associated with accepting engagements which you have studied previously.

Knowledge brought forward from earlier studies

From paper F8 *Audit and Assurance* (or equivalent)

Procedures before accepting nomination

(a)   Ensure that there are **no ethical issues** which are a **barrier** to accepting nomination

(b)   Ensure that the auditor is **professionally qualified** to act and that there are no legal or technical barriers

(c)   Ensure that the existing **resources** are **adequate** in terms of staff, expertise and time

(d)   Obtain **references for the directors** if they are not known personally to the audit firm

(e)   **Consult the previous auditors** to ensure that there are not any reasons behind the vacancy which the new auditors ought to know. This is also a courtesy to the previous auditors

Procedures after accepting nomination

(a)   **Ensure** that the **outgoing auditors' removal** or **resignation** has been **properly conducted** in accordance with the law

The new auditors should see a valid notice of the outgoing auditors' resignation, or confirm that the outgoing auditors were properly removed

(b)   **Ensure** that the **new auditors' appointment is valid**. The new auditors should obtain a copy of the resolution passed at the general meeting appointing them as the company's auditors

(c)   Set up and **submit a letter of engagement** to the directors of the company (see below)

4.2 Requirements of ISQC 1

We touched on some of the bulk of the requirements of ISQC 1 *Quality control for firms that perform audits and reviews of financial statements, and other assurance and related services engagements* in Chapter 4. However, it sets out standards and guidance in connection with the acceptance and continuance of client relationships and specific engagements which we shall consider here.

ISQC 1.26 and 1.27

The firm shall establish policies and procedures for the acceptance and continuance of client relationships and specific engagements, designed to provide the firm with reasonable assurance that it will only undertake or continue relationships and engagements where the firm:

(a)   Is competent to perform the engagement and has the capabilities, including time and resources, to do so

(b)   Can comply with relevant ethical requirements, and

(c)   Has considered the integrity of the client, and does not have information that would lead it to conclude that the client lacks integrity.

Such policies and procedures shall require:

(a)   The firm to obtain such information as it considers necessary in the circumstances before accepting an engagement with a new client, when deciding whether to continue an existing engagement, and when considering acceptance of a new engagement with an existing client.

(b)   If a potential conflict of interest is identified in accepting an engagement from a new or an existing client, the firm to determine whether it is appropriate to accept the engagement.

The firm should carry out the following steps:

Step 1   Obtain relevant information

Step 2   Identify relevant issues

Step 3   If resolvable issues exist, resolve them and document that resolution

4.2.1 Obtain information

The standard outlines three general sources of information:

- The communications auditors must make with the previous auditors according to the IFAC code
- Other relevant communications, for example with other parties in the firm, bankers or legal counsel
- Searches on relevant databases

In deciding whether to continue an engagement with an existing client, or to accept a new engagement with an existing client, the firm should also consider significant matters that have arisen in the course of the previous/existing relationship, for example, expansion into a business area in which the audit firm has no experience.

4.2.2 Identify issues

The standard gives a list of matters that the auditors might consider in relation to the acceptance decision.

Matters to consider	
Integrity of a client	The identity and business reputation of the client's principal owners, key management, related parties and those charged with governance.
	Nature of the client's operations, including its business practices.
	Information concerning the attitude of the client's principal owners, key management, those charged with governance towards matters such as aggressive interpretation of accounting standards/internal control environment.
	Whether the client is aggressively concerned with maintaining the firm's fees as low as possible.
	Indications of an inappropriate limitation in the scope of work.
	Indications that the client might be involved in money laundering or other criminal activities.
	The reasons for the proposed appointment of the firm and non-reappointment of the previous firm.
Competence of the firm	Do firm personnel have knowledge of relevant industries/subject matters?
	Do firm personnel have experience with relevant regulatory or reporting requirements, or the ability to gain the necessary skills and knowledge effectively?
	Does the firm have sufficient personnel with the necessary capabilities and competence?
	Are experts available, if needed?
	Are individuals meeting the criteria and eligibility requirements to perform the engagement quality control review available where applicable?
	Is the firm able to complete the engagement within the reporting deadline?

In addition, the firm needs to consider whether acceptance would create any conflicts of interest.

ISQC 1.28

The firm shall establish policies and procedures on continuing an engagement and the client relationship addressing the circumstances where the firm obtains information that would have caused it to decline the engagement had that information been available earlier. Such policies and procedures shall include consideration of:

(a) The professional and legal responsibilities that apply to the circumstances, including whether there is a requirement for the firm to report to the person or persons who made the appointment or, in some cases, to regulatory authorities, and

(b) The possibility of withdrawing from the engagement or from both the engagement and the client relationship.

Such procedures might include discussions with client management and those charged with governance, and, if required, discussions with the appropriate regulatory authority.

Exam focus point

The examiner wrote an article on this area for the March 2011 edition of *student accountant*. The article discussed the engagement acceptance process, but with a particular emphasis on the importance of establishing whether the preconditions for an audit are present.

Preconditions for an audit (see section 5.2 below) were then examined in the next exam sitting. So make sure you read *student accountant*, as it is likely to give a good indication of the topics that will be examined, and the areas that will be emphasised.

Question

Accepting nomination

You are a partner in Hamlyn, Jones and Co, a firm of Chartered Certified Accountants. You have just successfully tendered for the audit of Lunch Co, a chain of sandwich shops across West London. The tender opportunity was received cold, that is, the company and its officers are not known to the firm. The company has just been incorporated and has not previously had an audit. You are about ready to accept nomination.

(a) Explain the procedures should you carry out prior to accepting nomination.

In the course of your acceptance procedures you received a reference from a business contact of yours concerning one of the five directors of Lunch Co, Mr V Loud. It stated that your business contact had done some personal tax work for Mr Loud ten years previously, when he had found Mr Loud to be difficult to keep in contact with, slow to provide information and he had suspected Mr Loud of being economical with the truth when it came to his tax affairs. As a result of this distrust, he had ceased to carry out work for him.

(b) Comment on the effect this reference would have on accepting nomination.

Answer

(a) The following procedures should be carried out:

(i) Ensure that I and my audit team are professionally qualified to act and consider whether there are ethical barriers to my accepting nomination.

(ii) Review the firm's overall work programme to ensure that there are sufficient resources to enable my firm to carry out the audit.

(iii) Obtain references about the directors as they are not known personally by me or anyone else in my firm.

(b) The auditor must use his professional judgement when considering the responses he gets to references concerning new clients. The guidance cannot legislate for all situations so it does not. In the circumstance given above there is no correct answer therefore, in practice an auditor would have to make a justified decision which he would then document.

Matters to be considered

The reference raises three issues for the auditor considering accepting nomination.

(i) The issue that the director has been difficult to maintain a relationship with in the past

(ii)   The issue that the director was slow to provide information in the past

(iii)   The suspicion of a lack of integrity in relation to his tax affairs.

The auditor must **consider** these **in the light of several factors**:

(i)   The length of time that has passed since the events

(ii)   What references which refer to the interim time say

(iii)   The difference between accepting a role of auditing a company and personal tax work

(iv)   The director's role in the company and therefore the audit

(v)   The amount of control exercised by the director

-       Relationships with other directors

-       Influence

At this stage he **should not be considering** how highly he **values** the **opinion** of the referee. That should have been considered before he sent the reference. At this stage he should only be considering the implications of the reference for his current decision.

Auditing a company is different from auditing personal affairs in terms of obtaining information and contacting personnel. In this case, the **key issue** is the question over the **integrity** of the director.

As we do not have information about interim references and details of the business arrangements it is difficult to give a definite answer to this issue. However, Mr Loud is likely to only have **limited control over decisions** of the entity being one of five directors, which might lead to the auditor deciding that the reference was insufficient to prevent him accepting nomination. If Mr Loud were the **finance director**, the auditor would be more inclined not to take the nomination.

4.3 Money laundering

As we discussed in Chapter 1, accountants are now required to carry out specific client identification procedures when accepting new clients.

'Know your client' (KYC) is an important part of being in a position to comply with the law on money laundering, because knowledge of the client is at the bottom of 'suspicion' in the context of making reports about money laundering.

It is important from the outset of a relationship with a new client to obtain KYC information, such as:

- Expected patterns of business
- The business model of the client
- The source of the client's funds

When the client's money is to be handled by the professional, there is a higher than normal risk to the professional, so even more detailed KYC procedures will be required.

4.4 Politically exposed persons (PEPs)

Being involved with PEPs may be particularly risky for firms, particularly in terms of reputation risks if things go wrong.

Key term

Politically exposed persons (PEPs) are individuals who are, or have been, entrusted with prominent public functions in a foreign country (for example, heads of state or senior politicians and officials).

Firms and institutions should have risk management systems set up to determine whether an individual is a PEP when client identification procedures are being carried out. When a person has been identified as a PEP, a member of senior management should approve establishing a business relationship with that person.

The firm should then take reasonable measures to establish the source of that individual's wealth and funds and conduct enhanced ongoing monitoring of the firm's relationship with that individual.

4.5 Client screening

Many audit firms use a client acceptance checklist to assist them in making the decision and ensuring that such requirements are met.

5 Terms of the engagement 6/11

FAST FORWARD

The auditor must agree terms of the audit engagement with relevant personnel at the client and must ensure that preconditions for an audit exist in order to agree to those terms.

5.1 Objective of ISA 210

ISA 210 *Agreeing the terms of audit engagements* sets out best practice concerning this issue.

ISA 210.3

The objective of the auditor is to accept or continue an audit engagement only when the basis upon which it is to be performed has been agreed, through:

(a)   Establishing whether the **preconditions for an audit** are present, and

(b)   Confirming that there is a **common understanding** between the auditor and management and, where appropriate, those charged with governance of the terms of the audit engagement.

Key term

The **preconditions for an audit** are the use by management (those charged with governance in the UK) of an acceptable financial reporting framework in the preparation of the financial statements and the agreement of management, and, where appropriate, those charged with governance to the premise on which an audit is conducted.

5.2 Preconditions for an audit

The auditor needs to carry out tests to ensure that the preconditions for an audit outlined above are met.

ISA 210.6

In order to establish whether the preconditions for an audit are present, the auditor shall determine whether the financial reporting framework to be applied in the preparation of the financial statements is acceptable.

ISA 210 then goes on to require the auditor to ensure that management understands its responsibilities for:

> **ISA 210.6**
>
> (i) For the preparation of the financial statements in accordance with the applicable financial reporting framework, including where relevant their fair presentation;
>
> (ii) For such internal control as management determines is necessary to enable the preparation of financial statements that are free from material misstatement, whether due to fraud or error;
>
> (iii) To provide the auditor with:
>
> – Access to all information of which management is aware that is relevant to the preparation of the financial statements
>
> – Additional information that the auditor may request from management for the purpose of the audit
>
> – Unrestricted access to persons within the entity from whom the auditor determines it necessary to obtain audit evidence

This will all be confirmed in the engagement letter.

If any of these conditions does not exist (eg the framework used is unacceptable or management does not acknowledge its responsibilities), the **auditor shall not accept the audit** unless legally required to so do.

In addition, the auditor should not accept the engagement if those charged with governance impose a limitation on the scope of the auditor's work likely to result in a disclaimer of opinion, again, unless the auditor is legally required to accept the audit.

5.3 Clarifying the agreement

It is important when entering into a contract to provide services to ensure that both parties fully understand their respective responsibilities and what the agreed services are. Misunderstanding could lead to a break down in the relationship, and eventually result in legal action being undertaken.

5.4 Engagement letter

An auditor will outline the basis for the audit agreement in his tender to provide services. However, once he has accepted nomination, it is vital that the basis of his relationship is discussed with the new client and laid out in contractual form. This is the role of the **engagement letter**, which you should be familiar with from your earlier studies.

Matters which SHALL be clarified in the audit agreement

- Objective and scope of the audit
- Auditor's responsibilities
- Management's responsibilities
- Identification of applicable financial reporting framework
- Expected form and contents of reports to be issued by the auditor and statement that there may be circumstances when a report may differ from this

Matters which MAY be clarified in the audit agreement

- More detail on the scope of the audit including references to law, auditing and other standards the auditor follows
- Form of other audit communications
- Limitation of audit and internal controls and resulting risk that material misstatements may not be detected
- Composition of the audit team and other practical arrangements
- Expectation the management will provide written representations
- Agreement of management to make draft financial statements and other documents available in good time

---

- Agreement of management to inform the auditors of facts that may affect the financial statements before the date of the audit report
- Basis on which fees are computed and billing arrangements
- A request for management to acknowledge receipt of audit engagement letter and agree to its terms
- Arrangements concerning the use of experts or other auditors
- Arrangements concerning the use of internal auditors and other entity staff
- Arrangements to be made with predecessor auditors (in the case of a new audit)
- Any restrictions of the auditor's liability
- References to any other agreements between parties
- Any obligations to provide working papers to other parties

An auditor shall not agree to a change in the terms of the engagement letter where there is no reasonable justification for the change. If the terms of the engagement *are* changed, this should be recorded. If the auditor is unable to agree to a change, he shall withdraw from the engagement and consider whether he has an obligation to report the circumstances to other parties.

In practice, the auditors and the new client will meet to negotiate the terms of the audit agreement which the auditor will later clarify in the engagement letter.

Question
Engagement letter

ISA 210 *Agreeing the terms of audit engagements* lists a series of matters which may be referred to in an engagement letter. What are they?

Answer

The ISA includes the following matters in paragraphs A22 to A24:

- The objective of the audit of financial statements
- Management's responsibility and auditor's responsibility for the financial statements
- The scope of the audit, including reference to applicable legislation, regulations, or pronouncements of professional bodies to which the auditor adheres
- The form of any reports or other communication of results of the engagement
- The fact that because of the test nature and other inherent limitations of an audit, together with the inherent limitations of internal control, there is an unavoidable risk that even some material misstatement may remain undiscovered
- Unrestricted access to whatever records, documentation and other information requested in connection with the audit.
- The agreement of management to make available to the auditor draft financial statements and any accompanying other information in time to allow the auditor to complete the audit in accordance with the proposed timetable.
- Arrangements regarding the planning and performance of the audit
- Expectation of receiving from management written confirmation concerning representations made in connection with the audit
- Request for the client to confirm the terms of engagement by acknowledging receipt of the engagement letter
- Description of any other letters or reports the auditor expects to issue to the client
- Basis on which fees are computed and any billing arrangements
- Arrangements concerning the involvement of other auditors and experts in some aspects of the audit
- Arrangements concerning the involvement of internal auditors and other client staff
- Arrangements to be made with the predecessor auditor, if any, in the case of an initial audit

- Any restriction of the auditor's liability when such possibility exists
- A reference to any further agreements between the auditor and the client

5.4.1 Recurring audits

In a recurring audit, the auditor is not required to send a new letter for each audit, but must ensure that the client still understands the existing terms.

It may be necessary to revise the terms in the event of new circumstances arising, as you are aware from previous studies.

5.5 Other changes in agreement terms

ISA 210.14

The auditor shall not agree to a change in the terms of the audit engagement where there is no reasonable justification for doing so.

If there is reasonable justification for changing the terms, the new terms should be agreed upon and recorded.

If the auditor is not able to agree to new terms, and management refuses to let the firm continue on the basis of the old ones, the auditors should:

- Withdraw, if legally entitled to

- Consider if it is necessary to report the circumstances to other parties such as the shareholders or regulators.

Chapter Roundup

- Common reasons behind companies changing their auditors include audit fee, auditor not seeking re-election and size of company.

- ACCA's general rule on advertising is 'the medium used should not reflect adversely on the member, ACCA or the accountancy profession'.

- It is generally inappropriate to advertise fees.

- Members may accept or pay referral fees if appropriate safeguards exist.

- When approaching a tender, it is important to consider both fees and practical issues.

- ISQC 1 sets out what a firm must consider and document in relation to accepting or continuing an engagement which is the integrity of the client, whether the firm is competent to do the work and whether the firm meets ethical requirements in relation to the work.

- The auditor must agree terms of the audit engagement with relevant personnel at the client and must ensure that preconditions for an audit exist in order to agree to those terms.

Quick Quiz

1   Name three reasons why an auditor might not seek re-election.

2   Fill in the blanks:

Advertising and promotional material should not:

–   .... the service offered ....

–   Be ...., either directly or by implication

–   Fall short of the requirements of the ....
    ....

3   Why should accountants not usually advertise fees?

4   List five practical issues that an auditor should consider when approaching a tender.

5   Draw a diagram showing the key stages in a tender, explaining what happens at each stage.

6   List three sources of information about a new client given in ISQC 1.

7   According to ISQC 1, when considering whether to accept an engagement with a new or existing client, the auditors must consider whether a .... arises.

8   List five matters which may be referred to in an engagement letter.

1. (1) Ethical reasons (eg fees)
   (2) Another client in competition
   (3) Disagreement over accounting policy

2. Discredit, by others, misleading, United kingdom Advertising Standard Authority's Code of Advertising and Sales Promotion.

3. The advert is unlikely to be detailed, and facts given about fees could mislead potential clients.

4. (1) Does the timetable fit with current work plan?
   (2) Are suitable personnel available?
   (3) Where will work be performed? Is it cost-effective?
   (4) Are specialist skills needed?
   (5) Will staff need further training? If so, what is the cost?

5.

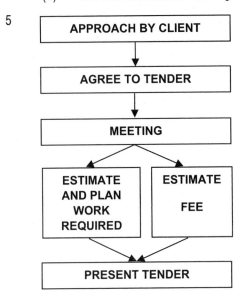

Auditor considers if it is possible to undertake work at a reasonable fee

Arrange meeting to obtain information prior to tender

Obtain knowledge of the business and the service required

Allocate potential staff to work plan and calculate fee by reference to standard charge out rates

This could be in the form of:

- – Letter
- – Report
- – Presentation

6. (1) Communications with existing/previous auditors
   (2) Communications with other third parties (eg bankers/legal counsel)
   (3) Relevant databases

7. Conflict of interest

8. See the answer to the question in Section 5.4 in the body of the chapter.

Now try the question below from the Exam Question Bank

Number	Level	Marks	Time
Q4	Examination	20	36 mins

Audit of historical financial information

Planning and risk assessment

Topic list	Syllabus reference
1 Revision: overview of audit planning	D1(i)
2 Audit methodologies	D1(i)
3 Materiality	D1(i)
4 Risk	D1(i)
5 Analytical procedures	D1(i)
6 Planning an initial audit engagement	D1(i)

Introduction

The issue of audit planning should not be new to you. You learnt how to plan an audit in your previous auditing studies. Why then is this chapter here? There are three key reasons:

- To provide you with a technical update

- To **revise** the details that should be included in an **audit plan** and the general considerations included in planning

- To **consider** some of the **finer points of planning** from the point of view of the engagement partner, specifically to consider the issue of the **risk associated with the assignment** (which is a personal risk to the partner in the event of litigation arising)

Risk is an important factor in the audit. It falls into two categories:

- Specific **assignment risk** (known as audit risk), which you have studied previously

- **Business risk** associated with the client, which may form a part of inherent risk and therefore impacts on the audit

Risk is a key issue in an audit, and the most common approach to audits incorporates a recognition of those risks in the approach taken. This and other audit methodologies are compared in Section 2.

Study guide

		Intellectual level
D	**Audit of historical financial information**	
D(i)	**Planning, materiality and assessing the risk of misstatement**	
(a)	Define materiality and performance materiality and demonstrate how it should be applied in financial reporting and auditing	2
(b)	Identify and explain business risks for a given assignment	3
(c)	Identify and explain audit risks for a given assignment	3
(d)	Identify and explain risks of material misstatement for a given assignment	3
(e)	Discuss and demonstrate the use of analytical procedures in the planning of an assignment	3
(f)	Explain how the result of planning procedures determines the relevant audit strategy	2

Exam guide

Exam case study questions are often set in the context of audit planning, identifying risk areas and considering the audit strategy to apply to the audit. This is the case in the pilot paper and questions of this type appeared very regularly under the previous syllabus.

1 Revision: overview of audit planning

FAST FORWARD

Auditors must plan their work so that it is undertaken in an effective manner.

One of the competencies you require to fulfil performance objective 17 of the PER is the ability to prepare audit programmes. You can apply the knowledge you gain from this chapter of the text to help demonstrate this competence,

1.1 ISA 200 *Overall objectives of the independent auditor and the conduct of an audit in accordance with international standards on auditing*

ISA 200.11

In conducting an audit of financial statements, the overall objectives of the auditor are:

(a) To obtain reasonable assurance about whether the financial statements as a whole are free from material misstatement, whether due to fraud or error, thereby enabling the auditor to express an opinion on whether the financial statements are prepared, in all material respects, in accordance with an applicable financial reporting framework; and

(b) To report on the financial statements, and communicate as required by the ISAs, in accordance with the auditor's findings.

ISA 200 states that the key requirements for the auditor to obtain reasonable assurance and to express an opinion are:

*   **Ethics**: comply with relevant ethical requirements. (ISA 200.14);

- **Professional scepticism**: plan and perform an audit with professional scepticism, recognising that circumstances may exist that cause the financial statements to be materially misstated (ISA 200.15);

- **Professional judgement**: exercise professional judgement in planning and performing an audit (ISA 200.16);

- **Sufficient appropriate audit evidence and audit risk**: obtain sufficient appropriate audit evidence to reduce audit risk to an acceptably low level (ISA 200.17).

The auditor then fulfils these requirements by conducting the audit in accordance with ISAs.

1.2 ISA 300 *Planning an audit of financial statements*

ISA 300 *Planning an audit of financial statements* states that the objective of the auditor is to plan the audit so that it will be performed in an effective manner.

The ISA refers to two documents, the **overall audit strategy** and the **audit plan**. The overall audit strategy sets out in general terms how the audit is to be carried out. Considerations in establishing the overall audit strategy include:

- Characteristics of the engagement
- Reporting objectives, timing of the audit and nature of communications
- Significant factors, preliminary engagement activities and knowledge gained on other engagements
- Nature, timing and extent of resources

The audit plan details specific procedures to be carried out to implement the strategy and complete the audit.

In the case of a smaller entity the strategy is likely to be a brief memorandum and the audit plan a series of tailored standard audit programs.

1.3 ISA 315 *Identifying and assessing the risks of material misstatement through understanding the entity and its environment*   6/09

The objective of ISA (UK and Ireland) 315 *Identifying and assessing the risks of material misstatement through understanding the entity and its environment* is as follows:

> **ISA 315.3**
>
> The objective of the auditor is to identify and assess the risks of material misstatement, whether due to fraud or error, at the financial statement and assertion levels, through understanding the entity and its environment, including the entity's internal control, thereby providing a basis for designing and implementing responses to the assessed risks of material misstatement.

1.3.1 Obtaining an understanding of the entity

In order to satisfy this objective the auditor is required to perform risk assessment procedures. These include the following:

- Inquiries of management
- Analytical procedures
- Observation and inspection

The following related activities are also required:

- Consider information obtained from the client acceptance/continuance process
- Consider information gathered from performance of other engagements for the entity (if relevant)
- Consider whether changes have occurred that may affect the relevance of information obtained from previous audits

- Discussion between the engagement partner and other key engagement team members of the susceptibility of the entity's financial statements to material misstatement

The ISA sets out a number of areas of the entity and its environment that the auditor should gain an understanding of. These are summarised below.

- Industry, regulatory and other external factors
- Nature of the entity
- Selection, application and reasons for changes of accounting policies
- Objectives, strategies and related business risks
- Measurement and review of the entity's financial performance
- Internal control

1.3.2 Risk assessment procedures

The ISA sets out various methods by which the auditors may obtain this understanding:

- Inquiries of management and others within the entity
- Analytical procedures
- Observation and inspection
- Audit team discussion of the susceptibility of the financial statements to material misstatement
- Prior period knowledge (subject to certain requirements)

The auditors must use a combination of the top three techniques, and must engage in the discussion for every audit. The auditor may use his prior period knowledge, but must carry out procedures to ensure that there have not been changes in the year meaning that it is no longer valid.

The purpose of obtaining the understanding is to **assess the risks of material misstatement** in the financial statements for the current audit. The ISA says that 'the auditor shall identify and assess the risks of material misstatement at the financial statement level, and at the assertion level for classes of transactions, account balances and disclosures'. It requires the auditor to take the following steps:

Step 1   **Identify risks** throughout the process of obtaining an understanding of the entity

Step 2   Assess whether the identified risks potentially affect many assertions

Step 3   **Relate the risks** to what can go wrong at the **assertion level**

Step 4   Consider the likelihood of misstatement and whether the risks are of a **magnitude** that **could result in a material misstatement**

Throughout this process the size of the entity being audited must be considered. For example, in a small entity there is likely to be limited segregation of duties. This may be compensated for by increased management oversight, however this in turn increases the risk of override of controls.

 Case Study

The audit team at Ockey Co has been carrying out procedures to obtain an understanding of the entity. In the course of making enquiries about the inventory system, they have discovered that Ockey Co designs and produces tableware to order for a number of high street stores. It also makes a number of standard lines of tableware, which it sells to a number of wholesalers. By the terms of its contracts with the high street stores, it is not entitled to sell uncalled inventory designed for them to wholesalers. Ockey Co regularly produces 10% more than the high street stores have ordered, in order to ensure that they meet requirements when the stores do their quality control check. Certain stores have more stringent control requirements than others and regularly reject some of the inventory.

The knowledge above suggests two risks, one that the company may have obsolescent inventory, and another that if their production quality standards are insufficiently high, they could run the risk of losing custom.

We shall look at each of these risks in turn and relate them to the assertion level.

Inventory

If certain of the inventory is obsolescent due to the fact that it has been produced in excess of the customer's requirement and there is no other available market for it, then there is a risk that inventory as a whole in the financial statements will not be carried at the appropriate value. Given that inventory is likely to be a material balance in the statement of financial position of a manufacturing company, and the value could be up to 10% of the total value, this has the capacity to be a material misstatement.

The factors that will contribute to the likelihood of these risks causing a misstatement are matters such as:

- Whether management regularly review inventory levels and scrap items that are obsolescent
- Whether such items are identified and scrapped at the inventory count
- Whether such items can be put back into production and changed so that they are saleable

Losing custom

The long-term risk of losing custom is a risk that in the future the company will not be able to operate (a going concern risk, which we shall revise later). It could have an impact on the financial statements, if sales were attributed to them that they dispute, sales and receivables could be overstated, that is, not carried at the correct value. However, it appears less likely that this would be a material problem in either area, as the issue is likely to be restricted to a few number of customers, and only a few number of sales to those customers.

Again, review of the company's controls over the recording of sales and the debt collection procedures of the company would indicate how likely these risks to the financial statements are to materialise.

Some risks identified may be **significant risks** (indicated by the following factors), in which case they present **special audit considerations** for the auditors.

- Risk of **fraud**
- Its relationship with **recent developments**
- The degree of **subjectivity** in the financial information
- The fact that it is an **unusual** transaction
- It is a significant transaction with a **related party**
- The **complexity** of the transaction

Routine, non-complex transactions are less likely to give rise to significant risk than unusual transactions or matters of director judgement because the latter are likely to have more management intervention, complex accounting principles or calculations, greater manual intervention or there is a lower opportunity for control procedures to be followed.

When the auditor identifies a significant risk, if he hasn't done so already, he should evaluate the design and implementation of the entity's controls in that area.

1.4 ISA 330 *The auditor's responses to assessed risks*

ISA 330 *The auditor's responses to assessed risks* states that the objective of the auditor is to 'obtain sufficient, appropriate audit evidence about the assessed risks of material misstatement, through designing and implementing appropriate responses to these risks'.

Overall responses include emphasising to the audit team the need for professional scepticism, assigning additional/alternative staff to the audit, using experts, providing more supervision on the audit and incorporating more unpredictability into the audit.

The evaluation of the control environment that will have taken place as part of the assessment of the client's internal control systems will help the auditor determine whether they are going to take a **substantive approach** (focusing mainly on substantive procedures) or a **combined approach** (tests of control and substantive procedures).

In accordance with this approach, the auditor should then determine **further audit procedures** designed to answer the assessed risks.

The auditor **must** carry out substantive procedures on material items. In addition, the auditor must carry out the following substantive procedures:

- Agreeing the financial statements to the underlying accounting records
- Examining material journal entries
- Examining other adjustments made in preparing the financial statements

1.5 Documentation requirements

ISAs 315 and 330 contain a number of documentation requirements. The following matters should be documented:

- The discussion among the audit team concerning the susceptibility of the financial statements to material misstatements, including any significant decisions reached
- Key elements of the understanding gained of the entity including the elements of the entity and its control specified in the ISA as mandatory, the sources of the information gained and the risk assessment procedures carried out
- The identified and assessed risks of material misstatement
- Significant risks identified and related controls evaluated
- The overall responses to address the risks of material misstatement
- Nature, extent and timing of further audit procedures linked to the assessed risks at the assertion level
- If the auditors have relied on evidence about the effectiveness of controls from previous audits, conclusions about how this is appropriate

Question
Revision of audit planning

You have been informed by the senior partner of your firm that you are to be in charge of the audit of a new client, Peppermint Chews, for the year ended 31 December 20X4. She tells you that the company is engaged in the manufacture and wholesaling of sweets and confectionery, with revenue of approximately $10,000,000 and a workforce of about 150. The company has one manufacturing location, sells mainly to the retail trade but also operates 10 shops of its own. The senior partner asks you to draw up an outline audit plan for the assignment showing when you anticipate visits to the client will be made and what kind of work will be carried out during each visit. The deadline for your audit report is 28 February 20X5.

Required

Draw up an outline plan for the audit of Peppermint Chews for the year ended 31 December 20X4, including:

(a) Approximate timing in the company's year of each stage of the audit of this new client. State why you have selected the approximate timing

(b) The objective of each stage

(c) The kind of work that will be carried out at each stage.

Answer

Initial visit

(a) Timing. As this is a new client, this visit should take place as soon as possible after the terms of engagement have been agreed with and accepted by the directors of Peppermint Chews.

(b) Objective. To build up a background knowledge of the company to assist in the more detailed planning of audit work that will be required at a later stage.

(c) Audit work. We shall need to obtain details of the following:

   (i) The history and development of the company

   (ii) The nature of the commercial environment within which the company operates

   (iii) The nature of the company's products and manufacturing processes

   (iv) The plan of organisation within the company

   (v) The accounting and internal control systems operating within the company

   (vi) The accounting and other records of the company and how they are maintained

The above will be obtained using such techniques as interview, observation, reviewing client's systems documentation, and so on.

We shall not at this stage carry out detailed tests of controls on the company's systems, but we should carry out 'walk-through' tests to gain confirmation that the systems outlined to them in theory appear to operate that way in practice.

Interim visit(s)

(a) Timing. As this is the first audit of Peppermint Chews, it may, in view of the extra work involved, be necessary to have more than one interim visit. If we decided that only one such visit would be needed, however, then ideally it should take place reasonably close to the year end, in, say, October 20X4. If it were decided that more than one visit were needed, then perhaps the first interim visit should take place in April/May 20X4.

(b) Objective. The purpose of interim audits is to carry out detailed tests on a client's accounting and internal control systems to determine the reliance that may be placed thereon.

(c) Audit work. Following the initial visit to the client, we should have completed our documentation of the client's systems using narrative notes and flowcharts. We should also have assessed the strengths and deficiencies of the systems and determined the extent to which we wish to place reliance on them.

Given effective controls, we shall select and perform tests designed to establish compliance with the system. We shall therefore carry out an appropriate programme of tests of controls. The conclusion from the results may be either:

(i) That the controls are effective, in which case we shall only need to carry out restricted substantive procedures; or

(ii) That the controls are ineffective in practice, although they had appeared strong on paper, in which case we shall need to carry out more extensive substantive procedures.

After carrying out tests of controls, it is normal practice, as appropriate, to send management a letter identifying any deficiencies and making recommendations for improvements.

Final visit

(a) Timing. This may well be split into a pre-final visit in December 20X4 and a final audit early in 20X5, or it could be a continuous process.

(b) Objective. We should visit the client prior to the year end to assist in the planning of the final audit so as to agree with the client detailed timings such as year end inventory count and trade receivables circularisation, preparation of client schedules, finalisation of accounts and so forth.

The object of the final audit is to carry out the necessary substantive procedures, these being concerned with substantiating the figures in the accounting records and, eventually, in the financial statements themselves. The completion of these tests, followed by an overall review of the financial statements, will enable us to decide whether they have obtained 'sufficient appropriate audit evidence to be able to draw reasonable conclusions' so that they are in a position to express an opinion on the company's financial statements, the expression of an opinion in their audit report being the primary objective of the audit.

(c) Audit work. The audit work to be carried out at this final stage would include the following:

(i) Consideration and discussion with management of known problem areas
(ii) Attendance at inventory count
(iii) Verification of assets and liabilities/income and expenditure
(iv) Following up interim audit work
(v) Carrying out review of events after the reporting period
(vi) Analytical procedures
(vii) Obtaining representations from management
(viii) Reviewing financial statements
(ix) Drafting the audit report

2 Audit methodologies

The audit strategy document will describe the audit methodology to be used in gathering evidence. This section describes the main methodologies currently used by auditors.

2.1 Risk-based audit

Risk-based auditing refers to the development of auditing techniques that are responsive to risk factors in an audit. As we set out in Section 4, the auditors apply judgement to determine what level of risk pertains to different areas of a client's system and devise appropriate audit tests.

This approach should ensure that the greatest audit effort is directed at the areas in which the financial statements are most likely to be misstated, so that the chance of detecting errors is improved and time is not spent on unnecessary testing of 'safe' areas.

The increased use of risk-based auditing reflects two factors.

(a) The growing complexity of the business environment increases the danger of fraud or misstatement. Factors such as the developing use of computerised systems and the growing internationalisation of business are relevant here.

(b) Pressures are increasingly exerted by audit clients for the auditors to keep fee levels down while an improved level of service is expected.

The risk approach is best illustrated by a small case study.

 Case Study

Audit risk approach

Your audit firm has as its client a small manufacturing company. This company owns the land and buildings in its statement of financial position, which it depreciates over 50 years (buildings only) and has always been valued at cost.

The other major item in the statement of financial position is inventory.

Looking at these two items from the point of view of the audit firm, the following conclusions can be drawn.

There is only a small chance that the audit engagement partner will draw an inappropriate conclusion about land and buildings.

In a manufacturing company, inventory is likely to be far more complex. There may be a significant number of lines to count and value, the quantity will change all the time, inventory may grow obsolete. The chance of the audit engagement partner drawing an inappropriate conclusion about inventory is higher than the risk in connection with land and buildings.

The auditors will have to do less work to render audit risk acceptable for land and buildings than on inventory. The audit risk approach will mean doing less work on land and buildings than inventory.

2.2 'Top-down' approach

 FAST FORWARD

With a 'top-down' approach (also known as the business risk approach) controls testing is aimed at high level controls and substantive testing is reduced.

ISA 315 requires that auditors consider the entity's process for assessing its own business risks, and the impact that this might have on the audit in terms of material misstatements. Auditors consider:

* What factors lead to the problems which may cause material misstatements?
* What can the audit contribute to the business pursuing its goals?

 BPP LEARNING MEDIA

This 'business risk' approach was developed because it is sometimes the case that the auditors believe the risk of the financial statements being misstated arises predominantly from the business risks of the company.

The table below highlights some of the factors that exist.

Principal risk	Immediate financial statement implications
(1) Economic pressures causing reduced unit sales and eroding margins	Inventory values (IAS 2) Going concern
(2) Economic pressures resulting in demands for extended credit	Receivables recoverability
(3) Product quality issues related to inadequate control over supply chain and transportation damage	Inventory values – net realisable value and inventory returns
(4) Customer dissatisfaction related to inability to meet order requirements	Going concern
(5) Customer dissatisfaction related to invoicing errors and transportation damage	Receivables valuation
(6) Unacceptable service response call rate related to poor product quality	Going concern Litigation – provisions and contingencies Inventory – net realisable value
(7) Out of date IT systems affecting management's ability to make informed decisions	Anywhere

Exam focus point

> Exam scenarios often contain two requirements linked to business risk – first, to identify business risks in a scenario and second, to link those risks to potential misstatements in the financial statements. Looking at this issue in **practice** is the best way to learn.

The business risk audit approach tries to mirror the risk management steps that have been taken by the directors. In this way, the auditor will **seek to establish that the financial statement objectives have been met**, through an investigation into whether all the other business objectives have been met by the directors.

This approach to the audit has been called a **'top-down' approach**, because it starts at the business and its objectives and works back down to the financial statements, rather than working up from the financial statements which has historically been the approach to audit.

The other key element of a business risk approach is that as it is focused on the business more fully, rather than the financial statements, there is greater opportunity for the auditor to add value to the client's business and to assist him in managing the risks that the business faces.

2.2.1 Advantages of business risk approach

There are a number of reasons why firms who use the business risk approach prefer it to historic approaches.

- Added value given to clients as the approach focuses on the business as a whole
- Audit attention focused on high level controls and high use of analytical procedures increase audit efficiency and therefore cost
- Does not focus on routine processes, which technological developments have rendered less prone to error than has historically been the case
- Responds to the importance that regulators and the government have placed on corporate governance in recent years
- Lower engagement risk (risk of auditor being sued) through broader understanding of the client's business and practices

2.3 Other audit strategies

In addition to the 'top-down' or business risk approach, a variety of different audit strategies may be adopted. These have been covered in your previous studies, and will only be mentioned briefly here. They include:

- Systems audit
- Balance sheet approach
- Transaction cycle approach
- Directional testing

2.3.1 Systems audit

An auditor may predominantly test controls and systems, but substantive testing can never be eliminated entirely.

2.3.2 Balance sheet approach

This is the most common approach to the substantive part of the audit, after controls have been tested.

The balance sheet shows a snapshot of the financial position of the business at a point in time. It follows that it if is fairly stated and the previous snapshot was fairly stated then it is reasonable to undertake lower level testing on the transactions which connect the two snapshots, for example, analytical review.

Under this approach, therefore, the auditors seek to concentrate efforts on substantiating the closing position in the year, shown in the balance sheet, having determined that the closing position from the previous year (also substantiated) has been correctly transferred to be the opening position in the current year.

In some cases, particularly small companies, the business risks may be strongly connected to the fact that management is concentrated on one person. Another feature of **small companies** may be that their **balance sheet** is **uncomplicated** and contains one or two material items, for example, debtors or stock. When this is the case, it is **often more cost-effective** to undertake a **highly substantive balance sheet audit** than to undertake a business risk assessment, as it is relatively simple to obtain the assurance required about the financial statements from taking that approach.

However, when not undertaken in conjunction with a risk based approach or systems testing, the level of detailed testing can be high in a balance sheet approach, rendering it costly.

2.3.3 Transaction cycle approach

Cycles testing is in some ways closely linked to systems testing, because it is based on the same systems. However, here we are looking at them in terms of **substantive testing**.

When auditors take a cycles approach, they test the transactions which have occurred, resulting in the entries in the profit and loss account (for example, sales transactions, stock purchases, asset purchases, wages payments, other expenses).

They would select a sample of transactions and test that each transaction was complete and processed correctly throughout the cycle. In other words, they substantiate the transactions which appear in the financial statements.

Point to note

> The auditors may assess the systems of a company as **ineffective**. In this case, they would carry out extensive substantive procedures. The substantive approach taken in this situation could be a cycles approach. In fact, if systems have been adjudged to be ineffective, the auditor is more likely to take a cycles approach, as it will be essential that the auditor substantiates that the transactions have been recorded properly, despite the poor systems.

2.3.4 Directional testing

Directional testing is a method of undertaking detailed substantive testing. Substantive testing seeks to discover errors and omissions, and the discovery of these will depend on the direction of the test.

Broadly speaking, substantive procedures can be said to fall into two categories:

- Tests to discover **errors** (resulting in over- or under-statement). These tests will **start with the accounting records** in which the transactions are recorded and check from the entries to supporting documents or other evidence. Such tests should detect any over-statement and also any under-statement through causes other than omission.

- Tests to discover **omissions** (resulting in under-statement). These tests must **start from outside the accounting records** and then check back to those records. Understatements through omission will never be revealed by starting with the account itself as there is clearly no chance of selecting items that have been omitted from the account.

The concept of directional testing derives from the principle of **double entry** bookkeeping, in that for every **debit** there is a **corresponding credit**, (assuming that the double entry is complete and that the accounting records balance). Therefore, any **misstatement** of a **debit entry** will result in either a **corresponding misstatement** of a **credit entry** or a **misstatement** in the opposite direction, of **another** debit entry.

By designing audit tests carefully the auditors are able to use this principle in drawing audit conclusions, not only about the debit or credit entries that they have directly tested, but also about the corresponding credit or debit entries that are necessary to balance the books. Tests are therefore designed in the following way.

The matrix set out below demonstrates how directional testing is applied to give assurance on all account areas in the financial statements.

Type of account	Purpose of primary test	Primary test also gives comfort on			
		Assets	Liabilities	Income	Expenses
Assets	Overstatement (O)	U	O	O	U
Liabilities	Understatement (U)	U	O	O	U
Income	Understatement (U)	U	O	O	U
Expense	Overstatement (O)	U	O	O	U

A test for the overstatement of an asset simultaneously gives comfort on understatement of other assets, overstatement of liabilities, overstatement of income and understatement of expenses.

So, by performing the primary tests shown in the matrix, the auditors obtain audit assurance in other audit areas. Successful completion of the primary tests will therefore result in them having tested all account areas both for overstatement and understatement.

The major advantage of the directional audit approach is its cost-effectiveness.

(a)   Assets and expenses are tested for overstatement only, and liabilities and income for understatement only, that is, items are not tested for both overstatement and understatement.

(b)   It audits directly the more likely types of transactional misstatement, ie unrecorded income and improper expense (arising intentionally or unintentionally).

Exam focus
point

Directional testing is particularly useful when there is a high level of detailed testing to be carried out, for example, when the auditors have assessed the company's controls and accounting system as ineffective.

As audit senior, you have recently attended a meeting with the managing director of Go Shop Co (audit client) and the new audit partner assigned to the audit, who has recently joined your firm, Eastlake and Pond. The audit partner is familiarising himself with the client.

Go Shop Co is a large limited liability building company set up by John Yeams, who has been managing director since incorporation. It operates in the south of the country, purchasing land outside of major towns and building retail parks, which the company then manages. You are familiar with the client, as you have taken part in the audit for the last three years. The other key member of the board is Kathleen Hadley, who set up the business with John Yeams and is finance director. Kathleen is a qualified accountant, and the accounting systems and procedures at Go Shop Co have always appeared sound.

You took minutes of the meeting, which are given below.

Minutes of a meeting between Mike Kenton and John Yeams, 30 March 20X0

MK introduced himself to JY and asked for a brief history of the business, which was given. Currently, the majority of income is from the property management side, as building market is becoming saturated. With interest rates set to rise, JY is less keen to borrow and build in the current climate.

MK asked JY whether a recent spate of terrorist bomb attacks had had any effect on business. JY commented that he had been given the impression that retail was down and that customers were staying

away from the retail centres – but he felt that some of that could be attributed to a rise in interest rates and was likely to be temporary. First months of the year are always poor for retail...

MK asked whether there had been a rise in empty units in the retail centres. JY said there had been a small rise.

MK asked JY about his views in relation to the current proposed legislation before the government concerning quality standards in the building trade. JY commented that it seemed like a 'load of nonsense' to him, and expressed some dissatisfaction with the current political situation... MK pressed the matter, enquiring as to JY's opinion on the likely effects on his business were more stringent standards to be required in the future. JY is of the firm belief that it would not be passed. MK expressed his fear that the legislation was more than likely to be passed, and would have far-reaching and expensive effects on most builders in the country. JY repeated some of his previous comments about politicians.

MK enquired as to whether there were any anticipated developments in the business, which he should know about. JY made reference to KH's plans to retire from full-time work in the business. MK asked how JY was going to replace her. JY commented that he was hoping to persuade her to stay on as she deals with all the financial side, he'd be lost without her. MK tried to enquire how firm her retirement plans were, but JY was not forthcoming.

After the meeting, Mike Kenton asked you to ring Kathleen and discuss her plans. She confirmed that she does plan to retire. She informed you that she plans to emigrate to Australia, and is not keen to put back her plans. She asked about the possibility of Eastlake and Pond assisting in the recruitment process for her replacement, as she does not feel that John Yeats has the technical ability to recruit someone without her, and has not accepted her plans enough to recruit before her retirement. She said that she has even wondered about the possibility of someone being seconded to the company from Eastlake and Pond to cover her position after she has left and before her replacement is found.

Mike is keen to reappraise the audit strategy taken towards the audit of Go Shop, as he feels the audit could be conducted more efficiently than it has in the past. Historically the audit has been highly substantive.

Required

(a)   Identify and explain the key business risks that exist at Go Shop

(b)   Explain what is meant by the 'business risk approach' to an audit

(c)   Propose and justify a strategy for the audit of Go Shop

(d)   Discuss the ethical implications for the audit of the two suggestions made by Kathleen.

Approaching the answer

| Question | Audit strategy |

As audit senior, you have recently attended a meeting with the managing director of Go Shop Co (audit client) and the new audit partner assigned to the audit, who has recently joined your firm, Eastlake and Pond. The audit partner is familiarising himself with the client.

> **Cumulative knowledge and understanding**

> **Volatile industry**

Go Shop Co is a large limited liability building company set up by John Yeams, who has been managing director since incorporation. It operates in the south of the country, purchasing land outside of major towns and building retail parks, which the company then manages. You are familiar with the client, as you have taken part in the audit for the last three years. The other key member of the board is Kathleen Hadley, who set up the business with John Yeams and is finance director. Kathleen is a qualified accountant, and the accounting systems and procedures at Go Shop Co have always appeared sound.

> **Good control environment**

You took minutes of the meeting, which are given below.

Minutes of a meeting between Mike Kenton and John Yeams, 30 March 20X0

> **Going concern**

> **Impact on any borrowing**

MK introduced himself to JY and asked for a brief history of the business, which was given. Currently, the majority of income is from the property management side, as building market is becoming saturated. With interest rates set to rise, JY is less keen to borrow and build in the current climate.

> **Knock on going concern issues?**

MK asked JY whether a recent spate of terrorist bomb attacks had had any effect on business. JY commented that he had been given the impression that retail was down and that customers were staying away from the retail centres – but he felt that some of that could be attributed to a rise in interest rates and was likely to be temporary. First months of the year are always poor for retail.

> **Pressure on major customers**

MK asked whether there had been a rise in empty units in the retail centres. JY said there had been a small rise.

> **Compliance risk if legislation is passed – likely? And going concern?**

MK asked JY about his views in relation to the current proposed legislation before the government concerning quality standards in the building trade. JY commented that it seemed like a 'load of nonsense' to him, and expressed some dissatisfaction with the current political situation… MK pressed the matter, enquiring as to JY's opinion on the likely effects on his business were more stringent standards to be required in the future. JY is of the firm belief that it would not be passed. MK expressed his fear that the legislation was more than likely to be passed, and would have far-reaching and expensive effects on most builders in the country. JY repeated some of his previous comments about politicians.

MK enquired as to whether there were any anticipated developments in the business, which he should know about. JY made reference to KH's plans to retire from full time work in the business. MK asked how JY was going to replace her. JY commented that he was hoping to persuade her to stay on as she deals with all the financial side, so he'd be lost without her. MK tried to enquire how firm her retirement plans were, but JY was not forthcoming.

> **Operational risk – loss of key staff member, and implications for FS and control environment**

After the meeting, Mike Kenton asked you to ring Kathleen and discuss her plans. She confirmed that she does plan to retire. She informed you that she plans to emigrate to Australia, and is not keen to put back her plans. She asked about the possibility of Eastlake and Pond assisting in the recruitment process for her replacement, as she does not feel that John Yeats has the technical ability to recruit someone without her, and has not accepted her plans enough to recruit before her retirement. She said that she has even wondered about the possibility of someone being seconded to the company from Eastlake and Pond to cover her position after she has left and before her replacement is found.

Mike is keen to reappraise the audit strategy taken towards the audit of Go Shop, as he feels the audit could be conducted more efficiently than it has in the past. Historically the audit has been highly substantive.

> Link with senior's cumulative knowledge and understanding – analytical review? Use of business risk approach. Control environment is sound …

Answer plan

(a)   Business risks

Operational – industry

(i)   Building industry volatile and apparently saturated

(ii) Retail management – retail industry volatile and affected by bomb threats/ interest rates

Operational – personnel

About to lose key management on the financial side and no current plans to replace her. Could severely affect systems in the finance department – could have knock on effects on sales and purchases relationships – suppliers/customers.

Finance

Likely that Go Shop has high borrowings against buildings built and managed – therefore increase in interest rates could be bad – particularly if they have borrowed lots while interest rates were low.

Compliance

Potential statute concerning quality standards:

(i)   Far reaching
(ii) Expensive
(iii) Going concern?

(b)   Business risk approach

Define BRA – link to ARA, etc…

Indicator of going concern problem?

Receivables' recoverability

Tangible non-current assets impairment

Effect on FS themselves – more prone to error?

Also, impact on control environment?

GC

Interest rates

GC

(c)   **Strategy**

BRA – have identified BR

Key risks to FS as identified above – linked strongly...seems reasonable to extend audit risk approach in this way.

Control environment strong – therefore reasonable to do controls testing – but question if this will still be the case if KH leaves.

Also, senior has cumulative knowledge and understanding – therefore analytical procedures will be good. Explanations available for analytical review.

BRA is generally more efficient than highly substantive – due to top-down procedures.

(d)   **Ethical implications**

Recruitment – mustn't make management decisions.

Secondment – must ensure that there are 'Chinese walls' between staff on audit team and seconded staff – may represent too great a loss of objectivity due to familiarity.

Answer

(a)   **Key business risks at Go Shop**

Operational – industry

The building industry is generally considered to be a volatile industry and sensitive to changes in economic climate. The managing director has identified that the particular market that the company operates in, retail parks, has become saturated. Go Shop's business is therefore likely to be volatile generally and the market for the services Go Shop provides is saturated. This is an operational risk – what will Go Shop do if it does not do what it has done historically?

The company is not only strongly connected with the building industry, but also the retail industry. This is another industry that is volatile. It has recently been affected by higher interest rates and reduced consumer spending. It has also suffered due to the bomb threats made against retail parks, which have discouraged consumers from shopping.

Operational – personnel

The business is about to lose a key member of personnel on the financial side, and there appear to be no current plans to replace her. This could severely affect systems in the finance department, which could have a knock on effect on crucial supply and customer relations and hence the operations of the wider business.

Finance

It is likely that Go Shop has a **high level of borrowings secured** on the buildings that they have built and now managed. If this is the case, the **increase in interest rates** will adversely affect their business directly in the form of **interest** on these loans. This may be particularly severe if they have over-borrowed when interest rates were low.

Compliance

There is currently legislation before the government that is likely to have far-reaching effects on the operations of Go Shop's building arm. The law relates to quality standards in the building industry and is likely to be costly to implement. It is possible that Go Shop will struggle to **afford to implement such standards**. An even more significant concern is that it appears that the director has taken **no steps to mitigate this risk** and has put **no action plans into place** to ensure that the law would be complied with, if passed. This could mean that the company could be liable to legal action and fines.

(b) **Business risk approach**

The business risk approach is an extension of the audit risk approach. When using an audit risk approach, the auditors focus their attention on matters that they feel are the most significantly risky to the financial statements so that they can provide a cost-effective audit.

The audit risk approach concentrates on three areas of risk; inherent risk, control risk and detection risk.

> In a business risk approach, the auditors determine that the risks that are most likely to adversely affect the financial statements are the business risks of the company, hence they direct their testing to the business risks apparent in the business.

This can be illustrated in the given scenario by looking at the significant links between the business risks identified and the financial statements:

Operational – industry	
Volatile industry	Significant issues relating to **going concern** arising, auditors should direct their audit work in this area.
Retail units affected by bomb threats	Potential issues relating to **receivables' recoverability**. Retail units may not be able to pay rent/honour leases if they are not receiving sufficient income from sales. The potential fall in income related to the retail units could affect the valuation **of tangible non-current assets** – is there a need for an impairment review?
Operational – personnel	
Loss of FD	This could have a significant impact on the **calculation and presentation of the financial statements** if they are now drafted by an inexperienced person. There is also a significant impact on the **control environment**, which will affect assessment of control risk.
Finance	
Interest rates	The issues relating to high interest will affect the **interest figure** in the income statement. It might also impact on the **going concern** assumption.
Compliance	
New law	Depending on the timing of the new legislation and the outcomes discussed above, this could affect **events after the reporting period**, contingencies or **provisions**. It could also potentially affect going concern.

(c) **Audit strategy**

The audit strategy will depend on certain matters such as the date when Kathleen Hadley leaves the business. Assuming that she leaves after the audit, a **business risk approach** would be appropriate.

This is because business risks have already been identified, and, as outlined above, there are **significant links between the business risks and the financial statements.**

The **control environment has historically been strong**, so making use of controls testing would appear to be appropriate. This in particular is highly dependent on the presence of Kathleen Hadley at the audit date.

The **audit senior** has **experience** of the client and significant **knowledge** of the business therefore it seems appropriate given this, that a high use be made of **analytical procedures**. It also appears that strong explanations will be available for movements on accounts over the period. Again, this is dependent on the presence of Kathleen Hadley.

Lastly, the business risk approach is considered an **efficient approach** as it uses 'top-down' procedures, so as strong evidence appears to be available, it is sensible to take the most efficient approach possible, while ensuring that a quality audit is conducted.

(d) **Ethical implications**

(i) *Recruitment*

It is very important that the audit firm does not take management decisions on behalf of the entity. Hence it would be appropriate for it to take a role in the recruitment process, perhaps reviewing CVs and advising as to qualifications and factors to look for. However, it should not get heavily involved in the interviewing process, as this could lead it to, in effect, make management decisions on behalf of the directors.

(ii) *Secondment*

If a staff member of the audit firm is to be seconded to the audit client to work in this significant role, the firm would have to be very clear that there were boundaries in place between that staff member and the audit team. This may in practice be impossible.

However, provided that objectivity can be retained for the audit team and that there is not a problem of familiarity, a secondment might be appropriate.

A problem of familiarity could arise if:

– Either, the person seconded had previously worked on the audit and the strategy and approach were not changed

– The audit team were familiar with the person seconded and had a personal relationship with him that presented a significant risk to objectivity

3 Materiality   12/10

FAST FORWARD

> Materiality considerations are important in both planning and performing the audit. An item might be material due to its nature, value or impact on the users of the financial statements as a group.

3.1 ISA 320 (UK and Ireland) *Materiality in planning and performing an audit*

Materiality issues are dealt with in two standards:

• ISA 320 *Materiality in planning and performing an audit*; and

• ISA 450 *Evaluation of misstatements identified during the audit*.

Significant developments include the formalisation of the concept of 'Performance materiality' and clarification on the need for the users of the financial statements to be treated as a group. There are also further guidelines for the determination of materiality and more stringent documentation and communication requirements.

**Key terms
(ISA 320)**

> **Materiality.** Misstatements, including omissions, are considered to be material if they, individually or in the aggregate, could reasonably be expected to influence the economic decisions of users taken on the basis of the financial statements
>
> **Performance materiality** means the amount or amounts set by the auditor at less than materiality for the financial statements as a whole to reduce to an appropriately low level the probability that the aggregate of uncorrected and undetected misstatements exceeds materiality for the financial statements as a whole.

> **ISA 320.11**
>
> The auditor shall determine performance materiality for purposes of assessing the risks of material misstatement and determining the nature, timing and extent of further audit procedures.

Materiality considerations during **audit planning** are extremely important. The assessment of materiality and performance materiality at this stage should be based on the most recent and reliable financial information and will help to determine an effective and efficient audit approach. Materiality assessment will help the auditors to decide:

- **How many** and **what items** to examine
- Whether to use **sampling techniques**
- What **level of misstatement** is likely to lead to a modified audit opinion

The resulting combination of audit procedures should help to reduce audit risk to an appropriately low level.

Materiality criteria	
An item might be material due to its	
Nature	Given the definition of materiality as an item that would affect the readers of the financial statements, some **items** might **by their nature affect readers.** Examples include **transactions related to directors,** such as remuneration or contracts with the company.
Value	Some items will be significant in the financial statements by virtue of their **size,** for example, if the company had bought a piece of land with a value which comprised three quarters of the asset value of the company, that would be material. That is why materiality is often expressed in terms of **percentages** (of assets, of profits).
Impact	Some **items may by chance have a significant impact** on financial statements, for example, a proposed journal which is not material in itself could convert a profit into a loss. The difference between a small profit and a small loss could be material to some readers.

3.2 Rules on materiality

It is clear from the points made about materiality criteria that materiality is judgemental, and an issue that auditors must be aware of when approaching all their audit work.

However, you will know from your previous studies that generally accepted rules about materiality exist. Examples are:

- Items relating to directors are generally material
- Percentage guidelines are often given for materiality

While materiality **must always be a matter of judgement** for the auditor, it is **helpful to have some rules** to bear in mind. Reasons for this are:

- The rules give the auditor a **framework** within which to base his thoughts on materiality
- The rules provide a **benchmark** against which to assess the quality of auditing, for example, in the event of litigation or disciplinary action.

The following figures are appropriate starting points for the consideration of materiality.

Value	%
Profit before tax	5
Gross profit	½ – 1
Revenue	1 – 2
Total assets	1 – 2
Net assets	2 – 5
Profit after tax	5 – 10

3.3 Problems with materiality

As discussed above, materiality is a matter of judgement for the auditor. Therefore, prescriptive rules will not always be helpful when assessing materiality. A **significant risk** of prescriptive rules is that a **significant matter**, which **falls outside the boundaries of the rules**, could be overlooked, leading to a **material misstatement in the financial statements**.

The percentage guidelines of assets and profits that are commonly used for materiality must be handled with care. The auditor must bear in mind the **focus** of the company being audited.

In some companies, **post tax profit** is the key figure in the financial statements, as the level of dividend is the most important factor in the accounts.

In **owner managed businesses**, if owners are paid a salary and are indifferent to dividends, the key profit figure stands higher in the income statement, say at **gross profit** level. Alternatively in this situation, the auditor should consider a figure that does not appear in the income statement: **profit before directors' salaries and benefits**.

Some companies are **driven by assets** rather than the need for profits. In such examples, higher materiality might need to be applied to assets. In some companies, say charities, **costs** are the driving factor, and materiality might be considered in relation to these.

While rules or guidelines are helpful to auditors when assessing materiality, they must always keep in mind the **nature** of the business they are dealing with. Materiality must be **tailored to the business and the anticipated user** of financial statements, or it is not truly materiality. Refer back to the definition of materiality and consider **all the elements** of it.

Exam focus point

> In earlier studies, you may have calculated materiality by taking a weighted average of the calculated percentages of revenue (1-2%), profit before tax (5%) and net assets (2-5%). This is appropriate when calculating preliminary (planning) materiality. In this paper, you will often be calculating materiality in relation to a specific item. You must only use the relevant comparator, for example, total assets if the matter relates to the statement of financial position, profit before tax if the matter impacts upon profit, and both if it relates to the statement of financial position and impacts on profit, for example, a provision.
>
> Also remember that where materiality is an issue and figures are provided you are expected to calculate materiality. Simply stating that materiality needs to be considered will gain no marks.

Question — Materiality

You are the manager responsible for the audit of Albreda Co. The draft consolidated financial statements for the year ended 31 March 20X8 show revenue of $42.2 million (20X7 $41.8 million), profit before taxation of $1.8 million (20X7 $2.2 million) and total assets of $30.7 million (20X7 $23.4 million). In March 20X8, the management board announced plans to cease offering 'home delivery' services from the end of the month. These sales amounted to $0.6 million for the year to 31 March 20X8 (20X7 $0.8 million). A provision of $0.2 million has been made at 31 March 20X8 for the compensation of redundant employees (mainly drivers).

Required

Comment upon the materiality of these two issues.

Home delivery sales

The appropriate indicator of materiality with regard to the home delivery sales is revenue, as the home delivery sales from part of the total revenue of the company.

$0.6 million is 1.4% of the total revenue for 20X8 (see Working 1).

An item is generally considered to be material if it is in the region of 1% of revenue, so the home delivery services are material.

Provision

The appropriate indicators of materiality with regard to the provision are total assets and profit, as the provision impacts both the statement of financial position (it is a liability) and the statement of comprehensive income (it is a charge against profit).

$0.2 million is 0.65% of total assets in 20X8 (see Working 2). As an item is generally considered to be material if it is the region of 1-2% of total assets, the provision is not material to the statement of comprehensive income.

However, $0.2 million is 11% of profit before tax for 20X8 (see Working 3 below). An item is considered material to profit before tax if it is in the region of 5%. Therefore, the provision is material to the statement of comprehensive income.

Working 1	*Working 2*	*Working 3*
$\dfrac{\$0.6\text{million}}{\$42.2\text{million}} \times 100\% = 1.4\%$	$\dfrac{\$0.2\text{million}}{\$30.7\text{million}} \times 100 = 0.65\%$	$\dfrac{\$0.2\text{million}}{\$1.8\text{million}} \times 100 = 11\%$

Exam focus point

This question is taken from an old syllabus exam paper. Had you calculated this materiality and commented upon whether these matters were material in the exam, then you could have earned up to two marks out of the twenty available in this question. Given that the question had two further parts which also required analysis of materiality, you could have earned a substantial number of marks for calculating relevant materiality indicators and commenting on them.

In the exam it is not necessary to give such a comment about the relevant indicator of materiality. The bits that would have earned two marks in the exam are shown in grey shade above. When attempting exam questions, when you are given the information to calculate and comment on materiality, you must do so.

3.3.1 Revision as audit progresses

The auditor will revise the materiality level during the audit if he becomes aware of information that would have caused a different materiality level to have been set in the first place.

3.4 Documentation

The auditor must document:

- Materiality for the financial statements as a whole
- Materiality for particular balances, classes of transactions or disclosures
- Performance materiality
- Any revisions to the above

3.5 Evaluating material misstatements

ISA 450 Evaluation of misstatements identified during the audit provides more specific guidance on the documentation and communication of errors identified.

> **ISA 450.5**
>
> The auditor shall accumulate misstatements identified during the audit, other than those that are clearly trivial.

Whereas immaterial misstatements were not required to be communicated in the past, now all misstatements must be communicated on a timely basis to management with a request that the misstatements are corrected. In the event that these errors remain uncorrected, the auditor is obliged to communicate the individual uncorrected errors to those charged with governance (above management) together with the effects on the audit opinion. Finally, for those errors that remain uncorrected, management must provide written representations that they believe that the effects of the errors (individually and in aggregate) are immaterial.

> **ISA 450.15**
>
> The auditor shall include in the audit documentation:
>
> (a)   The amount below which misstatements would be regarded as clearly trivial
>
> (b)   All misstatements accumulated during the audit and whether they have been corrected
>
> (c)   The auditors conclusion as to whether uncorrected misstatements are material, individually or in aggregate, and the basis for that conclusion

> One of the competencies you require to fulfil performance objective 18 of the PER is the ability to review the completed audit work, considering the significance of any errors or misstatements. You can apply the knowledge you gain from this chapter of the text to help demonstrate this competence.

4 Risk   12/07, 6/08, 6/09, 12/10

As you know from your earlier auditing studies, the auditor must be aware of two types of risk.

- **Audit risk** (sometimes known as assignment or engagement risk)
- **Business risk**

Exam focus point

> You must be able to distinguish between audit risk and business risk. Whilst many business risks will have consequences for the audit by increasing audit risk, they are two separate issues. For example the fact that a company has foreign exchange transactions is not an audit risk in itself. The audit risk is the potential for material misstatement in the financial statements.

4.1 Audit risk

FAST FORWARD

> Auditors must assess the risk of material misstatements arising in financial statements and carry out procedures in response to assessed risks.

ISA 200 *Overall objectives of the independent auditor and the conduct of an audit in accordance with international standards on auditing* states that 'the auditor shall obtain sufficient appropriate evidence to reduce audit risk to an acceptably low level'. As discussed in Section 1, the way he does this is by carrying out risk assessment procedures, and then further audit procedures to respond to the risk assessment. We shall look in detail at audit risk here.

> **ISA 200.5**
>
> ...ISAs require the auditor to obtain reasonable assurance about whether the financial statements as a whole are free from material misstatement... It is obtained when the auditor has obtained sufficient appropriate audit evidence to reduce audit risk to an acceptably low level.

Key terms

> **Audit risk** is the risk that auditors may give an inappropriate opinion on the financial statements when the financial statements are materially mistated. Audit risk has two key components – the risk of material misstatement in financial statements (**risk of material misstatement**) and the risk of the auditor not detecting the material misstatements in financial statements (**detection risk**). Risk of material misstatement breaks down into inherent risk and control risk.
>
> **Inherent risk** is the susceptibility of an account balance or class of transactions to material misstatement, either individually or when aggregated with misstatements in other balances or classes, irrespective of related internal controls.
>
> **Control risk** is the risk that a misstatement:
>
> - Could occur in an account balance or class of transactions
> - Could be material, either individually or when aggregated with misstatements in other balances or classes, and
> - Would not be prevented, or detected and corrected on a timely basis, by the accounting and internal control systems
>
> **Detection risk** is the risk that the auditors' substantive procedures do not detect a misstatement that exists in an account balance or class of transactions that could be material, either individually or when aggregated with misstatements in other balances or classes.

Consider an oil company which has abandoned one of its oil rigs. This abandonment is a risk of material misstatement because the abandonment gives rise to an impairment in the value of the rig, which might not be reflected in the financial statements. In other words, there is a risk that the financial statements are misstated in respect of this oil rig.

4.1.1 Inherent risk

Inherent risk is the risk that items will be misstated due to characteristics of those items, such as the fact that they are estimates or that they are important items in the accounts. The auditors must use their professional judgement and the understanding of the entity they have gained to assess inherent risk. If no such information or knowledge is available then the inherent risk is assessed as **high**.

Factors affecting client as a whole	
Integrity and **attitude to risk** of directors and management	Domination by a single individual can cause problems
Management experience and **knowledge**	Changes in management and quality of financial management
Unusual pressures on management	Examples include tight reporting deadlines, or market or financing expectations
Nature of business	Potential problems include technological obsolescence or over-dependence on single product
Industry factors	Competitive conditions, regulatory requirements, technology developments, changes in customer demand
Information technology	Problems include lack of supporting documentation, concentration of expertise in a few people, potential for unauthorised access

Factors affecting individual account balances or transactions	
Financial statement **accounts prone to misstatement**	Accounts which require adjustment in previous period or require high degree of estimation
Complex accounts	Accounts which require expert valuations or are subjects of current professional discussion
Assets at risk of being **lost or stolen**	Cash, inventory, portable non-current assets (computers)
Quality of **accounting systems**	Strength of individual departments (sales, purchases, cash etc)
High volume transactions	Accounting system may have problems coping
Unusual transactions	Transactions for large amounts, with unusual names, not settled promptly (particularly important if they occur at period-end)
	Transactions that do not go through the system, that relate to specific clients or processed by certain individuals
Staff	Staff changes or areas of low morale

4.1.2 Control risk

Control risk is the risk that client controls fail to detect material misstatements. A **preliminary assessment** of **control risk** at the planning stage of the audit is required to determine the level of controls and substantive testing to be carried out.

If the auditor judges that the internal control system is good then control risk will probably be low. The appendix to ISA 315 contains a summary of the components of a good system of internal controls. Here is a summary of the summary:

Control environment. This encompasses:

- Communication and enforcement of integrity and ethical values
- Commitment to competence
- Participation by those charged with governance
- Management's philosophy and operating style
- Organizational structure
- Assignment of authority and responsibility
- Human resource policies and practices.

Entity's Risk Assessment Process. The entity should have a process for identifying risks that may affect its financial reporting, assessing these risks and then responding to them. Examples of risks that might affect financial reporting include:

- Changes in operating environment. Changes in the regulatory or operating environment can result in changes in competitive pressures and significantly different risks

- New personnel. New personnel may have a different focus on or understanding of internal control

- New or revamped information systems. Significant and rapid changes in information systems can change the risk relating to internal control

- Rapid growth. Significant and rapid expansion of operations can strain controls and increase the risk of a breakdown in controls.

Information system. The information system relevant to financial reporting objectives, which includes the financial reporting system, encompasses methods and records that:

- Identify and record all valid transactions
- Describe on a timely basis the transactions in sufficient detail to permit proper classification of transactions for financial reporting
- Measure the value of transactions in a manner that permits recording their proper monetary value in the financial statements
- Determine the time period in which transactions occurred to permit recording of transactions in the proper accounting period
- Present properly the transactions and related disclosures in the financial statements.

Control activities, which include:

- Performance reviews. These control activities include reviews and analyses of actual performance versus budgets, forecasts, and prior period performance
- Information processing
- Physical controls, encompassing eg the physical security of assets
- Segregation of duties.

Monitoring of controls. In addition to putting controls in place, management must monitor that they are operating effectively, and that they continue to be appropriate when there are changes in circumstances.

4.1.3 Detection risk

Detection risk is the risk that audit procedures will fail to detect material errors. Detection risk relates to the inability of the auditors to examine all evidence. Audit evidence is usually persuasive rather than conclusive so some detection risk is usually present, allowing the auditors to seek 'reasonable assurance'.

The auditors' **inherent and control risk assessments** influence the **nature, timing and extent of substantive procedures** required to reduce detection risk and thereby audit risk.

Exam focus point

The P7 examniner has commented again and again in her examiner's reports that students often fail to get the marks in questions on risk by not being specific enough about the **audit** risk being discussed.

Her examiner's report for the Decem ber 2010 sitting is instructive in this regard. It identifies the following **common weaknesses** in answers to a question asking for an evaluation of business risk in a scenario, identification & explanation of risks of material misstatement:

- Repeating large chunks of text from the scenario with no explanation provided
- Not actually explaining or evaluating a risk identified – just saying 'this is a risk'
- Providing detailed definitions of business risk, which was not asked for
- Providing audit procedures for risks, again not asked for
- Providing recommendations for mitigating the risk, not asked for

4.2 Business risk Pilot paper, 6/09

FAST FORWARD

Business risk is the risk arising to companies through being in operation.

One of the competencies you require to fulfil performance objective 3 of the PER is the ability to evaluate activities in your area and identify potential risks, the nature of the risks, the probability of occurrence and consequence. You can apply the knowledge you have obtained from this chapter of the text to help demonstrate this competence.

Key terms

Business risk is the risk inherent to the company in its operations. It is risks at all levels of the business. It is split into three categories:

Financial risks are the risks arising from the financial activities or financial consequences of an operation, for example, cash flow issues or overtrading.

Operational risks are the risks arising with regard to operations, for example, the risk that a major supplier will be lost and the company will be unable to operate.

Compliance risk is the risk that arises from non-compliance with the laws and regulations that surround the business. The compliance risk attaching to environmental issues, for example, is discussed in Chapter 16.

Later in this Study Text, we will discuss the Turnbull Guidelines that highlight the importance of risk management in a business. The above components of business risk are the risks that the company should seek to mitigate and manage.

The **process of risk management** for the business is as follows:

- Identify significant risks which could prevent the business achieving its objectives
- Provide a framework to ensure that the business can meet its objectives
- Review the objectives and framework regularly to ensure that objectives are met

A key part of the process is therefore to **identify the business risks**. There are various tools used to do this that you may have come across before. They are listed below.

- SWOT analysis
- The five forces model
- The PEST analysis
- Porter's value chain

Exam focus point

The study guide states that you should be able to identify business risks in a question. If you have previously used any of the above techniques they may be useful to you, but in the exam it will be better to **use common sense** as you work through any given question, bearing in mind the three components of business risk given above.

4.2.1 Relationship between business risk and audit risk

On the one hand, business risk and audit risk are completely unrelated:

- Business risk arises in the operations of a business
- Audit risk is focused on the financial statements of the business
- Audit risk exists only in relation to an opinion given by auditors

In other ways, the two are strongly connected. The strong links between them can be seen in the inherent and control aspects of audit risk. In audit risk these are limited to risks pertaining to the financial statements.

Business risk includes all risks facing the business. In other words, inherent audit risk may include business risks.

In response to business risk, the directors institute a system of controls. These will include controls to mitigate against the financial aspect of the business risk. These are the controls that audit control risk incorporates.

Therefore, although audit risk is very financial statements focused, business risk does form part of the inherent risk associated with the financial statements, not least because if the risks materialise, **the going concern basis of the financial statements could be affected**.

4.3 Business risks from current trends in IT

4.3.1 The increasing risk of cyber incidents

Increasing connectivity and the openness of computer networks in the global business environment exposes businesses to system and network failures and to cyber attack. In a study titled 'The Economic Impact of Cyber Attacks' the US Congressional Research Service reported that recent estimates of the total worldwide losses due to hostile attacks range from US$13 billion (for worms and viruses only) to US$ 226 billion (for all forms of attacks). The study also noted that cyber incidents had the effect of wiping 1% to 5% off the share price of targeted companies.

4.3.2 Audit considerations

Auditors must assess their clients' procedures for identifying and addressing these risks. Some main considerations are:

- Has management established an information and Internet security policy?
- How does the entity identify critical information assets and the risk to these assets?
- Does the entity have cyber insurance (many general policies now exclude cyber events)?
- Is there a process for assuring security when linked to third party systems (eg partners/ contractors)?
- What controls are in place to ensure that employees only have access to files and applications that are required for their job?
- Are regular scans carried out to identify malicious activity?
- Are procedures in place to ensure that security is not compromised when the company's systems are accessed from home or on the road?
- What plans are in place for disaster recovery in case of an incident?

These issues will be built into the auditor's assessment of the control environment of the entity and in some cases may influence the auditor's view as to whether there are any uncertainties relating to the going concern status of the entity.

4.3.3 E-commerce

IAPS 1013 *Electronic commerce – effect on the audit of financial statements* emphasises the importance of risk identification where an entity undertakes e-commerce.

Specific business risks include:

- Loss of transaction integrity
- Pervasive e-commerce security risks
- Improper accounting policies for example capitalisation of website development costs
- Non-compliance with tax, legal and regulatory requirements
- Over-reliance on e-commerce

- Systems and infrastructure failures

Audit procedures regarding the integrity of the information in the accounting system relating to e-commerce transactions will be concerned with evaluating the reliability of the system for capturing and processing transactions.

Therefore in contrast to audit procedures for traditional business activities which focus separately on control processes relating to each stage of transaction processing, audit procedures for sophisticated e-commerce often focus on automated controls.

 Case Study

Risk in an e-commerce environment

Tripper Co is a travel agency operating in three adjacent towns. The directors have recently taken the decision that they should cease their operations and convert into a dot.com. The new operation, Trippers.com, will benefit from enlarged markets and reduced overheads, as they will be able to operate from single, cheaper premises.

Such a business decision has opened Tripper Co up to significant new business risks.

Customers

Converting to a dot.com company in this way enforces a loss of 'personal touch' with customers. Trippers staff will no longer meet the customers face to face. In a business such as a travel agency, this could be a significant factor. Customers may have appreciated the service given in branches and may feel that this level of service has been lost if it is now redirected through computers and telephones. Trippers should be aware of the possibility of, and mitigate against, loss of customers due to perceived reduction in service.

Competition

By leaving the local area and entering a wider market, Trippers is opening itself up to much more substantial competition. Whereas previously, Trippers competed with other local travel agents, it will now be competing theoretically with travel agents everywhere that have Internet facilities.

Technology issues

As Trippers has moved into a market that necessitates high technological capabilities, a number of business risks are raised in relation to technological issues:

Viruses

There is a threat of business being severely interrupted by computer viruses, particularly if the staff of Trippers are not very computer literate or the system the company invests in is not up to the standard required.

Viruses could cause interrupted sales and loss of customer goodwill, which could have a significant impact on the going concern status of the company.

Loss of existing custom

Technology could be another reason for loss of existing customers. Their existing customers might not have Internet access or ability to use computers. We do not know what Trippers' demographic was prior to conversion.

However, if conversion means that Trippers lose their existing client base completely and have to rebuild sales, the potential cost in advertising could be excessive.

Cost of system upgrades

Technology is a fast moving area and it will be vital that Trippers' website is kept up to current standards. The cost of upgrade, both in terms of money and business interruption, could be substantial.

New supply chain factors

Trippers may keep existing links with holiday companies and operators. However, they will have new suppliers, such as Internet Service Providers to contend with.

Personnel

Due to the conversion, Trippers.com will require technical staff and experts. They may not currently have these staff. If this is the case, they could be at risk of severe business interruption and customer dissatisfaction.

If the directors are not computer literate, they may find that they are relying on staff who are far more expert than they are to ensure that their business runs efficiently.

Legislation

There are a number of issues to consider here. The first is data protection and the necessity to comply with the law when personal details are given over the computer. It is important that the website is secure.

E-commerce is also likely to be an area where there is fast moving legislation as the law seeks to keep up with developments. Trippers must also keep up with developments in the law.

Lastly, trading over the Internet may create complications as to what domain Trippers are trading in for the purposes of law and tax.

Fraud exposure

The company may find that it is increasingly exposed to fraud in the following ways:

*   Credit card fraud relating from transactions not being face to face
*   Hacking and fraud relating from the website not being secure
*   Over-reliance on computer expert personnel could lead to those people committing fraud

Trippers' auditors will be regarding the conversion with interest. The conversion will also severely affect audit risk.

Impact on audit risk

Inherent risk

Many of the business risks identified above could have significant impacts on going concern.

Control risk

The new operations will require new systems, many of which may be specialised computer systems.

Detection risk

The conversion may have the following effects:

*   Create a 'paperless office' as all transactions are carried out online – this may make use of CAATs essential
*   The auditors may have no experience in e-commerce which may increase detection risk
*   There are likely to be significant impacts on analytical review as results under the new operations are unlikely to be very comparable to the old
*   There may be a significant need to use the work of experts to obtain sufficient, appropriate audit evidence

Point to note

In this case study, e-commerce has been used to illustrate the issue of risks. E-commerce is a topical area, and you should be familiar with the issues arising for audit and assurance from e-commerce. However, you need to be able to recognise issues for any business scenario you are given.

Try to learn to let key phrases trigger your thoughts about particular issues such as systems and going concern. Above all, think about the nature of the business in the scenario and the strengths and deficiencies likely to exist within it.

You should attempt the next question, which is a case study question on risks. The answer to this question includes an 'approach' to answering such questions, which you can look at if you struggle to identify risks in the scenario.

4.4 Risk of material misstatement

12/08, 12/09, 6/11

4.4.1 Definition

This is the risk that the financial statements are materially misstated. The material misstatement could involve:

- Errors in the amounts recorded in the statement of comprehensive income or statement of financial position
- Errors in or omissions from the disclosure notes

4.4.2 Link with business risk

Many, if not all, business risks will produce a risk of material misstatement.

Exam focus point

In scenario questions you could be asked to explain either business risk or the risk of material misstatement. It is important to use the scenario in the correct way and answer the exact question that is being asked.

Using the information in the previous case study to illustrate the link:

Business risk	Risk of material misstatement
The business may lose sales as a result of computer viruses, which could threaten the company's going concern status.	Uncertainties over going concern may not be fully disclosed.
Breaches of data protection law and other regulations could result in the company suffering financial penalties.	Provisions relating to breaches of regulations may be omitted or understated.
The business may suffer losses from credit card fraud.	Losses arising from frauds may not be recognised in the financial statements.

Question

Audit risk

Forsythia is a small limited liability company offering garden landscaping services. It is partly owned by three business associates, Mr Rose, Mr White and Mr Grass, who each hold 10% of the shares. The major shareholder is the parent company, Poppy Co. This company owns shares in 20 different companies, which operate in a variety of industries. One of them is a garden centre, and Forsythia regularly trades with it. Poppy Co is in turn owned by a parent, White Holdings Co.

The management structure at Forsythia is simple. Of the three non-corporate shareholders, only Mr Rose has any involvement in management. He runs the day-to-day operations of the company (marketing, sales, purchasing etc) although the company employs two landscape gardeners to actually carry out projects. The accounts department employs a purchase clerk and a sales clerk, who deal with all aspects of their function. The sales clerk is Mr Rose's daughter, Justine. Mr Rose authorises and produces the payroll. The company ledgers are kept on Mr Rose's personal computer. Two weeks after the year end, the sales ledger records were severely damaged by a virus. Justine has a single print out of the balances as at year end, which shows the total owed by each customer.

Forsythia owns the equipment which the gardeners use and they pay them a salary and a bonus based on performance. Mr Rose is remunerated entirely on a commission basis relating to sales and, as a shareholder he receives dividends annually, which are substantial.

Forsythia does not carry any inventory. When materials are required for a project, they are purchased on behalf of the client and charged directly to them. Most customers pay within the 60 day credit period, or take up the extended credit period which Forsythia offer. However, there are a number of accounts that appear to have been outstanding for a significant period.

Justine and her father do not appear to have a very good working relationship. She does not live at home and her salary is not significant. However, she appears to have recently purchased a sports car, which is not a company car.

The audit partner has recently accepted the audit of Forsythia. You have been assigned the task of planning the first audit.

Required

Identify and explain the audit and engagement risks arising from the above scenario.

Approaching the answer

 Question

Audit risk

Try to apply the two points mentioned in the exam focus point above. Look for **key words** and **ask questions** of the information given to you. This is illustrated here:

> Receivables likely to be significant

Forsythia is a small limited company offering garden landscaping services. It is partly owned by three

business associates, Mr Rose, Mr White and Mr Grass, who each hold 10% of the shares. The major

> Complicated corporate structure – why?

shareholder is the parent company, Poppy Co. This company owns shares in 20 different companies,

which operate in a variety of industries. One of them is a garden centre, and Forsythia regularly trades with

> Controlling party?

it. Poppy Co is in turn owned by a parent, White Holdings Co.

> Key man? Over-reliance?

The management structure at Forsythia is simple. Of the three non-corporate shareholders, only

Mr Rose has any involvement in management. He runs the day-to-day operations of the company

> Is it slightly odd that a landscape gardening business isn't owned by landscape gardeners?

(marketing, sales, purchasing etc) although the company employs two landscape gardeners to actually

carry out projects. The accounts department employs a purchase clerk and a sales clerk, who deal

with all aspects of their function. The sales clerk is Mr Rose's daughter, Justine. Mr Rose authorises and

> No segregatio of duties

produces the payroll. The company ledgers are kept on Mr Rose's personal computer. Two weeks

> Poor controls

after the year end, the sales ledger records were severely damaged by a virus. Justine has a

single print out of the balances as at year end, which shows the total owed by each customer.

> Limitation? And given below, a suspicion of fraud?
> Teeming and lading?

Forsythia owns the equipment which the gardeners use and they pay them a salary and a bonus based on performance. Mr Rose is remunerated entirely on a commission basis relating to sales and, as a shareholder he receives dividends annually, which are substantial.

> Very profit related focused – management bias?

> How accounted for?

Forsythia does not carry any inventory. When materials are required for a project, they are purchased on

behalf of the client and charged directly to them. Most customers pay within the 60 day credit period, or

BPP
LEARNING MEDIA

take up the extended credit period which Forsythia offer. However, there are a number of accounts that appear to have been outstanding for a significant period.

| Problem with |
| receivables fraud? |

Justine and her father do not appear to have a very good working relationship. She does not live at home and her salary is not significant. However, she appears to have recently purchased a sports car, which is not a company car.

| Fraud? |

The audit partner has recently accepted the audit of Forsythia. You have been assigned the task of planning the first audit.

| Any group |
| planning |
| issues? |

| Why not all the other group |
| companies? Why do they |
| have different auditors? |

| Detection risk |
| Opening balances |
| Comparatives – audited or not? |

Answer plan

Not all the points you notice will necessarily be **relevant** and you may also find that you do not have **time** to mention all the points in your answer. Now you should prioritise your points in a more formal answer plan and then write your answer:

Audit risks

Inherent

Related party transactions/group issues
Receivables
Fraud – possible indicators, professional scepticism
Profit driven management
Credit extended – accounting/law and regs

Control

Lack of segregation of duties
PC/virus
Suspicion of fraud?
Key man

Detection

First audit
Opening bals and comparatives – audited?

Engagement risks

Some questions raised which makes business look odd

- Group (complex/different auditors/who controls?)
- Nature of business – yet landscape gardeners hired

Indicators of potential fraud

Possible indicators of money laundering (complex structure/cash business)

These may be overstated, but auditor must   (a) consider them
                                            (b) be prepared for consequences

Answer

The following matters are relevant to planning Forsythia's audit:

Audit risks – inherent

Related parties and group issues

Forsythia is part of a **complicated group structure**. This raises several issues for the audit:

- There is a risk of related party transactions existing and not being properly disclosed in the financial statements in accordance with IAS 24 *Related party disclosures*.
- Similarly, there is a risk that it will be difficult to ascertain the controlling party for disclosure.
- There is likely to be some group audit implications. My firm may be required to undertake procedures in line with the group auditors' requirements if Forsythia is to be consolidated.

Receivables

Forsythia is a **service provider**, and it **extends credit** to customers. This is likely to mean that **trade receivables** will be a significant audit balance. However, there is **limited audit evidence** concerning trade receivables due to the effects of a computer virus. There are also indicators of a **possible fraud**.

Fraud

There are various factors that may indicate a sales ledger fraud has taken/is taking place:

- Lack of segregation of duties
- Extensive credit offered
- The virus only destroyed sales ledger information – too specific?
- Poorly paid sales ledger clerk – with expensive lifestyle
- Sales ledger clerk is daughter of rich shareholder and they do not have a good relationship

None of these **factors** necessarily point to a fraud individually, but **added together raise significant concerns**.

Profit driven management

Mr Rose is motivated for the financial statements to show a profit for two reasons:

- He receives a commission (presumably sales driven, which impacts on profit)
- He receives dividends as shareholder, which will depend on profits

There is a risk that the **financial statements** will be **affected by management bias**.

Credit extended

We should ensure that the credit extended to customers is standard business credit. There are unlikely to be any **complications**, for example, interest, but if there were, we should be aware of any **laws and regulations** which might become relevant, and any **accounting issues** which would be raised.

Audit risk – control

There are three significant control problems at Forsythia.

Segregation of duties

There appears to be a **complete lack of segregation of duties** on the three main ledgers. This may have led to a **fraud** on the sales ledger. The fact that there is no segregation on payroll is also a concern as this is an area where frauds are carried out.

Lack of segregation of duties can also lead to **significant errors** arising and not being detected by the system. This problem means that **control risk** will have to be assessed as **high** and **substantial substantive testing** be undertaken.

Personal computer

A PC is used for the accounting system. This is likely to have **poor built-in controls** and further exacerbate the problems caused by the lack of segregation of duties.

The **security** over PCs is also often poor, as has been the case here, where a **virus** has destroyed evidence about the sales ledger.

Key man

The fact that Mr Rose is dominant in management may also be a control problem, particularly if he were ever to be absent.

Audit risk – detection

The key detection risk is that this is the **first audit**, so we have no CAKE (cumulative audit knowledge and experience) of this client. We have not audited the **opening balances** and **comparatives**. We should have contacted any previous auditors and therefore be aware of whether these have been audited. If there were no previous auditors, these are unaudited. We must ensure that our audit report is clear on this issue.

There is also significant detection risk in relation to **related parties**, as discussed above.

Engagement risk

There are several indicators that Forsythia may be an 'odd' company.

The first indicator is that it is part of a **complex and unexplained group**, and that the group is not audited by the same firm of auditors, although it is unclear how many firms of auditors are involved in the group audit. There may be good reasons for this audit policy, but we should **investigate those reasons**, in case any other issues arise.

Another indicator is that it seems slightly odd that a small company should exist to provide landscape gardening services, when it appears that the owners are not landscape gardeners, or at least, if they are, they do not work in the business. Again, there may be valid reasons for this, but we should **discover and document them**.

It is particularly important that these issues are cleared up. A complex group structure and a company dealing in cash transactions (Forsythia's potentially are) could indicate the possibility that the owners are trying to **launder money**. There are also indicators of **fraud**. If either of these issues exist, the auditor may have **significant responsibility** to report and co-operate with relevant authorities, and the **professional relationship of client and auditor could be compromised**. Therefore, the audit firm must ensure that it has suitable 'know your client' procedures in place and the appropriate systems for making suspicion reports should a suspicion arise. The partners must ensure that staff have appropriate training so that they are able to comply fully with legal requirements in relation to money laundering.

5 Analytical procedures
6/09

FAST FORWARD Analytical procedures are important at all stages of the audit.

Knowledge brought forward from previous studies

> Guidance on analytical procedures is given in ISA 520 *Analytical procedures*
>
> Analytical procedures can be used at three stages of the audit:
>
> - Planning
> - Substantive procedures
> - Overall review
>
> Analytical procedures consist of comparing items, for example, current year financial information with prior year financial information, and analysing predictable relationships, for example, the relationship between receivables and credit sales.

5.1 Use of analytical procedures generally

There are a number of occasions and assignments when an auditor will look to take an analytical procedures approach. One has already been mentioned in this chapter. When auditors use the business risk approach they seek to use a high level of analytical procedures. Other examples include:

- Reviews (Chapter 12)
- Assurance engagements (Chapter 12)
- Prospective financial information (Chapter 13)

5.2 Use of analytical procedures on an audit

ISA 520.3

The objectives of the auditor are:

(a)   To obtain relevant and reliable audit evidence when using substantive analytical procedures

(b)   To design and perform analytical procedures near the end of the audit that assist the auditor when forming an overall conclusion as to whether the financial statements are consistent with the auditor's understanding of the entity

Exam focus point

You should note that whether or not auditors choose an analytical procedure approach for an audit, the knowledge you already have of analytical procedures **still applies**. In any audit, analytical procedures are used at the three stages mentioned. If the analytical procedures approach is taken, the use of analytical review at the second stage is expanded.

There are a number of factors which the auditors should consider when deciding whether to use analytical procedures as substantive procedures.

Factors to consider	Example
The **plausibility and predictability** of the relationships identified for comparison and evaluation	The strong relationship between certain selling expenses and revenue in businesses where the sales force is paid by commission
The **objectives** of the analytical procedures and the extent to which their results are reliable	
The **detail** to which information can be **analysed**	Analytical procedures may be more effective when applied to financial information or individual sections of an operation such as individual factories or shops
The **availability of information**	Financial: budgets or forecasts Non-financial: eg the number of units produced or sold
The **relevance of the information** available	Whether the budgets are established as results to be expected rather than as tough targets (which may well not be achieved)
The **comparability of the information** available	Comparisons with average performance in an industry may be of little value if a large number of companies differ significantly from the average
The **knowledge gained during previous audits**	The effectiveness of the accounting and internal controls The types of problems giving rise to accounting adjustments in prior periods

Factors which should also be considered when determining the reliance that the auditors should place on the results of substantive analytical procedures are:

Reliability factors	Example
Other audit procedures directed towards the same financial statements assertions	Other procedures auditors undertake in reviewing the collectability of receivables, such as the review of subsequent cash receipts, may confirm or dispel questions arising from the application of analytical procedures to a profit of customers' accounts which lists for how long monies have been owed.

Reliability factors	Example
The **accuracy** with which the expected results of analytical procedures can be predicted	Auditors normally expect greater consistency in comparing the relationship of gross profit to sales from one period to another than in comparing expenditure which may or may not be made within a period, such as research or advertising.
The **frequency** with which a relationship is observed	A pattern repeated monthly as opposed to annually

Reliance on the results of analytical procedures depends on the auditors' assessment of the **risk** that the procedures may identify relationships (between data) do exist, whereas a material misstatement exists (that is, the relationships, in fact, do not exist). It depends also on the results of investigations that auditors have made if substantive analytical procedures have highlighted significant fluctuations or unexpected relationships (see below).

5.3 Practical techniques

When carrying out analytical procedures, auditors should remember that every industry is different and each company within an industry differs in certain aspects.

Important accounting ratios	Gross profit margins, in total and by product, area and months/quarter (if possible)
	Receivables ratio (average collection period)
	Inventory turnover ratio (inventory divided into cost of sales)
	Current ratio (current assets to current liabilities)
	Quick or acid test ratio (liquid assets to current liabilities)
	Gearing ratio (debt capital to equity capital)
	Return on capital employed (profit before tax to total assets less current liabilities)
Related items	Payables and purchases
	Inventory and cost of sales
	Non-current assets and depreciation, repairs and maintenance expense
	Intangible assets and amortisation
	Loans and interest expense
	Investments and investment income
	Receivables and bad debt expense
	Receivables and sales

Ratios mean very little when used in isolation. They should be calculated for **previous periods** and for **comparable companies**. The permanent file should contain a section with summarised accounts and the chosen ratios for prior years.

In addition to looking at the more usual ratios the auditors should consider examining **other ratios** that may be **relevant** to the particular **client's business,** such as revenue per passenger mile for an airline operator client, or fees per partner for a professional office.

Exam focus point

At this level, you are more likely to be required to **justify** why an analytical procedures approach should be taken than to calculate a series of ratios.

However, if you are asked to perform analytical procedures in the exam, remember that it is vital that you analyse any calculation you have made in your answer. It is very important to make comments and draw conclusions.

Other analytical techniques include:

(a) **Examining related accounts** in conjunction with each other. Often revenue and expense accounts are related to statement of financial position accounts and comparisons should be made to ensure relationships are reasonable.

(b) **Trend analysis**. Sophisticated statistical techniques can be used to compare this period with previous periods.

(c) **Reasonableness tests**. These involve calculating **expected value** of an item and comparing it with its actual value, for example, for straight-line depreciation.

(Cost + Additions – Disposals) × Depreciation % = Charge in statement of comprehensive income

Question

Analytical procedures

Copthalls is a ladies fashion retailer operating a chain of shops from a small head office. Your firm has been the auditor of Copthalls for some years.

During the current year one shop was closed and the product range of the remaining eight shops was extended to include accessories and footwear.

The company has a computerised accounting system and the audit manager is keen to ensure that the audit is as efficient as possible.

As senior in charge of the audit you are currently planning the audit work for trade payables and you have obtained the following draft financial statements from the client.

	Draft 20X7	Actual 20X6
	$'000	$'000
Summary income statement		
Revenue	8,173	5,650
Gross profit	1,717	1,352
Summary statement of financial position		
Non-current assets	2,799	2,616
Current assets	1,746	1,127
Trade payables	991	718
Other payables	514	460

Required

State what observations you can draw from the extracts from the draft financial statements and how they may affect your audit of trade payables.

Answer

Observations	Impact on audit of trade payables
Gross profit margin has fallen from 24% last year to 21% this year.	Business strategy and performance must be discussed with the directors.
	The lower margin could arise from genuine business factors including some relating to payables such as new suppliers charging higher prices increases in the cost of raw materials used by suppliers.
	These factors would have to be confirmed during the audit of payables.
Cost of sales has increased by 50% whilst revenue has increased by 45%.	Where the decline in margin cannot be adequately explained by business factors, accounting errors must be considered. These could include

Observations	Impact on audit of trade payables
	– An inaccurate cut-off on goods received which misstates purchases and trade payables – Misclassification between purchases and other expenses. Potential errors would increase the level of work required on payables.
Trade payables have increased by 38%, which is less than the increase in cost of sales.	The scope of circularisation and/or supplier statement reconciliation work may have to be extended if there are trade payables that have not been recorded
The trade payables payment period has been reduced slightly from 61 days last year to 56 days this year.	Information on payment terms with new suppliers (eg for footwear) must be obtained to establish expectations. There is a risk of unrecorded liabilities (eg due to omission of goods received not invoiced or inaccurate cut-off in the purchase ledger). Review of subsequent cash payments to payables should cover the two months after the year end.
Other payables have risen by 12% – this does not seem consistent with a reduction in the number of shops.	Payables for purchases may be misclassified as other payables.

5.3.1 Trend analysis

Trend analysis is likely to be very important if an analytical procedure approach is taken. Information technology can be used in trend analysis, to enable auditors to see trends graphically with relative ease and speed.

Methods of trend analysis include:

- 'Scattergraphs'
- Bar graphs
- Pie charts
- Any other visual representations
- Time series analysis
- Statistical regression

Time series analysis involves techniques such as eliminating seasonal fluctuations from sets of figures, so that underlying trends can be analysed. This is illustrated below.

Example

Line 1 in the diagram shows the actual sales made by a business. There is a clear seasonal fluctuation before Christmas. Line 2 shows a level of sales with 'expected seasonal fluctuations' having been stripped out. It shows that sales were lower than expected for December and continued to be low, despite December sales being higher than the other months.

In this analysis the seasonal fluctuations have been estimated. This analysis is useful however, because the estimate is likely to be based on past performance, so the conclusion from this is that there might be a problem:

- Sales are below the levels of previous years
- Sales are below expectation

5.4 Investigating results

If analytical procedures produce results that are inconsistent with other relevant information or expected values, the auditors should investigate this by making inquiries of management and performing other audit procedures as necessary.

6 Planning an initial audit engagement

FAST FORWARD

An initial audit engagement will often involve more work at the planning stage than a recurring audit engagement.

Auditors must make special considerations at the planning stage when they are auditing an entity for the first time, whether because the entity has never required an audit before, or whether the entity has simply changed auditor.

New audits generally require a little more work than recurring engagements. But it is important to note that this is not because the auditor needs to do a first-time audit more thoroughly than other audits. Rather, it is because there are specific risks in relation to an auditor's relative lack of knowledge of new audit clients.

6.1 Audit strategy and audit plan

ISA 300.A20 states that the overall audit strategy and audit plan may include the following in an initial audit engagement:

- Arrangements to be made with the predecessor auditor, eg to review their working papers

- Any major issues discussed with management, eg relating to the application of IFRS, and how these issues affect the audit strategy & plan

- The audit procedures necessary in relation to opening balances (see Chapter 8)

- Any other procedures required by the firm for initial engagements, eg review of the audit strategy by another senior partner within the firm.

It is likely that more audit work will need to be performed in order to lower detection risk (and thus audit risk) to the required level. This may result in a **higher audit fee** being charged for an initial engagement, since fees should relate to the amount of time spent on the engagement.

6.2 Understanding the entity

ISA 315 requires the auditor to obtain an understanding of the entity and its environment in order to identify and assess the risks of material misstatement. In the case of an initial audit engagement this will tend to require more work, because the auditor will have less experience of the client.

6.3 Other considerations

Detection risk may be higher for an initial audit engagement, as the auditor may not have the knowledge to design and perform procedures to obtain sufficient appropriate audit evidence.

Materiality is likely to be set at a lower level for initial engagements. The auditor will generally be less familiar with the entity's internal controls, which means that a comparatively small misstatement could be indicative of a pervasive failure of internal control.

Chapter Roundup

- Auditors must plan their work so that it is undertaken in an effective manner.

- With a 'top down' approach (also known as the business risk approach) controls testing is aimed at high level controls and substantive testing is reduced.

- Materiality considerations are important throughout the audit process. An item might be material due to its nature, value or impact on the users of the financial statements as a group.

- Auditors must assess the risk of material misstatements arising in financial statements and carry out procedures in response to assessed risks.

- Business risk is the risk arising to companies through being in operation.

- Analytical procedures are important at all stages of the audit.

- An initial audit engagement will often involve more work at the planning stage than a recurring audit engagement.

Quick Quiz

1 What is the purpose of an audit strategy document?

2 What are the effects of a 'top-down' audit approach on:

   (a) Tests of controls   (c) Detailed testing

   (b) Analytical procedures

3 Name four key control objectives for sales.

   (1) ....   (3) ....

   (2) ....   (4) ....

4 When undertaking a cycles approach to auditing, the auditor is ensuring that transactions are processed through the cycle.

   True ☐   False ☐

5 A balance sheet approach should never be combined with a business risk approach.

   True ☐   False ☐

6 Complete the matrix.

Type of account	Purpose of primary test	Primary test also gives comfort on			
		Assets	Liabilities	Income	Expenses
Assets		U	O	O	U
Liabilities		U	O	O	U
Income		U	O	O	U
Expense		U	O	O	U

7 Complete the definition.

.... is an expression of the ....

or .... of a particular matter in the context of financial statements.

8 Identify whether the following matters, which represent potential business risks to the company are financial, operational or compliance risks.

Item	Potential business risk
Going concern	
Physical disasters	
Breakdown of accounting systems	
Loss of key personnel	
Credit risk	
Breach of legislation	
Sales tax problems	
Currency risk	
Poor brand management	
Environmental issues	

Answers to Quick Quiz

1   The audit strategy document sets out in general terms how the audit is to be carried out.

2   (a)   Tests of control focused on high level controls

       (b)   Analytical procedures used more extensively

       (c)   Detailed testing consequently reduced

3   Any of:

Ordering and granting of credit

- **Goods** and **services** are **only supplied** to **customers** with **good credit ratings**
- **Customers** are encouraged to **pay promptly**
- **Orders** are **recorded correctly**
- **Orders** are **fulfilled**

Despatch and invoicing

- All **despatches** of goods are **recorded**
- All **goods and services** sold are **correctly invoiced**
- All **invoices** raised **relate to goods and services** that have been **supplied** by the business
- **Credit notes** are only given for **valid reasons**

Recording, accounting and credit control

- All sales that have been **invoiced** are **recorded** in the general and sales ledgers
- All **credit notes** that have been **issued** are **recorded** in the general and sales ledgers
- All **entries** in the sales ledger are **made** to the **correct** sales ledger **accounts**
- **Cut-off** is applied correctly to the sales ledger
- Potentially **doubtful debts** are **identified**

4   True

5   False

6

		Primary test also gives comfort on			
Type of account	**Purpose of primary test**	**Assets**	**Liabilities**	**Income**	**Expenses**
Assets	Overstatement (O)	U	O	O	U
Liabilities	Understatement (U)	U	O	O	U
Income	Understatement (U)	U	O	O	U
Expense	Overstatement (O)	U	O	O	U

7   Materiality, relative significance, importance

8

Item	Potential business risk
Going concern	Financial
Physical disasters	Operational
Breakdown of accounting systems	Financial
Loss of key personnel	Operational
Credit risk	Financial
Breach of legislation	Compliance
Sales tax problems	Compliance
Currency risk	Financial
Poor brand management	Operational
Environmental issues	Compliance

Now try the questions below from the Exam Question Bank

Number	Level	Marks	Time
Q7	Examination	25	45 mins
Q8	Examination	20	36 mins

Evidence

Topic list	Syllabus reference
1 Audit evidence	D1(ii)
2 Related parties	D1(ii)
3 Written representations	D1(ii)
4 Reliance on the work of an auditor's expert	D1(ii)
5 Reliance on the work of internal audit	D1(ii)
6 Documentation	D1(ii)

Introduction

Audit evidence is a vital part of any audit. The basic issues relating to evidence are that:

- Auditors must obtain evidence to support financial statement assertions. This evidence must be sufficient and appropriate.

- Audit evidence must be documented sufficiently.

Related parties are a difficult area to obtain audit evidence on. The auditor must bear in mind who the evidence is from and how extensive it is. Obtaining evidence about related party transactions is considered in Section 2 of this chapter.

Often the auditors will have to rely on written representations about related parties and other issues. Written representations are subjective evidence, and the auditor must proceed with caution when dealing with them. This is discussed in Section 3.

Sometimes, the evidence the auditor requires is beyond the expertise of the auditor, and he will need to rely on the work of an expert. The relevant procedures that the auditor must undertake are outlined in Section 4. Similar considerations arise if the external auditor intends to rely on the work of internal audit.

Study guide

D(ii)	Evidence	Intellectual level
(a)	Identify and describe audit procedures to obtain sufficient audit evidence from identified sources.	2
(b)	Identify and evaluate the audit evidence expected to be available to:	3
	(i) support the financial statement assertions and accounting treatments (including fair values)	
	(ii) support disclosures made in the notes to the financial statements.	
(c)	Apply analytical procedures to financial and non-financial data.	2
(d)	Explain the specific audit problems and procedures concerning related parties and related party transactions.	2
(e)	Recognise circumstances that may indicate the existence of unidentified related parties and select appropriate audit procedures.	2
(f)	Evaluate the use of written management representations to support other audit evidence.	2
(k)	Recognise when it is justifiable to place reliance on the work of an expert (eg a surveyor employed by the audit client)	2
(l)	Assess the appropriateness and sufficiency of the work of internal auditors and the extent to which reliance can be placed on it	2

Exam guide

Specific audit issues examined in this paper are likely to be at a higher level than in your previous auditing exams. Therefore, the more complex evidence issues of related parties, written representations and using the work of others are important. You should consider how they link in with specific accounting issues in Chapters 9 and 10.

1 Audit evidence

FAST FORWARD   Auditors need to obtain sufficient, appropriate audit evidence.

1.1 Obtaining evidence

You should be aware of the key points of audit evidence from your previous auditing studies. We shall revise them briefly here. Substantive procedures are designed to obtain evidence about the financial statement assertions.

Exam focus point

It is essential that you tailor audit procedures depending on the specific scenario given in the question. After virtually every sitting, the examiner comments in her Examiner's Report that vague suggestions do not answer the requirement adequately.

Key term

Financial statement assertions are the representations of the directors that are embodied in the financial statements. By approving the financial statements, the directors are making representations about the information therein. These representations or assertions may be described in general terms in a number of ways.

Guidance on assertions is found in *ISA 315 Identifying and assessing the risks of material misstatement through understanding the entity and its environment.*

ISA 315.25

The auditor shall identify and assess the risks of material misstatement at:

(a)   the financial statement level, and
(b)   the assertion level for classes of transactions, account balances, and disclosures

to provide a basis for designing and performing further audit procedures.

It gives examples of assertions in these areas.

Assertions used by the auditor	
Assertions about **classes of transactions** and events for the period under audit	**Occurrence**: transactions and events that have been recorded have occurred and pertain to the entity. **Completeness**: all transactions and events that should have been recorded have been recorded. **Accuracy**: amounts and other data relating to recorded transactions and events have been recorded appropriately. **Cut-off**: transactions and events have been recorded in the correct accounting period (see measurement, above). **Classification**: transactions and events have been recorded in the proper accounts.
Assertions about **account balances** at the period-end	**Existence**: assets, liabilities and equity interests exist. **Rights and obligations**: the entity holds or controls the rights to assets, and liabilities are the obligations of the entity. **Completeness**: all assets, liabilities and equity interests that should have been recorded have been recorded. **Valuation and allocation**: assets, liabilities and equity interests are included in the financial statements at appropriate amounts and any resulting valuation or allocation adjustments are appropriately recorded.
Assertions about **presentation and disclosure**	**Occurrence and rights and obligations**: disclosed events, transactions and other matters have occurred and pertain to the entity. **Completeness**: all disclosures that should have been included in the financial statements have been included. **Classification and understandability**: financial information is appropriately presented and described, and disclosures are clearly expressed. **Accuracy and valuation**: financial and other information is disclosed fairly and at appropriate amounts.

You may find the following mnemonic useful when remembering the financial statement assertions: ACCA COVER

A ccuracy
C ompleteness
C ut-off
A llocation
C lassification (understandability)
O ccurrence
V aluation
E xistence
R ights and obligations

(Each letter of ACCA COVER is the first letter of each of the assertions listed above.)

ISA 500 *Audit evidence* outlines the objective of the auditor and procedures used by auditors to obtain evidence.

ISA 500.4

The objective of the auditor is to design and perform audit procedures in such a way as to enable the auditor to obtain sufficient appropriate audit evidence to be able to draw reasonable conclusions on which to base the auditor's opinion.

Procedures	
Inspection of assets	Inspection of assets that are recorded in the accounting records confirms **existence**, gives evidence of **valuation**, but does not confirm **rights and obligations**. Confirmation that assets seen are recorded in the accounting records gives evidence of **completeness**.
Inspection of documentation	Confirmation to documentation of items recorded in accounting records confirms that an asset **exists** or a transaction **occurred**. Confirmation that items recorded in supporting documentation are recorded in accounting records tests **completeness**. Cut-off can be verified by inspecting reverse population, that is, checking transactions recorded **after** the end of the reporting period to supporting documentation to confirm that they occurred after the end of the reporting period. Inspection also provides evidence of **valuation/measurement**, **rights and obligations** and the nature of items **(presentation and disclosure)**. It can also be used to **compare** documents (and hence test **consistency** of audit evidence) and confirm **authorisation**.
Observation	Observation involves watching a procedure being performed (for example, post opening). It is of limited use, as it only confirms the procedure took place when the auditor is watching.
Enquiries	Seeking information from **client staff** or **external sources**. Strength of evidence depends on knowledge and integrity of source of information.
Confirmation	Seeking confirmation from another source of details in client's accounting records for example, confirmation from bank of bank balances.
Recalculations	Checking arithmetic of client's records, for example, adding up ledger account.
Reperformance	Reperformance is the auditor's independent execution of procedures or controls originally performed as part of the entity's internal control, either manually or using CAATs. CAATs are covered in the next section.
Analytical procedures	Analytical procedures consist of evaluations of financial information made by a study of plausible relationships among both financial and non-financial data. Analytical procedures are covered in Section 1.4.

1.2 Sufficient and appropriate audit evidence

'Sufficiency' and 'appropriateness' are interrelated and apply to both tests of controls and substantive procedures.

- **Sufficiency** is the measure of the **quantity** of audit evidence.
- **Appropriateness** is the measure of the **quality** or **reliability** of the audit evidence.

Auditors are essentially looking for enough reliable audit evidence. Audit **evidence usually indicates what is probable** rather than what is definite (is usually persuasive rather than conclusive) so different sources are examined by the auditors. However, auditors can only give **reasonable assurance** that the financial statements are free from misstatement, so **not all sources of evidence will be examined**.

When assessing the sufficiency and appropriateness of audit evidence, auditors must consider whether the evidence is consistent. Where **contradictory evidence** is discovered, for example, where one piece of evidence suggests that a specific liability has been settled prior to the year end whilst another piece of evidence throws doubt on this, the auditors must perform any other procedures necessary to resolve the inconsistency.

ISA 500.11

If audit evidence obtained from one source is inconsistent with that obtained from another, or the auditor has doubts over the reliability of information to be used as audit evidence, the auditor shall determine what modifications or additions to audit procedures are necessary to resolve the matter, and shall consider the effect, if any, on other aspects of the audit.

ISA 530 *Audit sampling* is based on the premise that auditors do not normally examine all the information available to them, as it would be impractical to do so and using audit sampling will produce valid conclusions.

Key terms

Audit sampling involves the application of audit procedures to less than 100% of the items within a population of audit relevance such that all sampling units have a chance of selection in order to provide the auditor with a reasonable basis on which to draw conclusions about the entire population.

Statistical sampling is any approach to sampling that involves random selection of a sample, and use of probability theory to evaluate sample results, including measurement of sampling risk.

Population is the entire set of data from which a sample is selected and about which an auditor wishes to draw conclusions.

Sampling units are the individual items constituting a population.

Stratification is the process of dividing a population into sub-populations, each of which is a group of sampling units, which have similar characteristics (often monetary value).

Tolerable misstatement is a monetary amount set by the auditor in respect of which the auditor seeks to obtain an appropriate level of assurance that the monetary amount set be the auditor is not exceeded by the actual misstatement in the population.

Tolerable rate of deviation is a rate of deviation from prescribed internal control procedures set by the auditor in respect of which the auditor seeks to obtain an appropriate level of assurance that the rate of deviation set by the auditor is not exceeded by the actual rate of deviation in the population.

Anomaly. A misstatement or deviation that is demonstrably not representative of misstatements or deviations in a population.

Sampling risk arises from the possibility that the auditor's conclusion, based on a sample, may be different from the conclusion if the entire population were subjected to the same audit procedure.

Non-sampling risk arises from factors that cause the auditor to reach an erroneous conclusion for any reason not related to the sampling risk. For example, most audit evidence is persuasive rather than conclusive, the auditor might use inappropriate procedures, or the auditor might misinterpret evidence and fail to recognise an error.

Some testing procedures do **not** involve sampling, such as:

- Testing 100% of items in a population
- Testing all items with a certain characteristic (for example, over a certain value) as the selection is not representative

The ISA distinguishes between **statistically based sampling**, which involves the use of random selection techniques from which mathematically constructed conclusions about the population can be drawn, and **non-statistical methods**, from which auditors draw a judgemental opinion about the population. However the principles of the ISA apply to both methods. You should be aware of the major methods of statistical and non-statistical sampling.

The auditors' judgement as to what is sufficient appropriate audit evidence is influenced by a number of factors.

- **Risk assessment**
- The **nature** of the **accounting and internal control systems**
- The **materiality** of the item being examined
- The **experience gained during previous audits**
- The auditors' **knowledge of the business** and **industry**
- The **results of audit procedures**
- The **source** and **reliability of information** available

If they are unable to obtain sufficient appropriate audit evidence, the auditors should **consider the implications for their report**.

1.2.1 External confirmations

The reliability of audit evidence is affected by its source. Audit evidence is more reliable when it is obtained from independent sources outside the entity.

Both ISA 330 *The auditor's responses to assessed risks* and ISA 505 *External Confirmations* address the need for external confirmations in gathering sufficient and appropriate audit evidence.

> **ISA 330.19**
>
> The auditor shall consider whether external confirmation procedures are to be performed as substantive audit procedures.

ISA 330 identifies the following situations where external confirmations are appropriate:

- Bank balances and other information from bankers
- Accounts receivable balances
- Inventories held by third parties
- Property deeds held by lawyers
- Investments held for safekeeping by third parties or purchased from stockbrokers but not delivered at the balance sheet date.
- Loans from lenders
- Accounts payable balances

ISA 505.7 states that "**the auditor** shall maintain **control** over **external confirmation requests**". So to take the example of a receivables circularisation, it is the auditor who should be in control of sending and receiving the requests & the responses from customers.

If management refuses to allow the auditor to send an external confirmation request, the auditor must consider whether this is reasonable and whether audit evidence can be obtained in another way. If evidence cannot be obtained from another source, the auditor should communicate this to those charged with governance, and consider the impact on the audit report (there is a possibility that the auditor's opinion will have to be modified (qualified) on the basis of an inability to obtain sufficient appropriate audit evidence, or that a disclaimer of opinion will be issued).

In November 2009 the IAASB issued a Practice Alert in this area, *Emerging Practice Issues Regarding the Use of External Confirmations in an Audit of Financial Statements*. In addition to re-emphasising the points contained in ISA 505, the alert made the following points:

It is important that consideration is given to whether the confirmation request **provides evidence** on the **specific assertion being tested**, as it may provide evidence for some assertions but not others.

All confirmation responses carry some **risk of interception, alteration or fraud**. Such risk exists regardless of whether a response is obtained in paper form, or through electronic or other medium. Accordingly, it is essential that the auditor maintain control over the confirmation process. It is also important that the auditor **maintain appropriate professional scepticism** throughout the confirmation process, particularly when evaluating the confirmation responses.

The ISAs do not preclude the use of electronic confirmations, as they can, if properly managed, provide appropriate audit evidence.

Disclaimers and other restrictions included in confirmation responses do not necessarily invalidate the reliability of the responses as audit evidence.

One of the competencies you require to fulfil performance objective 17 of the PER is the ability to test and evaluate evidence and draw conclusions. You can apply the knowledge you obtain in this section of the text to help demonstrate this competence.

Question

Audit evidence

'The objective of the auditor is to design and perform audit procedures in such a way as to enable the auditor to obtain sufficient appropriate audit evidence to be able to draw reasonable conclusions on which to base the auditor's opinion.' (ISA 500.4)

Discuss the extent to which each of the following sources of audit evidence is sufficient and appropriate.

(a) Oral representation by management in respect of the completeness of sales where the majority of transactions are conducted on a cash basis

(b) Flowcharts of the accounting and control system prepared by a company's internal audit department

(c) Year end suppliers' statements

(d) Physical inspection of a non-current asset by an auditor

(e) Comparison of income statement items for the current period with corresponding information for earlier periods

Answer

Appropriate – relevance

The relevance of audit evidence should be considered in relation to the overall audit objective of forming an opinion and reporting on the financial statements. The evidence should allow the auditor to conclude on the following:

- Statement of financial position items (existence, rights and obligations, completeness, valuation and allocation).

- Income statement items (occurrence, completeness, accuracy, cut-off and classification).

(a) The representations by management in respect of the completeness of sales is relevant to the first of the objectives when gathering evidence on income statement items. Depending on the system operated by the client and the controls over cash sales there may be no other evidence as to the completeness of sales.

(b) The flowcharts prepared by the internal audit department will not be directly relevant to the auditor's opinion on individual figures in the financial statements, but rather when the auditor is following the requirement in ISA 315 to ascertain the enterprise's system of recording and processing transactions. The auditor will wish to assess the adequacy of the system as a basis for the preparation of financial statements so the flowcharts will be relevant only if they are sufficiently detailed to allow the auditor to carry out this assessment. The auditor would also wish to make an initial assessment of internal controls at this stage so the flowcharts will be more relevant for control procedures that are specifically identified.

(c)   Year end suppliers' statements provide evidence relevant to the auditor's conclusions on:

    (i)   The completeness of payables, as omissions from the purchase ledger listing would be identified by comparing statements received to that listing

    (ii)   The existence of payables recorded in the purchase ledger

    (iii)   The fact that the liabilities are properly those of the enterprise (for example, the statements are not addressed to, say, the managing director in his own name)

    (iv)   The valuation of payables at the year end with respect to cut-off of invoices and credit notes, and discounts or allowances.

(d)   The physical inspection of a non-current asset is clearly relevant to the auditor's opinion as to the existence of the asset, and to some extent the completeness of recording of assets, that is, the auditor can check that all the assets inspected have been recorded. In certain circumstances evidence relevant to valuation might be obtained, for example, where a client has written down a building due to permanent diminution in value and the auditor sees it standing unused and derelict.

(e)   The comparison of income statement items with prior periods will provide evidence as to:

    (i)   Completeness of recording, as omissions can be identified and investigated

    (ii)   Valuation, in cases where the auditor has appropriate information on which to base expectations, for example, if the number of workers has doubled during the year and a set percentage wage increase had been effected in the year

    (iii)   Disclosure, as the comparison should highlight any inconsistencies of classification and treatment from year to year

Appropriate – reliable

Reliability of audit evidence depends on the particular circumstances but the guideline offers three general presumptions

- Documentary evidence is more reliable than oral evidence.
- Evidence obtained from independent sources outside the enterprise is more reliable than that secured solely from within the enterprise.
- Evidence originated by the auditor by such means as analysis and physical inspection is more reliable than evidence obtained by others.

(a)   The oral representations by management would be regarded as relatively unreliable using the criteria in the guidelines, as they are oral and internal. In the absence of any external or auditor-generated evidence, the auditor should ensure that these representations are included in the letter of representation so that there is at least some documentary evidence to support any conclusions.

(b)   The assessment of how reliable the flowcharts are would depend on the auditor's overall assessment of the internal audit department. The factors to be considered would include its degree of independence, the scope of its work, whether due professional care had been exercised, the technical competence and level of resource available to the internal audit department. This assessment should be documented by the external auditor if he is to make use of the flowcharts in his audit planning and design of tests.

(c)   Suppliers' statements would generally be seen as reliable evidence, being documentary and from sources external to the enterprise. If the auditor had doubts as to the reliability of this evidence, it could be improved by the auditor originating similar evidence by means of a payables' circularisation rather than relying on suppliers' statements received by the client.

(d)   Physical inspection of a non-current asset is a clear example of auditor-originated evidence, so would usually be considered more reliable than that generated by others.

(e)   Analysis such as this comparison of income statement items with the prior periods would again be termed auditor-generated evidence, and would be considered more reliable than evidence generated by others. Ultimately the reliability of such audit evidence depends on the reliability of the underlying data, which should be checked by compliance or substantive testing.

Sufficiency

The auditor needs to obtain sufficient relevant and reliable evidence to form a reasonable basis for his opinion on the financial statements. His judgements will be influenced by factors such as:

- His knowledge of the business and its environment
- The risk of misstatement
- The persuasiveness of the evidence

(a)   To decide if the representations were sufficient with regard to concluding on the completeness of sales the auditor would consider:

   (i)   The nature of the business and the inherent risk of unrecorded cash sales
   (ii)   The materiality of the item; in this case it would appear that cash sales are material
   (iii)   Any possible management bias
   (iv)   The persuasiveness of the evidence in the light of other related audit work, for example, testing of cash receipts

If the auditor believes there is still a risk of material understatement of sales in the light of the above, he should seek further evidence.

(b)   Client-prepared flowcharts are **not** sufficient as a basis for the auditor's evaluation of the system. To confirm that the system does operate in the manner described, the auditor should perform 'walk through' tests, tracing a small number of transactions through the system. There is, however, no need for the auditor to prepare his own flowcharts if he is satisfied that those produced by internal audit are accurate.

(c)   The auditor's decision as to whether the suppliers' statements were sufficient evidence would depend on his assessment of materiality and the risk of misstatement. Its persuasiveness would be assessed in conjunction with the results of other audit work, for example, substantive testing of purchases, returns, and cash payments, and compliance testing of the purchases system.

(d)   Inspection of a non-current asset would be sufficient evidence as to the existence of the asset (provided it was carried out at or close to the period end). Before concluding on the non-current asset figure in the accounts, the auditor would have to consider the results of his work on other aspects, such as the ownership and valuation of the asset.

(e)   In addition to the general considerations such as risk and materiality, the results of a 'comparison' alone would not give very persuasive evidence. It would have to be followed by a detailed investigation of variances (or lack of variances where they were expected). The results should be compared to the auditor's expectations based on his knowledge of the business, and explanations given by management should be verified. The persuasiveness of the evidence should be considered in the light on other relevant testing, for example, compliance testing of payments systems, or substantive testing of expense invoices.

1.3 Computer assisted audit techniques (CAATs)

1.3.1 Audit software

Audit software performs the sort of checks on data that auditors might otherwise have to perform by hand. Examples of uses of audit software are:

- Interrogation software, which accesses the client's data files

- Comparison programs, which compare versions of a program
- Interactive software for interrogation of online systems
- Resident code software to review transactions as they are processed

Although audit interrogation software may be used during many tests of controls and substantive procedures, its use is particularly appropriate during substantive testing of transactions and especially balances. By using audit software, the auditors may **scrutinise large volumes of data** and concentrate skilled manual resources on the investigation of results, rather than on the extraction of information and **selection** of **samples**.

Major considerations when deciding whether to use file interrogation software are as follows:

(a) As a minimum auditors will require a **basic understanding** of data processing and the enterprise's computer application, together with a detailed knowledge of the audit software and the computer files to be used.

(b) Depending on the complexity of the application, the auditors may need to have a sound appreciation of **systems analysis**, operating systems and, where program code is used, experience of the programming language to be utilised.

(c) Auditors will need to consider how easy it is to **transfer** the **client's data** onto the auditors' PC.

(d) The client may **lack full knowledge** of the **computer system**, and hence may not be able to explain fully all the information it produces.

1.3.2 Test data

An obvious way of seeing whether a system is **processing** data in the way that it should be is to input some valid test data and see what happens. The expected results can be calculated in advance and then compared with the results that actually arise. Test data can also be used to check the controls that prevent processing of **invalid data** by entering data with say a non-existent customer code or worth an unreasonable amount, or transactions which may if processed breach limits such as customer credit limits.

A significant problem with test data is that any resulting corruption of the data files has to be corrected. This is difficult with modern real-time systems, which often have built in (and highly desirable) controls to ensure that data entered **cannot** easily be removed without leaving a mark.

Other problems with **test data** are that it only tests the operation of the system at a **single point of time**, and auditors are only testing controls in the programs being run and controls which they know about. The problems involved mean that test data is being used less as a CAAT.

1.3.3 Embedded audit facilities

The results of using test data would, in any case, be completely distorted if the programs used to process it were not the ones **normally** used for processing. For example a fraudulent member of the IT department might substitute a version of the program that gave the correct results, purely for the duration of the test, and then replace it with a version that siphoned off the company's funds into his own bank account.

To allow a **continuous** review of the data recorded and the manner in which it is treated by the system, it may be possible to use CAATs referred to as 'embedded audit facilities'. An embedded facility consists of audit modules that are incorporated into the computer element of the enterprise's accounting system.

Two frequently encountered examples are Integrated Test Facility (ITF) and Systems Control and Review File (SCARF). Such systems allow auditors to give frequent and fast audit reports on a wide variety of subject matters, key performance indicators and critical success factors.

The use of IT to produce such reports means additional risk to auditors. They need to ensure that the reports are replaced properly (ie that no one relies on yesterday's report today) and are protected from interference (hacking). It also widens the amount of expertise needed from auditors, as they will need IT skills as well as expertise in a number of different areas being reported on.

1.4 Substantive analytical procedures

1.4.1 Role of analytical procedures

Chapter 6 covered the use of analytical procedures at the planning stage of the audit, in assessing risk. Analytical procedures are also widely used as a substantive procedure and can be much more cost-effective than carrying out high volumes of tests of detail.

1.4.2 Examples

Simple comparisons

A simple year-on-year comparison could provide very persuasive evidence that an expense such as rent is correctly stated, providing that the auditor has sufficient knowledge of the business, for example knowing that the same premises have been leased year-on-year and that there has been no rent review.

Comparisons with estimates prepared by the auditors

A common example of this is where a business may have a large number of items of plant and machinery that are depreciated at different rates. The auditor could perform a quick calculation:

| Closing balance of plant and machinery (cost) | × | Average depreciation rate |

If this estimate was similar to the actual depreciation charge, it would go some way to allowing the auditor to conclude that the charge was materially correct.

Relationship between financial and non-financial information

In making an estimate of employee costs, probably for one specific department, such as manufacturing, the auditor might use information about the number of employees in the department, as well as rates of pay increases. The estimate might be

$$\text{Prior year wages expense} \times \frac{\text{Average no. of employees current year}}{\text{Average no. of employees prior year}} \times \% \text{ pay increase}$$

If the actual expense does not make sense when compared to the estimate, explanations would need to be sought and corroborated. For example, management might explain that for several months of the year the factory ran double shifts, so a higher proportion of hours worked were paid at higher overtime rates.

Further examination of production records for those months would be required.

If no explanation is available, then more detailed substantive testing will be required, directed towards possible misstatements such as mispostings or frauds such as payments to dummy employees.

1.4.3 Suitability of using analytical procedures

ISA 520 *Analytical procedures* notes that auditors should not rely on analytical procedures alone in respect of material balances but should combine them with tests of detail. Tests of detail are also required in areas where significant risks have been identified at the planning stage.

2 Related parties   6/08, 6/11

FAST FORWARD ▶▶

> It can be a difficult to gain audit evidence about related party transactions.

2.1 Importance of related parties

Central to a number of government investigations in various countries have been companies trading with organisations or individuals **other than at arm's length**. Such transactions were made possible by a degree of control or influence exercised by directors over both parties to the transactions. ISA 550 *Related parties* covers this area.

Key terms

> **Related party**: a person or entity that is either
>
> (a)   A person or a close member of that person's family is related to a reporting entity if that person:
>
> (i)   has control or joint control over the reporting entity;
> (ii)   has significant influence over the reporting entity; or
> (iii)   is a member of the key management personnel of the reporting entity or of a parent of the reporting entity.
>
> (b)   An entity is related to a reporting entity if any of the following conditions applies:
>
> (i)   The entity and the reporting entity are members of the same group (which means that each parent, subsidiary and fellow subsidiary is related to the others).
> (ii)   One entity is an associate or joint venture of the other entity (or an associate or joint venture of a member of a group of which the other entity is a member).
> (iii)   Both entities are joint ventures of the same third party.
> (iv)   One entity is a joint venture of a third entity and the other entity is an associate of the third entity.
> (v)   The entity is a post-employment benefit plan for the benefit of employees of either the reporting entity or an entity related to the reporting entity. If the reporting entity is itself such a plan, the sponsoring employers are also related to the reporting entity.
> (vi)   The entity is controlled or jointly controlled by a person identified in (a).
>
> Related party transactions are a transfer of resources or obligations between related parties, regardless of whether a price is charged.

Management is responsible for the identification of related party transactions. Such transactions should be properly approved as they are frequently not at arm's length. Management is also responsible for the **disclosure** of related party transactions.

It may not be self-evident to management whether a party is related. Furthermore, many accounting systems are not designed to either distinguish or summarise related party transactions, so management will have to carry out additional analysis of accounting information.

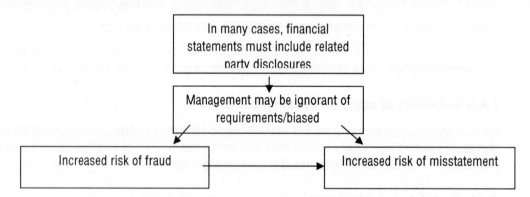

An audit cannot be expected to detect all material related party transactions. The risk that undisclosed related party transactions will not be detected by the auditors is especially high when:

*   **Related party transactions** have **taken place without charge**.
*   **Related party transactions** are **not self-evident** to the auditors.
*   Transactions are with a party that the auditors could **not reasonably** be expected to **know** is a **related party**.
*   **Active steps** have been taken by **management** to **conceal** either the full terms of a transaction, or that a transaction is, in substance, with a related party.
*   The **corporate structure** is **complex**.

> **ISA 550.9**
>
> The objectives of the auditor are:
>
> (a)   Irrespective of whether the applicable financial reporting framework establishes related party requirements, to obtain an understanding of related party relationships and transactions sufficient to be able:
>
>   (i)   To recognise fraud risk factors, if any, arising from related party relationships and transactions that are relevant to the identification and assessment of the risks of material misstatement due to fraud, and
>
>   (ii)   To conclude, based on the audit evidence obtained, whether the financial statements, insofar as they are affected by those relationships and transactions:
>
>   –   Achieve fair presentation (for fair presentation frameworks), or
>   –   Are not misleading (for compliance frameworks)
>
> (b)   In addition, where the applicable financial reporting framework establishes related party requirements, to obtain sufficient appropriate audit evidence about whether related party relationships and transactions have been appropriately identified, accounted for and disclosed in the financial statements in accordance with the framework.

2.2 Assessment and identification of risks

As part of the risk assessment procedures required by ISA 315, the auditor must carry out the following procedures to obtain information relevant to identifying risks associated with related parties.

- Audit team discussion of risk shall include specific consideration of susceptibility of financial statements to material misstatement through related parties and their transactions

- Auditor shall inquire of management:

  –   The identity of related parties including changes from prior period
  –   The nature of the relationships between the entity and its related parties
  –   Whether any transactions occurred between the parties, and if so, what
  –   What controls the entity has to identify, account for and disclose related party relationships and transactions
  –   What controls the entity has to authorise and approve significant transactions and arrangements with related parties
  –   What controls the entity has to authorise and approve significant transactions and arrangements outside the normal course of business

  (The auditor may have to perform risk assessment procedures in addition in respect of the latter three points.)

- Maintain alert for evidence of related party transactions when obtaining other audit evidence, in particular, when scrutinising bank and legal confirmations and minutes of meetings

- If significant transactions outside the normal course of business are discovered, inquire of management the nature of the transactions and whether related parties could be involved

- Share information obtained about related parties with the audit team

The following procedures may be helpful:

- **Enquire of management** and the directors as to whether transactions have taken place with related parties that are required to be disclosed by the disclosure requirements that are applicable to the entity
- **Review prior year working papers** for names of known related parties
- **Review minutes** of meetings of shareholders and directors and other relevant statutory records such as the register of directors' interests
- **Review accounting records** for large or unusual transactions or balances, in particular transactions recognised at or near the end of the financial period
- **Review confirmations of loans receivable** and payable and confirmations from banks. Such a review may indicate the relationship, if any, of guarantors to the entity
- **Review investment transactions**, for example purchase or sale of an interest in a joint venture or other entity
- **Enquire** as to the **names** of all pension and other trusts established for the benefit of employees and the names of their management and trustees
- **Enquire** as to the **affiliation** of directors and officers with other entities
- **Review the register of interests in shares** to determine the names of principal shareholders
- **Enquire of other auditors** currently involved in the audit, or predecessor auditors, as to their knowledge of additional related parties
- **Review the entity's tax returns**, returns made under statute and other information supplied to regulatory agencies for evidence of the existence of related parties
- **Review invoices and correspondence** from lawyers for indications of the existence of related parties or related party transactions

If risks relating to related parties and their transactions are identified, they should be treated as **significant risks** in accordance with ISA 315. Also, due to the close connection between related parties and possible fraud, the auditor must consider the overlap with ISA 240 here as well.

2.3 Responses to the risks

> **ISA 550.20**
>
> As part of the ISA 330 requirement that the auditor respond to assessed risks, the auditor designs and performs further audit procedures to obtain sufficient appropriate audit evidence about the assessed risks of material misstatement associated with related party relationships and transactions....

The audit procedures discussed above must include the following:

Further audit procedures: risk of misstatement due to related parties	
Situation	**Actions by auditor**
Auditor suspects existence of related parties not disclosed by management.	Determine whether the information does confirm the existence of related parties.

Auditor identifies related parties not disclosed by management.	• Tell the rest of the audit team
	• Request management to identify all transactions with identified related party
	• Inquire as to why company controls failed to identify related party
	• Perform substantive procedures relating to related party and its transactions with entity
	   – Making enquiries of third parties presumed to have knowledge, such as legal counsel
	   – Conducting an analysis of accounting records for transactions with the related party (using a CAAT?)
	   – Verifying terms and conditions of transactions by looking at the contract
	• Reconsider the risk of further related parties existing and not being disclosed to the auditor
	• If non disclosure appears intentional, and therefore indicative of fraud, evaluate implications for audit.

Auditor identifies related party transactions outside normal course of business	• Inspect contracts/agreements and evaluate whether
	   – The business rationale (or lack thereof) suggests a fraudulent purpose (is it overly complex, does it have unusual terms of trade, does it lack a logical business purpose?)
	   – The terms of the transactions are consistent with management's explanations
	   – The transactions have been accounted for and disclosed properly

Management has asserted in the financial statements that related party transactions were conducted at arm's length	• Obtain sufficient appropriate evidence that this is true by looking at the terms of the contract and assessing:
	   – Price
	   – Credit terms
	   – Contingencies
	   – Specific charges

2.4 Written representations

ISA 550.26

Where the applicable financial reporting framework establishes related party requirements, the auditor shall obtain written representations from management, and where relevant, those charged with governance, that they have disclosed to the auditor the identity of the entity's related parties and all the related party relationships and transactions of which they are aware, and they have appropriately accounted for and disclosed such relationships and transactions in accordance with the requirements of the framework.

2.5 Audit conclusions and reporting

If the auditor is unable to obtain sufficient appropriate audit evidence concerning related parties and transactions with such parties or concludes that their disclosure in the financial statements is not adequate, the auditor should modify the audit report appropriately.

The auditor must communicate all significant matters arising during the audit in connection with the entity's related parties (unless all those charged with governance are involved in managing the entity).

Exam focus point

The June 2011 exam asked candidates to explain the inherent limitations to the identification of related parties and related party transactions (4 marks), and to recommend audit procedures that are appropriate to the situation given in the question (4 marks). To score well, students needed to show a specific awareness of the requirements of ISAs in this area – specifically ISA 500.

The June 2008 exam contained a very similar requirement, asking candidates to discuss why the identification of related parties and material related party transactions can be difficult for auditors. The examiner's report commented that few candidates mentioned the existence of ISA 550. **Students should always refer to ISAs where appropriate for a strong technical answer.**

Problems with applying ISA 550	
Identification of controlling party	Auditors may find it very difficult to identify the controlling party if the entity is part of a multi-national group. If the controlling party is a trust, auditors may have problems determining who if anyone controls the trust.
	Alternatively the directors may state that they do not know the identity of the controlling party or that there is no controlling party. These statements may be difficult to disprove.
Materiality	This problem has two aspects:
	(a) Auditors may not be able to determine **whether transactions** are **material** to related parties who are individuals (directors, key management and their families).
	(b) Auditors may have particular problems **applying** the **definition** of **materiality** (an item is material if it affects the decisions of the users of the accounts). As materiality depends on circumstances as well as amounts, auditors have to decide whether the fact that certain transactions are on normal commercial terms influences whether they are disclosed.

2.6 Transactions with directors and management

Auditors may find it difficult to obtain sufficient assurance that they have identified all disclosable transactions because of:

(a) The **low value of certain transactions**, making them difficult to detect when using normal audit procedures

(b) Any **requirements** for **disclosure of transactions** between the company and the connected persons of a director, given that it may not always be easy for the auditors to identify such connected persons

(c) The fact that there may be little or no **documentary evidence** of **transactions** requiring disclosure

The complexity of the relevant legislation may give rise to difficulties of interpretation. For example, advances of expenses or remuneration on account may constitute a disclosable loan if the monies are outstanding for a long time.

2.6.1 Company procedures

Auditors should enquire as to the company's procedures for ensuring that all disclosable transactions are properly identified and recorded. Such procedures are likely to include the following.

- **Advise** all **directors** and **officers** that they have a **responsibility** to disclose transactions in which they have an interest, either directly or through connected persons. (Such disclosure should take place at a meeting of the directors)

- **Record** all **transactions** notified in the minutes of directors' meetings

- **Maintain** a **register** in which details of all transactions requiring disclosure are recorded

- **Establish** some **method** of:

    - **Identifying proposed transactions** which will require the approval of the members in general meeting
    - **Ensuring** that the **company does not enter** into any **illegal transaction**

- **Monitor the system** by checking on a regular basis (as a minimum, once a year) that each director is in agreement with the company's record of his disclosable transactions and is satisfied that such records are both complete and accurate

- **Obtain** from **each director** at the end of each financial year a **formal statement** indicating the disclosures necessary for the purposes of the statutory accounts

With smaller organisations, auditors may well find that there may be no formalised procedures or that they are inadequate. Auditors should **advise each director** of his statutory responsibilities, and make a **written request** for **confirmation** of any disclosable transaction in which he has an interest.

2.6.2 Audit procedures

Further audit procedures to be adopted should include the following.

- **Inspect** the **board minutes** and other records of transactions with directors and connected persons to consider their adequacy and whether or not they appear to have been kept up to date

- **Examine** any **agreements** and **contracts** involving **directors and connected persons**, including tracing the details of such transactions to any source documentation available

- **Consider** whether **transactions** disclosed are on **commercial** terms

- **Assess** the **recoverability** of amounts due from directors or connected persons

- **Review** the **legality** of the disclosable transactions recorded by the company. Where auditors are of the opinion that a transaction is illegal, they should:

    - Immediately advise the directors of their view
    - Give careful consideration as to whether any reference to the matter will be required in the audit report

- **Advise** the **client** to **seek legal advice** in those cases where there are doubts as to the legality and/or disclosable nature of a transaction

- **Consider** the **possibility** that the **company's details** of **disclosable transactions** may be incomplete as regards those directors (and connected persons) who have not been in office throughout the year

- **Review subsequent events** in order to consider whether they might have any impact on the matters requiring disclosure

Finally, auditors should consider obtaining **written representations** from each director giving confirmation of any disclosable transaction which relates to himself and any persons connected with him.

You are the senior in charge of the audit of AB Milton Co for the year ended 31 May 20X1. Details of AB Milton Co and certain other companies are given below.

AB Milton Co

A building company formed by Alexander Milton and his brother, Brian.

AB Milton Co has issued share capital of 500 ordinary $1 shares, owned as shown below.

Alexander Milton	210	42%	Founder and director
Brian Milton	110	22%	Founder and director
Catherine Milton (Brian's wife)	100	20%	Company secretary
Diane Hardy	20	4%	
Edward Murray	60	12%	Director

Edward Murray is a local business man and a close friend of both Alexander and Brian Milton. He gave the brothers advice when they set up the company and remains involved through his position on the board of directors. His own company, Murray Design Co, supplies AB Milton Co with stationery and publicity materials.

Diane Hardy is Alexander Milton's ex-wife. She was given her shares as part of the divorce settlement and has no active involvement in the management of the company. Alexander's girlfriend, Fiona Dyson, is the company's solicitor. She is responsible for drawing up and reviewing all key building and other contracts, and frequently attends board meetings so that she can explain the terms of a particular contract to the directors. Her personal involvement with Alexander started in May 20X1 and, since that time, she has spent increasing amounts of time at the company's premises.

Cuts and Curls Co

A poodle parlour, of which 50% of the issued shares are owned by Diane Hardy and 50% by Gillian Milton, who is Alexander and Diane's daughter.

Cuts and Curls operates from premises owned by AB Milton Co for which it pays rent at the normal market rate.

Campbell Milton Roofing Co

A roofing company owned 60% by AB Milton Co and 40% by Ian Campbell, the managing director.

Campbell Milton Roofing Co carries out regular work for AB Milton Co and also does roofing work for local customers. Alexander Milton is a director of Campbell Milton Roofing Co and Catherine Milton is the company secretary. All legal work is performed by Fiona Dyson.

Required

(a) Based on the information given above, identify the potential related party transactions you expect to encounter during the audit of AB Milton Co and summarise, giving your reasons, what disclosure, if any, will be required in the full statutory accounts.

(b) Prepare notes for a training session for junior staff on how to identify related party transactions. Your notes should include:

(i) A list of possible features which could lead you to investigate a particular transaction to determine whether it is in fact a related party transaction, and

(ii) A summary of the general audit procedures you would perform to ensure that all material related party transactions have been identified.

Answer

(a)

Person/entity	Related party	Why	Transaction
Alex Milton	✓	Director	
Brian Milton	✓	Director	No transactions mentioned
Brian's wife	✓	Wife of director	
Edward Murray	✓	Director	Purchases of stationery
Murray Designs	✓	Sub of director	
Diane Hardy	✗	No longer close family and ≥ 20%	
Fiona Dyson	✓	Presumed close family and shadow director	Contracts drawn
Cuts and Curls	?	(see below)	Rental agreement
Campbell Milton Roofing	✓	Sub of AB Milton	Work done for AB (see below)
Ian Campbell	✓/✗	Could be considered key management of group	

Cuts and Curls is not clear cut. For it to be a related party Gillian Milton would need to be in a position to control Cuts and Curls and then due to her relationship with Alex Milton her company would come under the related party umbrella. Gillian only holds 50% and therefore holds joint control with her mother.

Disclosure

Once a related party has been identified disclosure is required of any material transaction under IAS 24 *Related Party Disclosures*. Materiality is in most cases determined by considering both parties' perspective. For instance, the contracts drawn by Fiona Dyson may be material to her even if not to AB Milton.

Transactions with subsidiaries, that is, Campbell Milton Roofing:

Disclosure is not required of transactions which are cancelled on consolidation. However, if group accounts are not prepared due to a small/medium group exemption material transactions between the two companies would need to be disclosed.

Disclosure should include:

(i)   Names of the transacting related parties

(ii)   A description of the relationship

(iii)   A description of the transaction and the amounts included

(iv)   The amounts due to or from the related party at the end of the year

(v)   Any other element of the transaction necessary for an understanding of the financial statements

(b)   Notes for staff training sessions:

(i)   A logical place to start the audit of related party transactions would be to identify all possible related parties. This would always include

- Directors and shadow directors
- Group companies
- Pension funds of the company
- Associates

It is likely that the other related parties would include:

- Key management (perhaps identified by which staff have key man cover)
- Shareholder owning > 20% of the shares
- Close relatives associates of any of the above

A related party transaction needs to be reported if it is material either to the reporting entity or to the other party to the transaction.

Related party transactions do not necessarily have to be detrimental to the reporting entity, but those which are will be easier to find. Features which may indicate this may include:

- Unusually generous trade or settlement discounts
- Unusually generous payment terms
- Recorded in the nominal ledger code of any person previously identified as a related party (for example, director)
- Unusual size of transaction for customers (for example, if ABM were paying a suspiciously high legal bill for a building company)

(ii)   Audit steps to find related party transactions may include:

- Identification of excessively generous credit terms by reference to aged trade accounts receivable analysis
- Identification of excessive discounts by reference to similar reports
- Scrutiny of cash book/cheque stubs for payments made to directors or officers of the company (probably more realistic for smaller entities)
- Review of Board minutes for evidence of approval of related party transactions (directors are under a fiduciary duty not to make secret profits)
- Written representations from directors to give exhaustive list of all actual/potential related parties (that is, allow us to make the materiality assessment, not them)
- Review of accounting rewards for large transactions, especially near the year end and with non-established customers/suppliers
- Identification of any persons holding > 20% of the shares in the entity by reference to the shareholders' register

3 Written representations

Management is required to give written representations regarding the preparation and presentation of the financial statements, information provided to the auditor and management responsibilities. Other representations may also be sought, but it is important to remember they do not provide sufficient appropriate audit evidence on their own..

3.1 Representations

The auditors receive many representations during the audit, both unsolicited and in response to specific questions. Some of these representations may be critical to obtaining sufficient appropriate audit evidence. Representations are also be required for general matters, eg full availability of accounting records. ISA 580 *Written representations* covers this area.

This ISA was issued in April 2008 as part of the IAASB Clarity Project.

> **ISA 580.6**
>
> The objectives of the auditor are:
>
> (a) To obtain appropriate representations from management and, where appropriate, those charged with governance that they believe that they have fulfilled their responsibility for the preparation of the financial statements and for the completeness of the information provided to the auditor
>
> (b) To support other audit evidence relevant to the financial statements or specific assertions in the financial statements by means of written representations if determined necessary by the auditor or required by other ISAs, and
>
> (c) To respond appropriately to written representations provided by management and, where appropriate, those charged with governance, or if management or, where appropriate, those charged with governance do not provide the written representations requested by the auditor.

Written representations should be requested from management or directors with appropriate responsibilities for the financial statements and knowledge of the matters concerned.

3.2 Management from whom written representations are requested

> **ISA 580.9**
>
> The auditor shall request written representations from management with appropriate responsibilities for the financial statements and knowledge of the matters concerned.

ISA 580 requires the auditor to determine the appropriate individuals from whom to seek written representations. In most cases this is likely to be management, as they would be expected to have sufficient knowledge of the way in which the entity's financial statements have been prepared. However, the ISA goes on to point out that in circumstances where others are responsible for the financial statement, for example, those charged with governance then they should be requested to provide the representations.

The ISA emphasises the need for management to make **informed representations**. In some cases the auditor may request that management confirms that it has made appropriate enquires to enable it to do so.

3.3 Written representations concerning management responsibilities

> **ISA 580.10**
>
> The auditor shall request management to provide a written representation that it has fulfilled its responsibility for the preparation of the financial statements in accordance with the applicable financial reporting framework, including where relevant their fair presentation, as set out in the terms of the audit engagement.
>
> **ISA 580.11**
>
> The auditor shall request management to provide a written representation that:
>
> (a) It has provided the auditor with all the relevant information and access as agreed in the terms of the audit engagement, and
>
> (b) All transactions have been recorded and are reflected in the financial statements

This can be done when the auditors receive a signed copy of the financial statements which incorporate a relevant statement of management responsibilities. Alternatively, the auditors may obtain such evidence in the form of a **written representation** from management, or a document written by the auditors and signed by the management.

The responsibilities of management should also be set out as they are in the terms of engagement.

3.4 Other written representations

In addition to written representations relating to responsibility for the financial statements, the auditors may wish to rely on written representations from management as audit evidence, and several other ISAs require them.

> **ISA 580.13**
>
> Other ISAs require the auditor to request written representations. If, in addition to such required representations, the auditor determines that it is necessary to obtain one or more written representations to support other audit evidence relevant to the financial statements or one or more specific assertions in the financial statements, the auditor shall request such other written representations.

As written representations do not form sufficient audit appropriate evidence on their own, when the auditors receive such representations they should:

- Seek **corroborative audit evidence** from sources inside or outside the entity
- **Evaluate** whether the **representations** made by management appear reasonable and are consistent with other audit evidence obtained, including other representations
- **Consider whether the individuals** making the representations can be expected to be **well-informed** on the particular matters

The table below suggests areas where written representations may be required.

Other written representations	
Required by ISAs	The following ISAs require specific written representations: • ISA 240 • ISA 250 • ISA 450 • ISA 501 • ISA 540 • ISA 550 • ISA 560 • ISA 570 • ISA 710
Other management responsibility issues	• Whether the selection of accounting policies is appropriate • Whether the following matters have been recognised, measured, presented or disclosed correctly: – Plans or intentions affecting values of assets – Liabilities – Title to or control over assets – Aspects of laws and regulations that may affect the FS • Whether all deficiencies of internal controls have been communicated to the auditor
Concerning specific assertions	• Matters of director judgement and intention (corroborated to meeting minutes for example)

3.4.1 Doubt as to the reliability of written representations

The auditor will have to determine the effect of the following on the reliability of written representations (if one of the following arises):

- Concerns over the competence, integrity, ethical values or diligence of management

- Inconsistency of written representations with other evidence obtained

The auditor will seek to resolve the latter by performing audit procedures. However, if it remains unresolved, particularly in addition to the first point, the auditor will have to take appropriate actions, which may include modifying the audit report in accordance with ISA 705 .

3.4.2 Requested written representations not provided

If requested representations are not provided, the auditor must:

- Discuss the matter with management

- Re-evaluate the integrity of management and the effect that this may have on other representations and audit evidence in general

- Take appropriate actions, including determining the possible effect on the auditor's report per ISA 705 .

3.5 Form, timing and documentation of representations by management

The auditors should include in audit working papers evidence of management's representations in the form of a summary of oral discussions with management or written representations from management.

A written representation shall take the form of a **representation letter** from management.

The date of the letter should be as near as practicable to the date the audit report is signed, **but not after it**.

You have seen an example of a written representation letter in your previous studies, so should be familiar with the form they should take.

Question   Written representations

You are an audit manager reviewing the completed audit file of Leaf Oil Co.

(a)   There have been no events subsequent to the period-end requiring adjustment in the financial statements.

(b)   The company has revalued two properties in the year. The directors believe that the property market is going to boom next year, so have decided to revalue the other two properties then.

(c)   The directors confirm that the company owns 75% of the newly formed company, Subsidiary Co, at the year end.

(d)   The directors confirmed that the 500 gallons of oil in Warehouse B belong to Flower Oil Co.

Required

Comment on whether you would expect to see these matters referred to in the written representation letter.

Answer

(a)   I would expect to see this referred to in a representation letter. ISA 580 gives this as an example of a matter to be included in the letter, as management should inform auditors of relevant subsequent events.

(b)   This should not appear on a representation letter, even though management opinion is involved. This indicates an incorrect accounting treatment which the auditors should be in disagreement with the directors over.

(c)   This should not appear on a representation letter as there should be sufficient alternative evidence for this matter. The auditor should be able to obtain registered information about Subsidiary Co from the companies' registrar.

(d)   This should not appear on a representation letter. The auditors should be able to obtain evidence from Flower Oil Co that the inventory belongs to them.

4 Reliance on the work of an auditor's expert 12/08

> Sometimes auditors may need to use the work of an auditor's expert to obtain sufficient, appropriate audit evidence.

4.1 Experts

Professional audit staff are highly trained and educated, but their experience and training is limited to accountancy and audit matters. In **certain situations** it will therefore be necessary to employ someone else with **different expert knowledge** to gain sufficient, appropriate audit evidence.

Key term

> An **expert** is a person or firm possessing special skill, knowledge and experience in a particular field other than accounting and auditing.

Auditors have **sole responsibility** for their opinion, but may use the work of an expert in order to obtain **sufficient audit evidence** regarding certain financial statement assertions.

ISA 620 *Using the work of an auditor's expert* distinguishes between the 'auditor's expert' and 'management's expert'. The latter is used by the entity in the form of assistance in the preparation of financial statements.

Key terms

> **Auditor's expert** – An individual or organisation possessing expertise in a field other than accounting or auditing, whose work in that field is used by the auditor to assist the auditor in obtaining sufficient appropriate audit evidence. An auditor's expert may be either an auditor's internal expert (who is a partner or staff, including temporary staff, of the auditor's firm or a network firm), or an auditor's external expert.
>
> **Management's expert** – An individual or organisation possessing expertise in a field other than accounting or auditing, whose work in that field is used by the entity to assist the entity in preparing the financial statements.

4.2 Determining the need to use the work of an auditor's expert

> **ISA 620.3**
>
> …if the auditor using the work of an auditor's expert… concludes that the work of that expert is adequate for the auditor's purposes the auditor may accept that expert's findings or conclusions in the expert's field as appropriate audit evidence.

The following list of examples is given by the ISA of the audit evidence which might be obtained from the opinion, valuation etc of an expert.

- **Valuations of certain types of assets**, for example complex financial instruments, land and buildings, plant and machinery
- **Determination of quantities or physical condition of assets**
- **Determination of amounts** using specialised techniques, for example pensions accounting
- **The measurement of work completed** and **work in progress** on contracts
- **Legal opinions**

When considering whether to use the work of an expert, the auditors should review:

- The **importance** of the matter being considered in the context of the accounts
- The **risk of misstatement** based on the nature and complexity of the matter
- The **quantity** and **quality** of other available **relevant audit evidence**

ISA 620 requires that a written agreement exists covering instructions to the auditor's expert.

Engaging an auditor's expert is a costly business and the client and auditors will only want to if there is a real need to do so, in other words, in circumstances where other relevant and reliable audit evidence is not available. When recommending audit procedures in the exam, only recommend using an expert if it is a relevant test. It is not a substitute for alternative tests.

Once it is decided that an auditor's expert is required, the approach should be discussed with the management of the entity. Where the management is unwilling or unable to engage an expert, the auditors should consider engaging an expert themselves **unless sufficient alternative audit evidence can be obtained.**

ISA 620 distinguishes between 'internal' and 'external' auditor's experts.

- Auditor's internal experts   –   members of the engagement team
- Auditor's external experts   –   are not members of the engagement team. They are *engaged* but not employed by the auditor

4.3 Competence and objectivity of the auditor's expert

ISA 620.9

The auditor shall evaluate whether the auditor's expert has the necessary competence, capabilities and objectivity for the auditor's purposes. In the case of an auditor's external expert, the evaluation of objectivity shall include inquiry regarding interests and relationships that may create a threat to that expert's objectivity.

This will involve considering:

- The expert's **professional certification**, or licensing by, or membership of, an appropriate professional body
- The expert's **experience and reputation** in the field in which the auditors are seeking audit evidence

The risk that an expert's **objectivity is impaired** increases when the expert is:

- **Employed** by the entity
- **Related** in some other manner to the entity, for example, by being financially dependent upon, or having an investment in, the entity

If the auditors have **reservations** about the competence or objectivity of the expert they may need to carry out **other procedures** to obtain **evidence from another expert.**

4.4 The scope of work of the auditor's expert

ISA 620.11

The auditor shall agree, in writing when appropriate, on ... the nature, scope and objectives of that expert's work.

Written instructions usually cover the auditor's expert's terms of reference and such instructions may cover such matters as follows.

- The **objectives** and **scope** of the expert's work
- A **general outline** as to the specific matters the expert's report is to cover
- The **intended use** of the expert's work
- The **extent** of the **expert's access** to appropriate records and files
- Clarification of the expert's relationship with the entity, if any
- Confidentiality of the entity's information
- Information regarding the **assumptions and methods intended** to be used by the expert and their consistency with those used in prior periods

4.5 Assessing the work of the auditor's expert

> **ISA 620.12**
>
> The auditor shall evaluate the adequacy of the auditor's expert's work for the auditor's purposes including ... the relevance and reasonableness of that expert's findings or conclusions.

Auditors should assess whether the substance of the auditor's expert's findings is properly reflected in the financial statements or supports the financial statement assertions. It will also require consideration of:

- The **source data used**
- The **assumptions and methods used**
- **When** the expert carried out the work
- The reasons for any **changes in assumptions and methods**
- The **results** of the expert's work in the light of the auditors' overall knowledge of the business and the results of other audit procedures

The auditors do **not** have the expertise to judge the assumptions and methods used; these are the responsibility of the expert. However, the auditors should seek to obtain an understanding of these assumptions, to consider their reasonableness based on other audit evidence, knowledge of the business and so on.

Relevant factors when evaluating the relevance and reasonableness of the findings or conclusions of the auditor's expert, whether in a report or other form, may include whether they are:

- Presented in a manner that is consistent with industry standards
- Clearly expressed, including reference to the objectives agreed and standards used
- Based on an appropriate period and take into account any subsequent events
- Subject to any reservation, limitation or restriction on use
- Based on appropriate consideration of errors or deviations encountered by the auditor's expert.

> **ISA 620.13**
>
> If the auditor determines that the work of the auditor's expert is not adequate for the auditor's purposes, the auditor shall:
>
> (a)   Agree with that expert on the nature and extent of further work to be performed by that expert, or
> (b)   Perform additional audit procedures appropriate to the circumstances

4.6 Reference to an auditor's expert in the audit report

> **ISA 620.14**
>
> The auditor shall not refer to the work of an auditor's expert in an auditor's report containing an unmodified opinion unless required by law or regulation to do so.

Such a reference may be misunderstood and interpreted as a modification of the audit opinion or a division of responsibility, neither of which are appropriate.

If the auditors issue a modified audit report, then they may refer to the work of the expert. In such cases, auditors may need to obtain permission in advance from the expert. If such permission is not given, then the auditors may have to seek legal advice.

Question

The following situations are both extracted from an exam on the previous syllabus.

(a) 'The useful life of each oil platform is assessed annually on factors such as weather conditions and the period over which it is estimated that oil will be extracted.' You are auditing the useful lives of the oil platforms.

(b) 'Piles of copper and brass, that can be distinguished with a simple acid test, have been mixed up.' You are attending the inventory count.

Required

Explain whether it is necessary to use the work of an auditor's expert in these situations. Where relevant, you should describe alternative procedures.

Answer

(a) **Platforms**

It is not necessary to use an auditor's expert to audit the useful lives of the platforms as there are many other available sources of evidence. Relevant procedures include:

(i) Obtaining weather reports to see whether management's determination of useful lives is consistent with them

(ii) Comparing budgeted oil against actual oil extracted (if the budget was optimistic, so might the useful life be)

(iii) Reviewing published industry comparators (such as Shell and BP). If the useful lives of their platforms as published in financial statements is significantly different, discuss with management why that might be

(iv) Considering whether management's determination of useful lives in the past has been proved accurate

(b) It is not necessary to use an auditor's expert, as the question states that a 'simple' test is available. The auditors should confirm that the company will be making use of this test during the inventory count to separate the inventory. The auditor should reperform the test on a sample of 'brass' and 'copper' as counted to ensure it has been separated correctly.

Exam focus point

> The exam question will often give a clear indicator of whether an auditor's expert is required or not. For instance in (a) above, information was given on what the useful lives were based on – which the auditor should be able to interpret himself. In (b), the words '**simple** acid test' imply an auditor's expert is not required.

5 Reliance on the work of internal audit   6/10

The principles of relying on work done by anyone other then the audit firm are always the same. The role of internal audit is studied in depth in the earlier paper.

Knowledge brought forward from earlier studies

Reliance on the work of internal auditors by external auditors

The external auditors may make use of the work of internal audit. The guidance over when this appropriate is given to them in ISA 610 *Using the work of internal auditors*.

The ISA states that the external auditors must give consideration first to the scope and organisation of the internal audit function and then evaluate the specific audit work they are interested in.

The following factors must be considered.

- Proficiency and training of the people who have undertaken the work
- Level of supervision, review and documentation of the work of assistants
- Sufficiency and appropriateness of evidence to draw conclusions
- Appropriateness of conclusions drawn
- Consistency of any reports prepared with the work performed
- Whether the work necessitates amendment to the external audit programme

Where an entity has only recently developed an internal audit function (or has outsourced internal audit to eg a reliable service organisation), this may have an impact on the **audit strategy** adopted, perhaps reducing the level of substantive procedures employed.

Internal auditors are likely to suggest changes to systems and controls, and it is crucial that these are documented and evaluated by the external auditors. It is also arguable that any new procedure cannot be relied upon as heavily as an old procedure, as it may take time for procedures to bed in and for potential flaws in them to be rectified. Moreover, the work of documenting and evaluating any new procedure will take time to do, which may exert some upward pressure on the audit fee.

6 Documentation

 FAST FORWARD

All evidence obtained should be documented.

6.1 Document what?

 PER alert

One of the competencies you require to fulfil performance objective 18 of the PER is the ability to ensure the audit files accurately document the opinion, together with any relevant discussions before the report is signed or issued. You can apply the knowledge you obtain in this chapter of the text to help demonstrate this competence.

All audit work must be documented: the working papers are the **tangible evidence of all work done in support of the audit opinion.** ISA 230 *Audit documentation* provides guidance on documentation.

In the case of areas where the evidence is difficult to obtain, such as related parties, and may arise through discussions with management, it is vital that notes are made of conversations and that, as discussed earlier in this chapter, representations on material matters are confirmed in writing.

In your previous studies, you have learnt the practical issues surrounding how audit papers should be completed.

A key requirement of ISA 230 concerns what to include on a working paper as follows.

ISA 230.8

'The auditor shall prepare audit documentation that is sufficient to enable an experienced auditor, having no previous connection with the audit, to understand:

(a) The nature, timing and extent of the audit procedures performed to comply with the ISAs and applicable legal and regulatory requirements.

(b) The results of the audit procedures performed, and the audit evidence obtained.

(c) Significant matters arising during the audit, the conclusions reached thereon, and significant professional judgements made in reaching those conclusions.

The key reason for having audit papers therefore is that they provide evidence of work done. They may be required in the event of litigation arising over the audit work and opinion given.

The ISA sets out certain requirements about what should be recorded, such as the identifying characteristics of the specific items being tested.

It also sets out points an auditor should record in relation to significant matters, such as the extent of professional judgement exercised in performing the work and evaluating the results.

If an auditor felt it necessary to depart from customary audit work required by audit standards, he should document why, and how the different test achieved audit objectives.

The ISA also contains details about how the audit file should be put together and actions in the event of audit work being added after the date of the audit report (for example, if subsequent events results in additional work being carried out).

Specific consideration is given to **smaller entities**. The ISA recognises that the documentation of a smaller entity will be less extensive, but emphasises the overriding requirement that it should be capable of being understood by an experienced auditor.

We shall briefly revise here the review of working papers. **Review** of working papers is important, as it allows a more senior auditor to **evaluate the evidence obtained** during the course of the audit for sufficiency and reliability, so that more evidence can be obtained to support the audit opinion, if required.

6.2 Review of audit working papers

FAST FORWARD

Working papers should be reviewed by a more senior audit staff member before an audit conclusion is drawn.

Work performed by each assistant should be reviewed by personnel of appropriate experience to consider whether:

- The work has been performed in accordance with the audit programme.
- The work performed and the results obtained have been adequately documented.
- Any significant matters have been resolved or are reflected in audit conclusions.
- The objectives of the audit procedures have been achieved.
- The conclusions expressed are consistent with the results of the work performed and support the audit opinion.

The following should be reviewed on a timely basis.

- The **overall audit strategy** and the **audit plan**
- The **assessments of inherent and control risks**
- The **results** of **control** and **substantive procedures** and the conclusions drawn including the results of consultations
- The **financial statements,** proposed audit adjustments and the proposed auditors' report

In some cases, particularly in large complex audits, personnel not involved in the audit may be asked to review some or all of the audit work, the auditors' report etc. This is sometimes called a **peer review** or **hot review**.

Chapter Roundup

- Auditors need to obtain sufficient, appropriate audit evidence.

- It can be a difficult to gain audit evidence about related party transactions.

- Management is required to give written representations regarding the preparation and presentation of the financial statements, information provided to the auditor and management responsibilities. Other representations may also be sought, but it is important to remember they do not provide sufficient appropriate audit evidence on their own.

- Sometimes auditors may need to use the work of an auditor's expert to obtain sufficient appropriate audit evidence.

- All evidence obtained should be documented.

- Working papers should be reviewed by a more senior audit staff member before an audit conclusion is drawn.

1   Give five examples of financial statement assertions.

   (1)   ....

   (2)   ....

   (3)   ....

   (4)   ....

   (5)   ....

2   Which of the following is not a procedure designed to obtain evidence?

                    documents

      Inspection   **Observation**

                   assets

                    Analytical procedures

      Computation   **Deduction**

                 Enquiries

                               Confirmation

          management   external

                             sources

3   Give five reasons why the nature of related party relationships and transactions may give rise to increased risk.

   (1)   ....

   (2)   ....

   (3)   ....

   (4)   ....

   (5)   ....

4   Written representations from management might take the form of a letter from the auditors acknowledged and signed by the director.

   True   ☐

   False   ☐

5   Complete the definition.

   An .... is a person or organisation possessing ....,

   in a field other than .... or ....

6   Give three examples of audit evidence which can be obtained from an auditor's expert.

   (1)   ....

   (2)   ....

   (3)   ....

7   What is a hot review?

Answers to Quick Quiz

1   From:

   (1) Existence
   (2) Rights and obligations
   (3) Occurrence
   (4) Completeness
   (5) Valuation
   (6) Cut-off
   (7) Classification
   (8) Accuracy
   (9) Allocation

2   Deduction

3   (1) Related parties may operate through a **wide** and **complex** range of relationships and structures
   (2) **Management unaware** of the existence of all related party relationships and transactions
   (3) **Information systems may be ineffective** at identifying or summarising transactions and outstanding balances between an entity and its related parties
   (4) Related party transactions may not be conducted under **normal market terms and conditions**.
   (5) Related party relationships provide a greater opportunity for **collusion, concealment or manipulation** by management.

4   True

5   Expert, expertise, accounting, auditing

6   (1) Valuations of assets
   (2) Determination of quantities of assets
   (3) Legal opinions

7   A hot review is when a member of staff who has not been involved in the audit is asked to review all the working papers before the audit report is signed.

Now try the questions below from the Exam Question Bank

Number	Level	Marks	Time
Q10	Examination	20	36 mins

Evaluation and review (I)

Topic list	Syllabus reference
1 Revision: review procedures and evaluation of findings	D1(iii)
2 Revision: opening balances	D1(iii)
3 Revision: comparatives	D1(iii)
4 Revision: other information	D1(iii)
5 Revision: subsequent events	D1(iii)
6 Revision: going concern	D1(iii)

Introduction

Towards the end of an audit, a series of review and evaluations are carried out. You should be familiar with them from your previous auditing studies.

Section 1 outlines the **overall review** which is undertaken on the financial statements as a whole and the review of errors and potential errors.

In Sections 2 and 3, the issue of **opening balances and comparatives** is discussed. In the event of a recurring audit, both these items are audited by review. In special circumstances, notably the first audit, different considerations and procedures must be followed.

The auditor must review **other information** to establish whether it contradicts the audit report. The detailed procedures and requirements are discussed in Section 4.

The auditor conducts reviews of the **going concern** presumption and the period between the period end and the signing of the audit report **(subsequent events)**. There is guidance given on both these areas in ISAs, and they are dealt with in Sections 6 and 5 respectively.

Study guide

D1(iii)	Evaluation and review	Intellectual level
(b)	Explain the use of analytical procedures in evaluation and review	3
(c)	Explain how the auditor's responsibilities for corresponding figures, comparative financial statements and 'other information' are discharged	3
(d)	Apply the further considerations and audit procedures relevant to initial engagements	2
(e)	Discuss the courses of action available to an auditor if a material inconsistency or misstatement of fact exists in relation to other information	2
(f)	Specify audit procedures designed to identify subsequent events that may require adjustment to, or disclosure in, the financial statements of a given entity	2
(g)	Identify and explain indicators that the going concern basis may be in doubt and recognise mitigating factors	2
(h)	Recommend audit procedures, or evaluate the evidence that might be expected to be available and assess the appropriateness of the going concern basis in given situations	3
(i)	Assess the adequacy of disclosures in financial statements relating to going concern and explain the implications for the auditor's report with regard to the going concern basis	3
(j)	Evaluate the matters (eg materiality, risk, relevant accounting standards, audit evidence) relating to: (xxiii) events after the end of the reporting period	3

Exam guide

Going concern is a particularly important audit review which could be relevant in risks or evidence questions. Bear in mind the links with planning, knowledge of the business and analytical procedures. Subsequent events, corresponding figures and other information could also come up in an exam question in the context of audit reports.

1 Revision: review procedures and evaluation of findings

FAST FORWARD

> The auditors must perform and document an overall review of the financial statements before they can reach an opinion.

Once the bulk of the substantive procedures have been carried out, the auditors will have a draft set of financial statements which should be supported by appropriate and sufficient audit evidence. At the beginning of the end of the audit process, it is usual for the auditors to undertake an **overall review** of the financial statements. This review of the financial statements, in conjunction with the conclusions drawn from the other audit evidence obtained, gives the auditors a reasonable basis for their opinion on the financial statements. It should be carried out by a senior member of the audit team, with appropriate skills and experience.

 One of the competencies you require to fulfil performance objective 18 of the PER is the ability to review the completed audit work, considering the significance of any errors or misstatements. You can apply the knowledge you have obtained from this chapter of the text to help demonstrate this competence.

1.1 Compliance with accounting regulations

The auditors should consider whether:

(a) The information presented in the financial statements is in accordance with local/national statutory requirements

(b) The accounting policies employed are in accordance with accounting standards, properly disclosed, consistently applied and appropriate to the entity.

When examining the **accounting policies**, auditors should consider:

- Policies **commonly adopted in particular industries**
- Policies for which there is **substantial authoritative support**
- Whether any **departures from applicable accounting standards** are necessary for the financial statements to conform to the IASB *Framework*'s requirement of 'fair presentation'
- Whether the **financial statements reflect the substance** of the underlying transactions and not merely their form.

When compliance with local/national statutory requirements and accounting standards is considered, the auditors may find it useful to use a **checklist**.

1.2 Review for consistency and reasonableness

The auditors should consider whether the financial statements are consistent with their knowledge of the entity's business and with the results of other audit procedures, and the manner of disclosure is fair. The principal considerations are as follows.

(a) Whether the financial statements adequately reflect the **information** and **explanations** previously obtained and conclusions previously reached during the course of the audit

(b) Whether it reveals any **new factors** which may affect the presentation of, or disclosure in, the financial statements

(c) Whether analytical procedures applied when completing the audit, such as comparing the information in the financial statements with other pertinent data, **produce results** which assist in arriving at the overall conclusion as to whether the financial statements as a whole are consistent with their knowledge of the entity's business

(d) Whether the **presentation** adopted in the financial statements may have been unduly influenced by the **directors' desire** to present matters in a favourable or unfavourable light

(e) The potential impact on the financial statements of the **aggregate of uncorrected misstatements** (including those arising from bias in making accounting estimates) identified during the course of the audit and the preceding period's audit, if any

1.3 Analytical procedures

Exam focus point

Your examiner has indicated that you may **sometimes** be required to perform **specific tasks** in relation to analytical procedures. See the article in the January 2011 edition of *student accountant*.

Do not spend too much time rote-learning all of the formulae given below. For one thing, using these formulae is unlikely to form a major part of a P7 exam. Furthermore, **it is far more important that you understand what the numbers in financial statements mean** than that you can calculate lots of ratios. You need to show that you can 'make the numbers talk'.

In Chapter 6 we discussed how analytical procedures are used as part of the overall review procedures at the end of an audit. Remember the areas that the analytical procedures at the final stage must cover.

- Important accounting ratios
- Related items
- Changes in products; customers
- Price and mix changes

- Wages changes
- Variances
- Trends in production and sales
- Changes in material and labour content of production
- Other income statement expenditure
- Variations caused by industry or economy factors

As at other stages, significant fluctuations and unexpected relationships must be investigated and documented.

You should be familiar with all of the following from your previous studies. You should read through the material here and make sure that you are comfortable calculating the ratios.

1.3.1 Revision of key ratios: profitability

$$\text{ROCE} = \frac{\text{Profit before interest and taxation}}{\text{Total assets less current liabilities}} \times 100\%$$

| Capital employed | = | Shareholders' equity plus non-current liabilities (*or* total assets less current liabilities) |

What does ROCE mean? There are three main possibilities:

(a) The **change in ROCE from one year to the next** can be examined.

(b) The **ROCE being earned by other companies**, if this information is available, can be compared with the ROCE of this company.

(c) A comparison of the ROCE with **current market borrowing rates** may be made.

You also need to be familiar with **profit margin** and **asset turnover**, which both tie in nicely with the ROCE. The relationship between the three ratios can be shown mathematically.

Profit margin × Asset turnover = ROCE

$$\therefore \quad \frac{\text{PBIT}}{\text{Sales}} \times \frac{\text{Sales}}{\text{Capital employed}} = \frac{\text{PBIT}}{\text{Capital employed}}$$

It might be tempting to think that a high profit margin is good, and a low asset turnover means sluggish trading. In broad terms, this is so. But there is a trade-off between profit margin and asset turnover, and you cannot look at one without allowing for the other.

(a) A **high profit margin** means a high profit per £1 of sales, but if this also means that sales prices are high, there is a strong possibility that sales revenue will be depressed, and so asset turnover lower.

(b) A **high asset turnover** means that the company is generating a lot of sales, but to do this it might have to keep its prices down and so accept a low profit margin per £1 of sales.

1.3.2 Revision of key ratios: debt

The **debt ratio** is the ratio of a company's total debts to its total assets.

There is no absolute guide to the maximum safe debt ratio, but as a very general guide, you might regard 50% as a safe limit to debt. In practice, many companies operate successfully with a higher debt ratio than this, but 50% is nonetheless a helpful benchmark. In addition, if the debt ratio is over 50% and getting worse, the company's debt position will be worth looking at more carefully.

$$\text{Gearing} = \frac{\text{Interest bearing debt}}{\text{Shareholders' equity} + \text{interest bearing debt}} \times 100\%$$

As with the debt ratio, there is **no absolute limit** to what a gearing ratio ought to be. A company with a gearing ratio of more than 50% is said to be high-geared (whereas low gearing means a gearing ratio of less than 50%). Many companies are high geared, but if a high geared company is becoming increasingly high geared, it is likely to have difficulty in the future when it wants to borrow even more, unless it can also boost its shareholders' capital, either with retained profits or by a new share issue.

$$\text{Interest cover} = \frac{\text{Profit before interest and tax}}{\text{Interest charges}}$$

An interest cover of 2 times or less would be low, and should really exceed 3 times before the company's interest costs are to be considered within acceptable limits.

Debt ratios could very easily be combined with an examination question on **insolvency**.

$$\text{Current ratio} = \frac{\text{Current assets}}{\text{Current liabilities}} \qquad \text{Quick ratio} = \frac{\text{Current assets less inventory}}{\text{Current liabilities}}$$

Both the current ratio and the quick ratio offer an indication of the company's liquidity position, but the absolute figures **should not be interpreted too literally**. It is often theorised that an acceptable current ratio is 1.5 and an acceptable quick ratio is 0.8, but these should only be used as a guide.

Finally, you should also be comfortable with the ratios of the cash operating cycle – receivables days, payables days, inventory holding period.

1.3.3 Revision of key ratios: shareholders' investment ratios

$$\text{Dividend cover is a ratio of: } \frac{\text{Earnings per share}}{\text{Dividend per (ordinary) share}}$$

It shows the **proportion of profit for the year that is available for distribution to shareholders that has been paid (or proposed) and what proportion will be retained in the business to finance future growth.** A dividend cover of 2 times would indicate that the company had paid 50% of its distributable profits as dividends, and retained 50% in the business to help to finance future operations. Retained profits are an important source of funds for most companies, and so the dividend cover can in some cases be quite high.

The **Price/Earnings (P/E) ratio** is the ratio of a company's current share price to the earnings per share.

A high P/E ratio indicates strong shareholder **confidence** in the company and its future, eg in profit growth, and a lower P/E ratio indicates lower confidence.

$$\text{Dividend yield} = \frac{\text{Dividend on the share for the year}}{\text{Current market value of the share (ex div)}} \times 100\%$$

(a)   The dividend per share is taken as the dividend for the previous year.
(b)   Ex-div means that the share price does *not* include the right to the most recent dividend.

Shareholders look for **both dividend yield and capital growth**. Obviously, dividend yield is therefore an important aspect of a share's performance.

1.4 Summarising errors

During the course of the audit, errors will be discovered which may be material or immaterial to the financial statements. It is very likely that the client will adjust the financial statements to take account of material and immaterial errors during the course of the audit. At the end of the audit, however, some errors may still be outstanding and the auditors will summarise these **unadjusted errors**.

The summary of errors will not only list errors from the current year, but also those in the previous year(s). This will allow errors to be highlighted which are reversals of errors in the previous year, such as in the valuation of closing/opening inventory. Cumulative errors may also be shown, which have increased from year to year. It is normal to show both the statement of financial position and the statement of comprehensive income effect, as in the example given here.

SCHEDULE OF UNADJUSTED ERRORS

	20X2 Statement of comprehensive income Dr $	20X2 Cr $	20X2 Statement of financial position Dr $	20X2 Cr $	20X1 Statement of comprehensive income Dr $	20X1 Cr $	20X1 Statement of financial position Dr $	20X1 Cr $
(a) ABC Co receivable unprovided	10,470			10,470	4,523			4,523
(b) Opening/ closing inventory under-valued*	21,540			21,540		21,540	21,540	
(c) Closing inventory undervalued		34,105	34,105					
(d) Opening unaccrued expenses Telephone*		453	453		453			453
Electricity*		905	905		905			905
(e) Closing unaccrued expenses Telephone	427			427				
Electricity	1,128			1,128				
(f) Obsolete inventory write off	2,528			2,528	3,211			3,211
Total	36,093	35,463	35,463	36,093	9,092	21,540	21,540	9,092
*Cancelling items	21,540			21,540				
		453	453					
		905	905					
	14,553	34,105	34,105	14,553				

1.4.1 Evaluating the effect of misstatements

FAST FORWARD

As part of their completion procedures, auditors should consider whether the cumulative effect of unadjusted errors is material.

ISA 450.11

The auditor shall determine whether uncorrected misstatements are material, individually or in aggregate.

The aggregate of uncorrected misstatements comprises:

(a) **Specific misstatements** identified by the auditors, including the net effect of uncorrected misstatements identified during the audit of the previous period if they affect the current period's financial statements

(b) Their **best estimate** of **other misstatements** which cannot be quantified specifically (ie projected errors)

If the auditors consider that the aggregate of misstatements may be material, they must consider reducing audit risk by extending audit procedures or requesting management to adjust the financial statements (which management may wish to do anyway).

ISA 450.12

The auditor shall communicate with those charged with governance uncorrected misstatements and the effect that they, individually or in aggregate, may have on the opinion in the auditor's report.

If the aggregate of the uncorrected misstatements that the auditors have identified approaches the materiality level, the auditors should consider whether it is likely that undetected misstatements, when taken with aggregated uncorrected misstatements, could exceed the materiality level. Thus, as aggregate uncorrected misstatements approach the materiality level the auditors should consider reducing the risk by

- **Performing additional audit procedures**
- By **requesting management** to adjust the financial statements for identified misstatements

The schedule will be used by the audit manager and partner to decide whether the client should be requested to make adjustments to the financial statements to correct the errors.

1.5 Completion checklists

Audit firms frequently use checklists which must be signed off to ensure that all final procedures have been carried out, all material amounts are supported by sufficient appropriate evidence, etc.

2 Revision: opening balances 6/11

FAST FORWARD

Specific procedures must be applied to opening balances.

2.1 Audit procedures

Key term

> **Opening balances** are those account balances that exist at the beginning of the period. Opening balances are based upon the closing balances of the prior period and reflect the effects of transactions and events of prior periods and accounting policies applied in the prior period.

ISA 510 *Initial audit engagements – opening balances* provides guidance on opening balances.

- When the financial statements for the prior period were not audited
- When the financial statements for the prior period were audited by a predecessor auditor

ISA 510.6

The auditor shall obtain sufficient appropriate audit evidence about whether the opening balances contain misstatements that materially affect the current period's financial statements by:

(a) Determining whether the prior period's closing balances have been correctly brought forward to the current period or, when appropriate, have been restated;

(b) Determining whether the opening balances reflect the application of appropriate accounting policies; and

(c) Performing one or more of the following:

(i) Where the prior year financial statements were audited, reviewing the predecessor auditor's working papers to obtain evidence regarding the opening balances;

(ii) Evaluating whether audit procedures performed in the current period provide evidence relevant to the opening balances; or

(iii) Performing specific audit procedures to obtain evidence regarding the opening balances.

The nature and extent of audit procedures necessary to obtain sufficient appropriate audit evidence on opening balances depends on matters such as the following.

- The **accounting policies** followed by the entity
- The **nature of the account balances, classes of transactions and disclosures** and the risks of material misstatement in the current period's financial statements
- The **significance** of the opening balances relative to the current period's financial statements
- Whether the **prior period's financial statements were audited** and, if so, whether the predecessor auditors' opinion was modified

If the auditor obtains audit evidence that the opening balances contain **misstatements** that could materially affect the current period's financial statements, the auditor shall perform such **additional audit**

procedures as are appropriate in the circumstances to determine the effect on the current period's financial statements.

2.1.1 Specific audit procedures

For **current assets and liabilities** some audit evidence may be obtained as part of the current period's audit procedures. For example, the **collection** (payment) of opening accounts **receivable** (accounts payable) during the current period will provide some audit evidence of their existence, rights and obligations, completeness and valuation at the beginning of the period.

In the case of **inventories**, however, the current period's audit procedures on the closing inventory balance provide little audit evidence regarding inventory on hand at the beginning of the period. Therefore, additional procedures may be necessary, such as:

- **Observing a current physical inventory count** and reconciling it back to the opening inventory quantities
- **Performing audit procedures on the valuation** of the opening inventory items
- **Performing audit procedures on gross profit** and cut-off

A combination of these procedures may provide sufficient appropriate audit evidence.

For **non-current assets and liabilities**, some audit evidence may be obtained by examining the accounting records and other information underlying the opening balances. In certain cases, the auditor may be able to obtain some audit evidence regarding opening balances through confirmation with third parties, for example, for long-term debt and investments. In other cases, the auditor may need to carry out additional audit procedures.

2.1.2 Consistency of accounting policies

The auditor shall obtain **sufficient appropriate audit evidence** about whether the **accounting policies** reflected in the opening balances have been **consistently applied** in the current period's financial statements, and whether changes in the accounting policies have been appropriately properly accounted for and adequately presented and disclosed in accordance with the applicable financial reporting framework.

2.1.3 Prior period balances audited by a predecessor auditor

When the prior period's financial statements were audited by a predecessor auditor, the current auditor must **read the most recent financial statements and predecessor auditor's report** for information relevant to opening balances. The current auditor may be able to obtain sufficient appropriate evidence regarding opening balances by performing this review depending on the professional competence and independence of the predecessor auditor. Relevant ethical and professional requirements guide the current auditor's communications with the predecessor auditor.

If there was a **modification** to the opinion, the auditor must evaluate the effect of the matter giving rise to the modification in assessing the risks of material misstatement in the current period's financial statements.

2.2 Audit conclusion and reporting

ISA 510.10/11

If the auditor is unable to obtain sufficient appropriate audit evidence regarding the opening balances, the auditor shall express a qualified opinion or disclaim an opinion on the financial statements, as appropriate.

> If the auditor concludes that the opening balances contain a misstatement that materially affects the current period's financial statements, and the effect of the misstatement is not appropriately accounted for or not adequately presented or disclosed, the auditor shall express a qualified opinion or an adverse opinion, as appropriate.

The report will also be modified if **accounting policies** are **not consistently applied**.

> **ISA 510.12**
>
> If the auditor concludes that:
>
> (a)   the current period's accounting policies are not consistently applied in relation to opening balances in accordance with the applicable financial reporting framework; or
>
> (b)   a change in accounting policies is not appropriately properly accounted for or not adequately presented or disclosed in accordance with the applicable financial reporting framework,
>
> the auditor shall express a qualified opinion or an adverse opinion as appropriate.

If the prior period auditor's report was modified, the auditor should **consider the effect on the current period's financial statements**. For example, if there was a scope limitation in the prior period, but the matter giving rise to the scope limitation has been resolved in the current period, the auditor may not need to modify the current period's audit opinion. The ISA finishes:

> **ISA 510.13**
>
> If the predecessor auditor's opinion regarding the prior period's financial statements included a modification to the auditor's opinion that remains relevant and material to the current period's financial statements, the auditor shall modify the auditor's opinion on the current period's financial statements.

3 Revision: comparatives

FAST FORWARD

> The auditor's responsibilities for comparatives vary depending on whether they are corresponding figures or comparative financial statements.

3.1 Auditor objectives

ISA 710 *Comparative information – corresponding figures and comparative financial statements* establishes standards and provides guidance on the auditor's responsibilities regarding comparative information.

> **ISA 710.5**
>
> The objectives of the auditor are:
>
> (a)   To obtain sufficient appropriate audit evidence about whether the comparative information included in the financial statements has been presented, in all material respects, in accordance with the requirements for comparative information in the applicable financial reporting framework, and
>
> (b)   To report in accordance with the auditor's reporting responsibilities.

Key term

> **Comparative information** is the amounts and disclosures included in the financial statements in respect of one or more prior periods in accordance with the applicable financial reporting framework.

3.2 What type of comparative information?

Comparatives are presented differently under different countries' financial reporting frameworks. Generally comparatives can be defined as **corresponding amounts** and **other disclosures** for the preceding financial reporting period(s), presented for comparative purposes. Because of these variations in countries' approach to comparatives, the ISA refers to the following frameworks and methods of presentation.

- ISA 710 has been restructured under the Clarity Project to indicate that the auditor's procedures are the same in respect of corresponding figures and comparative financial statements. The only difference is in the audit report as outlined below.

> **Corresponding figures** are amounts and other disclosures for the preceding period included as part of the current period financial statements, which are intended to be read in relation to the amounts and other disclosures relating to the current period (referred to as 'current period figures'). These corresponding figures are not presented as complete financial statements capable of standing alone, but are an integral part of the current period financial statements intended to be read only in relationship to the current period figures.
>
> **Comparative financial statements** are amounts and other disclosures of the preceding period included for comparison with the financial statements of the current period, but do not form part of the current period financial statements.

Comparatives are presented in compliance with the relevant financial reporting framework. The essential audit reporting differences are that:

- For **corresponding figures**, the auditors' report only refers to the financial statements of the current period.
- For **comparative financial statements**, the auditors' report refers to each period that financial statements are presented.

3.3 Corresponding figures

3.3.1 The auditor's responsibilities

Audit procedures performed on the corresponding figures are usually limited to checking that the corresponding figures have been correctly reported and are appropriately classified. Auditors must assess whether:

- **Accounting policies** used for the corresponding figures are **consistent** with those of the current period or whether appropriate adjustments and/or disclosures have been made.
- **Corresponding figures agree** with the **amounts** and other disclosures presented in the prior period or whether appropriate adjustments and/or disclosures have been made.

When the financial statements of the prior period:

- Have been audited by other auditors
- Were not audited

the incoming auditors assess whether the corresponding figures meet the conditions specified above and also follow the guidance in ISA 510.

If the auditors become aware of a possible material misstatement in the corresponding figures when performing the current period audit, then they must perform any necessary additional procedures.

The auditor must request written representations for all periods referred to in the auditor's opinion. In the case of corresponding figures written representations are requested for the current period only because the auditor's opinion is on those financial statements which include the corresponding figures.

3.3.2 Reporting

> **ISA 710.10**
>
> When corresponding figures are presented, the auditor's opinion shall not refer to the corresponding figures.

The auditor's report will only make specific reference to corresponding figures in the circumstances described below. We will look at specific examples of the wording of the auditor's report in such circumstances.

Firstly, there is the problem of what happens when the auditor's report for the previous period was modified.

> **ISA 710.11**
>
> If the auditor's report on the prior period, as previously issued, included a qualified opinion, a disclaimer of opinion, or an adverse opinion and the matter which gave rise to the modification is unresolved, the auditor shall modify the auditor's opinion on the current period's financial statements.
>
> In the Basis for Modification paragraph in the auditor's report, the auditor shall either:
>
> (a) Refer to both the current period's figures and the corresponding figures in the description of the matter giving rise to the modification when the effects or possible effects of the matter on the current period's figures are material, or
>
> (b) In other cases, explain that the audit opinion has been modified because of the effects or possible effects of the unresolved matter on the comparability of the current period's figures and the corresponding figures.

In performing the audit of the current period financial statements, the auditor in certain unusual circumstances, may become aware of a material misstatement that affects the prior period financial statements on which an unmodified report has been previously issued.

> **ISA 710.12**
>
> If the auditor obtains audit evidence that a material misstatement exists in the prior period financial statements on which an unmodified opinion has been previously issued, and the corresponding figures have not been properly restated or appropriate disclosures have not been made, the auditor shall express a qualified opinion or an adverse opinion in the auditor's report on the current period financial statements, modified with respect to the corresponding figures included therein.

In these circumstances, if the prior period financial statements have not been revised and an auditor's report has not been reissued, but the corresponding figures have been properly restated and/or appropriate disclosures have been made in the current period financial statements, the auditors may include an emphasis of matter paragraph describing the circumstances and referencing the appropriate disclosures. In this regard, the auditors also consider the guidance in *ISA 560 Subsequent Events*.

ISA 710 requires that the auditor obtains written representations for all periods referred to in the audit opinion. This also applies where there is a current year restatement to correct a material misstatement in prior period financial statements that affects the comparative information.

3.3.3 Incoming auditors: additional requirements

When the prior period financial statements have been audited by other auditors, in some countries the incoming auditors can refer to the predecessor auditors' report on the corresponding figures in the incoming auditor's report for the current period.

> **ISA 710.13**
>
> If the financial statements of the prior period were audited by a predecessor auditor and the auditor is not prohibited by law or regulation from referring to the predecessor auditor's report on the corresponding figures and decides to do so, the auditor shall state in an Other Matter paragraph in the auditor's report:
>
> (a) That the financial statements of the prior period were audited by the predecessor auditor;
>
> (b) The type of opinion expressed by the predecessor auditor and, if the opinion was modified, the reasons therefore; and
>
> (c) The date of that report.

The situation is slightly different if the prior period financial statements were **not audited**.

> **ISA 710.14**
>
> If the prior period financial statements were not audited, the auditor shall state in an Other Matter paragraph in the auditor's report that the corresponding figures are unaudited. Such a statement does not, however, relieve the auditor of the requirement to obtain sufficient appropriate audit evidence that the opening balances do not contain misstatements that materially affect the current period's financial statements.

3.4 Comparative financial statements

3.4.1 The auditor's responsibilities

This effectively involves the auditors following the same procedures on the prior period statements as noted above.

3.4.2 Reporting

> **ISA 710.15**
>
> When comparative financial statements are presented, the auditor's opinion shall refer to each period for which financial statements are presented and on which an audit opinion is expressed.

The auditors may therefore express a **modified opinion** or include an **emphasis of matter** paragraph with respect to one or more financial statements for one or more period, whilst issuing a different report on the other financial statements.

The auditors may become aware of circumstances or events that materially affect the financial statements of a prior period during the course of the audit for the current period.

> **ISA 710.16**
>
> When reporting on prior period financial statements in connection with the current period's audit, if the auditor's opinion on such prior period financial statements differs from the opinion the auditor previously expressed, the auditor shall disclose the substantive reasons for the different opinion in an Other Matter paragraph.

3.4.3 Incoming auditors: additional requirements

Again, there are additional considerations where the prior period financial statements are audited by other auditors.

ISA 710.17

If the financial statements of the prior period were audited by a predecessor auditor, in addition to expressing an opinion on the current period's financial statements, the auditor shall state in an Other Matter paragraph:

(a)   That the financial statements of the prior period were audited by a predecessor auditor,

(b)   The type of opinion expressed by the predecessor auditor and, if the opinion was modified, the reasons therefore, and

(c)   The date of that report,

unless the predecessor auditor's report on the prior period's financial statements is reissued with the financial statements.

In performing the audit on the current period financial statements, the incoming auditors may become aware of a material misstatement that affects the prior period financial statements on which the predecessor auditors had previously reported without modification.

ISA 710.18

....the auditor shall communicate the misstatement with the appropriate level of management and, unless all of those charged with governance are involved in managing the entity, those charged with governance and request that the predecessor auditor be informed. If the prior period financial statements are amended, and the predecessor auditor agrees to issue a new auditor's report on the amended financial statements of the prior period, the auditor shall report only on the current period.

In certain circumstances the prior period financial statement may not have been audited.

ISA 710.19

If the prior period financial statements were not audited, the auditor shall state in an Other Matter paragraph that the comparative financial statements are unaudited. Such a statement does not, however, relieve the auditor of the requirement to obtain sufficient appropriate audit evidence that the opening balances do not contain misstatements that materially affect the current period's financial statements.

Question   Opening balances and comparatives

Auditing standards have been issued on opening balances for initial engagements and comparatives, and one of the matters considered is where one firm of auditors takes over from another firm. You have recently been appointed auditor of Lowdham Castings, a limited liability company which has been trading for about thirty years, and are carrying out the audit for the year ended 30 September 20X0. The company's revenue is about $500,000 and its normal profit before tax is about $30,000. Comparatives are shown as corresponding figures only.

Required

Explain your responsibilities in relation to the comparatives included in the accounts for the year ended 30 September 20X0. You should also outline the information you would require from the retiring auditors.

Consideration of the financial statements of the preceding period is necessary in the audit of the current period's financial statements in relation to three main aspects.

(a) Opening position: obtaining satisfaction that those amounts which have a direct effect on the current period's results or closing position have been properly brought forward.

(b) Accounting policies: determining whether the accounting policies adopted for the current period are consistent with those of the previous period.

(c) Comparatives: determining that the comparatives are properly shown in the current period's financial statements.

The auditors' main concern will therefore be to satisfy themselves that there were no material misstatements in the previous year's financial statements which may have a bearing upon their work in the current year.

The new auditors do not have to 're-audit' the previous year's financial statements, but they will have to pay more attention to them than would normally be the case where they had themselves been the auditors in the earlier period. A useful source of audit evidence will clearly be the previous auditors, and, with the client's permission, they should be contacted to see if they are prepared to co-operate. Certainly, any known areas of weakness should be discussed with the previous auditors and it is also possible that they might be prepared to provide copies of their working papers (although there is no legal or ethical provision which requires the previous auditors to co-operate in this way).

4 Revision: other information   12/10

FAST FORWARD

Auditors should always seek to resolve inconsistencies or misstatements of fact between financial statements and other published information.

> ISA 720 *The auditor's responsibilities relating to other information in documents containing audited financial statements* was redrafted in December 2007 in accordance with the clarity conventions as part of the Clarity Project. No significant changes have resulted.

4.1 What other information?

ISA 720 *The auditor's responsibilities relating to other information in documents containing audited financial statements* sets out the requirements of the auditor with respect to other information, on which the auditors have **no obligation to report,** in documents containing financial statements.

> **ISA 720.6**
>
> The auditor shall read the other information to identify material inconsistencies if any with the audited financial statements.

Key terms

> **Other information** is financial and non-financial information *other than* the financial statements and the auditor's report, which is included, either by law, regulation or custom, in a document containing audited financial statements and the auditor's report thereon.
>
> An **inconsistency** exists when other information contradicts information contained in the audited financial statements. A **material inconsistency** may raise doubt about the audit conclusions drawn from audit evidence previously obtained and, possibly, about the basis for the auditor's opinion on the financial statements.

Here are some examples of other information:

- A report by management or the board of directors on operations
- Financial summaries or highlights
- Employment data
- Planned capital expenditures
- Financial ratios
- Names of officers and directors
- Selected quarterly data

Auditors have no responsibility to report that other information is properly stated because an audit is only an expression of opinion on the truth and fairness of the financial statements. However, they may be **engaged separately**, or **required by statute**, to report on elements of other information. In any case, the auditors should give consideration to other information as inconsistencies with the audited financial statements may undermine their report.

Some countries require the auditors to apply specific procedures to certain other information, for example, required supplementary data and interim financial information. If such other information is omitted or contains deficiencies, the auditors may be required to refer to the matter in their report.

When there is an obligation to report specifically on other information, the auditors' responsibilities are determined by the **nature of the engagement** and by **local legislation** and professional standards. When such responsibilities involve the review of other information, the auditors will need to follow the guidance on **review engagements** in the appropriate ISAs.

4.2 Access to other information

Timely access to other information will be required. The auditors therefore must make arrangements with the client to obtain such information prior to the date of their report. In circumstances where all the other information may not be available prior to that date, the auditors should follow the guidance below.

4.3 Material inconsistencies

> **ISA 720.8/9/10**
>
> If, on reading the other information, the auditor identifies a material inconsistency, the auditor shall determine whether the audited financial statements or the other information needs to be revised.
>
> If revision of the audited financial statements is necessary and management refuses to make the revision, the auditor shall modify the opinion in accordance with ISA 705.
>
> If revision of the other information is necessary and management refuses to make the revision, the auditor shall communicate this matter to those charged with governance unless all of those charged with governance are involved with managing the entity and:
>
> (a) Include in the auditor's report an Other Matter(s) paragraph describing the material inconsistency in accordance with ISA 706, or
>
> (b) Withhold the auditor's report, or
>
> (c) Withdraw from the engagements, where withdrawal is possible under applicable law or regulation

The actions taken by the auditors will depend on the individual circumstances and the auditors may consider taking legal advice.

4.4 Material misstatements of fact

A 'misstatement of fact' in other information exists when such information, not related to matters appearing in the financial statements, is incorrectly stated and presented. A material misstatement of fact may undermine the credibility of the document containing audited financial statements.

ISA 720.14

If, on reading the other information for the purpose of identifying material inconsistencies the auditor becomes aware of an apparent material misstatement of fact, the auditor shall discuss the matter with management.

When discussing the matter with the entity's management, the auditors may not be able to evaluate the validity of the other information and management's responses to the auditors' enquiries, and would need to consider whether valid differences of judgement or opinion exist.

ISA 720.15/16

If, following such discussions, the auditor still considers that there is an apparent material misstatement of fact, the auditor shall request management to consult with a qualified third party, such as the entity's legal counsel, and the auditor shall consider the advice received.

If the auditor concludes that there is a material misstatement of fact in the other information which management refuses to correct, the auditor shall notify those charged with governance, unless all of those charged with governance are involved in managing the entity, of the auditor's concern regarding the other information and take any further appropriate action.

Such an action could include such steps as notifying those ultimately responsible for the overall direction of the entity and obtaining legal advice.

The effects of material inconsistencies and misstatements of fact on the auditor's report can be summarised as follows.

Problem	Revision needed to	Action
Material inconsistency	Other information	Other matter paragraph in auditor's report
	Financial statements	Modified opinion in accordance with ISA 705
Material misstatement of fact	Other information	Other matter paragraph in auditor's report Take further appropriate action, eg obtain legal advice, speak at AGM, resign from engagement
	Financial statements	Modified opinion in accordance with ISA 705

5 Revision: subsequent events

FAST FORWARD

> Auditors should consider the effect of subsequent events (after the end of the reporting period) on the accounts.

5.1 Events after the reporting period

'Subsequent events' include:

- Events occurring between the period end and the date of the auditor's report
- Facts discovered after the date of the auditor's report

ISA 560 *Subsequent events* deals with this issue. It is also worth recalling basic requirements of the accounting standard in this area, IAS 10 *Events after the reporting period* identifies two types of event:

Type of event	Definition (IAS 10)	Example
Adjusting	Events that provide further evidence of conditions that existed at the end of the reporting period	Customer becomes insolvent after period end – trade receivable at period end is uncollectible. Settlement of a court case after period end – confirms entity's obligation at the period end.
Non-adjusting	Events that are indicative of conditions that arose after the reporting period	Inventory lost in fire after period end – non-adjusting because the inventory still existed at the period end (but needs to be disclosed, with possible EoM).

Between the end of the reporting period and the date the financial statements are authorised (ie for issue outside the organisation), events may occur which show that assets and liabilities at the end of the reporting period should be adjusted, or that disclosure of such events should be given.

In relation to **going concern**, ISA 560 states that, where operating results and the financial position have deteriorated after the reporting period, it may be necessary to reconsider whether the going concern assumption is appropriate in the preparation of the financial statements.

Note that, while they may be non-adjusting, some events after the reporting period will require disclosure.

5.2 Events occurring up to the date of the auditor's report

ISA 560.6

The auditor shall perform audit procedures designed to obtain sufficient appropriate audit evidence that all events occurring between the date of the financial statements and the date of the auditor's report that require adjustment of, or disclosure in, the financial statements have been identified.

These procedures should be applied to any matters examined during the audit which may be susceptible to change after the year end. They are in addition to tests on specific transactions after the period-end, eg cut-off tests.

The ISA lists procedures to identify subsequent events which may require adjustment or disclosure. They should be performed as near as possible to the date of the auditor's report.

Procedures testing subsequent events	
Inquiries of management	New **commitments**, borrowings or guarantees
	Sales or **acquisitions of assets** occurred or planned
	Issues of **shares** or **debt instruments**, or an **agreement to merge** or **liquidate** made or planned
	Assets destroyed or appropriated by government
	Developments regarding **contingencies**
	Unusual accounting adjustments made or contemplated
	Events (eg going concern problems) bringing into question appropriateness of accounting policies
	Events relevant to measurement of **estimates** and **provisions**
	Events relevant to the **recoverability of assets**
Other procedures	**Consider procedures** of management for identifying subsequent events
	Read minutes of general board/committee meetings
	Review latest accounting records and financial information

ISA 560.8

[When] the auditor identifies events that require adjustment of, or disclosure in the financial statements, the auditor shall determine whether each such event is appropriately reflected in those financial statements in accordance with the applicable financial reporting framework.

Written representations will be sought that all events occurring subsequent to the date of the financial statements which require adjustment or disclosure have been adjusted or disclosed.

5.3 Facts discovered after the date of the auditor's report but before the financial statements are issued

The financial statements are the management's responsibility. They should therefore inform the auditors of any material subsequent events between the date of the auditor's report and the date the financial statements are issued. The auditors do **not** have any obligation to perform procedures, or make enquires regarding the financial statements **after the** date of their report.

ISA 560.10

The auditor has no obligation to perform any audit procedures regarding the financial statements after the date of the auditor's report. However, if after the date of the auditor's report but before the date the financial statements are issued, a fact becomes known to the auditor that, had it been known to the auditor at the date of the auditor's report, may have caused the auditor to amend the auditor's report, the auditor shall:

(a)   Discuss the matter with management and where appropriate, those charged with governance
(b)   Determine whether the financial statements need amendment and, if so
(c)   Inquire how management intends to address the matter in the financial statements

When the financial statements are amended, the auditors should **extend the procedures** discussed above to the **date of their new report**, carry out any other appropriate procedures and issue a new audit report. The new report should not be dated earlier than the date of approval of the amended financial statements.

The situation may arise where the statements are not amended but the auditors feel that they should be.

If the auditor's report has already been issued to the entity then the auditor should notify those who are ultimately responsible for the entity (the management or possibly a holding company in a group), not to issue the financial statements or auditor's reports to third parties. If management issues the financial statements despite the auditor's notification the auditor will take action to prevent reliance on the audit report. The action taken will depend on the auditor's legal rights and obligations and the advice of the auditor's lawyer.

5.4 Facts discovered after the financial statements have been issued

Auditors have no obligations to perform procedures or make enquiries regarding the financial statements after they have been issued.

However, when after the financial statement have been issued, the auditor becomes aware of a fact that had it been known to the auditor at the date of the auditor's report may have caused the auditor to amend the auditor's report, the auditor will carry out the following procedures:

(a)   Discuss the matter with management and where appropriate, those charged with governance
(b)   Determine whether the financial statements need amendment and if so
(c)   Inquire how management intends to address the matter in the financial statements

The ISA gives the appropriate procedures which the auditors should undertake when management revises the financial statements.

(a)   **Carry out the audit procedures** necessary in the circumstances

(b)   **Review the steps taken by management** to ensure that anyone in receipt of the previously issued financial statements together with the auditors' report thereon is informed of the situation

(c)   **Extend the audit procedures** to the date of the new auditor's report

(d)   **Issue a new report** on the revised financial statements

> **ISA 560.16**
>
> The auditor shall include in the new or amended auditor's report an Emphasis of Matter paragraph or Other Matters paragraph referring to a note to the financial statements that more extensively discusses the reason for the amendment of the previously issued financial statements and to the earlier report provided by the auditor.

> In our opinion, the revised financial statements give a true and fair view (or 'present fairly, in all material respects'), as at the date the original financial statements were approved, of the financial position of the company as of December 31, 20X1, and of the results of its operations and its cash flows for the year then ended in accordance with [relevant national legislation].
>
> In our opinion the original financial statements for the year to December 31, 20X1, failed to comply with [relevant national standards or legislation].
>
> Date   AUDITOR
> Address

Where local regulations allow the auditor to restrict the audit procedures on the financial statements to the effects of the subsequent event which caused the revision, the new auditor's report should contain an emphasis of matter paragraph referring to a note in the financial statements which explains the situation fully.

Where management does **not** revise the financial statements but the auditors feel they should be revised, or if management does not intend to take steps to ensure anyone in receipt of the previously issued financial statements is informed of the situation, then the auditors should consider steps to take, on a timely basis, to prevent reliance on their report. The actions taken will depend on the auditors' legal rights and obligations (for example, to contact the shareholders directly) and legal advice received.

Exam focus point

> Subsequent events have previously appeared in an audit reports question with five easy marks for outlining the auditors' responsibilities for subsequent events and then practical application in part (b).

You are auditing the financial statements of Hope Engineering, a limited company, for the year ending 31 March 20X8. The partner in charge of the audit instructs you to carry out a review of the company's activities since the financial year end. Mr Smith, the managing director of Hope Engineering, overhears the conversation with the partner and is surprised that you are examining accounting information which relates to the next accounting period.

Mr Smith had been appointed on 1 March 20X8 as a result of which the contract of the previous managing director, Mr Jones, was terminated. Compensation of $500,000 had been paid to Mr Jones on 2 March 20X8.

As a result of your investigations you find that the company is going to bring an action against Mr Jones for the recovery of the compensation paid to him, as it had come to light that two months prior to his dismissal, he had contractually agreed to join the board of directors of a rival company. The company's lawyer had informed Hope Engineering that Mr Jones' actions constituted a breach of his contract with them, and that an action could be brought against the former managing director for the recovery of the money paid to him.

Required

(a) Explain the nature and purpose of a subsequent events review.

(b) Describe the audit procedures which would be carried out in order to identify any material subsequent events.

(c) Discuss the audit implications of the company's decision to sue Mr Jones for the recovery of the compensation paid to him.

Answer

(a) The auditors' active responsibility extends to the date on which they sign their audit report. As this date is inevitably after the year-end, it follows that in order to discharge their responsibilities, the auditors must extend their audit work to cover the period after the year end.

The objective of this review is to ascertain whether management has dealt correctly with any events, both favourable and unfavourable, which occurred after the end of the reporting period and which need to be reflected in the financial statements, if those statements are to show a true and fair view.

The general rule is that, in the preparation of year end financial statements, no account should be taken of subsequent events unless to do so is required by statute or to give effect to retrospective legislation, or to take into account an event which provides information about a condition existing at the end of the reporting period, for example realisable values of inventory, or indicates that the going concern concept is no longer applicable. Additionally, certain events may have such a material effect on the company's financial condition, for example a merger, that disclosure is essential to give a true and fair view.

(b) (i) Ask management if there have been any material subsequent events.

(ii) Identify and evaluate procedures implemented by management to ensure that all events after the end of the reporting period have been identified, considered and properly evaluated as to their effect on the financial statements.

(iii) Review relevant accounting records to identify subsequent cash received in relation to accounts receivable, to check items uncleared at the year end on the bank reconciliation, and to check NRV of inventories from sales invoices.

(iv) Review budgets, profit forecasts, cash flow projections and management accounts for the new period to assess the company's trading position.

(v) Consider known 'risk' areas and contingencies, whether inherent in the nature of the business or revealed by previous audit experience, or by lawyers' letters.

(vi) Read minutes of shareholders' and management meetings, and correspondence and memoranda relating to items included in the minutes to identify any matters arising.

(vii)   Consider relevant information which has come to the auditors' attention from sources outside the enterprise, including public knowledge of competitors, suppliers and customers.

(viii)   Obtain written representations concerning subsequent events from management.

(c)   The compensation paid to Mr Jones would be disclosed as part of directors' remuneration for the year ended 31 March 20X8. However, the question then arises as to whether or not the financial statements need to take any account of the possible recovery of the compensation payment.

The auditors should first ascertain from the board minutes that the directors intend to proceed with the lawsuit and should then attempt to assess the outcome by consulting the directors and the company's legal advisors. Only if it seems probable that the compensation will be recovered should a contingent gain be disclosed in the notes to the accounts, along with a summary of the facts of the case. A prudent estimate of legal costs should be deducted.

It could be argued that Mr Jones' breach of contract existed at the year end and that the compensation should therefore be treated as a current asset, net of recovery costs. However, this would not be prudent, given the uncertainties over the court case.

6 Revision: going concern   Pilot paper, 12/08, 6/11

FAST FORWARD

Auditors should consider whether the going concern basis is appropriate, and whether disclosure of any going concern problems is sufficient.

6.1 The going concern assumption

Key term

Under the '**going concern assumption**' an entity is viewed as continuing in business for the foreseeable future. General purpose financial statements are prepared on a going concern basis, unless management either intends to liquidate the entity or to cease operations, or has no realistic alternative but to do so. When the use of the going concern assumption is appropriate, assets and liabilities are recorded on the basis that the entity will be able to realise its assets and discharge its liabilities in the normal course of business.

ISA 570 *Going concern* states that the preparation of the financial statements requires management to **assess** the entity's ability to continue as a going concern even if the financial reporting framework does not include an explicit requirement to do so.

When management are making the assessment, the following factors should be considered.

(a)   The **degree of uncertainty** about the events or conditions being assessed increases significantly the further into the future the assessment is made.

(b)   Judgements are affected by the **size** and **complexity** of the entity, the **nature** and **condition** of its business and the **degree** to which it is **affected** by **external factors**.

(c)   Judgements are made on the basis of the **information available** at the time.

ISA 570.9

The objectives of the auditor are:

(a)   To obtain sufficient appropriate audit evidence regarding the appropriateness of management's use of the going concern assumption in the preparation of the financial statements;

(b)   To conclude, based on the audit evidence obtained, whether a material uncertainty exists related to events or conditions that may cast significant doubt on the entity's ability to continue as a going concern; and

(c)   To determine the implications for the auditor's report.

The following are examples of events or conditions that may cast significant doubt about the going concern assumption.

(a) **Financial**

    (i) Net liabilities or net current liability position

    (ii) Fixed-term borrowings approaching maturity without realistic prospects of renewal or repayment, or excessive reliance on short-term borrowings to finance long-terms assets

    (iii) Indications of withdrawal of financial support by lenders

    (iv) Negative operating cash flows indicated by historical or prospective financial statements

    (v) Adverse key financial ratios

    (vi) Substantial operating losses or significant deterioration in the value of assets used to generate cash flows

    (vii) Arrears or discontinuance of dividends

    (viii) Inability to pay creditors on due dates

    (ix) Inability to comply with the terms of loan agreements

    (x) Change from credit to cash-on-delivery transactions with suppliers

    (xi) Inability to obtain financing for essential new product development or other essential investments

(b) **Operating**

    (i) Management intends to liquidate the entity or to cease operations

    (ii) Loss of key management without replacement

    (iii) Loss of a major market, key customer(s), franchise, licence, or principal supplier(s)

    (iv) Labour difficulties or shortages of important supplies

    (v) Emergence of a highly successful competitor

(c) **Other**

    (i) Non-compliance with capital or other statutory requirements

    (ii) Pending legal or regulatory proceedings against the entity that may, if successful, result in claims that the entity is unlikely to be able to satisfy

    (iii) Changes in law or regulation or government policy expected to adversely affect the entity

    (iv) Uninsured or underinsured catastrophes when they occur

The significance of such events and conditions often can be **mitigated** by other factors. For example, the loss of a key supplier may be mitigated by the availability of a suitable alternative source of supply. It is worth noting that the **size** of an entity may affect its ability to withstand adverse conditions. Small entities may be able to react quickly to exploit opportunities but may lack reserves to sustain operations.

<table>
<tr><td>**Exam focus point**</td><td>The June 2011 exam featured a 27 mark question which combined a requirement on going concern with prospective financial information (covered in Chapter 13). Candidates first had to review a draft statement of financial position and a draft cash flow forecast, identifying and explaining factors casting significant doubt over going concern. They then had to recommend procedures in relation to the cash flow forecast, before explaining the matters to consider in relation to the audit report if there are material uncertainties on going concern.</td></tr>
</table>

6.2 Evaluating management's assessment

ISA 570.10

When performing risk assessment procedures as required by ISA 315, the auditor shall consider whether there are events or conditions that may cast significant doubt on the entity's ability to continue as a going concern. In so doing, the auditor shall determine whether management has already performed a preliminary assessment of the entity's ability to continue as a going concern, and:

(a) If such an assessment has been performed, the auditor shall discuss the assessment with management and determine whether management has identified events or conditions that, individually or collectively, may cast significant doubt on the entity's ability to continue as a going concern and, if so, management's plans to address them; or

(b) If such an assessment has not yet been performed, the auditor shall discuss with management the basis for the intended use of the going concern assumption, and inquire of management whether events or conditions exist that, individually or collectively, may cast significant doubt on the entity's ability to continue as a going concern.

These procedures allow for more **timely discussions with management**, including a discussion of management's plans and resolution of any identified going concern issues.

The auditor shall remain **alert** throughout the audit for audit evidence of events or conditions that may cast significant doubt on the entity's ability to continue as a going concern. It may be necessary to revise the auditor's assessment of the risks of material misstatement if these are found.

ISA 570.12

The auditor shall evaluate management's assessment of the entity's ability to continue as a going concern.

The auditors may evaluate:

- The **process** management followed to make its assessment
- The **assumptions** on which management's assessment is based
- Management's **plans** for future action and whether these are feasible in the circumstances

Management do not need to make a detailed analysis, and auditors should not need to carry out detailed procedures, if the entity has a **history of profitable operations** and **ready access** to **financial resources.**

In evaluating management's assessment of the entity's ability to continue as a going concern, the auditor shall cover the **same period** as that used by management to make its assessment as required by the applicable financial reporting framework, or by law or regulation if it specifies a longer period.

If management's assessment covers a period of **less than twelve months** from the date of the financial statements, the auditor shall request management to extend its assessment period to at least twelve months from that date.

In evaluating management's assessment, the auditor shall consider whether management's assessment includes **all relevant information** of which the auditor is aware as a result of the audit.

ISA 570.15

The auditor shall inquire of management as to its knowledge of events or conditions beyond the period of management's assessment that may cast significant doubt on the entity's ability to continue as a going concern.

Because the time period is some way into the future, the indications of potential going concern problems would have to be significant. Auditors do not have to carry out specific procedures to identify potential problems which may occur after the period covered by management's assessment. However they should be alert during the course of the audit for any **indications** of future problems.

6.2.1 Additional audit procedures

ISA 570.16

If events or conditions have been identified that may cast significant doubt on the entity's ability to continue as a going concern, the auditor shall obtain sufficient appropriate audit evidence to determine whether or not a material uncertainty exists through performing additional audit procedures, including consideration of mitigating factors. These procedures shall include:

(a) Where management has not yet performed an assessment of the entity's ability to continue as a going concern, requesting management to make its assessment.

(b) Evaluating management's plans for future actions in relation to its going concern assessment, whether the outcome of these plans is likely to improve the situation and whether management's plans are feasible in the circumstances.

(c) Where the entity has prepared a cash flow forecast, and analysis of the forecast is a significant factor in considering the future outcome of events or conditions in the evaluation of management's plans for future action:

    (i) Evaluating the reliability of the underlying data generated to prepare the forecast; and
    (ii) Determining whether there is adequate support for the assumptions underlying the forecast.

(d) Considering whether any additional facts or information have become available since the date on which management made its assessment.

(e) Requesting written representations from management and, where appropriate, those charged with governance, regarding their plans for future action and the feasibility of these plans.

When events or conditions are identified which cast doubt on the appropriateness of the going concern assumption, auditors may also have to carry out **additional procedures**. The ISA lists various procedures which the auditors may carry out in this context.

- **Analysing and discussing cash flow**, profit and other relevant forecasts with management
- **Analysing and discussing** the entity's latest available **interim financial statements**
- **Reading the terms of debentures and loan agreements** and determining whether any have been breached
- **Reading minutes** of the meetings of shareholders, those charged with governance and relevant committees for reference to financing difficulties
- **Enquiring** of the entity's legal counsel regarding **litigation and claims**
- **Confirming the existence, legality and enforceability** of arrangements to provide or maintain financial support with related and third parties and **assessing** the **financial ability** of such parties to **provide additional funds**
- Evaluating the entity's plans to deal with **unfilled customer orders**
- **Performing audit procedures regarding subsequent events** to identify those that either mitigate or otherwise affect the entity's ability to continue as a going concern
- Confirming the existence, terms and adequacy of **borrowing facilities**
- Obtaining and reviewing reports of **regulatory actions**
- Determining the adequacy of **support for any planned disposal of assets**

Evaluating management's **plans for future actions** may include inquiries of management as to its plans for future action, including, for example, its plans to liquidate assets, borrow money or restructure debt, reduce or delay expenditures, or increase capital.

Where management's assumptions include **continued support by third parties**, and such support is important to an entity's ability to continue as a going concern, the auditor may need to consider requesting written confirmation to obtain evidence of their ability to provide such support.

6.3 Audit conclusions and reporting

> **ISA 570.17**
>
> Based on the audit evidence obtained, the auditor shall conclude whether, in the auditor's judgment, a material uncertainty exists related to events or conditions that, individually or collectively, may cast significant doubt on the entity's ability to continue as a going concern.

6.3.1 Use of going concern appropriate but a material uncertainty exists

The auditor shall determine whether the financial statements adequately describe the principal events or conditions that may cast significant doubt on the entity's ability to continue as a going concern and management's plans to deal with these events or conditions. They shall also make sure the financial statements disclose that there is a material uncertainty clearly and, therefore, that the entity may be unable to realise its assets and discharge its liabilities in the normal course of business.

> **ISA 570.19**
>
> If adequate disclosure is made in the financial statements, the auditor shall express an unmodified opinion and include an Emphasis of Matter paragraph in the auditor's report to:
>
> (a)　Highlight the existence of a material uncertainty relating to the event or condition that may cast significant doubt on the entity's ability to continue as a going concern; and to
>
> (b)　Draw attention to the note in the financial statements that discloses the matter

The auditors may consider it appropriate in extremely rare cases to express a disclaimer of opinion if there are multiple material uncertainties.

6.3.2 Adverse opinion

> **ISA 570.20**
>
> If adequate disclosure is not made in the financial statements, the auditor shall express a qualified opinion or adverse opinion, as appropriate, in accordance with ISA 705. The auditor shall state in the auditor's report that there is a material uncertainty that may cast significant doubt about the entity's ability to continue as a going concern.

If the financial statements have been prepared on a going concern basis, but in the auditor's judgement this is inappropriate, the auditor must express an adverse opinion. This applies regardless of whether the financial statements include disclosure of the inappropriateness of management's use of the going concern assumption.

6.3.3 Disclaimer of opinion

In certain circumstances, the auditor may believe it necessary to **request management to make or extend its assessment**. If management is unwilling to do so, a qualified opinion on the grounds of an inability to obtain sufficient appropriate audit evidence, or a disclaimer of opinion in the auditor's report may be appropriate.

6.4 Communication with those charged with governance

Unless all those charged with governance are involved in managing the entity, the auditor shall communicate with those charged with governance events or conditions identified that may cast significant doubt on the entity's ability to continue as a going concern. This communication must include the following

- Whether the events or conditions constitute a material uncertainty
- Whether the use of the going concern assumption is appropriate in the preparation and presentation of the financial statements
- The adequacy of related disclosures in the financial statements

6.5 Significant delay

When there is a significant delay in approving the accounts, auditors shall enquire as to the **reasons** for the delay. If the auditor believes that the delay could be related to events or conditions relating to the going concern assessment, the auditor shall **perform those additional audit procedures necessary**, as well as consider the **effect on the auditor's conclusion** regarding the existence of a material uncertainty.

6.6 Current issues

The global recession may affect management's assessment of going concern. Increased uncertainty and difficult economic conditions could mean the going concern basis is not appropriate for many companies. Auditors should take extra care when reviewing management's assessment of going concern in such circumstances.

The ACCA has issued *Technical factsheet 143*, which contains a useful summary of the effect of the 'credit crunch' on auditors:

> "If there is **increased risk** of material misstatement **at the overall economy level**, such as that arising from the credit crunch, the auditor should **assess the specific risk** of misstatement **for each audited entity** and limit the detection risk by designing and performing appropriate audit procedures"

Exam focus point

The P7 examiner wrote an article for the February 2010 edition of *Student accountant* on going concern. It focused on the IAASB's Practice Alert *Audit Considerations in Respect of Going Concern in the Current Economic Environment.*

The question that follows includes numerical information. In such a question it is vital that you attempt to use the figures in your answer.

Question

Going concern

You are planning to audit of Truckers whose principal activities are road transport and warehousing services, and the repair of commercial vehicles. You have been provided with the draft accounts for the year ended 31 October 20X5

	Draft 20X5 $'000	Actual 20X4 $'000
Summary income statement		
Revenue	10,971	11,560
Cost of sales	(10,203)	(10,474)
Gross profit	768	1,086
Administrative expenses	(782)	(779)
Interest payable and similar charges	(235)	(185)
Net (loss) profit	(249)	122
Summary statement of financial position		
Non-current assets	5,178	4,670
Current assets		
Inventory (parts and consumables)	95	61
Receivables	2,975	2,369
	3,070	2,430
Current liabilities		

	Draft 20X5	Actual 20X4
	$'000	$'000
Bank loan	250	–
Overdraft	1,245	913
Trade payables	1,513	1,245
Lease obligations	207	–
Other payables	203	149
	3,418	2,307
Long-term liabilities		
Bank loan	750	1,000
Lease obligations	473	–
	1,223	1,000
Net assets	3,544	3,793

You have been informed by the managing director that the fall in revenue is due to:

(1)   The loss, in July, of a long-standing customer to a competitor, and
(2)   A decline in trade in the repair of commercial vehicles.

Due to the reduction in the repairs business, the company has decided to close the workshop and sell the equipment and spares inventory. No entries resulting from this decision are reflected in the draft accounts.

During the year, the company replaced a number of vehicles funding them by a combination of leasing and an increased overdraft facility. The facility is to be reviewed in January 20X6 after the audited accounts are available.

The draft accounts show a loss for 20X5 but the forecasts indicate a return to profitability in 20X6 as the managing director is optimistic about generating additional revenue from new contracts.

(a)   State the circumstances particular to Truckers which may indicate that the company is not a going concern. Explain why these circumstances given cause for concern.

(b)   Describe the audit work to be performed in respect of going concern at Truckers.

Approaching the answer

> Question   Going concern

Look for **key words** and **key balances**. Ask questions of the information given to you. This is illustrated here:

> Remember the stage of the audit you are at will determine the kind of procedures you are concerned with

> Reliability? analysis of information? key ratios?

You are planning to audit of Truckers whose principal activities are road transport and warehousing services, and the repair of commercial vehicles. You have been provided with the draft accounts for the year ended 31 October 20X5

		Draft 20X5	Actual 20X4
		$'000	$'000
Summary income statement			
Revenue		10,971	11,560
Cost of sales	Change in GPM?	(10,203)	(10,474)
Gross profit		768	1,086
Administrative expenses		(782)	(779)
Interest payable and similar charges		(235)	(185)
Net (loss) profit	Significant losses this year	(249)	122
Summary statement of financial position			
Non-current assets		5,178	4,670
Current assets			
Inventory (parts and consumables)	Change in receivables ageing	95	61
Receivables		2,975	2,369
		3,070	2,430

Increase in short-term finance

Current liabilities		
Bank loan	250	–
Overdraft	1,245	913
Trade payables	1,513	1,245
Lease obligations	207	–
Other payables	203	149
	3,418	2,307
Long-term liabilities		
Bank loan	750	1,000
Lease obligations	473	–
	1,223	1,000
Net assets	3,544	3,793

Additional debt

Is this information reliable?

You have been informed by the managing director that the fall in revenue is due to:

Possible wider consequences?

(1)   The loss, in July, of a long-standing customer to a competitor, and

(2)   A decline in trade in the repair of commercial vehicles.

Need to remember this when analysing the financial information

Further negative business trends

Due to the reduction in the repairs business, the company has decided to close the workshop and sell the equipment and spares inventory. No entries resulting from this decision are reflected in the draft accounts.

Shortage of cash

During the year, the company replaced a number of vehicles funding them by a combination of leasing and an increased overdraft facility. The facility is to be reviewed in January 20X6 after the audited accounts are available.

Pressure on management? Reliance by 3rd parties

On what is this optimism based?

The draft accounts show a loss for 20X5 but the forecasts indicate a return to profitability in 20X6 as the managing director is optimistic about generating additional revenue from new contracts.

Your answer must be tailored to the question

(a)   State the circumstances particular to Truckers which may indicate that the company is not a going concern. Explain why these circumstances given cause for concern.

(b)   Describe the audit work to be performed in respect of going concern at Truckers.

What is the potential effect?

Answer plan

Remember the key issue is likely to be assessing future events

Not all the points you notice will necessarily be relevant and you may find that you do not have time to mention all the points in your answer. Now you should prioritise your points in a more formal answer plan and then write the answer.

(a)

Circumstances	Why cause for concern
(i) From review of financial information	
Fall in GP	Why? Calls into question future optimisms. Lack of control over expenses and increased finance costs
Loss	Significant in relation to previous year. Impact on bank overdraft review
Increased receivables ageing	Cash flow problems Debt write offs may be required
Increased short-term finance	Impact on continuing support from the bank
Liquidity ratio	Problems re commitments in future
Gearing	Finance cost Problems obtaining further finance

(ii)	**From other information**	
	Loss of major customer	Potential that others will follow?
	Loss of commercial customers	Provided regular income source
	Draft accounts	Impact of additional adjustments
	Review of overdraft	Increased pressure/risk
	Assessment of future by MD	Potentially too optimistic

(b) **Procedures**

- (i) Analyse subsequent events
- (ii) Review debt ageing
- (iii) Discuss future plans with MD
- (iv) Review bank records/correspondence particularly re overdraft facility
- (v) Review sales orders/scrutinise new orders
- (vi) Procedures on cash flow forecast
- (vii) Written representations

Answer

(a)

Circumstances	Why cause for concern?
Fall in gross profit % achieved	Whilst the fall in absolute revenue has been explained the fall in gross profit margin is more serious. This will continue to be a problem as expenses seem constant and interest costs are growing. This will make a future return to profitability difficult.
Losses $249,000	Such levels of losses by comparison to 20X4 profits will make negotiations with the bank difficult, especially with the loss of a major customer.
Increased receivables balance and increased ageing 20X5 96.7 days 20X4 74.8 days	Worsening debt collection is bad news when the company is making losses and has a deteriorating liquidity position. The increase in average debt collection period may be due to a bad debt on the account of the major customer lost in the year. A bad debt write-off would cause increased losses.
Worsening liquidity ratio 20X4 1.03 20X5 0.85	This is a significant fall which will worsen further if a bad debt provision is required. The company has loan and lease commitments which possibly may not be met.
Increasing reliance on short-term finance	This does not secure the future. With the company going through so much change this may cause difficulties for the bank overdraft facility negotiations.
Gearing will have increased	This leads to an interest commitment which is a drain on future profits. This may also cause a problem in negotiating new finance arrangements.
Loss of major customers to competitor	Risk of unprovided bad debts in the accounts. Other customers could follow suit worsening the company's future prospects.
Loss of commercial customers	Commercial customers normally provide regular income which is important for a company with repayment commitments.

Circumstances	Why cause for concern?
Loss of major customers to competitor	Risk of unprovided bad debts in the accounts. Other customers could follow suit worsening the company's future prospects.
Loss of commercial customers	Commercial customers normally provide regular income which is important for a company with repayment commitments.
Draft accounts – final adjustments are outstanding	The company's net asset position could be worsened considerably if non-current assets are written down to recoverable amount, repairs inventory is written down to net realisable value. As mentioned before further bad debt provisions may be necessary. The closure may necessitate redundancy provisions. All of these factors could increase losses considerably.
Overdraft facility to be reviewed 3 months after the year end	This time period is probably not long enough to see a real improvement in the company's fortunes. As auditors we will be reporting when faced with fundamental uncertainty. Trying to anticipate the bank's likely reaction to the financial statements would be a high risk.
Future return to profits anticipated at a time when competitors are achieving success	The concern should be whether this is over optimistic. If so too much reliance being placed upon written representations would be high risk strategy.

Summary – If the company is not a going concern the accounts would be truer and fairer if prepared on a break-up basis. Material adjustments may then be required to the accounts.

(b) (i) Analyse sale proceeds for non-current assets, inventory and cash received from customers occurring after the end of the reporting period.

(ii) Review the debt ageing and cash recovery lists. Ask directors if outstanding amounts from lost customer are recoverable.

(iii) Discuss the optimistic view of likely future contracts with the MD. Orders received after the end of the reporting period should be reviewed to see if they substantiate his opinion.

(iv) Obtain his opinion about future contracts in a written representation letter.

(v) Review bank/loan records to assess the extent to which the company has met its loan and lease commitments in the period after the end of the reporting period.

(vi) Review sales orders/sales ledger for evidence of additional lost custom after the year end.

(vii) Obtain cashflow and profit forecasts:

– Discuss assumptions with the directors

– Perform sensitivity analysis flexing the key assumptions ie interest rates, date of payment of payables and receipts from customers

– Check all commitments have been cleared in accordance with legal agreements

– Agree budgets to any actual results achieved after the year end

– Assess reasonableness of assumptions in the light of the success of the achievement of the company's budgets set for 20X5. Discuss with the directors any targets not achieved

– Reperform calculations

– Ensure future budgeted profits are expected to meet likely interest charges

(viii) Review bank records to ensure that the company is operating within its overdraft facility after the end of the reporting period. Review bank certificate for terms and conditions of the facility. Review bank correspondence for any suggestion the bank is concerned about its current position.

(ix) Ask management whether the new vehicle fleet is attracting new contracts as anticipated. Scrutinise any new contracts obtained and check improved gross profit margins will be achieved.

(x) Obtain written representations as to the likelihood of the company operating for 12 months from the date of approval of the financial statements.

Chapter Roundup

- The auditors must perform and document an overall review of the financial statements before they can reach an opinion.

- As part of their completion procedures, auditors should consider whether the cumulative effect of unadjusted errors is material.

- Specific procedures must be applied to opening balances.

- The auditor's responsibilities for comparatives vary depending on whether they are corresponding figures or comparative financial statements.

- Auditors should always seek to resolve inconsistencies or misstatements of fact between financial statements and other published information.

- Auditors should consider the effect of subsequent events (after the end of the reporting period) on the accounts.

- Auditors should consider whether the going concern basis is appropriate, and whether disclosure of going concern problems is sufficient.

1   Name eight items that analytical review at the final stage must cover.

(1) ....   (5) ....

(2) ....   (6) ....

(3) ....   (7) ....

(4) ....   (8) ....

2   The auditor will maintain a schedule of unadjusted errors. This will include:

  • Specific misstatements identified by the auditors
  • Best estimate of other misstatements

True   ☐

False ☐

3   Where prior period financial statements were unaudited, the auditor should make no reference to the comparatives in his report.

True   ☐

False ☐

4   Which of the items on the following list are not part of the 'other information' within the scope of ISA 720?

  • Directors' report
  • Financial ratios
  • Statement of cash flows
  • Employment data
  • Auditor's report
  • Financial summaries

5   Name two elements of 'subsequent events'.

(1)...

(2)...

6   List five enquiries which may be made of management in testing subsequent events.

(1)...

(2)...

(3)...

(4)...

(5)...

7   Complete the definition.

Under the .... assumption an entity is viewed as continuing in business for the ....

8   The 'foreseeable future' is always a period of 12 months.

True   ☐

False ☐

1   From:

- Important accounting ratios
- Related items
- Changes in products; customers
- Price and mix changes
- Wages changes
- Variances
- Trends in production and sales
- Changes in material and labour content of production
- Other income statement expenditure
- Variations caused by industry or economy factors

2   True

3   False

4   Statement of cash flows and auditor's report

5   (1)   Events occurring between the period end and the date of the auditors' report
     (2)   Facts discovered after the date of the auditors report

6   From:

     (1)   Status of items involving subjective judgement
     (2)   Any new commitments
     (3)   Sales of assets
     (4)   Issues of shares or debentures
     (5)   Developments in risk areas
     (6)   Unusual accounting adjustments
     (7)   Other major events

7   Going concern, foreseeable future

8   False

Now try the questions below from the Exam Question Bank

Number	Level	Marks	Time
Q11	Examination	20	36 mins
Q12	Introductory	25	45 mins

Evaluation and review (II) matters relating to specific accounting issues

Topic list	Syllabus reference
1 Fair value	D1(iii)
2 Inventory and construction contracts	D1(iii)
3 Tangible non-current assets	D1(iii)
4 Intangible non-current assets	D1(iii)
5 Financial instruments	D1(iii)
6 Investment properties	D1(iii)
7 Foreign exchange rates	D1(iii)

Introduction

You must be able to consider four key matters in relation to items appearing in financial statements: risk, materiality, relevant accounting standards and audit evidence. In this chapter, we shall focus primarily on the last two of these, as the first two will depend more on the scenario presented in any given question.

You have previously studied the audit of a basic set of financial statements. At this level, the issues you are presented with will be more complex, but remember that key basic points apply. Bear in mind the relevant **assertions** for the financial statement items.

You need a strong knowledge of all the accounting standards you learnt up to 3.6 *Advanced Corporate Reporting*/P2 *Corporate Reporting* to apply in this paper. BPP suggests you keep your previous Study Texts as a reference point when working through this chapter and accounting issues questions.

Study guide

		Intellectual level
D1(iii)	**Evaluation and review**	
(j)	Evaluate the matters (eg materiality, risk, relevant accounting standards, audit evidence) relating to:	3
	(i) Inventory and construction contracts	
	(ii) Standard costing systems	
	(vii) Non-current assets	
	(viii) Fair value	
	(xv) Impairment	
	(xvii) Intangible assets	
	(xviii) Financial instruments	
	(xix) Investment properties	
	(xxii) Assets held for sale and discontinued operations	
	(xxiv) The effects of foreign exchange rates	

Exam guide

At this level it is assumed that you can audit all of the items listed above and all items audited at the earlier auditing level. This is likely to be tested in a scenario-based long case study type question, typically in Section A, the compulsory part of the P7 paper.

1 Fair value

12/08

 FAST FORWARD

> Key assertions relating to assets are existence, completeness, valuation and rights and obligations.

Key term

> **Fair value** the price that would be received to sell an asset or paid to transfer a liability in an orderly transaction between market participants at the measurement date.

Fair value accounting is increasingly important and affects the audit of valuation for both assets and liabilities. In May 2011 the IASB issued IFRS 13 *Fair value measurement*, as a result of a joint project with the US FASB.

Exam focus point

> Fair value is a very topical area at the moment, and is therefore likely to be tested, possibly as part of a requirement to discuss the difficulties involved in auditing fair value estimates.

Other examples of accounting treatments where fair values are relevant include financial instruments and share-based payments.

For auditors, the determination of fair value will generally be more difficult than determining historical cost. It will be more difficult to establish whether fair value is reasonable for complex assets and liabilities than for more straightforward assets or liabilities which have a market and therefore a market value. For example, for an apartment held as an investment property, a fair value might be relatively easy to estimate, as there may be a large and active market for similar properties that can be used as a guide to the value of the property in question. If, on the other hand, an entity holds a large number of derivative financial instruments for which there is no active market, then the fair value will be extremely difficult to measure and hence to audit.

Generally speaking, the trend towards fair value accounting will increase audit work required, not only because determining fair values is more difficult, but because fair values fluctuate in a way that historical costs do not, and will need vouching each audit period.

1.1 Accounting estimates including fair value

In February 2008 the IAASB issued a revised and redrafted ISA 540 *Auditing accounting estimates, including fair value accounting estimates and related disclosures*.

Key term

Accounting estimate. An approximation of a monetary amount in the absence of a precise measurement. This term is used for an amount measured at fair value where there is estimation uncertainty as well as for other amounts that require estimation.

1.2 Requirements of ISA 540

These are as follows:

- The auditor shall obtain an understanding of the following as part of the process of understanding the business:
    - The requirements of the applicable financial reporting framework.
    - The means by which the management identifies transaction, events and conditions that may give rise to the accounting estimates.
    - How management makes the accounting estimate.
      This means that the auditor must have a sound knowledge of the accounting requirements relevant to the entity and when fair value is allowed, for example, IAS 16 allows fair value provided 'it can be measured reliably'.
- The auditor should evaluate the degree of estimation uncertainty associated with the accounting estimate and assess whether this gives rise to significant risks.
- Based on the assessed risks the auditor will determine whether the financial reporting framework has been properly applied and whether methods for making estimates are appropriate and have been applied consistently.
- The auditor will also:
    - Determine whether events occurring up to the date of the audit report provide evidence regarding the accounting estimate
    - Test how management made the accounting estimate
    - Test the operating effectiveness of controls together with appropriate substantive procedures
    - Develop a point estimate or a range to evaluate the management's point estimate.

Key term

Management's point estimate is the amount selected by management for recognition or disclosure in the financial statements as an accounting estimate.

- For accounting estimates which give rise to significant risks the auditor should also evaluate the following:
    - How management has considered alternative assumptions or outcomes
    - Whether the significant assumptions used are reasonable
    - Management intent to carry out specific courses of action and its ability to do so, where these affect the accounting estimate
    - Management's decision to recognise, or to not recognise the accounting estimate
    - The selected measurement basis
- The possibility of management bias must be considered by the auditor
- Written representations will be obtained from management as to whether management believes that significant assumptions used in making accounting estimates are reasonable.

1.3 Risk procedures: fair value

The auditor is required to assess the entity's process for determining accounting estimates including fair value measurements and disclosures and the related control activities and to assess the arising risks of material misstatement.

Management's processes for determining fair values will vary considerably from organisation to organisation. Some companies will habitually value items at historical cost where possible, and may have very poor processes for determining fair value if required. Others may have complex systems for determining fair value if they have a large number of assets and liabilities which they account for at fair value, particularly where a high degree of estimation is involved in determining the fair value.

Once the auditors have assessed the risks associated with determining fair value, they should determine further procedures to address those risks.

1.4 Audit procedures: fair value

Audit procedures will depend heavily on the complexity of the fair value measurement. Where the fair value equates to market value, the auditor should be able to verify this with reference to the market, for example, published price quotations for marketable securities, or by using the work of an expert, for example, an estate agent in the case of land and buildings.

However, in some cases, there may be a great deal of estimation and management assumption related to a fair value. Where this is the case, the auditor needs to consider matters such as the intent and ability of management to carry out certain actions stated in the assumptions. This includes:

*   Considering management's past history of carrying out its stated intentions with respect to assets or liabilities
*   Reviewing written plans and other documentation, including, where applicable, budgets, minutes etc
*   Considering management's stated reasons for choosing a particular course of action
*   Considering management's ability to carry out a particular course of action given the entity's economic circumstances, including the implications of its contractual commitments

If there are alternative allowable methods for measuring fair value, or a particular method is not prescribed by the relevant accounting standard, the auditor should consider whether the entity's method is consistent with other fair value measurements in the financial statements and whether it is applied consistently.

The auditor should consider the following when considering fair value measurements:

*   The length of time any assumptions cover (the longer, the more subjective the value is)
*   The number of assumptions made in relation to the item
*   The degree of subjectivity in the process
*   The degree of uncertainty associated with the outcome of events
*   Any lack of objective data
*   The timings of any valuations used
*   The reliability of third party evidence
*   The impact of subsequent events on the fair value measurement

Where a fair value measurement is based on assumptions reflecting management's intent and ability to carry out certain actions, then the auditor should obtain **written representations from management** that these assumptions are reasonable and achievable.

1.5 IAASB Practice Alert *Challenges in Auditing Fair Value Accounting Estimates in the Current Market Environment*

In October 2008 the IAASB issued a Practice Alert, *Challenges in Auditing Fair Value Accounting Estimates in the Current Market Environment*. It discussed the following key points:

*   Challenges faced in accounting on the basis of fair value;

- Requirements and guidance in standards that are particularly relevant to fair values;
- Other considerations in audits of fair value accounting estimates;
- Initiatives of the International Accounting Standards Board; and
- Recent revisions to extant standards on auditing accounting estimates and fair value measurements and disclosures which, while not yet effective, may be helpful to auditors.

2 Inventory and construction contracts 6/11

FAST FORWARD

> When standard costing is used, the auditor must assess whether the valuation is reasonable.

IAS 2 *Inventories*

Inventory should be measured at the lower of cost and net realisable value. Costs include costs of purchase, conversion and others incurred in bringing inventory to its present location and condition.

2.1 Inventory count

ISA 501 *Audit evidence - specific considerations for selected items* contains specific guidance on inventory. It says that **attending the inventory count is compulsory where inventory is material**. The auditor must then perform procedures to determine whether inventory in the financial statements accurately reflects the inventory actually counted.

2.2 Standard costing

You studied the audit of inventory in detail in your studies for 2.6 *Audit and Internal Review/F8 Audit and Assurance*. You should be able to design procedures to verify the existence and valuation of inventory. If you are in any doubt in this area, go back to your earlier study material and revise.

An additional thing to consider in the audit of inventory is what **evidence** to obtain about **cost**, when there is a **standard costing system** in operation. Remember that IAS 2 allows standard costs to be used where prices are fluctuating.

Where standard costing is being used the auditor will have **two objectives**:

- Ensure that standard costing is an **appropriate basis** for valuing inventory
- Ensure that the **calculation** of the standard cost is **reasonable**

In evaluating whether standard costs are an appropriate basis, the auditor must:

<ul><li>**Establish whether prices have fluctuated**. This can be done by reviewing purchase invoices, consulting a price index and enquiry of management.</li><li>**Consider if the use of standard costing is the best accounting policy to use**. This should be discussed with the directors.</li><li>If the accounting policy has changed from the previous year, he must **consider the comparability of the accounts**.</li><li>There should also be **disclosure** about any changes of accounting policy in the accounts, which he should ensure is sufficient.</li></ul>

In ensuring that the calculation of the standard cost is reasonable, the auditor must:

<ul><li>Obtain a copy of the calculation of standard cost</li><li>Check the additions and calculations</li><li>Consider whether the calculation is reasonable (for example, based on averages of costs over the year)</li></ul>

- Verify elements of the calculation to appropriate documentation, for example,
  - Purchase prices to invoices
  - Wages and salaries to personnel records
  - Overheads to expenses in the financial statements where possible
- Alternatively, the standard cost may be verifiable by analytical review with comparison to total expense figures in the income statement, for example, wages should be based on the total wage cost divided by the production total for the year.

Exam focus point

The June 2011 exam examined the audit of inventory not in isolation, but in relation to ISA 510 *Initial Audit Engagements – Opening Balances*. Candidates had to explain the audit procedures on inventory in the context of an entity whose prior year financial statements had not been audited, for seven marks. To score well, candidates needed to combine their knowledge of the two areas (ISA 510 and inventory) to come up with relevant procedures in the context of the scenario.

2.3 Construction contracts

Before addressing the issue of audit evidence with regard to long term contracts, it is useful to revise the accounting requirements of IAS 11 *Construction contracts*.

IAS 11 *Construction contracts*

Construction contract. A contract specifically negotiated for the construction of an asset or a combination of assets that are closely interrelated or interdependent in terms of their design, technology and function or their ultimate purpose or use.

The accounting treatment is as follows:

- Recognise **contract revenue** as revenue in the accounting period in which the work is performed.
- Recognise **contract costs** as an expense in the accounting period in which the work to which they relate is performed.
- Any **expected excess** of total contract costs over total contract revenue should be recognised as an expense immediately.
- Any costs incurred which relate to **future activity** should be recognised as an asset if it is probable that they will be recovered (often called contract work in progress, that is, amounts due from the customer).
- Where amounts have been recognised as contract revenue, but their **collectability** from the customer becomes doubtful, such amounts should be recognised as an expense, not a deduction from revenue.

The auditor will have to audit the calculation of attributable profit or loss and assess if it is reasonable. He will then have to verify all the movements on the statement of financial position to that calculation.

The auditor should undertake the following procedures:

- Obtain a copy of the calculation and check the additions and calculations
- Assess whether the basis of calculation is comparable with prior years
- He should then verify the figures in the calculation:
  - Revenue to certification of work completed to date
  - Total contract price to original contract
  - Cost of work completed to invoices also payroll/clock cards/wage rates
  - Payments on account to remittance advices
- He should discuss with management if there is any chance of a loss arising on the contract

From the auditor's point of view, the **% stage of completion** and the **assessment of the overall profitability of the contract** are **particularly risky areas** to audit, as they involve management exercising its **judgement**.

3 Tangible non-current assets   6/09, 12/09, 6/11

FAST FORWARD

Auditors should ensure that both tangible and intangible assets have been subjected to an annual impairment review.

You covered all the key aspects relating to tangible non-current assets in your earlier studies. If you are in any doubt in this area, go back to your previous material and revise. The issue of fair value discussed in Section 1.1 is likely to affect the audit of non-current assets.

3.1 Recognition of non-current assets

The key risk in relation to initial recognition is of costs being incorrectly recognised as assets, when they should in fact have been expensed to the income statement.

IAS 16 *Property, plant and equipment* lists the following as components of cost:

- Purchase price, less any trade discount or rebate

- Import duties and non-refundable purchase taxes

- Directly attributable costs of bringing the asset to working condition for its intended use, eg:
    - The cost of site preparation
    - Initial delivery and handling costs
    - Installation costs
    - Testing
    - Professional fees (architects, engineers)

- Initial estimate of the unavoidable cost of dismantling and removing the asset and restoring the site on which it is located

However, the following should **not be included** in the cost of the **asset, and should be recognised as an expense**:

- Administration and other general overhead costs
- Start-up and similar pre-production costs
- Initial operating losses before the asset reaches planned performance
- Any incidental costs.

3.2 Valuation of non-current assets

Non-current assets will be carried at cost or valuation (if an item has been revalued). **Cost is straightforward to audit**, it can be verified to original purchase documentation. **Valuation** may be straightforward to audit – **it can be verified to the valuation certificate**. The carrying value of non-current assets is therefore depreciated cost, or depreciated valuation.

Once a company has revalued assets, it is required to continue revaluing them regularly so that the valuation is not materially different from the fair value at period end. The auditors should therefore check that valuation is comparable to market value. They would do this by comparing the existing valuation to current market values (for example, in an estate agent's window).

Part D Audit of historical financial statements | **9: Evaluation and review (II) matters relating to specific accounting issues**   **243**

Assets are depreciated, so their carrying value will not be original cost or valuation. **Depreciation** can be verified by reperforming the depreciation calculations. Often a '**proof-in-total**' check will be sufficient, where auditors calculate the relevant depreciation percentage on the whole class of assets to see if it is comparable to the depreciation charged for that class of assets in the year.

The depreciation rate is determined by reference to the useful life of the asset. This is determined by management based on expectations of how long the asset is expected to be in use in the business. The auditors will audit this by scrutinising those expectations and verifying them where possible – for example, to the minutes of the meeting where management decided to buy the asset, to capital replacement budgets, to past practice in the business.

<table>
<tr><td>**Exam focus
point**</td><td>In a real exam paper, the examiner asked candidates for principal audit procedures to obtain evidence about the useful lives of oil platforms. A significant amount of information about what management based their expectations on was given in the question and the examiner expected candidates to use that information. For example, management considered weather conditions that the rigs were subject to. Therefore, to audit the useful life, auditors should obtain weather reports to see if they corroborated the useful life. A platform severely affected by wind and storms will have a shorter useful life than one in calmer conditions.</td></tr>
</table>

3.3 Impairment of non-current assets   12/10

An asset is impaired when its carrying amount (depreciated cost or depreciated valuation) exceeds its recoverable amount. You should be familiar with the following key terms from your accounting studies.

<table>
<tr><td>**Key terms**</td><td>The **recoverable amount** of an asset or cash-generating unit is the higher of its fair value less costs to sell and its value in use.

A **cash-generating unit** is the smallest identifiable group of assets that generates cash inflows that are largely independent of the cash inflows from other assets or groups of assets.

Value in use is the present value of the future cash flows expected to be derived from an asset or cash-generating unit.</td></tr>
</table>

Management are required to determine if there is any indication that the assets are impaired. IAS 36 *Impairment of assets* specifies the following indicators of possible impairment:

External sources of information regarding possible impairment:

- market value declines significantly;

- negative changes in technology, markets, economy, or legal environment;

- increases in market interest rates that are likely to affect the discount rate using to calculate value in use;

- company stock price is below book value.

Internal sources of information regarding possible impairment:

- obsolescence or physical damage;

- significant changes with an adverse effect on use, eg asset will become idle, is part of a restructuring, or is held for disposal;

- internal evidence shows worse economic performance of the asset than was expected..

The auditors will consider whether there are any **indicators of impairment** when carrying out risk assessment procedures. They will use the same impairment criteria laid out in IAS 36 as management do. If the auditors believe that impairment is indicated, **they should request that management show them the impairment review that has been carried out. If no impairment review has been carried out**, then the auditors should discuss the need for one with management, and if management refuse to carry out an impairment review, **qualify their opinion** on grounds of a material misstatement in respect of IAS 36 as a result of management not carrying out an impairment review.

If an impairment review has been carried out, then the auditors should audit that impairment review. Management will have estimated whether the recoverable amount of the asset/cash generating unit is lower than the carrying amount.

For auditors, the key risk is that **recoverable amount requires estimation**, which involves **management** using its **judgement**. Auditors will need to consider whether the judgement made by management is reasonable in accordance with IAS 36.

Management have to determine if recoverable amount is higher than carrying amount. It may not have been necessary for them to estimate both fair value and value in use, because if one is higher than carrying amount, then the asset is not impaired. If it is not possible to make a reliable estimate of net realisable value, then it is necessary to calculate value in use.

Net realisable value is only calculable if there is a active market for the goods, and would therefore be audited in the same way as fair value which was set out in paragraph 1.2. Costs to sell such as taxes can be recalculated by applying the appropriate tax rate to the fair value itself. Delivery costs can be verified by comparing costs with published rates by delivery companies, for example, on the Internet.

If management have calculated the value in use of an asset or cash-generating unit, then the auditors will have to audit that calculation. The following procedures will be relevant.

Value in use

- Obtain management's calculation of value in use
- Reperform calculation to ensure that it is mathematically correct
- Compare the cash flow projections to recent budgets and projections approved by the board to ensure that they are realistic
- Calculate/obtain from analysts the long term average growth rate for the products and ensure that the growth rates assumed in the calculation of value in use do not exceed it
- Refer to competitors' published information to compare how much similar assets are valued at by companies trading in similar conditions
- Compare to previous calculations of value in use to ensure that all relevant costs of maintaining the asset have been included
- Ensure that the cost/income from disposal of the asset at the end of its life has been included
- Review calculation to ensure cash flows from financing activities and income tax have been excluded
- Compare discount rate used to published market rates to ensure that it correctly reflects the return expected by the market

---

If the asset is impaired and has been written down to recoverable amount, the auditors should review the financial statements to ensure that the write down has been carried out correctly and that the IAS 36 disclosures have been made correctly.

Point to note

Although this section has been focused on impairment of tangible non-current assets, these considerations apply equally to intangibles, which can be impaired too.

3.4 Held for sale non-current assets   6/11

IFRS 5 *Non-current assets held for sale and discontinued operations* applies to **non-current assets and disposal groups**. A disposal group is a group of assets and associated liabilities that are to be disposed of in a single transaction.

IFRS 5 requires that non-current assets and disposals groups that are 'held for sale' should be presented separately in the statement of financial position. 'Held for sale' here means that the non-current asset/disposal group's carrying amount will be recovered principally through a sale rather than through continuing use. A number of detailed **criteria** must be met:

(a)   The asset must be available for immediate sale in its present condition

(b)   The sale must be highly probable

For sale to be highly probable the following must apply:

(a)   Management must be committed to a plan to sell the asset

(b)   There must be an active plan to locate a buyer

(c)   The asset must be marketed at a price that is reasonable in relation to its current fair value

(d)   The sale should be expected to take place within one year from the date of classification

(e)   It is unlikely that significant changes to the plan will be made or that the plan will be withdrawn

A non-current asset held for sale should be measured at the lower of its carrying amount and fair value less costs to sell. An impairment loss should be recognised where fair value less costs to sell is lower than the carrying amount.

Non-current assets held for sale should not be depreciated even if they are still being used by the entity.

The following audit procedures will therefore be relevant.

Confirm that the asset meets the definition of an asset held for sale:

- Discuss with management the availability of asset for sale
- Assess management commitment, eg minuted in board minutes
- Evaluate and assess practical steps being taken to sell the asset eg appropriate real estate agents appointed
- Determine when the sale is expected to take place by assessing progress to date
- Determine and assess the basis on which the sale price has been set
- Discuss with management any significant changes to the plans

Confirm that the asset has been valued as held for sale in accordance with IFRS 5 and assess how fair value has been determined.

Check that the asset has not been depreciated from the date of reclassification.

Confirm separate disclosure in accordance with IFRS 5.

---

4 Intangible non-current assets   12/07, 6/09, 12/10

Accounting guidance for intangibles is given in IAS 36 *Intangible assets* and IFRS 3 *Business combinations*. The types of asset we are likely to encounter under this heading include patents, licences, trademarks, development costs and goodwill. All intangibles should be subject to an annual impairment review.

IAS 38 *Intangible assets*

An **intangible asset** is an identifiable non-monetary asset without physical substance. It may be held for using in the production and supply of goods or services, or for rental to others, or for administrative purposes. The asset must be:

- Controlled by the entity as a result of events in the past, and
- Something from which the entity expects future economic benefits to flow.

Examples of items that might be considered as intangible assets include computer software, patents, copyrights, motion picture films, customer lists, franchises and fishing rights. An item should not be recognised as an intangible asset, however, unless it **fully meets the definition** in the standard. The guidelines go into great detail on this matter.

Internally generated goodwill may **not** be recognised as an **asset**.

The auditor should carry out the following procedures.

Completeness

Prepare analysis of movements on cost and amortisation accounts

Rights and obligations

- **Obtain confirmation** of all **patents** and **trademarks** held by a patent agent
- **Verify payment** of **annual renewal fees**

Valuation

- **Review specialist valuations** of intangible assets, considering:
  - Qualifications of valuer
  - Scope of work
  - Assumptions and methods used
- **Confirm carried down balances** represent **continuing value**, which are proper charges to future operations

Additions (rights and obligations, valuation and completeness)

- **Inspect purchase agreements, assignments** and **supporting documentation** for intangible assets acquired in period
- **Confirm purchases** have been **authorised**
- **Verify amounts capitalised** of patents developed by the company with supporting costing records

Amortisation

- **Review amortisation**
  - Check computation
  - Confirm that rates used are reasonable

Income from intangibles

- **Review sales returns** and **statistics** to verify the reasonableness of income derived from patents, trademarks, licences etc
- **Examine audited accounts** of third party sales covered by a patent, licence or trademark owned by the company

4.1 Goodwill

Key tests are as follows.

- **Agree consideration** to a **sales agreement**
- **Confirm valuation** of assets acquired is reasonable
- **Check purchased goodwill** is **calculated correctly**
- **Check goodwill** does **not include non-purchased goodwill**
- **Review amortisation**
  - Test calculation
  - Assess whether amortisation rates are reasonable
- **Ensure valuation of goodwill is reasonable** by reviewing prior year's accounts and discussion with the directors
- If useful life is judged to be indefinite, ensure impairment review has been carried out
- Review impairment review for reasonableness

Goodwill is covered in more detail in the context of the audit of groups in Chapter 11.

Part D Audit of historical financial statements | **9: Evaluation and review (II) matters relating to specific accounting issues** 247

4.2 Development costs

> **IAS 38 Intangible assets**
>
> - Development costs may be included in the statement of financial position (that is to say, capitalised) only in 'special circumstances' laid out in IAS 38 **Intangible assets**.
> - IAS 38 defines research and development as follows.
>   - **Research** is original and planned investigation undertaken with the prospect of gaining new scientific or technical knowledge and understanding.
>   - **Development** is the application of research findings or other knowledge to a plan or design for the production of new or substantially improved materials, devices, products, processes, systems or services prior to the commencement of commercial production or use.
> - Expenditure on **research** is required to be recognised in profit or loss in the year of expenditure.
> - IAS 38 states that the **development costs** of a project should be recognised as an asset only when all of the following criteria are met.
>   - Completion of the asset will be technically feasible.
>   - The business intends to complete the asset and use or sell it.
>   - The business will be able to use or sell the asset.
>   - The business can demonstrate how future economic benefits will be generated, either by demonstrating a market exists or the internal usefulness of the asset.
>   - Adequate technical, financial and other resources will be available to complete the development and use or sell the intangible asset.
>   - Expenditure attributable to the development of the asset can be measured reliably. General overhead expenditure, costs of inefficiencies and operating losses, and expenditure on training staff to operate the asset should not be capitalised. Amortisation of development expenditure should not exceed 20 years and an appropriate method should be used.
>
> The development costs of a project recognised as an asset should not exceed the amount that is likely to be recovered from related future economic benefits, after deducting further development costs, related production costs, and selling and administrative costs directly incurred in marketing the product.
>
> - In all other circumstances development costs should be recognised in profit or loss in the year of expenditure.

The key audit tests largely reflect the criteria laid down in IAS 38.

> - **Check accounting records** to confirm:
>   - **Project** is **clearly defined** (separate cost centre or general ledger codes)
>   - **Related expenditure** can be **separately identified**, and certified to invoices, timesheets
> - **Confirm feasibility and viability**.
>   - Examine market research reports, feasibility studies, budgets and forecasts
>   - Consult client's technical experts
> - **Review budgeted revenues** and **costs** by examining results to date, production forecasts, advance orders and discussion with directors.
> - **Review calculations** of **future cash flows** to ensure resources exist to complete the project.
> - **Review previously deferred expenditure** to ensure IAS 38 criteria are still justified.
> - **Check amortisation:**
>   - Commences with production
>   - Charged on a systematic basis

The good news for the auditors in this audit area is that many companies adopt a prudent approach and write-off research and development expenditure in the year it is incurred. The auditors' concern in these circumstances is whether the income statement charge for research and development is complete, accurate and valid.

4.3 Brands

The key accounting issue with regard to brands is whether the asset is **internally generated** or not. Remember, IAS 38 forbids the capitalisation of internally generated brands.

If a brand has been purchased separately (that is, not as part of goodwill) then auditors should test the value of the brand according to the sales documentation.

5 Financial instruments 6/09

FAST FORWARD

When auditing financial instruments, the auditors will have to ensure that recognition and valuation is in accordance with IFRS 9 *Financial instruments*.

5.1 Background

If you read the financial press you will probably be aware of **rapid international expansion** in the use of financial instruments. These vary from straightforward, traditional instruments, eg bonds, through to various forms of so-called 'derivative instruments'. Some of the more complex instruments played a role in the financial audit crisis of 2007-8. This is a particularly risky area for auditors, as the accounting standards on financial instruments involve an unavoidable element of complexity, and are tricky to apply in practice.

Exam focus point

If you see a financial instrument in a scenario question, think 'risk'. The main risk is that they are not accounted for in accordance with IFRS. Also, management may not understand the business risks to which they may be exposing the entity (which may affect the assessment of going concern).

Key terms

Financial instrument. Any contract that gives rise to both a financial asset of one entity and a financial liability or equity instrument of another entity.

Financial asset. Any asset that is:

- Cash
- An equity instrument of another entity
- A contractual right to receive cash or another financial asset from another entity or to exchange financial instruments with another entity under conditions that are potentially favourable to the entity
- A contract that will or may be settled in the entity's own equity instruments and is:
  - A non-derivative for which the entity is or may be obliged to receive a variable number of the entity's own equity instruments
  - A derivative that will or may be settled other than by the exchange of a fixed amount of cash or another financial asset for a fixed number of the entity's own equity instruments.

Financial liability. Any liability that is:

- A contractual obligation:
  - To deliver cash or another financial asset to another entity
  - To exchange financial instruments with another entity under conditions that are potentially unfavourable

- A contract that will or may be settled in the entity's own equity instruments and is:
  - A non-derivative for which the entity is or may be obliged to deliver a variable number of the entity's own equity instruments or
  - A derivative that will or may be settled other than by the exchange of a fixed amount of cash or another financial asset for a fixed number of the entity's own equity instruments

Fair value is the price that would be received to sell an asset or paid to transfer a liability in an orderly transaction between market participants at the measurement date.

Derivative. A financial instrument or other contract with all three of the following characteristics:

(a) its value changes in response to the change in a specified interest rate, financial instrument price, commodity price, foreign exchange rate, index of prices or rates, credit rating or credit index, or other variable (sometimes called the 'underlying');

(b) it requires no initial net investment or an initial net investment that is smaller than would be required for other types of contracts that would be expected to have a similar response to changes in market factors; and

(c) it is settled at a future date.

(IAS 32, IFRS 9 and IFRS 13)

Examples of financial assets include:

- Trade receivables
- Options
- Shares (when used as an investment)

Examples of financial liabilities include:

- Trade payables
- Debenture loans payable
- Redeemable preference (non-equity) shares
- Forward contracts standing at a loss

Financial instruments include:

(a) Primary instruments, eg receivables, payables and equity securities
(b) Derivative instruments, eg options, futures and forwards, interest rate swaps and currency swaps

The accounting requirements for financial assets are found in four Standards:

(a) IAS 32 *Financial instruments: Presentation*, which deals with:

    (i) The classification of financial instruments between liabilities and equity
    (ii) Presentation of certain compound instruments

(b) IFRS 7 *Financial instruments: Disclosures*, which revised, simplified and incorporated disclosure requirements previously in IAS 32.

(c) IAS 39 *Financial instruments: Recognition and measurement,* which dealt with:

    (i) Recognition and derecognition
    (ii) The measurement of financial instruments
    (iii) Hedge accounting

IFRS 9 *Financial Instruments*, issued in November 2009, replaced parts of IAS 39, with respect to the classification and measurement of financial assets. In 2010, IFRS 9 was updated to include the classification and measurement of financial liabilities, and the derecognition of financial assets and liabilities. This standard is a work in progress and in due course will be developed further to fully replace IAS 39. It will come into force for accounting periods ending in 2013. This is Phase 1 of the project to replace IAS 39.

5.2 Accounting treatment recap

Exam focus point

The financial reporting standards in relation to financial instruments are currently in a state of flux. It is therefore important that you are familiar with the current requirements, as they may have changed since you sat Paper P2.

Financial instruments should be recognised in the statement of financial position when the entity becomes a party to the **contractual provisions of the instrument**.

Point to note

An important consequence of this is that all derivatives should be in the statement of financial position.

Notice that this is **different** from the recognition criteria in the *Framework* and in most other standards. Items are normally recognised when there is a probable inflow or outflow of resources and the item has a cost or value that can be measured reliably.

5.2.1 Financial assets

Initial recognition of a financial asset is at the fair value of the consideration. Subsequent to this initial recognition, IFRS 9 requires that **financial assets** are classified as measured at either:

- **Amortised cost, or**
- **Fair value**

The IFRS 9 classification is made on the basis of both:

(a) The **entity's business model** for managing the financial assets, and
(b) The **contractual cash flow** characteristics of the financial asset.

An application of these rules means that **equity investments may not be classified as measured at amortised cost** and must be measured at fair value. This is because contractual cash flows on specified dates are not a characteristic of equity instruments. In addition, **all derivatives are measured at fair value.**

A **debt instrument** may be classified as measured at either amortised cost or fair value **depending on whether it meets the criteria above.**

5.2.2 Financial liabilities

As with financial assets, a financial liability is initially measured at the fair value of the consideration received. Subsequent to this, IFRS 9 requires that financial assets are **classified as measured** at either:

(a) **Fair value through profit or loss**, or
(b) **Amortised cost** under the effective interest rate method

A financial liability is classified at **fair value through profit or loss** if:

(a) It is **held for trading**, or
(b) Upon initial recognition it is designated at fair value through **profit or loss.**

Derivatives are always measured at fair value through profit or loss.

Point to note

These classification rules are unchanged from those previously contained within IAS 39.

5.2.3 IFRS 7 *Financial instruments: disclosure*

The principles in IFRS 7 complement the principles for recognising, measuring and presenting financial assets and financial liabilities in IAS 32 *Financial instruments: Presentation* IAS 39 *Financial instruments: Recognition and measurement*, and IFRS 9 *Financial instruments.*

IFRS 7 requires entities to make extensive disclosures in relation to financial instruments, which we will recap briefly here. The standard requires qualitative and quantitative disclosures about exposure to risks arising from financial instruments and specifies minimum disclosures about credit risk, liquidity risk and market risk.

Two types of disclosure need to be made: about the **significance** of the financial instruments, and about the **nature and extent of risks arising** from the financial instruments.

IFRS 7 requires disclosures about the **significance** of financial instruments to be made in relation to the SOFP and the SOCI. For example, entities must disclose the carrying amounts included within each IAS 39/IFRS 9 category on the SOFP, and the reason for any reclassification between these categories. The SOCI must then disclose the net gain/loss that is attributable to each of these categories.

Regarding the **nature and extent of risks**, IFRS 7 requires disclosures in respect of credit risk, currency risk, interest rate risk, liquidity risk, loans payable, market risk, other price risks, and instruments that are past due.

<table>
<tr>
<td>Point to note</td>
<td>As with many areas of financial reporting, you are unlikely to be examined on any of these areas in much detail. What is important is that you are familiar with the issues involved with each standard, and are able to think about them from the point of view of somebody auditing them.

In relation to IFRS 7, the key audit risk is simply that the entity does not comply with IFRS 7 by making inadequate disclosures.</td>
</tr>
</table>

5.2.4 IAS 32 *Financial instruments: presentation*

One key requirement of IAS 32 relates to **compound financial instruments**. Convertible debt is a commonly-examined example here, where IAS 32 requires the debt and equity elements of the instrument to be presented separately in the financial statements. Accounting in this area requires a level of **judgement**, which can be **risky** from an auditor's point of view. For example, judgement is required when calculating the present value of debt repayments (eg in selecting an appropriate discount rate).

5.3 Audit risk

Financial instruments, particularly complex ones, increase audit risk. Factors which increase audit risk include the following:

(a) Lack of management understanding of financial instruments and therefore inadequate management control.

(b) Inappropriate classification of financial instruments, particularly between debt and equity may lead to off-balance sheet financing. This will affect gearing and therefore the risk profile of the business. This is particularly an issue where hybrid or compound instruments have been issued with both debt and equity elements.

(c) The use of fair values involves the use of valuation techniques including market estimates. Judgements will need to be made to determine whether the valuation techniques and any estimates made are reasonable.

(d) Recognition of the costs associated with the instrument is not necessarily straightforward. For example, the discount on a discounted debenture should be treated as part of the overall cost of the instrument and recognised over the life of the debenture.

5.4 Audit procedures

Although the issues and evidence sought will depend on the specific nature of the financial instrument, the following key considerations will normally apply:

Consideration	Evidence
Classification	Review the terms of the financial instrument and confirm that they have been classified in accordance with their substance.
	Enquire of management as to their intention ie to sell in the short term or hold to maturity. Corroborate any statements by a review of events after the reporting period, forecast and projections.
Existence	For listed shares the auditor can check the company exists by reviewing stock exchange listings.
	Unlisted companies can be verified by simple enquiries a the Companies Registry.
Valuation: Initial fair value	Confirm that all financial assets and liabilities have been valued at fair value where this is required by IFRS 9.
	Agree fair value to transaction price (the cost of shares can be verified by checking the purchase documentation).
	Where part of the consideration has been given for something other than the financial instrument, assess valuation technique adopted, eg discounting of future cash flows.
Valuation: Subsequent measurement	Verify the subsequent classification of financial instruments by enquiry of management, as to the business model according to which the instruments are being held (ie whether they are being held for trading or to maturity). This information should be corroborated by a review of events after the reporting period and of forecasts and projections.
	Confirm that all financial assets that are equity or are derivatives are held at fair value.
	Check calculation of amortised cost complies with IFRS 9:
	• The initial amount recognised for the financial asset • Less any repayments of the principal sum • Plus any amortisation
	Confirm that the amount of amortisation has been calculated using the effective interest method.
	Confirm that financial assets and liabilities at fair are remeasured to fair value at the end of the reporting period in accordance with IFRS 13.
	Where there is an active market agree fair value to quoted market price (current bid price).
	Where there is no active market assess the valuation technique adopted by management and any assumptions made.
Ownership	Ownership of shares in another company should be checked to the share certificate. The share certificate may be kept in a bank or at a brokers, in which case the auditor should confirm with these parties that the share certificate exists.
Presentation and disclosure	Check that disclosures comply with IFRS 7. This includes eg qualitative disclosures about exposure to risk and risk management, and quantitative disclosures of summary data about exposures.

On 1 January 20X8 Daniels Co issued a $20 million debenture at par, with a nominal rate of interest of 4%. The debenture is redeemable in five years' time at which point the holder will have the option to convert the debenture to 12 million $1 ordinary shares in Daniel Co. The debenture has been recorded in the financial statements as a long-term liability at the net proceeds of issue. The first payment of interest on 31 December 20X8 has also been recorded.

Required

(a)   Identify the audit issues
(b)   List the audit procedures you would perform

Answer

(a)   Audit issues

(i)   The treatment of the debenture does not comply with IFRS 9.

(ii)   It should be treated as a hybrid instrument, split into its equity and liability components.

(iii)   The liability component should be calculated as the discounted present value of the cash flows of the debenture

(iv)   The remainder of the proceeds should be reclassified as equity

(b)   Audit procedures

(i)   Check the nominal interest rate and conversion terms to the debenture deed

(ii)   Agree amount of initial proceeds and interest payment to cash book and bank statement

(iii)   Obtain schedule calculating the fair value of the liability at the date of issue and confirm that an appropriate discount rate has been used (assuming revised treatment adopted)

(iv)   Confirm whether disclosures are adequate and in accordance with IFRS 9 and IFRS 7.

5.5 Investment income

We shall look at income in more detail in Chapter 10. Investment income is accounted for under IAS 18 *Revenue*.

6 Investment properties

A key factor to consider when auditing investment properties is whether one **exists** according to the **criteria** of IAS 40 *Investment property*.

Key term

Investment property is property (land or a building – or part of a building – or both) held (by the owner or by the lessee under a finance lease) to earn rentals or for capital appreciation or both, rather than for:

*   Use in the production or supply of goods or services or for administrative purposes, or
*   Sale in the ordinary course of business

Type of non-investment property	Applicable IAS
Property held for sale in the ordinary course of business	IAS 2 *Inventories*
Property being constructed or developed on behalf of third parties	IAS 11 *Construction contracts*
Owner-occupied property	IAS 16 *Property, plant and equipment*

Substantive tests

- Verify **rental agreements**, ensuring that occupier is not a connected company and that the rent has been negotiated at arm's length.
- If the building has recently been built, check **architect's certificates** to ensure that construction work has been completed

The second important assertion in relation to investment properties is **valuation**. IAS 40 requires that investment properties either be held at **cost** (benchmark treatment) or at fair value. This approximates to open market value. The auditor should be able to verify this by reference to a valuer's certificate as professional valuation is encouraged under the IAS.

The last key issue with regard to investment properties is **disclosure**. The auditor should review the disclosures made in the financial statements in relation to investment properties to ensure that they have been made appropriately, in accordance with IAS 40.

Question

You are reviewing the file on the audit of Apollo Co, a listed company, which is nearing completion. Apollo produces two products; the X and the W. Apollo plc purchased two new pieces of plant in the year. Plant is valued at cost. The X103 was bought to replace the X102, which was scrapped at the start of the year. The W103 was bought to replace the W102. The W102 will no longer be used in producing the W, but will be used to test new products, particularly the V, which Apollo is hoping to be able to market and sell in the next two years.

Required

Describe matters you would consider and the audit evidence you would expect to see on file in respect of the valuation of these pieces of plant.

Answer

Matters to consider

The main matter to consider here is the valuation of the W102. Now it will no longer be used in production, it may be impaired. The asset should be valued in the financial statements at the lower of carrying amount or recoverable amount. Recoverable amount will be fair value, as the W102 no longer has a value in use because it will not generate cash inflows until the V is marketed. Whether the W102 has a market (fair) value will depend on how specialised a machine it is. The fact that can be transferred to use on a different product to the W suggests that it is not highly specialised and that there may be a second hand market from which a valuation can be taken.

Evidence that should be contained on the audit file

- Indication that the value of the X103 and W103 has been agreed to purchase invoices
- Recalculation of profit/loss on scrapping of X102
- Note of physical inspection to ensure that X102 is no longer on premises
- Minutes of directors' meeting approving the scrapping of the X102 and change in use of the W102 reviewed
- Copy of management's impairment review with regard to the W102
- Fair value of W102 verified by reference to price lists of suppliers of such second-hand machines
- Note of observation of operation of machines to ensure W102 no longer used in production

Whilst exam questions will require you to use your knowledge of corporate reporting it is important that the accounting knowledge is applied (see the answer above). Few marks will be awarded for listing facts from accounting standards without adequate application and audit focus.

7 Foreign exchange rates

The presence of **foreign exchange** is likely to **increase audit risk**, so the auditor must perform procedures to reduce this risk.

You will have studied the accounting rules in relation to foreign exchange in depth at Paper P2. At P7 level you will need to revise this material, and then think about the area from the perspective of the external auditor. The key issue here is that the introduction of foreign exchange into a scenario increases the level of audit risk. This is most likely to be examined in the context of a **group** that includes an **overseas subsidiary**.

This area is relatively new to the P7 syllabus, so it is likely that the examiner will seek to test it. You are advised to revise it thoroughly.

7.1 Individual company

Perhaps the most immediate audit risk here is that the entity fails to comply with the accounting requirements of IAS 21 *The Effects of Changes in Foreign Exchange Rates*. For an individual company conducting trade in foreign currencies, there are two separate accounting issues: conversion and translation.

Conversion is uncontroversial, and relates to an entity conducting transactions in a foreign currency, and which incurs exchange gains/losses in relation to these transactions. The rule is simple: the gain or loss on conversion is recognised directly in profit and loss in the period in which it occurs. The principal risk here is of the wrong exchange rate being used, resulting in misstatement of the gain/loss in the financial statements.

Translation is more complex. Translation is required at the end of an accounting period when a company still holds assets or liabilities in its statement of financial position which were obtained or incurred in a foreign currency. IAS 21 distinguishes between **monetary items** and **non-monetary items**. The basic rule is that monetary items (eg cash, receivables) should be retranslated using the rate rule at the end of each accounting period. Non-monetary items are left at the amount recognised at the date of the transaction.

Audit procedures here would therefore include:

- Check that monetary items included in the statement of financial position at the year end are translated at the closing rate of exchange.

- Check that non-monetary items are translated at the historical rate of exchange.

- Check that items are included in the statement of comprehensive income at the historical rate of exchange.

7.2 Groups

It is also possible that a parent company may have overseas subsidiaries. It must translate the financial statements of those operations in to its own reporting currency before they can be consolidated in to group accounts. There are two methods of achieving this. The method used depends on whether the foreign operation has the same functional currency as the parent.

In a question on the audit of groups one of the issues you may need to consider is whether the correct treatment has been adopted for the translation of a foreign entity.

7.2.1 Same functional currency as the reporting entity

In this situation the foreign operation normally carries on its business as though it were an extension of the reporting entity's operations.

We can summarise the treatment as follows:

Income statement	Translate using actual rates. An average for a period may be used but not where there is a significant fluctuation and the average is therefore unreliable.
Non-monetary items	Translate using an historic rate at the date of purchase (or revaluation to fair value, or reduction to realisable/recoverable amount). This includes inventories and long-term assets (and their depreciation).
Monetary items	Translate at the closing rate
Exchange differences	Report as part of profit for the year

7.2.2 Different functional currency from the reporting entity

In this situation although the reporting entity may be able to exercise control, the foreign operation normally operates in a semi-autonomous way. It accumulates cash and other monetary items, generates income and incurs expenses, and may also arrange borrowings, all in its own local currency.

We can summarise the treatment as follows:

Assets and liabilities	Translate at the closing rate at the period end. (The balancing figure on the translated statement of financial position represents the reporting entity's net investment in the foreign operation.
Income statement	Translate items at the rate ruling at the date of the transaction (an average rate will usually be used for practical purposes)
Exchange differences	Taken to equity

7.3 Other issues

The table below outlines some of the other audit risks that may be present with an overseas subsidiary, along with some possible audit procedures to mitigate those risks.

Audit risk	Procedures
Potential misstatement due to the effects of **high inflation**. IAS 29 requires financial statements to be **restated** in terms of measuring units current at the **end of the reporting period**, and a **gain or loss** on the net monetary position included within net income	• Confirm that financial statements have been correctly restated • Check that disclosures have been made in line with IAS 29
Subsidiary may have been audited by **component auditors**.	Need to consider the extent to which their work can be relied upon, as per ISA 600
Different **accounting framework** may have been used by subsidiary	Confirm the accounting framework used, and that accounting policies are consistent with the rest of the group
Possible **difficulty** in the parent being able to **exercise control**, eg due to political instability, or laws and regulations	Need to consider whether there is still **control**, and whether it is correct to produce group accounts per IFRS 3
Currency **restrictions** limiting **payment of profits** to the parent	• Need to consider whether there is still control • Need to consider impact on parent's status as a **going concern**

Chapter Roundup

- Key assertions relating to assets are existence, completeness, valuation and rights and obligations.

- When standard costing is used, the auditor must assess whether the valuation is reasonable.

- Auditors should ensure that both tangible and intangible assets have been subjected to an annual impairment review.

- When auditing financial instruments the auditors will have to ensure that recognition and valuation is in accordance with IFRS 9 *Financial instruments*.

- The presence of foreign exchange is likely to increase audit risk, so the auditor must perform procedures to reduce this risk.

Quick Quiz

1   Match the accounting item with the relevant accounting standard(s)

    (a)   Construction contracts   (i)   IFRS 3
    (b)   Intangible non-current assets   (ii)   IAS 16
    (c)   Tangible non-current assets   (iii)   IAS 11
                                 (iv)   IAS 38

2   Complete the definition.

A .... is a contract specifically negotiated for the construction of an .... or a .... that are closely inter-related or interdependent in terms of their design, technology and function or their ultimate purpose or use.

3   Brands may never be capitalised.

    True   ☐

    False ☐

4   Financial assets are recognised initially at their fair value.

    True   ☐

    False ☐

5   Complete the definition.

.... is property held to earn.................................... or for .... or both, rather than for use in the .... or .... of goods or services or for administrative purposes, or .... in the ordinary course of business.

Answers to Quick Quiz

1   (a) (iii)
     (b) (iv)
     (c) (ii)

2   Construction contract, asset, combination of assets.

3   False. Internally generated brands may not be capitalised. Purchased brands with a separately identifiable value may be capitalised.

4   True. Subsequent measurement rules depend on the type of financial instrument being measured.

5   Investment property, rentals, capital appreciation, production, supply, sale

Now try the questions below from the Exam Question Bank

Number	Level	Marks	Time
Q13	Examination	25	45 mins
Q14	Examination	20	36 mins

Evaluation and review (III) matters relating to specific accounting issues

10

Topic list	Syllabus reference
1 Income	D1(iii)
2 Liabilities	D1(iii)
3 Expenses	D1(iii)
4 Disclosure	D1(iii)

Introduction

This chapter deals with further accounting issues that could appear in questions where you are required to consider materiality, risk, relevant accounting standards and audit evidence. As in Chapter 9, the content relates to the final two aspects on that list of matters.

Study guide

D1(iii)	Evaluation and review	Intellectual level
(j)	Evaluate the matters (eg materiality, risk, relevant accounting standards, audit evidence) relating to:	3
	(iii) Statements of cash flows	
	(iv) Changes in accounting policy	
	(v) Taxation (including deferred tax)	
	(vi) Segmental reporting	
	(ix) Leases	
	(x) Revenue recognition	
	(xi) Employee benefits	
	(xii) Government grants	
	(xiii) Related parties*	
	(xiv) Earnings per share	
	(xvi) Provisions, contingent liabilities and contingent assets	
	(xx) Share-based payment transactions	
	(xxi) Business combinations	
	(xxii) Assets held for sale and discontinued operations	
	(xxiv) The effects of foreign exchange rates	
	(xxv) Borrowing costs	

* Issues relevant to related parties were covered in Chapter 7, those relevant to business combinations will be covered in Chapter 11, and those relevant to events after the reporting period were covered in Chapter 8.

Exam guide

Scenario questions are likely to appear requiring you to apply your corporate reporting knowledge, to assess whether errors may have been made, determine materiality and identify appropriate evidence. These can feature any of the financial reporting topics you have studied in your ACCA exams.

1 Income

Revenue recognition is an extremely important issue and completeness is the key assertion to be audited.

1.1 Revenue recognition

IAS 18 *Revenue*

IAS 18 covers revenue from specific transactions/events

- Sale of goods
- Rendering of services
- Interest, royalties, dividends

Definitions

- **Revenue** is the gross inflow of economic benefits during the period arising in the course of the ordinary activities of an entity when those inflows result in increases in equity, other than increases relating to contributions from equity participants.
- **Fair value** is the amount for which an asset could be exchanged, or a liability settled, between knowledgeable, willing parties in an arm's length transaction.

Accounting treatment

- **Measurement**: at the fair value of consideration received, net of trade discounts/volume rebates.
- **Identification**: usually as a whole, but may need to break the transaction down into its **component parts** or put separate transactions together to obtain commercial meaning.

Sale of goods

An entity should only recognise when:

- **Significant risks/rewards** of ownership of goods are transferred
- It has **no continuing managerial involvement** over goods
- Revenue can be **measured reliably**
- Probable that **economic benefits will flow** to enterprise
- **Costs incurred** can be **measured reliably**

Rendering of services

An entity should recognise revenue depending on the **stage of completion of the transaction**. Outcome can only be reliably estimate when:

- Revenue can be **measured reliably**
- Probable **economic benefits** will flow to entity
- **Stage of completion** at year end can be measure reliably
- **Costs incurred** can be measured reliably

Reliable estimates will only be possible when these have been agreed:

- Each party's **enforceable rights**
- **Consideration** to be unchanged
- **Manner and terms** of settlement

Interest, royalties and dividends

- **Interest** is the charge for the use of cash or cash equivalents or amounts due to the entity.
- **Royalties** are charges for the use of long-term assets of the entity, eg patents, computer software and trademarks.
- **Dividends** are distributions of profit to holders of equity investments, in proportion with their holdings, of each relevant class of capital.

Revenue should be recognised when:

- Probable that **economic benefits** will flow to entity
- Revenue can be **measured reliably**

Recognise on these bases:

- **Interest**: time proportion basis (effective yield)
- **Royalties**: accruals basis, per agreement
- **Dividends:** when shareholders' gain right to receive payment

Disclosure

- **Accounting policy note**
- Amount of **each significant category** of revenue
- Amount of revenue from **exchange of goods/services**
- **Contingent gains/losses**, warranty costs

Part D Audit of historical financial information | **10: Evaluation and review (III) matters relating to specific accounting issues**   263

Revenue is commonly audited by analytical review. This is because revenue should be predictable and there are good bases on which to base analytical review, such as:

- Plenty of information, for example, last year's accounts, budget, monthly analyses (companies tend to keep a lot of information about sales)
- Logical relationships with items such as inventory and receivables

Unless complex transactions arise where revenue is not as clear cut as a product being supplied and invoiced for, revenue recognition is generally not an issue. However, in some companies, for example, those that deal primarily in construction contracts, revenue recognition can be a **material** issue. Examples of industries where this might be true:

- Building industry
- Engineering industry

In such industries, auditing revenue recognition will be part of auditing construction contracts. The auditor should:

- Consider whether the basis for recognition is reasonable
- Agree revenue recognised to relevant documents (for example, work certificates or contracts)

However, it should not be thought that revenue recognition is generally a low-risk area to audit. Far from it: **revenue recognition is one of the commonest areas of fraudulent financial reporting**. Indeed, ISA 240 *The Auditor's Responsibilities Relating To Fraud In An Audit Of Financial Statements* states that the auditor should presume that there is a risk of fraud in relation to revenue recognition ISA 240.26, and should obtain an understanding of the controls related to these risks (ISA 240.27). This presumption is 'rebuttable' (para A30) if the auditor concludes that there is no risk of material misstatement due to fraud, but unless this is the case, the auditor must presume that there is a possibility of revenue recognition fraud, and that the entity should have put in place controls to mitigate this risk.

Example: revenue recognition

You are an audit senior on the audit of a travel agency, Laxman Co.

Recognised within revenue are a series of credit sales of inventory totalling $200,000 that took place close to the year end. Laxman Co continues to hold the legal title to this inventory.

Laxman Co is a member of a trade organisation that imposes upon it a number of conditions, one of which is that its financial statements show an acid test ratio of more than one.

The following amounts are shown in Laxman Co's draft financial statements.

	$
Revenue	1,200,000
Current assets	1,000,000
Inventory	100,000
Current liabilities	800,000

Required

Identify and explain the principal matters to consider when auditing the revenue of Laxman Co.

Solution

The two principal matters to consider here are interrelated: whether IAS 18 has been properly applied to Laxman Co's inventory, and whether Laxman Co is in breach of the conditions of its membership of the trade organisation.

Inventory

IAS 18 states that revenue in respect of the sale of goods is recognised when the entity has transferred the risks and rewards of ownership of the goods to the buyer.

In this case, the transfer of title would appear to indicate that this has not happened, and that these items should not be recognised within revenue.

However, as auditors it will be necessary to obtain further information regarding the sale, as in accordance with IAS 18 the transfer of legal title is not sufficient evidence that the risks and rewards of ownership have been transferred. It is possible, for instance, that legal title has been retained in order to protect Laxman Co against the possibility of non-payment by the receivable, even though in substance a sale has in fact occurred.

Further audit evidence must be obtained in order to form a judgement over whether IAS 18 has in fact been breached.

Membership condition

Laxman Co appears to be within the criteria laid down by the trade organisation: it has an acid test ratio of 1.125 (= ($1,000,000 - $100,000) ÷ $800,000).

However, if the revenue recognised in respect of the inventory above has not been recognised in accordance with IAS 18, the financial statements may need to be amended. The amendment could be by as much as £200,000 (decreasing receivables and increasing inventory), which would change the acid test ratio to 0.625 (= ($800,000 - $300,000) ÷ $800,000).

If the conditions set by the organisation have been broken then it is likely that some negative consequence would result from this. This could range from a fine or penalty that would need to be recognised in the financial statements, to the possibility of Laxman Co being disbarred from membership of the organisation. If this were the case, it would be necessary to consider very carefully whether significant doubts exist over Laxman Co's ability to continue as a going concern.

Possibility of fraud

The auditor needs to consider the possibility that management has engaged in fraudulent financial reporting in respect of revenue recognition in order not to breach the conditions set by the trade organisation. If this were the case, the auditor will need to re-examine any representations it has already received from management.

 Case Study   Revenue recognition in an e-commerce environment

Companies that engage in e-commerce may have particular revenue recognition issues.

The entity may act as a **principal** or as an **agent**. They must determine whether to disclose their gross sales, or merely their commission. For example, Lastminute.com discloses a figure 'TTV', which does not represent statutory revenue, but represents the price at which goods and services have been sold across the group's platforms. Revenue itself is largely made up of commission on selling those goods and services.

The company may engage in **reciprocal arrangements** with other companies whereby they both advertise on each other's website. Whether such an arrangement results in 'revenue' must be considered. It must then be accounted for appropriately.

The company may deal in unusual **discounts** or voucher systems to encourage customers to buy. These must also be reflected.

Lastly, the company must determine a policy for **cut-off**. This may be complex if the company acts as an agent. When is the sale made? When the customer clicks 'accept', when the company emails acknowledgement, when the sale is made known to the principal, when the goods are despatched, when the customer receives the goods, when the customer has taken advantage of the services...? The company must determine a reasonable policy for when the sale has been made.

Case Study

Satyam Computer Services Ltd, an major Indian provider of IT services, was the subject of a major accounting scandal that has sometimes been referred to as "India's Enron".

Satyam manipulated its financial statements over a period of several years, from around 2002 to 2009, when the public announcement was made that the accounts had been falsified. A number of methods were used to do this, including producing false invoices, which inflated reported revenue and led to the creation of significant fictitious assets in the statement of financial position.

Satyam's auditors failed to detect this fraud, which had an ongoing and highly material impact on the financial statements. As a result of their failure to conduct the audit properly, and of the broader failure of quality control of which this was symptomatic, five Indian affiliates of PricewaterhouseCoopers were given a record fine of $7.5m by the SEC in the US. The firms were also required to set up employee training programmes, to reform audit policies, and to appoint an independent monitor.

It is important to note that this is not a question of auditors being held *liable* for audit failings, but rather of auditors being fined by a regulatory body for failing to conduct audits in accordance with the required standards.

Question
Revenue recognition and other matters

The senior partner of JLPN, a firm of auditors, has issued an 'Audit Risk Alert' letter to all partners dealing with key areas of concern which should be given due consideration by his firm when auditing public companies. The letter outlines certain trends in audit reporting that, if not scrutinised by the auditors, could lead to a loss of reliability and transparency in the financial statements. The following three key concerns were outlined in the letter.

(a) Audit committees play a very important role together with the financial director and auditor in achieving high quality financial control and auditing. Recently the efforts of certain audit committees have been questioned in the press.

(b) The Stock Exchange had reported cases of inappropriate revenue recognition practises including:

    (i) Accelerating revenue prior to the delivery of the product to the customer's site, or prior to the completion of the terms of the sales arrangement

    (ii) Recognition of revenue when customers have unilateral cancellation or termination provisions, other than the normal customary product return provisions

(c) It has been reported that the management of companies had intentionally violated IFRS. The reason for this has been the sensitivity of reported earnings per share in a market place where missing the market's expectation of earnings per share by a small amount could have significant consequences.

Required

(a) Explain the importance of the role of an 'Audit Risk Alert' letter to a firm of auditors.

(b) Discuss the way in which the auditor should deal with each of the key concerns outlined in the letter in order to ensure that audit risk is kept to an acceptable level.

Answer

(a) The '**risk alert letter**' is a memorandum used by the reporting partner to notify fellow partners of concerns emerging from dealings with clients, regulatory authorities or stock exchanges. It ensures that:

    (i) Key audit risk areas are reviewed
    (ii) Significant trends and irregularities are identified
    (iii) Quality is maintained
    (iv) Litigation risk is reduced

        (v)   Investor confidence is maintained as it reduces manipulation

(b)   (i)   **Audit committees** are held to secure good a quality of **internal control** and financial reporting in listed companies. If the auditor has doubts about the effectiveness of an audit committee then he should **review its structure, independence and membership** to ensure it meets its objectives. Any shortcomings should be reported to the board and/or the members.

        (ii)   **Revenue acceleration** is a **creative accounting device**. Revenue should **not be recognised until earned and realised** (realisable), so the practices described are not acceptable. Only if the risks of ownership have fully transferred to the buyer and the seller has not retained any specific performance obligation should revenue be recognised earlier.

              Extended audit tests concerning revenue recognition and 'cut-off' tests may be appropriate if the auditor suspects anomalies.

        (iii)   Where **intentional GAAP violations** have occurred, **materiality judgement** may be affected. The auditor must ensure the audit team is aware that violations of GAAP **can affect EPS** for certain clients, and that staff are sufficiently experienced and trained in order to detect such violations. It may be that the errors are individually immaterial, but the **aggregate effect** must be considered. Furthermore, the practice of intentional misstatements may indicate that the **management** of the company **lacks integrity** and the auditor should consider whether the client should be retained.

1.2 Government grants and assistance

Government grants and assistance are accounted for under IAS *20 Accounting for government grants and disclosure of government assistance*. They may be either revenue or capital grants relating to the assets or income.

IAS 20 *Accounting for government grants and disclosure of government assistance*

- **Government assistance.** Action by government designed to provide an economic benefit specific to an entity or range of entities qualifying under certain criteria.

- **Government grants.** Assistance by government in the form of transfers of resources to an entity in return for past or future compliance with certain conditions relating to the operating activities of the entity. They exclude those forms of government assistance which cannot reasonably have a value placed upon them and transactions with government which cannot be distinguished from the normal trading transactions of the entity.

- **Grants related to assets.** Government grants whose primary condition is that an entity qualifying for them should purchase, construct or otherwise acquire long-term assets. Subsidiary conditions may also be attached restricting the type or location of the assets or the periods during which then are to be acquired or held.

- **Grants related to income.** Government grants other than those related to assets.

- **Forgivable loans.** Loans which the lender undertakes to waive repayment of under certain prescribed conditions.

Accounting treatment

- **Recognise government grants and forgivable loans** once conditions complied with and receipt/waiver is assured.

- Grants are recognised under the **income approach**: recognise grants as income to match them with related costs that they have been received to compensate.

- Use a **systematic basis** of matching over the relevant periods.

- Grants for **depreciable assets** should be recognised as income on the same basis as the asset is depreciated.

- Grants for **non-depreciable assets** should be recognised as income over the periods in which the cost of meeting the obligation is incurred.
- A grant may be **split into parts** and allocated on different bases where there are a series of conditions attached.
- Where **related costs have already been incurred**, the grant may be recognised as income in full immediately.
- A grant in the form of a **non-monetary asset** may be valued at fair value or a nominal value.
- **Grants related to assets** may be presented in the statement of financial position *either* as a **separate credit** *or* deducted in arriving at the carrying value of the asset.
- **Grants related to income** may be presented in the statement of comprehensive income *either* as a **separate credit** *or* **deducted** from the related expense.
- Repayment of government grants should be accounted for as a **revision of an account estimate.**

Disclosure

- **Accounting policy** note.
- **Nature and extent** of government grants and other forms of assistance received.
- **Unfulfilled conditions** and other contingencies attached to recognised government assistance.

Grants where related costs have already been incurred offer no difficulties to account for or to audit. To audit them, the auditor should:

- Obtain documentation relating to the grant and confirm that it should be classified as revenue
- The value may be agreed to the documentation (for example, a letter outlining the details of the grant, or a copy of an application form sent by the client)
- The receipt of the grant can be agreed to bank statements

Capitalised grants can be more difficult to audit, particularly if a non-monetary government grant is being accounted for at fair value.

Audit procedures:

- Consider whether the basis of accounting is comparable to the previous year.
- Discuss the basis of accounting with the directors to ensure that the method used is the best method
- Ensure that any changes in accounting method are disclosed.

2 Liabilities

12/07, 6/09

The relevant financial statement assertions for liabilities are completeness, rights and obligations and existence. Liabilities must be tested for understatement.

Fair value is a key issue when considering certain liabilities. This should be borne in mind when auditing liabilities.

2.1 Leases

The classification of a lease can have a material effect on the financial statements.

First we shall look at the audit of **leases**. The relevant accounting standard for leases is IAS 17 *Leases*.

IAS 17 *Leases*

- **Lease**. An agreement whereby the lessor conveys to the lessee in return for a payment or series of payments the right to use an asset for an agreed period of time.
- **Finance lease**. A lease that transfers substantially all the risks and rewards incident to ownership of an asset. Title may or may not eventually be transferred.
- **Operating lease**. A lease other than a finance lease.

IAS 17 identifies five situations which would normally lead to a lease being classified as a finance lease:

- The lease **transfers ownership** of the asset to the lessee at the end of the lease term.
- The lessee has the **option to purchase** the asset at a price sufficiently below fair value at exercise date, that it is reasonably certain the option will be exercised.
- The lease term is for a **major part of the asset's economic life** even if title is not transferred.
- Present value of the minimum lease payments amounts to **substantially all** of the asset's fair value at inception.
- The leased asset is so **specialised** that it could only be used by the lessee without major modifications being made.

IAS 17 requires that a finance lease should be recorded in the statement of financial position of a lessee as an asset and as an obligation to pay future lease payments. At the inception of the lease the sum to be recorded both as an asset and as a liability should be the **fair value of the leased property** or, if lower, at the **present value of the minimum lease payments**. The latter are derived by discounting them at the interest rate implicit in the lease.

IAS 17 requires that the **rentals** under operating leases should be written off as an expense on a **straight line basis** over the lease term even if the payments are not made on such a basis, unless another systematic and rational basis is justified by the circumstances.

Sale and leaseback transactions

Sale and finance leaseback

The substance of the transaction is that there is no sale. Sale proceeds received are treated as a finance lease liability.

Any apparent profit or loss (that is the difference between the sale price and the previous carrying value) should be deferred and amortised in the financial statements of the seller/lessee over the lease term.

Sale and operating leaseback

BV = book value, SP = sale proceeds, FV = fair value

- If SP = FV (ie an arm's length transaction) recognise any profit/loss immediately
- If SP < FV recognise any profit/loss immediately unless the apparent loss is compensated by future rentals at below market price, in which case defer and amortise over period asset is expected to be used.
- If SP > FV
  - Defer excess over fair value and amortise over period asset is expected to be used
  - In substance this excess is a loan which would be held at amortised cost in accordance with IAS 39. Consequently, the operating lease rentals would need to be split between the fair market rental and the repayment of the loan plus interest.

Point to note

In all cases if FV < BV recognise the loss of BV − FV immediately.

You can see that the **classification** of the lease is **likely to have a material effect on the financial statements**. If the lease is a finance lease, the statement of financial position will show substantial assets and liabilities. The net effect will be minimal, but the face of the statement of financial position will be materially different from what it would be if it was an operating lease.

It is important that the auditor ensures that the **classification** (which would fall under the assertion existence) is correct. Other important assertions are valuation, and rights and obligations.

The following audit procedures are relevant.

Classification and rights and obligations

- Obtain a copy of the lease agreement
- Review the lease agreement to ensure that the lease has been correctly classified according to IAS 17

Valuation (finance leases)

- Obtain a copy of the client's workings in relation to finance leases
- Check the additions and calculations of the workings
- Ensure that the interest has been accounted for in accordance with IAS 17
- Recalculate the interest
- Agree the opening position
- Agree any new assets to lease agreements
- Verify lease payments in the year to the bank statements

Valuation (operating leases)

- Agree payments to the bank statements (if material)

Disclosure

- Ensure the finance leases have been properly disclosed in the financial statements

Question

Audit of leases

You are the manager responsible for the audit of Makepeace Co for the year ended 31 December 20X8. Makepeace Co has leased an asset from 1 January 20X8. The terms of the lease are as follows:

A non-refundable deposit of $5,800 on inception
Six annual instalments of $16,000 payable in arrears

The fair value of the asset (equivalent to the present value of the minimum lease payments) on 1 January 20X8 is $80,000 and the asset has a useful life to the company of five years.

As part of the lease agreement the company guaranteed to the lessor that the asset could be sold for $8,000 at the end of the lease term. It also incurred $2,000 of costs in setting up the lease agreement.

The lease has been classified as a finance lease in the books of Makepeace. The asset has been capitalised in the statement of financial position and is being depreciated straight-line over the life of the lease.

The interest rate implicit in the lease has been calculated at 10%.

The company has total assets of $1,600,000.

Required

List the audit issues you would consider in this situation.

Answer

Audit issues

The key risk is that the lease has been inappropriately classified as a finance lease. The fact that the present value of the minimum lease payments is equivalent to the fair value of the asset and that the residual value is guaranteed by the lessee would indicate that the treatment of the lease as a finance lease is correct. Further inspection of the lease agreement should be performed, however to determine which party bears the risks and rewards of ownership.

Materiality needs to be considered. As the asset was capitalised as a finance lease the statement of financial position should include a non-current asset stated at $67,200

$$\left[(80,000+2,000)-((80,000+2,000-8,000)/5)\right].$$

There should also be a financial lease liability of $65,620 in total (see Working). If the lease is an operating lease these balances would be removed. At 4.2% and 4.1% of total assets respectively these balances are material to the statement of financial position.

Profit figures are required to determine the potential materiality of interest and depreciation charges.

The period over which the asset is being depreciated needs to be considered. The depreciation period is normally the shorter of the useful life and the lease term. In this case the asset is being depreciated over the lease term (six years) when it will only be of use to the company for five years.

The treatment of the costs incurred in setting up the lease need to be considered. These can be capitalised as part of the non-current asset and depreciated.

There is a need to check whether the rate implicit in the lease has been calculated correctly. In accordance with IAS 17 this is the rate that gives a constant rate on the outstanding liability. This can be checked by using a market value for the asset to calculate the internal rate of return.

Disclosures must comply with the requirements of IAS 17. In particular the liability must be analysed to show the present value of the minimum lease payments in the categories < one year, two to five years, > five years. In this case the liability would be split as follows:

	$
< one year (65,620 – 56,182)(W)	9,438
Two to five years (W)	56,182

Working

		$
Year ended 31 December 20X8		
1 January 20X8	Asset at FV	80,000
1 January 20X8	Non-refundable deposit	(5,800)
		74,200
1 January 20X8 to 31 December 20X8	Interest at 10%	7,420
31 December 20X8	Instalment 1	(16,000)
Balance at 31 December 20X8		65,620
Year ended 31 December 20X9		
1 January 20X9 to 31 December 20X9	Interest at 10%	6,562
31 December 20X9	Instalment 2	(16,000)
Balance at 31 December 20X9		56,182

2.2 Deferred taxation   12/08

The auditor needs to audit the movement on the deferred tax liability.

Deferred tax is accounted for under IAS 12 *Income taxes*. This is revised briefly below.

IAS 12 *Income taxes*

- Deferred tax is the tax attributable to temporary differences, which are differences between the carrying amount of an asset or liability in the statement of financial position and its tax base.
- **Deferred tax liabilities** are the amounts of income taxes payable in future periods in respect of taxable temporary differences. All taxable temporary differences give rise to a deferred tax liability.
- **Deferred tax assets** are the amounts of income taxes recoverable in future periods in respect of:
  - Deductible temporary differences (eg provisions, unrealised profits on intra group trading

> - The carry forward of unused tax losses
> - The carry forward of unused tax credits
>
> All deductible temporary differences give rise to a deferred tax asset.
>
> - **Temporary differences** are differences between the carrying amount of an asset or liability in the statement of financial position and its tax base. Temporary differences may be either:
>   - **Taxable temporary differences**, which are temporary differences that will result in taxable amounts in determining taxable profit (tax loss) of future periods when the carrying amount of the asset or liability is recovered or settled.
>   - **Deductible temporary differences**, which are temporary differences that will result in amounts that are deductible in determining taxable profit (tax loss) of future periods when the carrying amount of the asset or liability is recovered or settled.
> - The **tax base** of an asset or liability is the amount attributed to that asset or liability for tax purposes.

Deferred tax is the **tax attributable to timing differences**. For example, where a company 'saves tax' in the current period by having accelerated capital allowances, a **provision for the tax charge** is **made in the statement of financial position**.

The provision is made is because over the course of the asset's life, the tax allowances will reduce until the depreciation charged in the accounts is higher than the allowances. This will result in taxable profit being higher than reported profit and the company will be 'suffering higher tax' in this period.

2.2.1 Types of taxable temporary difference

Accelerated capital allowances

The temporary difference is the difference between the carrying value of the asset in the statement of financial position at the end of the reporting period and its tax depreciated value.

Interest revenue (where interest is included in profit or loss on an accruals basis but taxed when received).

The temporary difference is equivalent to the income accrual in the statement of financial position at the end of the reporting period as the tax base of the interest receivable is nil.

Development costs (where development costs are capitalised for accounting purposes but deducted from taxable profit in the period incurred).

The temporary difference is equivalent to the amount capitalised in the statement of financial position at the end of the reporting period. The tax base is nil since they have already been deducted from taxable profits.

Revaluation to fair value (in jurisdictions where the tax base of the asset is not adjusted).

The temporary difference is the difference between the assets carrying value and tax base. A deferred liability is created even if the entity does not intend to dispose of the asset.

Fair value adjustments on consolidation

A temporary difference arises as for the revaluation above but the deferred tax effect is a consolidation adjustment in the same way as the revaluation itself.

| Question | Revision: taxable temporary differences |

Shelley Co purchased an asset costing $3,000. At the end of 20X8 the carrying amount is $2,000. The cumulative depreciation for tax purposes is $1,800 and the current tax rate is 25%.

Required

Calculate the deferred tax liability for the asset.

Tax base of the asset is $3,000 – $1,800 = $1,200

Deferred tax liability = $800 (2,000 – 1,200) × 25% = $200

2.2.2 Types of deductible temporary differences

Provisions

The provision is recognised for accounting purposes when there is a present obligation, but may not be deductible for tax purposes until the expenditure is incurred.

Losses

Current losses that can be carried forward to be offset against future taxable profits result in a deferred tax asset.

Fair value adjustments

For example, liabilities recognised on business combinations where the expenditure is not deductible for tax purposes until a later period.

Unrealised profits on intra-group trading

The profit is not realised from the group point of view until the items transferred are sold outside the group, but where the tax base is based on the cost to the individual receiving company and no equivalent adjustment for unrealised profit is made for tax purposes a temporary difference arises.

Revision: deductible temporary differences

Ontario Co recognises a liability of $20,000 for accrued product warranty costs on 31 December 20X8. These product warranty costs will not be deductible for tax purposes until the entity pays the claims. The tax rate is 25%.

Required

Calculate the deferred tax asset.

Tax base = Nil (carrying amount of $20,000 less the amount that will be deductible for tax purposes in respect of the liability in future periods).

Deferred tax asset = $20,000 (carrying amount) – Nil (tax base) = 20,000 × 25% = $5,000.

This should be recognised in accordance with IAS 12 (see Section 2.2.3 below).

2.2.3 Measurement of deferred tax

The key points to remember are as follows:

- IAS 12 adopts the **full provision** method of providing for deferred tax. This recognises that each timing difference at the period end has an effect on future tax payments.
- Deferred tax assets and liabilities are measured at the tax rates expected to apply to the period when the asset is realised or liability settled, based on the tax rates (and tax laws) that have been **enacted** (or substantively enacted) by the end of the reporting period.
- Deferred assets and liabilities **cannot be discounted**.
- Deferred tax assets are only recognised to the extent that it is **probable** that taxable profit will be available against which the deductible temporary difference can be utilised.

Part D Audit of historical financial information | **10: Evaluation and review (III) matters relating to specific accounting issues**   273

Point to note

In practice it is rare for a deferred tax asset to be recognised, as the asset only exists insofar as the entity's tax liability can be reduced in the future, which in turn depends on the entity being profitable enough to *have* a tax liability and thus to be able to 'use' any tax losses.

From the auditor's perspective deferred tax assets are risky because a significant degree of judgement must be exercised in determining whether tax losses will in fact result in reduced tax liabilities in the future. This is an illustration of the importance of the auditor approaching the audit with professional scepticism.

2.2.4 Audit issues and procedures

As part of the **planning process**, if the client receives tax services from the firm, the auditor should consult the tax department as to the company's future tax plans, to ascertain whether they expect a deferred tax liability to arise. This will assist any analytical review they carry out on the deferred tax provision.

Remember that **manipulating the deferred tax figure will not affect the actual tax position**. However, a **deferred tax charge** (the other part of the double entry for the statement of financial position provision) **is recognised in profit or loss before dividends**, even if it is not actually paid to HM Revenue and Customs.

The following procedures will be relevant:

- Obtain a copy of the deferred tax workings and the corporation tax computation
- Check the arithmetical **accuracy** of the deferred tax working
- Agree the **figures used** to calculate timing differences to those on the **tax computation** and the **financial statements**
- Consider the assumptions made in the light of your knowledge of the business and any other evidence gathered during the course of the audit to ensure reasonableness
- Agree the opening position on the deferred tax account to the prior year financial statements
- Review the basis of the provision to ensure:
  - It is line with accounting practice under IAS 12
  - It is suitably comparable to practice in previous years
  - Any changes in accounting policy have been disclosed

Question

Audit of deferred tax

Guido Co, a company producing domestic appliances for the retail market began trading on 1 January 20X7. Its draft accounts for the year ended 31 December 20X8 show profit before tax of $1,000,000, total assets of $5,200,000 and a deferred tax balance of $958,000.

You are the manager responsible for the audit of Guido Co and the following information relating to deferred tax has been provided by the client:

(1) The deferred tax balance in the financial statements is the brought forward balance from previous years. No deferred tax adjustment has been made for the current period.

(2) At the period end Guido Co have plant and equipment with a carrying amount of $5,200,000 and a tax base at that date of $2,400,000.

(3) The tax rate to be applied is 30%.

Required

(a) Identify the audit issues.

(b) List the procedures you would perform in respect of the amounts relating to deferred tax in the financial statements in relation to Guido Co.

(a)   **Audit issues**

   (i)   The deferred tax balance has not been adjusted to reflect current period balances.

   (ii)   Adjustment of deferred tax would result in the following balances:

   Deferred tax liability $840,000 (W)
   Credit in the income statement $118,000 (W)

   (iii)   With the change in liability representing approximately 11% of profit before tax and 2% of total assets the adjustment is material to both the income statement and the statement of financial position.

   (iv)   Whether the tax rate of 30% is the correct rate to apply.

   (v)   Whether the net book values and tax written down values provided are correct.

   (vi)   Whether there are any additional taxable temporary differences or deductible temporary differences that should be taken account of.

   (vii)   Whether adequate disclosure is provided in accordance with IAS 12.

(b)   **Audit procedures**

   (i)   Discuss with management why they have not adjusted the deferred tax liability for the period and request that they do so.

   (ii)   Agree the brought forward balance for deferred tax to the previous year's financial statements.

   (iii)   Obtain a schedule of the temporary differences relating to the plant and equipment and agree these to tax computations and asset registers.

   (iv)   Check that the rate applied of 30% is in accordance with IAS 12, ie the 'substantially enacted' rate of tax.

   (v)   Enquire of management and review tax computation to establish whether there are any further differences that need to be adjusted for.

   (vi)   Review disclosure notes to ensure that they comply with IAS 12 including disclosure of the components of the deferred tax liability, the change in the liability and the major components of the income tax expense.

Working

	$'000
Tax base of asset	2,400
Carrying amount	5,200
	$2,800 \times 30\% =$ 840
Brought forward liability	958
Decrease in liability	118

2.3 Provisions and contingencies   6/09, 12/09, 12/10

FAST FORWARD

A provision is accounted for as a liability, contingencies are disclosed, so auditors must ensure they have been classified correctly according to IAS 37.

Provisions are accounted for under IAS 37 *Provisions, contingent liabilities and contingent assets*.

> **IAS 37 *Provisions, contingent liabilities and contingent assets***
>
> A **provision** is a liability of uncertain timing or amount.
>
> A **liability** is a present obligation of the entity arising from past events, the settlement of which is expected to result in an outflow from the entity of resources embodying economic benefits.

An **obligating event** is an event that creates a legal or constructive obligation that results in an entity having no realistic alternative to settling that obligation.

A **legal obligation** is an obligation that derives from:

(a)   A contract (through its explicit or implicit terms)
(b)   Legislation or
(c)   Other operation of law.

A **constructive obligation** is an obligation that derives from an entity's actions where

(a)   By an established pattern of past practice, published policies and sufficiently specific current statement, the entity has indicated to other parties that it will accept certain responsibilities; and
(b)   As a result, the entity has created a valid expectation on the part of those other parties that it will discharge those responsibilities.

A **contingent liability** is:

(a)   A possible obligation that arises from past events and whose existence will be confirmed only by the occurrence or non-occurrence of one or more uncertain future events not wholly within the control of the entity, or
(b)   A present obligation that arises from past events but is not recognised because:
    (i)   It is not probable that an outflow of resources embodying economic benefits will be required to settle the obligation, or
    (ii)   The amount of the obligation cannot be measured with sufficient reliability.

A **contingent asset** is a possible asset that arises from past events and whose existence will be confirmed only by the occurrence or non-occurrence of one or more uncertain future events not wholly within the control of the entity.

Under IAS 37, an entity should not recognise a **contingent asset** or a **contingent liability**. However if it becomes probable that an outflow of future economic benefits will be required for a previous contingent liability, a provision should be recognised. A contingent asset should not be accounted for unless its realisation is virtually certain; if an inflow of economic benefits has become probable, the asset should be disclosed.

IAS 37 also gives guidance in regarding a number of specific provisions. These include the following:

Provisions for restructuring

A restructuring is a programme that is planned and is controlled by management and materially changes either:

•   The scope of the business undertaken by an entity.
•   The manner in which that business is conducted.

The IAS gives the following example of events that would fall under this definition.

•   The **sale or termination** of a line of business
•   The **closure of business locations** in a country or region or the **relocation** of business activities from one country region to another
•   **Changes in management structure**
•   **Fundamental reorganisations** that have a material effect on the **nature and focus** of the entity's operations.

In order to make a provision an obligation (legal or constructive) must exist at the period end. In this context, a constructive obligation exists only in the following circumstances:

•   An entity must have a **detailed formal plan** for the restructuring
•   It must have raised a **valid expectation** in those affected that it will carry out the restructuring by starting to implement that plan or announcing its main features to those affected by it.

A management or board decision alone would not normally be sufficient.

The IAS states that a restructuring provision should include only the **direct expenditures** arising from the restructuring.

Onerous contracts

An **onerous contract** is a contract in which the unavoidable costs of meeting the obligations under the contract exceed the economic benefits expected to be received under it. An example might be a vacant leasehold property.

If an entity has a contract that is onerous a provision must be made for the **net loss**.

Decommissioning provisions

A provision is only recognised from the date on which the **obligating event** occurs.

For example when an oil company initially purchases an oil field it is put under a legal obligation to decommission the site at the end of its life. The legal obligation exists therefore on the initial expenditure on the field and therefore the liability exists immediately. The IAS also takes into view that the decommissioning costs may be capitalised as an asset representing future access to oil reserves (ie an asset and a provision are recognised).

Contingent assets

Contingent assets are only very rarely recognised, as IAS 37 requires an entity to be virtually certain that it will receive an inflow of economic benefits. The recognition of contingent assets in financial statements therefore represents a **risk** for auditors, as it is only in rare circumstances that they should be recognised.

2.3.1 Audit procedures

The audit tests that should be carried out on provisions and contingent assets and liabilities are as follows.

- **Obtain details** of all **provisions** which have been included in the **accounts** and all **contingencies** that have been disclosed
- **Obtain** a **detailed analysis** of all **provisions** showing opening balances, movements and closing balances
- **Determine** for each material provision **whether** the **company** has a **present obligation** as a result of past events by:
  - **Reviewing** of **correspondence** relating to the item
  - **Discussion** with the **directors**, have they created a valid expectation in other parties that they will discharge the obligation?
- **Determine** for each material provision **whether** it is **probable** that a **transfer of economic benefits** will be required to settle the obligation by:
  - **Checking** whether any **payments** have been **made** after the year end in respect of the item
  - **Reviewing of correspondence** with solicitors, banks, customers, the insurance company and suppliers both pre and post year end
  - **Sending** a **letter** to the **solicitor** to obtain their views (where relevant)
  - **Discussing** the **position** of similar **past provisions** with the directors. Were these provisions eventually settled?
  - **Considering** the **likelihood** of **reimbursement**
- **Recalculate** all **provisions** made
- **Compare** the **amount provided** with any post year end payments and with any amount paid in the past for similar items
- In the event that it is not possible to estimate the amount of the **provision**, check that this **contingent liability** is **disclosed** in the accounts
- **Consider** the **nature** of the **client's business**. Would you expect to see any other provisions, for example, warranties?

- **Consider** whether disclosures of **provisions, contingent liabilities and contingent assets** are correct and sufficient

2.3.2 Obtaining audit evidence of contingencies

Part of ISA 501 *Audit evidence – specific considerations for selected items* covers contingencies relating to litigation and legal claims, which will represent the major part of audit work on contingencies. Litigation and claims involving the entity may have a material effect on the financial statements, and so will require adjustment to/disclosure in those financial statements.

ISA 501.9

The auditor shall design and perform audit procedures in order to identify litigation and claims involving the entity which may give rise to a risk of material misstatement.

Such procedures would include the following.

- **Make appropriate inquiries of management** including obtaining representations
- **Review board minutes** and correspondence with the entity's lawyers
- **Examine legal expense** account
- **Use any information** obtained regarding the entity's business including information obtained from discussions with any in-house legal department

ISA 501.10

If the auditor assesses a risk of material misstatement regarding litigation or claims that have been identified, or when audit procedures performed indicate that other material litigation or claims may exist, the auditor shall … seek direct communication with the entity's external legal counsel.

This will help to obtain sufficient appropriate audit evidence as to whether potential material litigation and claims are known and management's estimates of the financial implications, including costs, are reliable.

The ISA discusses the form the letter to the entity's external legal counsel should take.

ISA 501.10 (cont'd)

The auditor shall do so though a letter of inquiry, prepared by management and sent by the auditor, requesting the entity's external legal counsel to communicate directly with the auditor.

If it is thought unlikely that the external legal counsel will respond to a general enquiry, the letter should specify the following.

(a)   A list of **litigation and claims**

(b)   **Management's assessment** of the outcome of the litigation or claim and its estimate of the financial implications, including costs involved

(c)   A request that the **external legal counsel confirm the reasonableness** of management's assessments and provide the auditor with further information if the list is considered by the lawyer to be incomplete or incorrect

The auditors must consider these matters up to the date of their report and so a further, updating letter may be necessary. Written representations must be provided that all actual or possible litigations and claims have been disclosed to the auditor.

A meeting between the auditors and the external legal counsel may be required, for example where a complex matter arises, or where there is a disagreement between management and the external legal counsel. Such meetings should take place only with the permission of management, and preferably with a management representative present.

Question   Provisions

In February 20X0 the directors of Newthorpe Engineering Co, a listed company, suspended the managing director. At a disciplinary hearing held by the company on 17 March 20X0 the managing director was dismissed for gross misconduct, and it was decided the managing director's salary should stop from that date and no redundancy or compensation payments should be made.

The managing director has claimed unfair dismissal and is taking legal action against the company to obtain compensation for loss of his employment. The managing director says he has a service contract with the company which would entitle him to two years' salary at the date of dismissal.

The financial statements for the year ended 30 April 20X0 record the resignation of the director. However, they do not mention his dismissal and no provision for any damages has been included in the financial statements.

Required

(a)   State how contingent liabilities should be disclosed in financial statements according to IAS 37 *Provisions, contingent liabilities and contingent assets.*

(b)   Describe the audit work you will carry out to determine whether the company will have to pay damages to the director for unfair dismissal, and the amount of damages and costs which should be included in the financial statements.

      Note. Assume the amounts you are auditing are material.

Answer

(a)   IAS 37 states that a provision should be recognised in the accounts if:

    (i)   An entity has a **present obligation** (legal or constructive) as a result of a past event

    (ii)   A **transfer** of **economic benefits** will **probably** be **required** to settle the obligation

    (iii)   A **reliable estimate** can be **made** of the amount of the obligation.

    Under IAS 37 contingent liabilities should not be recognised. They should however be disclosed unless the prospect of settlement is remote. The entity should disclose:

    (i)   The **nature** of the liability

    (ii)   An estimate of its **financial effect**

    (iii)   The **uncertainties** relating to any possible payments

    (iv)   The likelihood of any **re-imbursement**

(b)   The following tests should be carried out to determine whether the company will have to pay damages and the amount to be included in the financial statements.

    (i)   **Review** the director's **service contract** and **ascertain** the **maximum amount** to which he would be entitled and the **provisions** in the service contract that would **prevent** him making a **claim**, in particular those relating to grounds for justifiable dismissal.

Part D Audit of historical financial information | **10: Evaluation and review (III) matters relating to specific accounting issues**   **279**

(ii) **Review** the results of the **disciplinary hearing. Consider** whether the company has acted in accordance with **employment legislation** and its **internal rules,** the **evidence** presented by the **company** and the defence made by the **director.**

(iii) **Review correspondence** relating to the case and **determine** whether the **company** has **acknowledged** any **liability** to the director that would mean that an amount for compensation should be accrued in accordance with IAS 37.

(iv) **Review correspondence** with the company's **solicitors** and **obtain legal advice**, either from the company's solicitors or another firm, about the likelihood of the claim succeeding.

(v) **Review** correspondence and contact the company's solicitors about the likely **costs** of the case.

(vi) **Consider** the **likelihood** of **costs** and **compensation** being **re-imbursed** by **reviewing** the company's **insurance arrangements** and contacting the insurance company.

(vii) **Consider** the **amounts** that should be **accrued** and the **disclosures** that should be made in the accounts. Legal costs should be accrued, but compensation payments should only be accrued if the company has admitted liability or legal advice indicates that the company's chances of success are very poor. However the claim should be disclosed unless legal advice indicates that the director's chance of success appears to be remote.

(viii) Obtain **written representations** that all details relating to actual cases and other possible litigations have been disclosed to the auditor.

3 Expenses

Borrowing costs must be capitalised as part of the cost of an asset if they are directly attributable to acquisition/construction/production. Other borrowing costs must be expensed.

3.1 Borrowing costs

IAS 23 *Borrowing costs* gives guidance on how to account for borrowing costs.

IAS 23 *Borrowing costs*

IAS 23 deals with the treatment of borrowing costs, often associated with the construction of **self-constructed assets**, but which may also be applied to an asset purchased that takes time to get ready for use/sale.

Definitions

- **Borrowing costs.** Interest and other costs incurred by an entity in connection with the borrowing of funds.

- **Qualifying asset.** An asset that necessarily takes a substantial period of time to get ready for its intended use or sale.

Accounting treatment

- Borrowing costs should be **capitalised** as part of the cost of the asset if they are directly attributable to acquisition/construction/production. Other borrowing costs must be expensed.

- **Borrowing costs eligible for capitalisation** are those that would have been avoided otherwise. Use judgement where a range of debt instruments is held for general finance.

- **Amount of borrowing costs available for capitalisation** is actual borrowing costs incurred less any investment income from temporary investment of those borrowings.

- For borrowings obtained generally, apply the **capitalisation rate** to the expenditure on the asset (weighted average borrowing costs). It must not exceed actual borrowing costs.

- **Capitalisation is suspended** if active development is interrupted for extended periods. (Temporary delays or technical/administrative work will not cause suspension.)
- **Capitalisation ceases** (normally) when physical construction of the asset is completed, capitalisation should cease when each stage or part is completed.
- Where the carrying amount of the asset falls below cost, it must be **written down/off**.

Disclosure

- **Accounting policy** note.
- Amount of **borrowing costs capitalised** during the period.
- **Capitalisation rate** used to determine borrowing costs eligible for capitalisation.

The **cost of borrowing is interest**, which is disclosed in the statement of comprehensive income.

Interest can often be audited by **analytical review**, as it has a predictable relationship with loans (for example, bank loans or debentures).

Alternatively it can be **verified to payment records** (bank statements) **and loan agreement** documents.

However, if borrowing costs are capitalised in accordance with IAS 23 the auditor should carry out the following procedures:

- Agree figures in respect of interest payments made to statements from lender and/or bank statements
- Ensure interest is directly attributable to construction

3.2 IAS 19 *Employee benefits*

IAS 19 *Employee benefits* covers the accounting for post-employment benefits, and was revised in 2011. Pension schemes are the most obvious example, but an employer might provide post-employment death benefits to the dependants of former employees, or post-employment medical care.

Post-employment benefit schemes are often referred to as 'plans'. The 'plan' receives regular contributions from the employer (and sometimes from current employees as well) and the money is invested in assets, such as stocks and shares and other investments. The post-employment benefits are paid out of the income from the plan assets (dividends, interest) or from money from the sale of some plan assets.

There are two types or categories of post-employment benefit plan: defined contribution plans and defined benefit plans.

3.2.1 IAS 19 recap

Accounting for payments into defined contribution plans is straightforward.

(a) The obligation is determined by the amount paid into the plan in each period.
(b) There are no actuarial assumptions to make.
(c) If the obligation is settled in the current period (or at least no later than 12 months after the end of the current period) there is no requirement for discounting.

IAS 19 requires the following.

(a) Contributions to a defined contribution plan should be recognised as an expense in the period they are payable (except to the extent that labour costs may be included within the cost of assets).
(b) Any liability for unpaid contributions that are due as at the end of the period should be recognised as a liability (accrued expense).
(c) Any excess contributions paid should be recognised as an asset (prepaid expense), but only to the extent that the prepayment will lead to, eg a reduction in future payments or a cash refund.

(d)   Disclosure is required of a description of the plan and the amount recognised as an expense in the period.

Accounting for defined benefit plans is much more complex. The complexity of accounting for defined benefit plans stems largely from the following factors.

(a)   The future benefits (arising from employee service in the current or prior years) cannot be estimated exactly, but whatever they are, the employer will have to pay them, and the liability should therefore be recognised now. To estimate these future obligations, it is necessary to use actuarial assumptions.

(b)   The obligations payable in future years should be valued, by discounting, on a present value basis. This is because the obligations may be settled in many years' time.

(c)   If actuarial assumptions change, the amount of required contributions to the fund will change, and there may be actuarial gains or losses. A contribution into a fund in any period is not necessarily the total for that period, due to actuarial gains or losses.

An outline of the method used for an employer to account for the expenses and obligation of a defined benefit plan is given below.

Step 1   **Determine the deficit or surplus**:

(a)   An **Actuarial technique** (the **Projected Unit Credit Method**), should be used to make a reliable estimate of the amount of future benefits employees have earned from service in relation to the current and prior years. The entity must determine how much benefit should be attributed to service performed by employees in the current period, and in prior periods. Assumptions include, for example, assumptions about employee turnover, mortality rates, future increases in salaries (if these will affect the eventual size of future benefits such as pension payments).

(b)   The benefit should be **discounted** to arrive at the present value of the defined benefit obligation and the current service cost.

(c)   The **fair value** of any **plan assets** should be deducted from the present value of the defined benefit obligation.

Step 2   The surplus or deficit determined in Step 1 may have to be adjusted if a net benefit asset has to be restricted by the **asset ceiling**.

Step 3   Determine the amounts to be recognised in **profit or loss**:

(a)   **Current service cost**

(b)   Any **past service cost** and **gain or loss on settlement**

(c)   **Net interest** on the **net defined benefit (asset)**

Step 4   Determine the **remeasurements** of the **net defined benefit (asset)**, to be recognised in **other comprehensive income**:

(a)   **Actuarial gains and losses**

(b)   **Return on plan assets** (excluding amounts included in net interest on the net defined benefit liability (asset)

(c)   Any change in the effect of the **asset ceiling** (excluding amounts included in net interest on the net defined benefit liability (asset)

In the statement of financial position, the amount recognised as a **defined benefit liability** (which may be a negative amount, ie an asset) should be the following.

(a)   The **present value of the defined obligation** at the year end, **minus**

(b)   The **fair value of the assets of the plan** as at the year end (if there are any) out of which the future obligations to current and past employees will be directly settled.

Plan assets are:

(a)   Assets such as stocks and shares, held by a fund that is legally separate from the reporting entity, which exists solely to pay employee benefits.

(b)   Insurance policies, issued by an insurer that is not a related party, the proceeds of which can only be used to pay employee benefits.

Investments which may be used for purposes other than to pay employee benefits are not plan assets.

The standard requires that the plan assets are measured at fair value, as 'the price that would be received to sell an asset in an orderly transaction between market participants at the measurement date.

IAS 19 includes the following specific requirements:

(a)   The plan assets should exclude any contributions due from the employer but not yet paid.

(b)   Plan assets are reduced by any liabilities of the fund that do not relate to employee benefits, such as trade and other payables.

All of the gains and losses that affect the plan obligation and plan asset must be recognised. The **components of defined benefit cost must be recognised as follows** in the statement of profit or loss and other comprehensive income:

Component	Recognised in:
(a) **Service cost**	Profit or loss
(b) **Net interest on the net defined benefit liability**	Profit or loss
(c) **Remeasurements of the net defined benefit liability**	Other comprehensive income

3.2.2 Audit evidence

Area	Procedures
Scheme assets (including quoted and unquoted securities, debt instruments, properties)	• Ask directors to reconcile the scheme assets valuation at the scheme year end date with the assets valuation at the reporting entity's date being used for IAS 19 purposes • Obtain direct confirmation of the scheme assets from the Investment custodian • Consider requiring scheme auditors to perform procedures

Scheme liabilities	• Auditors must follow the principles of ISA 620 *Using the work of an expert* to assess whether it is appropriate to rely on the actuary's work
	• Specific matters would include
	  – The source data used
	  – The assumptions and methods used
	  – The results of actuaries' work in the light of auditors' knowledge of the business and results of other audit procedures

	Actuarial source data is likely to include: • Scheme member data (for example, classes of member and contribution details) • Scheme asset information (for example, values and income and expenditure items)

Area	Procedures
Actuarial assumptions (for example, mortality rates, termination rates, retirement age and changes in salary and benefit levels)	Auditors will not have the same expertise as actuaries and are unlikely to be able to challenge the appropriateness and reasonableness of the assumptions. Auditors can, however, through discussion with directors and actuaries: • Obtain a general understanding of the assumptions and review the process used to develop them • Compare the assumptions with those which directors have used in prior years • Consider whether, based on their knowledge of the reporting entity and the scheme, and on the results of other audit procedures, the assumptions appear to be reasonable and compatible with those used elsewhere in the preparation of the entity's financial statements • Obtain written representations from directors confirming that the assumptions are consistent with their knowledge of the business
Items charged to operating profit (current service cost, past service cost, gains and losses on settlements and curtailments, interest)	• Discuss with directors and actuaries the factors affecting current service cost (for example, a scheme closed to new entrants may see an increase year on year as a percentage of pay with the average age of the workforce increasing)

Where the results of actuaries' work is inconsistent with the directors', additional procedures, such as requesting directors to obtain evidence from another actuary, may assist in resolving the inconsistency.

3.3 Share-based payment   12/08

IFRS 2 *Share-based payment* sets out rules for the measurement of expenses relating to share-based payment schemes. These arise most commonly in relation to payments for employee services and professional services.

3.3.1 IFRS 2 Recap

IFRS 2 requires entities to recognise the goods or services received as a result of share-based payment transactions.

There are three types of share-based payment transactions.

(a)   **Equity-settled share-based payment transactions**, in which the entity receives goods or services in exchange for equity instruments of the entity.

(b)   **Cash-settled share-based payment transactions**, in which the entity receives goods or services in exchange for amounts of cash that are based on the price (or value) of the entity's shares or other equity instruments of the entity.

(c)   Transactions in which the entity receives or acquires goods or services and either the entity or the supplier has a **choice** as to whether the entity settles the transaction in cash (or other assets) or by issuing equity instruments.

An entity should recognise goods or services received or acquired in a share-based payment transaction when it obtains the goods or as the services are received. They should be recognised as expenses unless they qualify for recognition as assets. Transactions are measured at fair value.

•   Equity-settled transactions:

DEBIT   Assets/expense
CREDIT   Equity

- Cash-settled transactions:

  DEBIT   Asset/expense
  CREDIT   Liability

3.3.2 Audit risks and evidence

The general audit risk here is that the requirements of IFRS 2 are not adhered to. This is a complex area of financial reporting, particularly in practice, and is therefore risky to audit. The risk is that the share-based payment is not measured correctly in relation to any conditions attached to the scheme.

The auditor will require evidence in respect of all the estimates feeding into the IFRS 2 calculation, in addition to reperforming the calculation itself for the expense for the current year.

Issue	Evidence
Number of employees in scheme/**number of instruments per employee/length of vesting period**.	Revenue scheme details set out in a contractual documentation
Number of employees estimated to benefit	• Enquire of directors • Compare to staffing numbers per forecasts and prediction
Fair value of instruments	• For equity-settled schemes check that fair value is estimated at **measured date** • For cash-settled schemes check that the fair value is recalculated at the **year end** and at the **date of settlement** • Check that model used to estimate fair value is in line with IFRS 2
General	Obtain written representations from management confirming their view that: • The assumptions used in measuring the expense are reasonable, and • There are no share-based payment schemes in existence that have not been disclosed to the auditors.

Exam focus point

A question in the December 2008 exam asked for a description of audit procedures in relation to share-based payments.

4 Disclosure

FAST FORWARD

The auditor must ensure disclosures in the financial statements are fairly stated.

4.1 Segment reporting

The disclosure of segmental information is governed by IFRS 8 *Operating segments*.

IFRS 8 *Operating segments*

An **operating segment** is a component of an entity:

• That engages in business activities from which it may earn revenues and incur expenses (including revenues and expenses relating to transactions with other components of the same entity);

- Whose operating results are reviewed regularly by the entity's chief operating decision maker to make decisions about resources to be allocated to the segment and assess its performance; and
- For which discrete financial information is available.

IFRS 8 requires an entity to report financial and descriptive information about its reportable segments. **Reportable segments** are operating segments or aggregations of operating segments that meet specified criteria:

- Its reported revenue, from both external customers and intersegment sales or transfers, is 10% or more of the combined revenue, internal and external, of all operating segments; or
- The absolute measure of its reported profit or loss is 10% or more of the greater, in absolute amount, of (i) the combined reported profit of all operating segments that did not report a loss and (ii) the combined reported loss of all operating segments that reported a loss; or
- Its assets are 10% or more of the combined assets of all operating segments.

If the total external revenue reported by operating segments constitutes less than 75% of the entity's revenue, additional operating segments must be identified as reportable segments (even if they do not meet the quantitative thresholds set out above) until at least 75% of the entity's revenue is included in reportable segments.

ISA 501 *Audit evidence - specific considerations for selected items* contains specific guidance on segment reporting.

ISA 501.13

The auditor shall obtain sufficient appropriate audit evidence regarding the presentation and disclosure of segment information in accordance with the applicable financial reporting framework by:

(a) Obtaining an understanding of the methods used by management in determining segment information, and:

   (i) Evaluating whether such methods are likely to result in disclosure in accordance with the applicable financial reporting framework; and

   (ii) Where appropriate, testing the application of such methods; and

(b) Performing analytical procedures or other audit procedures appropriate in the circumstances.

The following procedures are relevant:

- Obtain a client schedule of revenue workings
- Discuss with management the basis for the segmentation and ensure that the basis for segmentation mirrors that used for internal reporting purposes (IFRS 8)
- Verify a sample of items to backing documentation (invoices) to ensure disclosure is correct.

A key risk for auditors here is **management bias** in disclosure. This risk is particularly pronounced because IFRS 8 takes a **management approach** to reportable segments, which opens up the possibility of management adjusting its approach in order to change the way segment information is disclosed. For example there is a risk that loss-making segments could effectively go unreported or be hidden within other segments,

4.2 Earnings per share   6/09

Accounting for earnings per share is governed by IAS 33 *Earnings per share*. It requires that companies of a certain size disclose their earnings per share for the year.

Basic earnings per share should be calculated by dividing the net profit or loss for the period attributable to ordinary equity holders by the weighted average number of ordinary shares outstanding during the period as follows:

$$\frac{\text{Net profit /(loss) attributable to ordinary shareholders}}{\text{Weighted average number of ordinary shares outstanding during the period}}$$

Fontmell Co has profit of $1.5 million for the year ended 31 December 20X8. On 1 January 20X8 the company had 500,000 shares in issue. During 20X8 the company announced a rights issue as follows:

Rights: One new share for every five outstanding (100,000 new shares in total)

Exercise price : $5.00

Last date to exercise rights: 1 March 20X8

Market (fair) value of one share in Fontmell immediately prior to exercise on 1 March 20X8: $11.00

The EPS for 20X7 as originally stated was $2.20.

Answer

Computation of theoretical ex-rights price

$$\frac{\begin{array}{c}\text{Fair value of all outstanding shares +}\\ \text{total received from exercise of rights}\end{array}}{\begin{array}{c}\text{Number of shares outstanding prior to exercise +}\\ \text{number of shares issued in exercise}\end{array}} = \frac{(\$11.00 \times 500,000) + (\$5.00 \times 100,000)}{500,000 + 100,000} = \$10.00$$

20X8 EPS

$$\frac{\$1,500,000}{(500,000 \times {}^{2}\!/_{12} \times {}^{11}\!/_{10}) + (600,000 \times {}^{10}\!/_{12})} = \$2.54$$

20X7 EPS (restated)

$$2.20 \times {}^{10}\!/_{11} = \$2.00$$

Diluted earnings per share is calculated by adjusting the net profit attributable to ordinary shareholders and the weighted average number of shares outstanding for the effects of all dilutive potential ordinary shares.

These include:

- A **separate class of equity shares** which at present is not entitled to any dividend, but will be entitled in future.
- **Convertible loan** stock or **convertible preferred shares**.
- **Options** or **warrants**.

The calculation would be as follows:

$$\frac{\text{Diluted earnings}}{\text{Diluted weighted average number of shares}}$$

		$
Diluted earnings =	Basic earnings	X
	Interest saved on convertible debt (net of tax saving)	X
		X
Diluted shares =	Basic weighted average	X
	Convertible debt: additional shares on conversion	X
	Share options: potential shares less shares purchasable at FV	X
		X

Finally, if an entity reports a **discontinued operation** under IFRS 5 (see below), then it must **disclose the basic and diluted EPS** for the discontinued operation.

4.2.1 Audit issues

The size of the figure is unlikely to be material in itself, but it is a key investor figure. As it will be of **interest to all the investors** who read it, it is **material by its nature**.

When considering earnings per share, the auditor must consider **two issues**:

- Whether it has been disclosed on a comparable basis to the prior year, and whether any changes in accounting policy have been disclosed, and
- Whether it has been calculated correctly

A key audit risk is that the entity fails to meet IAS 33's disclosure requirements. These are:

(a)   The amounts used as the **numerators** in calculating basic and diluted EPS, and a **reconciliation** of those amounts to the net profit or loss for the period

(b)   The weighted average number of ordinary shares used as the **denominator** in calculating basic and diluted EPS, and a **reconciliation** of these denominators to each other.

The audit procedures are as follows:

> - Obtain a copy of the client's workings for earnings per share. (If a simple calculation has been used, this can be checked by re-doing the fraction on the face of the income statement.)
> - Compare the calculation with the prior year calculation to ensure that the basis is comparable.
> - Discuss the basis with the directors if it has changed to ascertain if it is the best basis for the accounts this year and whether the change has been adequately disclosed.
> - Recalculate to ensure that it is correct.

4.3 Discontinued operations

Discontinued operations are accounted for under IFRS 5 *Non-current assets held for sale and discontinued operations*. The IFRS requires that certain disclosures are made for discontinued operations in the statement of comprehensive income or in the notes. This may well be material for the following reasons:

- Potentially material through **size**
- May be **inherently material** if the change in operations is a sign of management policy or a major change in focus of operations

Essentially, the fact that some operations have been discontinued is of interest to shareholders, which is why the IFRS 5 disclosures came about.

IFRS 5 requires that assets which meet the criteria 'held for sale' are shown at the lower of carrying amount and fair value less costs to sell, and that held for sale assets are classified separately on the statement of financial position and the results of discontinued operations are presented separately in the statement of comprehensive income. Held for sale assets are discussed in Chapter 9.

To require separate classification in the statement of comprehensive income, discontinued operations must be:

> - A component (ie separately identifiable)
> - Which represents a separate major line of business/geographical area
> - In part of a single co-ordinated plan to dispose of a separate major line of business/geographical area
> - Or is a subsidiary acquired exclusively with a view to resale

An entity should **present and disclose information** that enables users of the financial statements to evaluate the financial effects of **discontinued operations** and disposals of non-current assets or disposal groups.

This allows users to distinguish between operations which will continue in the future and those which will not and makes it more possible to predict future results.

An entity should disclose a **single amount** in the statement of comprehensive income comprising the total of:

(a)   The **post-tax profit or loss** of discontinued operations and

(b)   The post-tax gain or loss recognised on the **measurement to fair value less costs to sell** or on the disposal of the assets or disposal group(s) constituting the discontinued operation.

An entity should also disclose an **analysis** of this single amount into:

(a)   The revenue, expenses and pre-tax profit or loss of discontinued operations

(b)   The related income tax expense

(c)   The gain or loss recognised on the measurement to fair value less costs to sell or on the disposal of the assets of the discontinued operation

(d)   The related income tax expense

This may be presented either in the statement of comprehensive income or in the notes. If it is presented in the statement of comprehensive income it should be presented in a section identified as relating to discontinued operations, ie separately from continuing operations. This analysis is not required where the discontinued operation is a newly acquired subsidiary that has been classified as held for sale.

An entity should disclose the **net cash flows** attributable to the operating, investing and financing activities of discontinued operations. These disclosures may be presented either on the face of the statement of cash flows or in the notes.

Relevant audit procedures include:

- Obtaining accounting records for component to ensure it is separately identifiable
- Review company documentation (such as annual report) to ensure it is separately identifiable
- Review minutes of meetings/make enquiries of management to ascertain management's intentions

To audit whether the disclosures have been made correctly, the auditor should undertake the following procedures:

- Obtain a copy of the client's workings to disclose the discontinued operations.
- Review the workings to ensure that the figures are reasonable and agree to the financial statements.
- Trace a sample of items disclosed as discontinuing items to backing documentation (invoices) to ensure that they do relate to discontinued operations.

4.4 Statements of cash flows

Statements of cash flows are accounted for under the provisions of IAS 7 *Statement of cash flows*. The statement of cash flows is essentially a reconciliation exercise between items in the statement of comprehensive income (operating profit) and the statement of financial position (cash).

As such, the statement of cash flows is often audited **by the auditor reproducing it from the audited figures in the other financial statements**. This can be done quickly and easily in the modern era by use of computer programmes.

However, if the auditor wished to audit it another way, he could check and recalculate each reconciliation with the financial statements. This would involve checking each line of the statement by working through the client's workings and agreeing items to the accounting records and backing documentation (for example, tax paid to the bank statements) and the other financial statements.

Question

Why is the statement of cash flows relevant to the auditors?

Answer

Report on the statement of cash flows

The statement of cash flows is specified in the audit report, as a statement the auditors are reporting on. Financial reports are obliged to include a statement of cash flows under IAS 7 in order to show a true and fair view. The auditors must therefore assess the truth and fairness of the statement of cash flows as required by IAS 7.

Analytical review

The information in the statement of cash flows will be used by the auditors as part of their analytical review of the accounts, for example, by adding further information on liquidity. This will be particularly helpful when comparing the statement to previous periods.

Going concern

The statement of cash flows may indicate going concern problems due to liquidity failings, overtrading and overgearing. However, the statement is an historical document, prepared well after the year-end, and is therefore unlikely to be the first indicator of such difficulties.

Audit evidence

The auditors will obtain very little direct audit evidence from the statement of cash flows. It has been prepared by the company (not the auditors or an independent third party) from records which are under scrutiny by the auditors in any case. Thus the auditors will already have most of this information, although in a different format.

However, the statement of cash flows should provide additional evidence for figures in the accounts, for example, the purchase or sale of tangible non-current assets. Consistency of evidence will be important and complementary evidence is always welcome.

Question

You work for Pitmans, a firm of chartered certified accountants. Tinga Co is a long-standing client of your firm, but this is the first year that Pitmans has carried out the audit. The firm also provides a number of other services to Tinga, including a range of tax planning services and business advisory services. Recently, the firm undertook a review of some forecast financial statements, which Tinga was required to present to the bank.

You have been asked to plan the forthcoming audit of the financial statements for the period ending 31 March 20X8. You have been given the following draft statement of financial position.

	20X8		20X7	
	$'000	$'000	$'000	$'000
ASSETS				
Non-current assets				
Tangible non-current assets		10,101		12,378
Investments		10,000		2,000
Current assets				
Inventory	196		191	
Receivables	1,012		678	
Bank	–		149	
Prepayments	4		5	
		1,212		1,023
		21,313		15,401
EQUITY AND LIABILITIES				
Equity				
Share capital		100		100
Share premium		1,000		1,000
Revaluation reserve		2,000		–
Retained earnings		(5,217)		(8,601)
		(2,117)		(7,501)
Long-term liabilities				
Bank loan		12,325		17,002
Deferred tax		5,000		5,000
Current liabilities				
Trade payables	938		900	
Bank overdraft	1,168		–	
Bank loan	3,999		–	
		6,105		900
		21,313		15,401

Required

Comment on any points arising for your planning of the audit for the year end 31 March 20X8. Your comments should include issues relating to risk and materiality, accounting issues and audit evidence issues and any limitations of the review you have undertaken to date. You should also highlight any further information that you intend to seek.

Approaching the answer

Question Accounting issues and audit evidence

You work for Pitmans, a firm of chartered certified accountants. Tinga Co is a long-standing client of your firm, but this is the first year that Pitmans has carried out the audit. The firm also provides a number of other services to Tinga, including a range of tax planning services and business advisory services. Recently, the firm undertook a review of some forecast financial statements, which Tinga was required to present to the bank.

You have been asked to plan the forthcoming audit of the financial statements for the period ending 31 March 20X8. You have been given the following draft statement of financial position.

	20X8		20X7	
	$'000	$'000	$'000	$'000
ASSETS				
Non-current assets				
Tangible non-current assets		10,101		12,378
Investments		10,000		2,000
Current assets				
Inventory	196		191	
Receivables	1,012		678	
Bank	–		149	
Prepayments	4		5	
		1,212		1,023
		21,313		15,401
EQUITY AND LIABILITIES				
Equity				
Share capital		100		100
Share premium		1,000		1,000
Revaluation reserve		2,000		–
Retained earnings		(5,217)		(8,601)
		2,117		7,501
Long-term liabilities				
Bank loan		12,325		17,002
Deferred tax		5,000		5,000
Current liabilities				
Trade payables	938		900	
Bank overdraft	1,168		–	
Bank loan	3,999		–	
		6,105		900
		21,313		15,401

Required

Comment on any points arising for your planning of the audit for the year end 31 March 20X8. Your comments should include issues relating to risk and materiality, accounting issues and audit evidence issues and any limitations of the review you have undertaken to date. You should also highlight any further information that you intend to seek.

Answer

Matters arising from preliminary review

Going concern

The statements of financial position show a worsening cash position over the year. There are some classic indicators of going concern problems.

- Substantial liabilities
- Excess of current liabilities over current assets
- Bank overdraft
- Substantial increase in receivables
- Bank requiring future profit forecasts, which have been verified by our firm

A profit has been made in the year, but it does not appear that sales are readily being converted into cash.

Sources of audit evidence

- Profit forecasts
- Correspondence with bank
- Any business plans in existence (consult with business advisory department)

Further information required

- We need to confirm for the audit file why the bank required profit forecasts
- We need to review for audit purposes the results of our work on those forecasts
- For the purposes of our audit we must satisfy ourselves that Tinga is a going concern

Three items on the accounts stand out as being particularly interesting at a planning stage. These are:

- Deferred tax
- Increase in investments
- Revaluation in the year

Deferred tax

We will need to confirm what the deferred tax relates to, particularly as the non-current assets in the statement of financial position do not seem particularly high. The deferred tax balance does not appear to have moved, despite the movements on non-current assets. We will have to check that deferred tax has been accounted for correctly in accordance with IAS 12.

Increase in investments

Investments are usually a straightforward area to audit with good audit evidence existing in terms of share certificates and valuation certificates.

However, as investments have increased, we must ensure that they have been accounted for correctly. We must also ensure that the increase does not represent a holding in another company that would require the results being consolidated into group results.

Revaluation

There appears to have been a revaluation in the year, although non-current assets have in fact decreased. We must discover what the revaluation reserve relates to, and ensure that it has been accounted for correctly.

Materiality

All the accounting issues discussed above are potentially material to the statement of financial position. Non-current assets is the key balance which does not show a liability. As the statement of financial position shows high liabilities, any as yet unrecorded impairment in either tangible non-current assets or investments could make the position of the company significantly worse. Conversely, if the liability shown in deferred tax was overstated, this would have the reverse effect.

Limitations of current review

The current review has only taken account of the statement of financial position, so is an incomplete picture. At present, we can only guess at factors in the statement of comprehensive income which have had implications for the statement of financial position.

As this is a first year audit, and the audit department is not familiar with this client, we have little knowledge of the business to apply to this review.

It is important as part of the planning process that the audit partner and/or manager enter into discussions with the various departments which have dealings with Tinga to increase their knowledge of the business and to obtain audit evidence on issues such as going concern.

However, it is also important for the audit team to bear in mind that, as auditors, they must maintain their independence towards the audit. There is a danger to the audit firm of loss of objectivity in respect of this audit due to the other services offered to the client, which must not be forgotten.

4.5 Changes in accounting policy

Where accounting standards allow alternative treatment of items in the accounts, then the accounting policy note should declare which policy has been chosen. It should then be applied consistently.

The effect of a change in accounting policy is treated as a retrospective adjustment to the opening balance of each affected component of equity as if the accounting policy had always applied.

IAS 8 *Accounting policies, changes in accounting estimates and errors* states that changes in accounting policies are rare, and only allowed if required by statute or if the change results in more reliable and relevant information.

Take care not to confuse a change in **accounting policy** with a **change in accounting estimate**. A change in policy is rare and per IAS 8 should be accounted for retrospectively, but a change in estimate (such as the method for calculating depreciation) is accounted for going forward (prospectively).

An example of a change in **accounting estimate** is a change to an entity's **depreciation policy**. In this case, the entity's accounting *policy* is *to depreciate non-current assets*, and the 'depreciation policy' (which would include eg reducing balance or straight line depreciation, estimates of useful lives, etc) is merely the policy chosen by management in order to estimate how much depreciation should be charged.

Changes in accounting policy will be rare and should be made only if :

(a)   The change is required by an IFRS; or

(b)   The change will result in a **more appropriate presentation** of events or transactions in the financial statements of the entity, providing more reliable and relevant information.

The standard highlights two types of event which do not constitute changes in accounting policy.

(a)   Adopting an accounting policy for a **new type of transaction** or event not dealt with previously by the entity.

(b)   Adopting a **new accounting policy** for a transaction or event which has not occurred in the past or which was not material.

Chapter Roundup

- Revenue recognition is an extremely important issue and completeness is a key assertion to be audited.

- The relevant financial statement assertions for liabilities are completeness, rights and obligations and existence. Liabilities must be tested for understatement.

- The classification of a lease can have a material effect on the financial statements.

- The auditor needs to audit the movement on the deferred tax liability.

- A provision is accounted for as a liability, contingencies are disclosed, so auditors must ensure they have been classified correctly according to IAS 37.

- Borrowing costs must be capitalised as part of the cost of an asset if they are directly attributable to acquisition/construction/production. Other borrowing costs must be expensed.

- The auditor must ensure disclosures in the financial statements are fairly stated.

Part D Audit of historical financial information | **10: Evaluation and review (III) matters relating to specific accounting issues**   295

1   Complete the definition.

A .... lease is one that transfers substantially all the .... and .... incident to ownership of an asset.

2   Sort the following valuation tests into those relevant for finance leases and those relevant to operating leases.

- Obtain client's workings
- Ensure interest calculated in accordance with IAS 17
- Agree the opening position
- Agree new assets to lease agreements
- Verify payments to bank statements

3   Name three types of contingency often disclosed by companies.

(1)   ....

(2)   ....

(3)   ....

4   The auditor may request information directly from the client's solicitors.

True   ☐   False   ☐

5   Link the disclosure issue with the accounting guidance

(a)	Segmental information	(i)	IAS 18
(b)	EPS	(ii)	IFRS 8
(c)	Discontinued operations	(iii)	IFRS 5
(d)	Revenue recognition	(iv)	IAS 33

6   Why is EPS disclosure likely to be material?

7   Which of the following is not a reason why revenue is often audited by analytical review?

(1)   Availability of good, comparable evidence
(2)   Statement of comprehensive income is not as important as statement of financial position
(3)   It is quicker than detailed substantive testing
(4)   Revenue has logical relationships with other items in the financial statements

8   Which of the following audit procedures relate to capitalised grants and which to grants put straight to income?

- Obtain relating documentation and ensure classification is correct.

- Agree value receipt of grant to:

    – Documentation (above)
    – Bank statements

- Consider reasonableness of transfers to revenue

- Ensure capitalisation method is comparable

9   Auditors do not report on the statement of cash flows (only the statement of financial position and statement of comprehensive income as recorded in the opinion section of the report).

True   ☐   False   ☐

Answers to Quick Quiz

1   Finance, risks, rewards

2
- Obtain client's workings   F
- Ensure interest calculated in accordance with IAS 17   F
- Agree the opening position   F
- Agree new assets to lease agreements   F
- Verify payments to bank statements   F and O

3   From:

   (1)   Guarantees
   (2)   Discounted bills of exchange
   (3)   Uncalled liabilities on shares
   (4)   Lawsuits/claims pending
   (5)   Options to purchase assets

4   True. However the letter should be written by management and sent by the auditor.

5   (a)(ii), (b)(iv), (c)(iii), (d)(i).

6   It is of interest to the key readers of accounts – the shareholders.

7   (2) The statement of comprehensive income **is just as important.** However, (3) **is true,** because it is cost effective to use analytical review as a substantive procedure where good evidence is available.

8
- Obtain relating documentation and ensure classification is correct.   C/I

- Agree value receipt of grant to: C/I

  – Documentation (above)
  – Bank statements

- Consider reasonableness of transfers to revenue   C

- Ensure capitalisation method is comparable   C

9   False

Now try the questions below from the Exam Question Bank

Number	Level	Marks	Time
Q16	Examination	15	27 mins
Q17	Examination	20	36 mins

Part D Audit of historical financial information │ **10: Evaluation and review (III) matters relating to specific accounting issues**   **297**

Group audits and transnational audits

11

Topic list	Syllabus reference
1 Group accounting recap	D2
2 Associates and joint ventures recap	D2
3 Audit of groups	D2
4 The consolidation: problems and procedures	D2
5 Joint audits	D2
6 Transnational audits	G3

Introduction

This is a new auditing topic for you, one which is concerned with practical difficulties of communication between auditors and the issues of geography.

In auditing group accounts, as in so many other areas, the auditors require detailed accounting knowledge in order to fulfil their responsibilities.

Group audits fall into two categories:

(1) Where the same firm of auditors audits the whole group

(2) Where one firm of auditors has responsibility for the opinion on the consolidated accounts and a different firm audits part of the group

Even where the audit of each individual company in the group is carried out by the same firm, there may be administrative complications where some audits are carried out by different branches, perhaps overseas, with different practices and procedures.

Study guide

		Intellectual level
D2	**Group audits**	
(a)	Recognise the specific matters to be considered before accepting appointment as principal auditor to a group in a given situation.	3
(b)	Identify and explain the matters specific to planning an audit or group financial statements including assessment of group and component materiality, the impact of non-coterminous year ends within a group, and changes in group structure.	2
(c)	Justify the situations where a joint audit would be appropriate.	2
(d)	Recognise the audit problems and describe audit procedures specific to a business combination, including goodwill, accounting policies, inter-company trading, the classification of investments, equity accounting for associates, changes in group structure and accounting for a foreign subsidiary.	3
(e)	Identify and explain the audit risks, and necessary audit procedures relevant to the consolidation process.	3
(f)	Identify and describe the matters to be considered and the procedures to be performed at the planning stage when a group auditor considers the use of the work of component auditors.	3
(g)	Consider how the auditor should evaluate the audit work performed by a component auditor.	2
(h)	Explain the implications for the auditor's report on the financial statements of an entity where the opinion on a component is qualified or otherwise modified in a given situation.	2
G3	**Transnational audits**	
(a)	Define 'transnational audits' and explain the role of the Transnational Audit Committee (TAC) of IFAC.	1
(b)	Discuss how transnational audits may differ from other audits of historical financial information (eg in terms of applicable financial reporting and auditing standards, listing requirements and corporate governance requirements).	2

Exam guide

Group audits are likely to be tested in case study type questions. These are likely to include issues relating to acceptance of appointment and working with other auditors as well as specific matters relating to accounting for the consolidation.

1 Group accounting recap

You will have covered IFRS 3 *Business combinations* in your P2 studies. The other accounting standards relating to groups have recently been revised. They are:

- IAS 27 *(revised) Separate financial statements*
- IFRS 10 *Consolidated financial statements*
- IFRS 11 *Joint arrangements*
- IFRS 12 *Disclosure of interests in other entities*
- IAS 28 *Investments in associates*

The key points that you should be aware of are summarised below.

1.1 Content of group accounts

Consolidated (or group) accounts combine the information contained in the separate accounts of a holding company and its subsidiaries as if they were the accounts of a single entity.

- **Control**. An investor controls an investee when the investor is exposed, or has rights, to variable returns from its involvement with the investee and has the ability to affect those returns through power over the investee. *(IFRS 10)*

- **Power**. Existing rights that give the current ability to direct the relevant activities of the investee *(IFRS 10)*

- **Subsidiary**. An entity that is controlled by another entity. *(IFRS 10)*

- **Parent**. An entity that controls one or more subsidiaries. *(IFRS 10)*

- **Group**. A parent and all its subsidiaries. *(IFRS 10)*

- **Associate**. An entity over which an investor has significant influence and which is neither a subsidiary nor an interest in a joint venture. *(IFRS 10)*

- **Significant influence** is the power to participate in the financial and operating policy decisions of an investee but is not control or joint control over those policies. *(IAS 28)*

1.2 Investments in subsidiaries

The important point here is **control**. In most cases, this will involve the holding company or parent owning a majority of the ordinary shares in the subsidiary (to which normal voting rights are attached). There are circumstances, however, when the parent may own only a minority of the voting power in the subsidiary, *but* the parent still has control.

IFRS 10 provides a definition of control and identifies three separate elements of control:

An investor controls an investee if and only if it has all of the following:

1) Power over the investee

2) Exposure to, or rights to, variable returns from its involvement with the investee; and

3) The ability to use its power over the investee to affect the amount of the investor's returns

If there are changes to one or more of these three elements of control, then an investor should reassess whether it controls an investee.

Power (as defined under Key Terms) can be obtained directly from ownership of the majority of voting rights or can be derived from other rights, such as:

- Rights to appoint, reassign or remove key management personnel who can direct the relevant activities

- Rights to appoint or remove another entity that directs the relevant activities

- Rights to direct the investee to enter into, or veto changes to, transactions for the benefit of the investor

- Other rights, such as those specified in a management contract.

1.3 Investments in associates

This type of investment is something less than a subsidiary, but more than a simple investment. The key criterion here is **significant influence**. This is defined as the 'power to participate', but *not* to 'control' (which would make the investment a subsidiary).

Significant influence can be determined by the holding of voting rights (usually attached to shares) in the entity. IAS 28 states that if an investor holds **20% or more** of the voting power of the investee, it can be presumed that the investor has significant influence over the investee, *unless* it can be clearly shown that this is not the case.

Significant influence can be presumed *not* to exist if the investor holds **less than 20%** of the voting power of the investee, unless it can be demonstrated otherwise.

The **existence of significant influence** is evidenced in one or more of the following ways.

(a)   Representation on the **board of directors** (or equivalent) of the investee

(b)   Participation in the **policy making process**

(c)   **Material transactions** between investor and investee

(d)   Interchange of management personnel

(e)   Provision of essential technical information

IAS 28 requires the use of the **equity method** of accounting for investments in associates.

1.4 Goodwill and the non-controlling interest

1.4.1 Non-controlling interests

The total assets and liabilities of subsidiary companies are included in the consolidated statement of financial position, even in the case of subsidiaries which are only partly owned. A proportion of the net assets of such subsidiaries in fact belongs to investors from outside the group (**non-controlling interests**).

IFRS 3 allows two alternative ways of calculating non-controlling interest in the group statement of financial position. Non-controlling interest can be valued at:

(a)   Its proportionate share of the fair value of the subsidiary's net assets; or

(b)   Full (or fair) value (usually based on the market value of the shares held by the non-controlling interest).

1.4.2 IFRS 3 (revised) goodwill calculation

In words, IFRS 3 states:

Consideration paid by parent + non-controlling interest – fair value of the subsidiary's net identifiable assets = consolidated goodwill

1.4.3 Proforma goodwill calculation

The proforma goodwill calculation could be set out like this:

	£
Consideration transferred	X
Non-controlling interests (at % FV of net assets or at 'full' FV – see below)	X
	X
Less: net acquisition-date fair value of identifiable assets acquired	
And liabilities assumed	(X)
Less: Impairment losses on goodwill to date	(X)
	X

1.4.4 Non-controlling interest at fair value

IFRS 3 (revised) gives entities the option of valuing non-controlling interest (NCI) at fair value. The thinking behind this is that the non-controlling interest also owns some of the goodwill in the subsidiary, and that the traditional method of consolidation does not show this goodwill.

IFRS 3 revised suggests that the closest approximation to fair value will be the market price of the shares held by non-controlling shareholders just before acquisition by the parent.

1.4.5 Non-controlling interest at year end

Where the option is used to value non-controlling interest at fair value, the goodwill attributable to the NCI will also be added to the NCI at the year end. The most straightforward way to calculate this is to start with the fair value of the NCI at acquisition and add the NCI share of post-acquisition retained earnings.

1.4.6 Effect of non-controlling interest at fair value

The use of the fair value option increases goodwill and non-controlling interest by the same amount. That amount represents goodwill attributable to the shares held by non-controlling shareholders. It is not necessarily proportionate to the goodwill attributed to the parent. The parent may have paid proportionately more to acquire a controlling interest.

1.4.7 Goodwill impairment

The ACCA have given the following advice regarding allocation of impairment of goodwill. The advice relates to an example where the proportionate shareholding of the NCI is 25% (and so the parent controls 75%) and the amount of the impairment is £1 million:

IAS 36 requires a subsidiary's goodwill impairment to be allocated between the parent and the non-controlling interest on the same basis as the subsidiary's profits and losses are allocated. Thus of the impairment of £1 million, £750,000 would be allocated to the parent (and debited to group retained earnings reducing them to £29.55 million (30,300 - 750)) and £250,000 would be allocated to the NCI writing it down to £3.65 million (3,900 - 250).

It could be argued that this requirement represents an anomaly; of the recognised goodwill (before the impairment) of £5 million only £500,000 ie 10% relates to the NCI, but it suffers 25% (its proportionate shareholding in the subsidiary) of the goodwill impairment.

In other words, **the impairment of the goodwill is allocated proportionately, even if the goodwill on the non-controlling interest is not itself proportionate.**

1.4.8 Gain on a bargain purchase

Goodwill arising on consolidation is one form of **purchased goodwill**, and is governed by IFRS 3. As explained in an earlier chapter IFRS 3 requires that goodwill arising on consolidation should **be capitalised in the consolidated statement of financial position** and **reviewed for impairment every year**.

Goodwill arising on consolidation is the difference between the cost of an acquisition and the value of the subsidiary's net assets acquired. This difference can be **negative**: the aggregate of the fair values of the separable net assets acquired may **exceed** what the parent company paid for them. This is often referred to as **negative** goodwill. IFRS 3 refers to it as a **'gain on a bargain purchase'**. In this situation:

(a)   An entity should first **re-assess** the amounts at which it has measured both the cost of the combination and the acquiree's identifiable net assets. This exercise should **identify any errors.**

(b)   Any **excess remaining** should be **recognised immediately in profit or loss**.

1.4.9 Expenses and issue costs

Expenses of the combination, such as lawyers and accountants fees are written off as incurred. However, IFRS 3 requires that the costs of issuing equity are treated as a deduction from the proceeds of the equity issue. Share issue costs will therefore be debited to the share premium account. Issue costs of financial instruments are deducted from the proceeds of the financial instrument.

1.4.10 Contingent consideration

IFRS 3 requires the acquisition-date **fair value** of contingent consideration to be recognised as part of the consideration for the acquiree. In an examination question students will be told the acquisition-date fair value or told how to calculate it.

The acquirer may be required to pay contingent consideration in the form of equity or of a debt instrument or cash. A debt instrument should be presented as under IAS 32. Contingent consideration can also be an asset, if the consideration has already been transferred and the acquirer has the right to require the return of some of it, if certain considerations are met.

Note: The previous version of IFRS 3 only required contingent consideration to be recognised if it was **probable** that it would become payable. IFRS 3 (revised) dispenses with this requirement – **all contingent consideration is now recognised**. It is possible that the fair value of the contingent consideration may change after the acquisition date. If this is due to additional information obtained that affects the position at acquisition date, goodwill should be remeasured. If the change is due to events after the acquisition date (such as a higher earnings target has been met, so more is payable) it should be accounted for under IFRS 9 if the consideration is in the form of a financial instrument (such as loan notes) or under IAS 37 as an increase in a provision if it is cash. Any equity instrument is not remeasured.

1.4.11 Deferred consideration

An agreement may be made that part of the consideration for the combination will be paid at a future date. This consideration will therefore be discounted to its present value using the acquiring entity's cost of capital.

1.4.12 Consolidation adjustments

At the date of acquisition the parent recognises the assets, liabilities and contingent liabilities of the subsidiary at their fair value at the date when control is acquired. It may be that some of these assets or liabilities had not previously been recognised by the acquiree.

For instance, the subsidiary may have tax losses brought forward, but had not recognised these as an asset because it could not foresee future profits against which they could be offset. If the tax losses can now be utilised by the acquirer they will be recognised as an identifiable asset and included in the goodwill calculation.

1.5 Consolidation process

The following summaries provide revision of the basic consolidation technique updated for the changes resulting from the revision of IFRS 3 (revised) and IFRS 10.

Summary of technique: consolidated statement of financial position

- **Net assets**: 100% Plus 100% S.
- **Share capital**: P only.
- **Retained earnings**: 100% P plus group share of post-acquisition retained earnings of S less consolidation adjustments.
- **Non-controlling interest**: Fair value at acquisition plus share of post-acquisition retained profit (loss).

The method of consolidation is as follows.

- Read the question and draw up the group structure (W1), highlighting useful information:
  - The % owned
  - Acquisition date
  - Pre-acquisition reserves.

- Draw up a proforma taking into account the group structure identified:
  - Leave out cost of investment
  - Put in a line for goodwill
  - Put in a line for investment in associate
  - Remember to include non-controlling interests
  - Leave lines in case of any additions.
- Work methodically down the statement of financial position, transferring figures to proforma or workings:
  - 100% of all assets/liabilities controlled at the year end aggregated in brackets on face of proforma, ready for adjustments
  - Cost of subsidiary/associate and reserves to group workings, setting them up as you work down the statement of financial position
  - Share capital & share premium (parent only) to face of proforma answer
  - Open up a (blank) working for non-controlling interests.
- Read through the additional notes and attempt the adjustments showing workings for all calculations.

  Do the double entry for the adjustments onto your proforma answer and onto your group workings (where the group workings are affected by one side of the double entry).

  Examples:
  - Cancel any intragroup items e.g. current a/c balances, loans
  - Adjust for unrealised profits:

Unrealised profit on intragroup sales	X		
% held @ y/e	%		
= Provision for unrealised profit (PUP)	X	DR	Retained earnings
(adjust in company selling goods)		CR	Group inventories

- **Make fair value adjustments**

	Acq'n date	Movement	Year end
Inventories	X	X	X
Depreciable non-current assets	X	X	X
Non-depreciable non-current assets	X	X	X
Other fair value adjustments	X	X	X
	X	X	X

- **Complete goodwill calculation**

Consideration transferred	X
NCI	X
Less: Net assets acquired	
Share capital	(X)
Pre-acquisition reserves	(X)
Revaluation to fair value	(X)
Goodwill	X

- **Complete the consolidated retained earnings calculation**

	P	S
Per question	X	X
Adjustments	X(X)	X(X)
Fair value adjustment (% x adj)		X/(X)
Pre-acq'n retained earnings	–	(X)
	X	A

Group share of post-acq'n retained earnings:

Subsidiary (= A × %)	X
Less: group share of impairment losses to date	(X)
	X

- **Complete the non-controlling interests calculation**

NCI at acquisition (from goodwill working)	X
NCI share of post acq'n reserves (from reserves working × NCI %)	X
Less: NCI share of impairment losses (only if NCI at 'full' FV at acq'n)	(X)
	X

Summary of technique: consolidated statement of comprehensive income

Adjustments required for consolidation of a subsidiary are as follows.

- Eliminate **intra-group sales and purchases**.
- Eliminate any **unrealised profits** on intra-group purchases still in inventory at the year end.
- Eliminate any **intra-group** dividends received and paid, ie show only P's dividends.
- Analyse profit for the year between owners of the parent and NCI.

For the inclusion of a subsidiary carry out the following.

- **Combine all P and S results** from turnover to profit after tax (where the acquisition is mid-year, use a time-apportioned basis).
- Exclude any **investment income** that is intra-group.
- **Calculate NCI**:
  - Where there are no preferred shares: NCI = % × PROFIT FOR THE YEAR
  - Where there are preferred shares an additional working is required

Unrealised profits/losses

Only where **S sells to P**, allocate the unrealised profit between NCI and P: *Debit* group reserves, *Debit* non-controlling interest, *Credit* Inventory.

Question

Revision: group accounts

Hinge Co acquired 80% of the ordinary shares of Singe Co on 1 April 20X5. On 31 December 20X4 Singe Co's accounts showed a share premium account of $4,000 and retained earnings of $15,000. The statements of financial position of the two companies at 31 December 20X5 are set out below. Neither company has paid any dividends during the year. Non-controlling interest should be measured at fair value. The market price of the subsidiary's shares was $2.50 prior to acquisition by the parent.

You are required to prepare the consolidated statement of financial position of Hinge Ltd at 31 December 20X5. There has been no impairment of goodwill.

STATEMENT OF FINANCIAL POSITION AS AT 31 DECEMBER 20X5

	HINGE CO $	SINGE CO $
Assets		
Non-current assets		
Property, plant and equipment	32,000	30,000
16,000 ordinary shares of 50c each in Singe Ltd	50,000	
	82,000	
Current assets	85,000	43,000

Total assets	167,000	73,000
Equity and liabilities		
Equity		
Ordinary shares of $1 each	100,000	
Ordinary shares of 50c each		10,000
Share premium account	7,000	4,000
Retained earnings	40,000	39,000
	147,000	53,000
Current liabilities	20,000	20,000
Total equity and liabilities	167,000	73,000

Answer

Singe Co has made a profit of $24,000 ($39,000 – $15,000) for the year. In the absence of any direction to the contrary, this should be assumed to have arisen evenly over the year; $6,000 in the three months to 31 March and $18,000 in the nine months after acquisition. The company's pre-acquisition retained earnings are therefore as follows.

	$
Balance at 31 December 20X4	15,000
Profit for three months to 31 March 20X5	6,000
Pre-acquisition retained earnings	21,000

The balance of $4,000 on share premium account is all pre-acquisition.

The consolidation workings can now be drawn up.

1   Goodwill

	$	$
Consideration transferred		50,000
Non-controlling interest ($2.50 × 4,000)		10,000
Net assets acquired		
represented by		
Ordinary share capital	10,000	
Retained earnings (pre-acquisition)	21,000	
Share premium	4,000	
		(35,000)
Goodwill at acquisition		25,000

2   Retained earnings

	Hinge Co	Singe Co
	$	$
Per question	40,000	39,000
Pre-acquisition (see above)		(21,000)
		18,000
Share of Singe: $18,000 × 80%	14,400	
	54,400	

3   Non-controlling interest at reporting date

	$
NCI at acquisition	10,000
Share of post-acquisition retained earnings (18,000 x 20%)	3,600
	13,600

HINGE CO
CONSOLIDATED STATEMENT OF FINANCIAL POSITION AS AT 31 DECEMBER 20X5

	$	$
Assets		
Property, plant and equipment		62,000
Goodwill (W1)		25,000
Current assets		128,000
Total assets		215,000
Equity and liabilities		
Equity		
Ordinary shares of $1 each	100,000	
Share premium account	7,000	
Retained earnings (W2)	54,400	
		161,400
Non-controlling interest (W3)		13,600
		175,000
Current liabilities		40,000
Total equity and liabilities		215,000

Exam focus point

The P7 exam will not require you to produce a set of consolidated financial statements to the same level as in paper P2, but it is important that you are able to prepare group accounts and are aware of the audit risks arising in the context of group accounting.

2 Associates and joint ventures recap

2.1 Associates

We have already looked at how the **status** of an investment in an associate should be determined, in section 1.3 above. (Note that, as for an investment in a subsidiary, any **potential voting rights** should be taken into account in assessing whether the investor has **significant influence** over the investee.)

IAS 28 requires all investments in associates to be accounted for in the consolidated accounts using the equity method, *unless* the investment is classified as 'held for sale' in accordance with IFRS 5 in which case it should be accounted for under IFRS 5, or the exemption in the paragraph below applies.

An investor is exempt from applying the equity method if:

(a) It is a parent exempt from preparing consolidated financial statements under IFRS 10, or

(b) All of the following apply:

    (i) The investor is a **wholly-owned subsidiary** or it is a **partially owned subsidiary** of another entity and its other owners, including those not otherwise entitled to vote, have been informed about, and do not object to, the investor not applying the equity method;

    (ii) The investor's securities are **not publicly traded**

    (iii) It is **not in the process of issuing securities** in public securities markets; and

    (iv) The **ultimate or intermediate parent** publishes consolidated financial statements that comply with International Financial Reporting Standards.

IAS 28 **no longer allows** an investment in an associate to be excluded from equity accounting when an investee operates under severe long-term restrictions that significantly impair its ability to transfer funds to the investor. Significant influence must be lost before the equity method ceases to be applicable.

The use of the equity method should be **discontinued** from the date that the investor **ceases to have significant influence**. From that date, the investor shall account for the investment in accordance with IFRS

9 *Financial instruments*. The carrying amount of the investment at the date that it ceases to be an associate shall be regarded as its cost on initial measurement as a financial asset under IFRS 9.

The equity method should be applied in the consolidated financial statements:

Statement of comprehensive income	Profit before tax	Parent and subsidiary = associate's profit after tax
	Tax	Parent and subsidiary only
Statement of financial position	Interest in associated companies should be stated at:	$
		Cost X Share of post acquisition retained earnings X ———— X ════ Also disclose group's share of post-acquisition reserves of associated companies and movements therein

2.2 Joint arrangements

Joint arrangements (joint ventures and joint operations) are dealt with by IFRS 11 *Joint arrangements*.

> **Joint arrangement**. An arrangement of which two or more parties have joint control.
>
> A **joint venture** is a contractual arrangement whereby two or more parties undertake an economic activity that is subject to joint control.
>
> **Joint control** is the contractually agreed sharing of control which exists only when the strategic financial and operating decisions relating to the activity require the unanimous consent of the parties sharing the control.

Joint arrangements can be:

Joint ventures	A separate entity is created which needs to be consolidated.
Joint operations	No separate entity is created. Accounted for in the investor's own books.

2.2.1 Consolidating joint ventures

Prior to the new group accounting standards issued in 2011, the old standard on joint ventures (IAS 31) permitted either equity accounting or proportionate consolidation to be used for joint ventures. **The choice has now been removed, and the equity method must be used**. (Proportionate consolidation meant including the investor's share of the assets, liabilities, income and expenses of the joint venture, line by line).

2.2.2 Joint operations

IFRS 11 requires that a joint operator recognises line-by-line the following in relation to its interest in a joint operation:

(a) its assets, including its share of any jointly held assets

(b) its liabilities, including its share of any jointly incurred liabilities

(c) its revenue from the sale of its share of the output arising from the joint operation

(d)   its share of the revenue from the sale of the output by the joint operation, and

(e)   its expenses, including its share of any expenses incurred jointly.

This treatment is applicable in both the separate and consolidated financial statements of the joint operator.

3 Audit of groups

FAST FORWARD

> The group engagement partner is responsible for the direction, supervision and performance of the group audit.

Point to note

Your examiner wrote an article in the March 2008 edition of *Student Accountant*: 'Group audit issues: Objectives and responsibilities'. You should ensure that you read this article. Note in particular the emphasis on the importance of your understanding of accounting for groups.
There is another useful article on the audit of groups in the April 2011 edition of the magazine.

The Standard here is ISA 600 *Special considerations – audits of group financial statements (including the work of component auditors)*. The ISA conforms to the requirements of other ISAs, for example ISAs 220, 315 and 330, in respect of the procedures required to accept the group audit, obtaining knowledge about the group and assessing risk.

ISA 600 states that the **objectives** of the auditor are as follows.

ISA 600.8

The objectives of the auditor are:

(a)   Determine whether to act as the auditor of the group financial statements; and

(b)   If acting as the auditor of the group financial statements:

   (i)   To communicate clearly with component auditors about the scope and timing of their work on financial information related to components and their findings; and

   (ii)   To obtain sufficient appropriate audit evidence about the financial information of the components and the consolidation process to express an opinion on whether the group financial statements are prepared, in all material respects, in accordance with the applicable financial reporting framework..

The group auditor should gain an understanding of the group as a whole and assess risks for the group as a whole and for individually significant components. The group auditor has to ensure other auditors are professionally qualified, meet quality control and ethical requirements and will allow the group auditor access to working papers or components themselves.

3.1 Definitions

Key terms

Component. An entity or business activity for which the group or component management prepares financial information that should be included in the group financial statements.

Component auditor. An auditor who, at the request of the group engagement team, performs work on financial information related to a component for the group audit.

Component materiality. The materiality level for a component determined by the group engagement team.

Group. All the components whose financial information is included in the group financial statements. A group always has more than one component.

Group audit. The audit of the group financial statements.

> **Significant component**. A component identified by the group engagement team: (a) that is of individual significance to the group, or (b) that due to its specific nature or circumstances, is likely to include significant risks of material misstatement of the group financial statements.

3.2 Responsibilities

Group financial statements may include amounts derived from accounts which have not been audited by the group auditors, but by a different firm altogether: the **component auditor**. Components of group financial statements can include subsidiaries, associates, joint ventures and branches.

3.2.1 Audit opinion

FAST FORWARD

The group auditor takes sole responsibility for the group audit opinion.

Much of the debate during the development of ISA 600 related to the issue of whether the group engagement partner should be permitted to divide responsibility for the group audit opinion with component auditors if national laws permit this. The view taken in the final standard is that it is the **group auditor who is solely responsible**.

> **ISA 600.11**
>
> The group engagement partner is responsible for the direction, supervision and performance of the group audit engagement in compliance with professional standards and applicable legal and regulatory requirements, and whether the auditor's report that is issued is appropriate in the circumstances.

As a result the auditor's report on the group financial statements **shall not refer to a component auditor**. If a reference to a component auditor is required (eg by local laws or regulations), the report shall indicate that this reference does not diminish the group auditor's responsibility for the group audit opinion.

If the group auditor cannot obtain sufficient appropriate audit evidence, he will be unable to refer to another auditor but instead will have to consider whether there is a **limitation in the scope** of the group audit. (An example of an audit report with a qualified opinion where the group engagement team is not able to obtain sufficient appropriate audit evidence is provided in Appendix 1 of ISA 600.)

If the opinion on a component is qualified, the group audit opinion is only affected if the matter is material to the group. **Only a matter which is material in a group context will affect the group audit opinion**.

Example: Group audit opinion

Aristotle & Co is the group auditor of the Plato Group. At the planning stage of the audit, group materiality is determined at $250,000.

Plato Co is the parent company of the group, and has a subsidiary called Socrates Co. The group auditor considers Socrates to be a significant component for the purposes of the group audit. Socrates Co is audited by a component auditor.

The component auditor's report on Socrates Co is qualified as a result of a material misstatement. The amount of the misstatement is $120,000.

Required

What is the effect on the audit report given on the Plato Group?

Solution

The group audit report is not modified, as the amount of the misstatement is not material to the group.

3.2.2 Parent company accounts

Balances contained within just the parent company financial statements (but not the group accounts) will also have an effect on the group financial statements. For example, the parent's SOFP will include investments in subsidiaries as non-current assets; the parent's SOCI will include dividend receipts from subsidiaries. The group auditor must obtain sufficient appropriate evidence in respect of these, in order to express an opinion on the financial statements of the parent as well as the group opinion.

3.3 Rights

The group engagement team has the right to require from auditors of subsidiaries the information and explanations they require, and to require the group management to obtain the necessary information and explanations from subsidiaries.

The group engagement team has all the statutory rights and powers in respect of their audit of the holding company that we identified in the context of the audit of non-group companies in earlier chapters (for example, right of access at all times to the holding company's books, accounts and vouchers).

The group engagement team also has the following rights:

(a)   The **right to require from the group management auditors** such **information and explanations** as they may reasonably require

(b)   The right to **require the group management** to take all reasonable steps to **obtain reasonable information** and explanations from the subsidiary and this will include foreign subsidiaries

Even where their responsibilities in this regard are not set down by statute, the component auditors should appreciate that the component company's financial statements will ultimately form a part of the group financial statements. In principle, the component auditors should therefore be prepared to **co-operate** with the **group engagement team**.

3.4 Objectives

In practical terms in order to achieve the group audit objectives the auditor needs to obtain evidence in relation to the:

(1)   **Individual components** of the group – this is covered in the remainder of Section 3.
(2)   **Consolidation process** – this is covered in Section 4.

3.5 Acceptance and continuance

For significant components the group auditors should consider whether their involvement will be sufficient to obtain sufficient appropriate evidence.

When considering whether to accept appointment or continue as group auditor, the group engagement partner should determine whether 'sufficient appropriate audit evidence can reasonably be expected to be obtained in relation to the consolidation process and the financial information of the components on which to base the group audit opinion'. For this purpose the group engagement partner **must obtain an understanding of the group before acceptance**. This may be obtained from the following sources.

In the case of **a new engagement**:

•   Information provided by group management
•   Communication with group management

- Where applicable, communication with the previous group engagement team, component manager, or component auditors

Other matters to consider will include:

- The group structure
- Components' business activities including the industry and regulatory, economic and political environments in which those activities take place
- The use of service organisations
- A description of group-wide controls
- The complexity of the consolidation process
- Whether component auditors that are not from the group engagement partner's firm will perform work on the financial information of any of the components
- Whether the group engagement team will have unrestricted access to those charged with governance of the group, those charged with governance of the component, component management, component information and the component auditors (including relevant audit documentation sought by the group engagement team)

In the case of **continuing engagements** the group engagement team's ability to obtain sufficient appropriate audit evidence may be affected by **significant changes**, eg changes in group structure, changes in business activities and concerns regarding the integrity and competence of group or component management.

Where components within the group are likely to be **significant components** the group engagement partner evaluates the extent to which the group engagement team will be able to be involved in the work of those component auditors.

The group engagement partner must either refuse to accept, or resign from, the engagement if he/she concludes that it will not be possible to obtain sufficient appropriate audit evidence.

Exam focus point

In addition to these points the group engagement team should also consider the general points relating to acceptance of appointment discussed earlier in this Study Text.

3.6 Planning and risk assessment

The planning and risk assessment process will need to take into account the fact that all elements of the group financial statements are not audited by the group auditor directly. The group auditor will not be able to simply rely on the conclusions of the component auditor. ISA 600 requires the group auditor to evaluate the reliability of the component auditor and the work performed. This will then determine the extent of further procedures.

3.6.1 Understanding the component auditor

ISA 600 requires the group engagement team to obtain an understanding of the component auditor. This involves an assessment of the following:

(a) Whether the component auditor is **independent** and understands and will comply with the ethical requirements that are relevant to the group audit

(b) The component auditor's **professional competence**

(c) Whether the group engagement team will be **involved in the work of the component auditor** to the extent that it is necessary to obtain sufficient appropriate audit evidence

(d) Whether the component auditor operates in a **regulatory environment** that actively oversees auditors.

The group engagement team may obtain this understanding in a number of ways. In the first year, for example, the component auditor may be visited to discuss these issues. Alternatively the component auditor may be asked to confirm these matters in writing or to complete a questionnaire. Confirmations from professional bodies may also be sought and the reputation of the firm will be taken into account.

3.6.2 Materiality

The group auditor is responsible for setting the materiality level for the group financial statements as a whole. Materiality levels should also be set for components which are individually significant. These should be set at a lower level than the materiality level of the group as a whole.

3.6.3 Extent of work required on components

The ISA distinguishes between **significant components** and other components which are not individually significant to the group financial statements.

ISA 600.A5 states that a significant component can be identified by using a **benchmark**. If component assets, liabilities, cash flows, profit or turnover (whichever is the most appropriate benchmark) **exceed 15% of the related group figure**, then the auditor may judge that the component is a **significant component**.

If a component is financially significant to the group financial statements then the group engagement team or a component auditor will perform a full audit based on the component materiality level.

The group auditor should be involved in the assessment of risk in relation to significant components. If the component is otherwise significant due to its nature or circumstances, the group auditors will require one of the following:

- A full audit using component materiality
- An audit of specified account balances related to identified significant risks
- Specified audit procedures relating to identified significant risks

Components that are not 'significant components' will be subject to analytical procedures at a group level – a full audit is not required.

Example: Component audit

Plato Group has recently established a new subsidiary, Plotinus Ltd. The group auditor does not consider Plotinus Ltd to be a significant component in accordance with ISA 600. The auditor of Plotinus Ltd has not communicated any of the findings of its audit to the group auditor. Aristotle & Co, the group auditor, has performed analytical procedures on the final financial statements of Plotinus Ltd, and is satisfied that there are unlikely to be any misstatements therein that are material to the group.

Required

What is the effect on the audit report given on the Plato Group?

Solution

The group audit report is not modified, and the auditor's opinion is unmodified. ISA 600.29 specifies that where a component is not a significant component, then analytical procedures performed at a group level are sufficient.

3.6.4 Involvement in the work of a component auditor

The extent of involvement by the group auditor at the planning stage will depend on the:

- Significance of the component
- Identified significant risks of material misstatement of the group financial statements
- Group auditor's understanding of the component auditor

Based on these factors the group auditors may perform the following procedures:

(a) Meeting with the component management or the component auditors to obtain an understanding of the component and its environment
(b) Reviewing the component auditor's overall audit strategy and audit plan
(c) Performing risk assessment procedures to identify and assess risks of material misstatement at the component level. These may be performed with the component auditor or by the group auditor.

Where the component is a **significant component** the nature, timing and extent of the group auditor's involvement is affected by their understanding of the component auditor but at a minimum should include the following procedures:

- Discussion with the component auditor or component management regarding the component's business activities that are significant to the group
- Discussing with the component auditor the susceptibility of the component to material misstatement of the financial information due to fraud or error
- Reviewing the component auditor's documentation of identified significant risks of material misstatements. This may be in the form of a memorandum including the conclusions drawn by the component auditors.

3.7 Evaluating the work of the component auditor

For all companies in the group the group auditor is required to perform a review of the work done by the component auditor. This is normally achieved by reviewing a report or questionnaire completed by the component auditor which highlights the key issues which have been identified during the course of the audit (see Section 3.8). The effect of any uncorrected misstatements and any instances where there has been an inability to obtain sufficient appropriate audit evidence should also be evaluated. On the basis of this review the group auditor then needs to determine whether any additional procedures are necessary. These may include:

- Designing and performing further audit procedures. These may be designed and performed with the component auditors, or by the group auditor.
- Participating in the closing and other key meetings between the component auditors and component management.
- Reviewing other relevant parts of the component auditors' documentation.

Point to note

> In co-operating with the group auditor the component auditor would be expected to provide access to audit documentation unless prohibited to do so by law.

3.8 Communication

ISA 600 prescribes the types of information that must be sent by the group auditor to the component auditor and *vice versa*.

> **ISA 600.40**
>
> The group engagement team shall communicate its requirements to the component auditor on a timely basis. This communication shall set out the work to be performed, the use to be made of that work and the form and content of the component auditor's communication with the group engagement team.

These communications include the following:

- A request that the component auditor confirms their co-operation with the group engagement team
- The ethical requirements that are relevant to the group audit and in particular independence requirements
- In the case of an audit or review of the financial information of the component, component materiality and the threshold above which misstatements cannot be regarded as clearly trivial to the group financial statements
- Identified significant risks of material misstatement of the group financial statements, due to fraud or error that are relevant to the work of the component auditor. The group engagement team requests the component auditor to communicate any other identified significant risks of material misstatement and the component auditor's responses to such risks
- A list of related parties prepared by group management and any other related parties of which the group engagement team is aware. Component auditors are requested to communicate any other related parties not previously identified.

> **ISA 600.41**
>
> The group engagement team shall request the component auditor to communicate matters relevant to the group engagement team's conclusion with regard to the group audit.

These communications include the following:

(a) Whether the component auditor has complied with ethical requirements that are relevant to the group audit, including independence and professional acceptance

(b) Whether the component auditor has complied with the group engagement team's requirements

(c) Identification of the financial information of the component on which the component auditor is reporting

(d) Information on instances of non-compliance with laws and regulations that could give rise to material misstatement of the group financial statements

(e) A list of uncorrected misstatements of the financial information of the component (the list need not include items that are below the threshold for clearly trivial misstatements)

(f) Indicators of possible management bias

(g) Description of any material deficiencies identified in internal control over financial reporting at the component level

(h) Other significant matters that the component auditor communicated or expects to communicate to those charged with governance of the component, including fraud or suspected fraud involving component management, employees who have significant roles in internal control at the component level or others where the fraud resulted in a material misstatement of the financial information of the component

(i) Any other matters that may be relevant to the group audit or that the component auditor wishes to draw to the attention of the group engagement team, including exceptions noted in the written representations that the component auditor requested from component management

(j) The component auditor's overall finding, conclusions or opinion.

This communication often takes the form of a memorandum or report of work performed.

3.9 Communicating with group management and those charged with governance

ISA 600 identifies the following as matters which should be communicated to group management.

- Material deficiencies in the design or operating effectiveness of group-wide controls
- Material deficiencies that the group engagement team has identified in internal controls at components that are judged to be significant to the group
- Material deficiencies that component auditors have identified in internal controls at components that are judged to be significant to the group
- Fraud identified by the group engagement team or component auditors or information indicating that a fraud may exist

Where a component auditor is required to express an audit opinion on the financial statements of a component the group engagement team will request group management to inform component management of any matters that they, the group engagement team, have become aware of that may be significant to the financial statements of the component. If group management refuses to pass on the communication the group engagement team will discuss the matter with those charged with governance of the group. If the matter is still unresolved the group engagement team shall consider whether to advise the component auditor not to issue the audit report on the component financial statements until the matter is resolved.

3.10 Communication with those charged with governance of the group

The following matters should communicated to those charged with governance of the group:

- An overview of the type of work to be performed on the financial statements of the component
- An overview of the nature of the group engagement team's planned involvement in the work to be performed by the component auditors on significant components
- Instances where the group engagement team's evaluation of the work of a component auditor gave rise to a concern about the quality of that auditor's work
- Any limitations on the group audit, for example, where the group engagement team's access to information may have been restricted
- Fraud or suspected fraud involving group management, component management, employees who have significant roles in group-wide controls or others where fraud resulted in a material misstatement of the group financial statements.

3.11 Other aspects of the audit requiring consideration in a group context

3.11.1 Co-terminous year ends

It is possible that all of the entities within a group will not have **co-terminous reporting periods**. In this case, ISA 600.37 requires the group auditor to evaluate whether appropriate adjustments have been made to the financial statements that are not co-terminous, in accordance with the relevant financial reporting framework. In the case of IFRSs, IFRS 10 requires that the difference between period-end dates of the parent and a subsidiary is **no more than three months**. Adjustments must be made for any significant events which occur between the date of the subsidiary's and the parent's financial statements.

3.11.2 Changes in group structure

The group structure may have changed in the course of the period being audited. For instance, there may have been acquisitions, disposals, reorganisations, or changes in how the group financial reporting system is organised (ISA 600.A12). The auditor must obtain an understanding of any such changes, and must consider their impact on the auditor's understanding of the group.

For example, it is possible that a new subsidiary has been acquired, in which case the auditor needs to consider whether or not it is a 'significant component' in accordance with ISA 600, in order to determine the extent of audit work that will be required on the subsidiary. It may then also be necessary to obtain evidence regarding the application of IFRS 3, including the assessment of fair values in accordance with IFRS 13 *Fair value measurement*, which will carry audit risk because it may involve the exercise of judgement on the part of the audited entity.

There may be **'hidden' changes in the group structure**. For instance, it may be that there has been a **part-disposal** of a subsidiary, in which case the auditor will need to obtain evidence regarding the extent to which control is present, in addition to the evidence it will need in relation to the actual transactions involved.

A further possibility is that an already-existing subsidiary, which the auditor had not considered to be 'significant' in previous periods in accordance with ISA 600, might suddenly become so in the current period. In this case the auditor would need to assess carefully the audit evidence it will need to obtain in relation to the subsidiary.

3.11.3 Support (comfort) letters

It sometimes happens that a subsidiary, when considered in isolation, does not appear to be a going concern, even though the group as a whole is a going concern. In such a case, the auditor may request a 'letter of support' (or 'comfort letter) from the management of the parent company. This letter states that the intention of the parent is to continue to support the subsidiary, which makes it a going concern.

From the auditor's perspective, if the letter of support is crucial to the assessment of the going concern of the subsidiary, then it will usually be necessary to obtain *some* further evidence on going concern. This would usually include obtaining evidence about whether the parent company (& the group as a whole) is indeed able to provide the support that the subsidiary will need.

3.11.4 Developing countries

Consolidating a subsidiary from a developing country may be a problem, as the basis of preparation of the subsidiary's accounts may be so different to GAAP that the group auditor will not be able to conclude that the accounts show a true and fair view.

This is only a problem if the accounts, or the differences caused by the basis of preparation, are **material to the group**.

The problem can be averted by asking the directors to restate the accounts under GAAP. The group auditors might require that this restatement process is audited to ensure it is accurate.

Increased internationalisation of accounting practice is **reducing the risk** of this problem arising.

3.11.5 Control environment and systems

ISA 600 requires the auditor to enhance its understanding of the group, its components and their environments including group-wide controls, obtained during the acceptance or continuance stage.

Key term

> **Group-wide controls**. Controls designed, implemented and maintained by group management over group financial statements.

Group-wide controls may include a combination of the following:

* Regular meetings between group and component management to discuss business developments and to review performance
* Monitoring of components' operations and financial results
* Group management's risk assessment process
* Monitoring, controlling, reconciling and eliminating intra-group transactions, unrealised profits and intra-group balances
* A process for monitoring the timeliness and assessing the accuracy and completeness of financial information received from components
* Monitoring of controls including internal audit

Assessment of the control environment and systems will include assessment of the overall group control environment. Factors to consider include:

* Organisational structure of the group
* Level of involvement of the parent company in components
* Degree of autonomy of management of components
* Supervision of components' management by parent company
* Information systems, and information received centrally on a regular basis

Question

Component auditors

You are the main auditor of Mouldings Holdings, a listed company, which has subsidiaries in the UK and overseas, many of which are audited by other firms. All subsidiaries are involved in the manufacture or distribution of plastic goods and have accounting periods coterminous with that of the holding company.

Required

(a)   State why you would wish to review the work of the auditors of the subsidiaries not audited by you.
(b)   Describe the principal audit procedures you would carry out in performing such a review.

(a) **Reasons for reviewing the work of other auditors**

The main consideration which concerns the audit of all group accounts is that the holding company's auditors are responsible to the members of that company for the audit opinion on the whole of the group accounts.

It may be stated (in the notes to the financial statements) that the financial statements of certain subsidiaries have been audited by other firms, but this does not absolve the group auditors from any of their responsibilities.

The auditors of a holding company have to report to its members on the truth and fairness of the view given by the financial statements of the company and its subsidiaries dealt with in the group accounts. The group engagement team should have powers to obtain such information and explanations as they reasonably require from the subsidiary companies and their auditors, or from the parent company in the case of overseas subsidiaries, in order that they can discharge their responsibilities as holding company auditors.

The auditing standard ISA 600 *Special considerations – audit of group financial statements (including the work of component auditors)* clarifies how the group auditors can carry out a review of the audits of components including subsidiaries in order to satisfy themselves that, with the inclusion of figures not audited by themselves, the group accounts give a true and fair view.

The scope, standard and independence of the work carried out by the auditors of subsidiary companies (the 'component' auditors) are the most important matters which need to be examined by the group auditors before relying on financial statements audited by them. The group auditors need to be satisfied that sufficient appropriate audit evidence has been obtained and that all material areas of the financial statements of subsidiaries have been audited satisfactorily and in a manner compatible with that of the group auditors themselves.

(b) **Work to be carried out by group auditors in reviewing the component auditors' work**

(i) Send a questionnaire to all other auditors requesting detailed information on their work, including:

(1) An explanation of their general approach (in order to make an assessment of the standards of their work)

(2) Details of the accounting policies of major subsidiaries (to ensure that these are compatible within the group)

(3) The component auditors' opinion of the subsidiaries' overall level of internal control, and the reliability of their accounting records

(4) Any limitations placed on the scope of the auditors' work

(5) Any qualifications, and the reasons for them, made or likely to be made to their audit reports

(ii) Carry out a detailed review of the component auditors' working papers on each subsidiary whose results materially affect the view given by the group financial statements. This review will enable the group auditors to ascertain whether:

(1) An up to date permanent file exists with details of the nature of the subsidiary's business, its staff organisation, its accounting records, previous year's financial statements and copies of important legal documents.

(2) The systems examination has been properly completed, documented and reported on to management after discussion.

(3) Tests of controls and substantive procedures have been properly and appropriately carried out, and audit programmes properly completed and signed.

(4) All other working papers are comprehensive and explicit.

(5) The overall review of the financial statements has been adequately carried out, and adequate use of analytical procedures has been undertaken throughout the audit.

(6)   The financial statements agree in all respects with the accounting records and comply with all relevant legal requirements and accounting standards.

(7)   Minutes of board and general meetings have been scrutinised and important matters noted.

(8)   The audit work has been carried out in accordance with approved auditing standards.

(9)   The financial statements agree in all respects with the accounting records and comply with all relevant legal and professional requirements.

(10)   The audit work has been properly reviewed within the firm of auditors and any laid-down quality control procedures adhered to.

(11)   Any points requiring discussion with the holding company's management have been noted and brought to the group auditors' attention (including any matters which might warrant a qualification in the audit report on the subsidiary company's financial statements).

(12)   Adequate audit evidence has been obtained to form a basis for the audit opinion on both the subsidiaries' financial statements and those of the group.

If the group engagement partner is not satisfied as a result of the above review, he should arrange for further audit work to be carried out either by the component auditors on their behalf, or jointly with them. The component auditors are fully responsible for their own work; any additional tests are those required for the purpose of the audit of the group financial statements.

4 The consolidation: problems and procedures

Pilot paper, 6/08, 6/11

FAST FORWARD 〉〉

Consolidation procedures include checking consolidation adjustments have been correctly made, checking treatment of additions and disposals have been accounted for correctly and arithmetical checks.

4.1 Audit procedures

ISA 600 requires the auditor to identify and assess the risks of material misstatement through obtaining an understanding of the entity and its environment. Part of that process involves **obtaining an understanding of the consolidation process**, including instructions issued by group management to components.

To achieve uniformity and comparability of financial information the group management will normally issue instructions to components. The instructions ordinarily cover:

- The accounting policies to be applied

- Statutory and other disclosure requirements including:
    - The identification and reporting of segments
    - Related party relationships and reporting of segments
    - Intra-group transactions and unrealised profits
    - Intra-group account balances
- A reporting timetable

The group engagement team will consider:

- The clarity and practicality of the instructions for completing the reporting package
- Whether the instructions:
    - Adequately describe the applicable financial reporting framework
    - Provide for adequate disclosures
    - Adequately provide for the identification of consolidation adjustments
    - Provide for the approval of the financial information by component management

The group auditor is also responsible for the audit of the consolidation process itself.

After receiving and reviewing all the subsidiaries' (and associates') accounts, the group auditors will be in a position to audit the consolidated accounts. An important part of the work on the consolidation will be checking the consolidation adjustments. Consolidation adjustments generally fall into two categories:

- **Permanent consolidation adjustments**
- **Consolidation adjustments** for the **current year**

The audit steps involved in the consolidation process may be summarised as follows.

Step 1   Compare the audited accounts of each subsidiary/associate to the consolidation schedules to ensure figures have been transposed correctly, and that all components have been included

Step 2   Review the adjustments made on consolidation to ensure they are appropriate and comparable with the previous year. This will involve:

- **Recording** the **dates** and **costs** of **acquisitions** of subsidiaries and the assets acquired
- **Calculating goodwill** and **pre-acquisition reserves** arising on consolidation
- **Preparing** an overall **reconciliation** of movements on reserves and non-controlling interests
- **Reconciling** any inter-company balances, and eliminating intra-group items from profit or loss
- **Verifying** that where relevant, subsidiary balances have been included in the group accounts at **fair value**, eg properties, which may be carried at depreciated cost in the subsidiary, must be at fair value in the group accounts
- **Verifying** that the **deferred tax** consequences of consolidation and fair value adjustments have been accounted for correctly.

Step 3   For business combinations determine:

- Whether the combination has been **appropriately** treated as an acquisition
- The **appropriateness** of the **date** used as the date of combination
- The **treatment** of the **results** of **investments** acquired during the year
- If acquisition accounting has been used, that the **fair value** of acquired **assets** and **liabilities** is reasonable (to ascertainable market value by use of an expert)
- **Goodwill** has been **calculated correctly** and reviewed annually for indicators of impairment

Step 4   For disposals:

- Agree the **date** used as the date for disposal to sales documentation
- Review management accounts to ascertain whether the **results** of the **investment** have been **included** up to the date of disposal, and whether figures used are reasonable

Step 5   **Consider** whether **previous treatment** of **existing subsidiaries** or **associates** is still **correct** (consider level of influence, degree of support)

Step 6   Verify the **arithmetical accuracy** of the consolidation workings by recalculating them

Step 7   **Review** the **consolidated accounts** for **compliance** with the legislation, accounting standards and other relevant regulations. Care will need to be taken where:

- Group companies do not have coterminous accounting periods
- Subsidiaries are not consolidated
- Accounting policies of group members differ because foreign subsidiaries operate under different rules

Other important areas include:

- – Treatment of participating interests and associates
- – Treatment of goodwill and intangible assets
- – Taxation
- – Foreign currency translation
- – Treatment of loss-making subsidiaries
- – Treatment of restrictions on distribution of profits of a subsidiary

Step 8 **Review** the **consolidated accounts** to confirm that they give a true and fair view in the circumstances

The audit of related party transactions was considered earlier in this Study Text. Remember that when auditing a consolidation, the relevant related parties are those related to the **consolidated group.** Transactions with consolidated subsidiaries need **not** be disclosed, as they are incorporated in the financial statements.

The group auditors are often requested to carry out the consolidation work even where the accounts of the subsidiaries have been prepared by the client. In these circumstances the auditors are of course acting as accountants **and** auditors, and care must be taken to ensure that the **audit** function is carried out and documented.

IFRS 3 requires goodwill to be review annually for impairment, in accordance with IAS 36. This is the responsibility of management, and the auditor's role is to obtain audit evidence regarding the impairment review that management has already conducted. Impairment reviews were covered in Chapter 9 of this Study Text.

Exam focus point

> The June 2011 exam contained eight marks for explaining the principal audit procedures that are performed on the consolidation process. These were relatively easy marks, and you should be well prepared for a question like this.

Question
Intra-group balances/profits

Your firm is the auditor of Beeston Industries, a limited liability company, which has a number of subsidiaries in your country (and no overseas subsidiaries), some of which are audited by other firms of professional accountants. You have been asked to consider the work which should be carried out to ensure that inter-company transactions and balances are correctly treated in the group accounts.

Required

(a) Describe the audit work you would perform to check that intra-group balances agree, state why intra-group balances should agree, and the consequences of them not agreeing.

(b) Describe the audit work you would perform to verify that intra-group profit in inventory has been correctly accounted for in the group accounts.

Answer

(a) Intra-group balances should agree because, in the preparation of consolidated accounts, it is necessary to cancel them out. If they do not cancel out then the group accounts will be displaying an item which has no value outside of the group and profits may be correspondingly under or over-stated. The audit work required to check that intra-group balances agree would be as follows.

(i) Obtain and review a copy of the holding company's instructions to all group members relating to the procedures for reconciliation and agreement of year end intra-group balances.

Particular attention should be paid to the treatment of 'in-transit' items to ensure that there is a proper cut-off.

(ii) Obtain a schedule of intra-group balances from all group companies and check the details therein to the summary prepared by the parent company. The details on these schedules should also be independently confirmed in writing by the other auditors involved.

(iii) Nil balances should be confirmed by both the group companies concerned and their respective auditors.

(iv) The details on the schedules in (iii) above should also be agreed to the details in the financial statements of the individual group companies which are submitted to the parent company for consolidation purposes.

(b) Where one company in a group supplies goods to another company at cost plus a percentage, and such goods remain in inventory at the year end, then the group inventory will contain an element of unrealised profit. In the preparation of the group accounts, best accounting practice requires that a provision should be made for this unrealised profit.

In order to verify that intra-group profit in inventory has been correctly accounted for in the group accounts, the audit work required would be as follows.

(i) Confirm the group's procedures for identification of such inventory and their notification to the parent company who will be responsible for making the required provision.

(ii) Obtain and review schedules of intra-group inventory from group companies and confirm that the same categories of inventory have been included as in previous years.

(iii) Select a sample of invoices for goods purchased from group companies and check to see that, where necessary, these have been included in year end intra-group inventory. Obtain confirmation from other auditors that they have satisfactorily completed a similar exercise.

(iv) Check the calculation of the provision for unrealised profit and confirm that this has been arrived at on a consistent basis with that used in earlier years, after making due allowance for any known changes in the profit margins operated by various group companies.

(v) Check the schedules of intra-group inventory against the various inventory sheets and consider whether the level of intra-group inventory appears to be reasonable in comparison with previous years, ensuring that satisfactory explanations are obtained for any material differences.

5 Joint audits 6/08

FAST FORWARD

In joint audits, more than one auditor is responsible for the audit opinion and it is made jointly.

The relationship between group and component auditors discussed in the previous sections is **not** the same as that between the auditors involved in a joint audit.

key term

A **joint audit** is one 'where two or more auditors are responsible for an audit engagement and jointly produce an audit report to the client'.

5.1 Reasons for joint audits

Two or more firms of accountants could act as joint auditors for a number of reasons.

(a) **Takeover**. The parent company may insist that their auditors act jointly with those of the new subsidiary.

(b) **Locational problems**. A company operating from widely dispersed locations may find it convenient to have joint auditors.

(c)   **Political problems**. Overseas subsidiaries may need to employ local auditors to satisfy the laws of the country in which they operate. It is sometimes found that these local auditors act jointly with those of the holding company.

(d)   Companies may prefer to use **local accountants**, while at the same time enjoying the wider range of services provided by a large national firm.

5.2 Accepting a joint audit

There are several practical points that must be borne in mind before accepting a joint audit. In particular it will be necessary to assess the **experience** and **standards** of the other firm by looking at the audit techniques used, by scrutinising their working papers and establishing whether they have had experience in similar jobs.

Where there are joint auditors, the audit engagement should be explained in similar terms by each set of auditors. The auditors should agree whether joint or separate letters should be sent to the client. Separate letters would normally need to be sent where other services are provided.

Once a joint position has been accepted the **programme** to be adopted and the **split** of the **detailed work** will have to be discussed.

5.3 Problems with joint audits

One of the major criticisms of joint audits is that they may be expensive. This is probably true, but if the two firms have organised the work between them properly the difference should be minimal. Furthermore, an increase in the fees may be justified by improved services not least because the two firms of accountants are likely to work as efficiently as possible from a sense of professional pride.

Both firms must sign the audit report and both are responsible for the whole audit whether or not they carried out a particular area of the audit programme. It follows that both firms will be **jointly liable** in the event of litigation.

Point to note

> This is a topical area. At the time this study text went to print the European Union was in the process of drafting audit regulations which would stipulate **joint audits** for some entities. This is part of the re-examination of the role of audit in the wake of the financial crisis, and is related to concerns about the domination of the audit market by the 'Big Four' audit firms.
>
> You should keep an eye on the industry press in the run up to your exam, as this is sure to remain a hot topic for some time to come.

6 Transnational audits   6/09

> Transnational audits are audits of financial statements which may be relied upon outside an entity's home jurisdiction.

6.1 The Forum of Firms

In response to the trend towards globalisation an international grouping, the Forum of Firms (FoF) was founded by the following networks: BDO, Deloitte Touche Tohmatsu, Ernst & Young, Grant Thornton, KPMG and PricewaterhouseCoopers.

Membership is open to firms and networks that have transnational audit appointments or are interested in accepting such appointments.

These firms have a voluntary agreement to meet certain requirements that are set out in their constitution. These relate mainly to:

•   Promoting the use of high quality audit practices worldwide, including the use of ISAs

- Maintaining quality control standards in accordance with International Standards on Quality Control issued by the IAASB, and conducting globally coordinated internal quality assurance reviews

6.2 The Transnational Auditors Committee

The IAASB has set up the **Transnational Auditors Committee** (TAC) to provide guidance to the members of the FoF.

The TAC has issued the following definition of transnational audit.

Transnational audit means an audit of financial statements which are or may be relied upon outside the audited entity's home jurisdiction for purposes of significant lending, investment or regulatory decisions; this will include audits of all financial statements of companies with listed equity or debt and other public interest entities which attract particular public attention because of their size, products or services provided.

Guidance	**Other public interest entities** shall include those entities in either the public or the private sectors which **have significant transactions across national borders**, whether or not having either listed equity or debt. These would include, for example, large charitable organisations or trusts, major monopolies or duopolies, providers of financial or other borrowing facilities to commercial or private customers, deposit-taking organisations and those holding funds belonging to third parties in connection with investment or savings activities.
	Significant transactions across national borders shall include transactions such that there is a reasonable expectation that the financial statements of the entity may be relied upon by a user outside the entity's home jurisdiction for purposes of significant lending, investment or regulatory decisions. Significant in this context does not include use of financial statements to establish normal trade terms with vendors or to open accounts with financial institutions (ie accounts for purposes of collecting customer receipts or making vendor payments). For the avoidance of doubt, an office required solely for the purpose of legal formation and continuing legal existence in a particular jurisdiction does not constitute a significant transaction across national borders.
	In principle, the definition of transnational audit should be applied to the consolidated entity as a whole including the individual entities comprising the consolidated entity.

Examples to illustrate the definition.

Example	Explanation
Private company in US raising debt finance in Canada	This would qualify as a transnational audit as it is reasonable to expect that the financial statements of the company would be used across national borders in obtaining the debt financing.
Private Savings and Loans operating entirely in the US (ie only US depositors and US investments)	Although it could be considered a public interest entity, this would not qualify as a transnational audit assuming it can be demonstrated that there are no transnational users.
	In applying the definition of transnational audit, there should be a rebuttable presumption that all banks and financial institutions are included, unless it can be clearly demonstrated that there is no transnational element from the perspective of a financial statement user and that there are no operations across national borders. Potential transnational users would include investors, lenders, governments, customers, regulators, etc.

Example	Explanation
International charity taking donations through various national branches and making grants around the world	This entity can clearly be considered a public interest entity and operating across borders. Further, the international structure would create a reasonable expectation that the financial statements could be used across national borders by donors in other countries if not by others for purposes of significant lending, investment or regulatory decisions.
Private Internet betting company registered in BVI, which operates from Costa Rica and takes wagers by credit card on a worldwide basis via Internet	Assuming there is no restriction on gamblers then it would be public interest and operate across borders and therefore classified as a transnational audit.

6.3 Features of transnational audits

In the globalised business and financial environment, many audits are clearly transnational, and this produces a number of specific problems which can limit the reliability of the audited financial statements:

- Regulation and oversight of auditors differs from country to country
- Differences in auditing standards from country to country
- Variability in audit quality in different countries

6.4 Role of the international audit firm networks

The Big Four and other international networks of firms can be seen as being ahead of governments and institutions in terms of their global influence. They are in a position to establish consistent practices worldwide in areas such as:

- Training and education
- Audit procedures
- Quality control procedures

These firms may as a result be in a better position than national regulators to ensure consistent implementation of high quality auditing standards.

Membership of the Forum of Firms imposes commitments and responsibilities, namely:

- To perform transnational audits in accordance with ISAs
- To comply with the IFAC *Code of Ethics for Professional Accountants*
- Be subject to a programme of quality assurance

6.5 Current debate: dominance of the global accounting firms

6.5.1 Competition and choice

The preceding paragraphs have emphasised the strengths of the global accounting firms.

Questions have been raised recently as to whether the concentration in the audit market, with the Big Four firms supplying audit services to most large companies, creates any risks.

The study 'Competition and choice in the UK audit market' commissioned by the Financial Reporting Council (FRC) and the Department of Trade and Industry (DTI) in the UK identifies these potential problems:

- If one or more firms are ineligible due to independence rules, a company may have no effective choice of auditor in the short term.
- If one of the Big Four left the market a few large companies would be unable to find an auditor.
- Restricted choice may represent a risk to high quality and competitive prices.

6.5.2 Barriers to entry

The situation is unlikely to change in the short term as there are significant barriers to entry to the market for auditors of large companies. It may not be economical for other firms to break into this market given the need to demonstrate:

- A credible reputation with large companies, their investors and other stakeholders.
- Appropriate resources and expertise in place to carry out large company audits, including relevant sector-specific skills.
- An effective capability to secure timely and reliable audit opinions on overseas subsidiaries for audits of companies with significant international operations.

Chapter Roundup

- The group engagement partner is responsible for the direction, supervision and performance of the group audit.
- The group auditor takes sole responsibility for the group audit opinion.
- The group engagement team has the right to require from auditors of subsidiaries the information and explanations they require, and to require the group management to obtain necessary information and explanations from subsidiaries.
- For significant components the group auditors should consider whether their involvement will be sufficient to obtain sufficient appropriate evidence.
- Consolidation procedures include checking consolidation adjustments have been correctly made, checking treatment of additions and disposals have been accounted for correctly and arithmetical checks.
- In joint audits, more than one auditor is responsible for the audit opinion and it is made jointly.
- Transnational audits are audits of financial statements which may be relied upon outside an entity's home jurisdiction.

Quick Quiz

1   Define the term 'component auditor'.

2   Outline the responsibilities of the component auditor regarding co-operation with the group auditor.

3   If a component is significant due to its nature or circumstances one of three procedures will be required. List these three procedures.

  (1)   ....

  (2)   ....

  (3)   ....

4   List five matters which the component auditor should communicate to the group auditor.

  (1)   ....

  (2)   ....

  (3)   ....

  (4)   ....

  (5)   ....

5   What is a support letter?

6   List the eight steps involved in auditing a consolidation.

7   If two firms undertake a joint audit, they shall be jointly liable in the event of litigation.

  True   ☐

  False ☐

Answers to Quick Quiz

1   An auditor who, at the request of the group engagement team, performs work on financial information related to a component for the group audit.

2   ISA 600 gives a professional responsibility to the component auditor to co-operate unless there are legal restrictions on their ability to do so. In some jurisdictions, for example, the UK, component auditors may have a legal responsibility to co-operate in certain circumstances.

3   (1)   A full audit using component materiality

    (2)   An audit of specified account balances related to identified significant risks

    (3)   Specified audit procedures related to identified significant risks

4   Any five of the following:

- Compliance with ethical requirements
- Compliance with group engagement team's requirements
- Identification of component financial information
- Material non-compliance with laws and regulations
- Uncorrected misstatements
- Indicators of management bias
- Material weaknesses in internal control
- Other matters including fraud or suspected fraud
- Overall findings, conclusions or opinion

5   A letter to the auditors from the parent company of a subsidiary which individually does not appear to be a going concern, stating that it intends to continue to support the subsidiary, rendering it a going concern.

6

Step 1	Check the transposition from individual audited accounts to the consolidation workings.
Step 2	Check consolidation adjustments are correct and comparable with prior years
Step 3	Check for, and audit, business combinations
Step 4	Check for, and audit, disposals
Step 5	Consider whether previous treatment of subsidiaries and associates is still correct
Step 6	Verify the arithmetical accuracy of the workings
Step 7	Review the consolidated accounts for compliance with law and standards
Step 8	Review the consolidated accounts to ensure they give a true and fair view

7   True

Now try the questions below from the Exam Question Bank

Number	Level	Marks	Time
Q15	Examination	15	27 mins
Q18	Examination	15	27 mins
Q19	Examination	25	45 mins
Q20	Examination	15	27 mins
Q23	Examination	15	27 mins

Other assignments

Audit-related services and other assurance services

Topic list	Syllabus reference
1 Audit-related services	E1
2 Assurance engagements	E2
3 Risk assessments	E2

Introduction

In this chapter we look at audit-related services and other assurance services.

Audit-related services include review engagements, such as interim financial information reviews and due diligence reviews. We consider the differences between the external audit and audit-related services.

Assurance services are also considered in this chapter and we examine the different levels of assurance that can be provided on such engagements. In particular we look at risk assessments, performance measurement and value for money audits. Finally in this chapter we look at the ways in which companies are using IT in their organisations and how this affects business risks.

Study guide

		Intellectual level
E	**Other assignments**	
E1	**Audit-related services**	
(a)	Describe the nature of audit-related services, the circumstances in which they might be required and the comparative levels of assurance provided by professional accountants and distinguish between: (i) Audit-related services and an audit of historical financial statements (ii) An attestation engagement and a direct reporting engagement	2
(b)	Plan review engagements, for example: (i) a review of interim financial information (ii) a 'due diligence' assignment (when acquiring a company, business or other assets).	2
(c)	Explain the importance of enquiry and analytical procedures in review engagements and apply these procedures	2
E2	**Assurance services**	
(a)	Describe the main categories of assurance services that audit firms can provide and assess the benefits of providing these services to management and external users	
(b)	Justify a level of assurance (reasonable, high, moderate, limited, negative) for an engagement depending on the subject matter evaluated, the criteria used, the procedures applied and the quality and quantity of evidence obtained	3
(c)	Recognise the ways in which different types of risk (eg strategic, operating, information) may be identified and analysed and assess how management should respond to risk	3
F3	**Other reports**	
(a)	Analyse the form and content of the professional accountant's report for an assurance engagement as compared with an auditor's report	2
(c)	Discuss the effectiveness of the 'negative assurance' form of reporting and evaluate situations in which it might be appropriate to express a reservation or deny a conclusion.	3

Exam guide

Assurance and audit-related services are very important areas for auditors in practice. Areas such as e-commerce are also particularly topical. Most of these topics have featured in practical questions in the past and are likely to continue to do so.

1 Audit-related services   12/07, 6/08, 6/11

FAST FORWARD

> Audit-related services may be assurance services (reviews) or not (agreed-upon procedures).

1.1 Reviews

> **Review engagements**. The objective of a review engagement is to enable an auditor to state whether, on the basis of procedures which do not provide all the evidence that would be required in an audit, anything has come to the auditor's attention that causes the auditor to believe that the financial statements are not prepared, in all material respects, in accordance with an identified financial reporting framework.

There are two types of assurance engagements which can be applied to reviews since these are a type of assurance service.

- An **attestation** engagement where the accountant declares that a given premise is either correct or not

- A **direct reporting** engagement, where the accountant reports on issues that have come to his attention during the course of his review

A client would generally engage an auditor to undertake a review engagement either because the client needs to make use of expertise that the auditor possesses but the client itself does not, or because it needs a relatively independent third party to provide assurance regarding some specific matter. For example, the client may lack the expertise to carry out a financial due diligence assignment on a potential acquisition, and may therefore engage the auditor to do this for them. Or it may be that the client needs to obtain new finance in the form of a bank loan, and engages the auditor to provide assurance over its prospective financial information because this will help strengthen its case with the bank.

Example: attestation engagement

Auditors may sometimes be asked to **review interim financial information**. In such an engagement, the auditor is being asked to attest assertions made, such as:

- The accounting policies used are consistent with those used in the prior year financial statements.
- No material modifications to the interim financial information as it has been presented are required.

Example: direct reporting engagement

An example of a direct reporting engagement is a **'due diligence'** engagement.

> **Due diligence** reviews are a specific type of review engagement. A typical due diligence engagement is where an advisor (often an audit firm) is engaged by one company planning to take over another to perform an assessment of the material risks associated with the transaction (including validating the assumptions underlying the purchase), to ensure that the acquirer has all the necessary facts and that the perceived business opportunities are in fact real. This is important when determining purchase price. Similarly, due diligence can also be requested by sellers.

It may include some or all of the following aspects:

- Financial due diligence (a review of the financial position and obligations of a target to identify such matters as covenants and contingent obligations)
- Operational and IT due diligence (extent of operational and IT risks, including quality of systems, associated with a target business)
- People due diligence (key staff positions under the new structure, contract termination costs and cost of integration)
- Regulatory due diligence (review of the target's level of compliance with relevant regulation)
- Environmental due diligence (environmental, health and safety and social issues in a target)

In a review engagement, the auditor will rely more heavily on procedures such as **enquiry and analytical review** than on more detailed substantive testing. The reasons for this are as follows:

- He is seeking a **lower level of assurance than for an audit**, so these forms of evidence are sufficient due to risk being lower.
- Such techniques provide **indicators** to direct work to risk areas and from which to draw conclusions, and they are **quick** and, therefore, **cost-effective**.

What the enquiries are about and what matters are the subject of analytical procedures will depend on the specific situation. However, a typical due diligence review could include enquiries into:

- Structure, including how the target is owned and constituted and what changes will be necessary
- Financial health, based on a detailed examination of past financial statements and an analysis of the existing asset base
- Credibility of the owners, directors and senior managers, including validation of the career histories of all the main players in the business
- Future potential, reflected in the strengths of its products or services and the probability of earnings growth over the medium to long term
- Assessment of the risk to the acquiring business, in terms of their markets, strategy and likely future events
- The business plan, in terms of how realistic it is, how solid the assumptions used are and how well it conveys the potential

ISRE (International Standard on Review Engagements) 2400 *Engagements to review financial statements* contains guidance on review engagements.

> **ISRE 2400.7**
>
> For the purpose of expressing negative assurance in the review report, the practitioner should obtain sufficient appropriate evidence primarily through inquiry and analytical procedures to be able to draw conclusions.
>
> **ISRE 2400.8**
>
> The procedures required to conduct a review of financial statements should be determined by the practitioner having regard to the requirements of this ISRE, relevant professional bodies, legislation, regulation and, where appropriate, the terms of the review engagement and reporting requirements.

Many of the requirements of the ISRE are similar to the requirements of an audit.

Planning

- Obtain knowledge of the business
- Same materiality requirements
- Using the work of others

Evidence

- Document all important matters
- Apply judgement in determining nature, timing and extent of procedures
- Enquire about subsequent events
- Extend procedures if material misstatements are suspected

1.1.1 Reporting

The nature of reporting on reviews was outlined in your earlier auditing studies so you should be familiar with it. However, we shall revise it here.

An external review is an **exercise similar to an audit**, which is designed to give a **reduced degree of assurance** concerning the proper preparation of a set of financial statements.

As you know from your earlier studies **negative assurance** is given on review assignments.

Key term

> **Negative assurance** is assurance of something in the absence of any evidence arising to the contrary. In effect, this means the auditor is saying, 'I believe that this is reasonable because I have no reason to believe otherwise.'

When no matters have come to the attention of the auditor, he should give a **clear expression of negative assurance** in his report. An example of an unqualified review report is given in the appendix to the ISRE, and it is reproduced here.

Note. ISRE 2400 has not yet been updated for the changes in terminology introduced by the revision of IAS 1 *Presentation of financial statements*.

Form of Unqualified Review Report

REVIEW REPORT TO…

We have reviewed the accompanying balance sheet of ABC Company at December 31, 20XX, and the related statements of income and cash flows for the year then ended. These financial statements are the responsibility of the Company's management. Our responsibility is to issue a report on these financial statements based on our review.

We conducted our review in accordance with the International Standard on Review Engagements 2400 (or refer to relevant national standards or practices) applicable to review engagements. This Standard requires that we plan and perform the review to obtain moderate assurance as to whether the financial statements are free of material misstatement. A review is limited primarily to inquiries of company personnel and analytical procedures applied to financial data and thus provides less assurance than an audit. We have not performed an audit and, accordingly, we do not express an audit opinion.

Based on our review, nothing has come to our attention that causes us to believe that the accompanying financial statements do not give a true and fair view (or 'are not presented fairly, in all material respects,') in accordance with International Accounting Standards.

PRACTITIONER

Date   *Address*

If matters have come to the attention of the auditor, he should **describe those matters**. The matters may have the following effects.

Impact	Effect on report
Material	Express a **qualified** opinion of negative assurance
Pervasive	Express an **adverse** opinion that the financial statements do not give a true and fair view

The auditor may feel there has been a limitation in the scope of the work he intended to carry out for the review. If so, he should **describe the limitation.** The limitation may have the following effects.

Impact	Effect on report
Material to one area	Express a **qualified** opinion of negative assurance due to amendments which might be required if the limitation did not exist
Pervasive	Do not provide any assurance

1.2 Review of interim financial information performed by the independent auditor of the entity

This subject is covered by ISRE 2410 *Review of interim financial information performed by the independent auditor of the entity.*

1.2.1 General principles

The auditor should comply with **ethical principles** relevant to the audit when carrying out an interim review and should apply **quality control procedures** applicable to the individual engagement. In addition, the auditor he should plan and perform the engagement with an attitude of **professional scepticism**. The auditor should agree the terms of the engagement with the client (these will not be the same terms as for the audit, as the review will result in a lower level of assurance than the annual audit), with a view to providing negative assurance.

1.2.2 Procedures

The procedures outlined below follow the same pattern as an audit, but, because this is a review not an audit they are not as detailed as audit procedures.

The auditor should possess sufficient understanding of the entity and its environment to understand the types of misstatement that might arise in interim financial information and to plan the relevant procedures (mainly enquiry and analytical review) to enable him to ensure that the financial information is prepared in accordance with the applicable financial reporting framework. This will usually include:

- Reading last year's audit and previous review files
- Considering any significant risks that were identified in the prior year audit
- Reading the most recent and comparable interim financial information
- Considering materiality
- Considering the nature of any corrected or uncorrected misstatements in last year's financial statements
- Considering significant financial accounting and reporting matters of ongoing importance
- Considering the results of any interim audit work for this year's audit
- Considering the work of internal audit
- Asking management what their assessment is of the risk that the interim financial statements might be affected by fraud
- Asking management whether there have been any significant changes in business activity, and if so, what effect they have had
- Asking management about any significant changes in internal controls and the potential effect on preparing the interim financial information
- Asking how the interim financial information has been prepared and the reliability of the underlying accounting records

A recently appointed auditor should obtain an understanding of the entity and its environment as it relates to both the interim review and final audit.

The key elements of the review will be:

- **Enquiries** of accounting and finance staff
- **Analytical procedures**

Ordinarily procedures would include:

- Reading the minutes of meetings of shareholders, those charged with governance and other appropriate committees
- Considering the effect of matters giving rise to a modification of the audit or review report, accounting adjustments or unadjusted misstatements from previous audits
- If relevant, communicating with other auditors auditing different components of the business
- Analytical procedures designed to identify relationships and unusual items that may reflect a material misstatement
- Reading the interim financial information and considering whether anything has come to the auditors' attention indicating that it is not prepared in accordance with the applicable financial reporting framework
- Agreeing the interim financial information to the underlying accounting records

Auditors should make enquiries of members of management responsible for financial and accounting matters about:

- Whether the interim financial information has been prepared and presented in accordance with the applicable financial reporting framework
- Whether there have been changes in accounting policies
- Whether new transactions have required changes in accounting principle
- Whether there are any known uncorrected misstatements
- Whether there have been unusual or complex situations, such as disposal of a business segment
- Significant assumptions relevant to fair values
- Whether related party transactions have been accounted for and disclosed correctly
- Significant changes in commitments and contractual obligations
- Significant changes in contingent liabilities including litigation or claims
- Compliance with debt covenants
- Matters about which questions have arisen in the course of applying the review procedures
- Significant transactions occurring in the last days of the interim period or the first days of the next
- Knowledge or suspicion of any fraud
- Knowledge of any allegations of fraud
- Knowledge of any actual or possible non-compliance with laws and regulations that could have a material effect on the interim financial information
- Whether all events up to the date of the review report that might result in adjustment in the interim financial information have been identified
- Whether management has changed its assessment of the entity being a going concern

The auditor should evaluate discovered misstatements individually and in aggregate to see if they are material.

The auditor should obtain **written representations** from management that it acknowledges its responsibility for the design and implementation of internal control, that the interim financial information is prepared and presented in accordance with the applicable financial reporting framework and that the effect of uncorrected misstatements are immaterial (a summary of these should be attached to the representations). The auditor should also obtain representations that all **significant facts** relating to **frauds or non-compliance with law and regulations** has been disclosed to the auditor and that all **significant subsequent events** have been disclosed to the auditor.

The auditor should read the other information accompanying the interim financial information to ensure that it is not inconsistent with it.

If the auditors believe a matter should be adjusted in the financial information, they should **inform management** as soon as possible. If management does not respond within a reasonable time, then the auditors should inform those charged with governance. If they do not respond, then the auditor should consider whether to modify the report or to withdraw from the engagement and the final audit if necessary. If the auditors uncover fraud or non-compliance with laws and regulations, they should communicate that promptly with the **appropriate level of management**. The auditors should communicate matters of interest arising to those charged with governance.

1.2.3 Reporting

The ISRE gives the following example standard report.

Note. ISRE 2410 has not yet been updated for the changes in terminology introduced by the revision of IAS 1 *Presentation of Financial Statements*

Report on Review of Interim Financial Information

(Appropriate addressee)

Introduction

We have reviewed the accompanying balance sheet of ABC Entity as of March 31, 20X1 and the related statements of income, changes in equity and cash flows for the three-month period then ended, and a summary of significant accounting policies and other explanatory notes. Management is responsible for the preparation and fair presentation of this interim financial information in accordance with (indicate applicable financial reporting framework). Our responsibility is to express a conclusion on this interim financial information based on our review.

Scope of Review

We conducted our review in accordance with International Standard on Review Engagements 2410, 'Review of Interim financial Information performed by the Independent Auditor of the Entity'. A review of interim financial information consists of making inquiries, primarily of persons responsible for financial and accounting matters, and applying analytical and other review procedures. A review is substantially less in scope than an audit conducted in accordance with International Standards on Auditing and consequently does not enable us to obtain assurance that we would become aware of all significant matters that might be identified in an audit. Accordingly, we do not express an audit opinion.

Conclusion

Based on our review, nothing has come to our attention that causes us to believe that the accompanying interim financial information does not give a true and fair view of (or 'does not present fairly, in all material respects,') the financial position of the entity as at March 31, 20X1, and of its financial performance and its cash flows for the three-month period then ended in accordance with (applicable financial reporting framework, including a reference to the jurisdiction or country of origin of the financial reporting framework when the financial reporting framework used is not International Financial Reporting Standards).

AUDITOR

Date

Address

It also gives examples of modified reports:

Review report: Departure from the applicable financial reporting framework

Previous paragraphs as per standard report.

Basis for Qualified Conclusion

Based on information provided to us by management, ABC Entity has excluded from property and long-term debt certain lease obligations that we believe should be capitalised to conform with (indicate applicable financial reporting framework). This information indicates that if these lease obligations were capitalised at March 31, 20X1, property would be increased by $ _____, long-term debt by $ _____, and net income and earnings per share would be increased (decreased) by $ _____, $ _____, $ _____, and $ _____, respectively for the three-month period then ended.

> *Qualified Conclusion*
>
> Based on our review, with the exception of the matter described in the preceding paragraph, nothing has come to our attention that caused us to believe that the accompanying interim financial information does not give a true and fair view of *(or 'does not present fairly, in all material respects,')* the financial position of the entity as at March 31, 20X1, and of its financial performance and its cash flows for the three-month period then ended in accordance with (indicate applicable financial reporting framework, including the reference to the jurisdiction or country of origin of the financial reporting framework when the financial reporting framework used is not International Financial Reporting Standards).
>
> AUDITOR
>
> Date
>
> Address

> **Review report: Limitation on scope not imposed by management**
>
> Introduction paragraph – as per standard report
>
> *Scope paragraph*
>
> Except as explained in the following paragraph .... – as per standard report.
>
> *Basis for Qualified Conclusion*
>
> As a result of a fire in a branch office on (date) that destroyed its accounts receivable records, we were unable to complete our review of accounts receivable totalling $ _____ included in the interim financial information. The entity is in the process of reconstructing these records and is uncertain as to whether these records will support the amount shown above the related allowance for uncollectible accounts. Had we been able to complete our review of accounts receivable, matters might have come to our attention indicating that adjustments might be necessary to the interim financial information.
>
> *Qualified Conclusion*
>
> Except for the adjustments to the interim financial information that we might have become aware of had it not been for the situation described above, based on our review, nothing has come to our attention that causes us to believe that the accompanying interim financial information does not give a true and fair view of *(or 'does not present fairly, in all material respects,')* the financial position of the entity as at March 31, 20X1, and of its financial performance and its cash flows for the three-month period then ended in accordance with (indicate applicable financial reporting framework, including a reference to the jurisdiction or country of origin of the financial reporting framework when the financial reporting framework used is not International Financial Reporting Standards).
>
> AUDITOR
>
> Date
>
> Address

1.3 Agreed-upon procedures

Key term

> **Agreed-upon procedures assignment.** In an engagement to perform agreed-upon procedures, an auditor is engaged to carry out those procedures of an audit nature to which the auditor and the entity and any appropriate third parties have agreed and to report on factual findings. The recipients of the report must form their own conclusions from the report by the auditor. The report is restricted to those parties that have agreed to the procedures to be performed since others, unaware of the reasons for the procedures, may misinterpret the results.

Agreed upon procedures assignments are discussed in ISRS 4400 *Engagements to perform agreed-upon procedures regarding financial information.*

1.3.1 Accepting appointment

> **ISRS 4400.9**
>
> The auditor should ensure with representatives of the entity, and ordinarily, other specified parties who will receive copies of the report of factual findings, that there is a clear understanding regarding the agreed procedures and the conditions of the engagement.

1.3.2 Carrying out procedures and reporting

The auditors should plan the assignment. They should carry out the agreed-upon procedures, documenting their process and findings.

> **ISRS 4400.18**
>
> The report of factual findings should contain:
>
> (a) Title
>
> (b) Addressee (ordinarily the client who engaged the auditor to perform the agreed-upon procedures)
>
> (c) Identification of specific financial or non-financial information to which the agreed-upon procedures have been applied
>
> (d) A statement that the procedures performed were those agreed upon with the recipient
>
> (e) A statement that the engagement was performed in accordance with the International Standard on Auditing applicable to agreed-upon procedure engagements, or with relevant national standards or practices
>
> (f) When relevant a statement that the auditor is not independent of the entity
>
> (g) Identification if the purpose for which the agreed-upon procedures were performed
>
> (h) A listing of the specific procedures performed
>
> (i) A description of the auditor's factual findings including sufficient details of errors and exceptions found
>
> (j) Statement that the procedures performed do not constitute either an audit or a review, and, as such, no assurance is expressed
>
> (k) A statement that had the auditor performed additional procedures, an audit or a review, other matters might have come to light that would have been reported
>
> (l) A statement that the report is restricted to those parties that have agreed to the procedures to be performed
>
> (m) A statement (when applicable) that the report relates only to the elements, accounts, items or financial and non-financial information specified and that it does not extend to the entity's financial statements taken as a whole
>
> (n) Date of the report
>
> (o) Auditor's address
>
> (p) Auditor's signature

2 Assurance engagements   12/07, 12/10

 Assurance services improve the quality of decision-making for users of information.

Exam focus point

> The P7 examiner wrote an article in *Student Accountant* on this area which is essential reading: October 2007 'How to tackle audit and assurance case study questions – part 2: clear thinking'. An article 'Continue to be 'rest assured'' is also available on the ACCA website.

2.1 Elements of an assurance engagement

The definition of an assurance engagement is set out below but you should be familiar with it from your earlier auditing studies.

ey term

> An **assurance engagement** is one where a professional accountant evaluates or measures a subject matter that is the responsibility of another party against suitable criteria, and expresses an opinion which provides the intended user with a level of assurance about the subject matter.

Here, we shall focus on assurance engagements on subjects other than historical financial information (which we have already looked at in the form of audits and reviews) as we look at the guidance in ISAE 3000 *Assurance engagements other than audits or reviews of historical financial information.*

2.2 Assurance provided

FAST FORWARD ▷ Assurance engagements may give reasonable assurance or limited assurance.

The ISAE refers to two types of engagement: 'reasonable assurance engagement' and 'limited assurance engagement'. These levels of assurance were discussed in your earlier studies. Remember that absolute assurance can **never** be given on an assurance engagement due to the **inherent limitations** of such engagements.

2.3 Accepting and continuing appointment

FAST FORWARD ▷ Assurance engagements should only be accepted if the firm meets the requirements of the IFAC Code of Ethics for Professional Accountants and ISQC 1.

The standard requires that practitioners ensure they comply with the Code of Ethics for Professional Accountants and the Quality Control Standard (ISQC 1) with regard to the assignment. In addition, the standard specifies the following.

> **ISAE 3000.8/9**
>
> The practitioner should accept (or continue where applicable) an assurance engagement only if, on the basis of a preliminary knowledge of the engagement circumstances, nothing comes to the attention of the practitioner to indicate that the requirements of the Code or of the ISAEs will not be satisfied.
>
> The practitioner should accept (or continue where applicable) an assurance engagement only if the practitioner is satisfied that those persons who are to perform the engagement collectively possess the necessary professional competencies.

The engagement must also genuinely be an assurance engagement, that is, it must have the characteristics of an assurance engagement (a three party relationship between the practitioner, the intended user of the information and the party responsible for the information). The responsible party may be an intended user so long as he is not the sole intended user of the information.

> **ISAE 3000.7**
>
> The practitioner should accept (or continue where applicable) an assurance engagement only if the subject matter is the responsibility of a party other than the intended users or the practitioner.

Commonly, the practitioner would ask the responsible party to acknowledge their responsibility for the information in written form.

2.3.1 Agreeing terms

ISAE 3000.10

The practitioner should agree on the terms of the engagement with the engaging party.

For the avoidance of confusion, this should normally be done in writing.

Sometimes, the nature of an assignment being carried out by a practitioner might change, and the responsible party might request that the practitioner provides less or no assurance on an engagement.

ISAE 3000.11

A practitioner should consider the appropriateness of a request, made before the completion of an assurance engagement to change the engagement to a non-assurance engagement or from a reasonable assurance engagement to a limited assurance engagement, and should not agree to a change without reasonable justification.

2.4 Planning and performing the engagement

ISAE 3000.12

The practitioner should plan the engagement so that it will be performed effectively.

This involves developing:

- An overall strategy
- A detailed engagement plan

Matters to be considered

- The terms of the engagement
- The characteristics of the subject matter and identified criteria
- The engagement process and possible sources of evidence
- Understanding of the entity and its environment (risks of material misstatement)
- Identification of intended users and their needs
- Materiality
- Components of assurance engagement risk
- Personnel/expertise requirements (including the potential use of experts)

As with audits, the practitioner should maintain an attitude of professional scepticism.

ISAE 3000.15

The practitioner should obtain an understanding of the subject matter and other engagement circumstances, sufficient to identify and assess the risks of subject matter information being materially misstated, and sufficient to design and perform further evidence gathering procedures.

Obtaining such an understanding of the entity assists the practitioner in exercising professional judgement throughout the engagement.

2.4.1 Appropriateness of the subject matter and criteria

The subject matter of an assurance engagement must be appropriate to have assurance given on it. The Framework outlines the characteristics of such appropriateness, which include it being identifiable, capable of consistent evaluation and measurement and capable of being subject to procedures and evidence gathering.

> **ISAE 3000.18**
>
> The practitioner should assess the appropriateness of the subject matter.

Equally, the criteria must be appropriate. The Framework also lists characteristics of suitable criteria, including relevance, reliability, completeness, neutrality and understandability. For example, if an assurance subject matter was design of internal controls, internationally recognised criteria such as the COSO framework would be appropriate.

> **ISAE 3000.19**
>
> The practitioner should assess the suitability of the criteria to evaluate or measure the subject matter.

2.4.2 Materiality and engagement risk

> **ISAE 3000.22/24**
>
> The practitioner should consider materiality and assurance engagement risk when planning and performing an assurance engagement.
>
> The practitioner should reduce assurance engagement risk to an acceptably low level in the circumstances of the engagement.

The circumstances of the engagement here refers to the level of assurance that is anticipated, that is, reasonable assurance or limited assurance.

2.4.3 Using the work of an expert

> **ISAE 3000.26/30/32**
>
> When the work of an expert is used in the collection and evaluation of evidence, the practitioner and the expert should, on a combined basis, possess adequate skill and knowledge regarding the subject matter and the criteria for the practitioner to determine that sufficient appropriate evidence has been obtained.
>
> The practitioner should be involved in the engagement and understand the work for which an expert is used, to an extent that is sufficient to enable the practitioner to accept responsibility for the conclusion on the subject matter information.
>
> The practitioner should obtain sufficient appropriate evidence that the expert's work is adequate for the purposes of the assurance engagement.

The practitioner is not expected to have the same degree of skill or expertise as the expert, or there would be no point in using him. However, he is supposed to ensure that the expert is suitably qualified to do the required work, and that he (the practitioner) understands what work is being done, so that the practitioner can give an opinion on the assurance engagement.

2.4.4 Evidence

> **ISAE 3000.33**
>
> The practitioner should obtain sufficient appropriate evidence on which to base the conclusion.

You should be aware of the meaning of sufficiency and appropriateness from your knowledge of auditing. Assurance engagements will involve the use of selective testing methods.

Obtaining sufficient appropriate evidence is likely to include obtaining written representations from the responsible party where appropriate, particularly where knowledge of facts is confined to the responsible party or it is a matter of judgement of the responsible party.

2.4.5 Subsequent events

> **ISAE 3000.41**
>
> The practitioner should consider the effect on the subject matter information and on the assurance report of events up to the date of the assurance report.

2.5 Reporting

The ISAE makes the following observations about reporting:

> **ISAE 3000.45/46**
>
> The practitioner should conclude whether sufficient appropriate evidence has been obtained to support the conclusion expressed in the assurance report.
>
> The assurance report should be in writing and should contain a clear expression of the practitioner's conclusion about the subject matter information.

In a reasonable assurance engagement, a practitioner should be able to give a 'positive' expression of his conclusion. This does not mean that a report in a reasonable assurance engagement should not be modified, it means the practitioner should be able to draw a conclusion on the basis of the evidence gained.

This is in contrast to a negative opinion, given in a limited assurance engagement, where an auditor gives an opinion as no evidence has been received to the contrary.

2.6 References for a client

Sometimes an auditor will be asked for a reference concerning a client, particularly in relation to his ability to **service a loan**. Where **no additional work is required** to provide a reference, the following matters should be considered:

- Inherent uncertainty of future income and expenditure
- The difficulty of reporting on present solvency (given that the audit is a historic exercise. Such information might be available if a **separate engagement** was made)
- The possibility of a **duty of care** arising
- That clarification might be required (there has been no engagement and no fees, and that liability might have to be expressly disclaimed)

However, the accountants might be able to provide certain information without difficulty:

- The length of time they have acted for the client
- The results declared to the taxation authorities over past years
- A statement of a level of negative assurance given past performance

Where it is necessary to create a separate engagement in order to provide the relevant information, the auditor should consider the guidance in ISAE 3000, discussed above.

In the following sections we shall start to consider some examples of areas where the accountant can provide assurance services.

3 Risk assessments

> Risk assessment is important to investors and managers and therefore is an important area for assurance services.

We discussed business risk earlier in this Study Text. It has three elements; financial, operational and compliance. There are a number of specific risks within these elements, some of which are shown the diagram below.

3.1 Need for assurance

Why is there a need for assurance in relation to risk assessment? For what reason would people want an independent opinion that gives them assurance? What criteria should this assurance be in relation to?

The key answer to the first question is that **the risk that the company enters into has a direct impact on the risk of the investment** that anyone purchasing shares in a company or loaning money to a company is making.

Interested stakeholders, **particularly investors**, need assurance that the risk taken by the company, in effect with their investment, is acceptable to them and that the returns that they receive are in accordance with that level of risk.

It is this need for assurance about the risks the company enters into that has led to the **importance of the issue of corporate governance and internal control effectiveness** that we looked at earlier and will continue to look at in Chapter 16 in the context of internal audit.

Other stakeholders will also be interested in the effectiveness of risk management in a company. Examples are lenders and employees. This is because the **ultimate risk is that a business might fail**.

3.2 Possible assurance criteria

The criteria by which risk assessment is evaluated will depend on the specific needs of the company and the user. However, some possibilities are:

- The requirements of the UK Turnbull Guidelines
- Management's policy on risk management

There are no universally recognised criteria suitable for evaluating the **effectiveness** of an entity's risk evaluation. Assurance is likely to be limited to whether evaluation is carried out, rather than the quality of the evaluation.

3.3 Responsibility for risk assessment

There are three sets of people who can be involved in risk assessment in a company:

- Directors/management
- Internal audit
- External audit

We shall discuss the role of internal audit in Chapter 16. The responsibility of the directors has previously been discussed earlier, and the role of the auditors in risk assessment has been discussed in Chapter 6.

It is vital that you distinguish between the risk assessment carried out by the auditors and the directors. The directors are responsible for assessing and then managing the risks arising to the business, that is, the business risks.

As part of their audit, the auditors assess audit risk. Audit risk is the risk that the auditors make an inappropriate opinion on the financial statements. The auditors may consider business risk as part of their audit risk assessment. However, the **auditors are not responsible for risk management of their clients**.

3.4 Assessing risk

Methods of identifying risk were outlined in Chapter 6. You should be familiar with methods such as SWOT or PEST analysis. In practice, risk identification is likely to be done in all the various departments of a business.

These risks could include, for example:

- Contractual risks (important customers not agreeing to given contractual terms)
- Operational risks (scarce raw materials, risks arising through storage and use)
- Physical risks (for example, health and safety compliance)
- Product distribution (logistics, networks, outlets)
- Regulation (different jurisdictions, Internet trading)
- Reputation (brands and staff profile)

The directors of a company need to determine guidelines for assessing risk. Risk might be assessed in terms of

- Significance
- Likelihood
- Capacity to be managed

Mathematical methods could be used to assess risk, for instance using probability factors. Risks can be analysed using a grid such as the example given:

Low likelihood Low impact	Low likelihood High impact
High likelihood Low impact	High likelihood High impact

3.5 Responses to risk

There are several responses that management take to risk:

- **Accept** risk (particularly if it is low likelihood, low impact)
- **Reduce** risk (by setting up a system of internal control to prevent the risk arising)
- **Avoid** risk (by not entering that market or not accepting certain contracts)
- **Transfer** risk (by taking out insurance)

If management choose to accept risk, they must set **risk thresholds**, that is, determine levels of risk where they will stop accepting risk and choose one of the other strategies. These thresholds are important because if directors or management are reckless with regard to risk they may be breaching their fiduciary duties.

3.6 Assurance

As stated above, assurance services may be provided. These may relate to the reliability of systems of internal control, which is important both for the financial statements and for the general running of the business. Assurance services could also relate to performance management. This has been studied in earlier papers and is not on the P7 syllabus.

Chapter Roundup

- Audit-related services may be assurance services (reviews) or not (agreed-upon procedures).

- Assurance services improve the quality of decision-making for users of information.

- Assurance engagements may give reasonable assurance or limited assurance.

- Assurance engagements should only be accepted if the firm meets the requirements of the Code of Ethics for Professional Accountants and ISQC 1.

- Risk assessment is important to investors and managers and therefore is an important area for assurance services.

Quick Quiz

1   Name the three types of engagement which comprise audit-related services.

(1)   ....

(2)   ....

(3)   ....

2   Link the review assignment with its description.

Review assignment:

(a)   Attestation engagement

(b)   Direct reporting engagement

Descriptions:

(i)   The accountant is required to confirm whether:

–   Accounting policies are consistent with those in prior year financial statements
–   Any material modifications to the presented information are required.

(ii)   The accountant is required to conduct a review and report on issues arising.

3   In an assurance engagement, the responsible party can also be an intended user.

A   Never
B   If there is more than one intended user
C   If there are more than ten intended users
D   In exceptional circumstances

4   When carrying out an assurance engagement the practitioner must assess the appropriateness of the subject matter and the criteria.

True   ☐

False   ☐

5   The assurance report should be in writing.

True   ☐

False   ☐

Answers to Quick Quiz

1   Review assignments, agreed-upon procedures assignments and compilation assignments.

2   (a)(i)
    (b)(ii)

3   B

4   True

5   True

Now try the questions below from the Exam Question Bank

Number	Level	Marks	Time
Q21	Examination	20	36 mins
Q22	Examination	15	27 mins

13

Prospective financial information (PFI)

Topic list	Syllabus reference
1 Reporting on prospective financial information	E3
2 Accepting an engagement	E3
3 Procedures	E3
4 Expressing an opinion	E3

Introduction

Reporting on prospective financial information (PFI) is covered by ISAE 3400 *The examination of prospective financial information.*

Forecasts are of significant interest to users. Some would say that PFI is of more interest to users of accounts than historic information (HFI), which of course, auditors do report on in the statutory financial audit.

This is an area in which the auditors can therefore provide an alternative service to audit, in the form of a review or assurance engagement. This chapter looks at the factors that the auditor should think about when taking on such an engagement. The basis for this chapter has been laid in Chapter 12, but in this chapter, we consider issues specific to PFI.

Study guide

		Intellectual level
E5	**Prospective financial information**	
(a)	Define 'prospective financial information' (PFI) and distinguish between a 'forecast', a 'projection', a 'hypothetical illustration' and a 'target'	1
(b)	Explain the principles of useful PFI	1
(c)	Identify and describe the matters to be considered before accepting a specified engagement to report on PFI	2
(d)	Discuss the level of assurance that the auditor may provide and explain the other factors to be considered in determining the nature, timing and extent of examination procedures	1
(e)	Describe examination procedures to verify forecasts and projections	2
(f)	Compare the content of a report on an examination of PFI with reports made in providing audit-related services	2
F3	**Reporting**	
(b)	Discuss the content of a report on examination of prospective financial information.	2

Exam guide

The difficulties of reporting on PFI could be examined in an exam question. Case studies can easily be set in the context of a PFI assignment.

1 Reporting on prospective financial information

> Prospective financial information is difficult to give assurance about because it is highly subjective.

Key term

> **Prospective financial information (PFI)** is information based on assumptions about events that may occur in the future and possible actions by an entity.

From the definition given above, you can see that prospective financial information is highly subjective. This makes it a difficult area to examine and report on. Guidance on reporting on PFI is given in ISAE 3400 *The examination of prospective financial information*.

The key issues that projections relate to are:

- Capital expenditure
- Profits
- Cash flows

These are the key areas which we will focus on in the procedure part of this chapter.

1.1 Principles of prospective financial information

Increasingly, company directors are producing PFI, either voluntarily or because it is required by regulators, for example, in the case of a public offering of shares.

Markets and investors need PFI that is understandable, relevant, reliable and comparable. Some specific issues arise in applying these principles to PFI.

Principle	Issue arising
Understandable	Disclosure is required of sources of uncertainty, assumptions made, determining factors that will affect whether the assumptions will be borne out, and alternative outcomes.
Relevant	No PFI-specific issues arise other than the need for the information to be relevant to the decision-making of investors or other users of the information.
Reliable	The reliability of PFI cannot be confirmed by evidence of past transactions or events. Its reliability depends on it being supported by analysis of the entity's business, strategies and plans.
Comparable	The PFI should be capable of comparison with eventual outcomes in the form of historical financial information. The accounting policies used in its preparation should also be disclosed.

1.2 Types of prospective financial information

PFI can be of two types (or a combination of both):

Forecast. PFI based on assumptions as to future events which management expects to take place and the actions management expects to take (best-estimate assumptions).

Projection. PFI based on hypothetical assumptions about future events and management actions, or a mixture of best-estimate and hypothetical assumptions.

There are two other terms commonly associated with PFI:

Hypothetical illustration. PFI based on assumptions about uncertain future events and management actions which have not yet been decided on.

Target. PFI based on assumptions about the future performance of the entity.

2 Accepting an engagement

FAST FORWARD

The auditor should agree the terms of the engagement with the directors, and should withdraw from the engagement if the assumptions made to put together the PFI are unrealistic.

2.1 General considerations

The ISAE gives the following guidance about accepting an engagement to examine PFI.

ISAE 3400.11

The auditor should not accept, or should withdraw from, an engagement when the assumptions are clearly unrealistic or when the auditor believes that the prospective financial information will be inappropriate for its intended use.

ISAE 3400.12

The auditor and the client should agree on the terms of the engagement.

The ISAE also lists the following **factors** which the auditor should consider:

- The **intended use** of the information
- Whether the information will be for general or limited **distribution**
- The **nature of the assumptions**, that is, whether they are best estimate or hypothetical assumptions
- The **elements** to be **included** in the information
- The **period covered** by the information

It also states that the auditor should have sufficient knowledge of the business to be able to evaluate the significant assumptions made.

A firm must also consider practical matters, such as the time available to them, their experience of the staff member compiling the information, any limitations on their work, and the degree of secrecy required beyond the normal duty of confidentiality.

3 Procedures
12/09, 6/11

FAST FORWARD

Procedures could include:

- Analytical review (against similar historic projects)
- Verification of projected expenditure to quotes or estimates

3.1 General matters

In carrying out their review, the general matters to which attention should be directed are:

- The nature and background of the company's business
- The accounting policies normally followed by the company
- The assumptions on which the forecast is based
- The procedures followed by the company in preparing the forecast

3.1.1 The nature and background of the company's business

The accountants will review the company's character and recent history, with reference to such matters as the nature of its activities and its main products, markets, customers, suppliers, divisions, locations, and trend of results.

3.1.2 The accounting policies normally followed by the company

The accountant will wish to establish the accounting principles normally followed by the company and ensure that they have been consistently applied in the preparation of forecasts.

3.1.3 The procedure followed by the company in preparing the forecast

In carrying out their review of the accounting bases and calculations for forecasts, and the procedures followed by the company for preparing them, the main points which the reporting accountants will wish to consider include the following:

(a) Whether the forecast under review is based on forecasts regularly prepared for the purpose of management or whether it has been separately and specially prepared for the immediate purpose

(b) Where forecasts are regularly prepared for management purposes, the degree of accuracy and reliability previously achieved, and the frequency and thoroughness with which estimates are revised

(c) Whether the forecast under review represents the management's best estimate of results which they reasonably believe can and will be achieved rather than targets which the management have set as desirable

(d) The extent to which forecast results for expired periods are supported by reliable interim accounts

(e) The details of the procedures followed to generate the forecast and the extent to which it is built up from detailed forecasts of activity and cash flow

(f) The extent to which profits are derived from activities having a proven and consistent trend and those of a more irregular, volatile or unproven nature

(g) How the forecast takes account of any material extraordinary items and prior year adjustments, their nature, and how they are presented

(h)   Whether adequate provision is made for foreseeable losses and contingencies and how the forecast takes account of factors which may cause it to be subject to a high degree of risk, or which may invalidate the assumptions

(i)   Whether working capital appears adequate for requirements (normally this would require the availability of properly prepared cash flow forecasts) and where short-term or long-term finance is to be relied on, whether the necessary arrangements have been made and confirmed

(j)   The arithmetical accuracy of the forecast and the supporting information and whether forecast statements of financial position and statements of cash flows have been prepared (as these help to highlight arithmetical inaccuracies and inconsistent assumptions)

ISAE 3400.17

When determining the nature, timing and extent of examination procedures, the auditor's considerations should include:

(a)   The likelihood of material misstatement;

(b)   The knowledge obtained during any previous engagement;

(c)   Management's competence regarding the preparation of prospective financial information;

(d)   The extent to which the prospective financial information is affected by the management's judgement;

(e)   The adequacy and the reliability of the underlying data.

The ISAE goes on to say that the auditor should **seek appropriate evidence** on those areas which are **particularly sensitive to variation** and have a **material effect** on the information.

3.2 Specific matters

The following list of procedures may also be relevant when assessing prospective financial information. The auditor should undertake the review procedures discussed above in addition to these.

Profit forecasts

*   Verify projected **income** figures to suitable evidence. This may involve:
    *   Comparison of the basis of projected income to similar existing projects in the firm
    *   Review of current market prices for that product or service
*   Verify projected **expenditure** figures to suitable evidence. There is likely to be more evidence available about expenditure in the form of:
    *   Quotations or estimates provided to the firm
    *   Current bills for things such as services which can be used to reliably estimate
    *   Market rate prices, for example, for advertising
    *   Interest rate assumptions can be compared to the bank's current rates
    *   Costs such as depreciation should correspond with relevant capital expenditure projections

Capital expenditure

The auditor should check the capital expenditure for **reasonableness**. For example, if the projection relates to buying land and developing it, it should include a sum for land.

*   Projected costs should be **verified to estimates and quotations** where possible
*   The projections can be reviewed for **reasonableness**, including a comparison with prevailing **market rates** where such information is available (such as for property)

Cash forecasts

*   The auditors should review cash forecasts to ensure the **timings involved** are **reasonable**.
*   The auditor should check the cash forecast for **consistency with any profit forecasts** (income/expenditure should be the same, just at different times).

- If there is no comparable profit forecast, the income and expenditure items should be verified as they would have been on a profit forecast.

Working capital

- **Confirm sources** of short-term and long-term finance to evidence from external finance providers.
- Compare the reasonableness of **available** finance to cash flow forecasts.
- Assess the reasonableness of **projected working capital ratios** such as trade receivables days and the assumptions made in calculating these.
- Compare working capital projections to **historical trends** to assess reasonableness.

Exam focus point

When faced with a PFI question in the exam it is important to tailor your answer to the facts given in the question. For example, don't say 'verify projected building costs to builders' quote' if the question states no quote has been obtained.

4 Expressing an opinion   12/09

FAST FORWARD

It is impossible to give the same level of assurance about PFI as it is on historical financial information but negative assurance may be given.

4.1 Level of assurance

It is clear that as prospective financial information is subjective information, it is **impossible** for an auditor **to give the same level of assurance** regarding it, as he would on **historic financial information**.

The ISAE suggests that the auditor express an opinion including:

- A statement of **negative assurance** as to whether the **assumptions** provide a reasonable basis for the prospective financial information
- An opinion as to whether the prospective financial information is **properly prepared** on the basis of the assumptions and the relevant reporting framework
- Appropriate **caveats as to the achievability** of the forecasts

Key term

Negative assurance is assurance of something in the absence of any evidence arising to the contrary. In effect, this means the auditor is saying, 'I believe that this is reasonable because I have no reason to believe otherwise.'

4.2 Reports under ISAE 3400

ISAE 3400.27

The report by an auditor on an examination of prospective financial information should contain the following:

(a) Title

(b) Addressee

(c) Identification of the prospective financial information

(d) A reference to the ISAE or relevant national standards or practices applicable to the examination of prospective financial information

(e) A statement that management is responsible for the prospective financial information including the assumptions on which it is based

(f) When applicable, a reference to the purpose and/or restricted distribution of the prospective financial information

(g)   A statement of negative assurance as to whether the assumptions provide a reasonable basis for the prospective financial information

(h)   An opinion as to whether the prospective financial information is properly prepared on the basis of the assumptions and is presented in accordance with the relevant financial reporting framework

(i)   Appropriate caveats concerning the achievability of the results indicated by the prospective financial information

(j)   Date of the report which should be the date procedures have been completed

(k)   Auditor's address

(l)   Signature

ISAE 3400.31

When the auditor believes that the presentation and disclosure of the prospective financial information is not adequate, the auditor should express a qualified or adverse opinion in the report on the prospective financial information, or withdraw from the engagement as appropriate.

ISAE 3400.32

When the auditor believes that one or more significant assumptions do not provide a reasonable basis for the prospective financial information prepared on the basis of best-estimate assumptions or that one or more significant assumptions do not provide a reasonable basis for the prospective financial information given the hypothetical assumptions, the auditor should either express an adverse opinion in the report on the prospective financial information or withdraw from the engagement.

Question   Prospective financial information

A new client of your practice, Peter Lawrence, has recently been made redundant. He is considering setting up a residential home for elderly people as he is aware that there is an increasing need for this service with an ageing population (more people are living to an older age). He has seen a large house, which he plans to convert into an old people's home. Each resident will have a bedroom, there will be a communal sitting-room and all meals will be provided in a dining-room. No long-term nursing care will be provided, as people requiring this service will either be in hospital or in another type of accommodation for the elderly.

The large house is in a poor state of repair, and will require considerable structural alterations (building work), and repairs to make it suitable for an old people's home. The following will also be required:

*   New furnishings (carpets, beds, wardrobes and so on for the resident's rooms; carpets and furniture for the sitting-room and dining-room)
*   Decoration of the whole house (painting the woodwork and covering the walls with wallpaper)
*   Equipment (for the kitchen and for helping disabled residents)

Mr Lawrence and his wife propose to work full-time in the business, which he expects to be available for residents six months after the purchase of the house. Mr Lawrence has already obtained some estimates of the conversion costs, and information on the income and expected running costs of the home.

Mr Lawrence has received about $30,000 from his redundancy. He expects to receive about $30,000 from the sale of his house (after repaying his house loan). The owners of the house he proposes to buy are asking $50,000 for it, and Mr Lawrence expects to spend $50,000 on conversion of the house (building work, furnishing, decorations and equipment).

Mr Lawrence has prepared a draft capital expenditure forecast, a profit forecast and a cash flow forecast which he has asked you to check before he submits them to the bank, in order to obtain finance for the old people's home.

Required

Describe the procedures you would carry out on:

(a) The capital expenditure forecast
(b) The profit forecast
(c) The cash flow forecast

Answer

All three of the forecasts to be reviewed should be prepared on a monthly basis and the following work would be required in order to consider their reasonableness.

(a) **Capital expenditure forecast**

  (i) Read estate agent's details and solicitors' correspondence and compare to the capital expenditure forecast to ensure that all expenditure (including sale price, surveyors' fees, legal costs, taxes on purchase) is included

  (ii) Confirm the estimated cost of new furnishings by agreeing them to supplier price lists or quotations

  (iii) Verify any discounts assumed in the forecast are correct by asking the suppliers if they will apply them to this transaction

  (iv) Confirm projected building and decoration costs to the relevant suppliers' quotation

  (v) Confirm the projected cost of specialist equipment (and relevant bulk discounts) to suppliers' price lists or websites

  (vi) In the light of my experience of other such ventures, consider whether the forecast includes all relevant costs

(b) **Profit forecast**

  As a first step it will be necessary to recognise that the residential home will not be able to generate any income until the bulk of the capital expenditure has been incurred in order to make the home 'habitable'. However, whilst no income can be anticipated the business will have started to incur expenditure in the form of loan interest, rates and insurance.

  The only income from the new building will be rent receivable from residents. The rentals which Mr Lawrence is proposing to charge should be assessed for reasonableness in the light of rental charged to similar homes in the same area. In projecting income it would be necessary to anticipate that it is likely to take some time before the home is fully occupied and it would be prudent to allow for some periods where vacancies arise because of the 'loss' of some of the established residents.

  The expenditure of the business is likely to include the following.

  (i) **Wages and salaries.** Although Mr and Mrs Lawrence intend to work full-time in the business, they will undoubtedly need to employ additional staff to care for residents, cook, clean and tend to the gardens. The numbers of staff and the rates of pay should be compared to similar local businesses of which the firm has knowledge.

  (ii) **Rates and water rates.** The estimate of the likely cost of these can be confirmed by asking the local council and/or the estate agents dealing with the sale of property.

  (iii) **Food.** The estimate of the expenditure for food should be based on the projected levels of staff and residents, with some provision for wastage.

  (iv) **Heat and light.** The estimates for heat, light and cooking facilities should be compared to similar clients' actual bills.

  (v) **Insurance.** This cost should be verified to quotes from the insurance broker.

  (vi) **Advertising.** The costs of newspaper and brochure advertising costs should be checked against quotes obtained by Mr Lawrence.

  (vii) **Repairs and renewals.** Adequate provision should be made for replacement of linen, crockery and such like and maintenance of the property.

(viii) **Depreciation.** The depreciation charge should be recalculated with reference to the capital costs involved being charged to the capital expenditure forecast.

(ix) **Loan interest and bank charges.** These should be checked against the bank's current rates and the amount of the principal agreed to the cash forecast.

(c) **Cash flow forecast**

(i) Check that the timing of the capital expenditure on the cash flow forecast is consistent with that shown on the capital expenditure forecast

(ii) Compare the cash flow forecast to the details within the profit forecast to ensure they tie up, for example:

– Income from residents would normally be receivable weekly/monthly in advance.

– The majority of expenditure for wages etc would be payable in the month in which it is incurred.

– Payments to the major utilities (gas, electricity, telephone) will normally be payable quarterly, as will the bank charges.

– Rates and taxes are normally paid half-yearly.

– Insurance premiums will normally be paid annually in advance.

(iii) Redo the additions on the cash forecast and check that figures that appear on other forecasts are carried over correctly.

 Question   More prospective financial information

Gunthorpe Plumbing Supplies ('Gunthorpe') is a wholly owned subsidiary of Lucknow Builders Merchants ('Lucknow') and has been trading at a loss for a number of years. The recent bleak economic climate has led the directors of Lucknow to decide to put Gunthorpe into liquidation and make all the employees redundant, including its three directors.

The three directors of Gunthorpe have decided to form a new company, Gunthorpe Plumbing Supplies (2008) ('Gunthorpe (2008)'), and use their redundancy pay and personal savings to purchase all the shares in the company.

The board of directors of Lucknow have agreed to sell the following assets and liabilities of Gunthorpe to the new company.

(a) All the non-current assets except for one warehouse (see below)
(b) Trading inventory
(c) Trade receivables and payables

The price for the non-current assets has been agreed and the value of the trading inventory, receivables and payables, will be confirmed at the date of transfer by an independent valuer.

The directors of Gunthorpe (2008) propose to obtain additional finance in the form of a long-term loan from a merchant bank and working capital will be financed by a bank overdraft from their existing bankers.

The directors have asked you to assist them in preparing a profit forecast and cash flow forecast for submission to the two banks. They have provided you with copies of the detailed accounts of Gunthorpe for the past five years, and they point out the following changes which, in their opinion, will enable the new company to trade at a profit.

(a) The substantial management charge imposed by Lucknow will disappear. However, additional costs will have to be incurred for services which were provided by the parent company, such as maintaining the accounting records and servicing the company's vehicles.

(b) Initially fewer staff will be employed.

(c) Only one of the company's two premises is being taken over – the premises which are not being taken over will be sold by Lucknow on the open market.

The directors have provided you with the following brief details of Gunthorpe's trade. It currently has a revenue of about $1 million and is a wholesaler of plumbing equipment (copper pipes, pipe connections, water taps etc) which are sold mainly on credit to plumbers and builders. Trade discount is given to larger customers. There are some cash sales to smaller customers, but these represent no more than 10% of total sales.

Required

Describe the work you would perform to:

(a)   Verify that the value of items included in the profit forecast is reasonable

(b)   Verify that the value of items included in the cash flow forecast is reasonable

Answer

(a)   **Verification of items in profit forecast**

The main items appearing in the profit forecast and the required work in relation to them would be as follows:

(i)   The budgeted sales income should be considered against that which has actually been achieved in recent years. If the new management are forecasting any increase in the level of sales, the justification for this must be carefully reviewed. Tests should be made to ensure that all expenditure directly related to income is properly accounted for. Confirmation should be sought that the projected income takes proper account of the trade discounts that it is assumed will have to be granted.

(ii)   The major form of expenditure is likely to be the purchase of goods for resale. Enquiry should be made as to whether suppliers will continue to grant the new company the same level of trade discounts as the old company and also whether the volume of purchases is such that a similar mark-up will be attained. Management explanations should be sought for any material differences in the anticipated gross profit rate, such explanations being fully investigated as to their plausibility.

(iii)   The wages and salaries payable by the new company should be checked by asking management how many people they intend to employ and at what rates. The reasonableness of the projected charge for wages and salaries should be assessed by comparison with the figure for wages and salaries most recently paid by the old company.

(iv)   All other major items of expenditure included in the profit forecast (ie selling expenses, finance expenses and administration expenses) should be considered by comparison with the figures of the old company in previous years, ensuring that a reasonable allowance is made for the effects of inflation.

(v)   The charges for items previously covered by the management charge should be checked for their completeness and reasonableness.

(vi)   An overall review of the projected profits should be undertaken to ensure that it appears to be a realistic forecast and not merely an idealistic target figure.

(b)   **Verification of items in the cash flow forecast**

As well as generally checking to ensure that the cash flow forecast appears to be consistent with the profit forecast, specific checks should be made as follows.

(i)   The timing of payments due to the parent company.

(ii)   The period of credit granted to customers by the old company as it is unlikely that the new company will be in a position to insist on prompter payment by customers.

(iii)   The period of credit taken from suppliers should be dealt with in a similar way, although enquiry should be made as to whether creditors are prepared to trade with the new company on the same terms as the old.

(iv)   The timing of payment for overhead expenditure should be checked to see that it is reasonable and consistent with established practice.

(v)   Although in the early months one would not expect there to be any major purchase or sale of non-current assets, the position here should be confirmed by discussion with management of their long term plans.

- Prospective financial information is difficult to give assurance about because it is highly subjective.

- The auditor should agree the terms of the engagement with the directors, and should withdraw from the engagement if the assumptions made to put together the PFI are unrealistic.

- Procedures could include:

  – Analytical review (against similar historic projects)
  – Verification of projected expenditure to quotes or estimates

- It is impossible to give the same level of assurance about PFI as it is on historical financial information but negative assurance may be given.

Quick Quiz

1 Complete the definition.

A .... means PFI prepared on the basis of .... as to .... events which management expects to take place and .... management expects to take as of the .... the .... is ....

2 Complete the matters an auditor should consider when undertaking a PFI engagement.

- The intended .... of the information
- Whether the information will be general or limited ....
- The nature of the ....
- The .... to be included in the information
- The .... to be covered by the information

3 Identify whether the following procedures are relevant to profit forecasts, capital expenditure forecasts or cash forecasts.

- Ensure the timings are reasonable
- Projected costs should be verified to estimates and quotations
- Analytical review on income (based on comparable projects)
- Review for reasonableness
- Review for consistency with profit forecast

4 Complete the definition.

.... is assurance of something in the .... of any evidence arising to the ....

5 Reporting accountants are responsible for the PFI they are giving an opinion on.

True ☐

False ☐

Answers to Quick Quiz

1   Forecast, assumptions, future, actions, date, information, prepared.

2   Use, distribution, assumptions, elements, period.

3   • Ensure the timings are reasonable   Cash
     • Projected costs should be verified to estimates and quotations   P/CapEx
     • Analytical review on income (based on comparable projects)   P
     • Review for reasonableness   P/CapEx/Cash
     • Review for consistency with profit forecast   CapEx/Cash

4   Negative assurance, absence, contrary.

5   False

Now try the question below from the Exam Question Bank

Number	Level	Marks	Time
Q24	Examination	20	36 mins

14

Forensic audits

Topic list	Syllabus reference
1 Definitions	E4
2 Applications of forensic auditing	E4
3 Ethical principles	E4
4 Planning, procedures and evidence	E4

Introduction

In the current globalised business world there is an increasing demand for forensic services. Audit and assurance professionals are well-placed to provide these.

This chapter introduces forensic accounting and auditing and discusses its applications in practice. It also considers the ethical issues applicable to forensic accountants.

The chapter concludes with a look at investigative procedures and evidence.

Study guide

		Intellectual level
E4	**Forensic audits**	
(a)	Define the terms 'forensic accounting', 'forensic investigation' and 'forensic audit'	1
(b)	Describe the major applications of forensic auditing (eg fraud, negligence, insurance claims) and analyse the role of the forensic auditor as an expert witness	2
(c)	Apply the fundamental ethical principles to professional accountants engaged in forensic audit assignments	2
(d)	Plan a forensic audit engagement	2
(e)	Select investigative procedures and evaluate evidence appropriate to determining the loss in a given situation	3

Exam guide

As is illustrated in the pilot paper, this topic can be examined in a very practical way. It is important to have an understanding of the framework but case study questions will involve the application of very similar procedures to those used in traditional audits of financial statements. Some specific knowledge is required of basic definitions, but otherwise the application of audit-style procedures is used.

1 Definitions

Pilot paper, 12/07, 12/08

Key terms

> **Forensic auditing.** The process of gathering, analysing and reporting on data, in a pre-defined context, for the purpose of finding facts and/or evidence in the context of financial/legal disputes and/or irregularities and giving preventative advice in this area.
>
> **Forensic investigation.** Carried out for civil or criminal cases. These can involve fraud or money laundering.
>
> **Forensic accounting.** Undertaking a financial investigation in response to a particular event, where the findings of the investigation may be used as evidence in court or to otherwise help resolve disputes.

1.1 More general definitions

The range of assignments in this area is vast so to give specific definitions for each is not always practicable. In a publication by the Institute of Chartered Accountants of Canada *Standard practices for investigative and forensic accounting engagements* (November 2006) the following definition is established.

> **Investigative and forensic accounting engagements** are those that:
>
> (a) Require the application of professional accounting skills, investigative skills, and an investigative mindset; and
>
> (b) Involve disputes or anticipated disputes, or where there are risks, concerns or allegations of fraud or other illegal or unethical conduct

EForensic audit and accounting is a rapidly-growing area. The major accountancy firms all offer forensic services, as do a number of specialist companies. The demand for these services arises partly from the increased expectation of corporate governance codes for:

- Company directors to take seriously their responsibilities for the prevention and detection of fraud, and also from
- Governments concerned abut risks arising from criminal funding of terrorist groups.

The next section outlines a number of the main applications of forensic auditing.

2 Applications of forensic auditing

AST FORWARD

Forensic auditing can be applied to a number of situations, including fraud and negligence investigations.

2.1 Fraud

Forensic accountants can be engaged to investigate fraud. This could involve:

- Quantifying losses from theft of cash or goods
- Identifying payments or receipts of bribes
- Identifying intentional misstatements in financial information, such as overstatement of revenue and earnings and understatement of costs and expenses
- Investigating intentional misrepresentations made to auditors

Forensic accountants may also be engaged to act in an advisory capacity to assist directors in developing more effective controls to reduce the risks from fraud.

2.2 Negligence

When an auditor or accountant is being sued for negligence, either or both parties to the case may employ forensic accountants to investigate the work done to provide evidence as to whether it did in fact meet the standards required. They may also be involved in establishing the amount of loss suffered by the plaintiff.

2.3 Insurance claims

Insurance companies often employ forensic accountants to report on the validity of the amounts of losses being claimed, as a means of resolving the disputes between the company and the claimant.

This could involve computing losses following an insured event such as a fire, flood or robbery. If a criminal action arises over an allegation that an insured event was deliberately contrived to defraud the insurance company, the forensic accountant may be called upon as an expert witness (see Section 2.6).

 Case Study

The following example illustrates that investigating fraud is sometimes a matter of applying common sense.

A forensic accountant was asked by an insurance company to quantify the value of loss to a firm following a robbery of gold bars. From the security tapes it was known that the two men, of average height and build, only made one visit to the safe. The accountant compared the amount claimed with a calculation of the weight of gold bars the two men could have physically carried and found that the claim was vastly inflated!

2.4 Other disputes

Forensic accountants can be involved in the investigation of many other types of dispute such as:

- Shareholder disputes
- Partnership disputes
- Contract disputes
- Business sales and purchase disputes
- Matrimonial disputes, including:
    - Valuing the family business
    - Gathering financial evidence
    - Identifying 'hidden' assets
    - Advising in settlement negotiations

2.5 Terrorist financing

In Chapter 1 we saw the legal requirements imposed on professional accountants in this area. In addition, governments are increasingly turning to forensic accountants as part of their counter-terrorism strategy.

The following quote is taken from a speech made by Gordon Brown, when he was the UK Chancellor of the Exchequer, in October 2006:

'...forensic accounting of transaction trails across continents has been vital in identifying threats, uncovering accomplices, piecing together company structures, and ultimately providing evidence for prosecution. Most recently, forensic accounting techniques have tracked an alleged terrorist bomb maker, using multiple identities, multiple bank accounts and third parties and third world countries to purchase bomb making equipment and tracked him to and uncovered an overseas bomb factory.'

2.6 The forensic accountant as an expert witness

The preceding sections have identified a number of circumstances where the forensic accountant may be involved as an expert witness in civil or criminal cases. For civil cases in England and Wales the duties of expert witnesses are set out in the **Civil Procedure Rules (CPR)**.

2.6.1 Duties of experts

Experts always owe a duty to exercise reasonable skill and care to those instructing them, and to comply with any relevant professional code of ethics. However when they are instructed to give or prepare evidence for the purpose of civil proceedings in England and Wales they have an overriding duty to help the court on matters within their expertise. This duty overrides any obligation to the person instructing or paying them. Experts must not serve the exclusive interest of those who retain them.

Experts should be aware of the overriding objective that courts deal with cases justly. This includes dealing with cases proportionately, expeditiously and fairly. Experts are under an obligation to assist the court so as to enable them to deal with cases in accordance with the overriding objective. However the overriding objective does not impose on experts any duty to act as mediators between the parties or require them to trespass on the role of the court in deciding facts.

Experts should provide opinions which are independent, regardless of the pressures of litigation. In this context, a useful test of 'independence' is that the expert would express the same opinion if given the same instructions by an opposing party. Experts should not take it upon themselves to promote the point of view of the party instructing them or engage in the role of advocates.

Experts should confine their opinions to matters which are material to the disputes between the parties and provide opinions only in relation to matters which lie within their expertise. Experts should indicate without delay where particular questions or issues fall outside their expertise.

Experts should take into account all material facts before them at the time that they give their opinion. Their reports should set out those facts and any literature or any other material on which they have relied upon in forming their opinions. They should indicate if an opinion is provisional or qualified, or where they consider that further information is required or if, for any other reason, they are not satisfied that an opinion an be expressed finally and without qualification.

Experts should inform those instructing them without delay of any change in their opinions on any material matter and the reason for it.

Experts should be aware that any failure by them to comply with the Civil Procedure Rules or court orders or any excessive delay for which they are responsible may result in the parties who instructed them being penalised in costs and even, in extreme cases, being debarred from placing the experts' evidence before the court.

2.6.2 Expert witness reports

The UK's Expert Witness Institute has produced a model form of expert's report to help expert witnesses, of whatever profession, to meet their legal duties. The main contents are outlined below:

Index/list of contents	Optional, but desirable
Brief curriculum vitae	Including expert's name, qualifications (eg ACCA) and relevant experience
Summary of conclusions	Brief list of main facts from the evidence and the conclusions/opinions arrived at
Instructions	Must give the substance of all instructions received by the expert, whether written or oral
Issues	The issues to be addressed and the questions to be answered must be clearly set out
Documentation	Full list of all documents and material on which the report is based
Chronology	This must deal only with **factual** evidence, not any matter of opinion
Technical background	Where technical aspects of the issues are outside the general knowledge or experience of those who will have to deal with the report an explanation of the technical issues in this section may be necessary. For example, in a case involving fraudulent accounting, the requirements of specific accounting standards may have to be explained.
Opinion	This should be presented clearly and unambiguously. The reasons for the opinions given should be explicit.
References	A numbered list of all items of technical literature relied on. For example in a negligence case this may comprise a list of relevant accounting standards and auditing standards.
Declaration	The expert must sign a declaration confirming his understanding of his legal duties, and including the following 'Statement of Truth':
	'I confirm that insofar as the facts stated in my report are within my own knowledge I have made clear which they are and I believe them to be true, and the opinions I have expressed represent my true and complete professional opinion.'

Exam focus point

The current P7 examiner wrote an article entitled 'Forensic auditing' in the September 2008 edition of *Student Accountant*. This article can also be accessed via the ACCA website and covers some of the key issues relevant to forensic investigations.

FAST FORWARD

The fundamental principles of the *Code of Ethics and Conduct* apply to ACCA members in all professional assignments.

3.1 Example

The following table contains a recap of the fundamental principles. Take a few minutes to think and note down any special relevance you see in them in relation to forensic assignments.

Question   Ethical principles

Integrity	
Objectivity	
Professional competence and due care	
Confidentiality	
Professional behaviour	

Answer

Integrity	Forensic accountants are often, by definition, working in an environment and dealing with individuals who are dishonest and lack integrity. If there is any risk that their own integrity may be compromised they should decline or withdraw from the assignment.
Objectivity	The previous section on the role of the expert witness emphasised the need for independence and objectivity. Any perceived threats to objectivity will undermine the credibility of the accountant's opinion.
Professional competence and due care	Forensic assignments may require very specialised skills, for example, where evidence gathering requires specific IT skills. A firm should consider very carefully whether they have adequate skills and resources before accepting the assignment.
Confidentiality	Forensic accountants will often be working for one party to a dispute, and have access to very sensitive information. Subject, of course, to legal rules of disclosure in court cases, it is clearly essential to maintain the strictest confidentiality.
Professional behaviour	Fraud cases and other situations such as takeover disputes can be very much in the public eye. Any lapse in the professionalism of, say, an expert witness could do serious damage to the reputation of the profession as a whole.

FAST FORWARD

> Many of the techniques used in a forensic investigation will be similar to those used in the audit of financial statements but the different objectives and risks of the assignment require some differences in approach.

4.1 Planning

The broad process of conducting a forensic audit bears some similarity to an audit of financial statements, in that it will include a planning stage, a period when evidence is gathered, a review process, and a report to the client. However, forensic investigations are not all of the same sort, and it is essential that the investigation team considers carefully exactly what it is that they have been asked to achieve in this particular investigation, and that they plan their work accordingly. Professional judgement will be required to:

- Identify the objectives of the engagement
- Obtain sufficient understanding of the circumstances and events surrounding the engagement
- Obtain sufficient understanding of the context within which the engagement is to be conducted (eg any relevant laws or regulations)
- Identify any limitation on the scope of the engagement (eg where information is not available)
- Evaluate the resources necessary to complete the work, and identifying a suitable engagement team.

In order to meet these requirements, the engagement plan should include the following.

- Develop hypotheses to address the circumstances and context of the engagement
- Decide on the best approach to meet the engagement objectives within constraints such as cost and time
- Identify the financial (and other) information needed, and develop a strategy to acquire it
- Determine the impact of the nature and timing of any reporting requirements.

One key difference in emphasis from an audit of financial statements is that the forensic accountant is stepping into an arena that is defined by conflict. It is thus essential that the investigator obtains an understanding of the background and context to the engagement as well as of any limitations on its scope, as these will affect the extent of the conclusions that can be drawn. In the case of a matrimonial dispute, for example, the investigator would need to take a sceptical attitude towards all the information they are provided with, as it may be biased, false or incomplete.

Many forensic investigations involve investigating potential frauds. The objectives of a fraud investigation would include the following:

- Identifying the type of fraud that has been operating, how long it has been operating for, and how the fraud has been concealed
- Identifying the fraudster(s) involved
- Quantifying the financial loss suffered by the client
- Gathering evidence to be used in court proceedings
- Providing advice to prevent the recurrence of the fraud.

The investigators should then consider the best way to gather evidence in the light of these objectives.

4.2 Audit procedures

The specific procedures which would be performed as part of a forensic audit will depend on the specific nature of the investigation. However, using a fraud investigation as an example, the following would normally apply.

- Develop a profile of the entity under investigation including its personnel
- Identify weaknesses in internal control procedures and basic record keeping, eg bank reconciliations not performed
- Perform trend analysis and analytical procedures to identify significant transactions and significant variations from the norm
- Identify changes in patterns of purchases/sales, particularly where a limited number of suppliers/customers are involved
- Identify significant variations in consumption of raw materials and consumables, particularly where consumption appears excessive
- Identify unusual accounts and account balances, eg closing credit balances on debit accounts and *vice versa*
- Review accounting records for unusual transactions and entries, eg large numbers of accounting entries between accounts, transactions not executed at normal commercial rates
- Review transaction documentation (eg invoices) for discrepancies and inconsistencies
- Once identified trace the individual responsible for fraudulent transactions
- Obtain information regarding all responsibilities of the individual involved
- Inspect and review all other transactions conducted by the individual of a similar nature
- Consider all other aspects of the business which the individual is involved with and perform further analytical procedures targeting these areas to identify any additional discrepancies

Question

Forensic audit

You are a manager in the forensic investigation department of an audit firm. You have been approached by the financial director of Arnold Co to investigate a fraud. The finance director has identified a number of discrepancies between inventory records and the quarterly physical inventory counts which are performed. His suspicions have been increased by the fact that the discrepancy always relates to the same product line and approximately the same number of items appear to be missing each time.

Required

Explain the procedures you would perform to determine whether a fraud has taken place and to quantify the loss suffered by the company.

Answer

> **Tutorial note.** In this case the approach taken is likely to involve elimination of legitimate reasons why the discrepancies may have arisen.

Procedures would involve the following:

To establish whether a fraud has taken place

- Obtain an understanding of the business and in particular the roles and responsibilities of those involved in processing inventory transactions and those in the warehouse.
- Discuss with management the method adopted for conducting the quarterly inventory count and review the detail of the count instructions. Any weaknesses in the controls should be identified and considered as a possible explanation for the discrepancies, eg double counting of this particular line of inventory.

- Obtain confirmation of whether inventory is held at more than one location. If so confirm that this has been included in the physical inventory counts.
- Review procedures for the identification of obsolete and damaged items and in particular the disposal of such items. Determine who is responsible for making the decision and the procedures for updating records for these adjustments. If items have been disposed of but records not maintained this could explain the discrepancy.

- Obtain an understanding of the system for the processing and recording of despatches and in particular consider the effectiveness of controls regarding completeness of despatches. Trace transactions from order to despatch in respect of the inventory line in question to confirm that all goods out have been recorded.
- Obtain an understanding of the system for the processing and recording of goods received for this inventory line. Controls over the initial booking in of inventory should be reviewed. If inventory is double counted at this stage this could account for the discrepancy.
- Review the system for subsequent processing of goods received, in particular the controls and procedures regarding the accuracy of input. If goods in are processed more than once this would give rise to a discrepancy between the book records and actual inventory.
- Assess the existence of general controls affecting access to the warehouse and inventory.

To quantify the loss

The evidence obtained above should enable the auditor to determine the accuracy of the book record and the accuracy of the physical inventory records. A reconciliation of the two figures should provide the number of units missing. The cost of each unit should be agreed to recent purchase invoices.

4.3 Differences in approach

Whilst many of the techniques used in a forensic investigation will be similar to those used in an audit the different objectives and risks involved will require some differences in approach.

Materiality	In many investigations there will be no materiality threshold.
Timing	Clearly less predictable than audit
	Timing of procedures needs to be unpredictable
Documentation	Needs to be reviewed more critically than on an audit
	The example in this section shows what an experienced fraud investigator might identify in a fraudulent invoice.
Interviews	It may be appropriate to interview a suspected fraudster in the hope of obtaining an admission but this entails some problems:
	• Challenging and requires a high skill level
	• Legal issues including the risk of being sued for defamation
Computer-aided techniques	Data mining is a key part of many investigation processes. It allows the accountant to access and analyse thousands or millions of transactions that have passed through an accounting system, and identify, say, unusual trends far more quickly than by traditional documentary analysis.
	100% of an entity's transactions can be checked for characteristics such as date, time, amount, approval, payee etc.
	If possible, data should be gathered prior to the initial field visit to reduce the risk of the data being compromised.

4.4 Example

Porridge Associates   **Invoice**

Suite 214
The Castle
Lancaster
LA1 1YL

INVOICE NO: 000796
DATE: February 5, 20X7
Registered Sales Tax Number 394/8126/07

To: **Attn: Peter Kenworthy**
         Silverfin Enterprises Limited   Our Reference:
         Century House
         Brook Street
         London NW3 9HE   **For the period: 1.3.X7 to 31/3/X7**

CONSULTANT	DESCRIPTION		AMOUNT
JFB	Fees in relation to testing of electronic payment systems		
	Total fees:		£8,000.00
	Expenses	£500.00	£500.00
		SUBTOTAL	£8,500.00
		SALES TAX	1,487.50
		TOTAL DUE	£9,987.50

If you have any questions concerning this invoice, call: **0778 279 1789**
or write to **Porridge Associates, UK Head office, 127 Elm Avenue, Nottingham, N12 7PY**
THANK YOU FOR YOUR BUSINESS!

Remittance Advice   Invoice Number: **LIA 000796**

To: Porridge Associates
         Bank of Wealth (Jersey) Ltd
         St Helier
         Jersey   Enclosed please find our cheque for
         Account number   87620549   **£9,987.50**
         Sort Code   16-58-79

                                                                         in settlement of your account
                  Registered in Jersey: company Registration No. 02470290

'Porridge Associates'

There are fifteen potential 'Red Flags of Fraud' which, taken together, should prevent an invoice such as Porridge's from being paid. However, for the most part these indicators are not correctly recognised for what they really are. As a result fraudulent invoices get paid all the time.

1.   The Castle is in fact 'HM Prison, The Castle, Lancaster'. Fraud investigations routinely check to see whether invoices are generated from prisons. A second indicator in this address is the use of a 'Suite', which suggests temporary accommodation or the use of a business centre.

2.   This is a mobile telephone number. This again suggests a temporary operation or one which does not have a permanent address.

3.   A low invoice number suggests that the company may have begun trading only recently. A comparison against other invoices from the same company may reveal sequential invoice numbering which can indicate that an organisation is the only organisation being invoiced. This may indicate that the organisation is being specifically targeted for fraudulent purposes.

4.   The date of the invoice pre-dates that of the service provided. This may be part of the contract but it is worth checking for clarification.

5.   The sales tax number contains a check digit. In this case the number is valid but it does not belong to Porridge Associates. The sales tax number, therefore, has been stolen to make this invoice appear legitimate.

6.   All round value payments should be treated with caution. They should be reviewed in detail as they may be staged payments or commissions. They could also be completely false.

7.   Round value expense items may indicate a percentage charge and should be checked carefully.

8.   The address is that of a residential property and appears out of place for a company's UK Headquarters Building. Invoices which contain 'The Close', 'The Crescent', 'The Avenue' or other such locations may all indicate a home address. Fraudsters make mistakes and with care, these can be identified.

9.   Off-shore banking facilities may indicate that the supplier is trying to minimise its tax liability but, it may also be the first leg of transferring fraudulently obtained funds beyond UK legal jurisdiction. The sort code in this case refers to a bank in Gibraltar and not Jersey and this kind of manipulation may suggest a sophisticated money laundering operation.

10.   Company registration numbers follow specific formats and this number is not valid for Jersey.

11.   The absence of a Purchase Order number may indicate a bogus invoice of the type used by certain infamous telex directories. Bogus invoices are routinely sent out by mailshot to hundreds of companies. The fraudsters work on the basis that many low value invoices get paid without being checked.

12.   Vague descriptions of products, service and a lack of backup for expenses should always prompt further enquiries.

13.   There are also different address details which should be looked into further.

14.   Tear-off section at bottom is the only place that shows bank account details.

As a general point, any invoices which contain correction fluid or the use of sticky labels to change an address should be investigated further.

Chapter Roundup

- Forensic auditing can be applied to a number of situations, including fraud and negligence investigations.

- The fundamental principles of the *Code of Ethics and Conduct* apply to ACCA members in all professional assignments.

- Many of the techniques used in a forensic investigation will be similar to those used in the audit of financial statements but the different objectives and risks of the assignment require some differences in approach.

Quick Quiz

1   Define the terms forensic auditing, forensic investigation and forensic accounting.

2   State three applications of the use of forensic auditing.

3   State five items that should ideally be included in an expert's report.

Answers to Quick Quiz

1   Forensic auditing is the process of gathering, analysing and reporting on data in a pre-defined context, for the purpose of finding facts and/or evidence in the context of financial/legal disputes and/or irregularities and giving preventative advice in this area.

Forensic investigations are carried out for civil or criminal cases, which can involve fraud or money laundering.

Forensic accounting is undertaking a financial investigation in response to a particular event, where the findings of the investigation may be used as evidence in court or to otherwise help resolve disputes.

2   Any three of:
- Fraud
- Negligence
- Insurance claims
- Terrorist financing

3   Any five of:

- Index/list of contents
- Brief curriculum vitae
- Summary of conclusions
- Instructions
- Issues
- Documentation

- Chronology
- Technical background
- Opinion
- References
- Declaration

Now try the question below from the Pilot paper

Number	Level	Marks	Time
Q25	Examination	15	27 mins

15

Social and environmental auditing

Topic list	Syllabus reference
1 Importance for the company	G4
2 Measuring social and environmental performance	G4
3 Implications for the statutory audit	G4
4 Implications for assurance services	G4

Introduction

In this chapter we investigate the impact of social and environmental issues on the auditor. This takes two distinct forms:

- Impact on the statutory audit
- Impact on the provision of assurance services by the auditor

Increasing importance is placed on social and environmental issues in business. Recent years have seen a substantial weight of environmental legislation passed which puts a significant burden of compliance on companies. The danger of non-compliance (fines, bad publicity, impact on going concern) is an aspect of the environmental risk which companies face.

Study guide

		Intellectual level
E5	**Social and environmental auditing**	
(a)	Plan an engagement to provide assurance on performance measures and sustainability indicators	2
(b)	Describe the difficulties in measuring and reporting on economic, environmental and social performance and give examples of performance measures and sustainability indicators	2
(c)	Explain the auditor's main considerations in respect of social and environmental matters and how they impact on entities and their financial statements (eg impairment of assets, provisions and contingent liabilities)	2
(d)	Describe substantive procedures to detect potential misstatements in respect of socio-environmental matters	2
(e)	Discuss the form and content of an independent verification statement (eg on an environmental management system (EMS) and a report to society)	2

Exam guide

This topic could be the subject of a current issues discussion question. Measuring social and environmental performance can also be examined as part of a Section A case study question.

1 Importance for the company

FAST FORWARD

A company's stakeholders include employees, society and the environment.

1.1 Stakeholders

To recap, there are various **stakeholders** in a company. Traditionally auditors are concerned with one set, the shareholders, to whom they report on the financial statements. The diagram below shows various other stakeholders that a company might have.

In this chapter we are concerned with the needs of three of the above categories; employees, the environment and society, and the knock-on impact this has on the shareholders, directors and the company itself.

The diagram links the first three because in this context they are inextricably linked.

Environment   The environment is directly impacted by many of our corporate activities today. This may be

PRIMARY   ——————————▶   The impact of processes

SECONDARY ——————————▶   The impact of products

The primary impact is regulated by environmental legislation, which has been prolific in recent years. The secondary impact is governed partly by legislation and partly by consumer opinion.

Society   Society, from the point of view of the company, is made up of consumers or potential consumers. As recognised above, consumers increasingly have opinions about 'green', environmentally-friendly products and will direct their purchasing accordingly.

Society will also, through lobby groups, often speak out on behalf of the environment as it cannot speak out itself.

Employees   Employees have a relationship with the company in their own right, in terms of their livelihood and also their personal safety when they are at work.

However, from the company's perspective, they are also a small portion of society at large, as they may purchase the products of the company or influence others to do so.

In some ways it is easier to see why the company is important to these stakeholders than why they are important to the company.

Environment   The company can cause harm to natural resources in various ways, including:

- Exhausting natural resources such as coal and gas
- Emitting harmful toxins which destroy the atmosphere

Society   Is concerned with the harm to the natural resources as they and their children have to live on the planet and may suffer direct or indirect effects of pollution or waste.

Employees   Have all the concerns that society do and, more immediately, depend on the company for their livelihood and safety when at work.

For a company however, there is one simple need. Companies desire above all else to keep making their product and to keep making sales.

Employees are needed to keep making the product, as are natural resources, and consumers' (that is, society's) goodwill is required to keep selling it.

Obviously, loss of employees and consumers is going to make it impossible for companies to stay in business. Therefore it is important for companies to have policies in order to appease these stakeholders and to communicate the policies to them.

Companies are also constrained by extensive legislation regulating their behaviour towards the environment. Many countries have produced environmental legislation in recent years.

1.2 Implications for management

FAST FORWARD

Social and environmental issues might present a risk to the company, and, by implication, the shareholders' investment, which directors are required to mitigate as part of their corporate governance.

The UK's Turnbull Guidelines states that management is responsible for internal controls which must comprise a sound system to mitigate against risks to the business. For many companies, environmental and social issues might be a significant risk.

The overriding business risk is the risk that the business might fail.

(a) Describe the key environmental and social risks that a business might face.

(b) Explain why they might result in the failure of the business.

Answer

(a) The mindmap below shows the risks that the business faces.

(b) Any of these issues could be at a level serious enough to cause significant business interruption or even business failure, for the reasons given below.

(i) **Bad publicity**. This could lead to customers choosing other products, boycotts and loss of market share significant enough to prevent the business from continuing in operation.

(ii) **Legislation**. The company could be found not to be complying with legislation (through whistleblowing by employees or auditors, or investigation by a regulatory body). This could have the following effects:

- **Fines/compensation**. These could be significant enough to prevent the continuance of the business.

- **Disqualification of directors**. If the staff involved are key members of the organisation, this could threaten the ability of the company to continue.

- **Bad publicity**. See points made above.

1.3 Management controls

Key term

> An **envionmental management system (EMS)** is a system for managing an organisation's overall risk asociated with its environment, encompassing the organisational elements, the planning and the resources involved in developing, implementing and maintaining the organisation's policy in this area.

The specific controls that management will put into place in line with their duties under the corporate governance codes will vary according to the needs of the business.

They are likely to involve specific measures designed to ensure that environmental legislation is complied with, for example they may relate to protective clothing, disposal of waste etc. The human resources department is likely to design policies to ensure that employment legislation is complied with.

The directors may also seek to incorporate social and environmental values into the corporate culture of the company, so that all employees are aware of the risks arising in these areas, and are focused on avoiding them. This can be achieved by implementing a corporate code, or by setting targets of social and environmental performance.

One such target might be to obtain the British Standards Institute's ISO 14001, relating to Environmental Management Systems. This will involve having an assessment by the BSI, and may involve updating management systems to comply with the standard (ISO 14001).

ISO 14001 is often a formal condition for entry into supply chains and certain markets. It does not require the company to produce an environmental report however. The European equivalent, the Eco-Management and Audit Scheme (EMAS), does. This was introduced by a European Council regulation, requiring implementation in all EU member states. The scheme provides recognition for all those companies who have established a programme of environmental action designed to protect and continuously improve their environmental performance.

2 Measuring social and environmental performance
12/08, 12/10

> Measuring social and environmental performance can be a difficult area. Auditors can provide assurance services in this area, giving opinions as to whether directors' assertions about performance are fair.

2.1 The problem of measurement – What? and for whom?

As discussed in Chapter 6, a key part of risk management is monitoring and evaluating results.

Social and environmental performance is not such an easy thing to measure as financial performance. It is less easy to produce ratios and there is unlikely to be an obvious profit attributable to social and environmental activities.

The first step in deciding what to measure is to **identify** who the key **stakeholders** are. With financial performance the main stakeholders are clear: the users of the financial statements, as defined by accounting standards. When it comes to social and environment performance, the business will need to think about its own specific stakeholders. Once these have been identified, the business must **identify** their **needs** and the **performance measures** that best relate to those needs.

2.1.1 Identifying and engaging stakeholders

Stakeholders can be grouped according to various criteria, eg internal/external, corporate/operational. You should be familiar with these from your earlier studies. Examples of stakeholders include:

- Internal: employees
- External: financial institutions, pressure groups, local communities, regulatory bodies, customers.

A good way to do this in practice might be to map out the business' value chain, and to think of stakeholders at each point on the value chain.

The next step is to **engage stakeholders**, which means finding out their views on how they are affected by the business. This must be an active process, as it is possible that stakeholders will know more about the impact of the business than management do. The aim of this process is to prioritise the main that concern stakeholders, with a view to measuring the business' impact in these areas.

2.1.2 Generating performance measures

The next step is to translate the main stakeholder issues into performance measures. This could take the form of Key Performance Indicators (KPIs), which you should be familiar with from your earlier studies.

A simple example of this could be:

Stakeholder	Issue	KPI
Local community	Noise	Number of noise complaints each year
Employee groups	Work-related injuries	Number of injuries sustained at work each year
Environmental groups	Pollution	Quantity of CO_2 emitted each year.

2.2 Targets and indicators

One way to measure social performance is to set targets and sustainability indicators and then appraise whether the targets have been met and the indicators exist.

These targets will vary from business to business, depending on what the issues are. To illustrate the point, a case study based on Shell is given below.

 Case Study

Shell

Shell is a large multi-national group of companies that deals in oil, gas and chemicals. There are various issues which make social and environmental issues important to this company:

- It deals in the earth's natural resources
- Its business is heavily environmentally legislated
- It employs a significant number of people
- Some employees work in risky environments
- It operates in areas of the world where human rights issues are not given sufficient priority

Targets

In response to the social and environmental issues raised above, Shell has set targets of social and environmental performance which it evaluates and reports on to shareholders on an annual basis.

The following are examples of targets which the company has set:

Environmental

- Reduce emissions of carbon dioxide from refinery activity
- Continue to develop cleaner fuels
- Reduce emissions of nitrogen oxides from burning fuel in operations
- Reduce spills of crude oil, oil and chemicals

Social

- Zero employee fatalities in work-related incidents
- Not exploit children in any country where child labour exists, by

    – Employing children under the legal age of employment

    – Dealing with other companies who employ children illegally

- Pursue equal opportunities for men and women in all countries that this is legally possible

Sustainability principles

The company has also set general sustainability principles which all staff should apply in daily business:

- Respect and safeguard people
- Engage and work with stakeholders
- Minimise impact on the environment
- Use resources efficiently
- Maximise profitability
- Maximise benefits to the community

Reporting

The company reports on all these issues to its shareholders, and wherever possible, the facts included within this report are checked by independent verifiers.

The case study shows a number of targets and sustainability indicators. Some can be measured in mathematical terms, for example:

- Emissions
- Spills
- Elimination of work-related fatalities
- Employment of children

However, some of the targets are not specific enough to be able to measure in that way. For example, it is more difficult to identify where the company is in relation to achieving a target of developing cleaner fuels until the cleaner fuel appears. Such a development target cannot have a prescribed timescale.

Equally, it is difficult to measure the effect of the general principles which the company has included within the culture of the company.

2.3 Social audits

The process of checking whether a company has achieved set targets may fall within the scope of a social audit that a company carries out.

Social audits involve:

- Establishing whether the firm has a rationale for engaging in socially responsible activity
- Identifying that all current environment programmes are congruent with the mission of the company
- Assessing objectives and priorities related to these programmes
- Evaluating company involvement in such programmes past, present and future

Whether or not a social audit is used depends on the degree to which social responsibility is part of the **corporate philosophy**. A cultural awareness must be achieved within an organisation in order to implement environmental policy, which requires Board and staff support.

In the USA, social audits on environmental issues have increased since the Exxon Valdez catastrophe in which millions of gallons of crude oil were released into Alaskan waters.

The Valdez principles were drafted by the Coalition for Environmentally Responsible Economics to focus attention on environmental concerns and corporate responsibility.

- Eliminate pollutants and hazardous waste
- Conserve non-renewable resources
- Market environmentally safe products and services
- Prepare for accidents and restore damaged environments
- Provide protection for employees who report environmental hazards
- Appoint an environmentalist to the board of directors, name an executive for environmental affairs, and develop an environmental audit of global operations, which is to be made publicly available

2.4 Environmental audits

Environmental audits seek to assess how well the organisation performs in safeguarding the environment in which it operates, and whether the company complies with its environmental policies.

Environmental audits are not compulsory, but in practice they may be done as a result of stakeholder pressure.

An environmental audit encompasses three processes.

a) Agreeing metrics: determining in what areas targets should be set, and at what level they should be set. This might be influenced by, for instance, the need to meet legal requirements (so that the metrics would be set in areas that are relevant to those requirements). Examples of metrics include:

- Emissions (pollution, greenhouse gases, waste)
- Consumption (water, gas, electricity, non-renewable feedstocks)

b) Performance measurement: the measurement of actual performance in terms of the agreed metrics.

c) Reporting compliance: reporting on the implications of the results for compliance with the targets specified in (a).

In order to do this, the auditor will carry out the following steps:

- Obtain a copy of the company's environmental policy
- Assess whether the policy is likely to achieve objectives:
  - Meet legal requirements
  - Meet British Standards
  - Satisfy key customers/suppliers' criteria
- Test implementation and adherence to the policy by:
  - Discussion
  - Observation
  - 'Walk-though tests' where possible

Exam focus point

An article in the March 2009 edition of *Student Accountant* entitled 'Risk and environmental auditing' looks at what social and environmental audits are and why they are important. A copy of this article is also available on the ACCA website. Make sure you have looked at this useful background reading.

3 Implications for the statutory audit

FAST FORWARD

Social and environmental issues can affect the statutory audit at the planning stage (risk), while undertaking substantive procedures (impairment/provisions) and during audit reviews (going concern).

3.1 Why important?

We now turn from the importance of social and environmental issues to the company and look at why they are important to the auditor in the context of the statutory audit.

The key reason that the issues are important to the statutory audit is that they are important to the company and therefore **can potentially impact on the financial statements**.

In the introduction, the impact of the issues on an audit was divided into three specific areas, which were:

- Planning the audit
- Undertaking substantive procedures
- Audit reviews

Another important point to note is the duties of the auditor arising under ISA 250 *Consideration of laws and regulations in an audit of financial statements*. We shall also consider this below.

3.2 Planning the audit

IAPS 1010 *The consideration of environmental matters in the audit of financial statements* emphasises that social and environmental issues impact in two ways:

- Knowledge of the business (ISA 315)
- Inherent risk assessment (ISAs 315 and 330)

You should be aware of the principles involved in these two issues, so there is no need to go into a lot of further detail at this stage.

As part of his or her knowledge of the business, the auditor should have an awareness of any environmental regulations the business is subject to, and any key social issues arising in the course of the business.

The auditor may be able to obtain knowledge of this aspect of the business by reading the firm's procedures or reviewing any quality control documentation it has relating to standards. The auditor may be able to review the results of any environmental audits undertaken by the company.

This will then form part of the assessment of inherent risk.

3.3 Substantive procedures

Social and environmental issues, particularly environmental issues, may impact on the financial statements in a number of ways.

Examples of the impact of social and environmental matters on financial statements

- Provisions (for example, for site restoration, fines/compensation payments)
- Contingent liabilities (for example, in relation to pending legal action)
- Asset values (issues may impact on impairment or purchased goodwill/products)
- Capital/revenue expenditure (costs of clean-up or meeting legal standards)
- Development costs (new products)
- Going concern issues (considered later in this chapter, under reviews)

---

xam focus oint

When approaching a question about auditing specific items in financial statements, or issuing an audit opinion in respect of them, you should bear in mind whether there is an environmental/social issue which will impact on valuation or disclosure. Use your common sense, however do not make up such issues where no obvious indicators are given in the question.

The auditor will have to bear in mind the effects of social or environmental issues on the financial statements when designing audit procedures. We will now look at some potential audit procedures that would be relevant in three of the key areas above.

3.3.1 Substantive procedures: asset valuation

The key risk that arises with regard to valuation is that assets might be **impaired**. IAS 36 *Impairment of assets* requires an impairment review to be undertaken with regard to non-current assets if certain indicators of impairment exist. We have discussed the audit of impairments in Chapter 9, but shall consider the points specific to environmental and social issues here.

Knowledge brought forward from *Financial Reporting*

IAS 36 gives a list of indicators that an impairment review is required. The indicator relevant here is a significant change in the technological market, legal or economic environment of the business in which the assets are employed.

The auditor should be aware of the regulatory environment of the client as part of his knowledge of the business (as discussed above), but the following **general procedures** could be undertaken as part of the non-current asset testing to **establish whether an impairment review is required**.

- Review the board minutes for indications that the environmental regulatory environment has changed.
- Review relevant trade magazines or newspapers to assess whether any significant adverse change has taken place.
- Discuss the issue with management, particularly those nominated to have responsibility for environmental issues, if such a position exists.

If a significant adverse change has taken place, the directors may or may not have conducted an impairment review. If the directors have not, the auditors should discuss the matter with them. If the directors refuse to conduct an impairment review, the auditors should consider the result of that on their audit report.

If an impairment review has been undertaken, and the valuation of the asset has been adjusted accordingly, the auditor should **audit the impairment review**.

3.3.2 Substantive procedures: provisions

Guidance on accounting for provisions is given in IAS 37 *Provisions, contingent liabilities and contingent assets*. The audit of provisions has been discussed previously in Chapter 10. We shall consider the points specific to environmental and social issues here.

Knowledge brought forward from *Financial Reporting*

IAS 37 defines a **provision as a liability of uncertain timing or amount**. A liability is a present obligation of the entity arising from past events, the settlement of which is expected to result in an outflow from the entity of resources embodying economic benefits. A provision should be recognised when:

- An entity has a **present obligation** (legal or constructive) as a result of a past event
- It is probable that an outflow of resources embodying economic benefits will be required to settle the obligation
- A **reliable estimate** can be made of the obligation

The IAS provides some helpful examples of environmental issues that result in provisions being required. If a company has an environment policy such that the parties would expect the company to clean up contamination, or if the company has broken current environmental legislation then a provision for environmental damage must be made.

The auditor needs to be aware of any circumstances that might give rise to a provision being required, and then apply the recognition criteria to it.

The **general substantive procedures** for **establishing if a provision is required** are the **same as** they were for identifying whether an **impairment review** was required.

If the directors have included provisions in the accounts relating to environmental issues, the **audit procedures** will be the same as were discussed earlier. Specifically, the auditor may be able to **review correspondence** from any regulatory watchdog, or obtain a copy of the **relevant legislation** to review its requirements.

3.3.3 Substantive procedures: contingent liabilities

Accounting for contingent liabilities is also governed by IAS 37.

Knowledge brought forward from *Financial Reporting*

IAS 37 defines a contingent liability as either:

(a) A possible obligation that arises from past events and whose existence will be confirmed only by the occurrence or non-occurrence of one or more uncertain future events not wholly within the entity's control, or

(b) A present obligation that arises from past events but is not recognised because it is not probable that an outflow of resources embodying economic benefits will be required to settle the obligation or because the amount of the obligation cannot be measured with sufficient reliability.

Social and environmental issues may also impact here. In fact, a contingent liability is likely to arise through items being identified in a provision review, when the items highlighted do not meet the recognition criteria for a provision.

This was discussed earlier. Given their relationship with provisions, the **general audit procedures to establish if contingent liabilities exist** are the **same as** the ones for **provisions**, given above.

If the directors have made **disclosures relating to contingent liabilities** in respect of environmental and social issues, the **procedures** to test them were set out earlier. **Specific evidence** would be on similar lines to as for provisions in respect of social and environmental issues: **correspondence with a regulator or relevant legislation**.

3.4 Audit reviews

Environmental and social issues can impact on the ability of the company to continue as a going concern.

The auditor will need to aware of such issues when undertaking the going concern review. The procedures involved in going concern reviews were discussed earlier in Chapter 8.

3.5 Auditor responsibility in the event of non-compliance with law and regulations

FAST FORWARD

The auditor must bear in mind the requirements of ISA 250 *Consideration of laws and regulations in an audit of financial statements.*

The auditors' responsibility with regard to law and regulations is set out in ISA 250 *Consideration of laws and regulations in an audit of financial statements*. This was discussed in Chapter 1, so you should refer back to this to remind yourself of the actions the auditor should take in the event of discovering non-compliance.

Environmental obligations would be core in some businesses (for example, our oil and chemical company given in the case study above), in others they would not. ISA 250 talks of 'other laws and regulations' where compliance may be fundamental to the operating aspects of the business, to an entity's ability to continue its business or to avoid material penalties.

Clearly, in the case of a company which stands to lose its operating licence to carry on business in the event of non-compliance, environmental legislation is fundamental to the business.

In the case of social legislation, this will be a matter of judgement for the auditor. It might involve matters of employment legislation, health and safety regulation, human rights law and such matters which may not seem fundamental to the objectives of the company, but permeate the business due to the needs of employees.

The auditor is not expected to be a specialist in environmental law. However, as part of his professional duty, he must ensure that he has enough knowledge to undertake the assignment, or that he engages the use of an expert if necessary.

4 Implications for assurance services

FAST FORWARD

Many different assurance services could be offered within the broad context of social and environmental issues.

4.1 Types of service

Auditors can provide a variety of services in respect of environmental and social issues. Most of these services are familiar to us, so there is no need to revisit these in detail. Remember that most of the services we have discussed could be applied in an environmental and social context:

- Internal audit services (reviewing controls)
- Review of internal controls and procedures
- Management letter concerning controls as a by-product of statutory audit
- Assurance services (see below)

As discussed in the introduction, **management increasingly report to members on social and environmental issues**, and there is a growing public perception that this is an important area.

This means that it is an issue that can give rise to **assurance services**.

> An **assurance engagement** is one where a practitioner expresses a conclusion designed to enhance the degree of confidence of the intended users other than the responsible party about the outcome of the evaluation or measurement of a subject matter against criteria.

Assurance engagements give rise to assurance reports, which we outlined in Chapter 12. We shall consider the issue of specific verification reports in relation to social and environmental issues here.

If the directors issue an environmental and social report, it may contain figures and statements that are verifiable. Using the example of Shell (above), the directors could make the following assertions:

- Carbon dioxide emissions were x million tonnes in 2001, which represents a 2% decrease from 2000.
- We have implemented a strategy aimed at ensuring that in five years' time, no one we deal with will have an involvement in child labour.

These assertions can be reviewed and assurance given about them. For instance, in the first case, the level of emission could be traced to records of emission from the refineries, and the percentage calculation could be checked.

In the second instance, the accountants could obtain details of the strategy and ascertain how fully it has been implemented by making enquiries of the staff who should be implementing the strategy. They could also appraise the strategy and give an opinion of the chances of it achieving the objective within the given time frame.

4.2 Contents of an assurance report on environmental issues

There is no guidance in issue as to the contents of such a report. The box below shows some items that should be included as a minimum.

> - Note of the objectives of the review
> - Opinions
> - Basis on which those opinions have been reached
> - Work performed
> - Limitations to the work performed
> - Limitations to the opinion given

Question   Social and environmental audit

Your audit client, Naturascope Co, is a health food and homeopathic remedies retailer, with a strong marketing emphasis on the 'natural' elements of the products and the fact that they do not contain artificial preservatives.

The directors have decided that it would benefit the company's public image to produce a social and environmental report as part of their annual report. There are three key assertions which they wish to make as part of this report:

- Goods/ingredients of products for sale in Naturascope have not been tested on animals
- None of Naturascope's overseas suppliers use child labour (regardless of local laws)
- All Naturascope's packaging uses recycled materials

The directors have asked the audit engagement partner whether the firm would be able to produce a verification report in relation to the social and environmental report.

Required

(a) Identify and explain the matters the audit engagement partner should consider in relation to whether the firm can accept the engagement to report on the social and environmental report.

(b) Comment on the matters to consider and the evidence to seek in relation to the three assertions.

Answer

(a) **Acceptance considerations**

There are four key things that the audit engagement partner should consider:

(i) **Impact of the new engagement on the audit**

The audit engagement partner needs to ensure that the **objectivity of the audit is not adversely affected** by accepting any other engagements from an audit client. This is of primary importance.

Factors that he will consider include the impact that any fees from the engagement will have on total fees from the client and what staff will be involved in carrying out the new engagement (ie, will they be audit staff, or could the engagement be carried out by a different department?)

In favour of the engagement, he would consider that such an engagement should increase his knowledge of the business and its suppliers and systems, and might enhance the audit firm's understanding of the inherent audit risk attaching to the business.

(ii) **Competence of the audit firm to carry out the assignment**

The audit engagement partner needs to consider whether the firm has the **necessary competence** to carry out the engagement in a quality manner, so as to minimise the risk of being sued for negligence.

This will depend on the nature of the engagement and assurance required (see below) and on whether the auditor felt it would be cost-effective to use the work of an expert, if required.

(iii) **Potential liability of the firm for the report**

As the engagement is not an audit engagement, the partner should consider to whom he would be **accepting liability** in relation to this engagement, and whether the risk that that entails is worth it, in relation to the potential fees and other benefits of doing the work (such as keeping an audit client happy, and not exposing an audit client to the work of an alternative audit firm).

Unless otherwise stated, liability is unlikely to be restricted to the shareholders for an engagement such as this, indeed, it is likely to extend to all the users of the annual report. This could include:

– The bank
– Future investors making ethical investing decisions
– Customers and future customers making ethical buying decisions

The partner should also consider whether it might be possible to limit the liability for the engagement, and **disclaim liability** to certain parties.

(iv) **Nature of the engagement/criteria/assurance being given**

Before the partner accepts any such engagement on behalf of the firm, he should **clarify** with the directors the **exact nature** of the engagement, the degree of assurance required and the criteria by which the directors expect the firm to assess the assertions.

As the engagement is not an audit engagement, the audit rules of 'truth and fairness', and 'materiality' do not necessarily apply. The partner should determine whether the directors want the firm to verify that the assertions are '**absolutely correct**' or 'correct in x% of cases' and also, what **quality of evidence** would be sufficient to support the conclusions drawn – for example, confirmations from suppliers, or legal statements, or whether the auditors would have to visit suppliers and make personal verifications.

This engagement might be less complex for the audit firm if they could conduct it as an 'agreed-upon procedures' engagement, rather than an assurance engagement.

(b)   **Assertions**

(i)   **Animal testing**

The assertion is **complex** because it does not merely state that products sold have not been tested on animals, but that ingredients in the products have not been tested on animals.

This may mean a **series of links** have to be checked, because Naturascope's supplier who is the manufacturer of one of their products may not have tested that product on animals, but may source ingredients from several other suppliers, who may, in turn source ingredients from several other suppliers, etc.

The audit firm may also find that it is a **subjective issue**, and that the assertion 'not tested on animals' is not as clear cut as one would like to suppose. For example, the dictionary defines animal as either 'any living organism characterised by voluntary movement...' or 'any mammal, especially man'. This could suggest that the directors could make the assertion if they didn't test products on mammals, and it might still to an extent be 'true', or that products could be tested on 'animals' that, due to prior testing, were paralysed? However, neither of these practices are likely to be thought ethical by animal lovers who are trying to invest or buy ethically.

Potential sources of evidence include: assertions from suppliers, site visits at suppliers' premises, a review of any licences or other legal documents in relation to testing held by suppliers.

(ii)   **Child labour**

This assertion is less complex than the previous assertion because it is restricted to Naturascope's direct overseas suppliers.

However, it contains complexities of its own, particularly the definition of 'child labour', for example in terms of whether labour means 'any work' or 'a certain type of work' or even, 'work over a set period of time', and what the definition of a child is, when other countries do not have the same legal systems and practical requirements of schooling, marriage, voting etc.

There may also be a practical difficulty of verifying how old employees actually are in certain countries, where birth records may not be maintained.

Possible sources of evidence include: assertions by the supplier and inspection by auditors.

(iii)   **Recycled materials**

This may be the simplest assertion to verify, given that it is the least specific. All the packaging must have an element of recycled materials. This might mean that the assertion is restricted to one or a few suppliers. The definition of packaging may be wide, for example, if all goods are boxed and then shrink-wrapped, it is possible that those two elements together are termed 'packaging' and so, only the cardboard element need contain recycled materials.

The sources of evidence are the same as previously – assertions from suppliers, inspections by the auditors or review of suppliers' suppliers to see what their methods and intentions are.

Chapter Roundup

- A company's stakeholders include employees, society and the environment.

- Social and environmental issues might present a risk to the company, and by implication, the shareholders' investment, which the directors are required to mitigate as part of their corporate governance.

- Measuring social and environmental performance can be a difficult area. Auditors can provide assurance services in this area – giving opinions as to whether directors' assertions about performance are fair.

- Social and environmental issues can affect the statutory audit at the planning stage (risk), while undertaking substantive procedures (impairment/provisions), and during audit reviews (going concern).

- The auditor must bear in mind the requirements of ISA 250 *Consideration of laws and regulations in an audit of financial statements*.

- Many different assurance services could be offered within the broad context of social and environmental issues.

Quick Quiz

1   Draw a mindmap showing the major stakeholders in a company.

2   Management have a duty to monitor risks arising from social and environmental issues as part of their corporate governance.

    True   ☐

    False   ☐

3   Name three areas of a statutory audit where social and environmental issues are relevant.

    (1)   ....

    (2)   ....

    (3)   ....

4   Give an example of why social and environmental issues might impact on all of the following financial statement areas:

    - Provisions
    - Contingent liabilities
    - Asset values
    - Capital/revenue expenditure
    - Development costs
    - Going concern

5   List six items which should be covered in an assurance report relating to environmental issues.

    (1)   ....   (4)   ....

    (2)   ....   (5)   ....

    (3)   ....   (6)   ....

Answers to Quick Quiz

1

2   True

3   (1)   Planning (risks)
     (2)   Substantive testing (accounting issues arising)
     (3)   Reviews (going concern)

4   •   Provisions   (site restoration or fines/compensation payments)
     •   Contingent liabilities   (pending legal action)
     •   Asset values   (impairment due to new environmental legislation)
     •   Capital/revenue expenditure   (cost of clean-up or meeting legal standards)
     •   Development costs   (new, environmentally-friendly products)
     •   Going concern   (operational existence threatened by new/proposed
                                          environmental laws)

5   (1)   Objectives   (4)   Work performed
     (2)   Opinions   (5)   Limitations on work
     (3)   Basis of opinions   (6)   Limitations on opinion

Now try the question below from the Exam Question Bank

Number	Level	Marks	Time
Q26	Examination	15	27 mins

Internal audit and outsourcing

Topic list	Syllabus reference
1 Revision: internal audit	E5
2 Outsourcing	E6
3 Outsourcing specific functions	E6
4 Impact of outsourcing on an audit	E6

Introduction

In this chapter we revise internal audit which you studied in some detail in your earlier auditing studies. Internal auditors provide services to the management of a company.

In the second half of the chapter, we look at outsourcing. Outsourcing is a key issue in business today. However, the main issues for management are cost and control.

The two issues are linked simply because the question of outsourcing has become a key issue in internal audit. Businesses are being encouraged to invest in internal audit, because of the benefits that the internal audit department can provide to corporate governance. However, setting up an internal audit department can be costly and difficult. Outsourcing can overcome these problems.

Study guide

Exam guide

Outsourcing and internal audit could be examined together or separately. Either or both could feature in a planning scenario question.

1 Revision: internal audit

> Internal audit plays a key role in corporate governance, providing objective assurance on control and risk management.

1.1 Revision

The internal audit function was considered in detail in your earlier auditing studies. Work through the following question to ensure that you remember the basic principles of internal auditing.

Question   Revision: internal audit

(a) Describe the principal differences between internal and external auditors, considering the following factors.
   (i)   Eligibility
   (ii)   Security of appointment
   (iii) Main objectives and limitations on the scope of their work
(b) Explain how external auditors would evaluate specific work carried out by internal auditors.

Answer

(a) **Eligibility**

   In the UK, a person is ineligible to act as external auditor if he is an officer or employee of the company, a partner or employee of such a person or a partnership in which such a person is a partner. An internal auditor is an employee of the company.

   External auditors are also required to belong to a recognised supervisory body, and this means they must hold an appropriate qualification, follow technical standards and maintain competence.

By contrast anyone can act as an internal auditor even if they do not have a formal accounting qualification. It is up to the company's management who they appoint.

Security

In the UK, the external auditors are appointed to hold office until the conclusion of the next general meeting. They can be dismissed by an ordinary resolution of shareholders with special notice in a general meeting, and have the right to make representations.

External auditors cannot be dismissed by individual directors or by a vote of the board. The only influence directors can have on the removal of external auditors is through their votes as shareholders. The rules on security of tenure are there because of the need for external auditors to protect the interests of shareholders by reporting on directors' stewardship of the business.

By contrast, as internal auditors are employees of the company, they can be dismissed by the directors or lower levels of management, subject only to their normal employment rights.

Objectives and limitations on the scope of the audit work

The primary objective of external auditors is laid down by statute, to report on whether the company's accounts show a true and fair view of the state of the company's affairs at the period-end, and of its profit or loss for the period. External auditors are also required to report if certain other criteria have not been met, for example the company fails to keep proper accounting records or fails to make proper disclosure of transactions with directors.

Internal auditors' objectives are whatever the company's management decide they should be. Some of the objectives may be similar to those of external audit, for example to confirm the quality of accounting systems. Other objectives might be in areas which have little or no significance to the external auditor, for example recommending improvements in economy, efficiency and effectiveness.

Statutory rules mean that management cannot limit the scope of external auditors' work. External auditors have the right of access to all of a company's books and records, and can demand all the information and explanations they deem necessary. As the objectives of internal audit's work are decided by management, management can also decide to place limitations on the scope of that work.

(b) External auditors should consider whether:

(i) The work is performed by persons having adequate technical training and proficiency as internal auditors

(ii) The work of assistants is properly supervised, reviewed and documented

(iii) Sufficient appropriate audit evidence is obtained to afford a reasonable basis for the conclusions reached

(iv) The conclusions reached are appropriate in the circumstances

(v) Any reports prepared by internal audit are consistent with the results of the work performed

(vi) Any exceptions or unusual matters disclosed by internal audit are properly resolved

(vii) Amendments to the external audit programme are required as a result of matters identified by internal audit work

(viii) There is a need to test the work of internal audit to confirm its adequacy

---

Hopefully you could answer that question. If you struggled, you might want to refer back to your notes from your previous auditing studies, but here is a summary of the key revision points on internal audit in this syllabus.

> **Role of internal audit in corporate governance**
>
> Internal audit are perfectly placed to assist management in the assessment of risks and internal controls required by the Hampel and Turnbull reports in the UK. The Turnbull report in particular highlights the role internal audit can have in providing objective assurance and advice on risk and control.

The Turnbull report sets out some key guidelines for the Board.

TURNBULL GUIDELINES

- Have a **defined process** for the **review** of effectiveness of **internal control**
- Review **regular** reports on **internal control**
- Consider **key risks** and how they have been **managed**
- Check the **adequacy** of **action taken** to remedy weaknesses and incidents
- Consider the **adequacy** of **monitoring**
- Conduct an **annual assessment** of risks and the effectiveness of internal control
- Make a **statement** on this process in the **annual report**

The traditional definition of internal audit given at the start of the section shows how internal audit can help the directors achieve these objectives; the traditional purpose of internal audit was to review controls.

The third of the Turnbull guidelines refers to risk. All companies face risks arising from their operational activities. Risks arise in different areas.

- Risk the company will go bankrupt
- Risks arising from regulations and law
- Risks arising from publicity

Turnbull requires that risk be managed. This gives rise to another role for the internal audit function, **risk management**.

Risk awareness and management should be the role of everyone in the organisation. The extended role of internal audit with regard to risk is the monitoring of integrated risk management within a company, and the reporting of results to the Board to enable them to report to shareholders.

Internal auditor relationships

Internal auditors have relationships with the following people:

- **Management**: by whom they are employed and may report to
- **Audit committee**: to whom they report
- **External auditors**: who may make use of their work

Reliance on the work of internal auditors by external auditors

The external auditors may make use of the work of internal audit. The guidance over when this appropriate is given to them in ISA 610 *Using the work of internal auditors*.

The ISA is divided into two key parts. First, the **external** auditor shall determine whether, and to what extent, the work of internal auditors can be used. This is done at the planning stage of the audit, and means considering whether internal audit's work is adequate or appropriate for the external audit, and then what effect relying on internal audit's work will have on the external audit procedures.

To consider whether internal audit's work is likely to adequate for the audit, the auditor needs to evaluate internal audit's **objectivity**, the internal auditors' technical **competence**, and whether the work is done with due **professional care**. To determine the effect on audit procedures, the auditor needs to evaluate the **nature and scope of the work** performed relative to the **risk** of material misstatement (assessed by external audit).

When actually using the specific work done by internal auditors, the external audit must consider the following factors.

- Proficiency and training of the people who have undertaken the work
- Level of supervision, review and documentation of the work of assistants
- Sufficiency and appropriateness of evidence to draw conclusions
- Appropriateness of conclusions drawn
- Consistency of any reports prepared with the work performed
- Whether the work necessitates amendment to the external audit programme

1.2 Internal auditors and risk management

The issue of the Turnbull guidance and internal audit's role in relation to risk management was touched on briefly above. In response to the Turnbull guidance, directors need to ensure three steps are taken in their business.

- Identify risks
- Control risks
- Monitor risks

It is not internal audit's primary role to manage risk in a company. It is the responsibility of the directors, usually delegated to individual managers in various departments.

The risks are identified and assessed, and a policy is taken in respect of each of them. To recap, this policy is usually one of four:

- Accept risk (if it is low impact and likelihood)
- Reduce risk (by setting up a system of internal control)
- Avoid risk (by not entering a market, accepting contract etc)
- Transfer risk (by taking out insurance)

With their skills in business systems, internal auditors are ideally placed to **monitor** this process and add value to it. They can:

- Give advice on the best design of systems and monitor their operation
- Be involved in a process that continually improves internal control systems
- Provide assurance on systems set up in each department

The involvement of internal audit as a monitoring unit will help to ensure that the process of risk identification and management in a business is a **continual process** rather than a one-off exercise.

2 Outsourcing   12/07

> Outsourcing is the contracting out of certain functions. A business can outsource a small part of the function, or the entire function, or practically all its functions.

2.1 Why outsource?

> **Outsourcing** is the process of purchasing key functions from an outside supplier. In other words, it is **contracting-out** certain functions, for example, internal audit or information technology.
>
> **Insourcing** is when an organisation decides to retain a centralised department for the key function, but brings experts in from an external market on a short-term basis to account for 'peak' and 'trough' periods. It is a business decision that is often made to maintain control of certain critical production or competencies.

There are three general reasons for outsourcing:

- Financial efficiency
- Change management
- Strategy

2.1.1 Financial efficiency

It is often argued that outsourcing **reduces cost**. This **may not necessarily be the case**, but businesses often find that it is worth investigating. If outsourcing is never considered, it is often the case that the cost of maintaining the function in-house is never calculated, and therefore not considered either.

This fact links into the next point about financial efficiency. Outsourcing a function can lead to **greater cost control** over that function. This is as a result of the function now being subject to a contractual fee rather than a previously unidentified, cost of maintaining the function in-house. This aspect of outsourcing might substantially **improve budgeting and cost control**.

Outsourcing may considerably **reduce the number of employees** for whom the business is responsible. The logistics of shedding staff may make outsourcing a difficult legal and human issue, but the **cost savings** in this area (salary, tax, pension, for example) could be substantial.

Outsourcing can have a fundamental effect on the **shape of an entity's financial statements**, particularly if a function with a high capital investment (for example, information technology) is being outsourced. In some cases, it might be possible to sell the company's assets to the service provider, producing a cash injection, or reduced initial fees.

2.1.2 Change management

Outsourcing can be a way of managing change in a company. For example, if the company decides to change its software, outsourcing the software provision might mean that all **staff training** on the new system is incorporated into the service.

Outsourcing a function such as finance might facilitate the smooth running of a **merger** of two firms who have different accounting systems. This may also be true when a business is **restructured**.

2.1.3 Strategy

Outsourcing can also be part of a strategy to **refocus on the core competencies** of a business, or a thrust to **improve technical services**. It can be a way of **entering a market in the most low risk way**. For example, a previously low-tech business wanting to engage in e-commerce could outsource its website development and maintenance.

2.2 Outsource what?

Generally, if a company chooses to outsource, it will outsource functions which are not perceived to be key competencies. The different approaches which can be taken to outsourcing depend on the extent to which a company contracts out non-core functions. This can be seen by way of an example.

 Case Study

The Toy Company

The Toy Company is a small company, owned and run by Edward T. Bear. It was left to him by his father, T. Bear, who was a skilled toy maker. The business began as a one man operation in the garage and it now has 250 employees, technical computerised processes and is run from its own factory complex.

Edward joined the company on leaving school. He worked alongside his father for ten years. Last year his father died and left the shares in the company to Edward and his sister Victoria. Victoria has never had any role in the company, and is keen to continue that.

The company employed an accountant 20 years previously, and he is still an employee of the firm. In the intervening years, the accounts department has grown to now incorporate five other employees, with one having specific payroll duties. The accounts department has a computer system which is separate from the computer system used in operations.

In operations, there are several divisions: design, manufacture, packaging, sales and marketing.

The company also employs a part-time human resources manager who deals with staff matters and recruitment. The office cleaner is the longest serving member of staff. She has worked for Mr Bear since he set up in his first work shop 40 years ago.

In the example of the Toy Company, there are several areas where management could consider outsourcing. We will consider the advantages and disadvantages of this below. Here we are only looking to see where the potential lies.

The core competency of the company is the manufacture of toys. This means that there are several functions which do not fall within this competency:

- Accounting
- Human Resources
- Cleaning

Of the above areas, cleaning would be the least risky to outsource because the cleaning does not directly impact on the operation of the business. Cleaning is a common outsourced function in the private sector.

However, we are more interested in the accounting function, being accountants. The accounts department is not part of the core competency, so potentially, it could be outsourced. Within this decision, there are several others. The company could outsource:

- Pension functions
- Tax related functions
- The entire payroll function
- Invoicing
- Credit control
- The entire accounting function

When considering **the extent to which the company wants to adopt outsourcing**, it must consider the risk involved and the control which management want to maintain over the function. There is less risk involved in outsourcing a part of the payroll function (for example, pensions) than the whole finance function.

Similar subdivisions can be seen when considering the outsourcing of other functions:

Human Resources	Welfare
	Health and safety
	Recruitment
	The entire HR department
Information Technology	Maintenance
	Project management
	Network management
	The entire IT function

Just to extend the point about outsourcing to its furthest extremes, it is possible to consider outsourcing more of the business than has been discussed above.

In the first instance, Edward could critically appraise the core competency of his business (the manufacture of toys) and subdivide it further. He might decide that the production processes are the core competency and that functions such as design and sales and marketing should be outsourced.

In an extreme case, it is possible to create a **virtual organisation**. For example, Edward could decide that he has no particular personal interest in toy manufacture, but that he does wish to retain the business. In this case, he could outsource all the different functions of the business, but maintain control of the contracts and therefore ultimately the business.

2.3 Advantages and disadvantages of outsourcing

We will look in detail at the advantages and disadvantages of outsourcing some specific functions in the following sections. For now, however, we shall consider some general advantages and disadvantages of outsourcing that apply to them all.

Advantages of outsourcing
Cost. A key advantage of outsourcing is that it is often cheaper to contract a service out than it is to conduct it in-house. It may also significantly improve cost control.
Specialist service. Outsourcing results in specialist being used to provide the service when that would not have been the case if the function was performed in house.
Indemnity. The service organisation may provide indemnity in the event of problems arising. If problems arise in-house, there is no such comfort zone.

Cash flow. Obtaining the service through a contract may assist with cash flow, as the contract will represent a flat fee, whereas the cost of providing the service in-house might have led to fluctuating costs (for example, if temporary staff are required in a busy period).

The single biggest disadvantage of outsourcing, is the extent to which the company **loses control** over the function itself, although not over cost control

The **initial cost** of outsourcing may be **substantial,** if an aspect of the decision is to close a current department of the business. The question of **potential redundancies** may dissuade companies from considering outsourcing.

The contract has to be **managed** to ensure that the service being provided is appropriate and in accordance with the contract. This may take a disproportionate amount of **time**.

The contract might limit the **liability** of the contractor, leading to problems if the contract is not performed well. This might even result in **court action** being required.

Should these disadvantages be realised, the **cost** of outsourcing could outweigh the benefit, even though in theory outsourcing should reduce cost.

3 Outsourcing specific functions   6/11

FAST FORWARD   Internal audit is not a core competency and may be outsourced fairly easily.

3.1 Internal audit

Internal audit is rarely a core competency of a company. However, it is a valuable service to management. The corporate codes of recent years that we discussed earlier in this Study Text have emphasised the importance of internal audit in assessing controls and monitoring risks.

There are **problems associated with setting up an internal audit department**, however. These are:

- Cost of recruiting staff
- Difficulty of recruiting staff of sufficient skill and qualification for the company's preference or need
- The fact that management are not accounting specialists and therefore might struggle to direct the new department in their duties
- The time frame between setting up the department and seeing the results of having the department
- The fact that the work required may not be enough to justify engaging full time staff
- The fact that a variety of skills and seniority levels are required, but only one member of full-time staff can be justified

3.1.1 Advantages

The advantage of outsourcing internal audit is that outsourcing can overcome all these problems:

- Staff need not be recruited, as the **service provider has good quality staff**.
- The service provider has **specialist skill** and can assess what management require them to do. As they are external to the operation, this will not cause operational problems.
- Outsourcing can provide an **immediate** internal audit department.
- The service contract can be for the **appropriate time scale** (a two week project, a month, etc).
- Because the **time scale is flexible**, a **team of staff** can be provided if required.
- The service provider could also provide less than a team, but, for example, could provide one member of staff on a full-time basis for a short period, as a **secondment**.

A key advantage of outsourcing internal audit is that **outsourcing can be used on a short term basis** to:

- Provide immediate services
- Lay the basis of a permanent function, by setting policies and functions
- Prepare the directors for the implications of having an internal audit function
- Assist the directors in recruiting the permanent function

Outsourced internal audit services are provided by many audit firms, particularly the Big Four. This can range from a team of staff for a short-term project, or a single staff member on a long-term project.

3.1.2 Disadvantages

However, the fact that internal audit services are typically provided by external auditors can raise problems as well:

- The company might wish to **use the same firm** for internal and external audit services, but this may lead to **complications for the external auditors**.

- The **cost** of outsourcing the internal audit function might be high enough to make the directors choose not to have an internal audit function at all.

3.2 Outsourcing finance and accounting functions

Various functions will be considered in the table below. Remember, however, the key advantages and disadvantages set out in Section 3, are all likely to be true of the functions discussed more specifically below.

Function	
Data processing *Disadvantages*	There may be logistical difficulties in outsourcing data processing, due to the high level of paper involved (invoices, goods received notes etc). This information will have to be given to the service organisation. A secondary, and more important, effect is that the company might not always have control of their key accounting documentation and records. It is a legal requirement that the directors maintain this information. While they may delegate the practicalities, they are still responsible for maintaining the records.
Pensions *Advantages*	Pensions are a specialist area and there is merit in getting a specialist to operate the company's pension provision.
Disadvantages	Pensions are closely related to the payroll and the company will need to share sensitive information with the pension provider, which may make the situation complicated.
Information technology *Advantages*	A key advantage of outsourcing all, or elements of, the IT function is that this will enable the company to keep pace with **rapid technological advances**. It also allows the company to take advantage of the work of a specialist in a field that many people still find difficult but which they use regularly to carry out their business. Outsourcing can provide a useful **safety net** of a technical helpline or indemnity in the event of computer disaster. It is also possible that through outsourcing, the company will be able to obtain **added value,** such as new ways of doing business identified (for example, e-commerce).

Function	
Due diligence *Advantages*	A key advantage in relation to outsourcing due diligence is the high level of **expertise** that can be brought in. The company can expect **quality** from its service contractor, and can seek **legal compensation** from them in the event of negligence.
Taxes *Advantages* *Disadvantages*	In relation to taxes, the key advantage is also the buying in of **expertise**. The disadvantage of outsourcing tax work is that while the work can be outsourced, the **responsibility** cannot. The tax authorities will deal with the responsible person, not the agent, so the loss of control is particularly risky in this case.

Exam focus point

The June 2011 exam contained three marks for the potential benefits of an externally provided due diligence review. This requirement encompassed the benefits of the due diligence itself, and the benefits of outsourcing it.

4 Impact of outsourcing on an audit

FAST FORWARD ▶▶ When a company uses a service organisation, there are special considerations for the user auditors.

Exam focus point

There are both **ethical** and **practical audit implications** of outsourcing on an audit – either could be examined.

4.1 Use of service organisations

The impact of outsourcing on an external audit is considered in ISA 402 *Audit considerations relating to an entity using a service organisation*. This ISA was updated under the Clarity Project because of the increasing use of service organisations and the complexity of relationships between the two parties.

Key terms

Service organisation – A third-party organisation (or segment of a third-party organisation) that provides services to user entities that are part of those entities' information systems relevant to financial reporting.

User entity – An entity that uses a service organisation and whose financial statements are being audited.

User auditor – An auditor who audits and reports on the financial statements of a user entity.

Service auditor – An auditor who, at the request of the service organisation, provides an assurance report on the controls of a service organisation.

A **type 1 report** is a report on the description and design of controls at a service organisation. It comprises (i) a description, prepared by management of the service organisation, of the service organisation's system, control objectives and related controls that have been designed and implemented as at a specified date, and (ii) a report by the service auditor with the objective of conveying reasonable assurance that includes the service auditor's opinion on the description of the service organisation's system, control objectives and related controls and the suitability of the design of the controls to achieve the specified control objectives.

A **type 2 report** is a report on the description, design and operating effectiveness of controls at a service organisation. It comprises (i) a description, prepared by management of the service organisation, of the service organisation's system, control objectives and related controls, their design and implementation as at a specified date or throughout a specified period and, in some cases, their operating effectiveness throughout a specified period, and (ii) a report by the service auditor with the objective of conveying reasonable assurance that includes (a) the service auditor's opinion on the description of the service organisation's system, control objectives and related controls, the suitability of the design of the controls

to achieve the specified control objectives, and the operating effectiveness of the controls, and (b) a description of the service auditor's tests of the controls and the results thereof.

As we have discussed above, some companies choose to outsource activities necessary to the running of their business to **service organisations**. Examples of such activities that may be outsourced are:

- Information processing
- Maintenance of accounting records
- Facilities management
- Asset management (for example, investments)
- Initiation or execution of transactions on behalf of the other entity

---

ISA 402.7

The objectives of the user auditor, when the user entity uses the services of a service organisation, are:

(a)   To obtain an understanding of the nature and significance of the services provided by the service organisation and their effect on the user entity's internal control relevant to the audit, sufficient to identify and assess the risks of material misstatement, and

(b)   To design and perform audit procedures responsive to those risks.

4.2 Obtaining an understanding

A service organisation may establish and execute policies and procedures that affect a client organisation's accounting and internal control systems. These policies and procedures are physically and operationally separate from the client organisation.

(a)   When the services provided by the service organisation are **limited to recording** and **processing client transactions** and the client retains authorisation and maintenance of accountability, the client may be able to implement effective policies and procedures within its organisation.

(b)   When the service organisation **executes** the client's **transactions** and **maintains accountability**, the client may deem it necessary to rely on policies and procedures at the service organisation.

The auditor needs to understand how a user entity uses the services of the service organisation, including:

- The nature and significance of the service provided including the effect on the controls at the user entity
- The nature and materiality of the transactions processed or accounts/financial reporting processes affected
- The degree of interaction between the user entity and the service organisation
- The nature of the relationship between the two, including the contractual terms
- If the service organisation maintains accounting records for the user entity, whether the arrangements affect the auditors' responsibility to report concerning accounting records

Sources of information include:

- User manuals
- System overviews
- Technical manuals
- The contract/service level
- Reports by the service organisations, internal auditors or regulatory authorities
- Reports by the service organisation auditor

The user auditor must evaluate the control at the user entity that relate to the service organisation and determine whether this gives the auditor sufficient understanding to provide a basis for assessing risks of material misstatement in the user entity financial statements.

If the auditor concludes that this is insufficient, he must carry out one of the following four activities:

- Obtain type 1 or type 2 report from the service organisation, if available
- Contact the service organisation to get specific information (with permission)
- Visit the service organisation and perform procedures to obtain the information (with permission)
- Use another auditor to perform procedures at the service organisation (with permission)

It is likely that the auditor will be able to obtain a type 1 or 2 report, and this will be the most straightforward option. If this action is taken, the auditor needs to be sure that:

- The service organisation's auditor is competent and objective
- The standards under which the report was issued are adequate for the user entity's auditor's purposes
- The report is for an appropriate date (that is, it covers the period the user entity is reporting on)
- The evidence it is based on is sufficient and appropriate for the user entity's auditor's understanding of the internal controls
- If complementary user entity controls are relevant to the user entity, that the auditor has obtained an understanding of these.

4.3 Responding to assessed risks

The auditor needs to assess whether sufficient appropriate audit evidence is available from records at the user entity. If so, he should carry out **appropriate procedures** at the user entity. If not, he should carry out further audit procedures.

When the user auditor expects controls at the service organisation to be operating effectively, he must obtain evidence that this is the case, by one of the following three methods:

- Obtaining a type 2 report, if available
- Performing test of controls at the service organisation
- Using another auditor to perform tests of controls at the service organisation

Again, obtaining a type 2 report is the most likely option, in which case the entity auditor has to:

- Check that the report is made up to an appropriate date
- Ensure that he has tested complimentary controls at the user entity if necessary
- Check the adequacy of the time period covered by the tests of controls and the time elapsed since those tests of controls were performed
- Ensure the tests of controls performed for the purposes of the report are relevant and provide sufficient appropriate audit evidence for the user entity auditors' purposes

The auditor must also make **enquiries of management** if it is aware or suspects any fraud, non-compliance with law and regulations or uncorrected misstatements at the service organisation that could affect the financial statements of the user entity and evaluate the impact of any matters on his procedures and report.

4.4 Reporting

The key issue to remember is that if the user auditor cannot obtain sufficient appropriate evidence about the impact of the service organisation on the user entity, the auditor must **modify** the auditor's report as the scope of the audit has been **limited**.

4.5 Impact on internal audit

External auditors will be affected when outsourced functions impact on the financial statements. Internal audit will be interested in outsourced functions which affect the business (that is, any outsourced function).

Internal audit will be interested in the contractual arrangements made with the service organisation. They may want to pay a visit to the organisation and undertake a review of its systems to ensure that they are sufficient for the business's needs.

Question	Outsourcing

(a)   Explain the meaning of the word 'outsourcing' and distinguish it from 'insourcing'.

(b)   Discuss the risks and benefits of outsourcing the payroll function of a small business which currently employs a management accountant and an accounts clerk.

(c)   You are planning the audit of a company that has just outsourced its credit control function. Describe the planning issues that arise as a result of this action.

Answer

(a)   **Outsourcing** is the practice of purchasing a specific function from an outside service provider. In other words, it is the practice of contracting-out functions of the business to an expert.

Insourcing, by contrast, is the practice of maintaining a specialist function in-house, but buying in external expertise on a short-term basis to balance peaks and troughs in demand for that expertise.

(b)   Payroll is a complicated accounting area, particularly due to the issues of taxation arising. It is also susceptible to fraud in the absence of strong controls.

In a small company, such as the one described, there is **little scope for segregation of duties** in relation to payroll. It is likely that payroll would be managed by the accountant, as it the clerk is likely to have a full-time job in relation to sales and purchases, and the accountant has greater expertise. However, it is possible that an accountant in such a position, even in a small business, might **not have time to manage payroll** in addition to other accounting duties. In order for there to be **adequate authorisation** and segregation in relation to payroll, **another senior figure should be involved** in authorising the payroll.

In this situation, it might be **cost-effective to outsource** the payroll function to an **expert**. This might also **reduce the control problems** inherent in the small department. However, there are some disadvantages related to outsourcing the function. The key issue is one of **confidentiality**, as payroll records contain sensitive data about personnel (for example, their bank details). **Personnel might object** to this information being given to an outside provider. The company would also have to **institute controls over the transfer of data** (such as weekly hours worked) to the service provider.

(c)   The user auditors should determine whether the outsourced function is **relevant to the audit**. In the case of the credit control function, this is clearly **relevant to receivables** reported in the statement of financial position and to **sales and bad debts**.

The user auditor must ensure that he **understands the terms of the contract** between the client and the service provider. As part of planning the audit, therefore, he **must obtain a copy of the contract** and **become familiar with its terms**.

The user auditor must **ascertain whether he will have access to the records** that he will require as part of his audit evidence. As part of planning he must **make arrangements to enable this access**.

As part of the risk assessment at the planning stage, the user auditor must consider whether the outsourcing arrangements affect the risk of material misstatement in the financial statements. In doing so he will consider factors such as the contract (referred to above), the reputation of the service provider and the effectiveness of past controls when the function was maintained in-house and present controls over the outsourcing arrangements.

Chapter Roundup

- Internal audit plays a key role in corporate governance, providing objective assurance on control and risk management.

- Outsourcing is the contracting out of certain functions. A business can outsource a small part of the function, or the entire function, or practically all its functions.

- Internal audit is not a core competency and may be outsourced fairly easily.

- When a company uses a service organisation, there are special considerations for the user auditors.

Quick Quiz

1   List six factors which the external auditors should consider in relation to the work of internal audit.

(1) ....

(2) ....

(3) ....

(4) ....

(5) ....

(6) ....

2   Name five elements of the accounts function which could be outsourced.

(1) ....

(2) ....

(3) ....

(4) ....

(5) ....

3   Complete the table, putting the advantages of outsourcing under the right headings and naming the specific function, if relevant.

General advantages	Function-specific advantages

- Cost
- Keeping pace with technological advance
- Liability/indemnity
- Cash flow
- Specialist service
- Immediacy
- Flexibility (particularly with regard to time scale)

4   The auditor may refer to the responsibility of the service organisation when giving his opinion in financial statements.

True ☐

False ☐

Answers to Quick Quiz

1   (1)   Proficiency and training of staff
    (2)   Level of supervision, documentation and review of the work
    (3)   Sufficiency and appropriateness of evidence
    (4)   Appropriateness of conclusion
    (5)   Consistency of reports with work performed
    (6)   Whether work necessitates amendment to original audit plan

2   (1)   Pension
    (2)   Tax
    (3)   Payroll
    (4)   Invoicing
    (5)   Credit control

3

General advantages	Function-specific advantages
• Cost • Liability/indemnity • Cashflow • Specialist service • Flexibility	• Technological advance (IT) • Liability/indemnity (IT/due diligence) • Immediacy (IA) • Flexibility (IA)

4   False

    –   Responsibility for accounting records still lies with directors
    –   Responsibility for auditing them still lies with auditors

Now try the questions below from the Exam Question Bank

Number	Level	Marks	Time
Q27	Examination	20	36 mins

Reporting

Reporting

17

Reporting

Topic list	Syllabus reference
1 Critically appraising the standard unmodified auditor's report	F1
2 Forming and critiquing an audit opinion	F1
3 Reporting electronically	F1
4 Communication with those charged with governance	F2
5 Actions when audit report is modified	F1

Introduction

As a student at this stage of your studies, you will be familiar with the external audit opinion. If this is not the case, before you read any of this chapter, you must go back to your previous Study Text and revise the basic features of the report, the various modifications that can be made, the concept of a true and fair view and the statutory requirements in relation to the audit opinion.

At this level, students are expected not only to know what the audit opinion is and how it is presented. They are required to draw audit opinions and also assess the appropriateness of an audit opinion formed by another person.

In this chapter we shall also consider the form of the audit report, the criticism that it receives and whether it enables an auditor to express properly a true and fair view.

We shall also look at the auditors' requirements in relation to reporting to those charged with governance. We have already looked at the issue of reporting on assignments other than audit assignments in Chapter 12 of this Study Text.

Study guide

		Intellectual level
F	**Reporting**	
1	**Auditor's report**	
(a)	Critically appraise the form and content of an auditor's report in a given situation.	3
(b)	Recognise and evaluate the factors to be taken into account when forming an audit opinion in a given situation and justify audit opinions that are consistent with the results of audit procedures.	3
(c)	Assess whether or not a proposed audit opinion is appropriate.	3
(d)	Advise on the actions which may be taken by the auditor in the event that a modified audit report is issued.	3
(e)	Recognise when the use of an emphasis of matter paragraph and other matter paragraph would be appropriate.	3
2	**Reports to those charged with governance and management**	
(a)	Critically assess the quality of a report to those charged with governance and management.	3
(c)	Advise on the content of reports to those charged with governance and management in a given situation.	3

Exam guide

Audit reporting questions at this level tend to be challenging, but 'do-able', particularly if you have practised similar questions and have established a step-by-step approach to questions on forming an audit opinion. You are likely to encounter a question on audit reports in Section B of the exam paper.

1 Critically appraising the standard unmodified auditor's report

FAST FORWARD

A standard format is used to promote understandability because the audit report is widely available to both accustomed users and those who are not accustomed to audit and audit language.

1.1 The act of communication

In essence, the auditors' job is straightforward. They carry out tests and enquiries and evaluate evidence received with the purpose of drawing an audit opinion. They then **communicate** that opinion, in the form of an audit report, as we have been discussing. This can cause problems.

The communication problem is caused by a number of different problems that can be identified under three headings, although some of the issues are broadly linked between categories. The three problematic areas are:

- Understandability
- Responsibility
- Availability

1.2 Understandability

Although the essence of the auditors' role is simple, in practice it is surrounded by auditing standards and guidance as it is a **technical** art. It also involves **relevant language**, or 'jargon' that non-auditors may not understand.

This can be seen in a definition of what audit is. 'An audit is an exercise designed to show whether financial statements are free from **material misstatement** and give a **true and fair view**.' The highlighted words reveal the problem.

Communicating the audit opinion in a way that people can understand it is a challenge.

1.3 Responsibility

Connected with the problem of what the audit is and what the audit opinion means is the issue of what the auditors are **responsible** for. As far as the **law** is concerned, auditors have a restricted number of duties. **Professional standards** and other bodies place other duties on auditors.

Users of financial statements, and the public, may not have a very clear perception of what the auditors are responsible for and what the audit opinion relates to, or what context it is in.

The issue of **auditors' liability** ties in here. Audit reports are addressed to shareholders, to whom auditors have their primary and legal responsibility. However, audited accounts are used by significantly more people than that. Should this fact be addressed in the audit report? This issue is also considered in Chapter 3.

1.4 Availability

FAST FORWARD

The availability of audit reports has been increased by the trend to publish financial statements on companies' websites. Auditors should consider the risks of this.

The fact that a significant number of people use audited accounts has just been mentioned. Audit reports are publicly available, as they are often held on **public record**. This fact alone may add to any perception that exists that auditors address their report to more than just shareholders.

The problem of availability is exacerbated by the fact that many companies publish their **financial statements** on their **website**. The IAASB Paper *Financial reporting on the internet: responsibilities of directors and management* stresses the need for directors and senior management to ensure that any financial information provided has the same integrity as that published in paper form. This also means that millions of people around the world have access to the audit report. (Note that this IAASB Paper is not examinable but has been included here as background information). The IAASB paper states that management should implement procedures to ensure access.

However, this issue may add significant misunderstandings.

- **Language** barriers may cause additional understandability problems
- It may not be clear **which financial information** an audit report refers to
- The audit report may be subject to **malicious tampering** by hackers or personnel

If an audit report is published electronically, auditors lose control of the **physical positioning** of the report, that is, what it is published with. This might significantly impact on understandability and also perceived responsibility. We will look at reporting electronically in Section 3.

1.5 The standard report

The standard audit report under ISA 700 *Forming an opinion and reporting on financial statements* is set out below.

INDEPENDENT AUDITOR'S REPORT

Report on the financial statements

We have audited the accompanying financial statements of ABC Company which comprise, the balance sheet as at December 31, 20X1, and the income statement, statement of changes in equity and cash flow statement for the year then ended, and a summary of significant accounting policies and other explanatory information.

Management's responsibility for the financial statements

Management is responsible for the preparation and fair presentation of these financial statements in accordance with International Financial Reporting Standards, and for such internal control as management determines is necessary to enable the preparation of financial statements that are free from material misstatement, whether due to fraud or error.

Auditor's responsibility

Our responsibility is to express an opinion on these financial statements based on our audit. We conducted our audit in accordance with International Standards on Auditing. Those standards require that we comply with ethical requirements and plan and perform the audit to obtain reasonable assurance about whether the financial statements are free from material misstatement.

An audit involves performing procedures to obtain audit evidence about the amounts and disclosures in the financial statements. The procedures selected depend on the auditor's judgement, including the assessment of the risks of material misstatement of the financial statements, whether due to fraud or error. In making those risk assessments, the auditor considers internal control relevant to the entity's preparation and fair presentation of the financial statements in order to design audit procedures that are appropriate in the circumstances, but not for the purpose of expressing an opinion on the effectiveness of the entity's internal control. An audit also includes evaluating the appropriateness of accounting policies used and the reasonableness of accounting estimates made by management, as well as evaluating the overall presentation of the financial statements.

We believe that the audit evidence we have obtained is sufficient and appropriate to provide a basis for our audit opinion.

Opinion

In our opinion the financial statements present fairly, in all material aspects (or *give a true and fair view of*) the financial position of ABC Company as at December 31, 20X1, its financial performance and its cash flows for the year then ended in accordance with International Financial Reporting Standards.

Report on other legal and regulatory requirements

[Form and content of this section of the auditor's report will vary depending on the nature of the auditor's other reporting responsibilities.]

[Auditor's signature]

[Date of auditor's report]

[Auditor's address]

Point to note

ISA 700 has not yet been updated to take account of the changes in terminology introduced by the revision of IAS 1 *Presentation of financial statements*.

The audit report has certain elements designed to eliminate common misconceptions:

- It is clearly addressed to shareholders
- Introductory paragraphs outlining what the report refers to
- Paragraphs outlining the responsibilities of management and auditors
- An explanation of the basis on which the auditors have come to their conclusion
- An expression of opinion

However, some parties still argue that the audit report is a difficult document to understand. It still includes technical terms which require further explanation.

It is sometimes argued that the existence of a standard report adds complexity to the situation and that users would be better served by having audit reports tailored to each specific client.

1.5.1 Advantages of a standard report

The key advantages of having a standard report is that it is **easier for users to understand** an audit report that has **elements in common** with all other audit reports. It also means that audit reports can be more easily compared.

When a standard report is used, there is less chance of isolated misunderstanding caused by the way one firm of auditors chooses to express itself or in relation to the explanation of a particular issue.

One of the competencies you require to fulfil performance objective 18 of the PER is the ability to draft a report in accordance with current relevant standards, legislation, regulations and any terms of engagement. You can apply the knowledge you obtain in this chapter of the text to help demonstrate this competence.

2 Forming and critiquing an audit opinion   Pilot paper
12/07, 6/09, 12/09, 6/10, 12/10, 6/11

Auditors express an opinion on financial statements based on the work they have done, the evidence obtained and conclusions drawn in relation to that evidence.

2.1 Forming an audit opinion

When the auditors have gathered all the evidence required, the audit engagement partner will form the audit opinion as to truth and fairness of the financial statements as a whole.

The following standards apply for the various audit opinions that can be given:

- ISA 700 *Forming an opinion and reporting on financial statements*
- ISA 705 *Modifications to the opinion in the independent auditor's report*
- ISA 706 *Emphasis of matter paragraphs and other matter paragraphs in the independent auditor's report*

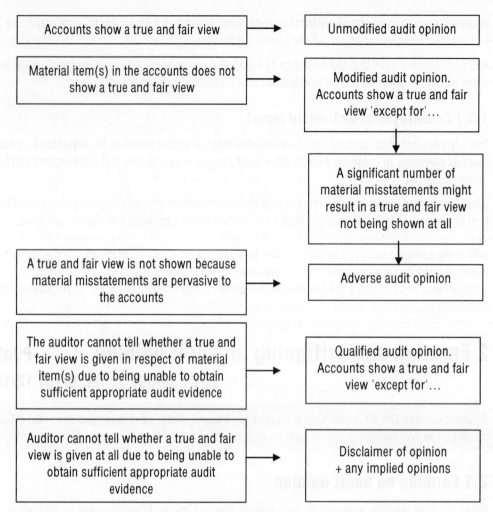

When forming their opinion, there are some key matters that the auditor must consider. These can be illustrated in the form of three questions:

Question 1 Have all the procedures necessary to meet auditing standards and to obtain all the information and explanations necessary for the audit been carried out?

Question 2 Have the financial statements been prepared in accordance with the applicable accounting requirements?

Question 3 Do the financial statements give a true and fair view?

Remember!

True: Information is factual and conforms with reality, not false. In addition the information conforms with required standards and law. The accounts have been correctly extracted from the books and records.
Fair: Information is free from discrimination and bias and in compliance with expected standards and rules. The accounts should reflect the commercial substance of the company's underlying transactions.

The process of forming an audit opinion in an exam question can be summarised in a step format, as follows:

Step 1 Read through all the information given in the question carefully.

Step 2 Analyse the requirement.

Step 3 Read through the information given in the question again in the light of the requirement, making notes of any key factors.

Step 4 Ascertain whether all the evidence reasonably expected to be available has been obtained and evaluated.

Step 5 If not, identify whether the effect of not gaining evidence is such that the financial statements could as a whole be misleading (disclaimer of opinion) or in material part could be misleading ('except for' opinion).

Step 6 Ascertain whether the financial statements have been prepared in accordance with generally accepted accounting principles (GAAP).

Step 7 If not, determine whether departure was required to give a true and fair view and if so, whether it has been properly disclosed.

Step 8 Decide whether any unnecessary departure is material to the financial statements ('except for' opinion) or is pervasive to them (adverse opinion).

Step 9 Conclude whether the financial statements as a whole give a true and fair view.

Even if the answers to steps 4 and 6 are yes, you must still carry out step 9 and make an overall assessment of the truth and fairness of the financial statements in order to conclude that an unmodified opinion is appropriate.

2.2 Emphasis of Matter and Other Matter paragraphs

ISA 706 *Emphasis of Matter paragraphs and Other Matter paragraphs in the Independent Auditor's report* is a new ISA addressing additional communication in the auditor's report where the audit opinion remains unaffected.

> **Emphasis of Matter paragraph.** A paragraph included in the auditor's report that refers to a matter appropriately presented or disclosed in the financial statements that, in the auditor's judgment, is of such importance that it is fundamental to users' understanding of the financial statements.
>
> **Other Matter paragraph.** A paragraph included in the auditor's report that refers to a matter **other than** those presented or disclosed in the financial statements that, in the auditor's judgment, is relevant to users' understanding of the audit, the auditor's responsibilities or the auditor's report.

2.2.1 Emphasis of Matter

The Emphasis of Matter paragraph can be used where the auditor considers it necessary (eg with regards to an uncertain outcome to litigation, early application of an accounting standard that has a pervasive effect on the financial statements in advance of its effective date, a major catastrophe that has had, or continues to have, a devastating effect on the entity's financial position). In certain circumstances, however, it must be used. That is when:

(a) The auditor has determined that the financial reporting framework prescribed by law or regulation would be unacceptable but for the fact that it is prescribed by law or regulation (*ISA 210 Agreeing the terms of audit engagements*).

(b) The auditor highlights the existence of a material uncertainty relating to the event or condition that may cast significant doubt on the entity's ability to continue as a going concern (ISA 570).

The Emphasis of Matter paragraph should be included immediately after the Opinion paragraph in the auditor's report and should be clearly identified as an Emphasis of Matter.

The following is an example of an Emphasis of Matter paragraph from ISA 706

> **Emphasis of matter**
>
> We draw attention to Note X to the financial statements which describes the uncertainty related to the outcome of the lawsuit filed against the company by XYZ Company. Our opinion is not qualified in respect of this matter.

2.2.2 Other Matter

The Other Matter paragraph can also be used when deemed necessary by the auditor (eg when the auditor is unable to withdraw from the engagement and yet is unable to obtain sufficient appropriate audit evidence, when the auditor has been requested to report on other matters or to provide more clarifications in line with the legal jurisdiction of the country). As above, there are specific circumstances where the Other Matter paragraph must be used:

(a)   Where prior period financial statements were audited by a predecessor auditor (ISA 710)

(b)   Where prior period financial statements were not audited (ISA 710) (note this does not relieve the auditor of obtaining sufficient appropriate audit evidence on opening balances)

(c)   When reporting on prior period financial statements in connection with the current period's audit, if the auditor's opinion on such prior period financial statements differs from the opinion the auditor previously expressed (ISA 710)

(d)   If revision of other information is necessary and management refuses to make the revision, the auditor shall include in the auditor's report an Other Matter paragraph describing the material inconsistency (ISA 720)

An example of an Other Matter paragraph from ISA 710 is

> *Other Matter*
>
> The financial statements of ABC Company for the year ended December 31, 20X0, were audited by another auditor who expressed an unmodified opinion on those statements on March 31, 20X1.

The Other Matter paragraph is included immediately after the Opinion paragraph and any Emphasis of Matter paragraph (or elsewhere in the auditor's report if the content of the Other Matter paragraph is relevant to the Other Reporting Responsibilities section).

In certain circumstances, a statement if required in **either an Emphasis of Matter or Other Matter paragraph**. These are required under ISA 560:

(a)   Where law, regulation or the financial reporting framework does not prohibit management from restricting the amendment of the financial statements to the effects of the subsequent event or events causing that amendment and those responsible for approving the financial statements are not prohibited from restricting their approval to that amendment, the auditor is permitted to restrict the audit procedures on subsequent events to that amendment

(b)   Where a reference is required referring to a note to the financial statements that more extensively discusses the reason for the amendment of the previously issued financial statements and to the earlier report provided by the auditor

2.3 Modified opinions

Sometimes it is necessary to modify the audit opinion. This is covered by ISA 705 *Modifications to the opinion in the independent auditor's report*.

> **ISA 705.4**
>
> The objective of the auditor is to express clearly an appropriately modified opinion on the financial statements that is necessary when:
>
> (a)   The auditor concludes, based on the audit evidence obtained, that the financial statements as a whole are not free from material misstatement, or
>
> (b)   The auditor is unable to obtain sufficient appropriate audit evidence to conclude that the financial statements as a whole are free from material misstatement.

The guidance in this standard is not significantly different from the guidance you may have already learned from the old ISA 700 (from before the IAASB Clarity Project).

The IAASB Clarity Project introduced a change in the terminology used in relation to modified audit opinions. This is a change in terminology only, and **does not affect the substance of the opinions being given.**

Type of opinion	Old ISA 700 (pre-Clarity Project)	New ISA 705 (post-Clarity Project)
Modified ('except for')	qualified due to a **disagreement**	qualified due to a **material misstatement**
Modified ('except for')	qualified due to a **limitation on scope**	qualified due to an **inability to obtain sufficient appropriate audit evidence**
Adverse	adverse opinion due to **material** and **pervasive disagreements**	adverse opinion due to **material** and **pervasive misstatements**
Disclaimer of opinion	disclaimed opinion due to a **material** and **pervasive limitation on scope**	disclaimed opinion due to a **material** and **pervasive inability to obtain sufficient appropriate audit evidence**

There are a number of other differences between the formats of the old and the new audit reports. The most significant of these relates to the naming of paragraphs. Previously, the paragraph giving the reason for a modified opinion would have contained this reason in the paragraph title, whereas the new ISA 705 requires the paragraph to be entitled simply "Basis for Qualified Opinion" (for example).

Qualified opinion

Auditor responsibility

Our responsibility is to express an opinion on these financial statements based on our audit. We conducted our audit in accordance with International Standards on Auditing. Those standards require that we comply with ethical requirements and plan and perform the audit to obtain reasonable assurance about whether the financial statements are free from material misstatement.

An audit involves performing procedures to obtain audit evidence about the amounts and disclosures in the financial statements. The procedures selected depend on the auditor's judgment, including the assessment of the risks of material misstatement of the financial statements, whether due to fraud or error. In making those risk assessments, the auditor considers internal control relevant to the entity's preparation and fair presentation of the financial statements in order to design audit procedures that are appropriate in the circumstances, but not for the purpose of expressing an opinion on the effectiveness of the entity's internal control. An audit also includes evaluating the appropriateness of accounting policies used and the reasonableness of accounting estimates made by management, as well as evaluating the overall presentation of the financial statements.

We believe that the audit evidence we have obtained is sufficient and appropriate to provide a basis for our qualified audit opinion.

Basis for Qualified Opinion

ABC Company's investment in XYZ Company, a foreign associate acquired during the year and accounted for by the equity method, is carried at xxx on the balance sheet as at December 31, 20X1, and ABC's share of XYZ's net income of xxx is included in ABC's income for the year then ended. We were unable to obtain sufficient appropriate audit evidence about the carrying amount of ABC's investment in XYZ as at December 31, 20X1 and ABC's share of XYZ's net income for the year because we were denied access to the financial information, management, and the auditors of XYZ. Consequently, we were unable to determine whether any adjustments to these amounts were necessary.

Qualified Opinion

In our opinion, except for the possible effects of the matter described in the Basis for Qualified Opinion paragraph, the financial statements present fairly, in all material respects, (or *give a true and fair view of*) the financial position of ABC Company as at December 31, 20X1, and (*of*) its financial performance and its cash flows for the year then ended in accordance with International Financial Reporting Standards.

Disclaimer of Opinion

Auditor's Responsibility

Our responsibility is to express an opinion on these financial statements based on conducting the audit in accordance with International Standards on Auditing. Because of the matter described in the Basis for Disclaimer of Opinion paragraph, however, we were not able to obtain sufficient appropriate audit evidence to provide a basis for an audit opinion.

Basis for Disclaimer of Opinion

The company's investment in its joint venture XYZ (Country X) Company is carried at xxx on the company's balance sheet, which represents over 90% of the company's net assets as at December 31, 20X1. We were not allowed access to the management and the auditors of XYZ, including XYZ's auditors' audit documentation. As a result, we were unable to determine whether any adjustments were necessary in respect of the company's proportional share of XYZ's assets that it controls jointly, its proportional share of XYZ's liabilities for which it is jointly responsible, its proportional share of XYZ's income and expenses for the year, and the elements making up the statement of changes in equity and cash flow statement.

Disclaimer of Opinion

Because of the significance of the matter described in the Basis for Disclaimer of Opinion paragraph, we have not been able to obtain sufficient appropriate audit evidence to provide a basis for an audit opinion. Accordingly, we do not express an opinion on the financial statements.

The following reports are given when the financial statements are **materially misstated**.

Qualified opinion

Basis for Qualified Opinion

The company's inventories are carried in the balance sheet at xxx. Management has not stated the inventories at the lower of cost and net realizable value but has stated them solely at cost, which constitutes a departure from International Financial Reporting Standards. The company's records indicate that had management stated the inventories at the lower of cost and net realizable value, an amount of xxx would have been required to write the inventories down to their net realizable value. Accordingly, cost of sales would have been increased by xxx, and income tax, net income and shareholders' equity would have been reduced by xxx, xxx and xxx, respectively.

Qualified Opinion

In our opinion, except for the effects of the matter described in the Basis for Qualified Opinion paragraph, the financial statements present fairly, in all material respects, (or *give a true and fair view of*) the financial position of ABC Company as at December 31, 20X1, and (*of*) its financial performance and its cash flows for the year then ended in accordance with International Financial Reporting Standards.

---

xam focus ◗int

It is vital for your exam performance that you can analyse a set of facts given to you and draw audit conclusions from them. This is a basic skill at this level. Work through the following question to practice this skill.

Question

Forming an audit opinion

You are an audit senior. You are nearing the end of the audit of Nesta Co for the year ended 30 June 20X8. Nesta Co owns a small chain of high-street clothing stores and also has a manufacturing division where it makes it own label brand 'Little Miss'. Own label clothing represents 50% of the inventory and sales of Nesta Co. The financial statements show a profit before tax of $7 million (20X7: $3 million) and a statement of financial position total of $23 million (20X7: $15 million). The following points have arisen on the audit:

(1)   Nesta Co owns a number of its retail premises, which it revalues annually. This year several of its shops did rise sharply in value due to inflated property prices in their locality. Nesta also capitalises refits of its shops. Two shops were refitted in the year. The total increase in assets due to refits and revaluations is $10 million. Nesta does not revalue its factory premises, which are held in the statement of financial position at $175,000.

(2)   Nesta values its inventory at the lower of cost or net realisable value. Cost is determined by deducting a suitable estimated profit margin from selling price. Inventory in the statement of financial position at 30 June 20X8 was $1,265,000.

(3)   Nesta Co has a refunds policy which states that a customer who is not satisfied with their purchase may return their goods within 28 days of purchase and obtain an exchange or a cash refund. Experience has shown that exchanges and refunds are common, as Nesta Co's shops do not provide fitting rooms, space being at a premium. Nesta does not make any provision in the financial statements for refunds.

Required

Comment on the matters you will consider in relation to the implications of the above points on the audit report of Nesta Co.

(1) **Non-current assets**

There are two issues here. The first is whether Nesta's policy of revaluations is correct and the second is whether Nesta should capitalise re-fit costs.

The most important issue to consider is materiality as only material items will affect the audit opinion. The revaluations and refit total is material to the statement of financial position. It is possible that any revaluation of the factory premises would also be material.

(i) **Revaluation policy**

Per IAS 16, non-current assets may be held at cost or valuation. Where a company applies a revaluation policy, IAS 16 requires that all revaluations are made with sufficient regularity that the carrying amount does not vary materially from that which would be determined if fair value were used. Nesta revalues annually, so meets the requirement.

Nesta revalues property and IAS 16 requires that all items in the same class of assets be revalued, so the question arises as to whether it should also revalue the factory. This might have a material effect on the statement of financial position.

IAS 16 states that a 'class' of property, plant and equipment is a grouping of assets of a similar nature and use in an entity's operations. Although the IAS implies that buildings comprise one class, in this case the **nature** and **use** of the two kinds of building are quite distinct. Therefore creating two classes (retail premises and manufacturing premises) would appear to be reasonable.

(ii) **Refits**

Assets should be held at cost or valuation as discussed above. However, in some cases, IAS 16 allows the cost of refits to be added to the original cost of the asset. This is when it is probable that future economic benefits **in excess** of the **originally assessed** standard of performance of the existing asset will flow to the entity. A retail shop will be subject to refitting and this refitting may enhance its value. However, it is possible in a shop that such refitting might be better classified as expenditure on fixtures and fittings. Nesta's policy should be consistent and comparable, so if they have followed a policy of capitalising refits into the cost of the shop in the past, this seems reasonable.

Conclusion

The issues relating to non-current assets were material and could have affected the auditors' report. However, having considered the issues, it appears that there are no material misstatements in the financial statements. As there appears to have been no inability to obtain sufficient appropriate audit evidence in relation to non-current assets, the audit opinion would be unqualified in relation to these issues.

(2) **Inventory**

IAS 2 requires that inventory be valued at the lower of cost or net realisable value. IAS 2 defines cost as all costs of purchase, conversion and other costs in incurred in bringing the inventory to its present location and condition.

The IAS outlines a number of methods of arriving at an approximation of cost in the absence of a satisfactory costing system. One such method is the use of a selling price less an estimated profit margin. This is a costing method commonly used in retail entities. However, this is reasonable only if it can be shown that the method gives a reasonable approximation of cost.

Given that 50% of Nesta's inventory is manufactured in-house, it appears to be unlikely that they cannot ascertain the cost of the inventory in a better way than the selling price method. The chain of shops is small, and there should be sufficient controls over inventory transfer to enable the company to establish the cost of inventory using a FIFO system.

While the auditors might suggest to the directors that they look into the costing systems and make improvements in future years, it is unlikely that they would modify the audit report in the current year over this matter, assuming that the directors have shown that the accounting policy gives a reasonable approximation of cost.

This is because if a reasonable approximation of cost is given, the difference is not going to be material to the financial statements. Also, if Nesta has had the policy for a long period, the policy is at least consistent with itself. If the auditors had made recommendations that the system was reviewed in future years and the directors refused to make any amendments to the system in future, the auditors might want to consider taking further action in future years.

Conclusion

If there are no other audit matters arising in relation to inventory, the audit report will be unmodified in this respect.

(3) **Provisions**

Nesta offers refunds and exchanges to unhappy customers and experience shows that this offer is commonly taken up. If a sale is refunded, it is as if the sale never took place. It is therefore not prudent for Nesta to recognise profits on such sales. If items are exchanged, the profit element would still exist, so only the inventory element would be potentially misstated.

As the refund period is 28 days, the issue is isolated to sales made in the last month of the year. In the absence of specific figures, this approximates to 1/12 of annual revenue and profit, and is therefore potentially material. Using these approximations, this would mean that if more than a quarter of June's sales were refunded, this could be material to revenue, and potentially to profit.

Given that the accounts are unlikely to be finalised before the end of July, the refunds figure for June should be available to both the directors and to the auditors. They should both be able to assess whether the potential provision required is material to the financial statements, and how much the provision should be, if one is required.

Conclusion

The audit report would only be modified in respect of this matter if the auditors felt that a material provision was required and the directors refused to include one in the financial statements. In this case, the auditors would issue an 'except for' opinion, on the grounds of material misstatement in the financial statements.

Overall conclusion

It appears likely that the auditors will issue an unmodified report for the year ended 30 June 20X8.

2.4 Critically appraising an audit opinion

Critiquing an audit opinion is an extension of forming an audit opinion. It is necessary to form an audit opinion yourself in order to ascertain whether someone else's conclusions on the same facts are fair and reasonable.

2.4.1 When will it be necessary to critically appraise an audit opinion?

The obvious answer to this is 'in exam questions'. However, the exams will be based on real-life scenarios and it is important for you to consider the genuine contexts in which audit opinions will be appraised. Consider the following situations:

* Engagement partner reviewing the audit work and conclusions drawn
* Auditor asked for second opinion about an audit opinion
* Second partner required to review an audit file

Probably the most common example is the engagement partner conducting his file review before drawing his opinion, which he will then give on the audit report that he takes responsibility for. His audit team have carried out the work, and in doing so have drawn audit conclusions about each aspect of the audit work. He must appraise these conclusions and determine whether they are correct or not.

Where a second partner review has been required, for instance, if the client is listed or public interest, one of the things the second partner is required to do is to review the audit opinion suggested and see whether it is reasonable.

The issue of second opinions, as you know, is a tricky one. It is rarely advisable for an auditor to give a second opinion on an audit opinion because he is unlikely to be in possession of the full facts.

2.4.2 How should an auditor critically appraise an audit opinion?

An auditor should form his own opinion on the basis of the facts and then evaluate the original audit opinion in the light of his own opinion. As this is a matter of judgement, it is possible that two different, yet reasonable conclusions could be drawn. For instance, auditors might disagree on whether a matter was material or not. If this was the case, further judgements and risk assessments would have to be made.

In exam questions, then, you should bear in mind the step process required to form an audit opinion in the first place. If you work through each step, you may be able to see that the person who formed the original opinion has missed out steps or failed to notice something important.

In the final analysis, this is a skill that you must practise to be able to do well. Try the following question.

| Question | Critically appraising an audit opinion |

You are an audit partner. Your firm carries out the audit of Branch Co, a listed company. Because the company is listed, you have been asked to perform a second partner review of the audit file for the year ended 30 June 20X8 before the audit opinion is finalised. Reported profit before tax is $1.65 million and the statement of financial position total is $7.6 million.

You have read the following notes from the audit file:

Earnings per share

As required by IAS 33 *Earnings per share*, the company has disclosed both basic and diluted earnings per share. The diluted earnings per share has been incorrectly calculated because the share options held by a director were not included in the calculations. Disclosed diluted earnings per share are 22.9c. Had the share options held by the director been included, this figure would have been 22.4c. This difference is immaterial.

Financial performance statement

The directors have currently not amended certain financial performance ratios in this statement to reflect the changes made to the financial statements as a result of the auditors' work. The difference between the reported ratios and the correct ratios is minimal.

Opinion

We recommend that an unqualified audit report be issued.'

You have noted that there is no evidence on the audit file that the corporate governance statement to be issued as part of the annual report has been reviewed by the audit team. You are aware that the company does not have an audit committee.

You are also aware that the director exercised his share options last week.

Required

Comment on the suitability of the proposed audit opinion and other matters arising in the light of your review. Your comments should include an indication of what form the audit report should take.

Earnings per share

The problem in the EPS calculation relates to share options held by a director. As they are held by a director, it is unlikely that they are immaterial, as matters relating to directors are generally considered to be material by their nature. The fact that EPS is a key shareholder ratio which is therefore likely to be material in nature to the shareholders should also be considered.

As the incorrect EPS calculation is therefore material to the financial statements, the audit report should be modified in this respect, unless the directors agree to amend the EPS figure. This would be an 'except for' modification, on the grounds of material misstatement.

Share options

The share options have not been included in the EPS calculations. The auditors must ensure that the share options have been correctly disclosed in information relating to the director both in the financial statements and the other information, and that these disclosures are consistent with each other. If proper disclosures have not been made, the auditor will have to modify the audit report due to lack of disclosure in this area.

Exercise of share options

The fact that the director has exercised his share options after the year-end does not require disclosure in the financial statements. However, it is likely that he has exercised them as part of a new share issue by the company and if so, the share issue would be a non-adjusting event after the reporting period that would require disclosure in the financial statements. We should check if this is the case and, if so, whether it has been disclosed. Non-disclosure would be further grounds for modification.

Financial performance statement

The financial performance statement forms part of the other information that the auditor is required to review under ISA 720. The ISA states that the auditors should seek to rectify any apparent misstatements in this information. The ratio figures are misstated, and the auditor should encourage the directors to correct them, regardless of the negligible difference.

The ISA refers to material items. The ratios will be of interest to shareholders, being investor information and this fact may make them material by their nature. However, as the difference is negligible in terms of value, on balance, the difference is probably not sufficiently material for the auditors to make any modifications or explanations in their audit report.

Corporate governance statement

For the company to meet listing requirements, the auditors must review the corporate governance statement. For our own purposes, we should document that we have done so. As having an audit committee is a requirement of the UK Corporate Governance Code and the company does not have one, the corporate governance statement should explain why the company does not have comply with the Code in this respect.

We would not modify our audit report over the corporate governance statement, although we might like to include a reference to it in an emphasis of matter paragraph, if we do not feel the disclosure is sufficient in respect of the non-compliance with the requirement to have an audit committee.

This emphasis of matter paragraph would be contained within the opinion section, after the opinion on the truth and fairness of the financial statements has been given. The opinion would not be modified in this respect.

Overall conclusion

None of the matters discussed above, either singly or seen together are pervasive to the financial statements. The audit report should be modified on the material matter of the incorrect EPS calculation. We should ensure that all the other disclosures are in order and also review the corporate governance statement. If the corporate governance statement does not adequately address the issue of the company not having an audit committee, we will need to include an emphasis of matter paragraph in the opinion section of our report. Our opinion will not be modified in this respect.

3 Reporting electronically

When financial information is available electronically, auditors must ensure that their report is not misrepresented.

3.1 Consent

The problems associated with audit reports being published on websites have been discussed in Section 1. The Auditing Practices Board in the UK has issued a bulletin to help the auditor respond properly to a request to publish the audit report electronically.

The Bulletin proposes that the directors should **obtain the consent** of the auditors to publish the audit report on a website. The matter should **ideally be referred to** in the **letter of engagement** between the parties.

The auditors may **reserve the right to decline** the report being so published, if they do not like the presentation of the report and the associated financial statements that the directors propose.

Guidance has been published by another body which advises directors to highlight statutory information given on the website.

3.2 Appropriate wording

The auditors should ensure that their report is worded so that it is appropriate for inclusion on a website. This will include reference to specific financial statements rather than the use of page numbers, for example.

3.3 Controls

Where the auditors' report is to be published electronically, the auditors should carry out a series of checks:

- They should **review the process** for deriving the electronic information from the hard copy financial statements
- They should **check** that the electronic copy is **identical** to the hard copy
- They should **check** that the **presentation** has **not** been **distorted** (ie, that certain items have not been given greater emphasis in the new presentation)

As the directors are responsible for controls in their business, they are responsible for ensuring that the report is not tampered with once it is on the website.

Exam focus point

You should read the accountancy press to follow any developments in this area.

4 Communicating with those charged with governance
6/08, 12/10

Auditors must report relevant audit matters to those charged with governance and will also sometimes produce a report to management detailing control deficiencies observed during the audit.

4.1 Report to those charged with governance

ISA 260 *Communication with those charged with governance,* gives guidance in this area and has been revised and redrafted as part of the Clarity Project.

ISA 260.9

The objectives of the auditor are:

(a) **To communicate clearly** with those charged with governance **the responsibilities of the auditor** in relation to the financial statement audit, and an **overview of the planned scope and timing of the audit**

(b) **To obtain** from those charged with governance **information relevant to the audit**

(c) **To provide** those charged with governance with **timely observations arising from the audit** that are significant and relevant to their responsibility to oversee the financial reporting process, and

(d) **To promote effective two-way communication** between the auditor and those charged with governance.

Those charged with governance are the persons or organisations with responsibility for overseeing the strategic direction of the entity and obligations related to the accountability of the entity. This includes overseeing the financial reporting process. […] For entities in some jurisdictions, this may include management personnel, for example, executive members of a governance board of a private or public sector entity, or an owner-manager.

(ISA 260.10)

The auditors may communicate with the whole board, the supervisory board or the audit committee depending on the governance structure of the organisation. To avoid misunderstandings, the engagement letter should explain that auditors will only **communicate matters** that come to their attention as a **result** of the **performance** of the audit. It should state that the auditors are **not required** to **design procedures** for the purpose of identifying matters of governance interest, however, if the auditors have agreed any specific matters of governance interest to be communicated, it will set these out.

The auditors will also explain:

- The **form** which any **communications** on governance matters will take (must be in writing)
- The **relevant persons** with whom such communications will be made
- The expected content of communications
- The expected timing of the communications (which should be on a timely basis)

4.1.1 Requirements

ISA 260.11

The auditor shall determine the appropriate person(s) within the entity's governance structure with whom to communicate.

Where the auditor communicates with a subgroup of those charged with governance, for example, an audit committee, or an individual the auditor should also consider the need to communicate with the governing body.

4.1.2 Matters to be communicated

Matters would include:

The **auditor's responsibilities** in relation to the financial statements	Including that: • The auditor is responsible for forming and expressing an opinion on the financial statements • The audit does not relieve management or those charged with governance of their responsibilities
Planned **scope and timing** of the audit	Including: • How the audit proposes to address the significant risks of material misstatement from fraud or error • The auditor's approach to internal control • Application of materiality • The extent to which the auditor will use the work of internal audit • Matters those charged with governance consider warrant particular attention
Significant findings from the audit	Including: • Selection of, or changes in, significant accounting policies • The potential effect on the financial statements of any significant risks and exposures, for example pending litigation, that are required to be disclosed in the accounts • Significant difficulties, if any, encountered during the audit (eg delays in provision of required information, brief time in which to complete audit, unavailability of expected information) • Material weaknesses, if any, in the design, implementation or operating effectiveness of internal control • Written representations the auditor is requesting • Other significant matters including material misstatements or inconsistencies in other information that have been corrected
Auditor independence	In the case of **listed entities** matters include: • A statement that relevant ethical requirements regarding independence have been complied with • All relationships (including total fees for audit and non-audit services) which may reasonably be thought to bear on independence • The related safeguards that have been applied to eliminate/reduce identified threats to independence

4.1.3 Communication process

The communication process will vary with the circumstances including:

- The size and governance structure of the entity
- How those charged with governance operate
- The auditor's view of the significance of the matters to be communicated

For example, reports of relatively minor matters to a small client may be best handled orally via a meeting or telephone conversation.

Before communicating matters with those charged with governance the auditor may discuss them with management, unless that is inappropriate. For example, it would not be appropriate to discuss questions of management's competence or integrity with management.

4.1.4 Timing

The auditor should communicate with those charged with governance on a timely basis.

4.1.5 Adequacy of the communication process

The auditor is required to evaluate whether the two-way communication between the auditor and those charged with governance has been adequate for the purposes of the audit. If not adequate and the situation cannot be resolved the auditor may take action as follows:

- Modifying the auditor's opinion on the basis of a inability to obtain sufficient appropriate audit evidence
- Obtaining legal advice
- Communicating with third parties (eg shareholders in a general meeting)
- Withdrawing from the engagement where permitted in the relevant jurisdiction

4.1.6 Documentation

Where matters are communicated orally the auditor is required to document them and when and to whom they were communicated.

xam focus **oint**

The April 2008 edition of *Student Accountant* included an article written by the current P7 examiner, 'Auditors' reports to those charged with governance'. This provides a useful summary of the issues contained in ISA 260.

4.2 Reporting deficiencies in internal control

ISA 265 *Communicating deficiencies in internal control to those charged with governance and management* deals with this area.

A **deficiency in internal control** exists when a control is designed, implemented or operated in such a way that it is unable to prevent, or detect and correct, misstatements in the financial statements on a timely basis or a control necessary to prevent or detect and correct misstatements in the financial statements on a timely basis is missing.

A **significant deficiency in internal control** is a deficiency or combination of deficiencies in internal control that, in the auditor's professional judgement, is of sufficient importance to merit the attention of those charged with governance.

The auditor determines whether any deficiencies in internal control have been identified during the audit, and if so, whether individually or in combination, they are significant deficiencies.

ISA 265.9

The auditor shall communicate in writing significant deficiencies in internal control identified during the audit to those charged with governance on a timely basis.

The communication should include a description of the deficiencies and an explanation of their potential effects. The communication should also make clear that the audit was for the purpose of identifying misstatements in financial statements, not identifying deficiencies in controls, and that the deficiencies identified have been identified as part of audit work, and are not comprehensive.

Auditors should also issue a report on control deficiencies to management. These reports were a key element in your earlier studies in auditing.

FAST FORWARD

The primary purpose of the report to management is to inform management of deficiencies in the system of internal controls, but the letter can also be used for other purposes.

4.2.1 Key qualities of a report

Recap of key qualities of a report to those charged with governance

- It should not **include language** that **conflicts** with the **opinion** expressed in the audit report.

- It should state that the **accounting and internal control** systems were **considered only** to the **extent necessary** to **determine** the **auditing procedures** to report on the financial statements and not to determine the adequacy of internal control for management purposes or to provide assurances on the accounting and internal control systems.

- It will state that it **discusses only deficiencies** in internal control which have **come to the auditors' attention** as a result of the **audit** and that other deficiencies in internal control may exist.

- It should also include a statement that the **communication is provided for use only** by **management** (or another specific named party).

- The auditors will usually ascertain the actions taken, including the reasons for those suggestions rejected.

- The auditors may encourage management to respond to the auditors' comments in which case any response can be included in the report.

4.2.2 Form of reports

The form of the report will depend on the type of organisation concerned. It may be appropriate to divide the report into sections, which cover significant and general points for senior management first, and then proceed to more specific, divisional points in subsequent sections. The report covering findings from the audit may typically be in the form of a covering letter (see below) and a schedule of points raised.

Case Study

Example: Reports to management covering letter

Private & Confidential

The Directors
XYZ Co
1 High Street
Anytown

24 June 20XX

Dear Sirs

XYZ Co

Following our recent audit of your company, we are writing to advise you of various matters which came to our attention.

We set out on the attached schedule the areas of significant deficiency which we noted, together with our recommendations. These recommendations have already been discussed with ... and their comments have been included.

As the purpose of the audit is to form an opinion on the company's financial statements, you will appreciate that our examination cannot necessarily be expected to disclose all shortcomings of the system and for this reason, the matters raised may not be the only ones which exist.

We should appreciate your comments as to how you propose to deal with the matters raised in this letter. If you require any further information or advice, please contact us.

We have prepared this letter for your use only. It should not be disclosed to a third party and we can assume no responsibility to any person to whom it is disclosed without our written consent.

We would like to take this opportunity to thank you and your staff for your help and co-operation during the course of our audit.

Your faithfully

ABC & Co

[margin notes, left:]
- ...uld be to ...dit committee
- ...ould be ...ted soon ...er ...mpletion of ...dit
- ...anaging ...pectations
- ...equesting ...edback
- ...sclaiming ...bility to third ...rties

4.2.3 Specific recommendations

The detailed recommendations included in the appendix would be structured as per the following example.

> Preparation of payroll and maintenance of personnel records
>
> *Deficiencies*
>
> Under your present system, just two members of staff are entirely and equally responsible for the maintenance of personnel records and preparation of the payroll. Furthermore, the only independent check of any nature on the payroll is that the chief accountant confirms that the amount of the wages cheque presented to him for signature agrees with the total of the net wages column in the payroll. This latter check does not involve any consideration of the reasonableness of the amount of the total net wages cheque or the monies being shown as due to individual employees.

[margin notes, left:]
- ...fficient detail ...enable ...rectors to ...llow up
- ...xplain ...tential effect ...n client ...usiness

Implications

It is a serious deficiency of your present system, that so much responsibility is vested in the hands of just two people. This situation is made worse by the fact that there is no clearly defined division of duties between the two of them. In our opinion, it would be far too easy for fraud to take place in this area (eg by inserting the names of 'dummy workmen' into the personnel records and hence on to the payroll) and/or for clerical errors to go undetected.

Recommendations

(i)   A person other than the two wages clerks should be made responsible for maintaining the personnel records and for periodically (but on a surprise basis) checking them against the details on the payroll.

(ii)   The two wages clerks should be allocated specific duties in relation to the preparation of the payroll, with each clerk independently reviewing the work of the other.

(iii)   When the payroll is presented in support of the cheque for signature to the chief accountant, he should be responsible for assessing the reasonableness of the overall charge for wages that week.

5 Actions when an audit report is modified   12/10

FAST FORWARD

When the auditor's report is expected to be modified, the auditor must communicate with those charged with governance, and must consider the effect of the modification on future audit engagements.

5.1 Communicate with those charged with governance

If the auditor expects that the audit opinion will be modified, then they must communicate the circumstances surrounding the modification with those charged with governance (TCWG) (ISA 705.28). This is in order:

*   To give TCWG notice of the modification and the reasons for it

*   To confirm the auditor's understanding with TCWG of the facts of any matters giving rise to modifications, and to confirm matters on which the auditor and TCWG disagree

*   To give TCWG a chance to provide the auditor with further information and explanations before the auditor's report is issued.

ISA 706 contains a similar requirement in relation to Emphasis of Matter and Other Matter paragraphs.

In addition, it is a specific requirement of ISA 260 that any 'significant difficulties' encountered are communicated with TCWG (see above) – this would include any matters that lead to a modified report being issued.

5.2 External consultation

If a modified opinion is expected to be expressed, then the auditor may need to consider consulting externally on the impact of this, eg with legal counsel under legal privilege, or anonymously with the ACCA.

5.3 Management integrity

The first thing to consider where the auditor's report is to be modified is whether the matter in question suggests that management may not have the requisite integrity. This is particularly relevant where the scope of the audit has been limited by management, eg if management refuses to allow auditors access to all necessary books and records.

If the auditor does consider management's integrity to be in doubt, then any **representations** (including written representations) provided by management during the course of the audit **need to be reconsidered** in this light.

It may also be necessary to **perform an engagement quality control review** on the audit, as a lack of management integrity would mean that the audit carries a higher level of risk than may have been envisaged at the planning stage of the audit.

5.4 Withdrawal from engagement

If the matter in relation to which the audit report is modified is sufficiently serious, then it may be necessary to seek to withdraw from the audit engagement. If the auditor does seek to withdraw then it will be necessary to obtain advice from legal counsel.

ISA 210 *Agreeing the terms of audit engagements* states that **if there has been a limitation on the scope of a prior audit** which leads the auditor to believe that the audit opinion expressed this year will likely be a **disclaimer of opinion**, then the **auditor must not accept the engagement** (unless required to do so by law).

Chapter Roundup

- A standard format is used to promote understandability because the audit report is widely available to both accustomed users and those who are not accustomed to audit and audit language.

- The availability of audit reports has been increased by the trend to publish financial statements on companies' websites. Auditors should consider the risks of this.

- Auditors express an opinion on financial statements based on the work they have done, the evidence obtained and conclusions drawn in relation to that evidence.

- When financial information is available electronically, auditors must ensure that their report is not misrepresented.

- Auditors must report relevant audit matters to those charged with governance and will also sometimes produce a report to management detailing control deficiencies observed during the audit.

- The primary purpose of the report to management is to inform management of deficiencies in the system of internal controls, but the letter can also be used for other purposes.

- When the auditor's report is expected to be modified, the auditor must communicate with those charged with governance, and must consider the effect of the modification on future audit engagements.

Quick Quiz

1   Name the various opinions auditors may give in their audit report.

    (1)   ....

    (2)   ....

    (3)   ....

2   Complete the definitions.

    (a)   .... information is free from .... and
            .... and in compliance with the expected standards and rules.

    (b)   .... is an expression of the relative .... or importance
            of a particular matter in the .... as a whole.

    (c)   .... information is .... and conforms with
            ...., not .... information conforms with required
            standards and law.

3   List the main contents of the ISA 700 standard, unmodified report.

4   Name four matters which might be covered in a letter to those charged with governance.

    (1)   ....

    (2)   ....

    (3)   ....

    (4)   ....

1   (1)   Unmodified
    (2)   Modified due to material misstatement
    (3)   Modified due to the inability to obtain sufficient appropriate audit evidence

2   (a)   Fair, discrimination, bias
    (b)   Materiality, significance, financial statements
    (c)   True, factual, reality, false, true

3   Title, addressee, introductory paragraph, responsibilities of management/auditors, opinion paragraph, other matters, date, signature, address

4   From:

- Auditor's responsibilities in relation to the financial statements

- The **general approach** or overall scope of the audit.

- Selection of, or changes in, **significant accounting policies**

- The potential effect on the financial statements of any **significant risks** and **exposures**, for example pending litigation, that are required to be disclosed in the accounts

- Significant difficulties encountered during the audit

- Other **significant matters** such as significant deficiencies in internal control, questions regarding management integrity, and fraud involving management

- Other **matters** mentioned in **terms** of **engagement**

Now try the questions below from the Exam Question Bank

Number	Level	Marks	Time
Q28	Examination	15	27 mins
Q29	Examination	15	27 mins

Current issues and developments

Current issues and
developments

18

Current issues

Topic list	Syllabus reference
1 Summary of current issues	Various
2 Update	G5
3 General issues	G5

Introduction

At this level in your studies you are expected to be familiar with current developments affecting the audit and assurance profession. Currently, many of these relate to international regulation.

You must read *Student Accountant* and the wider professional press to keep up to date with these.

Study guide

	Intellectual level
G5 **Other current issues**	
(a) Explain current developments in auditing standards including the need for new and revised standards and evaluate their impact on the conduct of audits	3
(b) Discuss other current legal, ethical, other professional and practical matters that affect accountants, auditors, their employers and the profession	3

Exam guide

You may be asked to discuss current developments and must be prepared to argue for or against any new proposals from the point of view of either a preparer or user of assurance reports.

1 Summary of current issues

This Study Text has covered the wide range of current issues within the relevant topic chapters. The following summary should remind you of the issues you have studied up to this point.

	Chapter(s)
Professional, ethical, regulatory and corporate governance topics	1 s1 2 s2 3 s4, s5.8
Going concern	8 s6
Audit documentation	6 s6
Social and environmental auditing	15

2 Update

2.1 The IAASB's Clarity project

As you know from earlier chapters in this Study Text, in 2009 the IAASB reviewed the drafting conventions used in its ISAs with a view to improving the clarity and therefore the consistent application of its ISAs. The IAASB also implemented a plan to complete the revision of certain ISAs and the redrafting of all ISAs in accordance with the new conventions. This project was completed in February 2009.

The following table shows the ISAs which have been issued and are included in your examinable documents listing. A summary of the key revisions is given here.

ISA	Key revisions
ISA 200 *Overall objectives of the independent auditor and the conduct of an audit in accordance with international standards on auditing*	Clarifies **objectives** of an audit and the auditor More detailed explanations of ethical requirements relating to an audit of financial statements, professional scepticism, conduct of an audit in accordance with ISAs and audit risk Requirement to obtain sufficient appropriate audit evidence has been moved here from ISA 500

ISA	Key revisions
ISA 210 *Agreeing the terms of audit engagements*	**Objective** of the auditor in accepting an audit engagement clarified
	Auditors have to establish whether the necessary **preconditions for an audit** are present
	Where the terms of an engagement are changed, management and the auditor must **record** the new terms in an engagement letter or other suitable written form
	Auditors cannot accept an engagement where a limitation of scope has been imposed that will result in a disclaimer of opinion (unless required by law)
ISA 220 *Quality control for an audit of financial statements*	Additional documentation requirements for the engagement quality control reviewer
ISA 265 *Communicating deficiencies in internal control to those charged with governance and management*	The term 'material weakness' has been replaced with **'significant deficiency'**
	Significant deficiencies in internal control must be brought to the attention, **in writing**, of those charged with governance
	The auditor must **communicate**, in writing, to management any significant deficiencies in internal control that are being communicated to those charged with governance (unless inappropriate)
	Other deficiencies in internal control which are not significant must be brought to the attention of management alone, and do not need to be reported in writing
ISA 320 *Materiality in planning and performing an audit*	Revised definition of materiality
	A new term 'performance materiality' introduced
	Considers matters that are **material to the users of financial statements as a group**, not individual users
	Additional detailed guidance on the use of benchmarks in calculating materiality
	New onus on documentation
ISA 402 *Audit considerations relating to an entity using a service organisation*	Definitions given for user entity, user auditor, service auditor and service organisation
	Service organisation prepares a Type 1 or Type 2 report
	The user auditor may use these reports to obtain an understanding of the nature and significance of the services provided by the service organisation
ISA 450 *Evaluation of misstatements identified during the audit*	**All** misstatements must be communicated to management on a timely basis, not just those which are material
	Auditors must request management to **correct** all misstatements
	If management refuse to correct misstatements, the auditor must **communicate** the individual misstatements to those charged with governance and request that these be corrected, mentioning any effect on the opinion in the auditor's report
	Written representations must be obtained from management, and where appropriate those charged with governance, that they believe the effects of any uncorrected mistakes are immaterial both individually and in aggregate
	More stringent documentation requirements for auditors

ISA	Key revisions
ISA 500 *Audit evidence*	New requirements dealing with the audit evidence implications of using a management's expert (an expert employed or engaged by the audited entity)
ISA 501 *Audit evidence-specific considerations for selected items*	Guidance on valuation and disclosure of long-term investments removed as the term is no longer prevalent under IFRS or any other major reporting framework
	Auditors must now request **written representations** that all actual or possible litigation and claims whose effects should be considered when preparing the financial statements have been disclosed to the auditor and correctly accounted for
ISA 505 *External confirmations*	External confirmations are **not** compulsory for the auditor
	Auditors must **communicate** with those charged with governance if management's refusal to send a confirmation is unreasonable
	Specific conditions must be present if **negative confirmations** are to the be only response to an assessed risk of material misstatement at the assertion level
	Increased guidance on the reliability and risks of **electronic confirmations**
	Auditor must consider the implication for the audit report if a positive confirmation is not received and the auditor has determined this is necessary to obtain sufficient appropriate audit evidence
	Auditors must obtain **audit evidence** to resolve any doubts over the reliability of external confirmations
ISA 520 *Analytical procedures*	No significant revisions
ISA 530 *Audit sampling*	Sample selection has moved to ISA 500
ISA 610 *Using the work of internal auditors*	No significant revisions
ISA 620 *Using the work of an auditor's expert*	Expert has been more clearly separated into two types
	An **auditor's expert** is used by the auditor to assist in obtaining sufficient appropriate audit evidence whereas a **management's expert** is used by the entity to assist in preparing financial statements
	Auditor's internal experts (permanent or temporary staff/partners of the audit firm/network firm) are members of the engagement team
	Auditor's external experts (expert engaged but not employed by the auditor) **are not** members of the engagement team
	Additional guidance is given detailing where it is appropriate that the auditor must agree certain items in writing with the expert
ISA 700 *Forming an opinion and reporting on financial statements*	Illustrative auditors reports in appendixes have been updated
ISA 705 *Modifications to the opinion in the independent auditor's report*	This ISA discusses the form and content of the audit report when a modification is already deemed necessary
	Limitation in scope becomes an '**inability to obtain sufficient appropriate audit evidence**'
	Disagreement is now '**financial statements are materially misstated**'
	Auditors are required to **communicate** to those charged with governance when they expect to modify the opinion in the audit report regarding the circumstances that led to the expected modification and the proposed wording of the modification

ISA	Key revisions
ISA 706 *Emphasis of matter paragraphs and other matter paragraphs in the independent auditor's report*	An ISA dealing with additional communication in the auditor's report when the auditor considers it necessary to include an emphasis of matter (EOM) or other matters (OM) paragraph EOM and OM paragraphs **do not affect the audit opinion** Standard highlights certain circumstances where the auditor may consider it necessary to include an EOM or OM paragraph Auditors must **communicate** with those charged with governance if they expect to include an EOM or OM paragraph in the auditor's report, letting them know the exact wording of the paragraph
ISA 710 *Comparative information-corresponding figures and comparative financial statements*	Auditors procedures are **similar** in respect of corresponding figure and comparative financial statements but the audit report differs for each The auditor must request written representations for **all** periods referred to in the audit opinion in respect of comparative financial statements In the case of corresponding figures written representations are requested for the financial statements of the current period only Specific written representations must be obtained regarding any restatement to correct a figure in prior period financial statements that affects the comparative information
International Standard on Quality Control (ISQC) 1 *Quality control for firms that perform audits and reviews of financial statements, and other assurance and related services engagements*	Definition of **engagement team** has been updated to exclude an auditor's external expert

Please note that this is **not** an exhaustive listing and that the clarity ISAs should always be referred to in full when carrying out future audit work.

2.2 Guidance on smaller audits

In general terms, the IAASB takes the view that 'an audit is an audit', and that all audits should be conducted in accordance with the same auditing standards. However, this does not mean that there will be special considerations for audits of smaller entities.

In August 2009 the IAASB issued a Questions & Answers publication, *Applying ISAs proportionately with the size and complexity of an entity*, focusing on matters relevant to the audit of SMEs in the context of implementing the new Clarity ISAs. The IAASB reiterated that the text of the ISAs is authoritative and must be followed, even in the audit of SMEs.

However, the IAASB did state that the work that an auditor will need to do in order to comply with an ISA will vary – a small, simple entity being likely to require less work than a large and complex one. The auditor needs to use professional judgement in applying the ISAs, in order to determine the procedures that are necessary to comply with their requirements.

To take a specific example, the IAASB stated that the requirement in ISA 315 to obtain an understanding of the entity and its environment is relevant to smaller entities, but that because smaller entities are typically simpler, it will be much easier to obtain this understanding.

Individual clarity ISAs include guidance on specific points relating to small entity audits. The purpose of this guidance is to assist in the application of the requirements of the ISA to a small entity audit. It does not limit or reduce the responsibility of the auditor to apply and comply with the requirements of the ISAs.

2.3 IAASB Practice Alert *Audit Considerations in Respect of Going Concern in the Current Economic Environment* (Jan 2009)

In January 2009 the IAASB issued a Practice Alert on going concern in the context of the global economic downturn. Its key message were as follows:

- The going concern assumption is a fundamental principle in the preparation of financial statements.

- The assessment of an entity's ability to continue as a going concern is the responsibility of the entity's management.

- The appropriateness of the use of the going concern assumption is a matter for the auditor to consider on every audit engagement.

- ISA 570 *Going Concern* establishes the relevant requirements and guidance with regard to the auditor's consideration of the appropriateness of management's use of the going concern assumption and auditor reporting.

- The credit crisis and economic downturn have led to a lack of available credit to entities of all sizes, which may affect an entity's ability to continue as a going concern; this and other factors may be relevant in the auditor's evaluation of forecasts prepared by management to support its going concern assessment.

- The extent of disclosures in the financial statements is driven by management's assessment of an entity's ability to continue as a going concern, coupled with the disclosure requirements of the applicable financial reporting framework.

Consideration of the need for an emphasis of matter paragraph in the auditor's report will be a difficult matter of judgment to be made in the context of the entity's circumstances; the mere existence of the credit crisis, though referred to in the financial statements, does not of itself create the need for an emphasis.

2.4 IAASB Practice Alert *Challenges in Auditing Fair Value Accounting Estimates in the Current Market Environment* (Oct 2008)

In October 2008 the IAASB issued a Practice Alert, *Challenges in Auditing Fair Value Accounting Estimates in the Current Market Environment.* It discussed the following key points:

- Challenges faced in accounting on the basis of fair value;

- Requirements and guidance in standards that are particularly relevant to fair values;

- Other considerations in audits of fair value accounting estimates;

- Initiatives of the International Accounting Standards Board; and

- Recent revisions to extant standards on auditing accounting estimates and fair value measurements and disclosures which, while not yet effective, may be helpful to auditors.

2.5 IAASB Q&A paper: *Auditor Considerations Regarding Significant, Unusual or Highly Complex Transactions*

Issued in August 2010, this IAASB Question & Answer paper dealt with significant/unusual/highly complex transactions, which may by nature carry a higher risk of material misstatement, and thus merit heightened attention from users. The IAASB emphasises the importance of the auditor exercising professional judgement and scepticism. The auditor is required to consider the susceptibility of the financial statements to material misstatement by fraud, which includes consideration of fraud risk factors (eg significant complex transactions, which may pose questions of 'substance over form' and fraudulent financial reporting). The auditor then needs to design audit procedures that gather audit evidence in relation to these risks.

2.6 IAASB Q&A paper: *XBRL: The Emerging Landscape*

In January 2010 the IAASB issued a Question & Answer paper to highlight the growing interest in, and use of, XBRL, and to raise awareness of how XBRL-tagged data is prepared and how it may affect financial reporting. The paper contained the following key messages:

- XBRL is an electronic business information format expected to provide benefits in the preparation, analysis and communication of business information.

- The use of XBRL can vary by jurisdiction and may be driven by regulatory requirements or voluntary application.

- Under the current ISAs, auditors are not required to perform procedures or provide assurance on XBRL-tagged data in the context of audited financial statements. Accordingly, the auditor's report in accordance with the ISAs on the financial statements does not cover the process by which XBRL data is tagged, the XBRL-tagged data that results from this process, or any representation of XBRL-tagged data.

- The IAASB is currently undertaking a consultation to determine the needs of preparers and users of XBRL-tagged data. This consultation will assist the IAASB in assessing whether it is necessary and in the public interest to develop a pronouncement addressing association with and/or assurance on XBRL-tagged data.

2.7 ISAE 3402: Assurance Reports on Controls at a Service Organization

In December 2009 the IAASB issued ISAE 3402 *Assurance Reports on Controls at a Service Organization*, which covers assurance reports given by outsourcers to the entities that use them. The ISAE effectively supersedes the commonly-used but older SAS 70 (issued by the Assurance Reports on Controls at a Service Organization).

3 General issues

3.1 FRC & FSA: *Enhancing the auditor's contribution to prudential regulation*

There has been a lot of discussion within the profession over the last few years on the related issues of the role of the audit generally, and the role that was played by auditors in the financial crisis.

In the UK, the Financial Review Council (FRC) recently issued a joint paper with the Financial Services Authority (FSA) entitled *Enhancing the auditor's contribution to prudential regulation*. The paper questioned aspects of the quality of audit work – in particular, whether the auditor has always been sufficiently sceptical and has paid sufficient attention to indicators of management bias. The paper then went on to make a number of suggestions of changes that could be made to the way auditors work. The paper has generated intense debate within the profession, with auditors strongly defending the view that they were independent in the run up to the financial crisis.

Fundamental questions are being asked about the very nature of audit and the value it provides. Many take the view that auditors have not been sufficiently independent from their clients. For example, in the UK a May 2009 Treasury Select Committee report stated that:

> We strongly believe that investor confidence, and trust in audit would be enhanced by a prohibition on audit firms conducting non-audit work for the same company [...]

This is a strongly-worded statement, made in the context of the recent financial crisis, which calls for a major review of all independence requirements relating to UK auditors. Needless to say, it has been strongly challenged by auditors. You should keep an eye on the financial press for any developments here, as this is an area of ongoing debate which is unlikely to be resolved for some time.

3.2 Audit referred to Competition Commission in UK

In July 2011 the UK's Office of Fair Trading referred the audit market to the Competition Commission. The referral was a result of concerns about lack of competition, and barriers to entry and switching. Needless to say, this referral has been controversial in the profession, as the Competition Commission is an extremely powerful body, which could require extreme measures to open up the UK audit market if it sees fit, such as the forced divestment of firms' assets, or large-scale break-up.

As ever, you should keep abreast of developments here, as it is possible that your exam might include a discussion question in this area, which links in well with other topical issues in relation to auditor independence.

3.3 EC green paper on audit

Considerable controversy has been caused within the profession by the proposals of EC Commissioner for Internal Markets, Michel Barnier. The proposals include:

- Severely restricting or banning the provision of non-audit services to audit clients (the draft paper covers, among others, tax advisory and consulting services, actuary, risk management, legal and valuation services, book-keeping and preparing accounting records);

- Mandatory auditor rotation;

- Mandatory joint audits for large companies;

- Audit quality certification;

- Expanded audit reports;

- EU-level regulatory oversight.

Many firms and institutes have reacted negatively to the proposals, arguing that although well-intentioned, they may not in fact result in an improvement in audit quality. The most controversial areas in this respect are the first three above. It is also disputed whether these proposals would have made any difference had they been in place in the run up to the financial crisis, since in the view of many auditors, audit quality was not a factor in the crisis.

Exam focus point

> The audit profession is currently going through a tumultuous period, with fundamental questions being asked about its future role. This makes it all the more crucial that you *read the financial press*. Doing this won't just help you with questions on 'current issues', but will also help you to develop the judgement and experience of audit that you need for the other parts of the P7 exam.

List of examiner's articles

List of examiner's articles

The P7 examiner, Lisa Weaver, has written a number of articles relevant to the P7 exam. It is highly recommended that you read these articles as they will provide you with an insight into the approach taken in examining P7, the best way for you to tackle exam questions, and an indication of areas of the syllabus the examiner considers to be important.

The examiner has commented that a common problem is that students tend only to read the most recent article written by the examiner, and fail to appreciate that articles published previous to the exam sitting they are preparing for are equally relevant.

A list of all the examiner's articles for P7 is provided in the table below.

Date published	Title	Overview
5 Apr 11	Audit and insolvency	Discusses the addition of insolvency to the P7 UK syllabus.
23 Mar 11	Acceptance decisions for audit and assurance engagements	Discussion of decisions to accept new clients in the light of IFAC/IESBA *Code of Ethics*, APB ES 5 and ISA 210.
1 Jan 11	Changes in question style for Paper P7	Examines the changes to the syllabus for exams in 2011 onwards.
8 Feb 10	Change in question requirements	Highlights the change in question style which affected UK paper from 2010 and INT paper from 2011.
8 Feb 10	Going concern	Discussion of guidance on going concern in the light of both ISA 570 and the IAASB Practice Alert on going concern and the current economic climate (Jan 09).
1 Sep 09	Exam technique	Explores some important exam technique points that are relevant to Paper P7.
1 Sep 09	Exam technique	Exam techniques specifically relevant to P7, focusing on questions on audit evidence, which tend to be tackled particularly poorly.
11 Aug 09	IAASB clarity project	Background to the clarity project, what changes have been made, why they have been made, and what their practical effect is likely to be.
11 Apr 09	Massaging the figures	Earnings management – what is it, when it becomes fraud, and the implications for auditors.
18 Nov 08	The importance of financial reporting standards to auditors	Guidance on financial reporting issues that require a detailed level of knowledge, and those for which less detailed knowledge will be expected.
21 Oct 08	The importance of financial reporting standards to the auditor	Provides guidance on financial reporting matters which are examinable from the auditor's point of view.
11 Sep 08	Forensic auditing	Explores some of the key issues relevant to forensic auditing.
10 Apr 08	Auditors' reports to those charged with governance	Discusses the important reporting 'output' produced as a result of the audit process, that of the auditors communication to those charged with governance.

Date published	Title	Overview
10 Mar 08	Group audit issues	Summarises some of the sections of ISA 600 (revised and redrafted)
15 Oct 07	Continue to be 'rest assured'	Looks at the topic of assurance, describing a framework for the classification of assurance and non-assurance engagements, and giving guidance on the practical approach needed.
14 Sep 07	How to tackle audit and assurance case study questions – part 2	Second part of a two part series outlining the recommended approach to answering typical section A case study questions.
1 Aug 07	How to tackle audit and assurance case study questions – part 1	An insight into the recommended approach for section A questions.
30 Jan 07	Examiner's approach to paper P7	The examiner provides her approach to the advanced audit and assurance paper.

All articles can be accessed on the ACCA's website in the following location:

http://www.accaglobal.com/students/acca/exams/p7/technical_articles/

Exam question and answer bank

1 Fundamental principles

27 mins

Fundamental principles require that a member of a professional accountancy body should behave with integrity in all professional, business and financial relationships and should strive for objectivity in all professional and business judgements. Objectivity can only be assured if the member is and is seen to be independent. Conflicts of interest have an important bearing on independence and hence also on the public's perception of the integrity, objectivity and independence of the accounting profession.

The following scenario is an example of press reports in recent years which deal with issues of objectivity and independence within a multinational firm of accountants:

'A partner in the firm was told by the regulatory body that he must resign because he was in breach of the regulatory body's independence rules, as his brother-in-law was financial controller of an audit client. He was told that the alternative was that he could move his home and place of work at least 400 miles from the offices of the client, even though he was not the reporting partner. This made his job untenable. The regulatory body was seen as 'taking its rules to absurd lengths' by the accounting firm. Shortly after this comment, the multinational firm announced proposals to split the firm into three areas between audit, tax and business advisory services; management consultancy; and investment advisory services.'

Required

Discuss the impact that the above events may have on the public perception of the integrity, objectivity and independence of the multinational firm of accountants. **(15 marks)**

2 Aventura International

27 mins

Aventura International, a listed company, manufactures and wholesales a wide variety of products including fashion clothes and audio-video equipment. The company is audited by Voest, a firm of Chartered Certified Accountants, and the audit manager is Darius Harken. The following matters have arisen during the audit of the group's financial statements for the year to 31 December 20X8 which is nearing completion:

(a) During the annual inventory count of fashion clothes at the company's principal warehouse, the audit staff attending the count were invited to purchase any items of clothing or equipment at 30% of their recommended retail prices.

(b) The Chief Executive of Aventura International, Armando Thyolo, owns a private jet. Armando invoices the company, on a monthly basis, for that proportion of the operating costs which reflects business use. One of these invoices shows that Darius Harken was flown to Florida in March 20X8 and flown back two weeks later. Neither Aventura nor Voest have any offices or associates in Florida.

(c) Last week Armando announced his engagement to be married to his personal assistant, Kirsten Fennimore. Before joining Aventura in September 20X8, Kirsten had been Voest's accountant in charge of the audit of Aventura.

Required

Discuss the ethical issues raised and the actions which might be taken by the auditor in relation to these matters.

Note. Assume it is 6 December 20X8. **(15 marks)**

3 Osbourne plc

27 mins

Andrews, a firm of Chartered Certified Accountants has 20 partners and 87 audit staff. The firm provides a range of audit, assurance, tax and advisory services. The firm has four offices around the country and clients ranging from sole traders to a number of small plcs (none of which are quoted companies).

The quality control partner has recently resigned to take up a position in industry. He has not yet been replaced as the managing board of Andrews have not been able to find a suitable replacement. On his departure the quality control partner was in the process of implementing a system of ethical compliance for assurance staff. Staff would be required to confirm in writing their compliance with ACCA Code of Ethics. Implementation of this system is incomplete.

Osbourne plc is one of the firm's largest clients for whom Andrews provides audit services, preparation of tax computations and other advisory services. A new engagement partner has been assigned to the audit as the previous partner has retired. The fee for the audit work and other services has been set at the same level as last year in spite of the fact that additional work will need to be performed as Osbourne has introduced a new computer system. The staring date of the audit has been delayed due to problems with the new system. The management of Osbourne was very insistent that the fee should not be increased because of this.

(a)   List the six elements of a firm's system of quality control identified by ISQC 1.   **(3 marks)**

(b)   Identify and explain the quality control issues in the scenario above and the action which should be taken by Andrews.   **(10 marks)**

(c)   Explain the ethical guidance in respect of the setting of fees for assurance services.   **(2 marks)**

(Total = 15 marks)

4 PLD Associates   36 mins

PLD Associates Co, a large quoted company, was founded and controlled by Mr J Scott. The principal business of the company was to develop derelict land in city centres into office accommodation. In 20X3, the taxation authorities became suspicious of the nature of the operations being carried out by the company and an investigation into its affairs commenced.

The resultant report stated that the organisation's internal controls had deficiencies and were non-existent in many cases. The investigators found payments to unknown persons, and fictitious consultancy firms. In addition, J Scott had maintained a secret expense account that was used to disburse funds to himself. The board of directors of PLD Associates Co did not know of the existence of this account. The expense account was maintained by the partner of the firm of accountants responsible for the audit of the company. The auditors were heavily criticised in the report of the investigators.

The firm of auditors, Allcost & Co, had an aggressive marketing strategy and had increased its audit fees by 100% in two years. The audit firm had accepted the appointment in 20X1 after the previous auditors had been dismissed. The audit report for the year ended 20X0 had been heavily qualified by the previous auditors on the grounds of poor internal control and lack of audit evidence. J Scott had approached several firms of auditors in order to ascertain whether they would qualify the audit report given the present systems of control in PLD Associates Co. Allcost & Co had stated that it was unlikely that they would qualify their report. They realised that J Scott was 'opinion shopping' but were prepared to give an opinion in order to attract the client to their firm.

PLD Associates plc subsequently filed for insolvency and Allcost & Co were sued for negligence by the largest loan creditor, its bankers.

Required

(a)   Describe the procedures which an audit firm should carry out before accepting a client with potentially high audit risk such as PLD Associates Co.   **(6 marks)**

(b)   Discuss the ethical problems raised by the maintenance of the secret expense account for Mr J Scott by the audit partner.   **(5 marks)**

(c)   Suggest measures that audit firms might introduce to try and minimise the practice of 'opinion shopping' by prospective audit clients.   **(5 marks)**

(d)   Explain how audit firms can reduce the risk of litigation and its effects upon the audit practice.   **(4 marks)**

(Total = 20 marks)

5 Professional responsibilities

27 mins

You are required to write an essay, in which you consider the extent to which an auditor should be responsible for detecting fraud and other irregularities when auditing the accounts of limited liability companies. Your essay should:

(a) Briefly outline the extent to which an auditor is responsible for detecting irregularities and fraud (as expressed in the auditing guidelines).

(b) Consider the extent to which it would be reasonable to extend the auditor's responsibilities beyond that and the practical problems of extending auditor's responsibilities.

(c) Reach a conclusion on and provide a definition of the extent to which you consider it reasonable for an auditor to be responsible for detecting irregularities and fraud. **(15 marks)**

6 CD Sales

36 mins

CD Sales, a limited liability company, was a growth orientated company that was dominated by its managing director, Mr A Long. The company sold quality music systems direct to the public. A large number of sales persons were employed on a commission only basis. The music systems were sent to the sales agents who then sold them direct to the public using telephone sales techniques. The music systems were supplied to the sales agents on a sale or return basis and CD Sales recognised the sale of the equipment when it was received by the sales agents. Any returns of the music systems were treated as re-purchases in the period concerned.

The company enjoyed a tremendous growth record. The main reasons for this apparent expansion were as follows.

(a) Mr A Long falsified the sales records. He created several fictitious sales agents who were responsible for 25% of the company's revenue.

(b) At the year end, Mr Long despatched nearly all of his inventories of music systems to the sales agents and re-purchased those that they wished to return after the year end.

(c) 20% of the cost of sales were capitalised. This was achieved by the falsification of purchase invoices with the co-operation of the supplier company. Suppliers furnished the company with invoices for non-current assets but supplied music systems.

(d) The directors of the company enjoyed a bonus plan linked to reported profits. Executives could earn bonuses ranging from 50% to 75% of their basic salaries. The directors did not query the unusually rapid growth of the company, and were unaware of the fraud perpetrated by Mr A Long.

Mr A Long spent large sums of money in creating false records and bribing accomplices in order to conceal the fraud from the auditor. He insisted that the auditor should sign a 'confidentiality' agreement which effectively precluded the auditor from corroborating sales with independent third parties, and from examining the service contracts of the directors. This agreement had the effect of preventing the auditor from discussing the affairs of the company with the sales agents.

The fraud was discovered when a disgruntled director wrote an anonymous letter to the Stock Exchange concerning the reasons for CD Sales's growth. The auditor was subsequently sued by a major bank that had granted a loan to CD Sales on the basis of interim accounts. These accounts had been reviewed by the auditor and a review report issued.

Required

(a) Explain the key audit tests which would normally ensure that such a fraud as that perpetrated by Mr A Long would be detected. **(7 marks)**

(b) Discuss the implications of the signing of the 'confidentiality' agreement by the auditor. **(4 marks)**

(c) Explain how the 'review report' issued by the auditor on the interim financial statements differs in terms of its level of assurance from the auditor's report on the year end financial statements.

(4 marks)

(d) Discuss where you feel that the auditor is guilty of professional negligence in not detecting the fraud. **(5 marks)**

(Total = 20 marks)

7 Marsden Manufacturing Co

45 mins

Marsden Manufacturing (MM) is an established audit client of your firm. You were involved with the audit last year as audit senior. This year, you are to act as audit supervisor. The engagement partner has asked you to plan the audit for the year ended 30 June 20X4. It is an old-fashioned audit, and the partner does not anticipate that you will require the use of the new laptops that the firm has just invested in.

MM has a sales ledger of approximately 100 customers, but in terms of value, 80% of the ledger is represented by just six. The company has just secured a new customer, Wallworths, which has only impacted on the sales ledger for 1 month in the current year, but is projected to represent 20% of sales in the year ending 30 June 20X5.

MM has a large bank loan with ABC Bank. There is a covenant attached to the loan. One of the conditions of the loan is that the company maintains certain financial ratios at the period end. The bank requires an interest cover of 2.5 and a current ratio of 1.5.

The major development in the year is that MM decided to factor their debts. In the past they had suffered a substantial bad debt expense when a major customer went bankrupt and they are concerned that the reoccurrence of such an event would affect their interest cover ratio. They sacked their sales ledger clerk at the end of the year, so have outsourced their sales ledger function to the factor.

The audit assistant attended the inventory count two days ago. She observed that there appeared to be a high level of old inventory. They were nevertheless added into the count.

The following draft figures have been provided:

Statement of financial position

	20X4		20X3	
	$'000	$'000	$'000	$'000
Non-current assets		210		243
Current assets				
Inventory	460		370	
Receivables	324		250	
Cash	15		69	
	799		689	
Payables: amounts falling due within one year				
Trade payables	381		367	
Bank loan	10		10	
	391		377	
Net current assets		408		312
Payables: amounts falling due in more than one year				
Bank loan		(250)		(260)
		368		295

Income statement

	20X4	20X3
	$'000	$'000
Revenue	2,534	2,967
Cost of sales	(1,583)	(1,823)
Gross profit (% 37.5/38.5)	951	1,144
Administrative expenses	(476)	(488)
Other expenses	(400)	(432)
Profit before interest and tax	75	224
Interest	14	14

Sally Forsyth, the sales ledger clerk has threatened to sue MM for unfair dismissal and sexual discrimination.

Wallworths is an audit client of the firm. You are aware that they were often in dispute with their previous supplier over their poor payment record and have changed supplier because the supplier broke off relations with them.

Required

(a)   Comment on the level at which you would set materiality.   **(4 marks)**

(b)   Identify and explain the audit risks in the above scenario for the audit for the year ended 30 June 20X4.   **(14 marks)**

(c)   Outline the key administrative planning matters that remain outstanding.   **(3 marks)**

(d)   Discuss whether an audit conflict of interest arises in this situation and what steps the auditor might take in this situation.   **(4 marks)**

(Total = 25 marks)

8 Gasoleum   36 mins

Your firm is the auditor of Gasoleum, a limited liability company which operates 15 petrol stations in and around London. You are the senior in charge of the audit for the year ending 31 January 20X1, and are engaged on the audit planning.

Most of the company's sites are long established and, as well as supplying fuel, oil, air and water, have a car wash and a shop.

Over the last few years, due to the intense price competition in petrol retailing, the shops have been expanded into mini-markets with a wide range of motor accessories, food, drinks and household products. They also sell state lottery tickets.

Point-of-sale microcomputers are installed in all the petrol stations, linked online via a network to the computer at head office. Sales and inventory data are input direct from the microcomputers.

The company has an internal auditor, whose principal function is to monitor continuously and test the operation of internal controls throughout the organisation. The internal auditor will also be responsible for co-ordinating the year end inventory count.

Required

Prepare notes for a planning meeting with the audit partner which:

(a)   Identify areas of potential risk which will have to be addressed by the audit   **(10 marks)**

(b)   Describe the extent to which the work performed by the internal auditor may affect your planning, and the factors that could limit the use you may wish to make of his work   **(5 marks)**

(c)   Detail the analytical review procedures that you would adopt to obtain audit evidence on revenue and gross profit as part of your substantive testing.   **(5 marks)**

(Total = 20 marks)

9 Audit

For the last few years your firm has helped Colin, a sole trader, prepare his accounts for the taxation authorities. Colin is about to incorporate his business and has asked your advice on a number of issues.

Required

Advise Colin on the following.

(a) The advantages to the company of having its accounts audited (you may assume that the company would be able to claim exemption from audit).

(b) Whether the audit undertaken on his small company would be the same as an audit undertaken on a large one.

(c) Whether he has any alternatives to audit that would still provide him with a degree of assurance.

10 Lambley Properties   36 mins

You are the manager in charge of the audit of Lambley Properties, a listed company, and you have been asked to prepare the written representation which will be signed by the company's directors.

You are aware that there are two material items in the accounts for the year ended 31 March 20X2 on which you want the company's directors to confirm that the treatment in the accounts is correct.

(a) One of the company's subsidiaries, Keyworth Builders Co, is experiencing going concern problems, and you want the directors' confirmation that they intend to support the company for the foreseeable future.

(b) Eastwood Manufacturing, a listed company, is in dispute with Lambley Properties over repairs required to a building they purchased from Lambley. Lambley Properties constructed the building for Eastwood, and three years after it was sold to Eastwood, the customer is claiming that repairs are required which will cost $3 million, and that Lambley is liable to pay for these repairs, as they are as a result of negligent construction of the building. In addition, Eastwood is claiming $2 million for the cost of disruption of the business due to the faults in the building and in the period when the repairs take place. Lambley Properties have obtained the advice of a lawyer and a surveyor, and the directors believe there are no grounds for the claim and any court action will find in their favour. However, Lambley Properties has included a note in its accounts concerning this contingency.

Required

(a) List the general representations which must be provided by management in a written representation.
(3 marks)

(b) Draft the relevant extracts of the written representation referring to the two items above. **(5 marks)**

(c) Discuss the reliability of a written representation as audit evidence and the extent to which the auditors can rely on this evidence. **(4 marks)**

(d) Describe the work you will perform to check whether a provision should be included in the accounts for the legal claim from Eastwood Manufacturing. **(5 marks)**

(e) Describe the matters you will consider and the further action you will take if the directors refuse to sign the written representation because of the legal claim from Eastwood Manufacturing.
(3 marks)

(Total = 20 marks)

11 Bestwood Electronics

36 mins

Your firm is the auditor of Bestwood Electronics Co, a listed company, which assembles microcomputers and wholesales them and associated equipment to retailers. Many of the parts for the computers and the associated equipment are bought from the Far East. These computers are used by businesses for accounting, word processing and other computing tasks.

You have been asked by the partner in charge of the audit to consider your firm's audit responsibilities in relation to subsequent events, and the audit work you will carry out on these matters.

Required

(a)   Describe the responsibilities of the auditors for detecting errors in the accounts during the following periods:

   (i)   From the period-end to the date of the auditors' report
   (ii)   From the date of the auditors' report to the issue of the financial statements
   (iii)   From the date the financial statements are issued to the date they are laid before the
           members   **(5 marks)**

(b)   Describe the audit work you will carry out in period (a)(i) above which involves consideration of subsequent events.   **(11 marks)**

(c)   Describe the work you will carry out in period (a)(ii) above to ensure no adjustments are required to the accounts.   **(4 marks)**

(Total = 20 marks)

12 Bingham Engineering

45 mins

You are auditing the accounts of Bingham Engineering Co for the year ended 31 March 20X7, which is experiencing going concern problems.

The company prepares monthly, as well as annual accounts and its accountant has supplied you with the following forecasts to enable you to assess whether the company will be a going concern. The forecasts have been prepared on a monthly basis for the year to 31 March 20X8, and are:

(a)   Capital expenditure/disposal forecast
(b)   Profit forecast
(c)   Cash flow forecast

The capital expenditure/disposal forecast and profit forecast have been used to prepare the cash flow forecast.

Required

(a)   Briefly describe what you understand by the term 'going concern' and state the minimum period you would expect the company to continue in business for it to be considered a going concern.

(3 marks)

(b)   List the factors which may indicate that a company is not a going concern.   **(9 marks)**

(c)   Describe the work you would perform to verify that the value of items in the following forecasts, prepared by the company's accountant, are reasonable:

   (i)   Capital expenditure/disposal forecast
   (ii)   Profit forecast
   (iii)   Cash flow forecast   **(10 marks)**

(d)   Briefly describe the further work, in addition to that described in (b) and (c) above, you would perform to enable you to determine whether the company is a going concern.   **(3 marks)**

(Total = 25 marks)

13 Locksley

45 mins

The following is the draft statement of financial position of Locksley Co for the year ended 31 January 20X3.

LOCKSLEY CO
STATEMENT OF FINANCIAL POSITION AS AT 31 JANUARY 20X3

	20X3 $	20X2 $
Non-current assets		
Development expenditure	59,810	–
Tangible assets	99,400	73,000
Investments	85,100	101,400
	244,310	174,400
Current assets		
Inventory	58,190	63,010
Receivables	184,630	156,720
Cash at bank and in hand	9,970	62,620
	252,790	282,350
Payables: amounts falling due within one year	231,510	170,900
Net current assets	21,280	111,450
Total assets less current liabilities	265,590	285,850
Payables: amounts falling due after more than one year	101,180	93,840
	164,410	192,010
Equity		
Share capital	89,700	89,700
Share premium account	11,300	11,300
Revaluation reserve	19,750	9,750
Retained earnings	43,660	81,260
	164,410	192,010

Locksley Co produces garden furniture and has incurred expenditure during the year ended 31 January 20X3 on the development of mouldings for a new range of plastic garden furniture. The directors wish to carry forward the development expenditure indefinitely as they feel that the company will benefit from the new moulding for many years. The product range is being developed because profits have been declining over the last few years owing to the uncompetitiveness of the products made by the company. The company has sold many of its non-current assets during the year and purchased new machinery which will enable the company's productivity to increase. The directors decided not to fund the above expenditure using outside finance but to generate the necessary resources internally by taking extended credit from its suppliers and utilising its liquid funds held at the bank. The company also sold part of its investments, which are made up of stocks and shares of public limited companies.

One of the reasons for this method of financing the expenditure was that the company already has a loan of $45,000 outstanding which has been included in the figure for 'payables: amounts falling due after more than one year'. This loan is secured on the non-current assets of the company and is repayable over ten years. The sale of non-current assets and investments did not yield as much as was expected and a small loss on sale of $1,200 has been included in the statement of comprehensive income as part of the amounts shown for 'other expenses'.

The company had the non-current assets revalued by a professional valuer, at the year end. The gain on revaluation of non-current assets has been credited by the company to the revaluation reserve.

The directors felt that the shareholders should share in the gain on the revaluation of the non-current assets and increased the proposed dividend accordingly. Over 90% of the shares of the company are held by the directors.

Required

(a) Describe the audit work to be performed to verify the value attributed to the development expenditure in the statement of financial position of Locksley Co. **(6 marks)**

(b) Describe the audit procedures which should be carried out to verify the gain arising on the revaluation of non-current assets. **(6 marks)**

(c) Explain to the directors why development expenditure should not be carried forward indefinitely in the financial statements, and describe the circumstances in which the costs maybe deferred to the future. **(8 marks)**

(d) Describe the implications for the company and the auditors of the directors' decision to generate internally the funds required for the development of the business. **(5 marks)**

(Total = 25 marks)

14 Bainbridge

36 mins

You are the auditor of Bainbridge, a regional-based limited liability company which manufactures top of the range kitchen units and accessories. The company is owned and run by the Bainbridge family who first set up the business in the 1950s. In recent years the company has experienced increasing success fuelled by the housing boom and the trend for home improvements. The draft accounts for the year ended 30 June 20X5 show revenue of $20.2 million, profit for the period of $1.6 million and total assets of $30 million. The following matters remain outstanding and have been brought to your attention:

Inventories

Inventories of finished goods are included in the draft accounts at a cost of $4.5 million. The majority of items are produced for inventories with the cost being calculated using a standard costing system. Standard costs are calculated for materials, labour, production overheads and other overheads.

The standards used have been kept the same as those applied last year and variance calculations have not been performed. Management have justified this by saying that costs have remained constant over the last two years and that historically variances have been negligible.

A small number of items in inventories have been made to customer specification. In respect of these management have included overheads relating to design. **(7 marks)**

Warehouse

On 1 July 20X4 Bainbridge entered into a 10-year lease for a warehouse. Under the terms of the lease the company have been given a one-year rent-free period after which the annual rental is $50,000 per year. At the end of the initial term Bainbridge has the option to extend the lease for a further two years at a notional rental.

Currently no charge has been included in the accounts in respect of the lease on the basis that the rent-free period means that no charge has been incurred for the year. In future management intend to account for the lease as an operating lease. **(7 marks)**

Convertible debenture

On 1 July 20X4 Bainbridge issued a $5m debenture at par. The debenture carries interest at 4% and is redeemable on 1 July 20X9 at which date the holder has the option to convert the debenture to 3 million $1 ordinary shares in Bainbridge.

Currently the only entries that have been made in relation to the debenture were to credit the net proceeds to a long-term liability account and to record the first payment of interest on 31 June 20X5. **(6 marks)**

Required

For each of the above issues:
(a) Comment on the matters you should consider, and
(b) The evidence you should expect to find,
in undertaking your review of the audit working papers and financial statements of Bainbridge.

(Total = 20 marks)

15 Griffin

36 mins

Griffin Co, a listed company, manufactures football kit. It has contracts with a number of league football teams. It also produces 'unbranded' football wear, which it sells to a number of wholesalers.

The profit before tax for the year is $1.2m (20X6 $3.5m). You are the manager responsible for the audit for the year end 30 June 20X7. Today you have visited the client's premises to review the audit team's work to date. The audit senior has drafted the following 'points for the attention of the manager':

(a)   Griffin is seeking to enter the market in women's leisure clothes. In light of that fact, during the year it purchased 30% of the share capital of Bees Co, a company that manufactures sporty leisurewear at a cost of $750,000. **(7 marks)**

(b)   During the year a major competitor emerged in the branded football kit market. Two of the contracts with nationwide clubs which came up during the year have not been renewed. A number of key personnel have been headhunted by the competitor. **(6 marks)**

(c)   A legal requirement to adjust the seats at which machinists sit was passed in December 20X6. The legislation required the seats to be adjusted by April 20X7. Griffin has not yet carried out any adjustment. Also in April 20X7, the government increased the national minimum wage. 5% of Griffin's employees receive less than the minimum wage. **(7 marks)**

Required

(a)   Comment on the matters you would consider.

(b)   State the evidence you would expect to find during your review of the working papers and financial statements of Griffin Co.

(Total = 20 marks)

16 Recognition

27 mins

Discuss the impact on the audit report of the proposed treatment of the following items in the financial statements.

(a)   Beak Co sells land to a property investment company, Wings Co. The sale price is $20 million and the current market value is $30 million. Beak Co can buy the land back at any time in the next five years for the original selling price plus an annual commission of 1% above the current bank base rate. Wings Co cannot require Beak Co to buy the land back at any time.

The accountant of Beak Co proposes to treat this transaction as a sale in the financial statements. You may assume that the amounts involved are material. **(6 marks)**

(b)   A car manufacturer, Gocar Co, supplies cars to a car dealer, Sparks Co, on the following terms.

Sparks Co has to pay a monthly fee of $100 per car for the privilege of displaying it in its showroom and is also responsible for insuring the cars. When a car is sold to a customer, Sparks Co has to pay Gocar Co the factory price of the car when it was first supplied. Sparks Co can only return cars to Gocar Co on the payment of a fixed penalty charge of 10% of the cost of the car. Sparks Co has to pay the factory price for the cars if they remain unsold within a four-month period. Gocar Co cannot demand the return of the cars from Sparks Co.

The accountant of Sparks Co proposes to treat the cars unsold for less than four months as the property of Gocar Co and not show them as inventory in the financial statements. At the year end the value of car inventory shown in the statement of financial position was $150,720. The total assets on the statement of financial position are $1.3m. The cars unsold for less than four months have a factory cost of $22,500.

(9 marks)

(Total = 15 marks)

17 Henshelwood

36 mins

You are employed as an audit manager by Viewstream, a firm of Certified Accountants. You are currently involved in planning the final audit of the financial statements of Henshelwood Co, a listed IT consultancy, for the year ended 31 March 20X7.

The draft financial statements show a profit before tax of $192m (20X6 $167m) and total assets of $553m (20X6 $510m).

The following disclosures have been extracted from the draft financial statements:

(a) **Share-based payments**

The fair value of all share-based remuneration is determined at the date of grant and recognised as an expense in the statement of comprehensive income on a straight-line basis over the vesting period, taking account of the estimated number of shares that will vest. The fair value is determined by use of the relevant valuation model. All share-based remuneration is equity-settled.

Notes made by the audit senior during some preliminary analytical review refer to a share-based payment expense of $4.8m and an equity reserve, relating to the share-based payment scheme, of $8.7m. **(5 marks)**

(b) **Pension costs**

Defined benefit schemes

(i) The scheme, the Henshelwood Pension Scheme, is a defined benefit scheme where the benefits are based on employees' length of service and final pensionable pay. It is a funded approved defined benefit scheme and closed to new members on 1 April 20X2. It is funded through a legally separate trustee administered fund.

The actuarial valuation was performed at 31 March 20X7 by the scheme actuary, an employee of Milton Human Resource Consulting.

The amounts recognised in the consolidated statement of comprehensive income for the defined benefit schemes are as follows:

	20X7
Current service cost	(8.1)
Past service costs	(0.1)
Total operating charge	(8.2)
Expected return on pension scheme assets	21.2
Interest on pension liabilities	(20.1)
Net financial income/(charge)	1.1
Total amount charged to the consolidated statement of comprehensive income	(7.1)

The actuarial gains and losses have been recognised in the other comprehensive income section of the statement of comprehensive income as follows:

	20X7
Actuarial gain on scheme assets	19.1
Actuarial (losses)/gain on scheme liabilities	(4.7)
Impact of changes in assumptions relating to the present value of scheme liabilities	1.4
Net income recognised in consolidated other comprehensive income	15.8

	20X7
Deficit in the scheme brought forward	(69.7)
Current service cost	(8.1)
Past service costs	(0.1)
Contributions	5.1
Net financial return	1.1
Actuarial gain	15.8
Deficit in the scheme carried forward	(55.9)

The amount included in the statement of financial position arising from the company's obligations in respect of its defined benefit retirement scheme is as follows:

	20X7
Present value of defined benefit obligations	(431.7)
Fair value of scheme assets	375.8
Defined benefit scheme deficit	(55.9)
Liability recognised in the statement of financial position	(55.9)

(9 marks)

(c) **Provisions**

	Property	Other	Total
Balance at 1 April 20X6	25.2	478	76.4
Exchange adjustments	–	0.1	0.1
Charged to statement of comprehensive income	–	0.2	0.2
Utilised	(8.2)	(14.3)	(22.5)
Balance at 31 March 20X7	17.0	33.8	50.8

Property provisions are for rents and other related amounts payable on certain leased properties for periods in which they are not anticipated to be in use by the company. The leases expire in periods up to 20Y3.

Other provisions comprise liabilities arising as a result of business disposals and the company transformation including the following items:

- Provisions of $7.1 million (20X6 – $8.9 million) relating to restructuring costs arising from the company transformation and closure of former shared service facilities and the closure of the former head office. These provisions are expected to be utilised over the next 12 – 36 months.

- Provisions of $6.2 million (20X6 – $160 million) for potential liabilities relating to the disposal of the European business including certain site restitution costs.

- Provisions of $19.1 million (20X6 – $19.4 million) relating to possible warranty and environmental claims in relation to businesses disposed. It is not possible to estimate the timing of payments against these provisions.

(6 marks)

Required

For each of the three issues identified above:

(a) Explain the matters you should consider to determine whether the amounts have been appropriately valued; and

(b) Describe the tests you should plan to perform to quantify the amount of any misstatement.

Note. The mark allocation is shown against each of the three issues.　　　　**(Total = 20 marks)**

18 Merger of audit firms　　　　　　　　　　　　27 mins

The increase in the size of audit firms has been a source of concern to regulators and clients alike. Some audit firms feel that mergers between the largest firms of auditors are necessary in order to meet the global demand for their services. However their clients are concerned that such mergers will create a monopolistic market for audit services which will not be in their best interests.

Required

(a) Explain the reasons why the largest audit firms might wish to merge their practices.　　**(7 marks)**
(b) Discuss the potential problems created by mergers of the largest firms of auditors.　　**(8 marks)**

(Total = 15 marks)

19 Annabella

45 mins

Annabella Co has been an audit client of your firm for 13 years. It is a business which manufactures soft furnishings. It also has a shop, from which it sells its own soft furnishings, and other manufacturers' soft furnishings and small items of furniture.

On the first day of the year ending 30 June 20X8, Annabella Co undertook a major reconstruction of its operations. It set up two subsidiary companies. Anna Co and Bella Co. It then transferred its trade to those companies. Anna Co took the manufacturing trade and Bella Co took the retail trade. On the same day, Annabella Co entered into a joint venture with its former chief designer. The joint venture, Annabella Designs Co, will provide designs for the soft furnishings manufactured by Anna Co and will also operate an interior design service, which will be advertised strongly by Bella Co.

Annabella Co is 100% owned by James Dancer, Annabella Co will charge Anna Co, Bella Co and Annabella Designs Co management charges.

The former chief designer, now a 50% shareholder in Annabella Designs Co is Annabel Dancer, James' only daughter. They make decisions about Annabella Designs jointly, and have agreed that the audit of Annabella Designs Co shall be carried out by David Turner and Co. David Turner is a friend of Annabel.

Required

(a)	Identify and explain the audit planning issues in the above scenario.	**(17 marks)**
(b)	Describe the principal audit procedures on a consolidation.	**(8 marks)**

(Total = 25 marks)

20 Anderson Group

27 mins

You are auditing the accounts of Anderson Group for the year ended 31 August 20X1. The group comprises Anderson, a public company and its wholly owned subsidiary Green, a limited liability company. The main activities of both companies are the manufacture and sale of household textiles. During the year under review Green made a substantial trading loss and the board of directors of Anderson has decided to sell the subsidiary. A suitable buyer was found and the sale which was approved and announced by the Board on 31 July 20X1, was legally completed on 31 August 20X1.

A summary draft income statement for the year ended 31 August 20X1 (which is shown below) has been prepared, which divides the group profit between continuing operations (those of Anderson) and discontinued operations (those of Green).

	Continuing operations $'000	Discontinued operations $'000	Total $'000
Revenue	25,700	10,000	37,500
Profit/(loss) before tax	1,300	(1,000)	300
Tax expense	(700)	450	(250)
Profit/(loss) before exceptional item	600	(550)	50
Loss on sale of subsidiary (note 1)	–	(450)	(450)
Loss for the period	600	(1,000)	(400)

Notes to the accounts (extract)

(a)   Loss on sale of subsidiary.

	$'000
Net assets of Green at 31 August 20X1	1,800
Cash proceeds	(1,350)
Loss arising on disposal of subsidiary	450

The results of Green, included above, have been obtained from the company's management accounts. No audited accounts of Green are available as Green's new owners have a different year end from Anderson and Anderson no longer has control over Green.

In view of the substantial loss of Green, the directors of Anderson do not want to include the trading results of Green in the group accounts. They have suggested that the loss on disposal of the subsidiary should be shown as an exceptional item.

You have approached Green, and in view of the change in ownership, they have said that they are not prepared to allow you to carry out an audit of their accounts or to answer questions on the management accounts to 31 August 20X1. However, the directors of Anderson are prepared to give you as much information about the preparation of Green's accounts as they are able.

Required

Assuming that the results of Green for the year ended 31 August 20X1 are consolidated into the accounts of Anderson, describe the audit work you would perform and the matters you would consider in relation to the income statement of Green which is included in the group accounts of Anderson as shown in the schedule above. Your answer should include consideration of:

(a)   The factors you would take into account in deciding whether the results of Green are sufficiently reliable to be included in the group accounts and receive an unqualified auditor's report   **(5 marks)**

(b)   The level of materiality (or acceptable error) you would accept in the results of Green which are included in the group income statement; and   **(5 marks)**

(c)   How you would audit the item in note 1 to the accounts: 'Loss on sale of subsidiary'.   **(5 marks)**

(Total = 15 marks)

Note. You should assume that the disposal of Green meets the criteria to be classed as a discontinued operation under IFRS 5 *Non-current assets held for sale and discontinued operations.*

21 Business assurance   36 mins

Audit practitioners have recently initiated substantive changes in the audit approach. It appears to be the strategy that audit firms are moving away from the audit of financial statements and more to the provision of assurances on financial data, systems and controls in those systems. Auditors are focusing on providing 'business assurance' and 'business risk' which gives clients wider assurance than the traditional audit has offered. Auditors are reviewing the business from a process standpoint utilising benchmarking, performance measurements and best control practices as the key criteria. It seems that the audit is moving more to the analysis of business risk and the alignment of the audit much more to the management perspective.

A wide range of risk assessment services is now part of the audit service. The provision of internal audit services is becoming an increasingly larger part of the 'business assurance' service offered by auditors. It seems that the audit is becoming a management consultancy exercise with internal audit, external audit and consultancy assignments being seen as complementary services.

Required

(a)   Discuss the implications of the external auditor providing an internal audit service to a client, explaining the current ethical guidance on the provision of other services to clients.   **(10 marks)**

(b)   Explain the principal effects of the external auditor providing wider assurance to the client.

(6 marks)

(c)   Critically evaluate the move by large auditing firms to providing 'business risk and assurance' services rather than the traditional audit assurance for investors and creditors.   **(4 marks)**

(Total = 20 marks)

22 Scenarios

27 mins

You are a partner in a medium sized firm of chartered certified accountants. The following opportunities have arisen.

(a) A major audit client, Lilac Co, is seeking loan finance from its bank to fund an expansion into a new factory. The expansion should result in an increase in capacity of 30%. Lilac has conducted market research and is confident that they will be able to sell the added output. The financial director has recently telephoned you and mentioned that the bank are keen to obtain a reference from the audit firm, relating to Lilac's ability to repay the loan and whether the business plan is reasonable. He said 'they just need their forms filled, for their files. They know we can repay. We're one of their best clients.' Your audit team is about to commence the audit for the year ended 31 March 20X8.

Required

Comment on the matters you would consider in relation to giving such a reference to the bank.

(7 marks)

(b) The finance director of Laurel Co, another audit client, telephoned you yesterday. He recently attended a half-day course on the importance of corporate governance run by your firm. Laurel's long term plans include the possibility of flotation on a stock exchange. The finance director has told the other directors the issues discussed at the course and they feel that it might be a good idea to engage the firm to undertake an assurance engagement to assess risk management and the internal control system at Laurel Co.

Required

Comment on the matters you would consider in relation to accepting and planning such an engagement.

(8 marks)

(Total = 15 marks)

23 Trendy Group

27 mins

Trendy Group Inc is an international group which manufactures costume jewellery and sells it through its own retail stores. It is a new client for your firm which was awarded the world-wide audit after submitting a competitive tender. You have just learnt that you are the senior assigned to the audit of Trendy Group Inc. As group audit senior, you will be responsible for the co-ordination of the world-wide audit for the year ending 30 September 20X2 and for the audits of the consolidation, the US parent entity, (Trendy Group Inc), and the US trading subsidiary, (Trendy (US) Inc). Your firm has offices in every country in which the Trendy Group has operations and you will instruct the relevant local offices to perform any overseas work required.

The audit manager has presented you with a copy of a background memorandum prepared in connection with the tender process **(Exhibit 1)**.

Required

Identify the key area of business risk associated with Trendy Group Inc. For each business risk area identified, include (perhaps in tabular format) the specific audit risks, if any, associated with that business risk, both at a group level and at an individual company level.

(15 marks)

EXHIBIT 1

To:	The Files
From:	Kim Welsby (Audit manager)
Date:	30 May 20X2
Subject:	Trendy Group Inc
	Invitation to tender for world-wide audit
	Background information

This memorandum summarises background information obtained at a meeting with Mary Pegg (Group Finance Director) on 27 May 20X2.

Group structure

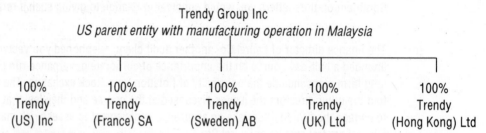

Trendy Group Inc
US parent entity with manufacturing operation in Malaysia

100%	100%	100%	100%	100%
Trendy	Trendy	Trendy	Trendy	Trendy
(US) Inc	(France) SA	(Sweden) AB	(UK) Ltd	(Hong Kong) Ltd

Local audit requirements

Full statutory audits are required for both US companies and for the subsidiaries in Sweden and Hong Kong. At all other locations, Mary wants the auditors to perform the minimum level of work necessary to give an overall opinion on the group financial statements.

Parent entity operations

The parent, Trendy Group Inc, has a factory in Malaysia. This factory manufactures costume jewellery using a local workforce and materials. All of the factory output is sold to Trendy Group Inc's trading subsidiaries at prices set in dollars at the beginning of each quarter. The prices charged by the factory include freight and are set to ensure that the factory makes a modest profit margin.

The parent is also responsible for design, international marketing and promotions, treasury management and certain other administrative activities. It charges the trading subsidiaries a royalty of 5% of retail sales to cover design costs and also levies management charges sufficient to recover its other overhead expenses.

Trading subsidiaries

The five trading subsidiaries each sell costume jewellery purchased from the Malaysian factory through retail stores in their own geographical area. All sales are made through the companies' own stores. Each trading subsidiary has a central warehouse at which deliveries from the Malaysian factory are received and distributed to individual retail stores. The subsidiaries are responsible for local marketing activities.

The US trading subsidiary, Trendy (US) Inc, also runs a factory outlet shop at which old inventories are sold at marked down prices. Any inventories held in the retail outlets at the end of a fashion season are first reduced in a shop sale. If it has not been sold by the end of the sale, the trading subsidiaries sell the obsolete lines to Trendy (US) Inc for 50% of their original cost. These inventories are then sold through the factory outlet or, if this proves unsuccessful, destroyed. In order to protect its reputation, the group will not sell obsolete inventories to market traders.

Kim Welsby

24 Verity

36 mins

Verity, a limited liability company, has a credit facility with Cranley Bank of $6 million. The facility is due to expire on 31 December 20X1. The overdraft in the recently audited statement of financial position at 30 September 20X1 is $5.5 million. The directors of Verity have started negotiations with their bankers for a renewal of the facility and to increase the amount to $9 million. To support this request the bank has asked Verity to provide a business plan for the coming 12 months consisting of a cash flow forecast supported by a forecast statement of comprehensive income and statement of financial position. The management of Verity has produced a cash flow forecast for the period 1 October 20X1 to 30 September 20X2 and, at the request of the bank, has asked the auditor to examine and report on it.

The audit manager, who has recently completed Verity's audit, has been asked to make a preliminary examination of the cash flow forecast and supporting material and she has noted the following observations.

(a) The cash flows from sales are based on the assumption of an overall increase in sales of 24% compared to the previous financial year. Analysis shows that this is based on an increase in selling price of 5% and an increase in the volume of sales of 18%. Just over a quarter of all Verity's sales are made to foreign customers.

(b) The cost of sales in the recently audited statement of comprehensive income to 30 September 20X1 was 80% of sales revenue, giving a gross profit of 20%. In the forecast statement of comprehensive income for the year to 30 September 20X2 the cost of sales has fallen to 72%, giving a gross profit of 28%. Manufacturing costs are made up of approximately one third each of materials, labour and production overheads.

(c) The trade receivables collection period used in the cash flow forecast to 30 September 20X2 is 61 days. In the year to 30 September 20X1 this period averaged 93 days. Management has stated that it is its intention to inform all customers of a new standard 60 day credit period. In addition an early settlement discount of 1% will apply to customers who settle their account within 30 days of the statement.

Conversely the credit period for trade payables has been extended from an average of 45 days in the current year to 90 days in the forecast.

(d) The cash flow forecast showed that the maximum credit required during the period would rise to nearly $9 million in August 20X2.

Required

(a) Describe the general matters an auditor should consider before accepting an engagement as a reporting accountant on forecast financial information. **(5 marks)**

(b) Detail the procedures that the reporting accountant should undertake in relation to the cash flow forecast of Verity for the year to 30 September 20X2. **(8 marks)**

(c) The negotiations with Cranley Bank resulted in a renewal of Verity's existing credit facility of $6 million, but the bank would not agree to increase it to $9 million. As a result of this Verity issued a circular to its existing shareholders inviting them to subscribe for a new $3 million issue of debentures. The purpose of the circular was to show the intended use and the future benefits from the debenture issue. It was supported by the same forecast financial information, including the accountant's report, that had been provided to Cranley Bank. However the directors of Verity had removed all references to its original purpose and restricted distribution.

The trading results of the first half of the year to 30 September 20X2 showed that the forecast information was proving to be over optimistic and that Verity was beginning to experience cash flow difficulties.

Discuss the basis on which a reporting accountant should form an opinion on forecast information, and consider whether the reporting accountants of Verity may be liable to:
(i) Cranley Bank; and
(ii) The investors who subscribe for the new debentures. **(7 marks)**

(Total = 20 marks)

Note. You are to assume that the accountant's report had expressed an unmodified opinion on the statement of cash flows.

25 Painswick Ltd

27 mins

(a) Define a forensic audit and explain how the definition applies to a fraud investigation. **(2 marks)**

(b) Compare the responsibilities of the auditor in respect of fraud when conducting a statutory audit and when conducting a forensic investigation. **(3 marks)**

(c) Explain how the fundamental principles of the *Code of Ethics and Conduct* apply to forensic assignments. **(5 marks)**

(d) Based on the following example of a fraud identify the procedures which would have enabled the forensic auditor to identify this fraud and quantify the loss to the company. **(5 marks)**

(Total = 15 marks)

Example of fraud

The purchase ledger clerk of Painswick Ltd has been channeling payments to suppliers in to his own bank account by altering bank account details of the relevant suppliers on the BACS masterfile. In order to disguise this activity the purchase ledger clerk has:

– Posted the relevant invoices to the purchase ledger twice. One entry has been made correctly to the relevant expense account whilst the other has been debited to a suspense account.

– Matched and removed the duplicate invoices and payments before the monthly reconciliation of supplier accounts is performed.

26 Harness

27 mins

(a) Briefly outline the reasons why social and environmental issues are of interest to an external auditor. **(5 marks)**

(b) Harness Co is a wind-farm situated on an island in the North Sea. Harness was set up a number of years ago by an energy fanatic who was also a millionaire. It is predominately owned by the millionaire Brewster Billings, who continues to loan it money, despite a history of loss-making.

Harness owns and operates 15 wind turbines which are situated on the island. The windmills are connected to a generator, which converts the wind power to electricity. The electricity is mainly supplied to Brewster's mansion on the east coast of Scotland, but some is sold to various power supply companies. One of these companies, Scot Power, has a small stake in Harness Co.

The company has suffered some problems this year. Firstly, the erosion, which has badly affected the island during the course of the company's occupation, has finally struck some of the windmills. One fell into the sea at the end of the year, and the foundations of another three appear to have been affected. The generator lies within 10 metres of the cliff.

During the year, Harness invested in a stake in an oil pipeline which runs near the island. The co-owners of the pipeline have just advised Brewster, as a director of Harness, that they have discovered a substantial crack in the pipeline.

Required

Comment on the implications of the above on the audit of Harness Ltd for the year end June 20X8.

(10 marks)

(Total = 15 marks)

27 Eastfield Distributors
36 mins

Your firm is the external auditor of Eastfield Distributors, a limited liability company which has revenue of $25 million and a profit before tax of $1.7 million. The company operates from a head office at Eastfield and has sales and inventory holding centres in different parts of the country. The directors have decided the company has reached a size when it needs an internal audit department. As is becoming increasingly common, the directors have asked your firm to provide this service to the company as well as being the external auditor of the company's annual financial statements.

In answering the question, you should consider:

(a)   The effects of the ACCA's *Code of Ethics and Conduct* in relation to providing an internal audit service to Eastfield Distributors

(b)   The extent to which your audit firm can rely on the internal audit work when carrying out the external audit of Eastfield Distributors

(c)   The arrangements over control of the work and reporting of the internal audit staff:

  (i)   The extent to which the internal audit staff should be responsible to Eastfield Distributors, and who should control their work

  (ii)   The extent to which the internal audit staff should be responsible to a manager or partner of the external audit firm, and whether the same manager and partner should be responsible for both the internal audit staff of Eastfield Distributors and the external audit.

Required

In relation to your audit firm becoming internal auditors of Eastfield Distributors:

(a)   Describe the matters you should consider and the action you will take to ensure your firm remains independent as external auditor of the annual financial statements   **(8 marks)**

(b)   Describe the advantages and disadvantages to Eastfield Distributors of your firm providing an internal audit service   **(7 marks)**

(c)   Describe the advantages and disadvantages to your *audit firm* of providing an internal audit service to Eastfield Distributors.   **(5 marks)**

(Total = 20 marks)

28 Maple
27 mins

(a)   Explain the auditor's responsibility in respect of fraud and error.   **(5 marks)**

(b)   Maple, a limited liability company, designs and manufactures high quality wooden furniture. The audit is nearing completion and you are in the process of reviewing the audit file in your capacity as audit manager.

Draft accounts for the year ended 30 September 20X5 show a profit before tax of $100,000 and total assets of $4,562,500.

The following matters are brought to your attention.

  (i)   The inventories figure of $675,000 includes $80,000 which has been valued based on the directors' estimate. This is due to the loss of the inventory counting sheets for the Sherwood depot. The audit team were unable to find any other means of validating these inventories.

  (ii)   During the year Maple made a loan to a director, Colin Wood, for $5,000. This is not disclosed in the accounts as the directors believe that the transaction is a personal issue.

  (iii) Trade receivables that total $525,000 include $47,000 due from Beech. This customer went into liquidation on 3 November 20X5. The audit senior has concluded that Maple is unlikely to recover the debt based on information provided by the liquidator.

The directors have refused to adjust the accounts.

The audit senior has drafted the auditor's report, extracts of which are as follows:

'*Modified opinion*

The inventories balance includes an amount of $80,000 based on the directors' estimate. This is because the inventory counting sheets for the Sherwood depot were lost and we were unable to find any other suitable means of confirming the inventory value. Also, included in receivables is an amount of $47,000 due from a company which is in liquidation. We believe that this amount should have been fully provided against as it is unlikely that the company will receive any payment in respect of this amount.

Except for the financial effects of the matters referred to in the preceding paragraph, in our opinion, the financial statements give a true and fair view, in accordance with Generally Accepted Accounting Practice, of the state of the company's affairs as at 30 September 20X5 and of its profit for the year then ended.'

The audit senior has also attached a note for you explaining that he has made no reference to the director's loan on the basis that the amount involved is not material.

Required

Comment on the suitability of this report. Your answer should include an assessment of the materiality of each of the three outstanding issues.   **(10 marks)**

(Total = 15 marks)

29 Reporting issues

27 mins

(a)   You are the engagement partner on the audit of Techie Co. The directors are developing the company's website and have intimated that they would like to provide access to the full financial statements, including the auditor's report through the site.

Required

Comment briefly on the issues this raises for the auditor.   **(5 marks)**

(b)   Later in the year, you undertake the audit of Techie Co.

The website is now operational, and Techie is trading through it. The website was developed by an external information technology expert. It will be maintained in the future by the company's IT staff. There is no continuing maintenance arrangement. The cost of developing the website, which was substantial, has been recognised in profit or loss as part of administrative expenses. Techie has a reciprocal arrangement with another company, Trekkie Co, whereby the companies have free advertising banners on each other's websites. No provision has been made for the above arrangement in the financial statements.

Required

(i)   Comment on any evidence you would seek in relation to the above items.
(ii)   Comment on the potential implications of the above items on the auditors' report.

(10 marks)

(Total = 15 marks)

1 Fundamental principles

> **Tutor's hint.** Don't let this scenario panic you in the long list of details it gives you. Deal with each point as it arises. Also, don't be afraid to draw a conclusion about the facts given to you, but remember to back your opinions up with justification. Consider what the fundamental principles and general guidance of the ACCA say, but also think about practical issues, such as ease of modern communication. Deal with the two issues raised in the scenario (the individual partner issue and the firm split) separately, there is no need to assume any connection between them. However, you may feel there is a point to be made about the juxtaposition of the two events.

Independence

It is important that auditors are, and are seen to be, independent. **Independence** is at the heart of the auditing profession as auditors claim to give an **impartial, objective** opinion on the truth and fairness of the financial statements.

Objectivity

A **family relationship** between an auditor and the client **can substantially affect the objectivity** of the audit, so auditors are advised not to build close personal relationships with audit clients and should not audit a company where family are employed in a capacity which is sensitive to the accounts, for example, in the finance department, although this is **not prohibited by law** unless the auditor's 'partner' is an employee of the company.

In this instance, the **partner was not the reporting partner** for the audit client in which his brother-in-law was a financial controller. According to generally accepted ethical practice then, the firm appeared to be independent of the audit client if the related partner did not have anything to do with the audit.

Resolution?

The regulatory body required the audit partner to move 400 miles. This presumably implies that the partner was requested to change offices within the firm by which he was employed. Given current levels of computer networking and other **communications** common in business, this would appear to be an **arbitrary distinction**, as a partner in an office in Glasgow could have similar access and influence over a single audit carried out by the firm as a partner in London.

Independence in appearance

However, in this situation, the regulatory body appears to be concerned about the appearance of independence. It appears to be concerned that the public will not perceive the distinction between a partner and a partner who reports on a specific engagement. This may or may not be fair. Arguably, it is only in publicising the problem that the public are likely to have a perception at all.

Also, given the comments made about modern communications above, the public are unlikely to be convinced that moving a member of staff to a different office will solve this independence problem, if they perceive that there is one.

Split of audit firm

The decision of the firm to split into three divisions could **enhance the public perception of the independence of the audit department**. While there might be **underlying scepticism** relating to the reasons behind the split (which could merely be for marketing purposes or to enable non-audit divisions to raise capital more easily), the **underlying benefit for objectivity still exists**.

However, some audit clients will be unhappy with the move of the firm as it will necessitate their engaging with several different service providers to gain the services they previously got from the one audit firm.

2 Aventura International

Ethical situations arising in connection with the audit of Aventura International

(a) **Offer of goods**

At the inventory count, the auditors attending were invited to purchase inventory at 30% of RRP, that is, at a 70% discount.

ACCA's guidance on accepting goods states that such benefits should only be accepted on 'normal commercial terms' or at a 'modest benefit'. What constitutes modest benefit will be a matter of judgement for the auditor.

Benefit

It is possible that this offer does approximate to offers made to staff at Aventura, as clothes commonly retail at prices with a substantial mark-up on cost. It would not be unreasonable for a clothes retailer to give staff a 'cost' benefit. The auditor should determine whether such a benefit is made available to staff. If it is not made to staff it should not be accepted by the auditor.

The term 'modest benefit' should be considered both in terms of materiality to the auditor and the company. The offer is not material to Aventura, for whom clothes retail is only one division. However, the offer of unlimited fashion at a 70% discount is extremely likely to be material to junior audit staff (who are the grade most likely to be allocated to the inventory count). In this context, the benefit is **not** clearly insignificant.

Timing

It would be inappropriate to take up the offer at the inventory count, not least because this would constitute movement of inventory during the count, which would be wrong.

Also, the junior staff members should not accept such goods without having discussed the matter with the audit partner (it is assumed in this answer that this is the first time such an offer has been made).

Lastly, if mistakes were to be made on the inventory count, the audit might be open to charges of negligence if it appeared its staff members indulged in a shopping trip when they should have been auditing.

Action to be taken

The staff members should not have taken up the offer at the inventory count.

The audit partner should discuss the matter with management, ascertain whether a similar benefit is offered to staff and decide whether he feels it is appropriate for his staff to take up the offer. It may be inappropriate as Aventura might become perceived to be a 'reward' job by audit staff. Alternatively, it might be appropriate if the audit firm imposed a financial limit to the benefits their staff could accept.

(b) **Hospitality**

An invoice to the company for business use of the Chief Executive's jet shows that the audit manager was flown to Florida and back for a stay of two weeks.

Issues arising

(i) If the invoice was ostensibly for 'business use', what was the business? (Neither the client nor the auditor have offices in Florida.)

(ii) If the invoice was not for business, the Chief Executive is wrong to invoice it to the company. Is this common practice?

(iii) If it was for business, the cost of the auditor's flight should not have been charged directly to the company, but the audit firm, who could then have re-charged it. Was Darius Harken working for the weeks in question, or is it recorded as holiday in the audit firm's records?

(iv) Does the invoice actually represent a significant example of hospitality being accepted by the audit manager?

(v) Did the audit manager travel alone, with family, or even with the Chief Executive? Does this indicate that the audit manager has a close personal relationship with the Chief Executive?

Hospitality/close personal relationship

It is possible that points (iv) and (v) above may be indicated by the invoice.

In terms of accepting hospitality, ACCA's guidance is the same as was discussed above in relation to accepting goods. It is unlikely that paying for an auditor's flight would be considered on normal commercial terms, because it would be traditional for the audit firm simply to recharge the cost of a business trip. Taking steps such as these would help to reduce the suggestion that something inappropriate has occurred, if the trip was genuinely business related.

If the trip was for pleasure (a) it should not have been charged to the company, which raises several auditing issues in its own right and (b) it does not come within the definition of 'modest commercial benefit'.

In terms of close business or personal relationships, ACCA's guidance states that these might adversely affect, or appear to affect, the objectivity of the auditor. It seems likely that in this instance, if the Chief Executive and the audit manager have been on holiday together, or at least a business 'jolly', then as a minimum, objectivity will **appear** to be threatened.

Action to be taken

(i) The audit firm should check their personnel records and see whether Darius Harken was working or holidaying at the relevant time.

(ii) If the trip was business-related, the audit partner should check why the cost has been invoiced to the company by the Chief Executive and not by the audit firm.

(iii) If the trip was personal, then the audit manager appears to have threatened the objectivity of the audit, and indeed, given that the trip appears to have been taken around the time the prior year audit was taking place, that audit is also adversely affected.

(iv) The prior year audit files should be subjected to a cold review and the audit manager should be replaced on this year's audit, which should also be subject to a quality control review.

(v) All invoices rendered to the company in respect of the jet should be scrutinised by the audit team, for further evidence of personal expenses being charged to the company.

(c) **The impending marriage of the Chief Executive**

The Chief Executive's assistant is the former accountant in charge of the audit of Aventura, who is likely to have been involved with the audit of the previous year end. She has just announced her engagement to the Chief Executive.

Issues arising

(i) Current year audit – there is a risk of loss of independence as the Chief Executive's assistant is aware of audit method.

(ii) Prior year audit – there is a suggestion that the accountant in charge of the audit may have been in a personal relationship with the Chief Executive which may have adversely affected her objectivity.

Movement of audit staff

ACCA does not cover the issue of audit staff moving between the employments of the audit firm and audit clients. However, it is clear that this might adversely affect objectivity, so members involved in such activity should bear in mind the general guidance on objectivity.

IESBA suggests a number of safeguards in this situation, such as:

● Considering the appropriateness of modifying the plan for the engagement

● Assigning the audit team to someone of sufficient experience in relation to the person who has left

● Involving an additional accountant not previously associated with the audit to review

Action to be taken

Although the accountant in charge was not the most senior staff member on the audit, it would have been prudent to modify the audit plan before this year's audit. However, this does not appear to have been done, and the audit is nearing completion.

Therefore, it is important that Voest implement the third bullet point above, and conduct a quality control review of this audit.

In relation to the suspicion that Ms Fennimore's objectivity may have been affected last year, it might also be a good idea to conduct a similar review of last year's audit work, evidence obtained and conclusions drawn. However, as the work should have been reviewed by an audit manager and partner after Ms Fennimore's involvement, the risk of a problem on last year's audit appears to be slight.

3 Osbourne plc

(a)   The six elements of a firm's system of quality control are:

- Leadership responsibilities for quality within the firm
- Relevant ethical requirements
- Acceptance and continuance of client relationships and specific engagements
- Human resources
- Engagement performance
- Monitoring

(b)   The issues are as follows:

Firm culture

ISQC 1 requires that firms implement policies such that the internal culture of the firm emphasizes the importance of quality control. It is the leaders of the firm who are responsible for creating and maintaining this culture through their actions and messages. In other words the entire business strategy of the firm should be driven by the need for quality in its operations. The personnel responsible for establishing and maintaining the firm's system of quality control must understand ISQC 1.

In this case two factors indicate that there is a lack of leadership on quality control:

(i)   The partner responsible for quality control has resigned and has not been replaced. While this may not have a direct impact on the audit of Osbourne plc, the fact that there is no one responsible for quality control in the firm increases the risk that quality control deficiencies will go undetected.

(ii)   The firm is under pressure to complete the audit and provide other services for the same fee as last year in spite of the fact that additional work will be required. There is a risk that quality will suffer as audit work will not be carried out as thoroughly as it should be in order to complete the work within budget. This problem is exacerbated by the potential lack of proper quality control review due to the departure of the quality control partner.

The quality control partner should be replaced as soon as possible. The budget for the audit of Osbourne should be monitored carefully. The audit should be conducted properly and in accordance with ISAs. Any cost overruns should be discussed with the client and additional fees negotiated if necessary.

Ethical requirements

A firm should have procedures in place to ensure that staff are aware of ethical requirements and comply with these. In this case the implementation of the system has not been completed. Whilst members of staff who are members of a professional body eg ACCA should be aware of their responsibilities they may not have all the relevant information to avoid an inadvertent breach of the regulations eg details of all companies who are clients of the firm.

The implementation of the system started by the previous ethics partner should be completed.

Monitoring

The fact that the auditor partner is new, and the previous partner is no longer with the firm increases the risk regarding audit monitoring. As the current audit partner is new he will not have an extensive knowledge of the audit client initially. The tight deadline for the audit accentuates this problem.

To decrease this risk the audit partner must gain an understanding of the business in accordance with ISAs. If possible, it may be appropriate to retain the audit manager and audit senior from the previous year to aid continuity. Andrews may also consider a second partner review to ensure that quality control standards have been maintained.

(c) Fees should be set on the basis of the time spent and the skills and experience of the personnel involved. They should not be undertaken on a contingency basis and should not be influenced by or determined by the provision of non-audit services.

4 PLD Associates

> **Tutor's hint.** The assessment of audit risk is a fundamental part of each audit and in considering whether to accept audit clients, it will *always* be necessary to carry out some kind of work to assess the overall risk at a client. Do not be tempted just to give a list of common risks, you must relate your answer to the situation given in the question. In this situation, you should have identified key words in the scenario, such as 'develop derelict land', 'taxation authorities became suspicious', 'internal controls had deficiencies'. This explains why the company was high risk and point you particularly to parts (iv) and (v) in the answer to (a). However, the requirement in (a) is not for you to identify the risk – so make sure you answer the question set and look past the risk to the procedures an audit firm would carry out to identify if the risk was too great to accept the audit. Remember also the importance of CDD procedures to avoid problems associated with clients who launder money.
>
> Part (b) requires assessment of information given in the question, but parts (c) and (d) can be answered without reference to the scenario. Do not fall into a trap of trying to relate your answer to these parts simply to this scenario. Use the scenario to prompt you if you wish, but you should use your general knowledge to answer much of this section.

(a) PLD Associates is a high-risk client on two counts:

 (i) The **nature of its business is property development**, a high-risk activity

 (ii) The **deficiencies of the company's internal control system** and the lack of integrity of the founder Mr J Scott

With such a potential client, the auditors must ensure that there are no independence or other ethical problems likely to cause conflict with the ethical code before accepting the appointment. They must also carry out customer due diligence to guard against accepting a client who launders money (remember, retaining the proceeds of any crime, eg tax evasion, is money laundering).

The procedures which an audit firm should carry out before accepting a potentially high audit risk client are as follows.

 (i) **Request** the prospective clients' **permission to communicate** with the **previous auditors**. If such permission is refused the appointment should be declined.

 (ii) On receipt of permission the prospective auditors should **request** in writing of the previous auditors all **information** which ought to be made available to them to enable them to decide whether they are prepared to accept nomination.

 The information requested from the old auditors could go as far as asking about the integrity of the management of PLD Associates.

 (iii) Ensure that the firm's **existing resources are adequate** to service the needs of the new client. This will raise questions of staff and time availability and the firm's technical expertise. This will be important in the case of PLD Associates as property development is a specialist area.

(iv) **Seek references** in respect of the new client company; it may be, as is often the case, that the directors of the company are already personally known to the firm; if not, independent enquiries should be made concerning the status of the company and its directors. Agencies such as Dun & Bradstreet might be of assistance together with a formal search at the Companies Registry. The search at the Companies Registry will uncover the qualified audit report if a copy of this has not already been obtained. It will be necessary to find out whether any regulatory authority has disciplined the company.

(v) A **preliminary assessment of audit risk** should be made. This will involve discussions with the management of the client and assessing the internal control structure (which in the case of the PLD Associates is obviously poor).

(vi) The **costs and benefits** of accepting the client should be estimated; this appointment may be considered too costly in terms of potential liability (or raised insurance premiums) and bad publicity.

(b) Ethical guidelines issued by the accountancy institutes require that the auditors are **independent and objective**. It is the integrity of the auditors which gives weight to the audit opinion. In this case the partner has shown a singular lack of integrity by maintaining this secret fund; his objectivity as an auditor has been impaired by his lack of independence. He has also contravened ethical guidelines by carrying out the **preparation** of **accounting records** for a **quoted company**.

The partner has, however, gone farther than this omission of fundamental ethical principles; he has in fact **colluded** with the **managing director** to conceal questionable transactions from fellow directors and shareholders. In the worst case this could be with a view to defrauding the company of which he is auditor. He has also concealed transactions which should have been disclosed to the taxation authorities. His position as auditor is untenable and his audit opinion, once knowledge of his involvement is known, is valueless. He may also face criminal prosecution for money laundering.

(c) The measures that audit firms might introduce to try to minimise the practice of 'opinion shopping' by prospective audit clients are as follows.

(i) To **establish why the question is being asked**. Is the prospective client looking for auditors who will confirm his views on the treatment of a particular transaction? He may be trying to use this against his current auditors with whom he is in dispute.

(ii) No **opinion** should be **given** until the **present auditors** have been **informed**. This is not only a matter of courtesy but may reveal other aspects to the problem which had not been forthcoming from the prospective client.

(iii) If an audit firm decides to give an opinion it should do so **in writing** giving the facts of the problem as it has been presented to them. This will protect the audit firm against the situation where an incorrect opinion is given because the facts have been misrepresented by the prospective client to order to get the opinion which concurred with their own.

Current legislation exists to protect auditors, allowing them to present their case against removal to the members. Similarly, when the auditors resign they are required to make a **statement** regarding the resignation which must be sent to the **Registrar** and everyone who is entitled to receive the financial statements.

In future the Review Panel might take a more active role in finding sets of accounts where an 'opinion shopper' has succeeded in obtaining an unqualified opinion which is unjustified.

(d) Audit firms can reduce the risk of litigation and its effects upon the audit practice by ensuring:

(i) **Auditing standards are applied** on all assignments

(ii) **Adequate quality control procedures** are in force

(iii) **Adequate review procedures** are in operation before a new client is accepted

(iv) **Adequate PI insurance** is obtained (this does not reduce the risk of litigation but limits the damage it causes)

5 Professional responsibilities

> **Tutor's hint.** You should expect at least one discussion question on your paper, which will probably be optional. This question requirement was not typical of a discussion question you could expect but is good practice for your essay skills.
>
> You should discuss who else has responsibilities in relation to fraud itself, given that actually auditors have no direct responsibility.
>
> Remember, when attempting an essay question, you should always set out all the sides to an argument, not just the ones you agree with, although you should always draw a conclusion at the end. Make sure your answer is justifiable given the arguments you have made. You should not introduce new arguments in your conclusions.

Responsibility of auditors

Before considering whether it is practical or desirable for auditors to accept a general responsibility to detect fraud and other irregularities it should be recognised that they already have a responsibility to obtain reasonable assurance that the financial statements are free from material misstatements whether caused by fraud or error.

It must also be acknowledged that the **primary responsibility** for preventing and detecting fraud must always **rest with the management of the entity.** It is they who have been given the responsibility to safeguard the assets of the enterprise while the auditor's primary responsibility is to express an opinion on the financial statements.

Extend responsibility?

However, it can be seen that the shareholders', the government's and the public's expectations of the auditor are changing and they are **increasingly calling on the auditor** to **widen his responsibility.**

One of the problems that may arise is the **difficulty of defining fraud.** Associated with this is the need for the auditor to determine an **appropriate level of materiality.**

Currently the auditor assesses materiality in relation to the true and fair view shown by the financial statements. This may no longer be the correct basis if all or most frauds have to be detected.

Fraud itself can cover several types of activities at various levels within the company. Should the auditor be expected to detect a petty theft committed by a junior employee? If not, how is a line drawn between insignificant and important frauds? The guidelines define fraud as involving the use of deception to obtain an unjust of illegal financial advantage.

The desirability of changing the auditor's responsibility has to be considered in the light of different types of organisations and different interested parties. It would seem to be reasonable for the auditor of a financial institution, where depositors' savings are at risk, to have a greater responsibility for the detection of fraud than the auditor of a small private company run by proprietors. Similarly the auditors of public companies should have a greater responsibility than those of private companies. This would reflect the public's expectations of the role of the modern auditor and legislation should react to these expectations.

Since fraud invariably has an impact on either the accounting records of the financial statements, it is generally accepted that auditors need to plan their audits so that they have a reasonable expectation of detecting material misstatements caused by fraud.

While few people would disagree that the auditor should have some responsibility for the detection of fraud, it may be that widening the auditor's role would mean that additional audit costs would be incurred by all organisations to detect fraud in a mere handful of cases.

Perhaps auditors should advise management how to prevent and detect fraud and penalties for it should be increased so that there is a greater deterrent. If organisations could prevent fraud more effectively there would not be such a need for auditors to try to detect it.

As to the practicalities of detection, fraud can be very difficult to detect where internal control systems are very weak. Some types of fraud may require special expertise to be detected. All auditors should already be detecting frauds and irregularities which give rise to material errors in financial statements. Procedures used to detect immaterial frauds would principally be an extension of the usual audit procedures but the time taken to **extend the level of testing** would be considerable.

The auditor judges the amount of work necessary on the need to obtain sufficient, reliable evidence on which to form an opinion on the view shown by the financial statements. If the auditor's objective was changed, whilst the **method would principally be the same**, the amount of **work necessary** would **increase significantly.** The auditor would not accept a greater responsibility for detecting fraud without a **substantial fee increase.** It is questionable whether this would be considered worthwhile for most organisations.

There is also the **practical difficulty** of **to whom the auditors reports a fraud.** If senior management is involved and the auditor has no real proof and there is no material effect on the financial statements, then the auditor will have to seek legal advice on what action should be taken. The auditor is bound by his **duty of confidentiality** from disclosing it to the appropriate authorities without the client's permission. However, the duty of confidence is not absolute, and the auditors may disclose matters to a proper authority either in the public interest or for other specific reasons.

An associated problem which might arise is a **deterioration in the relationship** between the auditor and the client. If he had to report directly to the authorities, the client may be reluctant to provide information which might cast suspicion over everyone.

Conclusion

Auditors have the skills necessary to detect most types of fraud but the **cost** of doing so **may exceed the likely benefits.** The approach I advise is for the auditor to make recommendations to management about how they could reduce the likelihood of fraud or irregularities and increase the possibility of detection.

6 CD Sales

(a) There are various key audit procedures which would have uncovered the fraud perpetrated by Mr A Long. Note that the first two tests would bring to the attention of the auditor the substantial inherent and control risk surrounding the accounts of CD Sales, thus increasing their perceived audit risk, and putting them on their guard.

Analytical review procedures

The auditor should perform analytical procedures in order to compare the company's results with those of other companies in the same business sector. In particular, the auditor should look at sales growth rates and gross profit margins, but also inventory holding levels, non-current assets and return on capital. This should indicate that the company's results are unusual for the sector, to a great extent.

Review of service contracts

The auditor should examine the directors' service contracts. It is unusual for *all* directors to be paid such substantial bonuses, although the payment of bonuses of some sort to directors is common business practice. It is the size of the bonuses in proportion to the directors' base salaries which is the problem here. It increases both the inherent and control risk for the auditor because it reduces the directors' objectivity about the performance of the company. Audit risk is thus increased.

Testing of sales, purchases and inventories

(i) The main audit test to obtain audit evidence for sales would be to require direct confirmations from the sales agents. These confirmations would also provide evidence for the balance owed to CD Sales at the year end and the inventories held by the agent at the year end. Replies to such confirmations should be sent direct to the auditor who would agree the details therein to the company's records or reconcile any differences. Where replies are not received alternative procedures would be carried out which might include visits to the agents themselves to examine their records.

(ii) A selection of agents should, in any case, be visited at the year end to confirm the inventories held on sale or return by physical verification. The auditor should count such inventories and consider obsolescence, damage etc.

(iii) Fictitious agents might be discovered by either of tests (iii) and (iv), but a further specific procedure would be to check authorisation of and contracts with all the sales agents. Correspondence could also be reviewed from throughout the year.

(iv) The practice of 'selling' all the inventory to the agents and them repurchasing it after the year end should be detected by sales and purchases cut-off tests around the year end. All transactions involving inventory items returned after the year end should be examined.

Testing of non-current assets

Non-current asset testing should help to identify inventory purchases which have been invoiced as non-current assets.

(i) Samples of additions to non-current assets can be checked to the non-current asset register and to the asset itself.

(ii) Physical verification will ensure that an asset is being used for the purpose specified, and this should be relatively straightforward to check as the computers will each have individual identification codes.

(iii) Where the assets cannot be found, then it may be possible to trace the asset to inventories, perhaps via the selling agents' confirmations, or to sales already made.

Related parties review

The level of collusion with suppliers makes detection of fraud difficult, but the auditor may be put on guard if he discovers that the suppliers are related parties to CD Sales. A related party review would normally take place as part of an audit.

(b) The type of 'confidentiality agreement' signed by the auditor of CD Sales has reduced the scope of the audit to such an extent that it has become almost meaningless.

While it is understandable that companies would wish to protect sensitive commercial information, the auditor has the right to any information he feels is necessary in the performance of his duties. This agreement clearly circumvents that right. Moreover, such information would still be protected if released to the auditor, because the auditor is under a duty of confidentiality to the client.

In reducing the scope of the audit to this extent, the agreement prevents the auditor obtaining sufficient appropriate evidence to support an audit opinion. The auditor's report should therefore be modified on the grounds of inability to obtain sufficient appropriate audit evidence, possibly to the extent of a full disclaimer.

In failing to issue such a modification, the auditor may well have acted negligently and even unlawfully in signing such an agreement.

(c) A review of interim accounts is very different from an audit of year end financial statements. In an auditor's report a positive assurance is given on the truth and fairness of the financial statements. The level of audit work will be commensurate with the level of the assurance given, that is it will be stringent, testing the systems producing the accounts and the year end figures themselves using a variety of appropriate procedures.

In the case of a review of interim financial statements, the auditor gives only negative assurance, that he has not found any indication that the interim accounts are materially misstated. The level of audit work will be much less penetrating, varied and detailed than in a full audit. The main audit tools used to obtain evidence will be analytical procedures and direct enquiries of the company's directors.

(d) It is not the duty of the auditor to prevent or detect fraud. The auditor should, however, conduct the audit in such a way as to expect to detect any material misstatements in the financial statements, caused by fraud. At the planning stage, the auditor should assess the risk that fraud is occurring both at the financial statement and the assertion level and plan his procedures accordingly. Where fraud is suspected or likely, the auditor should carry out additional procedures in order to confirm or deny this suspicion.

Even if a fraud is uncovered after an audit, the auditor will have a defence against a negligence claim if it can be shown that auditing standards were followed and that no indication that a fraud was taking place was received at any time.

Application of principles to this case

In this particular case, Mr A Long has taken a great deal of trouble to cover up his fraudulent activities, using accomplices, bribing people, cooking up fictitious documents etc. When such a high level fraud is carried out, the auditor might find it extremely difficult to uncover the true situation or even to realise anything was amiss. The auditor is also entitled to accept the truth of representations made to him and documents shown to him which purport to come from third parties.

On the other hand, the auditor should have a degree of professional scepticism. The auditor should be aware of the risks pertaining to the company and should recognise that controls can be overridden by collusion or by management actions. The suspicions of the auditor should have been aroused by the rapid growth rate of the company and fairly standard audit procedures on cut-off and non-current assets should have raised matters which required explanation.

Where the auditor has been most culpable, however, is in signing the confidentiality agreement. This restricted the scope of the audit to such an extent that the auditor should have known that there was insufficient evidence to support their opinion. The auditor will therefore find it difficult to defend a negligence claim.

7 Marsden Manufacturing Co

Tutor's hint. In part (a), it is vitally important that you do not just bang out the percentage indicators, but that you show the examiner that you are considering qualitative factors as well. You will probably get one mark for the calculations – the rest are available for considered comment.

In part (b) work through the scenario, looking out for items you think will be relevant or that raise questions (or exclamation) marks in your head. The examiner doesn't just include things in exam questions to take up paper. Think to yourself 'what does that mean for the company/the audit?'. However, you don't have to get 100% on this question to pass the paper, so don't waste time trying to think of points for every word in the question – if you really can't see anything relevant in the information, move on to the next thing you are told.

Part (c) should represent easy marks, as there are three or four key administrative matters which require attending to on every audit, none of which have been mentioned in the scenario. Remember lists such as 'administrative planning matters' so that you can always get easy marks like these. But don't mention things on your list that the question has discounted – that is obviously a waste of your time. For example, in this question, don't talk about deciding whether to use computers on this audit, because the question states that the partner has decided not to.

Part (d) is another source of useful marks on this question. You should be able to discuss the basic issues relating to conflicts of interest, draw a conclusion in this case and then discuss steps to take such as discussing it with both parties. It is unlikely in this case that the firm should divest either audit – don't fall into the trap of making over the top suggestions.

(a) **Materiality considerations**

Value indicators

The traditional indicators of materiality levels which would apply in this situation are as follows:

	Band A	Band B
	$	$
Revenue (1/2%/1%)	12,670	25,340
Profit before tax (5%)	3,050	–
Total assets (1%/2%)	10,090	20,180
Net assets (2%/5%)	7,360	18,400

A simple average of these indicators would give materiality of $13,870. This is a useful numerical indicator, but there are also some qualitative features that should be considered.

Qualitative features

As interest is an important figure to the company due to their agreements with the bank, it might be wise to include profit before interest and tax rather than profit before tax in the calculations. This would raise the average figure given above to $13,970.

Net assets are also important to the company, due to the bank agreement. The agreement requires current assets to be 1.5 times current liabilities. On the statement of financial position given, that would be $586,000. The current assets are well above that at the moment. However, when considering materiality, the auditor should look at matters cumulatively. The ratio is material to the statement of financial position, so any issues relevant to that ratio may be material, regardless of value.

Conclusion

I would therefore set planning materiality at $14,000. However, I would treat issues arising in relation to net current assets as potentially material, and consider the cumulative impact that any issues had.

(b) **Audit risks at Marsden Manufacturing**

Inherent risks

> Using the components of audit risk might help you identify the risks, or a greater breadth of risks, in the scenario in the first place.

The key issue relating to the statement of financial position in the year is the **factoring of receivables**. This raises a number of issues for the audit.

> [breaking up] your answer [to the] components of audit risk helps [you] structure your answer.

The first issue is questions behind the factoring of debt: **why have they been factored**? This is answered by the fact that the company is seeking a form of insurance against bad debts so that their interest cover will be maintained. However, it is important to check that this is the only reason, ie that the debt is not being factored because there are **cash flow** problems (which might also be indicated by the fall in cash in the year) which could in turn lead to suspicions of **going concern** issues.

> [yo]u do not [ne]ed to go into [lon]g details [he]re, but [sho]uld be [aw]are of the [iss]ues that [ma]ke this risky [for] the audit.

Specifically in relation to **receivables**, it raises issues of whether they have yet been accounted for in the statement of financial position and **properly disclosed** according to their substance. When there is a high transfer of all significant risks and rewards to the factor and as the entire sales ledger function has been outsourced to the factor, this needs investigation. Derecognising receivables would clearly be **material** to the statement of financial position, and could have an impact on the covenant with the bank although there would also be a significant influx of cash, so the net effect on net assets might not affect the net assets ratio too badly. If the factoring has already been accounted for, then cash appears to be dangerously low (given that an injection of cash should have just occurred). This would have serious implications for the going concern assumption. However, as there is a large debit balance in receivables, it appears more likely that the factoring has not yet been accounted for.

The **relationship with the bank** is clearly important to the business, and has been mentioned already. However, the whole issue of relationship with the bank must be considered for audit purposes, particularly as there appears to be a **worsening cash position** and there is a question mark over the factoring of receivables. **Going concern** is a risk on this audit, particularly if **accounting issues** such as the one mentioned above radically change the statement of financial position and have an **impact on the debt covenants**.

Connected to the issue of the factoring is the position of the former sales ledger clerk, Sally Forsyth. As part of the re-structuring, she has been dismissed. She appears to be bringing a claim against the company for unfair dismissal and sexual discrimination. It is unclear whether she has grounds for such action.

However, there is a **potential material contingent liability**. During the course of the audit it will be vital to investigate this affair and consider whether the potential liability falls within the **timing requirements of IAS 37** (when were the key dates?). If Ms Forsyth has been dismissed before the year end it is likely that there is a legal obligation arising, if she has a case. To consider whether she has a case or not, it may be necessary to **seek an expert legal opinion**.

Following up from the issues noted at the inventory count, there appears to a be problem with **possible inventory obsolescence**. In the absence of any further explanation for the inventory increase, this is borne out by the fact that inventory has risen on the statement of financial position from last year. It is unclear whether this may be material or not, however, given that current assets are material by their nature given the agreement with the bank and the possible effects of FRS 5 on receivables, **this matter may be material by its nature**.

> Facts such as the compensation limits for dismissal claims are not within your syllabus. However, they are cumulative general knowledge from your ACCA studies and here are relevant materiality considerations. An auditor would know or find out such details. For your purposes, being aware that they would be material is sufficient.

Control risk

As part of control risk evaluation, the auditor must consider the **effect of receivables factoring** on the systems of the business and the fact that the sales ledger function is now outsourced, and has been for a portion of the year under review. The **related controls must be assessed**. There is also a risk that the **controls over the transfer** from in house sales ledger to outsourced sales ledger may not have been strong, and that errors could have been made.

Detection risk

There are some key detection issues to consider. The first, as mentioned above, is that an **expert** may be required on this audit to obtain evidence about the contingent liability. The second is that the requirements of ISA 402 must be considered in relation to the outsourced sales ledger function. The auditor must ensure that he has all the **information he requires from the service provider**.

(c) **Administrative planning matters**

The engagement partner must organise a **planning meeting** to discuss the audit with the team.

The supervisor needs to obtain **key dates** relating to the audit, such as the dates of the manager and partner reviews, and client related dates such as when final accounts will be ready and when the accounts need to be signed by.

The supervisor needs to obtain **client permission to contact** the company's **solicitor** and the **factor** and he needs to **organise when the audit team will be able to liaise with them**.

(d) **Conflict of interest**

Does a conflict exist?

> It is important to set out that you are not in possession of enough details to come to a conclusion on this matter, stating what the relevant factors are.

The audit firm is in possession of information about Marsden's new client which Marsden would be interested in, which is sensitive information. However, it is also information they could have obtained by conducting a credit rating or search on the new customer, which they should have (and therefore may have) done for a customer of such magnitude.

It is obviously in Wallworth's best interests that their auditors do not share information about their poor payment history with their new supplier.

Whether a conflict exists depends on the size of the audit firm and the procedures put in place in the audit department to maintain the independence of the two audits. In a small department it is likely that it will be difficult in practice to keep matters completely confidential. (In other words, one audit team is likely to be aware of facts relating to the other audit client.)

What steps should the auditor take?

In this situation, it is probably best that the auditor makes both parties aware that they are the auditors for both companies and restate their duty of confidentiality to both. It may be wise to revisit the engagement letter for both clients to ensure that the duties and procedures in relation to this potential conflict are set out.

> Remember, draw a reasonable conclusion, based on the facts.

8 Gasoleum

Notes for planning meeting

(a)   Areas of potential risk to be addressed by the audit

Income

A substantial proportion of sales made at the stations will be cash based therefore making completeness of income difficult to establish.

Sales records are updated via an online computer ie records are updated automatically and instantly. Any deficiencies in the operation of the computer be it manual input or systematic error will directly impact income. The key risk is however weak control over manual input.

Income could be missed via deficiencies in controls over the sale of car wash and air tokens.

Misclassification of income would render management accounts meaningless for analytical review purposes.

Inventories

The nature of inventories (ie petrol) requires an unusual method to quantify – dipping of tanks. This increases the risk that the value is inaccurate.

All goods stocked within the mini markets are potentially desirable by both staff and customers. They are also easily moveable and thus inventory losses could occur. If this remains undetected, year end inventories and thus profit will be overstated.

Goods are also perishable. There is therefore a risk of inventory valuation being overstated where no provision/write-off is made.

State lottery outlet

There is a potential risk that income from sales of tickets is inappropriately included within the company's income.

Outlets receive commission per ticket sold. There is a risk of inappropriate classification and also overstatement if weak controls exist over the handling and storage of lottery tickets.

Inherent risk due to price competition

Intense price competition could significantly reduce margins which could in turn lead to management manipulation of financial information ie potential overstatement of income and understatement of expenses.

Multi-locations

With there being 15 garages to audit, there is increased risk of not detecting error as it is more complicated to control and co-ordinate the audit.

(b) The work performed by the internal auditor would impact planning to the extent that:

(i) The results of his work on the company's internal controls during the year could reduce the risk attached to particular parts of the audit and thus reduce the extent of our detailed testing on it.

For instance, evidence that the microcomputer has operated satisfactorily during the year would provide us with increased assurance as to the completeness and accuracy of both income and inventory records and thus allow a modification in the nature and timing and reduce the extent of our work. This is obviously only the case if the audit work was done thoroughly and competently.

(ii) Once we have determined that his work can be relied upon, the knowledge that he was responsible for co-ordinating the year end inventory count would again increase our confidence in inventory quantity figures, provided we are satisfied that he is suitably independent of the warehouse and of the normal inventory control procedures.

Before deciding to make use of his work we would first need to establish its relevance and reliability.

Relevance – Has he been engaged in projects whose results are of interest to us. Given what we have been told about his duties it would appear that we have some common objectives.

Reliability – His work is ultimately only reliable provided he is competent at what he does, carries out his work with due professional care and is suitably independent.

Once these have been determined, other factors would also need to be considered:

(i) Does management within the company act upon the results of his work?

(ii) The materiality of the area would need to be ascertained. For instance any work on the controls surrounding the sale of car wash and air tokens could reduce our testing to just a review of his working papers, whereas work on the operation of the online micro computers would give us confidence but not negate the need for some systems work to be done by our computer audit department.

(c) Analytical procedures on income and GP margin:

Income

(i) Obtain an analysis of income per petrol station and perform inter-branch comparisons to identify any branch with unusually high/low total income.

(ii) Obtain an analysis of income per source for each station and again carry out inter-branch comparisons to identify any branch with an unusual mix/split of income.

(iii) Compare income per source and per branch to last year. Are changes in line with our expectations and industry norms?

(iv) Obtain management accounts and do a month by month review of sales comparing with both previous years and other branches.

(v) For all the above we need to discuss fluctuations with management, follow up any discrepancies and confirm any statements made by the directors.

Gross profit

(i) Perform a comparison of gross profit percentage per branch.

(ii) Compare gross profit percentage this year to last year and against budget.

(iii) Review aged inventories analysis between this year and last year for slow-moving products, to identify any overstatement of closing inventories and thus gross profit.

(iv) Compare percentage of inventories written-off after inventory counts branch by branch and investigate branches with low gross profit percentages.

(v) Compare margins on petrol to industry norms.

(vi)   Consider the impact that fluctuations in oil prices would have on profits made.

(vii)   Again, for all of the above we would need to discuss fluctuations with management, follow up any discrepancies and confirm any statements made.

9 Audit

> **Tutor's hint**. This is not an exam standard question, but is a helpful exercise to remind yourself of the advantages of audit for a small company and also the alternative opinions available.

(a)   The advantages of having an audit include the following.

    (i)   **Shareholders** who are **not involved in management** gain **reassurance** from audited accounts about management's **stewardship** of the business.

    (ii)   Audited accounts are a reliable source for a **fair valuation of shares** in an unquoted company either for taxation or other purposes.

    (iii)   Some **banks** rely on accounts for the purposes of **making loans** and reviewing the value of security.

    (iv)   **Creditors and potential creditors** can use audited accounts to assess the potential strength of the company.

    (v)   The audit provides **management** with a **useful independent check** on the accuracy of the accounting systems; the auditors can recommend improvements in those systems.

(b)   **Audit of a small company**

The audit of a small company is still an exercise designed to express an opinion on the truth and fairness of the accounts.

However, the audit of a small company is often affected by certain factors:

- The concentration of ownership and management in one person
- The wider professional relationship between the auditor and the business
- The fact that small teams of auditors are involved with the audit

The methods of undertaking the audit will be the same, and the same auditing standards will be applied. However, the auditor must be aware of the different inherent risk in the audit of a small company and in applying auditing standards, consider all the relevant risks.

(c)   **Alternatives to audit**

A small company not requiring an audit could engage a firm of accountants to carry out a review instead.

A review is an engagement similar to audit, which is designed to give a lower level of assurance than would be given by an audit. Often this is expressed in terms of negative assurance. The procedures undertaken to express an opinion in a review engagement are therefore less detailed and often comprise enquiry and analytical procedures.

Colin needs to decide upon the level of assurance that is best for his business. This will involve him analysing the advantages of audit discussed above in part (a) and deciding whether his business requires the higher level of assurance or not. Some of the advantages of the audit will also be gained by a review.

10 Lambley Properties

> **Tutor's hint**. You should not just assume that if the directors refuse to sign the written representation a modification to the audit opinion is automatically required. There are other procedures to undertake first. Remember the circumstances (given in (b)) in which it is permissible to rely on a written representation.

(a)   ISA 580 specifies a number of general representations which management must provide.

These are as follows:

   (i)   That management has fulfilled its responsibility for the preparation and presentation of the financial statements as set out in the terms of the audit engagement.

   (ii)   Whether the financial statements are prepared and presented in accordance with the applicable financial reporting framework.

   (iii)   That management has provided the auditor with all the relevant information.

   (iv)   That all transactions have been recorded and are reflected in the financial statements.

   (v)   A description of management's responsibilities.

   (vi)   Significant assumptions in accounting estimates have been provided.

   (vii)   Related party relationships and transactions have been disclosed.

   (viii) All subsequent events information has been provided.

   (ix)   The effect of uncorrected mistakes is immaterial.

(b)   Extract from written representation letter

   Financial support

   Keyworth Builders Co, a subsidiary of the company, is experiencing going concern problems. We confirm that the company will continue to make financial support available to the subsidiary for the foreseeable future.

   Claim

   Eastwood Manufacturing Co has made a claim against the company for $5m arising from alleged negligent construction of a building. The claim comprises $3m for repairs and $2m for the cost of disruption to Eastwood's business. Following discussions with the company's professional advisers we consider that Eastwood has no claim on the company and hence no provision for these costs is required in the accounts for the year ended 31 March 20X2. However the contingency is fully explained in a note to the accounts.

(c)   **Reliability of written representation**

   The written representation is a written record of statements made by management to auditors during the audit. As it is a written record, it is stronger evidence than oral representations by themselves would be.

   However representations do not come from an independent source. They should not therefore be relied on when other evidence is available or expected to be available.

   Nevertheless representations may be the only available evidence when **based on management intent**, or the matter is **one of judgement** or opinion. Independent confirmation will not be available in these circumstances.

   Reliance on letter

   On receipt of a written representation the auditors will need to **ensure** that there is **no other evidence** that they have discovered during the course of their audit which conflicts with it. They will then have to **review the representations** made and decide, given the results of the audit testing and their assessment of risk, whether they are able to rely on them to give an unqualified opinion on the accounts.

(d)   Work to be performed to check whether a provision should be included in the accounts for the legal claim from Eastwood Manufacturing Co is as follows.

(i)   **Obtain and review all correspondence** relating to the claim.

(ii)   **Review written advice** obtained from the company's lawyer and surveyor.

(iii) **Review the original contract** between Eastwood and Lambley to assess the extent of Lambley's responsibility for repairs and any time period limitations.

(iv)   **Ascertain whether Lambley is covered by insurance** should the claim be payable.

(v)   **Examine minutes** of meetings of the Board and management which deal with this matter.

These procedures will allow the probability of the company having to meet the claim to be assessed. Disclosure and/or provision to comply with IAS 37 *Provisions, contingent liabilities and contingent assets* will be required.

(e)   In the circumstances where the directors refuse to sign the written representation because of the legal claim from Eastwood Manufacturing Co the following procedures could be considered.

(i)   A **meeting** between the auditors and directors to discuss a revision of the wording of the letter, so allowing the directors to sign.

(ii)   The integrity of management should be re-evaluated and the reliability of other representations (oral and written) and evidence in general reassessed.

(iii) Determine the possible effect on the audit opinion.

Assuming that satisfactory representations are not obtained, either because the original letter is amended in such a way that the situation concerning the claim is not properly explained or that the directors refuse to confirm the auditors' statement, then the auditors will need to **consider the implications** of this scope limitation **for their report**.

Given that refusal by the management to give satisfactory representations concerning the claim indicates that they may be uncertain as to the eventual outcome, the auditors would probably decide to qualify their opinion on the grounds of uncertainty.

11 Bestwood Electronics

(a)   (i)   Auditors should perform procedures designed to obtain sufficient appropriate audit evidence that all **material subsequent events** up to the date of their report which require adjustment of, or disclosure in, the financial statements have been **identified and properly reflected** therein.

These procedures should be applied to any **matters** examined during the audit which may be **susceptible to change** after the year end. They are in addition to tests on specific transactions after the period-end, eg cut-off tests.

Non-adjusting subsequent events should be disclosed in the notes to the accounts of the company, whereas all adjusting events should be incorporated in the accounts.

(ii)   The financial statements are the **directors' responsibility** and they would therefore be expected to inform the auditors of any material subsequent events between the date of the auditors' report and the date the financial statements are issued. The auditors do *not* have any obligation to perform procedures, or make enquires regarding the financial statements *after* the date of their report.

When, **after** the date of their **report** but **before** the **financial statements** are **issued**, the **auditors** become **aware** of **subsequent events** which may materially affect the financial statements, they should:

–   Establish whether the financial statements need amendment
–   Discuss the matter with the directors
–   Consider the implications for their report, taking additional action as appropriate

When the financial statements are amended, the auditors should extend the procedures discussed above to the date of their new report, carry out any other appropriate procedures and issue a new audit report. The new report should not be dated earlier than the date of approval of the amended financial statements.

The situation where the statements are not amended but the auditors feel that they should be is discussed below.

(iii) Auditors have no obligations to perform procedures or make enquiries regarding the financial statements **after** they have been issued.

When, after the financial statements have been issued, but before they have been laid before the members or equivalent, auditors become aware of subsequent events which, had they occurred and been known of at the date of their report, might have caused them to issue a different report, they should:

- **Consider** whether the financial statements need **amendment**
- **Discuss** the matter with the directors
- **Consider the implications** for their **report**, taking additional action as appropriate

There are two cases:

(1) An event which **occurred before** the **date** of the **auditors' report**, but which the auditors became aware of thereafter, and

(2) An **event** which **occurred after** the **date** of the **auditors' report**.

Under (1), the auditors and directors should consider whether the financial statements should be revised. In situation (2) there is no statutory provision for revising financial statements; the auditors might take legal advice on withdrawing their report. In **both** cases, a statement by the directors or auditors at the AGM may be feasible, but in any event legal advice may be helpful.

Where the directors do **not** revise the financial statements but the auditors feel they should be revised, and where the statements have been issued but not yet laid before the members; or if the directors do not intend to make an appropriate statement at the AGM, then the auditors should consider steps to take, on a timely basis, to prevent reliance on their report eg a statement at the AGM.

(b) The audit work for subsequent events will normally be concerned with asset values at and after the year end. The following procedures will be carried out.

(i) **Non-current assets**

(1) **Check for any sales** or proposed sales after the year end which may trigger a write down to net realisable value at the year end.

(2) **Consider obsolescence** of non-current assets, for example plant used to make a discontinue line, which might only become apparent after the year end.

(ii) **Inventory**

(1) **Check post year end selling price** of major items of inventory and compare to value in year end accounts. Consider write downs to net realisable value.

(2) **Consider the possible existence of obsolete, damaged or slow moving inventory** and the consequent value of any write down.

(3) **Perform a (limited) inventory count** after the year end **if the existence of all inventory is not known** for certain.

(iii) **Receivables**

(1) Review post year end receipts to determine recoverability.

(2) Take doubtful debts paid out of the provision and consider writing parts of the provision off for which no money has been received.

(3)   Review trade press and correspondence and consult the sales manager about any major customers who have become insolvent recently.

(4)   Check the issue of credit notes and return of goods after the year end to determine the provision for credit notes required in the accounts.

(iv)   **Cash at bank**

(1)   **Check that outstanding items** on the bank reconciliation have **cleared promptly after the year end** (to spot teeming and lading and late payment to payables).

(2)   **Write back any stale cheques** not cleared (over 6 months old).

(3)   **Check all material payments and receipts around the year end** to check the completeness of both accruals and prepayments.

(v)   **Trade payables**

(1)   **Check reconciling items** on suppliers' statements have **cleared promptly** after the year end.

(2)   If the payables circularisation has been carried out then **examining post year end payments** will help to verify balances where there was no supplier's statement and no reply.

(vi)   **Going concern problems and other matters**

The subsequent events review is important in terms of going concern investigations. The following procedures should be carried out as a matter of routine.

(1)   **Check profit and cash flow forecasts.**

(2)   **Review management accounts** and reports after the year end.

(3)   **Review board minutes** after the year end.

(4)   **Request any information** on subsequent events and going concern matters from the directors and check their information.

(5)   The **directors should also state** they have given all such information in the letter of representation.

(vii)   **Non-adjusting events**

Look for any matters which are non-adjusting but which should be disclosed in the accounts, for example, major sales of non-current assets, accidental losses and issues of shares and debentures.

(c)   I will check whether there have been any material events after the reporting period in this period, particularly if there is a significant delay between the date of the auditors' report and the issue of their financial statements. I will not undertake such detailed enquiries as in (b) above, but I will perform the following procedures.

(i)   **Ask the management or directors if any further material events have occurred** which might affect my opinion on the accounts.

(ii)   **Review the latest board minutes, reports and management accounts** issued since the end of the audit.

(iii)   Any **matters which were uncertain** at the end of the audit should be **reviewed** again to establish an outcome and any effect on the accounts. Examples would include doubtful debts, contingencies and inventory obsolescence (perhaps due to new developments).

(iv)   **Consider any matters** which have **arisen in the industry** or the economy which might affect the company.

12 Bingham Engineering

> **Tutor's hint**. This question combines the issue of the auditors' review of the going concern assumption in financial statements with the review of forecast information. Although you are given a brief scenario in the question, this question is largely based on your learning in these areas and you do not need to apply your knowledge to a scenario. As such, it is not exam standard, but it is a useful exercise to run through your knowledge on these important areas.

(a)   The 'going concern' concept assumes that the accounts are drawn up on the basis that the business will continue to exist as a viable commercial entity, without any need for any significant curtailment in its present level of activity for the 'foreseeable future'.

When forming his opinion at the conclusion of the subsequent events review the auditor should have regard to the term 'foreseeable future' in the context of going concern. While the foreseeable future must be judged in relation to specific circumstances, the auditors should normally expect the directors to have considered information which relates to a minimum of 12 months following the date of approval of the financial statements.

(b)   The most common factors indicating that a company may not be regarded as a going concern are as follows.

    (i)   Adverse financial figures or ratios:

- Recurring operating losses
- Financing to a considerable extent out of overdue suppliers and other payables
- Heavy dependence on short-term finance for long-term needs
- Working capital deficiencies
- Low liquidity rates
- Over-gearing, in the form of high or increasing debt to equity ratios
- Under capitalisation, particularly if there is a deficiency of share capital and reserves

    (ii)   Borrowing in excess of limits imposed by debenture trust deeds

    (iii)   Defaults on loans or similar agreements

    (iv)   Dividends in arrears

    (v)   Restrictions placed on usual trade terms

    (vi)   Excessive or obsolete inventory

    (vii)   Long overdue receivables

    (viii)   Non-compliance with statutory capital requirements

    (ix)   Deterioration of relationship with bankers

    (x)   Necessity of seeking new sources or methods of obtaining finance

    (xi)   The continuing use of old non-current assets because there are not funds to replace them

    (xii)   The size and content of the order book

    (xiii)   Potential losses on construction contracts

Other factors, not necessarily suggesting inability to meet debts, may be internal or external matters.

    (i)   **Internal matters**

- Loss of key management or staff
- Significantly increasing inventory levels
- Work stoppages or other labour difficulties
- Substantial dependence upon the success of a particular project or particular asset
- Excessive reliance on the success of a new product
- Uneconomic long-term commitments

(ii)   **External matters**

–   Legal proceedings or similar matters that may jeopardise a company's ability to continue in business

–   Loss of a key franchise or patent

–   Loss of a principal supplier or customer

–   The undue influence of a market dominant competitor

–   Political risks

–   Technical developments which render a key product obsolete

–   Frequent financial failures of enterprises in the same industry

The indications above vary in importance and some may only have significance as audit evidence when viewed in conjunction with others.

The significance of the indications above may diminish because they are matched by audit evidence indicating that there are mitigating factors. Indications that the business may be having to sell non-current assets to meet present cash demands may be mitigated by the possibility of obtaining new sources of finance or of renewing and expanding loan finance. Indications of problems that raise questions about the continuation of the business without suggesting inability to meet debts may be mitigated by factors relating to the enterprise's capacity to adopt alternative courses of action, for example, the likelihood of finding alternative sales markets where a principal customer is lost.

(c)   (i)   Under the present circumstances of the company, it is unlikely that the capital expenditure/disposal forecast will contain many items of capital expenditure because of the adverse effect that this would have on the company's cash flow. For such items as there are, the auditor should check that the quoted costs are reasonable, with any large value items being checked against price lists etc. Enquiries should be made of management as to whether there are any proposed items of capital expenditure not included in the forecast.

In relation to any intended disposals of non-current assets, the auditors should:

(1)   Check whether the proceeds of sale appear to be reasonable with particular care being taken to see that any estimates are arrived at on a prudent basis.

(2)   Consider whether the estimates of the timing of the receipt of sale proceeds appear to be reasonable and, once again, arrived at on a prudent basis.

(ii)   The audit work required in relation to the profit forecast would be as follows.

(1)   Check that the level of projected sales is reasonable, being similar to the previous year and consistent with current market conditions and the confirmed orders received from the company's customers.

(2)   Consider whether the gross profit margin appears reasonable in the light of the company's recent experiences and there has been consistency in the recognition of those items affecting the calculation of this key ratio.

(3)   Compare the level of income and expenditure items to the previous year, investigating carefully any areas of significant change. Any projected savings in expenditure must be justified and the auditor should take particular care to see that proper provision has been made for all bank charges and interest.

(4)   All castings and extensions in the profit forecast should be checked and comparison made with common items dealt with in the other two forecasts.

(iii)   The cash flow forecast which is based on the above two forecasts should be checked in the following way.

(1)   The opening balance should be checked to the draft financial statements and the company's cash book. For the expired period of the forecast, the month-end balance should also be checked to the cash book.

(2)   All receipts and payments for the elapsed period of the forecast should be checked against supporting documentation.

(3)   The reasonableness of the timing of future receipts and payments should be considered in the light of the normal period of credit taken by customers and extended by suppliers, due date for payment of income tax etc.

(4)   The consistency of items in the cash flow forecast with the other two forecasts should be considered, as well as consistency and accuracy of forecasts in previous years.

(5)   All castings and extensions in the forecast should be checked.

(d)   The reasonableness of the three forecasts referred to above and the willingness of the company's bankers and other creditors to supply the required funds will be the main factors to consider in assessing whether the company is a going concern.

If the work already carried out suggests that the forecasts are reasonable, then with the permission of the client, some direct confirmation of the future 'co-operation' of the bank and major suppliers should be sought. Such co-operation is more likely to be forthcoming if the company is forecast to make profits rather than losses and consideration should also be given to any security held by the various creditors and the chances of any single creditor precipitating a crisis by seeking to invoke his own security.

13 Locksley

> **Tutor's hint**. The audit of these assets is relatively straightforward, but it relies on your knowledge of the relevant accounting standards. You should cover every aspect of the audit of these items, perhaps by considering the statement of financial position and then the statement of comprehensive income effects.

(a)   The relevant audit tests are as follows.

(i)   The auditors should **obtain** from the client a **breakdown** of the figure for development expenditure which makes it possible to trace the amounts spent to the nominal ledger and the final accounts.

(ii)   **Tests of controls** should be performed to ensure that a system exists for controlling the authorising and recording of development expenditure, and that the system is operating adequately. (This work may be covered where practicable by the audit tests performed on the company's purchases and payroll systems.)

(iii)   Individual amounts should be **vouched** by reference to **supporting documentation**. The relevant documentation will vary according to the type of expenditure, but tests might include the following.

(1)   Agree purchases to requisitions, orders, goods received notes, invoices, cash book and bank statement.

(2)   Agree labour costs to the payroll and to supporting evidence, such as time sheets or job cards.

(3)   If overheads have been included in the development figure, ensure that they have been calculated on a basis consistent with that used generally by the company.

The auditors will wish to set a materiality level for testing individual items; this will have to be established when the breakdown of the total figure is known. For instance, it may be possible to restrict testing considerably if one or two large invoices represent the bulk of the relevant expenditure.

(iv)   The **arithmetical accuracy** of the schedule of expenditure should be **checked**.

(v)   The auditors should **ensure** that there has been **no double-counting**, that is, that development items capitalised have not also been charged as an expense in the income statement.

(vi)   Finally, the auditors should carry out a **review of the development figure** in order to be satisfied that it is reasonable and consistent with what else is known about the company and its business.

(b)   The following audit procedures may be performed to verify the revaluation gain arising on non-current assets.

(i)   Ensure that the **valuer** appears to be **appropriately qualified** and **independent** of the company. If these conditions are not fulfilled, the auditors will need to consider their possible impact on the results of the valuation.

(ii)   By reference to the instructions given to the valuer and the valuer's report, ensure that the **valuation** has been **performed on a basis reasonable and consistent** with previous valuations.

(iii)   Check that **profits or losses on individual non-current assets** have been **correctly calculated** by reference to the non-current asset register and the detailed analysis of the revaluation.

(iv)   **Check the arithmetical accuracy** of the compilation of the **revaluation schedule** and of the **calculation of asset profits and losses**.

(c)   IAS 38 lays down the basis on which development costs may be carried forward. They may be carried forward only if, and to the extent that, they represent an **asset** which is likely to generate income for the company in the future. It would contravene the prudence concept to carry forward expenditure which is not reasonably expected to generate future income.

According to IAS 38, development expenditure should be recognised in profit or loss in the year it is incurred, unless it meets all the following criteria:

(i)   The technical feasibility of completing the intangible asset so it will be available for use or sale can be demonstrated

(ii)   The entity can demonstrate its intention to complete the intangible asset and use or sell it

(iii)   The entity can demonstrate its ability to use or sell the asset

(iv)   The entity can show how the asset will generate probable future economic benefits

(v)   The availability of adequate technical, financial and other resources to complete the development and to use or sell the asset can be shown

(vi)   The entity can measure reliably the expenditure attributable to the asset during its development

If, taking a prudent view of the available evidence, these conditions are met, development costs may be deferred and amortised over the period expected to benefit.

(d)   The decision to finance development internally has resulted in a large increase in payables and a decrease in cash and bank balances. This may lead to liquidity problems, especially since the company will still need funds to finance the new product. These funds will have to be generated either by the sale of further investments, the raising of a loan from the directors or an outside investor, or by the issue of shares. If **funding** is **not available**, the **development expenditure** should be **recognised in profit or loss** on the basis that it will not be possible to complete the project. This would eliminate the retained earnings reserve and would create doubts about the company's status as a going concern.

The auditors should discuss with the directors their plans for obtaining **additional finance**, and request that they produce cash flow forecasts in support of these. If the auditors do not obtain satisfactory evidence of the company's ability to obtain finance, it may be necessary to qualify the audit report on the grounds of going concern problems which have not been fully disclosed.

14 Bainbridge

Inventories

Matters to consider

- Risk that items produced for inventories are misstated due to out of date standards being applied. Inventories are also potentially misstated if no comparison with NRV has been made.

- Risk that bespoke items are overstated due to the inclusion in cost of design fees.

- Inventory value as a whole is likely to be a material area of the accounts so this is an area where audit effort should be directed. The materiality of any adjustments required needs to be considered. The lowest level of materiality would be $16,000 (1% of profit).

- Whether management has considered the NRV of the inventories on a line by line basis as required by IAS 2 *Inventories*.

- Whether the standard costing approach provides the fairest practical approximation to actual cost as required by IAS 2.

- Whether the management is justified in maintaining the same standards as last year on the basis that they do reflect current prices. (IAS 2 states that standard costs should be reviewed regularly and revised where necessary).

- Whether overheads have been allocated to inventories based on the normal level of activity.

- Whether other overheads have been split between functions (ie production, administration) on a sensible basis.

- Whether the capitalisation of design fees relating to the bespoke items is in compliance with IAS 2. Such 'other costs' can be capitalised only to the extent that they are incurred in bringing the inventories to their present location and condition.

Evidence to seek

- Confirm with management that they have considered the need to write down certain inventory lines to their NRV. Review any schedules produced by the client to support their conclusions and check that any issues identified by the auditor at the inventory count or in the follow up work have been reflected in the final inventory valuation.

- Obtain a schedule of the standards applied and compare to last year to determine whether they have remained the same.

- Agree major components to supporting documentation eg materials can be agreed to purchase invoices, labour can be agreed to payroll records.

- Obtain an analysis of the production and other overheads allocated to inventories. Check that these costs are related to the production centre.

- For other overheads determine the way that management have allocated these costs between the different business centres. Determine whether the allocation is reasonable and consistent with previous years.

- Check the calculation of the 'normal' activity levels used to allocate the overheads to units of production. Establish that this does not include the effects of any abnormal events and that it is consistent with previous years.

- Obtain a schedule of design fees capitalised. Agree the details to sales contracts and establish the date on which they were incurred checking that this was before the commencement of production.

Lease

Matters to consider

- Risk that the lease is incorrectly classified. If it is a finance lease the lower of present value of the minimum lease payments and fair value should be capitalised and depreciated. If an operating lease the rentals should be expensed.

- Extent to which the risks and rewards of ownership have been transferred to the lessee (eg who is responsible for maintenance, insurance). According to IAS 17 *Leases* if the risks and rewards of ownership remain with the lessor the lease would be of an operating nature.

- Basis on which management have decided that the lease is an operating lease. IAS 17 states that the land element of a lease of land and buildings is not normally a finance lease unless title is expected to pass at the end of the lease, because, due to its indefinite economic life, the lessee does not receive substantially all the risks and rewards incidental to ownership. The building element, however, could be. This would suggest that the management have come to the right conclusion, at least for the land element.

- Treatment of the rent-free period. IAS 17 states that operating lease rentals should be charged on a straight line basis over the lease term, even if the payments are not made on such a basis unless another systematic basis is representative of the time pattern of the user's benefit. On this basis the benefit of the rent free period should be spread over the lease term rather than being taken upfront.

- The likelihood of management taking up the option to extend the lease. IAS 17 states that the lease term should include any further terms for which the lessee has the option to continue to lease the asset with or without payment if it is reasonably certain at the inception of the lease that the option will be exercised. This would affect the period over which the rentals would be spread.

- Materiality. Assuming that the option is to be exercised the total lease payments of $450,000 should be spread over the 12 year lease term. This would give a charge of $37,500. This represents 2.3% of profit so is likely to be material.

- Completeness and adequacy of disclosures. IAS 17 requires a lessee to disclose the amounts to which he is committed broken down into payments due not later than one year, later than one year and not later than five years and over five years.

- Impact on the auditor's report. If it was concluded a material adjustment was required which management refused to make, the auditor's opinion would be modified (qualified – 'except for') on the grounds of disagreement.

Evidence to seek

- The lease agreement. The terms should be reviewed to confirm that the risks and rewards of ownership remain with the lessor. Details of the rent-free period, the rentals and the option to extend should be confirmed.

- Discussions with management should be held to determine the likelihood of the option to extend the lease being exercised. Conclusions should be confirmed in writing.

- Experience of treatment of any existing leases ie whether the company normally takes up the extension period.

- A recalculation of the allocation of total rentals over the lease term should be performed.

- Disclosures should be checked to confirm that they are in accordance with IAS 17.

Convertible debenture

Matters to consider

- The par value of the debenture is material to the statement of financial position as it represents 16.7% of total assets. The coupon interest is material to the income statement as it amounts to 12.5 % of profit after tax.

- The treatment does not appear to comply with IFRS 9 *Financial instruments.* Under IFRS 9 it should be treated as a hybrid instrument, split into its equity and liability components. Normally the liability component should be calculated as the discounted present value of the cash flows of the debenture, discounted at the market rate of interest for a comparable borrowing with no conversion rights. The remainder of the proceeds represents the fair value of the right to convert and this element should be reclassified as equity.

- The treatment currently adopted by Bainbridge therefore appears to be incorrect.

- It is not possible from the information given to assess whether the reclassification would materially affect the view given by the statement of financial position, but if it does, and the directors are not willing to change the classification then the audit opinion may have to be qualified on the grounds of disagreement.

Evidence to seek

- A copy of the debenture deed showing the interest rate, and conversion terms.

- A schedule calculating the fair value of the liability at the date of issue, using interest rates for quoted for similar borrowings without conversion rights.

- A copy of any disclosures relating to the debenture that have been prepared by the directors.

- A schedule showing the initial proceeds and interest payment agreed to the cash book and bank statement.

15 Griffin

> **Tutor's hint**. This question requires a good accounting knowledge as well as good auditing knowledge. You must anticipate that there will be at least one question on the paper that has such a requirement. It is essential for auditors to understand accounting problems and the audit issues that such matters raise.
>
> It is also important that you show the examiner that you have used the details given to you to consider matters such as materiality. Whether an issue is material or not is critical to an audit manager, who will not want to waste audit time considering matters which are not material. Use the details given to you as much as you can. For example, in (1), the details about profits and cost of investment help you to make a sensible comment about the chances that the 'group' created by the investment in the associate will be large enough to require some sort of group accounts, or in this case, additional disclosures for the associate. Note that **consolidated** financial statements are **not** required – as there is no subsidiary involved.
>
> Lastly, it is perfectly legitimate for you to include current issues in your answer if they seem relevant, and you will receive credit for them if they are relevant and you use them well. For example it is reasonable in the answer to (2) where it touches on going concern to mention that if a lot of Griffin's revenue comes from these two nationwide clubs, the company may be facing ongoing financial difficulties as a result of problems with television revenues. You are training to be an accountant, you should be aware of current financial issues.

(a)   **Investment in Bees Co**

    (i)   *Matters to consider*

        Inclusion in Griffin's accounts

        Bees Co may meet the criteria to be accounted for as an associate under IAS 28. This states that an associate is an entity (other than a subsidiary) in which another entity (the investor) has a participating interest and over whose operating and financial policies the investor exercises a significant influence.

        A company holding 20% or more of the voting rights in a company is presumed to exercise a significant influence. The auditors must check whether the shares held are **voting shares**.

Assuming that the entity is an associate, it should be included in Griffin's accounts as a fixed asset investment at cost, assuming that cost does not overstate the value of the asset. It is unclear whether the investment is material to Griffin's statement of financial position.

roup
counts' here
es **not** mean
onsolidation
required.

Requirement for group accounts?

Griffin and Bees may represent a 'group' for which group financial statements are required, even though as there is no subsidiary involved, consolidated financial statements are not required.

If group accounts are required, a further set of accounts with the associate equity accounted is required. Alternatively, Griffin's accounts could contain additional disclosure of what the accounts would look like if Bees had been equity accounted.

The 'Griffin Group' would be exempt from group accounts if the group was small or medium sized. Pre-tax profit of $1.2 million and the cost of the investment to Griffin of $750,000 both indicate that the group is not small. The auditor needs to consider whether group accounts are required.

Component auditors

If group accounts are required, our firm would be the group auditors and would need to liaise with the auditors of Bees Co (the component auditors).

Related party transactions

There may be related party transactions requiring disclosure under IAS 24.

Dividends

Griffin may have received, or be due, dividend income from Bees Co which will require disclosure in the financial statements.

(ii) *Audit evidence required*

The investment in Bees Co should be verified to a **share certificate**. In order to determine whether the shares are voting or not, the auditors should obtain and review the **register of members** at Bees Co, which is open to the public for a fee.

The cost of the investment should be verified to purchase documentation, and the payment should be agreed to bank statements.

The auditors must **review the financial statements** or the most up to date financial information available **of Bees Co** to ensure that the cost figure used for the investment is still reasonable and that all dividends have been accounted for correctly in Griffin's financial statements. This information may be passed on by the other auditors.

The **sales and purchase ledgers** and the **bank statements** should be **scrutinised** to assess whether there are any related party transactions in the normal course of business. This should also be **discussed with the directors**.

(b) **Competitor**

(i) *Matters to consider*

Going concern

The entrance into the market of a major competitor, the failure of the clubs to renew their contracts and the loss of personnel to the competitor may raise issues relating to going concern. The auditors must assess whether the non-renewal of contracts was anticipated, and whether historic practice shows that such contracts are often swapped. They must also discover whether the directors have assessed the impact of the competitor on their business and consider whether these assessments have covered all the issues, and what the implications for the future of Griffin are.

Further indicators of going concern issues could be the large drop in profit, the plan to diversify (does this indicate the old market is shrinking?) and the football league clubs facing current financial problems, some of whom may be customers of Griffin. However, there appears to have been sufficient cash available to make a substantial investment in Bees Co, which may indicate that going concern is not an issue. The auditor needs to check these matters.

Receivables

If the income from contracts with the nationwide clubs has not been replaced, both revenue and receivables should have fallen on last year. We should check that this is the case.

Non-current asset impairment?

The entrance of a major competitor to the market could be considered under IAS 36 as a potential indicator of non-current asset impairment. The auditors need to consider whether non-current assets have been impaired, and whether the directors have considered if non-current assets have been impaired.

(ii) *Audit evidence required*

The auditors need to gain evidence about going concern issues. They should review the statement of cash flows and the financial statements generally and **assess the cash position** of the company. They should consider how the investment in Bees Co has been financed. They should review **arrangements with the bank** and ensure that Griffin has sufficient cash to operate.

The auditors must **discuss** (and document) the loss of the contracts and the new competitor with the directors, particularly the sales director. They should **review budgets and sales projections** and ensure that these factors have been taken into account in them. They should review the current order book for signs that the budgets are unrealistic.

The reasons for the plans to diversify into women's leisure wear must be discussed (and documented) with the directors. There must be evidence on file that the auditors have investigated the issue of going concern and satisfied themselves either that the entity will continue in the foreseeable future, or that the directors have made sufficient disclosures in the financial statements that the situation is explained to the users of the financial statements.

The auditors should **review any correspondence** relating to the non-renewal of contracts to ensure that the contract has not been renewed. If no such information is available, the former customers should be included as part of the **receivables' circularisation** to ensure that no money is owed by them at the end of the year. There must be evidence on file that the level of receivables has been analysed in the light of known facts about customers and loss thereof. The auditors should also have reviewed discussions in the press about the financial viability of any clubs that are customers to assess the **recoverability of current debt**.

The auditors should identify whether the directors have carried out an **impairment review** and should review it to see if it is reasonable if they have done so. If no impairment review has been carried out, the auditors should consider whether one is required and discuss this with the directors. They may want to obtain **written representation** from the directors that no impairment review is required.

(c) **Legal requirements**

(i) *Matters to consider*

IAS 37

The provisions of IAS 37 must be considered in relation to the requirement to amend machinist's working conditions and the increase in the national minimum wage.

IAS 37 states that a provision is required if

(1) An enterprise has a present obligation as a result of a past event

(2)　It is probable that an outflow of resources embodying economic benefits will be required to settle the obligation, and

(3)　A reliable estimate can be made of the amount of the obligation

Three situations arise for Griffin:

(1)　**Cost of adjustments**. As the adjustments have not yet been made, there is no present obligation to pay for them. The obligation to make the adjustments does not create a financial obligation to pay for them until a contract has been formed for the adjustments. No provision is therefore required for the cost of adjustment.

(2)　**Possibility of penalty**. As Griffin has not made the adjustments before the required date, it is possible that they are now subject to a penalty under the legislation. If this were to be in the form of a fine, this would result in the transfer of economic benefit. However, as it is only possible that such a penalty would occur (ie, no order has yet been made) no provision for fines would be required. However, the matter should be disclosed as a contingent liability, were it material.

(3)　**Liability to employees**. Some employees are not being paid the national minimum wage. If this is material, the auditor must consider whether there is a present obligation to pay those wages. However, as the shortfall is for 5% of employees and for two months of the year, it is extremely unlikely that this matter is material to the financial statements. Secondly, the auditor must consider whether any employees are taking action over the health and safety issue which has arisen over the seat adjustment.

ISA 250

Both issues arising here indicate that the entity is not complying with the laws and regulations concerning health and safety and to the national minimum wage.

Three considerations for the auditor result:

(1)　Material effect on the financial statements? The auditors must consider whether examples of non-compliance will affect the financial statements in a material way. Given the considerations linked to IAS 37 above, it appears that this is not the case in this situation.

(2)　Reporting on non-compliance. When the auditors become aware of non-compliance with laws and regulations, they must discuss them with those charged with governance. There may also be a requirement to report non-compliance to a third party, such as a regulator. In this instance, it is extremely unlikely that there is such a requirement.

(3)　Implications for other aspects of the audit. Now the auditors are aware of a possible non-compliance with laws and regulations, they must evaluate the implication of this on the rest of the audit on Griffin, including their original risk assessment.

> ou are unlikely to be *ı fait* with national ınimum wage law. emember the quirement to report is extreme cases, such terrorism and drug- afficking. Express a easured opinion.

(ii)　*Audit evidence required*

The auditor must identify whether a contract has been entered into to make the adjustments to the seats. This might become obvious from a review of board minutes, or discussions with directors.

The auditor should also review the minutes to establish whether any fines have been levied. There should also be correspondence on the legislation requirements to review, or correspondence from the company solicitor.

In terms of the national minimum wage, the auditors should review the payroll to assess the extent of the problem.

It may be necessary to contact the solicitors to establish whether any legal action has been threatened by employees over either the health and safety issues or the wage issues outlined. If so, the auditors might have to rely on the solicitor's expert opinion as to whether the claims were actionable and the possible outcomes.

16 Recognition

(a) **Accounting treatment**

Beak Co has sold the land to Wings Co at a price well under current market value for no discernible reason. It is able to repurchase that land at cost at any time in the next five years but cannot be forced to do so. Therefore unless the land value falls significantly it can be assumed that Beak Co will repurchase the land. Wings Co will not use the building or the land for redevelopment in that period otherwise on repurchase they would lose any investment they had made.

The **commercial effect** of this transaction, assuming land values do not fall significantly, is that of **a loan** to Beak Co secured on the land. The commission is in effect interest on the loan, payment being deferred until the repurchase takes place.

Hence Beak Co should not treat this transaction as a sale. The land should continue to be shown as an asset in the statement of financial position and a loan of $20m should be recorded. The statement of comprehensive income should be charged annually with the commission charge and the accrual shown as a deferral liability in the statement of financial position.

As this is a material transaction, the auditors should qualify their opinion on the grounds of a material misstatement.

(b) **Accounting treatment**

The **substance** of this transaction appears to be that the **cars are part** of the **inventory of Sparks Co** from the time they take delivery of them from Gocar Co. This is because Sparks Co bears the risks and rewards of ownership, ie it has to insure the cars, but only pays the wholesale price in force on the date the cars were first supplied, so avoiding subsequent price rises. The monthly rental is a form of interest charged by Gocar Co, varying with the length of time Sparks Co holds the inventory.

This interpretation of the transaction is also supported by the fact that Gocar Co cannot demand the return of the cars from Sparks Co.

The cars unsold for less than four months should be treated as inventory in the financial statements and the liability to Gocar Co for them recognised.

Materiality considerations

The auditors should make a judgement as to whether they feel the amounts are material. The value of the additional inventory represents 15% of their inventory already recognised on the statement of financial position. It is 1.7% of the statement of financial position total. Bearing in mind a general guideline for materiality of 1–2% of total assets, this is likely to be material.

Impact on audit report

If the matter is material to the statement of comprehensive income (these details are not given in the question), or there are other errors in inventory which would result in inventory being increased in the statement of comprehensive income, they should modify their opinion.

This would be on the grounds of disagreement, as before.

17 Henshelwood

(a) **Share-based payments**

   (i)   Matters to consider:

      (1)   The share-based payment expense for the year is not individually material being only 2.5% of the profit before tax; the related equity reserve is material to the statement of financial position being 1.6% of total assets.

      (2)   The nature of the share-based payment must be determined; the valuation of shares in a public company is likely to be easier to determine than the value of options.

      (3)   The terms of the share-based payment and the assumptions as to the number of equity instruments that will vest.

   (ii)   Tests:

      (1)   Obtain a copy of the terms of the scheme and verify the details used in the calculation of the expense, including the number of instruments granted, grant date, vesting date and any conditions attached to the scheme.

      (2)   If the fair value calculation has been performed by an expert, obtain a copy of the valuation report and

         –   Review the assumptions for reasonableness
         –   Consider professional qualification and reputation of the expert

      (3)   Discuss with management their assumptions about the number of instruments that will ultimately vest and consider their reasonableness in the light of

         –   Latest budgets and forecasts
         –   Board minutes, and
         –   Any subsequent events that might affect employee numbers or the likelihood of achieving any performance targets.

      (4)   Reperform the calculation of the expense for the year.

(b) **Pension costs**

   (i)   Matters to consider:

      (1)   The net amount charged to the statement of comprehensive income is not individually material being only 3.7 % of the profit before tax; the net deficit carried in the statement of financial position is material, amounting to 10.1% of total assets.

      (2)   Whether the pension scheme accounts have been audited as at Henshelwood's year end or a date close to that.

      (3)   Whether all the pension schemes operated within the group have been included in the figures in the draft financial statements.

      (4)   Whether the valuation of assets and liabilities have been performed on bases that are acceptable under IAS 19 *Employee benefits.*

      (5)   The expected return on assets and the finance charge relating to the unwinding of the discount on the scheme liabilities carry a high risk of misstatement as they are based on the directors' judgement and hence may be manipulated.

   (ii)   Tests:

      (1)   Obtain a copy of the latest audited accounts of the pension scheme and verify the asset valuation used in Henshelwood's draft financial statements.

      (2)   Obtain a copy of the actuarial valuation of the pension scheme liabilities and:

         –   Check that the actuary is a member of a relevant professional body
         –   Review the source data used relating to scheme members

- Consider whether the actuarial assumptions appear reasonable and consistent with assumptions made elsewhere in the financial statements.
- Compare the assumptions used with those used in previous years

(3) Obtain copies of all written communications from the actuary to the company directors concerning the findings of their work.

(4) Obtain explanations from the directors and actuary in respect of the expected rate of return for all main asset categories and consider whether these are consistent with, for example, changes in investment strategy.

(5) Compare the expected rate of return with market indices for fixed interest and index-linked securities.

(6) Discuss with directors the choice of discount rate and obtain explanations for any change in the rate.

(7) Compare the discount rate to the appropriate high-quality corporate bond rate at the start of the year.

(8) Perform a proof in total of the interest cost by applying the discount rate to an average of the liabilities at the beginning and end of the year and compare it to the actual charge.

(9) Discuss with directors and actuaries the factors affecting the current service cost.

(10) Discuss with directors and actuaries the underlying reasons for actuarial gains and losses.

(11) Obtain written representations from the directors confirming that all retirement benefits have been identified and properly accounted for and that the assumptions used in valuing the scheme liabilities are consistent with the directors' knowledge of the business.

(c) **Provisions**

(i) Matters to consider:

(1) The net effect of provision on the statement of comprehensive income, a credit of $22.2m, represents 11.6% of profit before tax so is clearly material. The total liability, being 9.2% of total assets is also highly material.

(2) The risk of misstatement is always high in respect of provisions because estimate and judgement is involved. In the case of Henshelwood where there has been a significant write back to the statement of comprehensive income there is a risk that the provisions could have been utilised incorrectly. IAS 37 *Provisions, contingent assets and contingent liabilities* requires that provisions are only used to offset those expenses for which they were originally established.

(3) There is also a risk that the company may have additional obligations that have not been provided for.

(ii) Tests:

(1) Agree the opening balance on all provisions to the prior year's audit file.

(2) Review the estimates used in the provisions with reference to:

- The latest rental agreement in respect of the unused leasehold properties
- Recent budgets and projections relating to the restructuring costs.
- Copies of any licences or other legal documentation relating to the site restitution in the European business.
- The terms of the sales agreements relating to the warranty and environmental claims, and also to any correspondence between the purchasers of those businesses and the directors of Henshelwood.

(3) Obtain a breakdown of the expenses against which the provisions have been utilised to verify that they have only been utilised against the appropriate expenses.

(4) Review board minutes, budgets and projections, and discuss with directors whether there are any plans to resume using the leasehold properties or to sublet them in which case the provision would no longer meet the criteria of IAS 37.

(5) Obtain written representations from the directors that no additional obligations exist that would require provisions and that there have been no events after the reporting period that would affect the carrying value of the provisions.

18 Merger of audit firms

(a) The reasons behind a merger could include the following.

(i) The desire to operate on a **global scale** and increase market shares

(ii) The wish to service **multinational clients** demanding an international presence

(iii) Increased **expertise** and professional experience

(iv) **Business expansion:** the competitive nature of auditing and consultancy services demands a larger firm to service clients globally

(v) **Increasing funds** available for investment. (Increasing investment in IT systems makes this necessary)

(vi) The need to **compete with banks** who are increasing management consultancy services

(vii) To **resist liability claims**

(viii) To reduce the ability of major clients to exert fee pressures and thus improve **financial independence**

(ix) To increase the **range of opportunities** available to skilled staff

(x) To take advantage of **cost savings** achievable

(b) Possible problems could include the following.

(i) A reduction in **choice of clients**

(ii) Possible **conflicts of interest** arising from mergers of firms providing services to competing clients

(iii) A reduction in **auditors' independence**, particularly as a result of increasing provision of consultancy services

(iv) The emergence of **'audit giants'** which weakens the arguments for limiting auditors' liability

(v) **Domination** of the profession by 'giant firms'

(vi) Increase in the **influence of large firms** on the standard setting process

(vii) **Redundancies** caused by elimination of overlapping departments

(viii) **Scrutiny of the mergers** by outside agencies

(ix) **Disputes** emerging between partners as to management styles leading to resignation of disaffected partners and loss of experience

(x) A **loss of the 'personal touch'** which is a feature of smaller firms

19 Annabella

(a) **Planning issues**

Engagement letters

The audit firm needs to ensure that **every entity** that it audits is **covered in an engagement letter** so that there is no confusion over the audit that is undertaken. Annabella Co requires a **new engagement letter** itself because of the **radical overhaul** of its business and the impact that that will have on its own audit. Both the auditor and management need to confirm their common understanding of the terms of the audit engagement and of their respective responsibilities.

Impact on Annabella Co's individual accounts

(i) **Accounting for the investment in subsidiaries**. The auditors need to establish what the credit accounting entries were in Annabella Co's financial statements. If the trade and assets have been transferred, Annabella's **statement of financial position is likely to be substantially different** from the previous year. As the firm were probably involved in the reconstruction and may have advised the journals, this information should be available at the firm.

(ii) **Profit on sale**. The auditors need to establish whether a profit on sale was made on the transfer of assets to the subsidiaries, as this may require special disclosure under IAS 8.

(iii) **Other items requiring special disclosure**. The auditors should consider whether any **costs of reconstruction** (for example, **legal fees or accountancy fees**) represent exceptional costs under the requirements of IAS 8. If this is the case, these would also require special disclosure.

(iv) **Discontinued operations**. Disclosures should have been made in the previous year's accounts for discontinued operations under IFRS 5. This should be checked in the **comparatives** for this year.

(v) **Accounting for the investment in a joint venture**. In the individual financial statements of Annabella, this should be **accounted at cost**. The auditors will need to check that the joint venture does **qualify** as a joint venture for accounting purposes under the requirements of IAS 31.

New subsidiaries

The audit firm will have to ensure that **financial statements** are being drafted for the new subsidiaries and that these are **to be audited**. They will have to determine an **audit approach** for these new audits. It is likely that they will be able to make use of **analytical evidence** from the previous business of Annabella, so while these will be first year audits, in many ways they will **not be a risky as first year audits can be**.

Related party transactions

In the individual company accounts there are going to be a number of related party transactions which **require disclosure** under IAS 24 . <90% subsidiaries are not required to make disclosures. If Annabella's parent accounts are published within the group accounts, the parent does not have to make disclosures either.

	Anna	Bella	Annabella Designs
Annabella	Transfer of assets and trade. Management charges.	Transfer of assets and trade. Management charges.	Management charges. Any transfer of assets and trade?
Anna		Trading on commercial terms?	Trading on normal commercial terms?
Bella			Advertising? Trading at all?

The relationships between the companies and directors and the ultimate controlling party will all require disclosure in the accounts. When the accounts are consolidated, intercompany trading will drop out, but the controlling party will still require disclosure.

Consolidation

(i) **Required?** The audit firm must determine whether the group will be required to publish group accounts. This will depend upon its **size**. If it qualifies as a small group, it may be exempt.

(ii) **Audited.** If the company is required to produce group accounts, then the consolidated accounts must be audited.

(iii) **Other auditors.** See below.

(iv) **Accounting.** The subsidiaries will require consolidating into the results of the group. The joint investment should be included in the group accounts under the gross equity method. Intercompany transactions will have to be stripped out.

(v) **Drafting.** The audit firm should determine who is to draft any required group accounts, in case the client would like them to. This would have to be included in the engagement letter and would also impact upon new fee quotes for the group.

Arrangements with the other auditors

(i) **Evaluation.** The firm is the group auditor, so it will need to evaluate the second audit firm (David Turner and Co) to assess **to what degree it is happy to rely on the audit of Annabella Designs**. It will need to satisfy itself particularly that the audit is going to be **objective** and independent, due to the personal relationship between the audit partner and the director of the firm. The firm may feel that the relationship is too close and the audit will not be objective, in which case they would have to discuss this matter with the directors of Annabella.

(ii) **Procedures.** If the auditors are happy that the audit will be objective and they are satisfied with the qualifications, resources and reputation of the other auditors, they will then have to **discuss the procedures and audit approach** with the other auditors.

(iii) **Timing.** The group auditors will also need to outline the **deadlines** that they are working to, so the **time requirement** for the audit of Annabella Designs Ltd to be agreed.

Costs and time budgets

As the group is new, it is **difficult to determine the time** that will be taken to complete the audit of the group, and this may **impact upon the fee**. The engagement partner should **discuss the fee level with the directors** and **possibly arrange** a margin by which it might rise, as it becomes apparent how long the audit will take.

The auditors will also require **good time budgets** upon which **to base future audits and billings**. The audit plan should require that **very detailed time records** are maintained, in particular, outlining time spent in the main because the audit of the group was **new** and on the **restructuring**.

(b) **Audit of a consolidation**

Step 1   Compare the audited accounts of each subsidiary/associate to the consolidation schedules to ensure figures have been transposed correctly.

Step 2   Review the adjustments made on consolidation to ensure they are appropriate and comparable with the previous year. This will involve:

- **Recording** the **dates** and **costs** of **acquisitions** of subsidiaries and the assets acquired

- **Calculating goodwill** and **pre-acquisition reserves** arising on consolidation

- **Preparing** an overall **reconciliation** of movements on reserves and minority interests

Step 3   For business combinations, determine:

- Whether acquisition accounting has been appropriately used

- The appropriateness of the date used as the date for acquisition

- The treatment of the results of investments acquired during the year

- If acquisition accounting has been used, that the fair value of acquired assets and liabilities is reasonable (to ascertainable market value by use of an expert)

- Goodwill has been calculated correctly and if amortised, period of amortisation is reasonable

Step 4   For disposals:

- Agree the **date** used as the date for disposal to sales documentation

- Review management accounts to ascertain whether the **results** of the **investment** have been **included** up to the date of disposal, and whether figures used are reasonable

Step 5   Consider whether previous treatment of existing subsidiaries or associates is still correct (consider level of influence, degree of control)

Step 6   Verify the arithmetical accuracy of the consolidation workings by recalculating them

Step 7   Review the consolidated accounts for compliance with the law and standards and other relevant regulations. Care will need to be taken where:

- Group companies do not have coterminous accounting periods.

- Subsidiaries are not consolidated.

- Accounting policies of group members differ because foreign subsidiaries operate under different rules.

Other important areas include:

- Treatment of participating interests and associates
- Treatment of goodwill and intangible assets
- Foreign currency translation
- Treatment of loss-making subsidiaries
- Treatment of restrictions on distribution of profits of a subsidiary

Step 8   **Review** the **consolidated accounts** to confirm that they give a true and fair view in the circumstances.

20 Anderson Group

(a)   **Availability and reliability of information**

Since no direct communication with subsidiary management is possible, and audit results are not available, the auditor should consider the results of Green in the light of:

(i)   The reliability of management accounts in previous years

(ii)   Any evidence that this year's management accounts have been prepared on a basis consistent with that applied in earlier years

(iii)   The amount of information and explanations which the management of Anderson are able to provide from their knowledge acquired whilst still in control of Green

(iv)   Any audit work carried out on an interim visit and the extent to which useful audit evidence may be obtained by reviewing the work of Anderson's internal auditors on the accounts of Green in respect of the year ended 31 August 20X1

(v)   Any year end audit work, such as attendance at inventory count and receivable circularisation, carried out before control of Green was lost

(b)   **Materiality level in relation to Green's results**

There is no reason to suppose that the reported revenue of Green is incorrect: the main question mark would be against the extent of the pre-tax loss. The reliability of the figure for the reported loss would be very dependent on the matters considered above.

Under the circumstances prevailing, over or understatement of the pre-tax loss would be offset by a corresponding decrease or increase in the exceptional item, loss on sale of subsidiary. In the light of this compensating effect, the auditor of Anderson would be able to accept a higher level of error than would have been the case if the group structure had continued as before.

(c)   **Audit of loss on disposal of subsidiary**

The auditor of Anderson should check the loss arising on the disposal of its subsidiary Green as follows.

(i)   Confirm that the net assets of Green at 31 August 20X1 are equivalent to the reported net assets at 31 August 20X0 less the reported trading loss for the year ended 31 August 20X1.

(ii)   The cash proceeds should be confirmed to any agreement in relation to the sale of Green and agreed to post year end receipts.

(iii)   The sale of the subsidiary should be confirmed to board minutes and a sales agreement.

(iv)   The journal posting the loss should be traced through to the nominal ledger.

(v)   The notes to the financial statements should be checked to ensure that adequate disclosure of the disposal is given.

21 Business assurance

> **Tutor's hint.** This question could have been answered with basic auditing knowledge and did not need an in-depth knowledge of the services currently performed by auditors. However, you need to feel confident and familiar with the subject.

(a)　Current ACCA guidance on the provision of other services to clients is generally based on the IESBA guidance which applies in an international basis.

The emphasis in the IESBA guidance is on the audit firm avoiding assuming a management responsibility when providing other services. However in the case of internal audit services the IESBA code prohibits internal audit services when the audit client is a public interest entity if they relate to:

- A significant part of the internal controls over financial reporting;
- Financial accounting systems generating information which is significant to the financial statements; or
- Amounts or disclosures which are material to the financial statements.

The view taken internationally by IESBA is that many companies would be restricted if they were unable to obtain the other services available from their auditors, provided these services do not interfere with the exercise of managerial functions and auditors' independence. It would seem that **IESBA guidance allows external auditors to act as internal auditors** of clients.

The view taken by the current ACCA guidelines is as follows.

(i)　The ACCA guidance states that **objectivity may be threatened** by the provision of non-audit services. Care must be taken not to give executive advice or to become part of the client's active management.

(ii)　Firms **should not provide accountancy services to listed clients.**

(iii)　If accounting records are prepared for a client, then the **client** must accept **responsibility for the records.**

(iv)　There is **no specific prohibition** from an external auditor undertaking the internal audit function.

Specific **problems** which could occur include the following.

(i)　The **difficulty of reporting deficiencies** in internal controls in systems designed by employees of the auditor acting as internal auditors of the client.

(ii)　The **perceived difficulties in testing work** carried out by internal auditors who are colleagues of the external auditors.

(iii)　Internal audit programmes designed to **reduce the work** of external auditors.

(iv)　The danger of **breaching ACCA rules** of conduct if the internal audit department is deemed to be **part of the management** of the client.

(v)　**Fee pressures** arising from the increase in fees for providing an internal audit service leading to breaching the fee guidelines.

(vi)　**Audit risk** assessed by the external auditor. The presumption is that control risk would reduce because of the involvement of the external auditor in the provision of internal audit services

(b)　The **effects** would be as follows.

(i)　Increased **risk of liability claims**

(ii)　**Additional costs** to the auditor incurred in employing suitable staff to provide wider assurance

(iii)　An impact upon **fees** charged to clients

(iv)　Possible **increased expectations** of audit clients

(v)　The difficulty in formulating and wording an appropriate **audit report** which could require legislative changes

(c)   The new approach could be seen as a **'repackaging'** of existing services where auditors concentrate
        upon providing services which add value to the audit fee in the eyes of the client. Basic audit work
        may be foregone as it is perceived as adding very little.

        The difficulty with this approach is that auditors are increasingly faced with **litigation claims** and
        should therefore provide more basic assurance based lower materiality thresholds. It may be that
        external auditors came to view the roles of audit committees and internal audit departments as
        crucial in reducing control risk.

        It is dangerous to assume that external audit is a consultancy exercise aimed at adding value
        because traditional audit assurance will be lost and overall levels of audit risk will rise.

22 Scenarios

> **Tutor's hint.** Both scenarios given in this question should help you explore the issues that would be
> considered in practice, if an audit firm was going to offer assurance services.
>
> Notice that you must think about a variety of issues: ethics, acceptance, planning, liability, reporting. You
> must be prepared to bring in all strands of your syllabus in questions set in scenarios.
>
> Part (a) considers the position of an audit firm asked to report on a client to a third party but with no
> engagement. The auditor must consider whether it is possible to provide assurance in this situation. Is
> there an official assurance service that can be offered in this situation? Above all, the auditor must ensure
> that he is not accepting liability on this reference. The bank is seeking to reduce its risk – but the auditor
> must not allow that risk to be transferred to him. That might have dangerous implications for his audit
> independence, apart from the issue of personal risk.
>
> Part (b) looks at the idea of providing assurance on the whole process of business systems. It is important
> that the terms of an engagement are settled. An assurance service cannot be undertaken if there is no
> clear requirement as to the nature of the service.

(a)   **Lilac**

        An audit engagement partner would have to consider the following things before issuing a
        reference on behalf of a client:

        (i)   Is any **additional work** required to give such a reference?

        (ii)   If so, the need to contact the bank and discuss whether a **separate engagement** might be
                appropriate.

        (iii)   The **inherent uncertainty** of future income and expenditure and therefore the **high risk**
                which is associated with giving such an opinion.

        (iv)   The **difficulty of issuing an opinion on current solvency**. The auditors are about to
                commence the audit for the past year, meaning they will be investigating information up to
                15 months' old.

        (v)   The fact that a **duty of care** to the bank is likely to arise if such a reference is given.

        (vi)   The need for **disclaimers of liability**, therefore, which will need to be reasonable in order to
                have legal force, perhaps the **need for legal advice** before such disclaimer is made.

        (vii)   Any need to negotiate a **liability cap**, although a disclaimer of liability should be
                sufficient/more appropriate.

        (viii) Need for **written clarification** of the status of the reference, that is, explanation that there
                has been no engagement between the parties, that no fee has been paid, that it is given to
                the best of knowledge at the time.

        (ix)   The **form of the reference**. It is likely to be inappropriate to sign a bank's pre-printed
                document. The audit firm may have a standard reference document of its own, or may
                choose to compose each one according to the facts of the situation.

(b)   **Laurel**

The directors of Laurel have expressed an interest in engaging the audit firm to undertake an assurance engagement in relation to their risk management and controls.

The following matters will be relevant:

Acceptance

Independence

The audit firm has to consider the issue of **independence**. It is vital that the provision of other services to the audit client does not **impair their objectivity towards the audit**. ACCA states that provision of other services may impair objectivity.

The IESBA guidance, which was revised in July 2009, states whether a of threat to objectivity exists when providing **any** professional service will depend upon the particular circumstances of the engagement, and on the nature of the work that the professional accountant in public practice is performing.

The amount that audit independence would be affected will depend on the exact nature of the service provided (see below). However, an assignment testing the operation of controls could be complimentary to the audit.

Nature of the service

The firm would not be able to accept the engagement as it has been currently set out. An assurance engagement should exhibit certain elements, key of which are subject matter, suitable criteria and an engagement process. It is very difficult to give assurance on the effectiveness of risk management, as there are no recognised criteria by which to judge it. However, the firm could provide an assurance service checking that controls are designed according to management criteria and they operate according to management policy, for example. This would need discussing and agreeing in writing before the engagement could be accepted.

Planning

In terms of planning such an engagement, once the details of the engagement had been agreed, the following matters would be relevant:

(i)   Is the firm **sufficiently independent** of the client to conduct the assurance service objectively? It may be that the fact that the company is an audit client would impair their objectivity towards this engagement.

(ii)   Are all the **elements** of an assurance engagement **present**? This has been discussed above.

(iii)   Have **the firm and the parties agreed terms**? In this case, the assurance service is likely to be carried out to benefit shareholders, so it may be necessary for a vote to be passed in general meeting to approve the service.

(iv)   Are the **criteria** for assessing the subject matter **suitable**? In this case, management policy would be a suitable criterion for evaluating the operation of systems.

(v)   The auditor must assess the **materiality and risk** of the engagement. These should be incorporated into a **fee** and into the **detailed procedures** planned for the engagement.

(vi)   What **form of report** is required by the parties? There is no such thing as a standard report, so it is important for the parties to agree upon the format of the report that will be produced at the end of the engagement.

23 Trendy Group

Business risks	Audit risks

(a) Fraud and loss

This obviously impacts on both the business and potentially affects the risk of an incorrect audit opinion if they result in material misstatements which go unadjusted.

As for business risk.

(b) Foreign currency transactions

The parent entity is responsible for treasury management but no details are given as to how group FX risk is being controlled. In fact the current procedures may for intragroup transactions be creating further currency exchange problems.

The audit of purchases may appear easier if costs are fixed at the beginning of the year but this may well increase audit work required in inventory provisioning and year end adjustments to reflect the inventories at their real cost to the group.

(c) Single sourcing manufacture

Currently adverse price movements in the Malay employment or raw material market, or indeed inflation or interest rate movements, may result in the group having significantly reduced profits.

Quality may reduce as only one supplier has a monopoly on sales. This has an audit impact due to the risk of overvaluation of poor quality inventories.

As prices are set each quarter guaranteeing a modest Malaysian operation profit margin, this does not lead to future cost control strategies being effective. There is the ability of local management to live rather lavishly without effectively controlling costs.

There is also a enhanced risk of fraud.

Political unrest may also cut-off supply and lead to significant going concern issues for the group.

Over-reliance on a single supplier would be a key non going concern indicator to be followed up by the auditors of the individual companies.

Non going concern risk

(d) Design risks

Potentially US designed goods produced in Malaysia may not sell abroad.

This may lead to further inventory provisioning to be required again increasing audit risk associated with inventory over valuation.

Design costs may have been capitalised in the parent entity's books. There is an audit risk of overstated intangible assets.

(e) Inventory obsolescence and valuation

The ability to achieve good sales in the countries of the individual trading operations depends upon

– the design capability of the parent entity team
– the local advertising spend.

Inventories purchased at the set transfer price may be over-valued if not saleable at the year end.

| | *Business risks* | *Audit risks* |

Business risks

As the US trading company ultimately buys the obsolete lines at 50% of original transfer price this company could end up with substantial losses and inventory provisions as a result of someone else's bad design and advertising decisions.

Audit risks

In the individual company's inventory provisions should bring inventories held down to the lower of cost and net realisable value.

There is a further audit risk that from a group perspective that the inventory valuation is not appropriate.

The transfer of inventories around the group means that the individual companies are not reflecting the inventories at original cost to the group.

In addition any provision to reduce inventories to NRV should be based upon the NRV expected to be achieved according to where it is likely the inventories are going to be sold. If it is expected to be the US at marked down prices then the group accounts should reflect the full loss on original cost to the group.

(f) **Cash rich environments**

The retail stores are carrying significant levels of cash, credit card receipts and cheques. There is exposure to loss, theft and human error in giving out change and entering sales details.

Risk from lack of reliable audit evidence. Material misstatement of cash balances.

(g) **Property**

With retail stores and the Malaysian factory the group has many responsibilities and commitments:

– Insurance
– Security offered on loans
– Repairs and maintenance
– Payments on mortgages
– Maintaining an acceptable level of return on the floor space
– Refurbishments to maintain market presence

There is an audit risk the financial statements include:

– Inflated revaluations to support loans and guarantees
– Inappropriate depreciation charges/ policies
– Wwrongly capitalised repairs expenditure
– Lack of necessary disclosures.

(h) **Tax**

The use of fixed transfer prices may expose the group to making profits in countries where the tax regime is not favourable.

24 Verity

(a)   The factors that will affect the accountants' decision on whether to accept appointment are as follows.

   (i)   **Previous experience of client**

   The accountants should draw on their knowledge of the client as gained during the audit. In particular they will be interested in the willingness of the client to provide information, the integrity and knowledge of the directors, and the reliability of the forecasts prepared for financial accounting purposes, for example for assessment of going concern or deferred tax.

   (ii)   **How prepared**

   The accountants will need to consider how the forecast is being prepared, in particular:

   (1)   How the forecast was compiled, and the staff who compiled it.

   (2)   The extent to which the forecast is based on assumptions consistent with past events. The details given suggest that a more optimistic view is being taken than is warranted by the company's record in recent years.

   (3)   Whether the forecast represents management's best estimate of achievable results, or whether it represents hopeful targets or is based on certain hypothetical events taking place.

   (4)   How the forecast takes account of factors which may invalidate the assumptions made.

   (5)   The level of detail available supporting the forecast.

   (iii)   **Terms of report**

   The accountants will need to consider the exact terms within which they are reporting, as this could have a bearing on their liability. This is discussed further in (c) below.

   (iv)   **Users**

   The accountants should consider carefully the use to which the report will be put, and its audience.

(b)   A major concern of the reporting accountant will be the assumptions on which the report is based. The level of evidence required will depend on the terms of the accountants' report, but some evidence will be required on the major assumptions made in the forecast.

   (i)   **Sales**. It might be expected that the price increase would result in some lost sales, so extra sales will be needed from other customers to make up for the sales lost as well as achieving the planned increase. The auditor will need to focus on the plans to achieve that increase. Increases might be a result of a change in the sales mix or new products or customers; if these changes have already occurred, the accountants should consider what effect they have already had. Increased marketing and promotional activity may also be necessary, and this would need to occur rapidly in order to achieve the desired effect. This activity will probably be reflected in increased costs, and the accountants will need to check that these have been included in the forecast.

   (ii)   **Cost of sales**. The accountants will need to consider whether economies have been planned to improve margins, whether these economies are likely to be achieved, and whether there will be consequential other costs that need to be reflected in the plan. For example reduction in the labour force is likely to mean redundancy costs, investment in more up-to-date plant and equipment to mean capital investment costs.

   (iii)   **Trade receivables**. The accountants should consider whether the decrease in settlement period is likely to be achieved. They should consider whether emphasising new credit limits and prompt settlement discounts will help achieve the required target, and also the effectiveness of any other measures the company takes, for example tighter checks on new customers and more rigorous pursuit of slow payers. In particular the accountants will need to review the position of foreign customers, as they may be less flexible in reducing settlement periods. The accountants should also check that the consequences of the prompt settlement discount, a reduction in amounts received, have been reflected in the forecast. For foreign customers, the accountants should also check any exchange rate effects have been reflected in the forecast.

(iv) **Trade payables**. The accountants should check that the increase in payable days will not breach terms of business with suppliers, leading to possible supply problems or withdrawal of credit terms and demands for immediate cash payments. They should also check that the forecast reflects other possible consequences of the increase, for example a loss of early settlement discounts.

(v) **Maximum finance**. The accountants should check whether the estimated increase in finance is reasonable or whether other sources will be required, either because the $9 million is an under-estimate or because other existing sources of finance will need to be repaid. The accountants should check that the consequences of the increase, particularly an increased interest burden, have been reflected. They should consider also whether the forecast shows that the company will be able to make the repayments comfortably, or whether the forecast margins are tight.

The accountants should also check that the forecast is internally consistent, for example that increased sales correspond with increased purchases, and reflects all non-trading cash flows. Consistency with forecasts made for other purposes, for example management accounting budgets, should also be checked.

(c) Liability will depend partly on the following general factors.

Extent of assurance

In this assignment accountants are focusing on uncertain future events, as opposed to an audit, where the report is based on a verification of data relating to past events. Therefore the level of assurance that can be given on this type of report is lower.

The exact level of assurance will depend on the form of the opinion given. Reporting under ISAE 3400 *The examination of prospective financial information* would require the accountants to report whether the forecast has been properly compiled on the basis of the stated assumptions and is presented in accordance with the relevant financial reporting framework. The report would state that nothing has come to the accountants' attention to suggest that the assumptions do not provide a reasonable basis for the prospective financial information. The accountants may go further, and make a positive report on the assumptions or less probably give a report on the achievability of the forecasts. If the report gives more positive assurance, this may increase the expectations of the report's readers as to the assurance given.

Other report issues

Whatever the exact terms of their opinion, the accountants should mention other matters in their report that will clarify for users what the accountants have done and hence what they are offering:

(i) The accountants should state why and for whom the report is being prepared.

(ii) Reference should be made to the work done, and whether the work has been done in accordance with ISAE 3400.

(iii) The report should state that the directors are responsible for the assumptions made.

(iv) The accountants may be able to include specific disclaimers on the assumptions made and achievability of the forecasts. Even if they do not, they should make a statement about the uncertainty of the forecast, and the possibility that the actual outcomes will differ from what is predicted.

Cranley Bank

The accountants were on notice that the forecast was being prepared for the purposes of the bank, and thus the degree of the proximity that the law relating to professional liability requires has been established. If a claim arises, the courts will consider whether the forecast was properly prepared and based on reasonable assumptions that took account of the information that should have been known at the time of the forecast. If it was not, the court would then consider whether the accountants should have drawn the conclusion that they did or allowed themselves to provide some degree of implicit assurance on the forecast because of their association with it.

Certainly some of the assumptions made would appear to be doubtful and the bank may have a case against the accountants. However if the company fails to meet the forecast, it may well be difficult to assess how much this was due to factors that could have been predicted, and how much it was due to factors that could not have been forecast when the forecast was made.

The debenture holders

The accountants will probably not be liable to the debenture holders, The accountants stated in their report that it was prepared solely for the bank. The fact that the directors omitted this statement makes no difference to the accountants' liability, although it may render the directors liable. In addition had the report been prepared for the purposes of obtaining debenture finance it would have been prepared on different assumptions.

25 Painswick Ltd

(a) A forensic audit can be defined as the process of gathering, analysing and reporting on data in a pre-defined context, for the purpose of finding facts and/or evidence in the context of financial/legal disputes and/or irregularities and giving preventative advice in this area.

Fraud is an example of an irregularity which may be investigated as part of a forensic audit. The main objective of the work is to determine whether a fraud has taken place, identify who has perpetrated the fraud and to calculate the loss incurred by the company.

The evidence obtained may be presented in a court of law.

(b) In accordance with ISA 240 the primary responsibility for the prevention and detection of fraud rests with management. An auditor conducting a statutory audit in accordance with ISAs is responsible for obtaining reasonable assurance that the financial statements are free from material misstatement as a result of fraud. However the ISA acknowledges that there are inherent limitations in an audit in this respect as the overall purpose of the audit is to form an opinion on the financial statements not to detect fraud. The auditor must maintain an attitude of professional skepticism but unless the auditor has reason to believe the contrary records and documents may be accepted as genuine.

When undertaking a fraud investigation the forensic auditor's role will be determined by the specific terms of the engagement agreed between the forensic auditor and the client. Normally this will refer specifically to the identification of whether fraud has occurred. Although many of the procedures involved will be similar to the audit of financial statements their purpose will be different and therefore the approach will differ. For example materiality will be viewed differently and documentation will be reviewed more critically than on an audit.

(c) The fundamental ethical principles apply to forensic assignments as follows:

- Integrity

    If there is any risk that the forensic accountant's integrity will be compromised they should decline or withdraw from the audit. This is a particular issue as forensic assignments will often involve dealing with individuals who are dishonest or lack integrity.

- Objectivity

    Objectivity is crucial particularly if the forensic accountant is taking the role of an expert witness. If the accountant is not seen to be objective the credibility of his evidence will be undermined.

- Professional competence and due care

  Specialist skills may be required to conduct forensic assignments. The accountant must ensure that he has the relevant capabilities.

- Confidentiality

  The general principle of confidentiality still applies particularly where the forensic accountant is working for one party in a dispute. In certain circumstances eg a court case the accountant may be required to disclose information and evidence obtained.

- Professional behaviour

  Professional behaviour is always important to protect the reputation of the individual and the profession as a whole.

(d)   The fraud could have been identified by carrying out the following procedures:

- Assess the overall control environment and controls, in particular segregation of duties
- Determine who is able to access all aspects of the purchase ledger system including posting of invoices, payments of cash and reconciliation of accounts
- Obtain a printout of masterfile amendments including those to BACS details and review for any unauthorised changes. Where unauthorised changes have been made obtain supporting documentation giving details of the amounts transferred and the details of the account holder.
- Review transactions on a number of supplier accounts and investigate duplicate posting of invoices
- Scrutinise the entries in the suspense account and obtain an explanation as to what each entry relates to.
- Review reconciliations of major supplier accounts and trace individual entries to invoices and cash payments

26 Harness

Tutor's hint. When it comes to the impact of social and environmental issues on the work of the external audit, two things are important. These two things are:

- Why the issues are relevant
- How the issues are relevant

These two issues were addressed in an essay question on the pilot paper for the old syllabus. In this question, the same issues are addressed, but the 'how' aspect is addressed through an auditing scenario. Notice that the question in part (b) does not ask you to comment on the implications of the environmental issues on the audit, but more generally asks you to comment on the above. You should not restrict your answer to environmental matters then.

This question is overtly aimed at environmental matters. However, in the exam, issues like these will not necessarily have a neon sign over them. You may find that they are thrown into a more general risks and planning question. In such a case, it is for you to identify that such matters are important.

Notice that this question also requires a solid accounting knowledge to discuss issues such as non-current asset impairment, contingent liabilities and joint ventures. Auditors must have a good accounting knowledge to be able to identify risk matters in financial statements.

(a) **Importance of social and environmental issues**

Social and environmental issues are important to the external auditor today for a variety of reasons.

(i) *Importance to companies*

The first reason is that these matters are **important to the companies on whom the auditor is reporting**. Social and environmental matters which are important to the company form a necessary part of knowledge of the business.

Companies are increasingly reporting to their shareholders on matters of corporate responsibility. The external auditors report to the shareholders and have responsibilities to review other information presented with the financial statements which they have audited. Social and environmental issues are a natural part of corporate reporting these days.

(ii) *Impact on the financial statements*

Social and environmental issues may well have financial implications which impact on the financial statements. Several examples can be given:

   – Non-current asset impairment (IAS 36)
   – Provisions (IAS 37)
   – Revenue recognition (IAS 18)
   – Development costs (IAS 38)
   – Going concern issues (IAS 1)

(iii) *ISA 250*

It will sometimes be the case that social and environmental issues will be regulated, in which case the auditing guidance contained in ISA 250 will become relevant to the auditor.

(b) **Audit of Harness**

ISA 250

As part of the understanding of the business exercise, when planning the audit, the auditors must ensure that they are **aware** of any **relevant regulations** relating to energy provision and/or piping oil which may impact on the financial statements.

Non-current assets

Harness appears to have accidentally **disposed** of a windmill in the year and three others show signs of being impaired. The auditors must ensure that the disposal has been **correctly accounted** for and whether any loss on disposal is an **item requiring special disclosure under IAS 8**. They must also discover whether Brewster has conducted an **impairment review** and, if so, whether the review is appropriate and reasonable.

Going concern

The loss of three or four windmills is likely to **severely affect operations** in terms of quantity of power generated. However, as the vast majority of the power goes to Brewster himself, it is likely that other customers will still be able to be accommodated.

However, the **generator also lies close to the eroding cliff**. The auditors must assess whether the generator is in danger of being affected by the erosion as this is more likely to impact severely on the going concern assumption. It appears that Brewster is happy to finance the loss-making business, but without a generator, it would not be able to operate anyway.

Cracked pipe line

Harness has invested in a pipeline which has a large crack in it. The auditors need to assess whether this gives rise to any **obligation to transfer economic benefits**.

If repair work has been commissioned, this might give rise to an obligation which might necessitate a **provision for repair costs**.

It is unclear whether the crack is going to result in **oil spill and resulting environmental contamination**. The auditors may need to obtain the opinion of an **expert engineer** as to the **likelihood** of that happening. If contamination is possible or probable, there may be a **contingent liability** arising in respect of fines or compensation.

Investment

Harness is the 'co-owner' of the pipeline. The auditors need to investigate the details of this **investment** to determine whether the pipeline is a non-current or current asset or whether it would constitute a joint venture or arrangement under IAS 31.

Going concern

The auditors need to investigate the potential impact the cracked pipeline could have on the business of Harness, because this could also impact upon the going concern basis, if fines or legal action was extensive.

27 Eastfield Distributors

> **Tutor's hint**. This answer is based on the ACCA Code in force at the time this study text went to print. The ACCA Code is designed to comply with the IESBA Code of Ethics for Professional Accountants and the IESBA Code was revised in July 2009.

(a)   The auditor should consider the following factors when assessing their independence.

   (i)   The level of fee income from Eastfield should not exceed 15% of the practice's total income. If Eastfield is listed, the fees should not exceed 10%.

   (ii)   As external auditor, the firm will be reviewing the work of internal audit; if the same staff were acting as external and internal auditors, they would be judging their own work. This obvious threat to objectivity can be lessened by different staff carrying out the detailed work, and different partners and managers being in charge of providing both services.

   (iii)   There is a specific threat to independence if preparing Eastfield's accounts is part of the desired internal audit service. If Eastfield is a listed company, the audit firm's staff should not be involved in preparing the accounting records unless their work is of a mechanical nature. If Eastfield is not listed, it must accept responsibility for its accounts and accounting records, and the practice must carry out sufficient audit work on the accounting records.

   (iv)   Similarly there is a threat to independence if the internal auditors become involved in the management of the company, because as external auditor the audit firm is reporting on the stewardship of management. However part of the internal audit service could be making recommendations about the design of systems and controls. The audit firm should thus ensure that the directors take responsibility for implementation of any recommendations, and their decisions are clearly recorded in board minutes.

   (v)   Internal audit staff may be particularly likely to breach other independence guidelines that are applicable to them as employees of the firm carrying out the external audit. They should be reminded that they should not own shares in the client, accept a loan from the client, or obtain goods or services on more favourable terms than are offered to Eastfield's own staff.

   (vi)   If Eastfield does fail to pay fees, there may be a greater danger of the amounts owing being akin to a loan because of their size and because they are amounts owed for a continuing service rather than an annual audit.

   (vii)   The engagement letter should set out clearly the respective responsibilities of the audit firm and Eastfield. It should separately identify the work that the audit firm should carry out as external and internal auditors, and how fees will be calculated for each service. It should make clear to whom the audit firm's internal audit team will report.

   (viii) The firm should consider as part of its annual review of independence whether it is still sufficiently independent to be able to continue to act as external auditor.

(b) The advantages for Eastfield of having the external auditor provide internal audit services are as follows.

(i) The audit staff will be qualified or partly qualified accountants who are subject to professional standards and guidelines.

(ii) Training costs will be saved, as the audit firm, not Eastfield will be responsible for staff training.

(iii) The audit firm may be able to provide a range of expertise which would not be available to Eastfield without incurring considerable extra costs.

(iv) The efficiency of external audit would be enhanced, and hence its costs lowered, because internal auditors are using the same procedures to record and assess systems. Therefore the external auditor would not have to spend time checking whether appropriate work has been performed.

The disadvantages for Eastfield of using the internal auditors are as follows.

(i) Eastfield may want to use internal audit for a variety of tasks on the non-financial areas of its business, and the audit firm may not have staff with the expertise necessary in these areas.

(ii) As discussed in (a), the ACCA's independence requirements place limitations on the work that the internal auditors can carry out as a result of their firm also acting as external auditor.

(iii) The audit firm may not be able to guarantee continuity of internal audit staff. There may be regular staff changes as staff leave or are involved in other work, and the learning curve for new staff may add to the costs of internal audit.

(iv) The audit firm may not be able to provide the staff that Eastfield wants at the time Eastfield needs them because of commitments to other clients.

(v) The costs of the audit firm's staff will be higher than if Eastfield employed its own internal audit staff, because the audit firm will be charging Eastfield a mark-up on the staff's time as well as their salaries.

(vi) There may be conflicts over the reporting arrangements for internal audit staff. Eastfield would want to maintain control over their activities, but there has to be a mechanism for reporting to the audit firm as well, because the external firm is responsible for the staff's professional development and hence will need to assess how staff have performed.

(c) The advantages for the audit firm of carrying out both the internal and external audit are as follows.

(i) The audit firm will be able to gain greater assurance from their own staff's work as internal auditors than they are likely to be able to gain if the internal audit staff were employed by Eastfield. The firm will know that its staff have the necessary levels of competence and independence. It will also not have to spend time assessing the methods used to record and evaluate controls.

(ii) The extent of the work done by internal audit is likely to go beyond that necessary to support an external audit opinion, so the firm will have more evidence available than it would aim to have if it was just carrying out an external audit.

(iii) Working on a variety of internal audit tasks will enhance the professional development of the audit staff concerned.

(iv) The internal audit work might be able to be carried out at times of the year when the amount of other work is low, and thus staff will be used more efficiently.

The disadvantages for the firm of carrying out both services are as follows.

(i) The firm may have problems exercising control over the internal audit staff, because of their responsibility to report to the client.

(ii) Problems over the internal audit work may jeopardise the firm's role as external auditor.

(iii) The potential problems discussed in (a) in guaranteeing independence may prove insurmountable.

28 Maple

(a)   **Auditor's responsibility in respect of fraud and error**

ISA 240 *The auditor's responsibilities relating to fraud in an audit of financial statements* states that the primary responsibility for the prevention and detection of fraud rests with both those charged with governance and the management of an entity. It is not the auditor's function to prevent fraud or error although the fact that an audit is carried out may act as a deterrent.

In respect of detection, ISA 240 states that the auditor should assess the risk of material misstatement due to fraud at both the financial statement and assertion level and determine overall responses to address the assessed risks. This might include changing the nature, timing and extent of audit procedures, eg more inspection, more work conducted during the year rather than at the year end and larger sample sizes.

The approach to error under ISA 315 *Identifying and assessing the risks of material misstatement through understanding the entity and its environment* and ISA 330 *The auditor's procedures in responses to assessed risks* is broadly similar to the approach outlined for fraud above.

In practical terms the likelihood of detecting errors will be much higher than that of detecting fraud as deliberate attempts are normally made to conceal fraud including collusion and falsification of records.

In either case an audit is subject to an unavoidable risk that some material misstatements will not be detected.

If the auditor identifies an instance of fraud or error, he should document his findings and report them to the appropriate level of management and possibly to those charged with governance of the entity depending on their significance.

The auditor also needs to consider the potential impact on the audit opinion. If the fraud or error has a material effect on the financial statements the auditor's report may need to be modified. The nature of the modification would depend on the specific circumstances.

The auditor may need to consider whether there is a legal duty to report the occurrence of fraud or material error to regulatory or enforcement authorities.

(b)   **Auditor's report**

Inventories in Sherwood

An exact calculation of the required adjustment to inventories cannot be performed as it is not possible to tell the extent to which the directors' valuation is incorrect. However the inventories figure of $80,000 overall is material to both the profit and total assets figure.

The issue here is a limitation on scope which is material (assuming that the audit manager agrees that no other procedures can be performed). In the draft auditor's report this has not been dealt with correctly. It appears that it has been dealt with as a disagreement.

The explanation of the problem has been correctly dealt with in the explanatory paragraph itself. The opinion paragraph should have acknowledged the limitation as follows:

'Except for the financial effects of such adjustments, if any, as might have been determined to be necessary had we been able to satisfy ourselves as to the validity of the inventories figure, in our opinion the financial statements......'

Director's loan

The audit senior has made no reference to the loan on the basis that $5,000 is not material to the financial statements. While this is true from a quantitative perspective, in this case the director's loan is material due to the sensitive nature of the balance. IAS 24 *Related party disclosures* requires disclosure of transactions with key management personnel.

If the directors of Maple still refuse to provide the necessary information the details of the loan should be included in the auditor's report. In addition the opinion would be modified (qualified – 'except for') on the grounds of a material disagreement for non compliance with legislation/IFRS.

Bad debt

If the debt in respect of Beech were recognised in profit or loss this would result in a reduction in profits of 47% and assets of 8.4%. On this basis it would have a material effect on the financial statements. While material, the matter is isolated to the receivables balance and does not affect the truth and fairness of the financial statements overall. The audit senior has modified the audit opinion on the grounds of material disagreement with the decision not to provide against the debt. This is the correct treatment and the report has been correctly drafted in respect of this issue.

29 Reporting issues

Tutor's hint. Part (a) involves a fairly straightforward run through of the issues covered in the Study Text on this issue.

Part (b) involves some more complex accounting and auditing issues. There is some advanced financial reporting knowledge and you might not have known about it. Don't worry too much about the exact financial reporting requirements for an issue such as a website, just show the examiner that you are aware of the relevant issues. You don't need to know detailed standards to raise the issue that the website is likely to qualify as a non-current asset of some description and to discuss the issues raised by that. You should be able to discuss issues of auditing evidence, whatever the accounting issues are. Don't spend too long on the first issue raised in the scenario to the detriment of the others.

(a)   **Electronic publication of auditors' report**

Publishing the auditors' report electronically will in practice make the report **available to a greater number of people** than is likely to have been the case previously. There are **three key risks** to which publication of the auditors' report on the website exposes the auditor:

(i)   The risk that users will **misunderstand** which financial statements the auditors' report refers to, or that the report will be disconnected from the correct statements

(ii)   The risk that people will **assume** that the auditors' report **gives assurance on any financial information available on the website**

(iii)   The risk that the report could be **amended by unauthorised persons**

These risks could result in two things:

(i)   **Increase in expectations gap.** Such lack of understanding about a widely available audit report (as discussed above) will only serve to expand the expectations gap between what auditors do and what people think they do, which is to the detriment of the auditing profession.

(ii)   **Impact on auditors' liability.** More pressingly for the auditor making public the information, it is possible that extending the audience of the audit report could impact on the liability of the auditor by having an effect on the auditors' duty of care. This would only be discovered in the courts (that is, if a case was brought).

(b)   **Issues arising at Techie**

(i)   *Audit evidence*

The website: The auditor should seek evidence about the assertions made by the directors in relation to the website. The key assertions are in relation to existence and valuation.

The auditors should **visit the website** to ensure that it exists and should perhaps check with an IT literate staff member whether the **complexity** of the website **bears out the cost** of developing it.

With regard to valuation, the auditors should **verify the cost to the invoices** tendered by the IT specialist who developed the website.

With regard to the **advertising**, the auditors should visit the other party's website to **vouch the existence** of the advertising. They should also review the **terms of the agreement** between the parties to verify that there is no liability or income on the arrangement.

(ii) *Implications for the audit report*

Website costs. The Framework states that **assets** are 'resources controlled by the enterprise as a result of past events and from which future economic benefits are expected to flow to the enterprise'.

As the website is an arena for trading, controlled by the entity, it would **appear to fall within this description**. If this website should be capitalised, which it seems to under the definition of an asset, it should be included in the statement of financial position.

As the matter is considered **material** (it has been disclosed) this matter would cause a **qualification due to material misstatement** (except for qualification) if the directors do not amend the financial statements. However, it is **not pervasive** to the accounts, so the qualification **would not need to be an adverse opinion**.

Advertising banner. It is **possible** that the advertising banner **also falls within the definition of an asset given above**. As it is maintained on someone else's website, it could be argued that it is not under the entity's control. However, there is likely to be an agreement with the other entity under which Techie controls the nature and form of the advert.

IAS 38 states that **non-purchased assets** may only be recognised if they are capable of being readily measured. This will be the case if it is a member of a group of homogenous assets with an active market. An advertising banner is **not comparable to a brand** which has no such market. **There is a market in advertising slots**.

The **engagement partner would have to take a view** on whether this advertising banner should be capitalised or not, **if the amounts involved were material** to the financial statements. **It is unlikely that they would be so**. However, if they were, and the directors disagreed with the auditors, another modification on the grounds of material misstatement might be required.

Index

Review Form – Paper P7 Advanced Audit and Assurance (10/11)

Please help us to ensure that the ACCA learning materials we produce remain as accurate and user-friendly as possible. We cannot promise to answer every submission we receive, but we do promise that it will be read and taken into account when we update this Study Text.

Name: _____   Address: _____

_____

_____

How have you used this Study Text?
(Tick one box only)

☐ Home study (book only)

☐ On a course: college _____

☐ With 'correspondence' package

☐ Other _____

Why did you decide to purchase this Study Text? *(Tick one box only)*

☐ Have used BPP Texts in the past

☐ Recommendation by friend/colleague

☐ Recommendation by a lecturer at college

☐ Saw information on BPP website

☐ Saw advertising

☐ Other _____

During the past six months do you recall seeing/receiving any of the following?
(Tick as many boxes as are relevant)

☐ Our advertisement in *ACCA Student Accountant*

☐ Our advertisement in *Pass*

☐ Our advertisement in *PQ*

☐ Our brochure with a letter through the post

☐ Our website www.bpp.com

Which (if any) aspects of our advertising do you find useful?
(Tick as many boxes as are relevant)

☐ Prices and publication dates of new editions

☐ Information on Text content

☐ Facility to order books off-the-page

☐ None of the above

Which BPP products have you used?

Text	☑	Success CD	☐
Kit	☐	i-Pass	☐
Passcard	☐	Interactive Passcard	☐

Your ratings, comments and suggestions would be appreciated on the following areas.

	Very useful	Useful	Not useful
Introductory section	☐	☐	☐
Chapter introductions	☐	☐	☐
Key terms	☐	☐	☐
Quality of explanations	☐	☐	☐
Case studies and other examples	☐	☐	☐
Exam focus points	☐	☐	☐
Questions and answers in each chapter	☐	☐	☐
Fast forwards and chapter roundups	☐	☐	☐
Quick quizzes	☐	☐	☐
Question Bank	☐	☐	☐
Answer Bank	☐	☐	☐
Index	☐	☐	☐

	Excellent	Good	Adeqate	Poor
Overall opinion of this Study Text	☐	☐	☐	☐

Do you intend to continue using BPP products?   Yes ☐   No ☐

On the reverse of this page is space for you to write your comments about our Study Text. We welcome your feedback.

The BPP Learning Media author of this edition can be e-mailed at: benjaminsmith@bpp.com

Please return this form to: Lesley Buick, ACCA Publishing Manager, BPP Learning Media Ltd, FREEPOST, London, W12 8BR

TELL US WHAT YOU THINK

Please note any further comments and suggestions/errors below. For example, was the text accurate, readable, concise, user-friendly and comprehensive?